Computer Vision for Multimedia Applications:
Methods and Solutions

Jinjun Wang
Epson Research and Development, USA

Jian Cheng
Chinese Academy of Sciences, China

Shuqiang Jiang
Chinese Academy of Sciences, China

INFORMATION SCIENCE REFERENCE
Hershey · New York

Director of Editorial Content: Kristin Klinger
Director of Book Publications: Julia Mosemann
Acquisitions Editor: Lindsay Johnston
Development Editor: David DeRicco
Publishing Assistant: Deanna Jo Zombro
Typesetter: Deanna Jo Zombro
Production Editor: Jamie Snavely
Cover Design: Lisa Tosheff

Published in the United States of America by
      Information Science Reference (an imprint of IGI Global)
      701 E. Chocolate Avenue
      Hershey PA 17033
      Tel: 717-533-8845
      Fax: 717-533-8661
      E-mail: cust@igi-global.com
      Web site: http://www.igi-global.com

Library of Congress Cataloging-in-Publication Data

Computer vision for multimedia applications : methods and solutions / Jinjun
Wang, Jian Cheng, and Shuqiang Jiang, editors.
      p. cm.
  Includes bibliographical references and index.
  Summary: "This book presents the latest developments in computer vision
methods applicable to various problems in multimedia computing, including new
ideas, as well as problems in computer vision and multimedia computing"--
Provided by publisher.
  ISBN 978-1-60960-024-2 (hardcover) -- ISBN 978-1-60960-026-6 (ebook) 1.
Computer vision. 2. Multimedia systems. I. Wang, Jinjun, 1977 Nov. 17- II.
Cheng, Jian, 1977- III. Jiang, Shuqiang, 1977-
  TA1634.C655 2011
  006.3'7--dc22
                              2010021446

British Cataloguing in Publication Data
A Cataloguing in Publication record for this book is available from the British Library.

Editorial Advisory Board

Table of Contents

Section 1
Computer Vision for Human Computer Interaction

Chapter 1

Wen Wu, Carnegie Mellon University, USA
Jie Yang, Carnegie Mellon University, USA
Xilin Chen, Chinese Academy of Sciences, China

Chapter 2

Yongmian Zhang, Rensselaer Polytechnic Institute, USA
Jixu Chen, Rensselaer Polytechnic Institute, USA
Yan Tong, GE Global Research, USA
Qiang Ji, Rensselaer Polytechnic Institute, USA

Chapter 3

Giancarlo Iannizzotto, University of Messina, Italy
Francesco La Rosa, University of Messina, Italy

Chapter 4

Richard M. Jiang, Loughborough University, UK
Abdul H. Sadka, Brunel University, UK

Section 4
Multimedia Authentication

Section 5
Biologically Inspired Multimedia Computing

Detailed Table of Contents

Section 1
Computer Vision for Human Computer Interaction

> *Wen Wu, Carnegie Mellon University, USA*
> *Jie Yang, Carnegie Mellon University, USA*
> *Xilin Chen, Chinese Academy of Sciences, China*

Human drivers often use landmarks for navigation. For example, we tell people to turn left after the second traffic light and to make a right at Starbucks. In our daily life, a landmark can be anything that is easily recognizable and used for giving navigation directions, such as a sign or a building. It has been proposed that current navigation systems can be made more effective and safer by incorporating landmarks as key navigation cues. Especially, landmarks support navigation in unfamiliar environments. This chapter aims to describe technologies for two intelligent vision systems for landmark-based car navigation: 1) labeling street landmarks in images with minimal human effort; the authors have proposed a semi-supervised learning framework for the task; 2) automatically detecting text on road signs from video; the proposed framework takes advantage of spatio-temporal information in video and fuses partial information for detecting text from frame to frame.

> *Yongmian Zhang, Rensselaer Polytechnic Institute, USA*
> *Jixu Chen, Rensselaer Polytechnic Institute, USA*
> *Yan Tong, GE Global Research, USA*
> *Qiang Ji, Rensselaer Polytechnic Institute, USA*

This chapter describes a probabilistic framework for faithful reproduction of spontaneous facial expressions on a synthetic face model in a real time interactive application. The framework consists of a coupled Bayesian network (BN) to unify the facial expression analysis and synthesis into one coherent structure. At the analysis end, the authors cast the facial action coding system (FACS) into a dynamic Bayesian network (DBN) to capture relationships between facial expressions and the facial motions as well as their uncertainties and dynamics. The observations fed into the DBN facial expression model are measurements of facial action units (AUs) generated by an AU model. Also implemented by a DBN, the AU model captures the rigid head movements and nonrigid facial muscular movements of a spontaneous facial expression. At the synthesizer, a static BN reconstructs the Facial Animation Parameters (FAPs) and their intensity through the top-down inference according to the current state of facial expression and pose information outputted by the analysis end. The two BNs are connected statically through a data stream link. The novelty of using the coupled BN brings about several benefits. First, a facial expression is inferred through both spatial and temporal inference so that the perceptual quality of animation is less affected by the misdetection of facial features. Second, more realistic looking facial expressions can be reproduced by modeling the dynamics of human expressions. Third, very low bitrate (9 bytes per frame) in data transmission can be achieved.

Chapter 3

Giancarlo Iannizzotto, University of Messina, Italy
Francesco La Rosa, University of Messina, Italy

This chapter introduces the VirtualBoard framework for building vision-based Perceptual User Interfaces (PUI). While most vision-based Human Computer Interaction applications developed over the last decade focus on the technological aspects related to image processing and computer vision, the main effort of this chapter is towards ease and naturalness of use, integrability and compatibility with the existing systems and software, portability and efficiency.

Chapter 4

Richard M. Jiang, Loughborough University, UK
Abdul H. Sadka, Brunel University, UK

This chapter introduces a robust human face tracking scheme for vision-based human-robot interaction, where the detected face-like regions in the video sequence are tracked using unscented Kalman filter (UKF), and face occlusion are tackled by using an online appearance-based scheme using principle component analysis (PCA). The experiment is carried out with the standard test video, which validates that the proposed PCA-based face tracking can attain robust performance in tackling face occlusions.

Chapter 5

Zahid Riaz, Technische Universität München, Germany
Suat Gedikli, Technische Universität München, Germany
Michael Beetz, Technische Universität München, Germany
Bernd Radig, Technische Universität München, Germany

This chapter focuses on the human robot joint interaction application where robots can extract the useful multiple features from human faces. The idea follows daily life scenarios where humans rely mostly on face to face interaction and interpret gender, identity, facial behavior and age of the other persons at a very first glance. The authors term this problem as face-at-a-glance problem. The proposed solution to this problem is the development of a 3D photorealistic face model in real time for human facial analysis.

Section 2
Computer Vision for Multimedia Content Summary and Retrieval

Video summary is very important for users to grasp a whole video's content quickly for efficient browsing and editing. This chapter proposes a novel video summarization approach based on redundancy removing and content ranking. Firstly, by video parsing and cast indexing, the approach constructs a story board to let user know about the main scenes and the main actors in the video. Then it removes redundant frames to generate a "story-constraint summary" by key frame clustering and repetitive segment detection. To shorten the video summary length to a target length, "time-constraint summary" is constructed by important factor based content ranking. Extensive experiments are carried out on TV series, movies, and cartoons. Good results demonstrate the effectiveness of the proposed method.

This chapter provides a survey of the major research efforts that have exploited computer vision tools to extend the content production industry towards automated infrastructures allowing contents to be produced, stored, and accessed at low cost and in a personalized and dedicated way.

This chapter describes an approach based human perception to content-based image representation and retrieval. The author considers textured images and proposes to model the textural content of images by a set of features having a perceptual meaning and their application to content-based image retrieval. The author presents a new method to estimate a set of perceptual textural features, namely coarseness, directionality, contrast and busyness. The proposed computational measures are based on two representations: the original images representation and the autocovariance function (associated with images) representation. The correspondence of the proposed computational measures to human judgments is shown using a psychometric method based on the Spearman rank-correlation coefficient. The set of computational measures is applied to content-based image retrieval on a large image data set, the well-known Brodatz database. Experimental results show a strong correlation between the proposed computational textural measures and human perceptual judgments. The benchmarking of retrieval performance, done using the recall measure, shows interesting results. Furthermore, results merging/fusion returned by each of the two representations is shown to allow significant improvement in retrieval effectiveness.

Section 3
Computer Vision for Multimedia Content Analysis

Chapter 9

Guoliang Fan, Oklahoma State University, USA
Yi Ding, Oklahoma State University, USA

Semantic event detection is an active and interesting research topic in the field of video mining. The major challenge is the semantic gap between low-level features and high-level semantics. This chapter advances a new sports video mining framework where a hybrid generative-discriminative approach is used for event detection. Specifically, the authors propose a three-layer semantic space by which event detection is converted into two inter-related statistical inference procedures that involve semantic analysis at different levels. The first is to infer the mid-level semantic structures from the low-level visual features via generative models, which can serve as building blocks of high-level semantic analysis. The second is to detect high-level semantics from mid-level semantic structures using discriminative models, which are of direct interests to users. This framework can explicitly represent and detect semantics at different levels. The use of generative and discriminative approaches in two different stages is proved to be effective and appropriate for event detection in sports video. The experimental results from a set of American football video data demonstrate that the proposed framework offers promising results compared with traditional approaches.

Chapter 10

Hong Lu, Fudan University, China
Xiangyang Xue, Fudan University, China

This chapter surveys the methods on video scene segmentation. Specifically, there are two kinds of scenes. One kind of scene is to just consider the visual similarity of video shots and clustering methods are used for scene clustering. Another kind of scene is to consider both the visual similarity and temporal constraints of video shots, i.e., shots with similar contents and not lying too far in temporal order. Also, the authors present their proposed methods on scene clustering and scene segmentation by using Gaussian mixture model, graph theory, sequential change detection, and spectral methods.

Kongqiao Wang, Nokia Research Center, China
Yikai Fang, Nokia Research Center, China
Xiujuan Chai, Chinese Academy of Sciences, China

Vision based gesture recognition is a hot research topic in recent years. Many researchers focus on how to differentiate various hand shapes, e.g. the static hand gesture recognition or hand posture recognition. It is one of the fundamental problems in vision based gesture analysis. In general, most frequently used visual cues human uses to describe hand are appearance and structure information, while the recognition with such information is difficult due to variant hand shapes and subject differences. To have a good representation of hand area, methods based on local features and texture histograms are attempted to represent the hand. And a learning based classification strategy is designed with different descriptors or features. This chapter mainly focuses on 2d geometric and appearance models, the design of local texture descriptor and semi-supervised learning strategy with different features for hand posture recognition.

Section 4
Multimedia Authentication

Lin Wu, Tianjin University, China
Yang Wang, Tianjin University, China

This chapter presents a framework for detecting fake regions by using various methods including watermarking technique and blind approaches. In particular, it describes current categories on blind approaches which can be divided into five: pixel-based techniques, format-based techniques, camera-based techniques, physically-based techniques and geometric-based techniques. Then, it takes a second look on the geometric-based techniques and further categorizes them in detail. In the following section, the state-of-the-art methods involved in the geometric technique are elaborated.

Bin Ma, Beihang University, China
Chun-Lei Li, Beihang University, China & Zhongyuan Institute of Technology, China
Yun-Hong Wang, Beihang University, China
Xiao Bai, Beihang University, China

Visual saliency, namely the perceptual significance to human vision system (HVS), is a quality that differentiates an object from its neighbors. Detection of salient regions which contain prominent features and represent main contents of the visual scene, has obtained wide utilization among computer vision based applications, such as object tracking and classification, region-of-interest (ROI) based image compression, etc. Specially, as for biometric authentication system, whose objective is to distinguish the identification of people through biometric data (e.g. fingerprint, iris, face etc.), the most important metric is distinguishability. Consequently, in biometric watermarking fields, there has been a great need of good metrics for feature prominency. This chapter presents two salient-region-detection based biometric watermarking scenarios, in which robust annotation and fragile authentication watermark are respectively applied to biometric systems. Saliency map plays an important role of perceptual mask that adaptively select watermarking strength and position, therefore controls the distortion introduced by watermark and preserves the identification accuracy of biometric images.

Section 5
Biologically Inspired Multimedia Computing

Chapter 14

Le Dong, University of Electronic Science and Technology of China, China
Ebroul Izquierdo, University of London, UK
Shuzhi Sam Ge, University of Electronic Science and Technology of China, China

In this chapter, research on visual information classification based on biologically inspired visually selective attention with knowledge structuring is presented. The research objective is to develop visual models and corresponding algorithms to automatically extract features from selective essential areas of natural images, and finally, to achieve knowledge structuring and classification within a structural description scheme. The proposed scheme consists of three main aspects: biologically inspired visually selective attention, knowledge structuring and classification of visual information.

Chapter 15

Jing Tian, South China University of Technology, China
Weiyu Yu, South China University of Technology, China

Visual saliency detection aims to produce saliency map of images via simulating the behavior of the human visual system (HVS). An ant-inspired approach is proposed in this chapter. The proposed approach is inspired by the ant's behavior to find the most saliency regions in image, by depositing the pheromone information (through ant's movements) on the image to measure its saliency. Furthermore, the ant's movements are steered by the local phase coherence of the image. Experimental results are presented to demonstrate the superior performance of the proposed approach.

Visual saliency, which distinguishes "interesting" visual content from others, plays an important role in multimedia and computer vision applications. This chapter starts with a brief overview of visual saliency as well as the literature of some popular models to detect salient regions. The authors describe two methods to model visual saliency – one in images and the other in videos. Specifically, they introduce a graph-based method to model salient region in images in a bottom-up manner. For videos, they introduce a factorization based method to model attention object in motion, which utilizes the top-down knowledge of cameraman for model saliency. Finally, future directions for visual saliency modeling and additional reading materials are highlighted to familiarize readers with the research on visual saliency modeling for multimedia applications.

Preface

The multimedia research mainly focused on images in the early of 1990s, and then multimedia became the synonymous of video in mid-1990s. Other modalities, such as audio and text, began to be added after 2000s. Today, the ever increasing variety and decreasing cost of various types of sensors enables the use of additional different media such as GPS location data, infrared, motion sensor information, optical sensor data, biological and physiological sensor signal etc. There were sporadic discussions on the merits and demerits of using single or joint media, and now it is being accepted that, the specific needs from different applications define the set of media, either single or multiple.

To process different type of media, the multimedia computing research have been borrowing methods from other domains, trimming and fusing them to fulfill the needs of individual multimedia application. For example, identifying audio keywords from sports video mainly uses the MFCC feature that is popular in the speech recognition field; analyzing the text streams in news video borrows many algorithms from the Natural Language Processing area. Among all the studied types of media, video is still the most fundamental one. This defines a coupled relationship between multimedia computing and computer vision, because the later provides necessary techniques to go from sequences of two-dimensional images to structural description of the visual content for modeling, such as edge/texture detection and SIFT/SURF local descriptor for low-level video feature extraction, image segmentation and object tracking for middle-level video keywords creation, and image understanding and object/scene recognition for high-level video semantic annotation.

Recovering the unknown structural representation from the video media is an inverse problem. There is, however, no standard formulation of how this inverse problem could be solved. In another word, although there exists an abundance of methods for solving various well-defined computer vision tasks, these methods are often task-specific and can seldom be generalized over a wide range of applications. In addition, many existing computer vision algorithms are still in the state of basic research, therefore it is not straightforward how computer vision methods can be applied to multimedia applications. At the same time, little literature is available to discuss the disciplines of computer vision for multimedia applications. This has motivated us to edit a book to address problems related to applying computer vision to multimedia computing. The book includes many latest developments in computer vision methods applicable to various problems in multimedia computing, and lists successful examples of multimedia modeling, system and application where computer vision techniques play an indispensible role. The whole book is organized as follows:

Section 1 focuses on introducing computer vision in human-computer interaction. Multimedia system is primarily designed with the human being as the user. This human-centered design is a distinctive feature and defines the necessity of the human-computer-interaction (HCI) functionality. The recent development in Internet media, streaming, gaming, etc fields has further demanded the next generation of HCI, i.e., Human Multimedia Interaction (HMI), where users may convey messages and emotions to the computer or eve*n to other users with the help of multimedia.* Human beings perceive the world with a three-dimensional representation, while most multimedia documents only convey the one-dimensional audio and/or two-dimensional visual signals. To let an automatic system perceive the world in the same way as human does, it is necessary to recover some unknowns given insufficient information to fully specify the solution. The computer vision research is the one that addresses this inverse problem. Although HCI using other modality, such as human speech, has already been made possible, the ability of existing computer vision techniques in modeling the visual world in all of its rich complexity is far more challenging than modeling the vocal tract that produces spoken sounds. Human being can perceive the object, shape, shading or other three-dimensional structures from the video with ease. Despites decades of research by perceptual psychologists trying to understand how the human visual system works, and computer vision researchers trying to develop mathematical techniques for recovering the three-dimensional shape and appearance of objects in imagery, many people still believe that it remains challenging to have a computer to interpret the visual content at the same level as a child. Fortunately, with physics-based and probabilistic models, existing computer vision techniques are already able to accomplish many tasks to a moderate success, and HMI tools and services based on these works are emerging. Section 1 of this book presents several representative works on face modeling, landmark recognition, expression analysis for HMI applications.

Section 2 and 3 discuss computer vision techniques for multimedia content analysis, summarization and retrieval. The problem arises with the explosive increasing of multimedia content, and automatic understanding of these contents has been demanding. Generally speaking, multimedia content is consisted of heterogeneous multi-modal media, such as the image, video, audio, text, etc. According to perception, these media can be roughly classified into two categories: visual content and audio content. As an inter-discipline of computer science, vision and statistics, computer vision has been investigated for near thirty years. A set of relatively mature theory and algorithms have been developed, which provides substantial foundation for multimedia content analysis. Some issues in multimedia content analysis are directly or indirectly derived from computer vision field. In this section, we selected several works that focus in three aspects: visual feature extraction, object detection/tracking/recognition, and video structuring. Feature extraction is the basis of multimedia content analysis. Low-level visual features extracted for multimedia content analysis are usually borrowed from computer vision community, such as color histogram, Gabor/Tamura texture descriptor, Fourier shape descriptor, etc; Object detection, tracking and recognition technologies are related to computer vision that deal with capturing and recognizing instances of semantic objects of a certain class. Some well-researched object categories, including face, hand, car, pedestrian, etc, have applications in many multimedia applications such as image/video retrieval and video surveillance; Video structuring aims at identifying semantic units from the multimedia data at different hierarchical level. It is usually domain specific, such as shot and story in news video and event in sports video. Video structuring relies on analyzing the temporal transition or motion pattern, which poses challenging topics in applying techniques available for static image.

Section 4 talks about multimedia authentication. Multimedia signal in electronic forms makes it easy to reproduce and manipulated, especially with the availability of versatile multimedia processing software and the wide coverage of the Internet. The existing HMI tools and content-based retrieval engines have also eased the way for large-scale multimedia applications. However, abuses of these technologies pose threats to multimedia security management and multimedia copyright protection. Multimedia authentication is to confirm the genuineness or truth of the structure and/or content of multimedia documents. However, the unique characteristic of multimedia data makes traditional authentication methods based on physical clues inapplicable. Nowadays, there are mainly two approaches for multimedia authentication, cryptograph and digital watermarking. The cryptograph method, or called the digital signature technique, depends on the multimedia content and certain secret information known only to the signer. The digital signature cannot be forged, and the authenticator can verify multimedia data by examining whether its content matches the information contained in the digital signature; the digital watermarking method is to modify the multimedia bitstream to embed some codes, called watermarks, without changing the meaning of the content. The embedded watermark may represent either a specific digital producer identification label or some content-based codes generated by applying certain rules. In the authenticator, the watermarks are examined to verify the integrity of the data. However, for both the two approaches, since the multimedia data are usually distributed and re-interpreted by many interim entities, the authentication information may get distorted or discarded. Hence it becomes challenging to guarantee trustworthiness between the origin source and the final recipient. In this section, we show two representative works related to multimedia watermarking and forgery detection.

Section 5 presents several biologically inspired methods for multimedia computing. The current Internet-scale multimedia database, highly distributed and orderless, brings difficulties for many multimedia applications. The solutions to these problems may lie in our nature. Many species exhibit collective movement patterns which are highly organized compared to the seemingly random individual behaviors. This shows that aggregate behaviors in these animals may have special group-level properties that go beyond the ability of an individual, and evidences show that the group behaviors are not coordinated by a centralized leader. This implies that there exists an intrinsic mechanism among insect aggregates that overcomes individuals' drawbacks and yields results that might be impossible for individuals to attain. The fact has inspired many algorithms and methods that, through cooperation between much simpler group members, more elegant and complicated tasks can be complimented. The biologically inspired algorithms have shown promising results in many domains, including distributed covering and searching, optimization, distributed localization and estimation, group pattern modeling and group formations. These algorithms have also found their usages in multimedia applications due to the similarity between multimedia computing environment and the animal's aggregation society structure. In this section, we include several works that utilized biologically inspired algorithms to solve a family of multimedia problems.

In summary, multimedia computing and computer vision are different but closely related domains. They both emerged around 1970s when computers could manage the processing of large data sets such as images. After decades of development, rich literature exists in both domains. In this book, we formally present the problems related to applying computer vision for multimedia computing. It's never like today where multimedia technology is requesting urgent computer vision algorithms and methods to support various multimedia applications. On the other side, the field of computer vision is still characterized as diverse (task-specific) and immature (in the state of basic research), and is expected to endure for the near future. Hence in this particular historic moment, we believe that a book to address the problem of applying computer vision into multimedia computing is high necessary. To a limited extent, the book can present existing works that pioneers the field; to a large extent, the book will let people in related areas be aware of the situation, and inspire them to develop systems with better performance.

Jinjun Wang
Epson Research and Development, USA

Jian Cheng
Chinese Academy of Sciences, China

Shuqiang Jiang
Chinese Academy of Sciences, China

Acknowledgment

Editors of this book sincerely thank Dr. Gao Wen, Peking University, China, Dr. Hanjalic Alan, Delft University of Technology, Netherlands, Dr. Izquierdo Ebroul, University of London, United Kingdom, Dr. Jin Jesse S., University of Newcastle, Australia, Dr. Lu Hanqing, Chinese Academy of Sciences, China, Dr. Pietikainen Matti, University of Oulu, Finland, Dr. Tian Qi, Microsoft Research Asia, China, and Dr. Xu Changsheng, Chinese Academy of Sciences, China, for serving as the Editorial Advisory Board Members. They contribute valuable ideas and suggestions in almost all aspects of the book.

The publication of this book could not have been possible but for the ungrudging efforts put in by a large number of individuals working in the circle. It is therefore only fair their contribution do not get unacknowledged. Thanks go to the authors of each chapter in presenting their cutting-edge research achievements.

Thanks are also due to Christine Bufton, Dave DeRicco and Myla Harty, the Editorial Assistants from IGI Global, for providing templates throughout every major step in the editing process, helping compiling and correcting each chapter to ensure the high-quality of the book.

We sincerely thank IGI Global for publishing this book.

Jinjun Wang
NEC Laboratories America, Inc., USA

Jian Cheng
Chinese Academy of Sciences, China

Shuqiang Jiang
Chinese Academy of Sciences, China

Section 1
Computer Vision for Human Computer Interaction

Chapter 1
Intelligent Vision Systems for Landmark–Based Vehicle Navigation

Wen Wu
Carnegie Mellon University, USA

Jie Yang
Carnegie Mellon University, USA

Xilin Chen
Chinese Academy of Sciences, China

ABSTRACT

Human drivers often use landmarks for navigation. For example, we tell people to turn left after the second traffic light and to make a right at Starbucks. In our daily life, a landmark can be anything that is easily recognizable and used for giving navigation directions, such as a sign or a building. It has been proposed that current navigation systems can be made more effective and safer by incorporating landmarks as key navigation cues. Especially, landmarks support navigation in unfamiliar environments. In this chapter, we aim to describe technologies for two intelligent vision systems for landmark-based car navigation: (1) labeling street landmarks in images with minimal human effort; we have proposed a semi-supervised learning framework for the task; (2) automatically detecting text on road signs from video; the proposed framework takes advantage of spatio-temporal information in video and fuses partial information for detecting text from frame to frame.

INTRODUCTION

Navigation is the process of planning, recording, and controlling the movement of a craft or vehicle from one place to another. Navigating a vehicle in dynamic environment is one of the most demand-

ing activities for drivers in daily life. American people drive 12,000 miles per year in average. Studies have long identified the difficulties that drivers have in planning and following efficient routes (King, 1986).

A vehicle navigation system (also termed route guidance system) is usually a satellite navigation system designed for use in vehicles. Most systems

DOI: 10.4018/978-1-60960-024-2.ch001

typically use a combination of Global Positioning System (GPS) and digital map matching to calculate a variety of routes to a specified destination such as a shortest route. They then present map overview and turn-by-turn instructions to drivers, using a combination of auditory and visual information. A typical turn-by-turn instruction is an auditory "turn right in 0.5 mile", accompanied by a visual right turn arrow plus a distance-to-turn countdown that reduces to zero as the turn is approached. Vehicle navigation systems generally function well although of course they are wholly dependent on the accuracy of the underlying map database and availability of GPS signal. However, from a human factors perspective, there are several potential limitations to the current design (May & Ross, 2006): mainly presenting procedural and paced navigation information to the driver, and relying on distance information to enable a driver to locate a turn.

Human drivers often use landmarks for navigation. The definition of landmark in navigation context has been studied from varying theoretical perspectives. Lynch described landmarks as external reference points that are easily observable from a distance (Lynch, 1960). Kaplan defined a landmark as "a known place for which the individual has a well formed representation", and described two theoretical factors that lead to a object or place acquiring landmark status: the frequency of contact with the object or place, and its distinctiveness (Kaplan, 1976). Based on the human factor studies using the above attributes Burnett has further identified the top scoring landmarks in United Kingdom (UK) (Burnett, 2000) such as traffic lights, petrol station, superstore, church, street name signs, etc. It is quite evident that in the United States, we observe that common navigation-useful landmarks include (1) road signs, (2) other signs (e.g., signs of gas stations, fast food restaurants, stores, subway stations, etc) and (3) buildings (e.g., churches, stores, etc). In this chapter, we only focus on detecting text on

road signs and how to semi-automatically acquire labeled image data. To learn about more relevant work on other landmarks, readers can read (Wu, 2009).

In order to learn a discriminative model of the landmark of interest for recognition, we need to first label the landmark versus its background in a given image. Manually labeling images is not only a labor intensive task, but also subject to human labeling and annotation errors. While efforts have been focused on online massive user labeling (e.g. MIT LabelMe (Russell, Torralba, Murphy, & Freeman, 2008), The ESP Game), limited attention has been paid to semi-automatically labeling objects in images or videos (Ayache & Qunot, 2007). Our proposed SmartLabel and SmartLabel-2 aim to let a user only mark a small region of interest inside the landmark (or object) on the image with simple input (e.g. dragging a rectangle), and our algorithms can then label the rest of the landmark (object) in the image (Wu & Yang, 2009) The evaluation of proposed SmartLabel-2 and comparison with other methods on a dataset of six object classes indicate that SmartLabel-2 not only works effectively with a small amount of user input (e.g., 1-5% of image size) but also achieve very promising results (macro-average F_1=0.84). In some cases, SmartLabel-2 even obtains nearly perfect performance.

Text on road signs carries much useful information for driving and describes the current traffic situation, defines right-of-way, provides warnings about potential risks, and permits or prohibits roadway access. Automatic detection of text on road signs can help to keep a driver aware of the traffic situation and surrounding environments by highlighting signs that are ahead and/or have been passed (Wu, Chen, & Yang 2005). We have introduced a novel framework that can incrementally detect text on road signs from video. The proposed framework takes advantage of spatio-temporal information in video and fuses partial information for detecting text from frame to frame. The feasibility of the proposed framework has been evaluated using video sequences captured from a moving vehicle. This new framework gives an overall text detection rate of 88.9% and a false hit rate of 9.2%.

BACKGROUND

In this section, we briefly review the most related works to landmark labeling and detection of text on road signs.

Landmark Labeling

Labeling landmarks or objects in images can also be called image segmentation, foreground extraction, object extraction or image editing, although they are slightly different in terms of applications and domains. Image segmentation has been an active area of research for decades and its application has been widely adopted in many research fields including content-based image retrieval. The goal is to create systems capable of segmenting foreground objects from the background accurately and to achieve good segments of the image. Recently, research has focused on the problem of interactive extraction of a foreground object from an image (Rother, Kolmogorov, & Blake, 2004). There are three key differences between our proposed SmartLabel framework and other state-of-the-art interactive segmentation tools. First, the goal of SmartLabel is to create labels for interesting object(s) in the image, not to segment the image into a number of blobs. Secondly, although SmartLabel is a semi-automatic labeling tool, it does not rely too much on user input; only initial specification and relevance feedback after the first iteration are required. Finally, SmartLabel can extract a foreground object at multiple locations in the image even though the user only specifies part of the object at one location, but most iterative segmentation tools extract objects within

or around the user specified region of interest. These properties make SmartLabel different from several state of the art interactive object extraction (segmentation) tools: Magic Wand, GrabCut (Rother et al., 2004), ClickRemoval (Nielsen & Nock, 2005), and central object extraction (Kim, Park, & Kim, 2003).

Detection of Text on Road Signs

Based on its origin, text in video can be classified into two classes: graphic text and scene text (Lienhart, 1996). Graphic text is text that is added to the video after the video is captured, such as captions added to news videos. Scene text exists as part of objects in a natural environment when it is directly captured by a camera, which includes billboards, and street names on road signs. A common assumption used by previous research in graphic text detection from video is that the text plane is perpendicular to the optical axis of the camera (Jain & Yu, 1998). This is suitable for some domains such as broadcast video where the camera is fixed or has relatively little motion. However, the assumption does not necessarily hold in the scene text detection task since road sign planes are often encountered at a non-perpendicular angle with respect to the camera optical axis. More general techniques for detecting scene text from still images have been developed in pattern recognition and computer vision fields. Recently, some researchers were able to detect scene text from still images (Chen, Yang, Zhang, & Waibel, 2002) and reported that edge features can better handle lighting and scale variations in scene images than texture features (Chen, Yang, Zhang, & Waibel, 2004), which are often used for detecting text in news video. Inspired by their work, we chose to use the edge-based features for text detection in this study. Myers et al. described a full perspective transformation model to detect 3D deformed text from still images (2001).

MAIN FOCUS OF THE CHAPTER

In this chapter we focus on two problems in designing an intelligent landmark-based vehicle navigation system: (1) semi-automatically labeling landmarks and objects in images and (2) detection of text on road signs from video. We will present our perspectives on these two problems in the following.

Semi-Automatically Labeling Landmarks and Objects in Images

The fast growth of visual data on the Internet has created new challenges for the image processing (IP) community. Most IP tasks such as image annotation (Volkmer, Smith, & Natsev, 2005), content based image retrieval (Rui & Huang, 1999) and object detection & recognition (Viola & Jones, 2001), require training data. Manually labeling images is not only a labor-intensive and time-consuming task but also subject to human operation errors and variances. There has been much attention on attracting Internet users to label images manually such as MIT LabelMe and ESPGame.org, but research on the semi-automatical manner has been limited. Our goal is to offer a semi-automatic framework to label objects in images effectively (focusing on things as opposed to stuff (Carson, Belongie, Greenspan, & Malik, 2002)).

We have introduced a family of semi-automatic labeling methods in this study based on a graph-based semi-supervised learning (SSL) algorithm (Zhu, Ghahramani, & Lafferty, 2003), which we refer to as Zhu's SSL method in the following. Zhu's SSL method represents labeled and unlabeled samples as vertexes in a weighed graph. Edge weights represent the similarity between connected vertexes. It adopts Gaussian fields over a continuous state space rather than random fields over a discrete label set. The mean of the field is characterized in terms of harmonic functions and its solution can be efficiently obtained using matrix methods or belief propagation. This relaxation to a continuous space has some attractive properties. For instance, lack of negative samples and continuous label values can be naturally handled by Zhu's SSL method. However, Zhu's SSL method was proposed for problems in other domains, and there are still difficulties in directly applying it to our problem. In (Wu & Yang, 2006), we have proposed SmartLabel based on Zhu's SSL method. SmartLabel has four novelties: (1) Real numbers from 0 to 1 are used as label values for positive patches. (2) The weighed graph is constructed from the input image using two spatial constraints. (3) Harmonic energy minimization is applied iteratively to estimate labels for patches in U and newly labeled patches are added to L for the next iteration. (4) It brings the human in the loop by plugging in relevance feedback (RF) to collect negative samples for learning. Unfortunately, SmartLabel has some shortcomings such as demand of human supervision for RF and zigzag object boundaries in resulting object areas. These issues limit SmartLabel's application to many tasks. To overcome these weaknesses, we have proposed SmartLabel-2 which improves in three aspects (Wu & Yang, 2009). In particular, we introduce a novel saliency-based method to sample negative samples. Secondly, we apply a quadtree structure to partition images instead of using regular gridding. Finally, we adopt image superpixel representation (Ren & Malik, 2003) to refine labeling results and extract smooth object boundaries.

Detection of Text on Road Signs from Video

Some previous research work has paid particular attention to detecting and recognizing symbols on road signs, particularly warning signs such as "STOP", "YIELD", and "DO NOT ENTER".

Since only a finite number of shapes and colors can be applied on these warning signs, color and edge-based shape features are normally used to train the detector (Fang, Chen & Fuh, 2003). In this chapter, we are interested in detecting not only symbols, but also text on road signs. Text appearing on road signs can have a variety of appearances. Color and shape features are not enough to train a robust detector. Without knowing text on the signs, drivers cannot obtain correct information about current traffic situation and appropriate driving instructions.

To improve the efficiency of the detection process while maintaining a low false hit rate in this task, we naturally employ a divide and conquer strategy to decompose the original task into the two subtasks: localizing road signs and detecting text. The key idea for realizing such an incremental framework is to exploit the temporal information available in video. This idea has been shown to be effective in other text detection tasks such as caption detection in broadcast video (Li, Doermann, & Kia, 2000). Moreover, because of government requirements on the design and placement of road signs (The Federal Highway Administration [FHWA], 2003), this task also has some auspicious properties for the new framework: (1) text on road signs is highly luminant compared to most sign background colors; (2) text on the same road sign always has similar foreground and background patterns; (3) most road signs exist on vertical planes; and (4) there are only a limited number colors used as background colors.

Solutions and Recommendations

Semi-Automatically Labeling Landmarks and Objects in Images

We first describe SSL notations and the application of Zhu's SSL method to label objects. SSL is about learning from labeled and unlabeled data. Given a data set, $X=\{x_1,\ldots,x_l,x_{l+1},\ldots,x_n\}$ and a label set, $C=\{1,\ldots,c\}$ the first l samples have labels $\{y_1,\ldots,y_l\}\in C$ and remaining samples are unlabeled. We call $L=\{(x_1,y_1),\ldots,(x_l,y_l)\}$ the labeled set and

$U=\{x_{l+1},y_{l+1}),\ldots,x_n,y_n)\}$ the unlabeled set. Graph-based SSL methods consider a connected graph, $G=(V, E)$, with n vertexes in V corresponding to n samples, where vertexes $L=\{1,\ldots,l\}$ are labeled samples and vertexes $U=\{l+1,\ldots,n\}$ are unlabeled samples. The edges, E, are weighted by an $n\times n$ affinity matrix, W, computed by certain distance metrics. In [129], W is defined as

$w_{ij} = \exp(-\sum_{d=1}^{n} \frac{(x_{id} - x_{jd})^2}{2\sigma_d^2})$ for the n-dimensional space, where x_{id} is d-th component of the feature vector $x_i \in \mathbb{R}^n$ and $\sigma_1,\ldots,\sigma_n$ are length scale hyperparameters for each dimension.

The goal of Zhu's SSL method is to compute a real-valued labeling function, $g(\cdot):V\rightarrow R$, on G with certain nice properties, and then to assign labels for U based on $g(\cdot)$. The labeling function is constrained to assign labels such as $g(i)=g_l(i)=y_i$, on $L, i=1,\ldots,l$. Gaussian field configuration aims to make unlabeled samples that are nearby in the graph have similar labels. This motivates choosing a quadratic energy function,

$$E\left(g\right) = \frac{1}{2}\sum_{i,j} w_{ij}(g\left(i\right) - g(j))^2. \qquad (1)$$

The harmonic property indicates $g(\cdot)$ at each unlabeled sample is average of $g(\cdot)$ at its nearby samples,

$$g\left(j\right) = \frac{1}{d_j}\sum_{i,j} w_{ij}g\left(i\right), \;\; for\, j = l+1,\ldots,n$$

$$(2)$$

which maintains the smoothness constraint of $g(\cdot)$ with respect to G. To compute the harmonic solution, W is split into 4 blocks based on the separation of L and U. $W_{n\times n} = \begin{bmatrix} W_{ll} & W_{lu} \\ W_{ul} & W_{uu} \end{bmatrix}.$

Denote the target labeling function $g(\bullet) = \begin{bmatrix} g_l(\bullet) \\ g_u(\bullet) \end{bmatrix}$ and $g_l(\cdot)$ denotes labels on L and $g_u(\cdot)$ denotes labels on U. From [129], we know that the unique harmonic is given as a $u \times c$ matrix $g_u(\cdot)$,

$$g_u\left(\bullet\right) = \left(D_{uu} - W_{uu}\right)^{-1} W_{ul} g_l(\bullet). \tag{3}$$

where $D = diag\left(d_i\right), d_i = \sum_j w_{ij}.$

To formulate our task as an SSL-based labeling problem, we construct L and U. Given an image and ROI(s) that is given by the user, we partition the image into non-overlapping patches of size $B \times B$ (pixels). ROI can be a rectangle drawn by the user or any other closed area(s) marked by the user. Each patch is treated as a sample. Patches that are in the ROI or overlap with it are treated as positive samples and added in L. Other patches are treated as unlabeled samples and put in U. The number of labeled samples is l and the number of unlabeled samples is u and n = l + u. Note L does not contain negative samples yet. Labeling objects in an SSL manner possess some unique properties which other SSL problems do not have. One property is that location and context are important in images. Intuitively, pixels or patches nearby tend to belong to one object instance rather than those far away. Regions at nearby locations are more likely to contain similar color distributions than those far away. By observing this location-dependent property, we propose two spatial constraints which we embed to build the weighed graph: a location-based similarity distance metric and separation of U into Ur and Un. We first define a new distance metric by introducing an additional spatial distance term.

$$w_{ij} = \exp(-\sum_{d=1}^{n} \frac{(x_{id} - x_{jd})^2}{2\sigma_d^2} \cdot \frac{\sum_{k=1}^{2}(x_i^k - x_j^k)^2}{\epsilon}),$$

$$\tag{4}$$

where the 1st term shows the feature distance as in Zhu's SSL method and the 2nd term measures the spatial distance between two samples. The new distance metric approximates the relevancy between two samples by combining Mahalanobis distance in the feature space and Euclidean distance in 2D. For separation of U into Ur and Un, we consider the regions around L as Ur (relevant unlabeled set) and the rest image regions are considered as Un (irrelevant unlabeled set).

SmartLabel introduces an iterated harmonic energy minimization in place of the one-shot minimization in Zhu's SSL method. This scheme allows an automatic increment of L after every iteration. Note in most SSL other algorithms L is fixed but in SmartLabel L is dynamically updated. Figure 1 shows the main elements of SmartLabel, here without the relevance feedback step.

SmartLabel is not perfect. Its limitations include lack of negative samples, demanding human feedback, zigzag object boundaries and holes in extracted regions. To overcome these issues we have proposed SmartLabel-2 by extending SmartLabel in three aspects (Wu & Yang, 2009):

1. SmartLabel needs human supervision to collect negative samples. With the goal of minimizing human effort, SmartLabel-2 revises a spectral residual approach (Hou & Zhang, 2007) to automatically sample negative examples from the input image.

2. Furthermore, SmartLabel-2 applies quadtree to partition instead of regular gridding used in SmartLabel. This not only increases granularity of patches to reach object boundaries but also improves labeling accuracy by reducing mixture of object and background in one patch.

3. Finally, SmartLabel-2 refines labeled object patches via superpixels (Ren & Malik, 2003). Each image's superpixels are computed offline and used with labeled patches to extract object boundaries.

Figure 1. Main steps of SmartLabel, without the relevance feedback step

Input An image (I) and input ROI(s).

Initialize Divide I in patches of $B \times B$ pixels. Create L and U. Set the max iteration as T and neighborhood size as H. $U_r = \emptyset, U_n = \emptyset$.

SmartLabel*

for $t = 1$ to T **do**

   1. Update U_r & U_n. Extract neighboring patches from L in H pixels and put them into U_r, and the rest unlabeled patches are put in U_n.

   2. Compute the matrix W' based on L and U_r. Form the weight matrix W' using certain weight measure and $W'_{ii} = 1$.

   3. Construct the Laplacian. Compute the matrix $\Delta = D' - W'$, in which D' is a diagonal matrix with D'_{ii} equal to the sum of the i-th row of W'.

   4. Compute the harmonic solution. Compute the label prediction on U_r using the following:
   $$g_{u_r} = (D_{u_r u_r} - W_{u_r u_r})^{-1} W_{u_r l} g_l.$$

   5. Augment L. Add newly predicted unlabeled patches from U_r to L using the predictions g_{u_r}.

Output results. Produce extracted object regions from patches in L.

To overcome the lack of negative data, we need an automatic robust scheme to sample negative examples from the input image. We have proposed to revise a spectral residual approach (Hou & Zhang, 2007) to detect uninformative image regions such as sky and sample negative patches from them. The spectral residual approach is first proposed to detect information rich regions. Using Inverse Fourier Transform, the method outputs the image's saliency map which contains the nontrivial image parts. We revise the method to detect less informative regions. We apply the inverse of saliency map to obtain a background map which mainly contains uninformative regions. Our scheme suffers when the object(s) contains uninformative regions decided by the spectral residual method. Fortunately, this happens only in few cases when labeling sky and ground among other uninformative objects. Even so, SmartLabel-2 works by skipping the step of sampling of negative samples step.

A quadtree [40] is a tree data structure in which each internal node has up to four children.

Quadtree is often used to partition a 2D space by recursively subdividing it into four quadrants or regions. A similar partitioning is also known as a Q-tree. All forms of quadtrees share some common features: (1) They decompose space into adaptable cells. (2) Each cell has a maximum capacity. When maximum capacity is reached, the cell splits. (3) The tree directory follows the spatial decomposition of the quadtree. SmartLabel-2 replaces regular gridding by quadtree based partitioning. We adopt *qtdecomp* function in Matlab to perform quadtree decomposition, which needs a preprocessing step to resize the input image to a square image at resolution of 2n. Resizing input images to be square changes the height-to-width, it does not affect patch-based feature extraction much. This resembles unaccessible selection of optimal size and ratio of sliding windows which are commonly used in the image processing and computer vision fields. Quadtree partitioning not only increases granularity of patches to reach arbitrary object boundaries but also improves accuracy by minimizing mixture of object and

Figure 2. Three novelties of SmartLabel-2. (a) input image; (b) automatically sampled negative samples (i.e., sky and part of lake) using a revised approach [51]; (c) quadtree portioning; (d) 100 superpixels

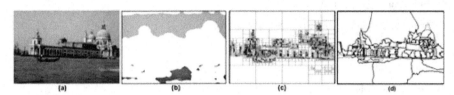

background in one patch. It is fast and takes 0.2 second to process a 512×512 image on a 3.2GHz CPU with the Matlab implementation.

Many existing image processing algorithms use image pixel as the basic representation unit. However, a pixel is not a natural representation unit of real scenes. It is only a representation unit of digital imaging. It would be more natural to work with perceptually meaningful units obtained from a low-level clustering process. One well-known way to achieve this natural representation (Ren & Malik, 2003) is to apply Normalized Cuts (NCut) (Shi & Malik, 2000) to partition an image into P segments, called superpixels. This method gives over-segmentation results, so most structures such as object boundaries and edges are conserved. NCut is a classical segmentation algorithm which uses spectral clustering to exploit pairwise brightness, color and texture affinities between pixels. As in (Ren & Malik, 2003), we apply NCut to over-segment the image to obtain superpixels. This is done offline because it normally takes 3 minutes to process a 320×240 image.

Figure 2 shows an example image's sampled negative regions, quadtree partitioning and 100 superpixels. In SmartLabel-2, the obtained labeled regions are compared with superpixels to generate refined object boundaries.

Detection of Text on Road Signs from Video

Figure 3 shows the architecture of our proposed framework for detection of text on road signs from

video, of which four main steps are summarized as follows:

1. Discriminative points detection and clustering - detecting discriminative feature points in every video frame using the algorithm proposed in (Shi & Tomasi, 1994) and partition them into clusters.
2. Road sign localization - selecting candidate road sign regions corresponding to clusters of feature points using a vertical plane criterion.
3. Text detection - detecting text on candidate road sign areas and track them.
4. Text extraction and recognition - extracting text in candidate sign plane(s) for recognition given a satisfactory size.

There are some interesting properties of the new framework. First, the number of selected points in step 1, N, balances the sign localization speed and system process rate because more feature point's likelihood that the sign is located early. A large number of feature points also mean intensive computation. Second, spatio-temporal information is extracted and used by the framework to recover the orientation of potential planes in the 3D space. Once a point cluster is classified as a vertical plane, the text detection algorithm will be run on it. Third, the framework applies a feature-based tracker which can track a feature point in a sub-pixel level. The corners of detected road sign areas are tracked to the next frame by averaging the motions of the nearest points of each corner. There are two reasons for tracking discriminative

Figure 3. The architecture of the incremental text detection framework

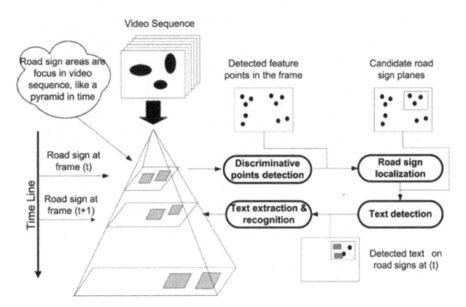

points instead of the boundary corners directly: (1) boundary corners may not be a good feature to track compared to those selected points; and (2) tracking the selected points on the road sign area can relieve the problem of partial occlusion when it happens in video.

The new framework possesses two unique merits: (1) By applying the divide and conquer strategy, the first two steps of the algorithm can significantly narrow down the search space for the later text detection step and thus reduce the majority of false hits which occur in the case of the whole-image text detection; 2) It takes advantage of both temporal and spatial information in video for detecting text on road signs over the timeline.

The key step in our proposed frameworks is to robustly and automatically localize road sign regions in video. In order to differentiate road signs from other objects, we have to use properties of road signs such as color distribution and geometric constraints. To recover the orientations rigid planes in videos, the system finds a number of discriminative feature points in the current video frame at any given frame. Features are found using the detector of Shi and Tomasi (1994). We are estimating the orientations of the candidate planes (signs) given three or more points in two successive frames. Here, we make two assumptions: (1) the optical axis of the camera is roughly horizontal and the motion of camera is also going along its optical axis; and (2) scene text lies on planar surfaces. These two assumptions are often true in the real world setting. Particularly, a camera is mounted on the vehicle in our task and its optical axis is calibrated to parallel to the horizontal plane of the vehicle. In Figure 4, the upper figure shows the side view of the scenario and the lower one shows the spatial constraints among the road sign plane, the image plane and the camera between two successive frames. Based on the property that most road signs are on vertical planes, the ratio of the component to the length of the normal vector should be smaller than a certain threshold. Thus, we can estimate the ratio and use it to localize vertical planes in video.

Figure 4 depicts that $\vec{A}$ is a vector from P_1 to P_2, and $\vec{B}$ is a vector from P_3 to P_2. Using the estimated coordinates, we further obtain the estimations of $\vec{A}$ and $\vec{B}$ as:

Figure 4. The basic spatial relationship between two frames

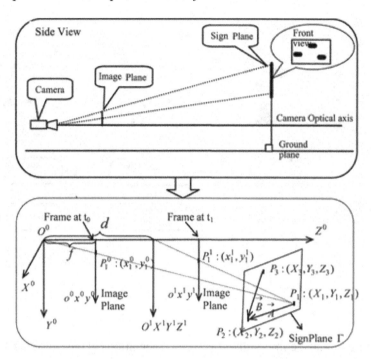

$$\vec{A}: \begin{pmatrix} X_1 - X_2 \\ Y_1 - Y_2 \\ Z_1 - Z_2 \end{pmatrix} = \begin{pmatrix} d \cdot \dfrac{x_1^{t_0}}{f} \cdot M_1 - d \cdot \dfrac{x_2^{t_0}}{f} \cdot M_2 \\ d \cdot \dfrac{y_1^{t_0}}{f} \cdot M_1 - d \cdot \dfrac{y_2^{t_0}}{f} \cdot M_2 \\ d \cdot (M_1 - M_2) \end{pmatrix},$$

(5)

$$\vec{B}: \begin{pmatrix} X_3 - X_2 \\ Y_3 - Y_2 \\ Z_3 - Z_2 \end{pmatrix} = \begin{pmatrix} d \cdot \dfrac{x_3^{t_0}}{f} \cdot M_3 - d \cdot \dfrac{x_2^{t_0}}{f} \cdot M_2 \\ d \cdot \dfrac{y_3^{t_0}}{f} \cdot M_3 - d \cdot \dfrac{y_2^{t_0}}{f} \cdot M_2 \\ d \cdot (M_3 - M_2) \end{pmatrix}.$$

where the ratios M_k are defined as:

$$M_k = \frac{x_k^{t_1}}{x_k^{t_1} - x_k^{t_0}} = \frac{y_k^{t_1}}{y_k^{t_1} - y_k^{t_0}}, \; k = 1, 2, 3.$$

(6)

In order to recover the orientation of the sign plane Γ, we need to further know the normal vector of Γ, noted as N, which can be obtained by the cross product of $\vec{A}$ and $\vec{B}$.

$$N = \vec{A} \times \vec{B} = \begin{pmatrix} X_\Gamma & Y_\Gamma & Z_\Gamma \end{pmatrix}^T,$$

(7)

Based on the property that most road signs are on vertical planes, the ratio of the Y component to the length of N is supposed to be smaller than a certain threshold. Thus, we can estimate the ratio and use it to localize vertical planes. The ratio is defined as follows:

$$R = \frac{|Y|}{\|N\|} = \frac{|C_Y|}{\sqrt{C_X^2 + C_Y^2 + C_Z^2}},$$

(8)

where C_X, C_y and C_z are components along each direction. Figure 5 shows the algorithm to localize road signs from video.

Even when sign locations are known in images, correctly detecting text on road signs is still not easy because of deformations, highlights, shadows and other factors. To work around these changes in an image, we use an edge-based cascade text detection method that integrates edge detection, adaptive searching, color analysis and geometry alignment analysis. This method was first proposed in (Chen et al., 2004). Figure 6 shows the basic flow of this schema. For more details about each step, please read (Chen et al., 2004).

EXPERIMENTAL RESULTS AND DISCUSSION

In this section, we present the experimental results of previously introduced systems. First, we present results of SmartLabel and SmartLabel-2 systems. Notations: Zhu's SSL method (Zhu's),

as a baseline, takes ROI(s) as positive samples and makes one-shot labeling prediction on all unlabeled patches. SmartLabel* utilizes the iterative labeling scheme without relevance feedback (RF). SmartLabel includes RF. SmartLabel-2 requires no human supervision during learning and incorporates quadtree partitioning and sampling of negative samples.

Figure 7 shows results by SmartLabel-2 on several classes. The 1st column lists input images with input ROIs. The 2nd column shows corresponding superpixel maps. The 3rd column shows labeling results produced by SmartLabel-2. The last column depicts ground truth. We have several interesting observations from the results. First, SmartLabel-2 generalizes very across manmade objects such as airplanes, buildings and text signs, and natural objects such as flowers and animals. Second, superpixels are proven to be effective in SmartLabel-2 to extract most of

Figure 5. The algorithm for the road sign localization

Input: Feature point clusters $C_1^t, C_2^t, ... , C_K^t$.

Output: $L^t = l_1^t, l_2^t, ... , l_K^t, l_i^t \in P, V, R, NV$ label for C_i^t. P is the perpendicular planes, V for vertical planes, R for rigid planes and NR for non-rigid planes.

Algorithms:

1. *R-plane identification step:* compute R_i and $Var(R_i)$. If $Var(R_i) < \varepsilon$, go to Step 2; otherwise, label $l_j^t = NR$. Get the next cluster. If all clusters have been examined, exit.

2. *V-plane identification step:* If $R_i < \delta$, which means it meets the vertical plane criterion, and then go to Step 3 to further verify it is a perpendicular plane; otherwise, label $l_j^t = R$; it is a rigid but not vertical plane. Go back to Step 1.

3. *P-plane identification step:* Compute the mean $\bar{\gamma}$ and variance $Var(\bar{\gamma})$. If $\bar{\gamma} < \xi$ and $Var(\bar{\gamma}) < \upsilon$, label $l_i^t = P$; otherwise, label $l_i^t = V$. Go back to Step 1.

Note: $\varepsilon, \delta, \xi, \upsilon$ are thresholds in the algorithm.

Figure 6. An edge-based text detection method

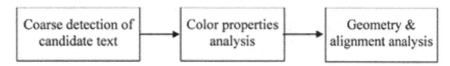

11

object boundaries despite its heavy computation. Third, the results suggest that SmartLabel-2 can assist humans to generate ground truth of object locations in images. Top two building examples in Figure 7 show that SmartLabel-2 even does a better job than a human labeler.

Figure 8 lists a comprehensive comparison on six classes. Numbers in the 1st column are numbers of images in each class. The average of 10 runs' FM 1 is shown for each method. Input images are resized to 512×512. Results of published methods are slightly different from those in (Wu & Yang, 2006) due to different experiment settings. We observe that large patches (B = 16) improve Zhu's because segmenting images into

small patches would create more patches which merely contain background and bring noise to L. We see that SmartLabel-2 with SP refinement achieves near SP-Limit performance on the flower class (according to the macro-averaging F_1^M score, which is average of F_1 scores). For other classes, SmartLabel-2 performs very well and better than SmartLabel. The car class is harder than others because its images are all gray so color info is not explored. SmartLabel runs for a few seconds processing an image of 384×256 using 16×16 patches on a 3.2GHz CPU. SmartLabel-2 requires a few seconds more. Computing superpixels takes several minutes per 320×240

Figure 7. Results by SmartLabel-2. (a) Input images with ROIs. (b) Superpixel maps (P =100). (c) SmartLabel-2's labeling results. (d) Ground truth

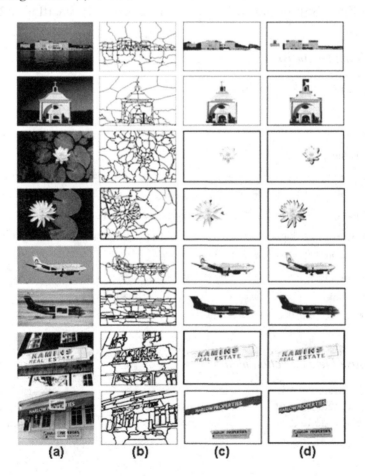

image, so it can be done offline or on a distributed cluster.

To make a qualitative comparison between SmartLabel-2 and SmartLabel, Figure 9 shows various labeling results by two methods. The 1st row shows input images with ROIs. The 2nd row shows SmartLabel's results and the third row is SmartLabel-2's results. SmartLabel obtains reasonable results but with zigzag boundaries, holes and some false positives. SmartLabel-2 gives results with smooth object boundaries and no holes. The quantitative improvement by F_1^M may not be significant on these results, but the qualitative improvement in terms of user satisfaction is distinctive.

Now we present the experimental results of detection of text on road signs from video. Figure 10 illustrates the process of incremental text detection. During a few initial video frames, no discriminative points are found on the road sign plane as shown in (a). In the frame (b), some feature points are detected in the frame, shown as blue points. The system then verifies the sign area by using the plane classification algorithm. Once the area is confirmed as a vertical plane it will be bounded with a yellow rectangle as in (c). The following frames, such as (d) - (h), show that more and more texts are detected on the road sign over the time. Newly detected text regions are merged with previously partial detection results. In the meantime, all detected text regions are

Figure 8. Comparing 3 methods proposed in (Wu & Yang, 2006) with SmartLabel-2 (S-Label2). For S-Label* and S-Label, H = 64 and B = 8 or B = 16. S-Label2 uses B = 16 and H = 64. SP: refinement by superpixels, SP-Limit: superpixel-based upper bound, C = 0:5: 50% overlap criterion for selecting a superpixel

Figure 9. Comparison between SmartLabel and SmartLabel-2. In two groups of three rows. The 1st row shows input images with ROIs. The 2nd row shows results by SmartLabel. The 3rd row shows results by SmartLabel-2

	Zhu's		S-Label*		S-Label		S-Label2		SP-Limit
	B=8	B=16	B=8	B=16	B=8	B=16	w/o SP	SP	C=0.5
Airplane (128)	0.56	0.60	0.71	0.72	0.78	0.77	0.78	0.82	0.91
Animal (59)	0.57	0.53	0.72	0.75	0.74	0.76	0.79	0.85	0.92
Building (42)	0.60	0.63	0.75	0.70	0.80	0.78	0.77	0.82	0.89
Car (123)	0.54	0.59	0.72	0.69	0.76	0.73	0.74	0.78	0.91
Flower (37)	0.66	0.70	0.82	0.81	0.85	0.83	0.85	0.90	0.91
Text (57)	0.64	0.61	0.73	0.71	0.78	0.78	0.80	0.84	0.94
Avg-F_1^M	0.60	0.61	0.74	0.73	0.79	0.78	0.79	0.84	0.91

tracked by averaging the optical flows of the feature points within the detected areas. Finally, all texts on the road sign are correctly detected as shown in (i). Note that there was a sign on the right at the beginning of the sequence (a)-(c),

however, our system did not detect it. The reason is that no feature points were found in that sign area.

Figure 11 summarizes the overall text detection performance. We compare two methods in the

Figure 10. An illustration of incremental text detection on a video sequence. Blue points are selected feature points, the yellow box bounds the localized road sign area and red boxes indicate the detected text lines

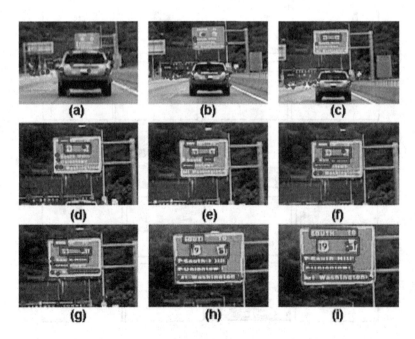

experiment: the baseline algorithm (which analyzes the whole image for every video frame) and our proposed algorithm. There are a total of 359 words in the testing videos, including numbers and symbols such as arrows on all road signs. The new framework significantly reduces the false hit rate and achieves a higher hit rate than the baseline algorithm. The low false hit rate is mainly because of the two-step strategy of the new framework and a higher hit rate is due to the sign localization step before detection. The total false hit rate of text detection is 9.2% as shown in the Figure 11. On average, there are about two false positives per minute in areas without traffic signs.

FUTURE RESEARCH DIRECTIONS

For labeling landmarks and objects in images, future directions might include: (1) directly using over-segmentation patches (superpixels) as the labeling units; (2) reinventing the SmartLabel-2 algorithm for labeling objects in videos. One question arises when using over-segmentation in SmartLabel-2 - why not use over-segmentation patches (superpixels) directly as the labeling units? We offer three thoughts for discussion: (1) Computation. Generating 100 superpixels on a 512×512 image can take >10 minutes on a current PC but quadtree normally takes <1 second, both using Matlab. (2) Feature representation (FR). FR is not well addressed for superpixels yet. Many current FR methods are for representing features on regular regions not arbitrary ones. Apart from the

FR issue, normalization and similarity measurement can be problematic too. (3) Effectiveness. Applying quadtree partitioning and refinement by superpixels has led to promising results in our experiments. We would like to leave this interesting direction for future audience.

For detection of text on road signs from video, future directions might include: (1) generalizing the proposed framework to detect scene text on other surfaces; (2) applying the proposed road sign detection algorithm to classify and analyze other objects in images and videos.

CONCLUSION

In this chapter, we have discussed two intelligent vision systems for landmark-based vehicle navigation: semi-automatically labeling landmarks and objects in images, and detection of text on road signs from video. We have first presented a family of semi-automatic object labeling methods based on Zhu's SSL method in a semi-supervised learning framework. Given an image with a small-size ROI, our methods can extract the contour of the object and also the same or similar objects at other locations in the image. In particular, we have proposed SmartLabel-2 to enhance SmartLabel by overcoming three of its limitations. Our experiments on various object classes have demonstrated that SmartLabel-2 not only outperforms SmartLabel but also achieves close-to-fine extraction of object contours in many classes.

Figure 11. Results of detection of text on road signs from video

Text Detection	Box-based		
	hit rate	false hits	miss rate
Refined baseline algorithm with text tracking	80.2%	307 (85.6%)	19.8%
Incremental algorithm with vertical-plane model	88.9%	33 (9.2%)	11.1%

Large amounts of information are embedded in natural scenes. Road signs are good examples of objects in natural environments that have rich information content. Here, we have presented a new framework for incrementally detecting text on road signs from video. The proposed framework efficiently embeds road sign plane localization and text detection mechanisms with feature-based tracking into an incremental detection framework. The framework can significantly improve the robustness and efficiency of text detection. The new framework has also provides a novel way to detect road sign text from video by integrating image features and the vertical plane properties of road signs. Experimental results have demonstrated the feasibility of the new incremental detection framework under real-world settings.

REFERENCES

Ayache, S., & Qunot, G. (2007). Evaluation of active learning strategies for video indexing. *Signal Processing Image Communication, 22*(7-8), 692–704. doi:10.1016/j.image.2007.05.010

Burnett, G. E. (1998). "Turn right at the King's Head": drivers' requirements for route guidance information. PhD thesis, Loughborough University, UK.

Chen, X., Yang, J., Zhang, J., & Waibel, A. (2002). Automatic detection of signs with affine transformation. In *Proceedings of the IEEE Workshop on Applications of Computer Vision* (pp. 32–36).

Chen, X., Yang, J., Zhang, J., & Waibel, A. (2004). Automatic detection and recognition of signs from natural scenes. *IEEE Transactions on Image Processing, 13*(1), 87–99. doi:10.1109/TIP.2003.819223

Fang, C.-Y., Chen, S.-W., & Fuh, C.-S. (2003). Road-sign detection and tracking. *IEEE Transactions on Vehicular Technology, 52*, 1329–1341. doi:10.1109/TVT.2003.810999

FHWA. (2003). Manual on uniform traffic control devices (MUTCD) for streets and highways. In *The Federal Highway Administration (FHWA), U.S. Dept. Transp.* Retrieved from http://www.fhwa.dot.gov/

Finkel, R., & Bentley, J. L. (1974). Quad trees: A data structure for retrieval on composite keys. *Acta Informatica, 4*, 1–9. doi:10.1007/BF00288933

Hou, X., & Zhang, L. (2007). Saliency detection: a spectral residual approach. In *Proceedings of the IEEE Conference on Computer Vision and Pattern Recognition (CVPR)*.

Jain, A. K., & Yu, B. (1998). Automatic text location in images and video frames. *Pattern Recognition, 31*, 2055–2076. doi:10.1016/S0031-3203(98)00067-3

Kaplan, S. (1976). Adaption, structure and knowledge. In Golledge, R. G., & Moore, G. T. (Eds.), *Environmental Knowing: theories, research and methods*.

Kim, S., Park, S., & Kim, M. (2003). Central object extraction for object-based image retrieval. In *Proceedings of the ACM Intl. Conference on Image and Video Retrieval (CIVR)*.

King, G. F. (1986). Driver performance in highway navigation tasks. *Transportation Research Record, 1093*, 1–11.

Li, H., Doermann, D., & Kia, O. (2000). Automatic text detection and tracking in digital video. *IEEE Transactions on Image Processing, 1*(9), 147–156.

Lienhart, R. (1996). Automatic text recognition for video indexing. *In Proceedings of the ACM Intl. Conference on Multimedia (ACM MM)* (pp. 11–20).

Lynch, K. (1960). *The Image of the City*. MIT Press.

May, A. J., & Ross, T. (2006). Presence and quality of navigational landmarks: Effect on driver performance and implications for design. *Human Factors: The Journal of the Human Factors and Ergonomics Society, 48*(2), 346–361. doi:10.1518/001872006777724453

Myers, G., Bolles, R., Luong, Q.-T., & Herson, J. (2001). Recognition of text in 3-D scenes. In *4th Symposium on Document Image Understanding Technology* (pp. 23–25).

Nielsen, F., & Nock, R. (2005). Clickremoval: Interactive pinpoint image object removal. In *Proceedings of the ACM Intl. Conference on Multimedia (ACM MM)*.

Ren, X., & Malik, J. (2003). Learning a classification model for segmentation. In *Proceedings of the IEEE Intl. Conference on Computer Vision (ICCV)*.

Rother, C., Kolmogorov, V., & Blake, A. (2004). Grabcut: Interactive foreground extraction using iterated graph cuts. In *Proceedings of the ACM SIGGRAPH*.

Rui, Y., & Huang, T. S. (1999). A novel relevance feedback technique in image retrieval. In *Proceedings of the ACM Intl. Conference on Multimedia (ACM MM)*.

Russell, B. C., Torralba, A., Murphy, K. P., & Freeman, W. T. (2008). LabelMe: a database and web-based tool for image annotation. *International Journal of Computer Vision, 77*(1-3), 157–173. doi:10.1007/s11263-007-0090-8

Shi, J., & Malik, J. (2000). Normalized cuts and image segmentation. *IEEE Transactions on Pattern Analysis and Machine Intelligence, 22*(8), 888–905. doi:10.1109/34.868688

Shi, J., & Tomasi, C. (1994). Good features to track. In *Proceedings of the IEEE Conference on Computer Vision and Pattern Recognition (CVPR)* (pp. 593–600).

Smeulders, A. W. M., Worring, M., Gupta, A., Santin, S., & Jain, R. (2000). Content-based image retrieval at the end of the early years. *IEEE Transactions on Pattern Analysis and Machine Intelligence, 22*(12), 1349–1380. doi:10.1109/34.895972

Viola, P., & Jones, M. (2001). Rapid object detection using a boosted cascade of simple features. In *Proceedings of the IEEE Conference on Computer Vision and Pattern Recognition (CVPR)*.

Volkmer, T., Smith, J. R., & Natsev, A. (2005). A web-based system for collaborative annotation of large image and video collections. In *Proceedings of the ACM Intl. Conference on Multimedia (ACM MM)*.

Wu, W. (2009). Multimedia Technologies for Landmark-Based Vehicle Navigation. Ph.D. thesis, CMU-LTI-09-014, Language Technologies Institute, School of Computer Science, Carnegie Mellon University, USA.

Wu, W., Chen, X., & Yang, J. (2005). Detection of text on road signs from video. *IEEE Transactions on Intelligent Transportation Systems, 6*(4), 378–390. doi:10.1109/TITS.2005.858619

Wu, W., & Yang, J. (2009). Semi-automatically labeling objects in images. *IEEE Transactions on Image Processing, 18*(6), 1340–1349. doi:10.1109/TIP.2009.2017360

Zhu, X., Ghahramani, Z., & Lafferty, J. (2003). Semi-supervised learning using Gaussian fields and harmonic functions. In *Proceedings of the Intl. Conference on Machine Learning (ICML)*.

ADDITIONAL READING

Ayache, S., & Qunot, G. (2008). Video corpus annotation using active learning. In *30th European Conference on Information Retrieval (ECIR)*.

Chen, Y., Wang, J. Z., & Krovetz, R. (2005). CLUE: Cluster-based retrieval of images by unsupervised learning. *IEEE Transactions on Image Processing*, *14*(8), 1187–1201. doi:10.1109/TIP.2005.849770

Clark, P., & Mirmehdi, M. (2001). Estimating the orientation and recovery of text planes in a single image. In *Proceedings of the British Machine Vision Conference (BMVC)*.

Deselaers, T., Keysers, D. & Ney, H. (2004). FIRE - flexible image retrieval engine: ImageCLEF 2004 evaluation (LNCS 3491).

Jing, F., Zhang, B., Lin, F., Ma, W. Y., & Zhang, H. J. (2001). A novel region-based image retrieval method using relevance feedback. In *ACM Workshops on Multimedia*. Multimedia Information Retrieval.

Kim, K. I., Jung, K., & Kim, J. H. (2003). Texture-based approach for text detection in images using support vector machines and continuously adaptive mean shift algorithm. [PAMI]. *IEEE Transactions on Pattern Analysis and Machine Intelligence*, *25*(12), 1631–1639. doi:10.1109/TPAMI.2003.1251157

Li, L., Huang, W., Gu, I. Y. H., & Tian, Q. (2003). Foreground object detection from videos containing complex background. In *Proceedings of the ACM Intl. Conference on Multimedia (ACM MM)*.

Lienhart, R., & Wernicke, A. (2002). Localizing and segmenting text in images and videos. *IEEE Transactions on Circuits and Systems for Video Technology*, *4*(12), 256–268. doi:10.1109/76.999203

Steinfeld, A., & Green, P. (1998). Driver responses to navigation information on full-windshield, head-up displays. *International Journal of Vehicle Design*, *19*(2), 135–149.

Streeter, L. A., & Vitello, D. (1986). A profile of drivers' map-reading abilities. *Human Factors*, *28*(2), 223–239.

Tom, A., & Denis, M. (2003). Referring to landmark or street information in route directions: What difference does it make? *COSIT 2003 (. LNCS*, *2825*, 362–374.

Torralba, A., Murphy, K. P., Freeman, W. T., & Rubin, M. (2003). Context-based vision system for place and object recognition. In *Proceedings of the IEEE Intl. Conference on Computer Vision (ICCV)*.

Vitabile, S., Gentile, A., & Sorbello, F. (2002). A neural network based automatic road signs recognizer. *In Proceedings of the International Joint Conference on Neural Networks*, *3*, 2315–2320.

Wang, J. Z., Li, J., & Wiederhold, G. (2001). SIMPLIcity: Semantics-sensitive integrated matching for picture libraries. [PAMI]. *IEEE Transactions on Pattern Analysis and Machine Intelligence*, *23*(9), 947–963. doi:10.1109/34.955109

Wierwille, W. W., Antin, J. F., Dingus, T. A., & Hulse, M. C. (1988). Visual attentional demand of an in-car navigation display system. In *Proceedings of the conference Vision in Vehicles* (pp. 307-316).

Winn, J., & Shotton, J. (2006). The layout consistent random field for recognizing and segmenting partially occluded objects. In *Proceedings of the IEEE Conference on Computer Vision and Pattern Recognition* (CVPR).

Wu, W., Blaicher, F., Yang, J., Seder, T., & Cui, D. (2009). A prototype of landmark-based car navigation using a full-windshield head-up display system. In *ACM Intl. Conference on Multimedia - Workshop on Ambient Media Computing*.

Wu, W., Chen, D., & Yang, J. (2005). Integrating co-training and recognition for text detection. In *Proceedings of the IEEE Intl. Conference on Multimedia & Expo (ICME)*.

Wu, W., Chen, X., & Yang, J. (2004). Incremental detection of text on road signs from video with application to a driving assistant system. In *Proceedings of the ACM Intl. Conference on Multimedia*.

Wu, W., & Yang, J. (2006). SmartLabel: An object labeling tool using iterated harmonic energy minimization. In *Proceedings of the ACM Intl. Conference on Multimedia*.

Wu, W., & Yang, J. (2008). Object fingerprints for content analysis with applications to street landmark localization. In *Proceedings of the ACM Intl. Conference on Multimedia*.

Wu, W., Yang, J., & Zhang, J. (2006). A multimedia system for route sharing and video-based navigation. In *Proceedings of the IEEE Intl. Conference on Multimedia & Expo (ICME)*.

KEY TERMS AND DEFINITIONS

Landmark: External reference points (objects) that are easily observable from a distance.

Landmark-Based Vehicle Navigation: Utilizing landmarks within vehicle navigation directions.

Road Sign: Signs erected at the side of roads to provide information to road users.

Semi-Supervised Learning: A class of machine learning techniques that make use of both labeled and unlabeled data for training - typically a small amount of labeled data with a large amount of unlabeled data.

SmartLabel and SmartLabel-2: Two semi-supervised learning-based image labeling tools proposed by Wen Wu and Jie Yang (2006, 2009).

Vehicle Navigation: The process of planning, recording, and controlling the movement of a vehicle from one place to another.

Vertical Plane Property: The property of most road signs in the world that they are vertical planes to the ground.

Chapter 2
Spontaneous Facial Expression Analysis and Synthesis for Interactive Facial Animation

Yongmian Zhang
Rensselaer Polytechnic Institute, USA

Jixu Chen
Rensselaer Polytechnic Institute, USA

Yan Tong
GE Global Research, USA

Qiang Ji
Rensselaer Polytechnic Institute, USA

ABSTRACT

This chapter describes a probabilistic framework for faithful reproduction of spontaneous facial expressions on a synthetic face model in a real time interactive application. The framework consists of a coupled Bayesian network (BN) to unify the facial expression analysis and synthesis into one coherent structure. At the analysis end, we cast the facial action coding system (FACS) into a dynamic Bayesian network (DBN) to capture relationships between facial expressions and the facial motions as well as their uncertainties and dynamics. The observations fed into the DBN facial expression model are measurements of facial action units (AUs) generated by an AU model. Also implemented by a DBN, the AU model captures the rigid head movements and nonrigid facial muscular movements of a spontaneous facial expression. At the synthesizer, a static BN reconstructs the Facial Animation Parameters (FAPs) and their intensity through the top-down inference according to the current state of facial expression and pose information output by the analysis end. The two BNs are connected statically through a data stream link. The novelty of using the coupled BN brings about several benefits. First, a facial expression is inferred through both spatial and temporal inference so that the perceptual quality of animation is less affected by the misdetection of facial features. Second, more realistic looking facial expressions can be reproduced by modeling the dynamics of human expressions in facial expression analysis. Third, very low bitrate (9 bytes per frame) in data transmission can be achieved.

DOI: 10.4018/978-1-60960-024-2.ch002

INTRODUCTION

Facial expressions provide various types of messages for human communications. Facial expression synthesis is clearly of interest for many multimedia applications such as human-computer interaction, entertainment, virtual agents, interactive gaming, computer based learning, video teleconferences, and animation. To interactively synthesize the facial expressions of a live person, we need an automated facial expression analysis system, which can recognize the spontaneous facial expressions, by explicitly modeling their temporal behavior so that the various stages of the development of a human emotion can be interpreted by machine. However, extending the existing methods to spontaneous facial behavior analysis and synthesis is a non-trivial problem due to the following challenges.

1. Thousands of distinct nonrigid facial muscular movements related to facial actions have been observed so far (Scherer, 1982), and most of them differ subtly in a few facial features.
2. Compared to the highly controlled conditions of posed facial expressions, spontaneous facial expressions often co-occur with natural head movement when people communicate with others.
3. Unlike the posed facial expressions, most of the spontaneous facial expressions are activated without significant facial appearance changes. In addition, the spontaneous facial expression often has a slower onset phase and a slower offset phase compared to the posed facial expression. (Cohn, 2004)
4. The spontaneous facial expression may have multiple facial expressions often occurring sequentially without always following a neutral-expression-neutral temporal pattern (Pantic, 2006) as for the posed facial expressions.

Since the MPEG-4 visual standard (MPEG4, 1998) will have a crucial role in forthcoming multimedia applications, the facial expression synthesis has gained much interest within the MPEG-4 framework. The MPEG-4 visual standard specifies a set of facial definition parameters (FDPs) and facial animation parameters (FAPs). The FAPs are used to characterize the movements of facial features defined over jaw, lips, eyes, mouth, nose, cheek, which are adequate to define the measurement of muscular actions relevant to AUs. Moreover, the FAPs can be placed on any synthetic facial model in a consistent manner with little influence by the inter-personal variations. For animating a person in a remote end, the FDPs are normally transmitted once per session and then followed by a stream of compressed FAPs. The animation of a virtual face is achieved by first transmitting the coded FAPs and then re-synthesizing on the client-side. To accommodate very low bandwidth constraint, the FAPs must be compressed. Despite significant progress, the current techniques in facial expression synthesis face several issues that still need to be resolved.

1. Although the discrete cosine transform (DCT) technique can achieve a high FAP compression, the DCT involves a large coding delay (temporal latency) that makes it unsuitable for real time interactive applications. The principal component analysis (PCA) is able to achieve a high FAP compression for intraframe coding, however, it compromises the reconstruction accuracy.
2. An automated video analyzer may often mis-detect some facial features. Consequently, this may create animation artifacts on the facial model, which affects the perceptual quality of facial animation.
3. The intensity of facial expressions reveals the emotional evolution. It is difficult for machine to extract the subtle variation of facial features. Consequently, a dynamic

behavior of human expressions is difficult to be animated. However, as indicated by physiologists, the temporal course information is necessary for lifelike facial animation (Allman, 1992).

Current technologies are still unable to synthesize human expressions in a realistic and efficient manner and with crucial emotional contents, in particular for spontaneous facial expressions. This work is to introduce an alternative approach to address the above issues by using a coupled Bayesian network (BN) to unify the facial expression analysis and synthesis into one coherent structure. The proposed approach allows real time faithful visual reproduction of spontaneous human expressions on a synthetic face model.

To address the issues in automated facial analysis, we cast the FACS (Ekman, 1978) into a dynamic Bayesian network (DBN) to account for the uncertainties of the observations and to model the dynamics of facial expressions. The observations fed into the DBN facial expression model are AUs. However, due to the low intensity, nonadditive effect, and individual difference of spontaneous facial action, it is not accurate and reliable to recognize AUs through measuring some local aspects of facial motion. Hence, understanding spontaneous facial action requires not only improving facial motion measurements, but more importantly, exploiting the spatiotemporal interactions among facial motions because it is these interactions that produce a synchronized, smooth, symmetrical, and consistent facial display. By explicitly modeling and using these inherent relationships, we can improve AU recognition performance by compensating erroneous or misdetected facial features.

To address the issues in the facial expression synthesis, we use a coupled Bayesian network that allows unifying the facial expression analysis and synthesis into one coherent structure to perform consistent reasoning and FAP reconstruction. Therefore, the temporal course of a facial

expression can be animated to achieve a lifelike animation. In addition, by taking advantage of Bayesian inference in handling missing data, the robust reconstruction of the facial expression is possible even in the absence of some FAPs. With a coupled Bayesian network, data communication between the analysis end and the synthesizer can be implemented as the dependency between the two BNs. Therefore, facial expressions are reproduced at the synthesizer without recourse to streaming the FAPs. Instead, we transmit only 9 bytes of data per frame to the synthesizer (6 bytes for the state of the six facial expressions and 3 bytes for face pose).

BACKGROUND

Automatic facial expression recognition had an early start with static face images. There have been several attempts to recognize facial expressions over time from video sequences. Black and Yacoob (Black, 1997) used local parameterized flow models to identify facial expressions. An affine model and a planar model represent head motion, and a curvature model represents nonrigid facial motion. Essa and Pentland (Essa, 1997) used the invariance between the motion energy template learned from ideal 2D motion views and the motion energy of the observed image to classify the facial expressions. Oliver et al. (Oliver, 1997) applied Hidden Markov model (HMM) to recognize mouth-related expressions. The facial expression is identified by computing the maximum likelihood of the input sequence with respect to all HMMs which are trained for each expression. Tian and Kanade (Tian, 2001) used the two separate neural networks to recognize the upper face AUs and the lower face AUs. Recently, Zhang and Ji (Zhang, 2005) proposed to use dynamic Bayesian networks for modeling both spatial and dynamic relationships among facial expressions, and for recognizing the six basic facial expressions through a probabilistic inference. Tong, Liao and Ji (Tong, 2007) proposed a DBN model to systematically account for the relationships among different AUs and their temporal evolutions to improve AU recognition in spontaneous facial expressions under more realistic environment including illumination variation, face pose variation, and occlusion.

The MPEG-4 visual standard has motivated intensive research in facial feature extraction for facial animation (Malciu, 2000; Chou, 2001; Cootes, 2001; Ahlberg, 2002). Substantial efforts in facial expression analysis with MPEG-4 FAPs have been made recently (Cowie, 2001; Raouzaiou, 2002; Pardas, 2002). Among these works, either rule-based approach or HMMs are used. The rule-based approach lacks the expressive power to capture the temporal behaviors and dependencies among facial actions. The HMMs are able to model time series with uncertainty, but they cannot represent variables at different levels of abstraction and the dependencies among facial actions.

In the area of multimedia, researchers have shown great interest in lifelike animated agents with realistic behavior. Eisert and Girod (Eisert, 1998) applied facial expression synthesis to virtual conference, whereby the optical flow is used to capture the motion information to estimate 17 FAPs for controlling a virtual head. A similar approach is presented by Valente and Dougelay (Valente, 2000). In facial animation, Tao and Huang (Tao, 1998), Lavagetto and Pockaj (Lavagetto, 1999), Goto et al. (Goto, 1999), Raouzaiou et al. (Raouzaiou, 2002), and Kshirsagar et al. (Kshirsagar, 2001) proposed a mesh-independent free-form deformation model. The animation of synthetic face is controlled by FAPs. Each FAP defines the animation by specifying feature points and geometric transformation. A thorough overview of MPEG-4 visual standard as related to facial animation technology can be found in (Abrantes, 1999).

The FAP compression can be categorized as intraframe coding and interframe coding. In intraframe coding, one way to achieve data reduction is to send only a subset of active FAPs to a synthesizer. The MPEG-4 visual standard (MPEG4, 1998) proposed a FAP interpolation table (FIT) that only use a subset of FAPs to interpret the values of other FAPs based on a set of fixed interpolating rules. However, it is generally difficult to adapt such rules to all faces. Tao et al. (Tao, 1999) and Ahlberg and Li (Ahlberg, 1999) use the PCA technique. By performing a linear transformation, each FAP is transformed into a new subspace. Although this technique can achieve efficient FAP compression, the reconstruction accuracy is often compromised. Two interframe coding schemes, predictive coding (PC) and discrete cosine transform (DCT), are adopted in the MPEG-4 animation technology. In the PC scheme, the difference of FAPs between consecutive frames are encoded and transmitted. Because the differences of FAPs between neighboring frames are usually in smaller quantities, fewer bits are needed to represent these differences. If the FAP sampling rate is high (>10 Hz), the DCT technique may be used. By performing the DCT in each temporal segment, high compression efficiency can be achieved; but it introduces a coding delay.

SYSTEM OVERVIEW

Figure 1 gives a block diagram of the system components. We introduce each of these components briefly below. In subsequent sections, we describe each of them in more detail.

Video Analysis: Video analysis is to generate the measurements of facial motion and face pose. The 3D facial shape model and eye detection technique makes our facial feature detection and pose estimation robust under the head motion and non-rigid facial expression. The detected facial feature points are used to produce the measurements of face pose estimation and the observations of AU model.

Figure 1. A block diagram shows the modules and their relationships of our facial expression animation system. The channel here represents a very low bitrate communication link

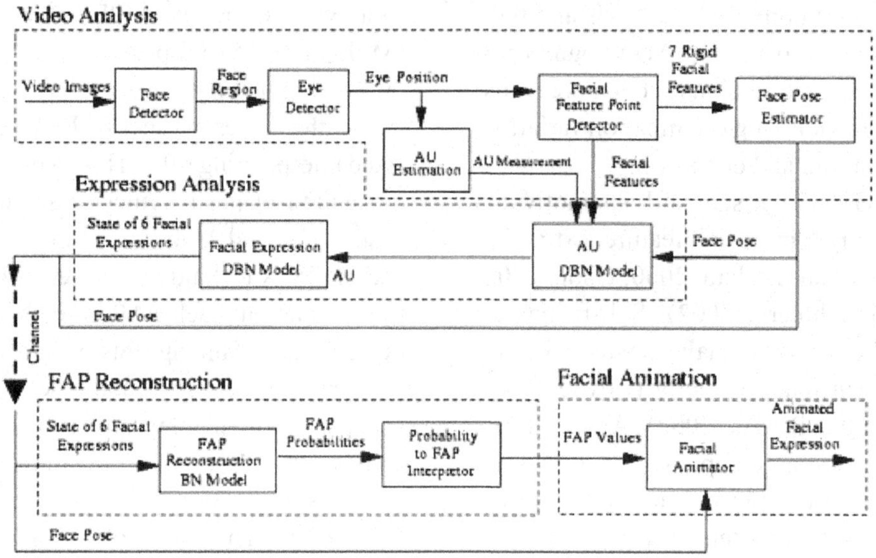

Expression Analysis: This module includes two dynamic Bayesian network models. One is for AU modeling and the other for facial expression modeling. The output from AU model is fed into facial expression model as the observations. The facial expression model integrates the current observed AUs and previous evidences to generate the probability distribution of the six facial expressions.

FAP Reconstruction: Using the probability distribution of six facial expressions produced by the analysis end, the facial expression synthesizer reconstructs the FAPs and their intensity through BN top-down inference to provide quantitative information about the facial expressions and their temporal behavior.

Facial Animation: This module uses the reconstructed FAPs to reproduce the facial expression on the facial model. The dynamics of facial expressions is characterized by the intensity development of the reconstructed FAPs. The BN model is interfaced with a 3D synthetic head model to perform facial animation.

VIDEO ANALYSIS

This section gives a brief introduction to our approach in facial feature extraction and face pose estimation. The details about this work may be found in (Tong, 2007).

Facial Feature Detection

Our technique in facial feature detection starts with face detection and then eye detection on the detected face. Both face and eye detector use AdaBoost classifier with non-linear discriminate features (Wang, 2007). Figure 2(a) shows an example of the detected eye positions. Given the detected eyes, the image is first normalized and the normalized image is then used to detect other facial features. Each feature point and its local neighborhood are represented by a set of multi-scale and multi-orientation Gabor wavelet coefficients. For each feature point, we compute a set of 18 complex Gabor wavelet coefficients. At each frame, the initial positions of each facial feature are located via Gabor wavelet matching in the approximate region constrained by the detected eyes. To achieve a robust and accurate detection, the initial feature positions are further refined by an active shape model (Cootes, 1995) that characterizes the spatial relationships between the detected facial features. The detected feature positions are shown in Figure 2(d).

Pose Estimation

The face pose may distort the motion measurements if they are computed directly from the 2D images, and such distortion needs to be eliminated in the facial expression analysis. Also, the face poses need be animated in order to generate a realistic facial expression on a synthetic face model.

To estimate the face pose, we use a 3D face shape model and 7 relatively rigid points including four eye corners and three points on the nose as control points to determine the 3D head movement, as shown in Figure 2(c). Given the detected image coordinates for the 7 points and their corresponding coordinates in the 3D model, the 3D face pose, i.e., the pan, tilt and roll angles as well as a scale factor can be estimated using

a robust pose estimation technique by assuming weak perspective projection. Figure 2(d) illustrates a facial tracking example, where the face normal perpendicular to the face plane is computed from the estimated.

AU Estimation

We first normalize the face image based on the detected eye positions. Given the normalized face image, we can extract the measurement for each AU based on Gabor wavelet-based feature representation and AdaBoost classification similar to the work in (Bartlett, 2006). However, since spontaneous facial action often produces subtle facial appearance changes, measuring each AU individually at low intensity levels is not accurate and reliable. In the following sections, we will describe how to incorporate these AU measurements into the facial action model to infer the state of AUs.

Figure 2. (a) An example of detected eyes (marked with white circles) by using the AdaBoost classifier. (b) A frontal face image; and (c) its 3D face shape model with 7 rigid facial features (marked with white dot) as control points. (d) Facial feature and pose tracking under facial expressions, where the face normal is represented by a dark line and the detected features are marked with white dots

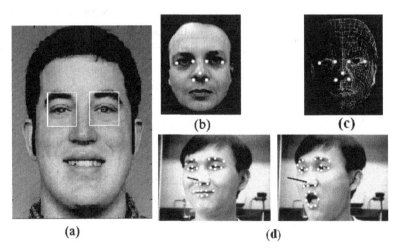

(a) (b) (c) (d)

FACIAL EXPRESSION ANALYSIS

In psychological studies (Ekman, 1978), it is generally believed that the six basic expressions, i.e., happiness, sadness, anger, disgust, fear and surprise, can be decomposed into culture and ethnics independent AUs. Our technique in understanding facial expressions starts with AU modeling and recognition. In this section, we first introduce a unified probabilistic AU model based on DBNs. Then, we give a brief description of our facial expression model for facial expression analysis.

Facial AU Modeling

Unlike a posed facial action, a spontaneous facial action consists of rigid motion, non-rigid motion and their spatiotemporal interactions. The rigid motion characterizes the 3D head pose, and the non-rigid motion characterizes the local facial muscular movement, which is described by AUs. The AUs we modeled here are listed in Figure 7 (a).

Overview of Facial Action Model

Our probabilistic AU model simultaneously models the rigid and non-rigid facial action, their relationships and their image measurements as shown in Figure 3.

In the view of facial action analysis from 2D images, the 2D facial shape (S_{2D}) is generated

Figure 3. A graphical model represents the causal relationships among the elements of facial actions

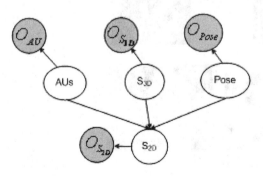

from three hidden causes: head pose (*Pose*), 3D facial shape (S_{3D}) and non-rigid facial motion (*AUs*). The directed links among the clear nodes in Figure 3 represent these causal relationships. The shaded nodes represent their measurements from the video analysis as described previously. Given this probabilistic model, facial action recognition is to find the optimal states of head pose and AUs by maximizing the posterior of pose and AUs given the measurements as follows:

$$Pose^{*}, \mathbf{AU}^{*} = \underset{Pose, \mathbf{AU}}{\arg\max}\, p(Pose, \mathbf{AU} \mid O_{pose}, O_{\mathbf{AU}}, O_{S_{3D}}, O_{S_{2D}})$$

where **AU** is the set of all AUs; $O_{pose}, O_{\mathbf{AU}}, O_{S_{3D}}, O_{S_{2D}}$ denote the measurements of head pose, AUs, 3D facial shape, and 2D facial shape, respectively. The details are given in the following sections.

Modeling Interactions between Rigid and Non-Rigid Facial Motions

The shape of a 3D face can be represented by a vector of 28 facial feature points, which are located around each facial component (e.g., mouth, eye, nose, and eyebrow), as shown in Figure 2(d). Given a 3D face, the deformation of a 2D facial shape reflects the action of both head pose and facial muscular movements. Specifically, head pose and facial muscular movements may affect different sets of facial feature points. As a result, the facial feature points are further divided into global feature points (Figure 2(b)), which are relatively invariant to facial muscular movements, and local feature points, which are affected by both head pose and facial muscular movements.

The 2D global shape denoted by S_g is the projection of the 3D global feature points on the image plane. Therefore, the 3D facial shape governs the shape of the 2D global shape, whereas the 3D head pose controls both the position and shape of S_g. This causal dependency can be represented by a directed link from head pose/3D facial shape to

S_g, as shown in Figure 4(a). Given S_g, the center of each 2D local facial component can be roughly estimated. For example, the center of eye can be determined, given the eye corners, which are parts of the global shape. Hence, this causal relationship can be represented by a directed link from S_g to each 2D local facial component shape (i.e., S_B, S_E, S_N, and S_M for eyebrow, eye, nose and mouth, respectively), as shown in Figure 4(a).

The non-rigid facial muscular movements produce significant changes in the 3D shape of the facial component. These 3D facial muscular movements can be systematically represented by AUs as defined in (Ekman, 1978). For example, activating AU27 (mouth stretch) will produce a widely open mouth; and activating AU4 (brow lower) makes the eyebrows lower and pushed together.

Besides rigid head movement, the 2D local facial component shape is controlled by the AUs since the 3D shape of each facial component is determined by the related AUs. We can model such causal relationship by directly connecting the related AUs to the corresponding facial component. For instance, AU1 (Inner brow raiser), AU2 (Outer brow raiser), and AU4 (Brow lowerer) control eyebrow movements, and can be connected to the eyebrow. However, directly connecting all related AUs to one facial component would result in too many AU combinations, most of which rarely occur in the daily life. Thus, only a set of common AUs or AU combinations are sufficient to control

the shape variations of the facial component. As a result, a set of intermediate nodes (i.e., "CB", "CE", and "CM" for eyebrow, eye, and mouth, respectively) are explicitly introduced to model the correlations among AUs and to reduce the number of AU combinations. For example, "CM" has 8 states, each of which represents a common AU or AU combination controlling mouth movement. Figure 4 (b) shows the modeling of the relationships between non-rigid facial motions (AUs) and the local facial component shapes.

Modeling Semantic and Dynamic Relationships among AUs

Tong et al (Tong, 2007) demonstrated that modeling the spatial and temporal dependencies among AUs is crucial for accurate AU recognition. There are two important spatial semantic relationships among the AUs: co-occurrence and mutually exclusive relationships. Additionally, AUs show strong temporal dependencies to represent different naturalistic facial behaviors. Generally speaking, there are two types of temporal dependencies among AUs: intra-dependency and inter-dependency. Intra-dependency characterizes the self-evolution of an AU, while inter-dependency captures temporal dependencies among different AUs, i.e., an AU will be activated following the activation of another AU. For example, in a spontaneous smile, AU6 (cheek raiser) is activated in an average of 0.4 second after the activation of AU12

Figure 4. Modeling the interactions between rigid and non-rigid facial motions. (a) Relationships between rigid facial motions and 2D shape. (b) Relationships between non-rigid facial motions and 2D shape

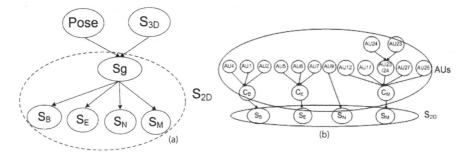

(lip corner puller) (Schmidt, 2001); after both actions reach their apexes simultaneously, AU6 is relaxed before AU12 is released. Furthermore, due to the variability among individuals and different contexts, the dynamic relationships among AUs are stochastic. Therefore, systematically capturing the spatiotemporal dependencies among AUs and incorporating them into facial action recognition process is especially important for spontaneous facial behaviors.

We use a DBN to model the spatiotemporal relationships among AUs. The structure and the parameters of this DBN are learned using the learning algorithms in (Tong, 2010). The learned DBN model is shown in Figure 5.

The Complete Facial Action Model

Based on the detailed models in Figure 4 and 5, we can extend and enrich the causal relationships in Figure 3 to a complete DBN model as shown in Figure 6. Specifically, the interactions among nonrigid facial muscular movements are

characterized by the static links among AUs in the same time slice and the temporal links among AUs across consecutive time slices. The 2D shape deformations of the facial components are controlled by both the head pose through the 2D global shape and the related AUs through the intermediate nodes. In this way, the interactions between head pose (rigid motion) and the AUs (nonrigid motions) are indirectly modeled through their relationships with 2D global and local facial component shapes. Finally, the facial motion measurements are systematically incorporated into the model through the shaded nodes. This model therefore characterizes the spatiotemporal dependencies between rigid and nonrigid facial motions and accounts for the uncertainties in facial motion measurements.

Facial Action Inference

The measurements for AUs, 2D Shape, and head pose in Figure 6 are obtained through the video analysis as described previously. The observed

Figure 5. The learned DBN for AU modeling. The self-arrow at each AU node indicates the intra-dependency. The dashed arrow across two time slices indicates the pair-wise inter-dependency between different AUs

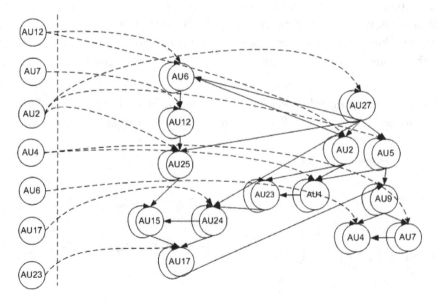

Figure 6. The complete DBN for spontaneous facial action understanding. The shaded nodes are the observations for the connected hidden node. The self-arrow at the hidden node represents its temporal evolution from time t − 1 to t. The link from AU$_i$ at time t − 1 to AU$_j$ (j≠i) at time t represents the dynamic inter-dependency between different AUs

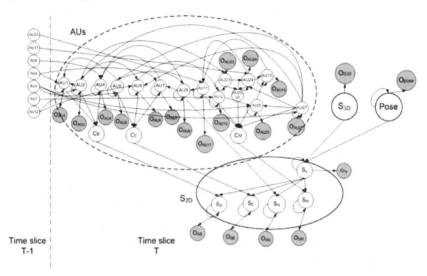

3D shape is obtained by personalizing a trained generic 3D shape model. Specifically, the x and y- coordinates of the generic 3D shape model are adapted to current subject based on the detected positions of facial feature points on the frontal view face. Due to the unknown depth information, the z-coordinates of the generic 3D shape model are scaled based on the size of the same frontal view face to approximate the face depth for each individual. Once the measurement nodes are observed, we can infer the states of pose and AUs by maximizing their joint probability given the measurements.

Facial Expression Modeling

Figure 7(a) gives the AUs which are relevant to the six facial expressions. AUs can be grouped as primary AUs and auxiliary AUs given a specific facial expression. By the primary AUs, we mean those AUs or AU combinations that can be clearly classified as or are strongly pertinent to one of the six facial expressions without ambiguity, while an auxiliary AU is the one that can only be combined

with the primary AUs to provide supplementary cue in distinguishing facial expressions. Figure 7(b) gives a summary of the primary and auxiliary AUs corresponding to a specific facial expression.

Figure 7 (a) and (b) deterministically characterize the relationships between facial expressions and the AUs. To account for the uncertainty in the feature measurement and the dependency among the AUs, we cast the deterministic relationships into a probabilistic framework using a BN, which provides us a mathematically rigorous foundation for consistent, coherent and efficient reasoning. Our BN model of facial expressions has three different abstractions: expression layer, facial AU layer and observation layer as shown in Figure 8. The values of observational variables are the output of AU model we discussed previously. The intensity of facial expressions is measured by its probability. The conditional probabilities required to parameterize the BN model are trained from subjects in the Cohn-Kanade database (Kanade, 2000).

To capture the temporal evolution of a facial expression, the static BN model is further ex-

Figure 7. (a) A list of AUs related to the six facial expressions; (b) the primary AUs and auxiliary AUs corresponding to a specific facial expression

AU	Description	AU	Description
AU1	Inner brow raiser	AU2	Outbrow raiser
AU4	Brow lower	AU5	Upper lid raiser
AU6	Cheek raiser	AU7	Lid tighter
AU12	Lip corner puller	AU9	Nose Wrinkler
AU17	Chin raiser	AU15	Lip Corner Depressor
AU24	Lip pressor	AU23	Lip tighter
AU27	Mouth stretch	AU25	Lip apart

(a)

Expressions	Primary AUs	Auxiliary AUs
Happiness	6, 12	25, 27, 15
Sadness	1, 15, 17	4, 7, 25, 27
Disgust	9	17, 25, 27
Surprise	5, 25, 27, 1+ 2	
Anger	2, 4, 7, 23, 24	17, 25, 27, 15
Fear	1+5, 5+7	4, 5, 7, 25, 27

(b)

tended to the DBN. Our DBN model of facial expressions is made up of interconnected time slices of a static BN and the dependency between two neighboring time slices are based on first order Hidden Markov Model (HMM). The DBNs enable to correlate and associate the continual arriving evidences through temporal dependencies to perform reasoning over time.

FACIAL EXPRESSION SYNTHESIS AND ANIMATION

The FAPs are a set of parameters defined in the MPEG-4 visual standard (MPEG4, 1998) for the animation of synthetic face models. There are 68 FAPs including 2 high-level FAPs used for visual phoneme and expression, and 66 low-level FAPs used to characterize the facial feature movements over jaw, lips, eyes, mouth, nose, cheek, ears, etc. We select 27 FAPs to characterize the six facial expressions, and they are measured by facial animation parameter units (FAPUs) that permit us to place the FAPs on any facial model in a consistent way. The FAPUs are defined with respect to the distances between key facial features in their neutral state such as eyes (ES0), eyelids (IRDS0), eye-nose (ENS0), mouth-nose (MNS0), and lip corners (MW0), as shown in Figure 9. The association between FAPs and AUs can be seen in (Zhang, 2008).

At the synthesizer, we use a static BN with FAPs added as the bottom layer of the network, as shown in Figure 10. The two BNs are coupled to unify the facial expression analysis and synthesis into one coherent structure so that the vi-

Figure 8. The BN model of the six facial expressions. HAP, ANG, SAD, DIS, FEA and SUP denote Happiness, Anger, Sadness, Disgust, Fear and Surprise, respectively. HP, AP, SDP, DP, FP and SPP denote the primary AUs and HA, AA, SDA, DA and FA denote the auxiliary AUs for the six expressions

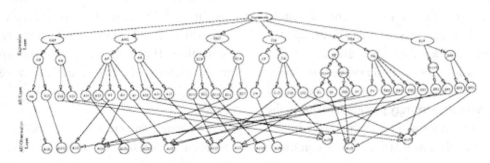

Figure 9. A neutral face model and feature points used to define facial animation parameter units (FAPUs). The feature points are numerated with MPEG-4 visual standard. Only the feature points marked with solid dots are tracked

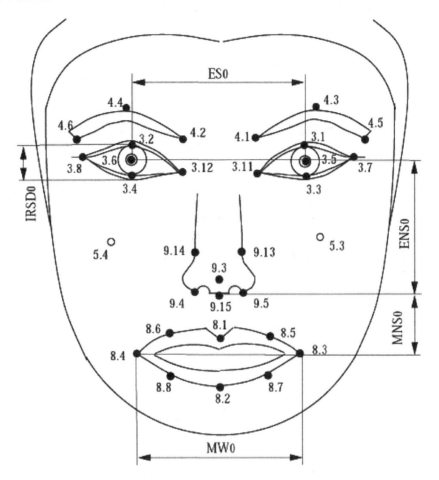

sual evidences observed at the analysis end can be propagated directly to the synthesizer for re-constructing the FAPs and their intensity. Figure 11 depicts the dependency graph of such a coupled BN. The BN model at the synthesis end is coupled with the DBN at analysis end by the conditional dependency link between their top nodes Θ and Θ' such that the probability distribution of the six facial expressions at analysis end passes to the BN at the synthesizer. Such a link acts like a data stream communication channel in the actual applications. At the analysis end, the hypothesis node Θ completely summarizes the continual arriving visual evidences by integrating them through Bayesian inference. At the synthesizer,

the FAPs are inferred given Θ' through the top-down predictive inference. Therefore, we only need to transmit the state of Θ (the probability distribution of the six facial expressions) and the values of the pose angles to the synthesizer for reconstructing the FAPs, which achieves very low bit-rate (9 bytes per frame). Since the dynamics of facial expression is modeled by a trained DBN model, the temporal course of facial expression can be also animated, which is necessary for those desiring lifelike facial animation.

Bayesian networks can also be used for causal reasoning to specify how causes generate effects. Specifically, through a top-down infer-ence, we can compute the probabilities of a set

Figure 10. The BN model of facial expression for reconstructing the FAPs through top-down inference

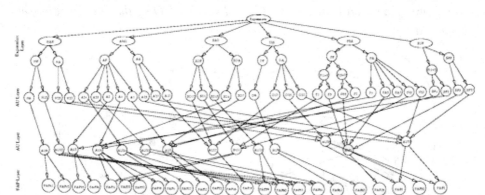

Figure 11. The dependency graph shows a coupled Bayesian network. The facial expression analysis end uses a dynamic Bayesian network and the facial expression synthesizer uses a static Bayesian network (see Figure 8 and 9 for the detail of the two models). The nodes Θ, Θ', S, and X denote the hypothesis nodes, a set of hidden nodes and a set of FAPs (or AUs), respectively

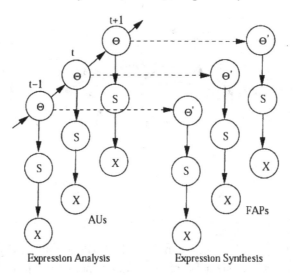

of FAPs given Θ' which equals to Θ if the data is completely transmitted to the synthesizer from the analyzer. At the synthesis end, the FAPs which are most relevant to the current state of facial expressions have a higher probability than others. In other words, the FAP intensity at the synthesis end evolves according to the continual arriving AU observations at the analysis end.

Now we need to translate FAP intensity to FAP amplitude in order to drive the facial animation. Let f be FAP amplitude and f_{max} be its maximal

amplitude. Let p_n, p_c and p_a be the intensity of this FAP when a facial expression is in neutral state, current expression and apex state, respectively. Then, the amplitude of a FAP can be simply computed by $f=f_{max}(p_c-p_n)/(p_a-p_n)$, where f_{max} can be predetermined based on the facial expression database, and f_n, f_a can be obtained from the BN model. Since f_{max} is measured by FAPU, it allows us to map f on any facial model. Given FAP amplitudes and face poses, facial expressions can be reproduced on a synthetic facial model.

EXPERIMENT RESULTS

In this section, we first evaluate the effectiveness of our approach in facial AU recognition. We then show how the dynamic nature of facial expression is modeled and how facial expressions are synthesized onto a facial model.

Facial Expression Analysis

AU Recognition

Figure 12 illustrates an exemplar of AU recognition results on an image sequence, where the subject performs smiling and simultaneously changes his head pose. It can be found that even the face pose changes significantly; the 2D facial shape and AUs still can be estimated accurately by the proposed model.

Expression Recognition

Figure 13 illustrates an output showing a temporal course of the six facial expressions. The images are sampled in every 7 frames from a 700-frame sequence containing the six facial expressions and the neutral state. Although, as we can see from the figure, there are a certain number of recognition errors due to feature detection errors, a visual inspection indicates that the expression evolvement

is well reconstructed. A quantitative performance evaluation of recovering the dynamics of facial expressions with DBN can be found in (Zhang, 2005). The ability of our approach to correlate and reason about facial temporal information over time allows capturing the dynamic behavior of facial expressions in an image sequence such that various stages of the emotional development can be analyzed by machine. This enables us to reproduce a realistic behavior of facial expressions at the synthesis end.

Facial Expression Synthesis and Animation

Figure 14(a) gives the probability distribution generated by our facial expression analysis model showing the subject's expression starts with the neutral, then gradually reaches the apex and finally releases; Figure 14(b) depicts the reconstructed FAPs and their intensities given the facial expression in Figure 14(a). A visual inspection shows that the reconstructed FAP intensities agree with the development of this facial expression. Based on the reconstructed FAPs, we reproduce the temporal course of this expression and the face pose on a facial model as shown in Figure 15 and the details of performance evaluation can be found in (Zhang, 2008).

Figure 12. A resulting example of AU recognition from an image sequence. The estimated 2D facial shape is displayed on the face; the numbers at the bottom represent the recognized AUs; the estimated pose is displayed at the upper-left corner (Left, Frontal and Right)

Figure 13. The emotional intensity (probability distribution over the six facial expressions) is plotted over time

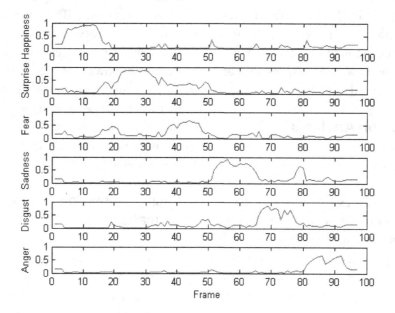

Figure 14. (a) The probability distribution generated by the facial expression analysis model showing the subject's expression starts with the neutral, then gradually reaches the apex and finally releases. (b) The intensity of FAPs reconstructed from Facial expression in (a). Only the FAPs associated with the facial expression are marked with line symbols

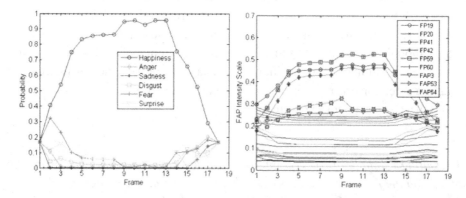

CONCLUSION

In light of MPEG-4 visual standard, a significant amount of research has been directed to MPEG-4 FAP compression and facial animation, but less emphasis has been placed on synthesizing the temporal course of facial expressions. However, the physiological studies show that temporal course information is necessary for those desiring lifelike facial animation. This is the key motivation of this work. This chapter explores the use of a coupled Bayesian network to unify the facial expression analysis and synthesis into one coherent structure to synthesize dynamic facial expressions. There are the following benefits with this approach:

Figure 15. A resulting example showing the temporal course of a facial expression is animated for the given facial expression in Figure 13(a)

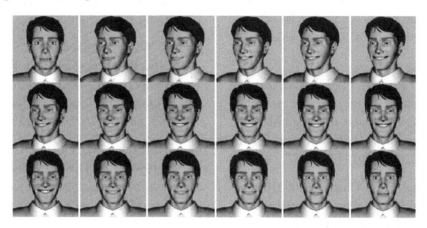

- To synthesize six pose-variable facial expressions, our approach needs to transmit only 9 bytes of data per frame to the synthesizer. It is particularly suitable for the interactive facial animation applications, where very low bitrate transmission is required.
- The temporal course of facial expressions can be synthesized by means of modeling dynamics of facial expressions. This is particularly important for the lifelike facial animation.
- Unlike streaming directly the FAPs to the synthesizer, the perceptual quality of animation in our approach is less affected by the misdetection of facial features.

However, our approach is incapable of reproducing the individuality of a facial expression because the semantic relations between the FAPs and the facial expressions are parameterized by facial muscular actions from psychological studies, and such relations are person-independent. Still for many animation applications, the individuality is not important as the facial model itself is synthetic. Finally, the evaluation of our method is mostly qualitative through visual inspection. A more quantitative performance evaluation of our

method is needed. This requires first to establish a quantitative measure to quantify the quality of the reconstructed FAPs and their temporal development. We will pursue this study in the future.

REFERENCES

Abrantes, G. A., & Pereira, F. (1999). MPEG-4 Facial Animation Technology: Survey, Implementation, and Results. *IEEE Transactions on Circuits and Systems for Video Technology, 9*(2), 290–305. doi:10.1109/76.752096

Ahlberg, J. (2002). An active model for facial feature tracking. *EURASIP Journal on Applied Signal Processing,* (6): 566–571. doi:10.1155/S1110865702203078

Ahlberg, J., & Li, H. (1999). Representation and Compressing Facial Animation Parameters Using Facial Action Basis Functions. *IEEE Transactions on Circuits and Systems for Video Technology, 9*(3), 405–410. doi:10.1109/76.754768

Allman, J., Cacioppo, J. T., Davidson, R. J., Ekman, P., Friesen, W. V., Lzard, C. E., & Phillips, M. (1992). *NSF Report - Facial Expression Understanding.* San Francisco: University of California.

Bartlett, M. S., Littlewort, G. C., Frank, M. G., Lainscsek, C., Fasel, I. R., & Movellan, J. R. (2006). Automatic recognition of facial actions in spontaneous expressions. *J. Multimedia, 1*(6), 22–35.

Black, M. J., & Yacoob, Y. (1997). Recognizing Facial Expression in Image Sequences Using Local Parameterized Models of Image Motion. *International Journal of Computer Vision, 25*(1), 23–48. doi:10.1023/A:1007977618277

Chou, J., & Chang, Y. Y. & Chen, Y. (2001) Facial feature point tracking and expression analysis for virtual conferencing systems, *IEEE International Conference on Multimedia and Expo*, 24–27.

Cohn, J. F., & Schmidt, K. (2004). The Timing of Facial Motion in Posed and Spontaneous Smiles. *International Journal of Wavelets, Multresolution, and Information Processing, 2*, 1–12. doi:10.1142/S021969130400041X

Cootes, T., Edwards, G., & Taylor, C. (2001). Active appearance models. *IEEE Transactions on Pattern Analysis and Machine Intelligence, 23*(6), 681–685. doi:10.1109/34.927467

Cootes, T. F., Taylor, C. J., Cooper, D. H., & Graham, J. (1995). Active shape models—their training and application. *Computer Vision and Image Understanding, 61*(1), 38–59. doi:10.1006/cviu.1995.1004

Cowie, R. (2001). D-Cowie, E., Tsapatsoulis, N., Votsis, G., Kollias, S., Fellenz, W., & Taylor, J. G. (2001) Emotion recognition in human computer interaction. *IEEE Signal Processing Magazine*, (1): 33–80.

Eister, S., & Girod, B. (1998). Analyzing Facial Expressions for Virtual Conferencing. *IEEE Computer Graphics and Applications, 18*(5), 70–79. doi:10.1109/38.708562

Ekman, P., & Friesen, V. (1978). *Facial Action Coding System (FACS): Manual*. Palo Alto, CA: Consulting Psychologists Press.

Essa, I. A., & Pentland, A. P. (1997). Coding, Analysis, Interpretation, and Recognition of Facial Expressions. *IEEE Transactions on Pattern Analysis and Machine Intelligence, 19*(7), 757–763. doi:10.1109/34.598232

Goto, T., Escher, M., Zanardi, C., & Thalmann, N. M. (1999). LAFTER: Lips and face real time tracker with facial expression recognition. In *Proceedings of IEEE Conf. on Erographics Workshop Computer Animation and Simulation*.

Kanade, T., Cohn, J., & Tian, Y. (2000). Comprehensive Database for Facial Expression Analysis. In *Proceedings of International Conference on Automatic Face and Gesture Recognition*.

Kshirsagar, S., Molet, T., & Magnenat-Thalmann, N. (2001). Principal Components of Expressive Speech Animation. In *Proceedings of International Conference on Computer Graphics*.

Lavagetto, & F., Pockaj, R. (1999). The facial Animation Engine: Toward a High-Level Interface for the Design of MPEG-4 Compliant Animation Faces. *IEEE Transaction on Circuits and Systems for Video Technology, 9*(2), 277-289.

Malciu, M. & F. Preteux, F. (2000) Tracking facial features in video sequences using a deformable model-based approach, *Proceding of SPIE International Society of Optical Engineering*, 4121, 51–62.

MPEG4, & the Moving Picture Experts Group. (1998). *ISO/IEC 14496-MPEG-4 International Standard*, Tokyo.

Oliver, N., Pentland, A., & Berard, F. (1997). LAFTER: Lips and face real time tracker with facial expression recognition. In *Proc. of IEEE Conf. on Computer Vision and Pattern Recognition*.

Pantic, M., & Patras, I. (2006). Dynamics of Facial Expression: Recognition of Facial Actions and Their Temporal Segments from Face Profile Image Sequences. *IEEE Transactions on Systems, Man, and Cybernetics. Part B, Cybernetics, 36*(2), 433–449. doi:10.1109/TSMCB.2005.859075

Pardas, M., & Bonafonte, A., A. (2002). Facial animation parameters extraction and expression recognition using hidden markov models. *Signal Processing Image Communication, 17,* 675–688. doi:10.1016/S0923-5965(02)00078-4

Raouzaiou, A., Tsapatsoulis, N., Karpouzis, K., & Kollias, S. (2002). Parameterized Facial Expression Synthesis Based on MPEG-4. *EURASIP Journal on Applied Signal Processing,* (10): 1021–1038. doi:10.1155/S1110865702206149

Scherer, K., & Ekman, P. (1982). *Handbook of Methods in Nonverbal Behavior Research.* Cambridge Univ. Press.

Schmidt, K., & Cohn, J. (2001). Dynamics of facial expression: Normative characteristics and individual differences. *IEEE Int'l Conf. on Multimedia and Expo* (pp. 728–731).

Tao, H., Chen, H. H., Wu, W., & Huang, T. (1999). Compression of MPEG-4 Facial Animation Parameters for Transmission of Talking Heads. *IEEE Transactions on Circuits and Systems for Video Technology, 9*(2), 264–276. doi:10.1109/76.752094

Tao, H. & Huang, T. S. (1998) Facial animation and video tracking, *Workshop Modeling and Motion Capture Techniques for Virtual Environments,* 242–253, 1998.

Tian, Y., Kanade, T., & Cohn, J. F. (2001). Recognizing Action Units for Facial Expression Analysis. *IEEE Transactions on Pattern Analysis and Machine Intelligence, 23*(2), 97–115. doi:10.1109/34.908962

Tong, Y., Chen, J., & Ji, Q. (2010). A Unified Probabilistic Framework for Spontaneous Facial Action Modeling and Understanding. *IEEE Transactions on Pattern Analysis and Machine Intelligence, 32*(2), 258–274. doi:10.1109/TPAMI.2008.293

Tong, Y., Liao, W., & Ji, Q. (2007). Facial Action Unit Recognition by Exploiting Their Dynamic and Semantic Relationships. *IEEE Transactions on Pattern Analysis and Machine Intelligence, 29*(10), 1683–1699. doi:10.1109/TPAMI.2007.1094

Tong, Y., Wang, Y., Zhu, Z., & Ji, Q. (2007). Robust Facial Feature Tracking under Varying Face Pose and Facial Expression. *Pattern Recognition Journal, 40*(11), 3195–3208. doi:10.1016/j.patcog.2007.02.021

Valente, S., & Dougelay, J.-L. (2000). Face Tracking and Realistic Animations for Telecommunicate Clones. *IEEE MultiMedia, 7*(1), 34–43. doi:10.1109/93.839309

Wang, P., & Ji, Q. (2007). Multi-View Face and Eye Detection Using Discriminant Features. *Computer Vision and Image Understanding, 105*(2), 99–111. doi:10.1016/j.cviu.2006.08.008

Zhang, Y., & Ji, Q. (2005). Active and Dynamic Information Fusion for Facial Expression Understanding from Image Sequence. *IEEE Transactions on Pattern Analysis and Machine Intelligence, 27*(5), 699–714. doi:10.1109/TPAMI.2005.93

Zhang, Y., Ji, Q., Zhu, Z., & Yi, B. (2008). Dynamic Facial Expression Analysis and Synthesis with MPEG-4 Facial Animation Parameters. *IEEE Transactions on Circuits and Systems for Video Technology, 18*(10), 1383–1396. doi:10.1109/TCSVT.2008.928887

Chapter 3
A Modular Framework for Vision–Based Human Computer Interaction

Giancarlo Iannizzotto
University of Messina, Italy

Francesco La Rosa
University of Messina, Italy

ABSTRACT

This chapter introduces the VirtualBoard framework for building vision-based Perceptual User Interfaces (PUI). While most vision-based Human Computer Interaction applications developed over the last decade focus on the technological aspects related to image processing and computer vision, our main effort is towards ease and naturalness of use, integrability and compatibility with the existing systems and software, portability and efficiency. VirtualBoard is based on a modular architecture which allows the implementation of several classes of gestural and vision-based human-computer interaction approaches: it is extensible and portable and requires relatively few computational resources, thus also helping in reducing energy consumption and hardware costs. Particular attention is also devoted to robustness to environment conditions (such as illumination and noise level). We believe that current technologies can easily support vision-based PUIs and that PUIs are strongly needed by modern applications. With the exception of gaming industry, where vision-based PUIs are already being intensively studied and in some cases exploited, more effort is needed to merge the knowledge from HCI and computer vision communities to develop realistic and industrially appealing products. This work is intended as a stimulus in this direction.

INTRODUCTION

Computer technology is rapidly saturating all aspects of our life and producing an epochal shift towards digital information management and communication; nevertheless, in many offices, laboratories and meeting rooms, when it's time for creativity, people prefer to share their ideas and present their theses by using traditional media – felt pens on whiteboards, paper sheets and even combinations of everyday-life objects like ashtrays or pencil holders, mugs, and so on,

DOI: 10.4018/978-1-60960-024-2.ch003

usually placed and moved on a desk to represent a graph or a schema and its evolution.

This choice is so common due to the prompt availability of such objects and to the naturalness and immediacy of interaction provided by physical objects. Unfortunately, the information generated during such interactions cannot be easily recorded in digital format and can easily be lost.

Perceptual User Interfaces (PUIs) adopt alternate sensing modalities to replace or complement traditional mouse and keyboard input: specialized devices are exploited to provide the user with alternate interaction channels, such as speech, hand gesture, eye-gaze tracking and even face or full-body gesture. Often those devices resemble everyday-life objects, both in shape and in usage. The computer can therefore be hidden, disappearing in the environment (Want, Borriello, Pering, & Farkas, 2002).

A number of points should be considered when building a new PUI:

- When collaborative use of the media is required, it might be necessary to discriminate between two or more users interacting with each medium. Moreover, when a user moves from one medium to another (for example, moves from a desk to another or to a whiteboard), the user interface of the first medium must be able to understand that the user has gone and the user interface of the second medium must be able to detect that the user is approaching.

- Even when invisibility is not strictly required, the user interface should be as much unobtrusive as possible. Wires, gloves, heavy or large head-mounted displays, user-perceivable sensors which make the user feel clumsy must be avoided. As mentioned by Norman (Norman, 1998), the aim of the user interface of a computerized system should be to let the user concentrate on the task at hand and forget about the tool being exploited (the computer).

- Initiating an interaction session (Engagement) with an user interface should be natural and fast. For example, initiating a user interaction with a mouse only requires the user to pick the device, while initiating an interaction with a sensorized glove requires the user to wear the glove (which takes more time and effort). Closing a session (Disengagement) should be equally easy and straightforward.

- The user-perceived predictability of the system is a main issue: a lack of predictability in responding to user input rapidly leads to user frustration. A good level of predictability requires adequate feedback, as the user needs to know whether the interface correctly decoded a command, if the command was executed or there was any error, and even if the command was received at all. For the system to be predictable, every user input must always have a corresponding response: if an user input does not have a matching response, i.e. it is an unexpected input, then adequate improvement in the sensing accuracy and, eventually, error detection and correction or recovery processes must be triggered (Bellotti et al., 2002). There must not be undefined states and each response must be perceived as coherent and intuitive by the user.

- The novel user interface should also support, at an initial stage (i.e. until the alternative interaction paradigm is fully accepted by software application developers), the legacy WIMP (Windows-Icons-Menu Pointers) applications, without forcing the user to revert to mouse and keyboard.

- For a user interface to be of interest for the industry, it should be reasonably cheap. This does not mean that we can expect an innovative perceptual interface to be as cheap as a mouse or a keyboard, of course (at least, at the initial phases of its commercial launch). But it should not cost more than (or as much as) the computer it connects to.

A very great deal of studies have been developed in the area of Human-Computer Interaction (HCI), addressing all the possible issues from usability to power consumption. Also, in the last decade the use of real-time computer vision for developing wireless, unobtrusive, relatively cheap PUIs has gained more and more interest and has led to popular industrial products.

In this chapter we introduce the VirtualBoard vision-based PUI framework, designed to allow single- and multi- user gesture-based human computer interaction. The user can interact with the computer by using bare hands gesture, full-body motion and by scribbling with a stylus on any plane surface, such as a wall or a desk. By exploiting infrared illumination and beaconing, the framework is able to operate in almost all kinds of lighting conditions. The adopted software technology is compatible with all WIMP (Windows-Icons-Menu Pointers) applications under both Microsoft Windows and Linux with X-Windows.

In the next sections we briefly review the literature related to PUIs with particular regard to vision-based approaches. After giving the necessary motivation for the work, the Virtual-Board framework is described and significant experimental results are reported. Final remarks conclude the chapter.

BACKGROUND

Perceptual User Interfaces can be roughly classified in two categories: *personal* and *active space*.

Personal PUIs are inherently single-user and are designed to allow a single user to interact with a computer, and can be either *immersive* or *non-immersive*. Immersive PUIs assume that the user is provided with some kind of head-mounted

display and are therefore based on a *subjective* perception of the user behavior (gesture, speech, eye gaze) from the user's point of view. Non-immersive personal PUIs do not require any special display: they allow – for example – an user to interact with a desktop pc or with a pc connected to a wall projector (during a presentation). Several "smart home" applications have also been developed, which allow the user to interact with a disappearing computer-based system able to control common electronic devices such as a television, a stereo or a video camera and even turn on and off the light.

Active space PUIs support *collaborative* applications and are designed to be multi-user, i.e. to support multiple users at the same time (Prante, Streitz, & Tandler, 2004). Multi-user interaction may be supported also by a combination of two or more coupled systems, each one featuring its own personal PUI. For example, the NTII virtual reality-based communication system (Towles et al., 2002) is composed by two or more individual stations, located in different places, connected by Internet and each one having its own personal PUI. Collaborative applications, on the other hand, require *the same PUI* to be able to support more than one user at the same time.

Three classes of technologies can be exploited for PUIs:

- *User-obtrusive* technologies are based on sensorized devices such as gloves, jackets (Wexelblat, 1999), finger- or wrist- mounted sensors (Rekimoto, 2001), which the user must wear before initiating an interaction session. Even though recent technologies enable wireless communication between those devices and the computer, thus freeing the user from being hampered by wiring, this approach still produces a strong feeling of clumsiness.
- *Environment-obtrusive* technologies rely on a series of sensors or sensorized devices connected (usually physically attached) to

common life objects, such as touch-sensitive flat panels attached to the usual whiteboard or on a desk, which communicate to the computer the needed information about the user interaction. For example, it is possible to transform a common whiteboard into a PUI by attaching a special touch-sensitive film on its surface: when the user draws something on the whiteboard, the draw is traced and this information is passed to the computer, which perceives the draw on the whiteboard as a "mouse draw" or as a special key associated to some command (currently commercially available). Recent works suggest to extend this approach to realize a "smart home" able to constantly monitor the behavior and health status of impaired or older people by receiving data from sensors attached to each one of the objects commonly and daily used (Ross, 2004).

- *Unobtrusive* technologies exploit some wireless, transparent, (ideally invisible) sensing approach to detect, trace and recognize user interaction.

An almost straightforward approach to unobtrusive interaction is using computer vision to process and analyze the video stream produced by a video camera pointing at the user. Vision-based PUIs are based on an intuition which dates back to the early '80s: human gesture tracking and recognition (either hand-gesture, face expression, or full-body gesture) have been studied very intensely and actively in the computer vision community since the first seminal works (Blake, Curwen, & Zisserman, 1994; Wren, Azarbayejani, Darrell, & Pentland, 1997).

Computer vision has been exploited to produce several "demonstration systems", as they are named in (Ye, Corso, Burschka, & Hager, 2003), for each of the classes listed above. An approach which resulted quite popular in the past years consists of placing visual markers or, in

poor lightning conditions, Infrared Light Emitting Diodes (IR-LED) on the user's hand and/or fingertips (or body, as well) to simplify vision-based detection and tracking (Piekarski, Avery, Thomas, & Malbezin, 2004; Dorfmuller & Wirth, 1998). Apart from its visual impact, which can reveal to be impressive and useful for scenic purposes (see, for example, the movie Minority Report, by S. Spielberg, 2002), the idea of having tiny lights shining from the fingertips cannot be considered particularly appealing for everyday use – and changing to IR lights does not completely solve the problem. We can thus classify this applications as user-obtrusive.

Another approach consists of bare-hand detection by applying color-based segmentation techniques (Starner & Pentland, 1995; Bretzner, Laptev, Lindeberg, Lenman, & Sundblad, 2001): regions presenting a color distribution similar to that of human skin are extracted from a scene. The main problem here is how to identify those regions of the image, given that skin color is not uniform, varying according to the user and the lighting conditions in the working environment. As a solution, some methods require the user to wear a fabric glove of a known, uniform color, while other methods such as the MIT "6th sense" project (Mistry, Maes, & Chang, 2009; Baldauf & Fröhlich, 2009) require color markers to be attached to the fingers of the user.

A number of studies rely on background image subtraction techniques to detect the user's hands: the background is removed by processing successive frames in the video sequence (Hardenberg & Bérard, 2001) or, in the case of stereo vision (Jojic, Brumitt, Meyers, Harris, & Huang, 2000; Grzeszczuk, Bradski, Chu, & Bouguet, 2000), by processing frames acquired by several video cameras from different points of view (Gavrila & Davis, 1995; Regh & Kanade, 1994). Once the background has been removed, the hand is searched in the pre-processed frame, for example by using a color-based segmentation technique. Here again, however, there are limitations, especially when the scene has a complex background and/or a variable illumination.

Several arm-tracking methods are based on the use of a simplified geometrical model of the arm (Di Bernardo, Goncalves, Perona, & Ursella, 1995). Other approaches combine depth from stereo and color information (Elmezian, Al-Hamadi, Appenrodt, & Michaelis, 2008) to obtain a more accurate tracking. Most of the solution based on 3D, however, are affected by problems of self-occlusion and involve very high computational costs, while those based on color classification require an adequate ambient illumination.

Other approaches based on fingertip detection, rely on the analysis of the shape of the objects identified in a previous segmentation phase, (Hardenberg & Bérard, 2001; Maggioni & Kammerer, 1998). These fingertip detection techniques make great use of a priori geometrical knowledge of the object being sought, for example the length and breadth of two or more fingers.

Many other methods have been proposed in addition to those mentioned above. A good review of hand tracking methods and hand gesture analysis algorithms can be found in (Erol, Bebis, Nicolescu, Boyle, & Twombly, 2007; Pavlovic, Sharma, & Huang, 1997) and (Wu & Huang, 1999; Crowley, Coutaz, & Bérard, 2000) describe a series of separated vision-based applications aimed at proofing the validity of several computer vision approaches to human tracking. They also significantly state that "in the near future we expect machine perception to converge with ubiquitous computing and communication".

Although, in our knowledge, the technologies to be exploited are not clearly stated and described, Microsoft claims it will exploit bare-hand and full-body visual tracking for user interaction purpose in its Project Natal (http://www.xbox.com/en-US/live/projectnatal/).

All the approaches just described (but the case requiring fabric gloves) are unobtrusive: only a laptop pc and one or two video cameras are required, eventually supported by an infrared illumination lamp. In some cases the algorithms are extremely optimised and can execute on a wearable computer (Gandy, Starner, Auxier, & Ashbrook, 2000; Iannizzotto, Villari, & Vita, 2001).

Several applications have been developed, which are able to visually track a graspable, physical object (Starner, Leibe, Singletary, & Jarrell, 2000; Leibe et al., 2000; La Rosa, Costanzo, & Iannizzotto, 2003). Some very popular commercial gaming devices launched in the last years, such as the Nintendo Wii (http://www.nintendo.com/wii), adopt the same approach.

None of the works cited above described a whole framework aimed at integrating the vision-based applications with the underlying system: in most cases ad-hoc applications were developed for demonstrating the presented approaches. Moreover, in most cases issues like computational complexity, cost and portability are neglected.

THE VIRTUALBOARD FRAMEWORK

The Framework Architecture

The VirtualBoard framework is a modular, simple and portable vision-based PUI environment. As shown in Figure 1, it is composed by several sensing modules, which can be functions called by a main application or stand-alone lightweight programs, and a central application – the dispatcher – which receives the information about the events related to user interaction and trigger the corresponding behaviour in the host operating system (OS).

The communication between each sensing module and the dispatcher is obtained by means of messages sent through *sockets*. The communication between the dispatcher and the host OS is obtained by pushing suitable messages in the event queue (for example, a MouseMoveTo(x,y) message). This approach allows each sensing module to reside in a different node respect to the dispatcher, for example in an embedded system

Figure 1. Structure of the VirtualBoard framework

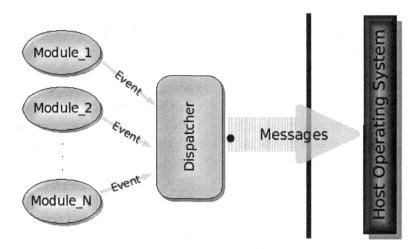

connected through Wireless Ethernet or Bluetooth with the controlled computer, and – at the same time – guarantees a considerable degree of portability. The sensing modules are completely autonomous: all the processing related to a module is entirely performed in the module itself, therefore the communication does not require high bandwidth and does not affect the processing performances. On the other hand, communication does affect the overall PUI effectiveness and reliability: since the feedback for the user is produced by the host OS, if the communication between a sensing module and the dispatcher is not timely, the user will experiment a lag in the OS reaction and the perceived quality of service will degrade. This raises some real-time communication and scheduling issues which are currently being assessed and dealt with.

It is also worth noticing that, since the communication between a module and the host OS is mediated by the dispatcher, the dispatcher itself acts as a scheduler from the point of view of the host OS. Indeed, depending on the selected process communication approach, the dispatcher can actually act as a real scheduler for the sensing modules.

The VirtualBoard framework has been ported to Linux and Windows: only ANSI C, gcc-compliant code has been used in order to keep the platform as portable as possible. The code was mainly developed from scratch to avoid compatibility issues but in some cases the OpenCV Open Source Computer Vision Library (Bradski & Kaehler, 2008) has been exploited.

In this chapter, four different sensing modules are described: the VirtualBoard module, the VisualPen module, the VisualGlove module and the VisualGrasp module.

The VirtualBoard Sensing Module

The VirtualBoard sensing module[1] is a vision system for real-time recognition of the hand gestures of a user interacting with the wall projection of a common PC desktop (either in Windows or Linux OS). Its applicability goes far beyond simply driving a Powerpoint presentation and – according to the classification stated above – it belongs to the active space class. The supported interaction covers all the functions of a mouse-driven interface, such as:

- Controlling the cursor position (*mouse move*);
- Selecting an icon (*click*);

- Dragging an icon and releasing it in a different position (*drag'n'drop*);
- Opening a folder or an application by double clicking it (*double click*);
- Opening the "right-button" menu (*right-click*).

Each function is controlled by performing very natural gestures like pointing at an icon with the forefinger (Figure 1a, "*mouse move*"), extending both the forefinger and the thumb (Figure 1b, "*click*"), or extending three fingers ("*right-click*").

Due to the peculiar architecture of the framework, exploiting message queues to communicate directly with the host OS, VirtualBoard can drive all standard WIMP applications and thanks to its immediate usability (only natural and simple gestures are required) is candidate for straightforward adoption without any need for user training. Figure 2 shows some examples of interaction with a Microsoft Windows Desktop, a Web browser and a screenshot of a user drawing free-hand with Microsoft Paint.

The hardware setup of VirtualBoard is extremely simple (see the schema in Figure 3a). The user stands in front of a wall-projected display and uses hand gesture to interact with the system. An off-the-shelf, commercial video camera able to work with IR light is used to acquire in real-time the scene and a common led-based infrared illuminator for video surveillance is used to obtain a suitably illuminated video. The ambient illumi-

nation can vary in a very wide range, from darkness to full light. A very cheap, off-the-shelf, IR filter taken from the proximity sensor of an automatic gate opener is used to partially reduce the light captured by the camera lenses. The whole system, comprising the wall projector, can be easily mounted and moved in a few seconds (see Figure 3b) and does not disturb the user operation with cables or other obtrusive devices.

A different setup can be adopted for VirtualBoard, named VirtualDesk: in this case the user interacts with a projection on a desk surface instead of a wall projection and perceives this setup as a virtual desktop. Apart from the different setup, in which the projector and the camera point to the desktop, nothing changes and the applicability is exactly the same as in VirtualBoard.

While interacting with VirtualBoard, the use of a keyboard is definitely not needed. A simple gesture calls the hand-writing window and the drawn text is automatically input in the underlying application (see Figure 5a). If the user is not familiar with stylus-based writing interfaces, a virtual keyboard can be invoked and one-finger typing is available (see Figure 5b).

The algorithm on which the VirtualBoard is based and the implementation issues related to its realization are better described in previous works (Costanzo, La Rosa, & Iannizzotto, 2003; Iannizzotto, Costanzo, La Rosa, & Lanzafame, 2005; Iannizzotto, La Rosa, Costanzo, & Lanzafame, 2005) and are beyond the scope of this paper,

Figure 2. VirtualBoard gestures

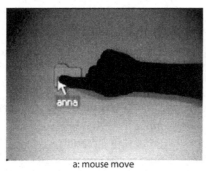 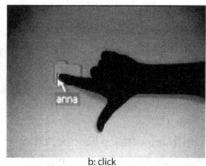

a: mouse move   b: click

Figure 3. User interaction with VirtualBoard

a: Desktop interaction

b: Internet Explorer interaction

c: Microsoft Paint interaction

Figure 4. VirtualBoard setup

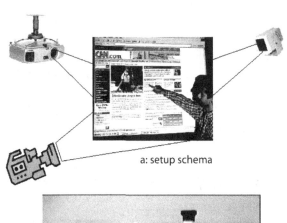

a: setup schema

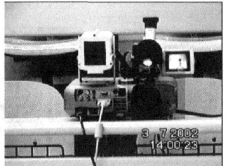

b: projector, camera and illuminator

Figure 5. VirtualDesk typing

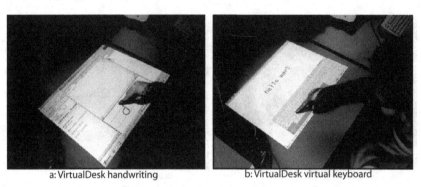

a: VirtualDesk handwriting | b: VirtualDesk virtual keyboard

aimed at reviewing the overall architecture and its applications. We therefore only illustrate here the main characteristics of the algorithm (see Figure 6a), referring to the VirtualBoard setup.

The scene is segmented by exploiting a modified background subtraction algorithm. After segmentation, a set of "foreground objects" is returned, each of them being a candidate representation of the user standing in the scene. A hierarchical approach is adopted to examine the shape of each of the candidate objects in order to assign each of them a probability of being the user: the final decision is then driven by either a tracking system, which takes in account the information deriving from the previous frames (the *past history*) or, if no past information is available (the user was not present in the previous frames), by relying on the last step of the hierarchical approach, i.e. the finger detection step.

Finger detection is performed by exploiting physiological information about shape and size proportions among hands, fingers and the full body of human beings (see Figure 6b).

Only after detecting – in the analysed object– the presence of a hand and of one or more extended fingers, the hierarchical process is reversed and the probabilities are updated and suitably increased in order to produce a final probability. Those objects which produce a probability higher than a threshold are marked as a representation of the user and thus tracked in the next instants. This threshold is not fixed but statistically learned from experimental observations at start-up and automatically adapted at run time.

After detecting the hand of the user, gesture identification is performed by taking in account the past history and reconstructing in time the gesture. Since the recognized gestures are extremely

Figure 6. VirtualBoard algorithm schematics

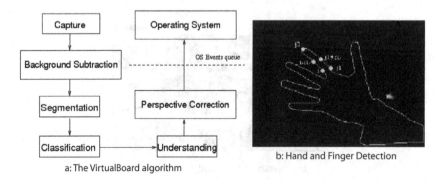

a: The VirtualBoard algorithm | b: Hand and Finger Detection

simple, we do not exploit complex approaches like Hidden Markov Models (HMM) which have proven to be very effective in complex gesture recognition (Starner et al., 1995; Elmezian et al., 2008). Instead, we only rely on a simple state model featuring a few states, thus largely reducing the overall computational complexity of the module.

A number of experimental tests have been made in different working conditions, mainly during lecturing and presenting demos and papers. Table 1 shows the results of one of those tests, in which the main interaction gestures were performed 100 times. The last column on the right of this table reports the number of times that the performed gesture was correctly identified but the spatial positioning was not exact, i.e. the location of the finger at the end of the gesture was not correctly tracked.

Long drag'n'drop gestures span almost the whole screen; short drag'n'drop gestures are shorter, in the range between the size of an icon on the desktop and about half the size of the screen.

As expected, long drag and drops show a lower hit percentage, as the probability that noise affects the tracking is higher when the gesture takes a longer time. To cope with this lower hit percentage, the user can reduce the speed of the gesture: this allows the system to gather more samples per second and increase the accuracy of the tracking.

VirtualBoard was designed to work also as a multiuser PUI: while multitouch PUIs are able to merely recognize that more than one input is being received (for example, two finger gestures

Table 1. Experimental results for VirtualBoard gesturing

Command	# Tests	Hits	Near-hits
Click	100	96	//
Double Click	100	93	//
Short Drag'n'drop	100	96	98
Long Drag'n'Drop	100	89	97

at the same time), during a multiuser interaction session each action is attributed to a specific user, thus allowing different users to perform, for example, *competitive* tasks. VirtualBoard is able to discriminate between two or more users in the scene by tracking each one of them and by relying on a rough texture analysis algorithm. Basically, a grey level histogram representation of each user is maintained and updated in time and this representation is exploited to disambiguate among different users in the scene. As a result, two or more users can interact with the same application, each user being identified as distinct from the others. Of course, since common WIMP applications do not support multiple users interfaces, to test this system we had to write our own applications (see Figure 7).

The VisualPen Sensing Module

VisualPen exploits a video camera to track in real time an IR-emitting stylus, that can be used to completely replace both mouse and keyboard and is able to work with all lightning conditions and on any surface (e.g. walls, writing desks, projection screens, a notepad,...). The pen is tracked while being moved on the surface and a button on it emulates the mouse button. It features two different IR LEDs, which are continuously tracked by the system through the video camera: one is exploited to trace the position of the pen, the other is connected to the button and its status is revealed and translated into mouse-button events.

The necessary feedback to the user can be provided by a video projector, a traditional CRT or LCD screen, or by more innovative devices such as head-mounted displays. The computational complexity of the exploited algorithms is so low that the system can be easily ported to a PDA without heavily affecting its power consumption.

VisualPen lets the user control the position of the cursor by moving the pen over the screen, generate the "click" and "double-click" events and therefore select and drag an icon, open a folder,

Figure 7. Multi-users VirtualBoard

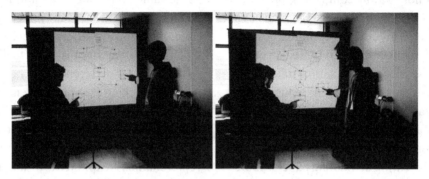

draw and write. It is a system as simple to use as the mouse, but at the same time it is much more natural.

We all have experienced the difficulty to draw using the mouse and the trouble to use keyboard and mouse in order to write a text. VisualPen puts together the naturalness of use of an everyday-life object, a pen, with the versatility of a personal computer and the possibility of a distance interaction and collaborative work (it is indeed possible to have more than a VisualPen working at the same time).

Again, we do not deal with algorithmic and implementation details here, as they are quite simple and were already described in a previous work (Costanzo, La Rosa, & Iannizzotto, 2003). We instead prefer to highlight some peculiarities of the chosen approach.

First of all is the simplicity and low computational complexity of the algorithms: the next implementation step will indeed be the porting of the module in hardware, by exploiting embedded and FPGA technologies.

The second point is accuracy: as we have shown with a wide testing campaign, the error related to this approach can be bounded within 0 and 1.5 pixels, which can be considered very accurate unless considering sub-pixel accuracy approaches, which tend to be computationally intensive.

The third point is robustness: after utilising it as a tool for lecturing and demonstrating it in

a number of different occasions, letting people test it freely and try to confuse it with malicious usage, we can assess that VisualPen is robust and fool proof.

Fourth point is ease of use. In all cases, the users never needed any previous training nor they needed any hints: they just picked up the pen and started using it and experimenting plotting, drawing, clicking and scribbling. Only the availability of a handwriting recognition software was advertised, in order to let people know that they did not need a keyboard to type-in the text.

Again, the setup can be either for on-wall or on-desk usage and compatibility is guaranteed by the VirtualBoard framework. Figure 8 shows user interaction with Microsoft Paint and text keying by using handwriting recognition software.

Recent studies (Forlines, Vogel, & Balakrishnan, 2006) have shown that when interacting with very large projection displays, direct interaction (i.e. when a displacement in the interaction space is mapped 1:1 to the display space) is outperformed by indirect interaction (i.e. when a displacement ΔX in the interaction space is mapped to a displacement $K*\Delta X$ with $K > 1$). We therefore introduced in VisualPen both interaction modalities: the user can switch from one modality to the other by clicking on an icon in the taskbar. Figure 9 shows an example of interaction with a large projection display with indirect interaction.

Figure 8. Using VisualPen

a: Interacting with Microsoft Paint   b: Handwriting recognition

c: Painting on a wall

Figure 9.Interacting with a large projection display in indirect mode

The VisualGlove Sensing Module

The computing power required by most gesture recognition applications to recognize, in real-time, human gestures, by no means corresponds to that of the CPUs currently available on most handheld or *wearable* devices, and the expressive potential of human gestures is by far greater than that provided by a pointer device. We therefore decided to investigate a vision system which, making use of very stable and low-complexity algorithms, could track the hand (actually, just two fingers) of the user, in order to recognize some simple and intuitive gestures thus substituting the mouse in almost any user operation: the Graylevel VisualGlove sensing module.

Once again, we focused on a grey-level approach as it can be used in a wider range of environmental situations including almost total darkness, thanks to the use of a small, economical infrared illuminator and an ordinary infrared filter like those used in television remote control receivers.

The typical usage situation should feature the user wearing a lightweight, head-mounted, see-through display, and a small *wearable* camera (for example, in the shape of a pendant (Gandy, Starner, Auxier, & Ashbrook, 2000)), in order to image approximately the same scene seen by the user. The user would then interact with the system in an extremely intuitive way, by gesturing with only two fingers. Unlike most systems described in the literature, indeed, Graylevel VisualGlove does not track the operator's whole hand: it only tracks the fingertips of the thumb and index finger positioned (see Figure 10.a) as if the user wants to clasp something between the two fingers. To be able to accurately track CPU usage, resource drain and timing issues, during the experimental tests we used a webcam connected to a low-end PC (Pentium II processor, 300MHz, 64MB RAM) to test the system (a more detailed description of the testbed is given in (Iannizzotto et al., 2001)). In Figure 10.a the webcam is clearly visible over the monitor. Given the generality of our approach, the results shown here can be directly applied to a wearable computer.

The two fingertips are tracked separately but in a co-operative fashion, in such a way that the information from one of the two trackers combines with and validates the information from the other tracker. This considerably reduces the effect of background noise, increasing the probability of correct detection and thus the reliability of the system. Contact between the two fingertips corresponds to the "mouse_click" event, which can easily become "double_click" via fast repetition of the joining of the fingertips. By keeping the index finger and thumb joined and moving the hand at the same time it is quite simple to simulate a "drag" or "draw" operation, while by separating the two Fingers after a "drag" operation it is possible to simulate "drag-and-drop". The user gestures detected by the VisualGlove sensing module are then communicated (thanks to the VirtualBoard framework) to the dispatcher and there translated into messages and inserted into the mouse event queue of the host OS, thus simulating the presence of an ordinary mouse.

Current graphical interfaces cannot be considered as the most suitable for free-hand interaction. They are designed to be driven by a mouse and thus the "sensitive spots" in icons and windows are often so small that it is hard to *pick* them with two fingers. This is especially true for menu items and window scrolling controls (the "sliders") and when interacting with small projections in the VirtualDesk setup.

To overcome this issues, we developed GestureTools, a set of widgets which can be "attached" to windows and icons to visually and functionally enhance them. The main feature of GestureTools widgets is that they are graspable: when attached to an element of a WIMP interface they enhance the ability of the user to interact with it, both by changing the graphical characteristics of its sensitive spots and by enriching its functionalities. Figure 10.b shows a screenshot of a Internet

Explorer window, enhanced by three Graspable GestureTools: two handles and a menu button. On the bottom-right is visible the GestureTools Toolbar. GestureTools have been developed by using standard, Open Source OpenGL libraries and are available for both Microsoft Windows and for Linux. The installation of GestureTools is extremely simple and follows the same rules as any other user-space application.

The VisualGrasp Sensing Module

Approaches like GestureTools can effectively help the user in interacting with legacy WIMP-based interfaces. Nevertheless, those interfaces cannot be considered as suited for hand gesture-based interaction. Better metaphors must be devised instead of the usual icons and widgets, and more usable command interfaces must be adopted. We developed the VisualGrasp module to experiment and explore this field. VisualGrasp is designed to allow single-user, gesture-based, human-computer interaction by using bare hands gestures on a plane surface. The use of machine vision technology and a user-centred approach exploiting large, realistic icons and widgets resembling real-life objects and supporting straightforward interaction produce a highly usable PUI, allowing a natural and relaxing experience for long and demanding tasks.

In order to demonstrate the characteristics of the VisualGrasp approach, we built two different applications, sharing the same basic technology and aimed at very peculiar tasks.

Figure 10. The VisualGlove setup (a) and an example of a GestureTools-enabled window

a: VisualGlove

b: GestureTools

The first application is a *video-surveillance control panel*: instead of using legacy interaction devices, such as joystick or mouse, the user can exploit natural gestures on a plane surface on which the control panel is projected, and interact with visual knobs, handles, and other "virtually graspable" objects (see Figure 11). The graphical interface is split in two sections, the first for rendering (and interacting with) a map of the region being surveilled and the second to show the video streams from the cameras we are looking by. The user can select an IP camera (Pan Tilt Zoom Focus PTZF) of interest, from a pool shown in the map, and control its pose and zoom, and can also switch between a set of different maps and browse the areas under control. The second section of the panel is devoted to display the video streams acquired by the IP cameras distributed in the regions under control.

With the second application (see Figure 12) we propose the use of vision-based PUIs to enable advanced interaction with Virtual Reality environments as an Augmented Reality application. We introduce an Augmented Reality-based communication and collaboration environment, able to provide multi-client and multimedia communication, which exploits a multimodal user interaction

paradigm based on hand gesture and other perceptual user interfaces.

The system is composed of a number of remote identical units connected to each other by a network infrastructure. The users, by means of these units, collaborate in design tasks. Each unit is composed by an entry-level PC, a video projector, a low intensity infrared spotlight, a network interface, a headset, two videograbbers and two videocameras. Two video streams are thus acquired: one containing the user's face, the other the user's hand gestures and the panel.

The graphical interface of each unit is split in two sections (see Figure 12), the first for rendering (and interacting with) 3D graphical objects and the second to show the remote collaborators we are working with.

The users can manage and "manipulate" the objects as they would do in a real environment with a real object. Once a new project has been created, all the remote users share a common virtual workspace in which different users can integrate or modify some components. A semaphore based policy has been implemented to manage the access and the interaction within the workspace.

For details about the implementation of the hand gesture recognition we refer to previously

Figure 11. The video surveillance control panel. The user can interact with the panel through natural hand gestures, such as rotating a virtual knob or grasping a virtual tool and dragging it to a specific position

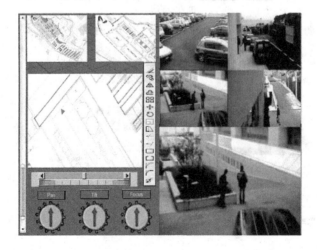

Figure 12. A collaborative interface. The users can manage and "manipulate" the virtual objects as they would do in a real environment with a real object. The videos in the floating windows show the remote collaborators we are working with

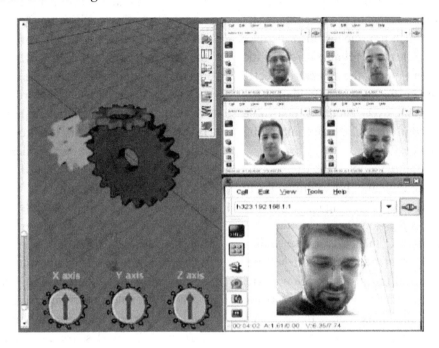

published works (Iannizzotto, Costanzo, La Rosa, & Lanzafame, 2005; Iannizzotto, La Rosa, Costanzo, & Lanzafame, 2005); as in the previous cases, our aim here is to show how such applications have been developed through a common framework which allows for high flexibility in terms of different user interaction patterns and wide applicability.

The usability of VisualGrasp was tested in several working conditions and with several sets of users (one of the tests involved 12 different users). The users were totally untrained and in most cases were mechanical engineering students. The reported experience was highly satisfying, even though in some cases the network lag was sensible.

Usability Issues

A widely accepted concept of HCI usability requires an ideal user interface to be reliable, user-predictable, self-explanatory (or at least highly

learnable and recallable), efficient and effective, and enjoyable, i.e., pleasant to use.

Reliability implies that the interface should be intrinsically as simple as possible, robust to noise and to other disturbing factors, self-calibrating and should correctly support changes in environment and setup.

User-perceived predictability regards how the system behaves in response to a user input in a given situation. The user naturally creates a model of the system he/she is interacting with: due to this model, the user expects a determined response from the system in each situation and to each set of inputs. Any deviation from this expected behavior induces in the user a certain level of frustration, proportional to the severity and frequency of the deviations.

User-perceived predictability is closely related to the ability of the interface to be self-explanatory, i.e., of not requiring any instructions or help to be used, or at least to be highly learnable and memorable. If an interface is highly learnable, i.e. it requires a very short learning time, and is highly memorable, i.e. when the user returns to the interface after a period of not using it, he/she can easily reestablish proficiency, then the user easily builds up a clear and reliable model of the system. With such a model, the user can correctly predict the behavior for the widest field of situations and user inputs, experiencing an enjoyable feeling of "full control" and actually improving performances and efficiency.

On the other hand, the interface can be self-explanatory but not reliable: for example, it can be very complex, so that building up a clear and simple model becomes too hard or too time expensive for the user. In this case the user builds a partial and simplified model, taking in account only some aspects of the system. Such a model will not be able to explain fully the behavior of the system in several situations, mainly those related to critical (and therefore less frequent) events. The confidence of the user will then decrease, the sense of frustration will increase, and the quality of the user experience will decrease accordingly.

The system can also behave unnaturally, even if it is generally easy to understand and to use: in this case the user tends to build an erroneous model, as he/she expects a natural behavior. When the unnatural behavior only shows up in response to some error or critical (therefore rare or not very frequent) event, the user is not able to correct the model. The consequences of such a situation closely match those described above.

In order to better model react to the dynamics of the user interaction, control theory has been widely adopted in literature (Blake et al., 1994). When this approach is fully exploited, the user is considered as being embedded in a closed-loop process control chain and his/her interaction with the interface and the underlying system is analyzed by means of well-known control theory mathematical instruments. While the appeal of such an approach is evident, it should be pointed out that the human user is far from being fully observable

and can reveal to be too complex to be modeled: therefore, embedding a human user in a closed-loop control chain model can be in some cases an unacceptable simplification. Other approaches only partially exploit the idea of modeling both the user and the interface, in order to analyze the interaction patterns in terms of expected, sensed and desired user actions (Benford et al., 2005).

While designing and developing the Virtual-Board framework, we tried to keep in mind and take into account all the issues described above. For each module, representing a different interaction paradigm and modality, we recruited a set of untrained users (mainly students) and observed their reactions while freely interacting with the interface. The objective was to assess the ability of the module to be self-explanatory and its degree of robustness and reliability. While a skilled user can heavily exploit a user interface for a long time without incurring in errors and therefore triggering bugs and critical issues, an inexperienced user typically incurs in severe bugs and critical patterns in a very short time. This happens because the experienced user unconsciously avoids those behavior patterns which can trigger erroneous (and therefore frustrating) system responses. In some cases, we set up public demonstration sessions (in one case during an international conference related to computer engineering topics but not to HCI issues) in which people from the public were invited to freely interact with our demo. We carefully recorded and annotated information from each demo session, and exploited the gathered knowledge to improve the modules.

A typical example of an issue, emerging from the tests performed "on the field" by inexperienced users, is the need for a natural, explicit and straightforward protocol for engagement and disengagement in an interaction session.

Let us consider the VirtualBoard sensing module: one of the experiments we prepared was used to let untrained users exploit the Virtual-Board to drive through gestures a MS PowerPoint presentation, introducing and illustrating some concept. When additional explanatory sketches were needed, the users were invited to use their fingers to draw on a MS Paint window, acting as a whiteboard (see Figure 3c).

The users often waved their hands and gestured while explaining some concepts to their audience: though being a straightforward and natural way of communicating, this behavior could become a source of severe impairment for our gesture recognition module, as hand gestures are also a mean to interact with the computer. Discriminating between gestures directed to the computer and gestures directed to the audience is a hard task for a software. Therefore, a better way to afford this problem is probably to give the user a way to initiate an interaction with the computer system (*engagement*), perform the interaction, and terminate the interaction (*disengagement*), in order to be free of gesturing to the human audience for the rest of the time. This engagement/disengagement protocol needs to be extremely simple, as it is supposed to be exploited very often during a presentation. Also, it must be natural, straightforward, and easy to be learned and performed. After a number of trials and tests, we realized that for most users it is very hard to remember to perform any kind of engagement/disengagement gestures (or, as some users defined them, rituals). They rather prefer the engagement/disengagement ritual in an implicit way: for example, if we look at the legacy mouse device, this protocol is:

- move the mouse, click the buttons (engagement and interaction);
- leave the mouse still (disengagement).

Clearly enough, there is no explicit protocol for session initiation/termination: the engagement is implicit in the interaction and disengagement is represented by the absence of interaction. We therefore choose to follow the same approach. We carefully devised a hand gesture detection algorithm, able to discriminate a predefined set of few gestures being performed right on the

projection surface (See Figure 2), while discarding those gestures being performed on different planes (for example, while gesturing at the audience). We also implemented a Kalman tracker in order to detect sensible changes in the user gestures and behavior, respect to the expected one. Finally, we studied a hierarchical full-body user detection algorithm (based on the same shape analysis technique described above, but applied to the whole user body), which ensures that the largest possible part of the whole user's body is detected and recognized, before trying to recognize the hand gesture.

All this complexity was introduced in order to obtain a very stable and robust gesture detection and tracking process. With this approach it is possible to reliably detect both the intention of the user to start an interaction session (when the user's hand approaches the projection surface while initiating a recognizable gesture) and the intention of closing a session (when the users does not perform a recognizable gesture for a given number of frames).

Now, what should the system do when the user initiates or terminates an interaction?

In our framework, when the interaction session is initiated, the cursor moves from its current position to the current detected (sensed) position of the user's hand (actually, forefinger fingertip for VirtualBoard, pen tip for VisualPen, and so on). The speed of the cursor while moving to this new position is intentionally set fast enough to avoid a sensation of sloppiness but slow enough to be seen while moving: this gives the user the feeling that the cursor is "coming to meet him/her", like a pet going toward the owner. Of course this speed can be varied.

When the user stops interacting, after a few frames the interaction session is terminated and the cursor remains in the last sensed (i.e. reliably detected) position. This gives the feeling that the cursor remains there where the user left it. When a new interaction is initiated, the cursor again moves from its position towards the user's hand.

The inactivity time threshold and the activity time threshold used, respectively, to detect session disengagement and engagement, were determined experimentally. VirtualBoard features a control widget which allows to easy setting those parameters (in analogy to the legacy mouse drivers, which allow the user to set the click speed and other parameters) but it was almost never used during our experiments, after the initial adjustments.

Similar approaches have been adopted for all the sensing modules: this produces a uniform "look and feel" to the framework and gives to the user the ability of creating a reliable and general behavior model, which in turn induces a good "full control" feeling.

FUTURE RESEARCH DIRECTIONS

Computer vision and image analysis technologies for human tracking and gesture recognition can be considered fully mature for entering HCI applications: recent and imminent commercial products (such as the cited Nintendo Wii and the Microsoft Natal Project) clearly demonstrate this fact.

Completely different is the state of the art from the point of view of the graphical user interfaces and – more in general – the user interfaces for most common operating systems and applications. As regards OS interfaces, the panorama is quite poor: even though both Microsoft and Apple claim since years that their products will soon fully exploit touch-based interfaces, at the time being touch interaction is merely supported at the hardware and device drivers level. Microsoft Surface technology seems not to find its way into Windows 7 and Apple OSX does not show anything similar to touch-based interaction. In the meanwhile, Linux is probably waiting to see if such interfaces will eventually come out in the market before spending open source resources on them, though being ready too for multitouch technology, at the hardware support level, through the cited MPX framework.

It seems that the cause preventing hand gesture interaction from being fully exploited is twofold: on one hand, there are probably not so many applications *really needing* gesture-based interaction; on the other hand, current *legacy* applications (much more than the operating systems) are designed so as to be near incompatible with touch and gesture interaction, and changing this would cost a lot of money. For this reason gesture based interaction is gaining momentum only in the gaming and mobile worlds, where novelty (in all regards) is a fundamental cause of success.

The situation pictured above is probably going to change soon with the introduction of devices such as Microsoft Natal and other home automation, highly pervasive, applications.

As regards future research issues in the area of computer vision applied to human-machine interaction, we suggest that improving stability and accuracy of *eye gaze direction tracking* and *user recognition* (either through face recognition or remote iris recognition) will probably become the next frontiers.

Eye gaze direction tracking allows to reveal and analyze the focus of interest of the user at a given instant and a long time, with a very wide range of applications from gaming to interaction with impaired users, from advertisement to commercial information gathering and so on. Virtual and enhanced reality would largely benefit from such technologies.

People recognition is basilar for two main reasons: user authentication and user discrimination during multiuser interaction. The introduction of such ability in the user interfaces would provide a very strong boost to applications in the area of smart home and pervasive computing.

CONCLUSION

In this chapter a complete vision-based Perceptual User Interface framework is presented, namely the VirtualBoard framework, supporting both personal and active-space and both bare hand and pen-mediated user interaction. The described architecture is simple and cheap, features low computational cost, high reliability and high robustness to noise and bad illumination conditions.

The main contribution of this framework is the effort of shifting the focus from the development of computer vision algorithms to usable and effective PUI interfaces, by addressing issues such as ease of use, low cost, portability, integrability and compatibility with existent applications, long-term usability.

REFERENCES

Baldauf, M., & Frohlich, P. (2009). Supporting Hand Gesture Manipulation of Projected Content with Mobile Phones. In *Proceedings of the Workshop on Mobile Interaction with the Real World*. New York: ACM Press.

Bellotti, V., Back, M., Edwards, W. K., Grinter, R. E., Henderson, A., & Lopes, C. (2002). Making sense of sensing systems: five questions for designers and researchers. In *Proceedings of the SIGCHI Conference on Human Factors in Computing Systems: Changing Our World, Changing Ourselves* (pp. 415-422). New York: ACM Press.

Benford, S., Schnädelbach, H., Koleva, B., Anastasi, R., Greenhalgh, C., & Rodden, T. (2005). Expected, sensed, and desired: A framework for designing sensing-based interaction. *ACM Transactions on Computer-Human Interaction*, *12*(1), 3–30. doi:10.1145/1057237.1057239

Blake, A., Curwen, R., & Zisserman, A. (1994). A framework for Spatio-Temporal Control in the Tracking of Visual Contours. In Brown, C. M., & Terzopoulos, D. (Eds.), *Real-Time Computer Vision*. Cambridge: Cambridge University Press.

Bradski, G., & Kaehler, A. (2008). *Learning OpenCV: Computer Vision with the OpenCV Library* (1st ed.). O'Reilly Media, Inc.

Bretzner, L., & Laptev, I. Lindeberg. T., Lenman. S., & Sundblad, Y. (2001). *A prototype system for computer vision based human computer interaction* (Tech. Report, KTH University, Stockholm, Sweden).

Costanzo, C., La Rosa, F., & Iannizzotto, G. (2003). VirtualBoard: Real-Time Visual Gesture Recognition for Natural Human-Computer Interaction. In. *Proceedings of IPDPS, 2003*, 112–119.

Crowley, J., Coutaz, J., & Berard, F. (2000). Things That See. *Communications of the ACM*, *43*(3), 54–64. doi:10.1145/330534.330540

Di Bernardo, E., Goncalves, L., Perona, P., & Ursella, E. (1995). Monocular Tracking of the Human Arm in 3-D. In *Proceedings of the Fifth International Conference on Computer Vision* (pp. 764a). Washington: IEEE Computer Society.

Dorfmuller, K., & Wirth, H. (1998). Real-Time Hand and Head Tracking for Virtual Environments Using Infrared Beacons. In *Proceedings of the International Workshop on Modelling and Motion Capture Techniques for Virtual Environments* (pp. 113-127). London: Springer-Verlag.

Elmezian, M., Al-Hamadi, A., Appenrodt, J., & Michaelis, B. (2008). A Hidden Markov model-based isolated and meaningful hand gesture recognition. In *Proceedings of World Academy of Science, Engineering and Technology* (pp. 394-401). World Academy of Science, Engineering and Technology.

Erol, A., Bebis, G., Nicolescu, M., Boyle, R. D., & Twombly, X. (2007). Vision-based hand pose estimation: A review. *Computer Vision and Image Understanding*, *108*(1-2), 52–73. doi:10.1016/j.cviu.2006.10.012

Forlines, C., Vogel, D., & Balakrishnan, R. (2006). Hybridpointing: fluid switching between absolute and relative pointing with a direct input device. In *Proceedings of the 19th ACM symposium on User interface software and technology* (pp. 211-220). New York: ACM Press.

Gandy, M., Starner, T., Auxier, J., & Ashbrook, D. (2000). The Gesture Pendant: A Self-illuminating, Wearable, Infrared Computer Vision System for Home Automation Control and Medical Monitoring. In *Proceedings of the Fourth International Symposium on Wearable Computers* (pp. 87-94).

Gavrila, D. M., & Davis, L. S. (1995). Towards 3D model-based tracking and recognition of human movement: A Multi-View Approach. In *Proceedings of the International Conference on Automatic Face and Gesture Recognition* (pp. 272-277). Los Alamitos: IEEE CS Press.

Grzeszczuk, R., Bradski, G., Chu, M. H., & Bouguet, J. Y. (2000). Stereo Based Gesture Recognition Invariant to 3D Pose and Lighting. *In Proceedings of the International Conference on Computer Vision and Pattern Recognition* (pp. 1826a). Los Alamitos: IEEE CS Press.

Hardenberg, C., & Bérard, F. (2001). Bare-Hand Human Computer Interaction. In *Proceedings of the workshop on Perceptual User Interfaces* (pp. 1-8). New York: ACM Press.

Iannizzotto, G., Costanzo, C., La Rosa, F., & Lanzafame, P. (2005). A Multimodal Perceptual User Interface for Collaborative Environments. In *Proceedings of the 13th International Conference on Image Analysis and Processing* (pp. 115-122). London: Springer-Verlag.

Iannizzotto, G., La Rosa, F., Costanzo, C., & Lanzafame, P. (2005). A Multimodal Perceptual User Interface for Video-Surveillance Environments. In *Proceedings of the 7th International Conference on Multimodal Interfaces* (pp. 45-52). New York: ACM Press.

Iannizzotto, G., Villari, M., & Vita, L. (2001). Hand Tracking for Human-Computer Interaction with Graylevel VisualGlove: Turning Back to the Simple Way. In *Proceedings of the workshop on Perceptual User Interfaces*. New York: ACM Press.

Jojic, N., Brumitt, B., Meyers, B., Harris, S., & Huang, T. (2000). Detection and Estimation of Pointing Parameters in Dense Disparity Maps. In *Proceedings of the Fourth International Conference on Automatic Face and Gesture Recognition.*

La Rosa, F., Costanzo, C., & Iannizzotto, G. (2003). VisualPen: A Physical Interface for natural human-computer interaction. *ACM MOBILE HCI'03, Physical Interaction (PI03) - Workshop on Real World User Interfaces.*

Leibe, B., Starner, T., Ribarsky, W., Wartell, Z., Krum, D., & Weeks, J. (2000). Toward Spontaneous Interaction with the Perceptive Workbench. *IEEE Computer Graphics and Applications, 20*(6), 54–65. doi:10.1109/38.888008

Maggioni, C., & Kammerer, B. (1998). Gesture-Computer - history, design and applications. In Cipolla, R., & Pentland, A. (Eds.), *Computer Vision for Human-Machine Interaction.* Cambridge: Cambridge University Press.

Mistry, P., Maes, P., & Chang, L. (2009). WUW - wear Ur world: a wearable gestural interface. In *Proceedings of the 27th International Conference on Human Factors in Computing Systems* (pp. 4111-4116). New York: ACM Press.

Norman, D. A. (1998). *The Invisible Computer.* Boston: MIT Press.

Pavlovic, V. I., Sharma, R., & Huang, T. S. (1997). Visual Interpretation of Hand Gestures for Human-Computer Interaction: a Review. *IEEE Transactions on Pattern Analysis and Machine Intelligence, 19*(7), 677–695. doi:10.1109/34.598226

Piekarski, W., Avery, B., Thomas, B. H., & Malbezin, P. (2004). Integrated Head and Hand Tracking for Indoor and Outdoor Augmented Reality. In *Proceedings of the IEEE Virtual Reality Conference* (p. 11). Los Alamitos: IEEE Computer Society.

Prante, T., Streitz, N. A., & Tandler, P. (2004). Roomware: Computers Disappear and Interaction Evolves. *IEEE Computer*, *37*(12), 47–54.

Regh, J., & Kanade, T. (1994). DigitEyes: Vision-Based Hand Tracking for human-computer interaction. In *Proceedings of the Workshop on Motion of Non-Rigid and Articulated Objects* (pp. 16-22). Los Alamitos: IEEE Computer Society.

Rekimoto, J. (2001). GestureWrist and Gesture-Pad: Unobtrusive Wearable Interaction Devices. In *Proceedings of the Fifth International Symposium on Wearable Computers* (pp. 21). Los Alamitos: IEEE Computer Society

Ross, P. E. (2004). Managing Care Through the Air. *IEEE Spectrum*, *4*(12), 14–19. doi:10.1109/MSPEC.2004.1265120

Starner, T., Leibe, B., Singletary, B., & Pair, J. (2000). MIND-WARPING: towards creating a compelling collaborative augmented reality game. In *Proceedings of the International Conference on Intelligent User Interfaces Conference* (pp. 256-259).

Starner, T., & Pentland, A. (1995). Visual Recognition of American Sign Language Using Hidden Markov Models. In *Proceedings of the International Workshop on Automatic Face and Gesture Recognition* (pp. 189-194).

Towles, H., Chen, W.-C., Yang, R., Kum, S.-U., Fuchs, H., Kelshikar, N., et al. (2002). 3D Tele-Collaboration Over Internet2. In *Proceedings of the International Workshop on Immersive Telepresence*.

Want, R., Borriello, G., Pering, T., & Farkas, K. I. (2002). Disappearing Hardware. *IEEE Pervasive Computing / IEEE Computer Society [and] IEEE Communications Society*, *1*(1), 36–47. doi:10.1109/MPRV.2002.993143

Wexelblat, A. (1995). An approach to natural gesture in virtual environments. *ACM TOCHI*, *2*(3), 179–200. doi:10.1145/210079.210080

Wren, C. R., Azarbayejani, A., Darrell, T. J., & Pentland, A. P. (1997). Pfinder: Real-Time Tracking of the Human Body. *IEEE Transactions on Pattern Analysis and Machine Intelligence*, *19*(7), 780–785. doi:10.1109/34.598236

Wu, Y., & Huang, T. (1999). Vision-Based Gesture Recognition: A review. In *Proceedings of the International Gesture Workshop on Gesture-Based Communication in Human-Computer Interaction* (pp. 103-115). London: Springer-Verlag.

Ye, G., Corso, J., Burschka, D., & Hager, D. (2003). VICs: A Modular Vision-Based HCI Framework. In *Proceedings of the 3rd International Conference on Computer Vision Systems* (pp. 257-267).

ENDNOTE

[1] This sensing module has the same name of the whole framework for historical reasons, but this should not confuse the reader: in the current Section the name "VirtualBoard" refers to the VirtualBoard Sensing Module, in the other Sections the name "VirtualBoard" refers to the whole framework.

Chapter 4
Robust Human Face Tracking in Eigenspace for Perceptual Human–Robot Interaction

Richard M. Jiang
Loughborough University, UK

Abdul H. Sadka
Brunel University, UK

ABSTRACT

This chapter introduces a robust human face tracking scheme for vision-based human-robot interaction, where the detected face-like regions in the video sequence are tracked using unscented Kalman filter (UKF), and face occlusion are tackled by using an online appearance-based scheme using principle component analysis (PCA). The experiment is carried out with the standard test video, which validates that the proposed PCA-based face tracking can attain robust performance in tackling face occlusions.

1. INTRODUCTION

Visual content analysis has become a hot topic in machine vision research due to its application in a number of practical robotic applications (Jensen *et al*, 2005; Hartley & Zisserman, 2004; Bucher *et al*, 2003; Lang *et al*, 2003; Alam & Bal, 2007). Intelligent machine vision analysis can enable machine or computer with at least two gifts in practical applications: one is automatic localization and mapping (SLAM) (Hartley, 2004) for scene structure understanding; another is the intelligent understanding of human activity in the visual scene for perceptual human-computer interaction. The

recognition of salient human objects (Bucher, 2003; Lang, 2003; Alam, 2007) presented in the visual scene then becomes a primary task in this kind of applications.

As for human motion tracking and analysis (Isard & Blake, 1998; Zhou *et al*, 2008; Vadakkepat *et al*, 2008; Heuring & Murray, 1999; Boheme *et al*, 1998; Feyrer & Zell, 1999; Hong & Jain, 1999), human head tracking is a useful technique for human-robot interaction applications, where computer or robotic systems need to detect human in the scene, understand human intention or behavior, and adapt their responsive actions to human activity promptly. With this viewpoint, an intelligent vision-based system need to track human motion and understand the events

DOI: 10.4018/978-1-60960-024-2.ch004

happened in the scene. Figure1 is an example of the walking robot controlled by computer, which may need the capability of smart perception in assigned tasks, such as finding the right person in the visual scene.

Vision-based head tracking usually means two tasks in its technical implementation. The first task in head tracking is to detect the head, a specific visual object in a cluttered scene. The second task is to track the head motion in a cluttered scene. The combination of these two tasks makes the problem challenging, while a bunch of methods have been investigated.

Head tracking can be carried out by motion segmentation and tracking (Alam & Bal, 2007; Isard & Blake, 1998), where the moving object is segmented from its background. More than using visual feature alone, multimodal tracking (Zhou *et al*, 2008; Vadakkepat *et al*, 2008) with stereo audio signal from audiovisual sensor network can also locate the position of speaker, while motion blob can be referred as inference assistance. However, not all moving objects are human. Therefore, clas-

sification of moving objects is requested in this kind of approach to discriminate a human face from other objects.

Finding a human face in the scene seems extremely easy for the human visual system. It is however a complex problem in computer-based systems. The difficulty resides in the fact that faces are non rigid objects. Face appearance may vary between two different persons but also between two photographs of the same person, depending on the light conditions, the emotional state of the subject and pose. Faces also vary apparently with added features, such as glasses, hat, moustache beards and hair style. A number of approaches have been developed for this task. Among them, Viola-Jones approach (Viola & Jones, 2001; Meynet, 2007) has been reported to attain great success in face detection. However, to be applied in practical applications, the detected faces need to be tracked consistently, which demands the robustness to challenges such as face occlusions.

In this chapter, in order to tackle with these challenges in practical applications, a robust human face tracking scheme is developed for vision-based human-robot interaction, where the detected face-like regions in the video sequence are tracked using unscented Kalman filter (UKF), and face occlusion are tackled by using an online appearance-based scheme where principle component analysis (PCA) (Schulz *et al*, 2001) is applied to measure the similarity between tracked faces. The experiment is carried out with test videos, which shows that the proposed PCA-based face tracking can attain robust performance in tackling face occlusions.

In the following sections, section 2 introduces the face detection and tracking scheme, where unscented Kalman filter is applied to face tracking, and section 3 presents the approaches to tackle with the face occlusion challenge, where a PCA-based scheme is developed for face tracking. Section 4 gives the experimental results, and Section 5 concludes this chapter.

Figure 1. A robot with camera eyes needs smart perception in assigned tasks, such as finding the right person's head in the visual scene

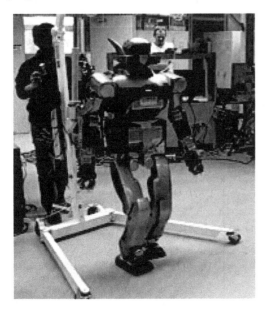

2. FACE DETECTION AND TRACKING

2.1. Face Detection in Cluttered Scene

Many approaches have been developed for face detection in the past decades. In early days, one intuitive approach is to use colour which takes the regions with the face-like color as face regions. Colour based approach (Funt *et al*, 1998; Jang & Kweon, 2001; Yang & Waibel, 1998; Saber & Tekalp, 1998; Juan *et al*, 2007) has been developed for face tracking as an intuitive and efficient approach. Juan (2007) uses mean-shift to track face in YUV space using a facial skin-colour model. A major drawback of colour based approach is its fragileness to illumination caused colour change as well as colour-similar non-face regions.

In comparison with geometric feature-based approach, detection algorithms using holistic representations have the advantage of finding small faces, pose-variant faces, or faces in poor-quality images (Lam & Yan, 1996). A combination of holistic and feature-based approaches (Lam & Yan, 1996) is a promising approach to face detection. However, the colour-based approach face difficulties in robustly detecting skin colours in the presence of complex background and different lighting conditions (Saber & Tekalp, 1998; Juan *et al*, 2007). Hsu & Jain (2002) proposed a robust face detection algorithm by combining holistic features with geometry features and semantic facial component maps of eyes, mouth using a parametric ellipse. Menser & Muller (1999) combines face colour approach with principle component analysis to achieve a high reliability in face detection. Yip & Sinha (2001) also exploits colour cues for face recognition while shape cues are degraded.

In comparison, geometric feature-based approaches (Feraud & Bernier, 2001; Sung 1996; Yow & Cipolla, 1996; Leung *et al*, 1995; Froba & Kublbeck 2001; Rowley *et al*, 1998; Osuna *et*

al, 1998; Pavlovic & Garg, 2001) usually ignore the colour information and apply the greyscale spatial variation as the primary cue for object detection, which may be sensitive to head pose variation but resistant to illumination-caused colour change. This advantage makes geometry-based approaches suitable for head pose tracking.

Among geometric feature-based approach, adaptive boosting (AdaBoost) presented by Jones & Viola (2001) achieves a great success in face detection. AdaBoost is an aggressive learning algorithm which produces a strong classifier by choosing visual features in a family of simple classifiers and combining them in a cascaded sequence. The family of simple classifiers contains simple rectangular wavelets which are reminiscent of the Haar wavelet basis.

In the machine learning community it is well known that more complex classification functions yield lower training errors yet run the risk of poor generalization. AdaBoost uses a cascaded scheme to overcome this problem and achieve the best of both worlds: high detection rates and extremely fast classification (Viola & Jones, 2001; Meynet 2007). The final classifier can be expressed as,

$$H(x) = \text{sign}\left(\sum_{t=1}^{T} \alpha_t h_t(x)\right) \qquad (1)$$

where, h_t is weak Haar classifiers in cascaded scheme, as shown in Figure 2.

In the cascaded classifier, using rectangular Haar features is a commonly adopted strategy for face detection. The wavelet function corresponding to Haar wavelet is:

$$\phi(x) = \begin{cases} 1, & if \ 0 \leq x \leq \dfrac{1}{2} \\ -1, & if \ \dfrac{1}{2} \leq x \leq 1 \\ 0, & \text{otherwise} \end{cases} \qquad (2)$$

Figure 2. Cascaded Haar Classifiers in AdaBoost

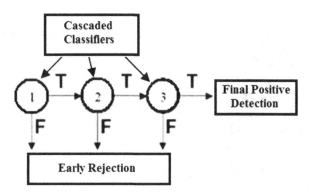

Haar features can be classified as three types, as shown in Figure 3, including center-surround features, edge features, and line features. Integral image technique which yields a fast feature computation is applied to extract Haar-like features for the classifier training.

However, geometric feature based Haar wavelet classifier usually fails to discern false positive regions which have a complex textures in clothes or backgrounds, as shown in Figure 4. This kind of false positive detection can usually ruin the face tracking accuracy in practical applications. To solve this problem, face tracking can be applied to solve this problem.

2.2. Face Tracking with Unscented Kalman Filter

After a possible face region is detected, a further decision diagram can be performed by tracking

the detected face in the following frames successively. There may exist several challenges in face tracking, such as,

1) As shown in Figure 2, the face detection approaches usually suffer from false positive detection.

2) Also, not all faces in every frame can be detected. A face detected in n-th frame may fail to be detected in (n+1)-th frame.

3) Besides, a face may be occluded by other objects in some frames.

To tackle with these challenges, face tracking needs to be performed to predict the position of a face in the next frame using the information obtained in previous frames (Schulz 2001). To achieve this, unscented Kalman filter (UKF) is used to perform the prediction of face positions.

Figure 3. Haar rectangular features for face detection

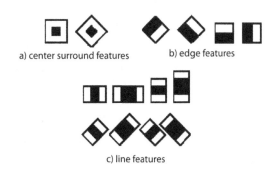

a) center surround features   b) edge features

c) line features

Figure 4. Classifier fails in false positive test (Meynet 2007)

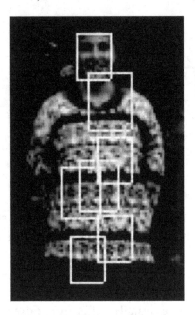

The UKF uses a deterministic sampling technique known as the unscented transform to pick a minimal set of data points around the mean. These sigma points are then propagated through the non-linear functions, from which the mean and covariance of the estimate are then recovered. UKF removes the requirement to explicitly calculate Jacobians, which can be a difficult task in itself for multiple face tracking modeling. The implementation of unscented Kalman filter for face position tracking can be divided into two steps: predict and update.

In the predict step, the estimated state and covariance are augmented with the mean and covariance of the process noise,

$$
x^a_{k|k} = \begin{bmatrix} x_{k|k} \\ E(W_k) \end{bmatrix},
$$
$$
P^a_{k|k} = \begin{pmatrix} P_{k|k} & 0 \\ 0 & Q_k \end{pmatrix}
\tag{3}
$$

A set of 2L+1 sigma points is then derived from the augmented state and covariance where L is the dimension of the augmented state,

$$
\begin{pmatrix} \chi^0_k \\ \dots \\ \chi^i_k \\ \dots \\ \chi^{L+i}_k \end{pmatrix} = \begin{pmatrix} x^a_{k|k} \\ \dots \\ x^a_{k|k} + \gamma_a R^a_k \\ \dots \\ x^a_{L+k} - \gamma_a R^a_k \end{pmatrix}, \quad i = 1,\dots,L
\tag{4}
$$

where, R is the root of covariance matrix,

$$
RR^T = P^a_{k|k}
\tag{5}
$$

The matrix square root should be calculated using the Cholesky decomposition. The sigma points are propagated through the transition function f,

$$
\widehat{\chi}^i_{k+1|k} = f\left(\chi^i_{k|k}\right),
$$
$$
i = 0,\dots,2L
\tag{6}
$$

The weighted sigma points are recombined to produce the predicted state and covariance.

$$
\widehat{x}^i_{k+1|k} = \sum_{i=0}^{2L} W^i x^a_{k+1|k},
$$
$$
P_{k+1|k} = \sum_{i=0}^{2L} W^i \left(x^a_{k+1|k} - \hat{x}^a_{k+1|k} \right)
\tag{7}
$$

where the weights for the state and covariance are given by:

$$
W^0 = 1 - \frac{L}{3},
$$
$$
W^i = \frac{1 - W^0_s}{2L}
\tag{8}
$$

Here, W^i are weights defined above to minimize the fourth-order errors for a Gaussian.

In the update step, the predicted state and covariance are augmented as before, except now with the mean and covariance of the measurement noise,

$$x_{k+1|k}^a = \begin{bmatrix} \hat{x}_{k+1|k} \\ E(V_k) \end{bmatrix}, P_{k+1|k}^a = \begin{pmatrix} P_{k+1|k} & 0 \\ 0 & G_k \end{pmatrix} \quad (9)$$

As before, a set of 2L + 1 sigma points is derived from the augmented state and covariance where L is the dimension of the augmented state,

$$\begin{pmatrix} \chi_{k+1}^0 \\ \dots \\ \chi_{k+1}^i \\ \dots \\ \chi_{k+1}^{L+i} \end{pmatrix} = \begin{pmatrix} x_{k+1|k}^a \\ \dots \\ x_{k+1|k}^a + \gamma_a S_k^a \\ \dots \\ x_{k+1|k}^a - \gamma_a S_k^a \end{pmatrix}, \ i = 1,...,L \quad (10)$$

The sigma points are projected through the observation function h.

$$\gamma_{k+1}^i = h(\chi_{k+1|k}^i), \\ i = 0,...,2L \quad (11)$$

The weighted sigma points are recombined to produce the predicted measurement and its covariance,

$$\hat{z}_{k+1|k}^i = \sum_{i=0}^{2L} W^i \gamma_{k+1|k}^i, \\ P_{z|z} = \sum_{i=0}^{2L} W^i \left(\gamma_{k+1|k}^a - \hat{z}_{k+1|k}^a \right) \left(\gamma_{k+1|k}^a - \hat{z}_{k+1|k}^a \right)^T \quad (12)$$

The cross-covariance matrix is,

$$P_{xz} = \sum_{i=0}^{2L} W^i \left(\chi_{k+1|k}^a - \hat{x}_{k+1|k}^a \right) \left(\gamma_{k+1|k}^a - \hat{z}_{k+1|k}^a \right)^T \quad (13)$$

Which is used to compute the UKF Kalman gain.

$$K_k = P_{xz} P_{zz}^{-1} \quad (14)$$

As with the Kalman filter, the updated state is the predicted state plus the innovation weighted by the Kalman gain,

$$\hat{x}_{k+1|k+1} = \hat{x}_{k+1|k} + K_{k+1} \left(z_{k+1} - \hat{z}_{k+1} \right) \quad (15)$$

And the updated covariance is the predicted covariance, minus the predicted measurement covariance, weighted by the Kalman gain,

$$P_{k+1|k+1} = P_{k+1|k} - K_{k+1} P_{zz} K_{k+1}^T \quad (16)$$

With the above iteration process of statistical fitting going through frame by frame, the face regions can be tracked frame by frame.

3. FACE OCCLUSION ANALYSIS

3.1 Face Occlusions

Face occlusion refers to a tracked face occluded by another human body or face, as shown in Figure 5, where two faces move closer and one face is then occluded by another. Unscented Kalman filter can tackle well with short period occlusion by assuming the face will appear somewhere after occluded. However, frequent face occlusions in a video sequence may greatly reduce the reliability of the conventional tracking algorithms, such as UKF.

Figure 5 gives the example of face occlusion, where faces of persons in red and blue shirts are occluded by another face. In this case, faces cannot be easily tracked using position/speed using Kalman filter. It's still a challenge for the state-of-art face tracking approaches. Also, it can be

Figure 5. Face occlusion problem: a face is hidden behind another one and appears again in the following frames

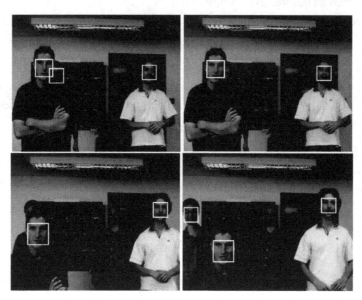

noticed that the face detection fails to detect the person in blue shirt.

To tackle with this kind of complete and frequent occlusions, a useful technique is to combine pattern recognition into face tracking to find out which face is the face in previous frames.

With this expectation, it has been proposed by Schulz *et al* (2001) to use principle component analysis (PCA) to recognize a face detected in current frame. With this recognition-based tracking, a face which is lost in previous frames and appears again in the following frames can still be identified which faces it corresponds to in previous frames.

In this chapter, we present a scheme that can take the advantage of appearance-based face tracking, where principle component analysis is applied to appearance-based face tracking. In face tracking, a number of face images with different poses in successive frames can correspond to the same subject.

3.2 PCA-Based Face Tracking

To tackle with face occlusion, it is necessary to find out which face is the previously occluded face. This means that a detected face needs to be compared with faces in previous frames. To compare one face with others, appropriate facial features need to be extracted. Usually, using Eigenfeatures is an efficient way for face image comparison (Wilhelm *et al*, 2004; Crowley, 1997).

Eigenfeatures of face images are extracted by principal component analysis (PCA), which involves a mathematical procedure that transforms a number of possibly correlated variables into a smaller number of uncorrelated variables called principal components. Invented in 1901 by Karl Pearson, PCA is also named the discrete Karhunen–Loève transform (KLT), the Hotelling transform or proper orthogonal decomposition (POD). Now it is mostly used as a tool in exploratory data analysis and for making predictive models.

For a covariance matrix X^T of 1D vectors of face images with zero empirical mean, where each row represents a different repetition of the experiment, and each column gives the results from a particular probe, the PCA transformation is given by:

$$Y^T = X^T W \qquad (17)$$
$$= V\Sigma$$

where $V\Sigma W^T$ is the singular value decomposition (SVD) of X^T. Given a set of face images of several subjects, the first principal component corresponds to a line that passes through the mean and minimizes sum squared error with those face images. Each eigenvalue indicates the portion of the variance that is associated with each eigenvector. Thus, the sum of all the eigenvalues is equal to the sum squared distance (SSD) of the points with their mean divided by the number of subspace dimensions. Figure 6 shows the detected faces in a frame and their corresponded Eigenfaces.

After the Eigenfeatures are extracted from the detected faces, the correspondence of detected faces against previously detected faces can be combined with UKF-based face tracking, while the appearance based matching is combined with position based prediction. Figure 7 shows the schematic diagram of the PCA-based face tracking procedure. The procedure can be described as following steps,

1) PCA face classifier is trained using previously dtected face samples of subjects in the scene.
2) UKF-based prediction is performed to estimate the face positions of all detected subjects in the (n-1)-th frame.

3) Faces in the n-th frames are detected;
4) The position of detected faces is used to updated UKF parameters, and the UKF based likelihood P_{UKF} of a face F_i^n in the n-th frame corresponding to F_j^{n-1} in the (n-1)-th frame is estimated.
5) The detected faces are projected into Eigenface subspace, and the appearance-based likelihood P_{PCA} of a face F_i^n in the n-th frame corresponding to F_j^{n-1} in the (n-1)-th frame is estimated.
6) The total likelihood in face corresponding is estimated as,

$$P\left(F_i^n \mid F_j^{n-1}\right)$$
$$= P_{UKF}\left(F_i^n \mid F_j^{n-1}\right) P_{PCA}\left(F_i^n \mid F_j^{n-1}\right) \qquad (18)$$

where F_j^{n-1} means the j-th face in the (n-1)-th frame, so does F_i^n. The pair of faces with maximum likelihood is considered as corresponded faces.

7) The corresponded faces are added to the train sample database.

After the above steps, the procedure moves on to the next frame, and begins to iterate from step (1).

Figure 6. Faces detected in the previous frame and their eigenfaces

a) detected faces from a fram

b) extracted eigenfaces

Figure 7. PCA-based scheme for occlusion problem

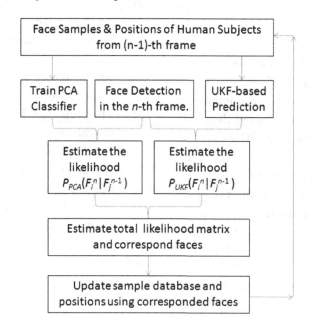

4. EXPERIMENTAL RESULTS

The presented two face tracking approaches were implemented by MATLAB, and compiled into executable files. The software runs on Windows-XP with Intel 3.00GHz Pentium microprocessor. The test video is a standard benchmark video provided by QMUL with four human objects walking across each other in the scene.

Figure 8 shows how the proposed scheme tackles with the face occlusion challenge. In the first frame, four faces are detected and labeled as subject 1, 2, 3 and 4. Faces of subject 1 and 3 are occluded in the following frames, where face 1 first hides behind face 3 from the right and then appears own in the left. The newly appeared face is then detected and identified as subject 1 again, as shown in the last image in Figure 8. While such kind of face occlusions cannot be solved by the conventional position-based face tracking algorithms (such as Kalman filter or particle filter), PCA-based approach can easily find the lost faces back in occlusion cases.

Figure 9 shows a comparison between the PCA-based face tracking scheme and the UKF-only face tracking scheme. As it is seen in the sequence, face occlusion happens while face 2 moves to behind face 1, and then appears in the left of face 1. While the re-appearing faces are wrongly classified by UKF-only face tracking, PCA-based scheme can correctly classify the moving face as shown in the last image in Figure 9-b.

Table 1 gives the statistic results of the experiment on the test video. Here, face tracking precision is defined as the ratio of correctly classified faces and all faces in all test frames,

$$\Pr = \frac{N_{Correct}}{N_{All}} \qquad (19)$$

From Table 1, it can be seen that PCA-based face tracking can attain a dramatic enhancement in face tracking accuracy. The tracking precision is enhanced from 35% in the UKF-only approach to 76% while PCA-based tracking is applied. Obviously, the proposed PCA-based face track-

Figure 8. Tackling occlusion in PCA-based face tracking

Figure 9. Comparison of UKF-only face tracking and PCA-based face tracking. While UKF-only labelling lose its tracked face after occlusion, PCA-based approach can tackle well with these occlusion cases

a) UKF-only Face Tracking   b) PCA-based Face Tracking

Table 1. Statistic results of face occlusion correction

	Face Tracking Precision
UKF-Only	35%
PCA-based	76%

ing approach can attain a robust performance in tackling face occlusion challenge.

5. CONCLUSION

In conclusion, a robust human face tracking scheme is developed for vision-based human-robot interaction, where the PCA-based face tracking scheme is developed in combination with unscented Kalman filter to overcome the challenge of face occlusions that happens frequently in practical robotic applications. The experiment is carried out with the standard test video, which validates that the proposed PCA based face tracking scheme can efficiently tackle with face occlusions to attain a robust performance.

REFERENCES

Alam, M. S., & Bal, A. (2007). Improved multiple target tracking via global motion compensation and optoelectronic correlation. *IEEE Transactions on Industrial Electronics, 54*(1), 522. doi:10.1109/TIE.2006.885513

Böhme, H. J., Braumann, U. D., Brakensiek, A., Corradini, A., Krabbes, M., & Gross, H. M. (1998). User localisation for visually-based human–machine interaction. In *Proceedings of the 1998 IEEE International Conference on Face and Gesture Recognition*, Nara, Japan (pp. 486–491).

Bucher, T., Curio, C., Edelbrunner, J., Igel, C., Kastrup, D., & Leefken, I. (2003). Image processing and behavior planning for intelligent vehicles. *IEEE Transactions on Industrial Electronics, 50*(1), 62–75. doi:10.1109/TIE.2002.807650

Crowley, J. L. (1997). Vision for man-machine interaction. *Robotics and Autonomous Systems, 19*, 347–358. doi:10.1016/S0921-8890(96)00061-9

Feraud, R., & Bernier, O. J. (2001). A Fast and Accurate Face Detection based on Neural Network. *IEEE Transactions on Pattern Analysis and Machine Intelligence, 23*(1), 42. doi:10.1109/34.899945

Feyrer, S., & Zell, A. (1999). Detection, tracking, and pursuit of humans with an autonomous mobile robot. In *Proceedings of the International Conference on Intelligent Robots and Systems* (pp.864–869).

Fröba, B., & Küblbeck, C. (2001). Face detection and tracking using edge orientation information. *SPIE Visual Communications and Image Processing*, 583-594.

Funt, B., Barnard, K. & Martin L. (1998). Is machine colour constancy good enough (LNCS 1406, pp. 445-459).

Hartley, R., & Zisserman, A. (2004). *Multiple View Geometry in Computer Vision*. Cambridge University Press.

Heuring, J. J., & Murray, D. W. (1999). Modeling and copying human face movements. *IEEE Transactions on Robotics and Automation, 15*(6), 1999. doi:10.1109/70.817672

Hong, L., & Jain, A. (1999). Multimodal biometrics. In *Biometrics: Personal Identification in Networked Society*. Kluwer.

Hsu, R., Abdel-Mottaleb, M., & Jain, A. K. (2002). Face detection in colour images. *IEEE Transactions on Pattern Analysis and Machine Intelligence, 24*(5), 696. doi:10.1109/34.1000242

Isard, M., & Blake, A. (1998). Condensation – conditional density propagation for visual tracking. *International Journal of Computer Vision, 29*(1), 5–28. doi:10.1023/A:1008078328650

Jang, G. J., & Kweon, I. S. (2001). Robust object tracking using an adaptive color model. In *Proceedings of the IEEE International Conference on Robotics and Automation* (pp. 1677–1682).

Jensen, B., Tomatis, N., Mayor, L., Drygajlo, A., & Siegwart, R. (2005). Robots meet humans— Interaction in public spaces. *IEEE Transactions on Industrial Electronics, 52*(6), 1530–1546. doi:10.1109/TIE.2005.858730

Juang, C., Chiu, S., & Shiu, S. (2007). Fuzzy System Learned Through Fuzzy Clustering and Support Vector Machine for Human Skin Color Segmentation. *IEEE Transactions on Systems, Man, and Cybernetics, 37*(6), 1077. doi:10.1109/TSMCA.2007.904579

Lam, K., & Yan, H. (1996). An Analytic-to-Holistic Approach for Face Recognition Based on Single Frontal View. *IEEE Transactions on Pattern Analysis and Machine Intelligence, 29*(5), 1771.

Lang, S., Kleinehagenbrock, M., Hohenner, S., Fritsch, J., Fink, G. A., & Sagerer, G. (2003). Providing the basis for human–robot interaction: a multi-modal attention system for a mobile robot. In *Proceedings of the 2003 International Conference on Multimodal Interfaces*, Vancouver, Canada, 2003 (p. 28).

Leung, T., Burl, M., & Perona, P. (1995). Finding Faces in cluttered scenes using labelled random graph matching. In *Proc. 5th Int. Conf. on Computer Vision* (p. 637). Boston, MA: MIT.

Menser, B., & Muller, F. (1999). Face detection in colour images using principal components analysis. In *Seventh International Conference on Image Processing and Its Applications* (Vol. 2, p. 620).

Meynet, J. (2007). *Information theoretic combination of classifiers with application to face detection*, PhD Thesis, EPFL, no 3951.

Osuna, E., Freund, E., & Girosi, F. (1998). Training support vector machines: an application to face detection, *IEEE Conf. Computer Vision and Pattern Recognition* (p. 45).

Pavlovic, V., & Garg, A. (2001), Efficient Detection of Objects and Attributes using Boosting. *IEEE Conf. Computer Vision and Pattern Recognition. QMUL database* (n.d.). Retrieved from http://www.elec.qmul.ac.uk /mmv

Rowley, H. A., Baluja, S., & Kanade, T. (1998). Neural network-based face detection. *IEEE Transactions on Pattern Analysis and Machine Intelligence, 20*(1), 23–38. doi:10.1109/34.655647

Saber, E., & Tekalp, A. M. (1998). Frontal-view face detection and facial feature extraction using colour, shape and symmetry based cost functions. *Pattern Recognition Letters, 19*(8), 669–680. doi:10.1016/S0167-8655(98)00044-0

Schulz, D., Burgard, W., Fox, D., & Cremers, A. B. (2001). Tracking multiple moving targets with a mobile robot using particle filters and statistical data association. *IEEE International Conference on Robotics and Automation.*

Sung, K. K. (1996). *Learning and Example Selection for Object and Pattern Detection*. PhD Thesis, Massachusetts Institute of Technology.

Vadakkepat, P., Lim, P., Liyanage, C., Silva, D., Liu, J., & Ling, L. (2008). Multimodal Approach to Human-Face Detection and Tracking. *IEEE Transactions on Industrial Electronics, 55*(3), 1385. doi:10.1109/TIE.2007.903993

Viola, P., & Jones, M. (2001). Robust real-time object detection. *Second International Workshop on Statistical Learning and Computational Theories of Vision Modeling, Learning, Computing and Sampling*, July 2001.

Wilhelm, T., Böhme, H. J., & Gross, H. M. (2004). A multi-modal system for tracking and analyzing faces on a mobile robot. *Robotics and Autonomous Systems, 48*, 31–40. doi:10.1016/j. robot.2004.05.004

Yang, J., & Waibel, A. (1998). Skin-color modeling and adaptation (LNCS 1352, pp. 687-694).

Yip, A., & Sinha, P. (2001). Role of color in face recognition. *MIT tech report (ai.mit.com)*, AIM-2001-035 CBCL-212, 2001.

Yow, K. C., & Cipolla, R. (1996). Scale and orientation invariance in human face detection. In *Proc. British Machine Vision Conference* (p. 745).

Zhou, H., Taj, M., & Cavallaro, A. (2008). Target detection and tracking with heterogeneous sensors. *IEEE Journal of Selected Topics in Signal Processing, 2*(4), 503–513. doi:10.1109/ JSTSP.2008.2001429

Chapter 5
3D Face Modeling for Multi-Feature Extraction for Intelligent Systems

Zahid Riaz
Technische Universität München, Germany

Suat Gedikli
Technische Universität München, Germany

Michael Beetz
Technische Universität München, Germany

Bernd Radig
Technische Universität München, Germany

ABSTRACT

In this chapter, we focus on the human robot joint interaction application where robots can extract the useful multiple features from human faces. The idea follows daily life scenarios where humans rely mostly on face to face interaction and interpret gender, identity, facial behavior and age of the other persons at a very first glance. We term this problem as face-at-a-glance problem. The proposed solution to this problem is the development of a 3D photorealistic face model in real time for human facial analysis. We also discuss briefly some outstanding challenges like head poses, facial expressions and illuminations for image synthesis. Due to the diversity of the application domain and optimization of relevant information extraction for computer vision applications, we propose to solve this problem using an interdisciplinary 3D face model. The model is built using computer vision and computer graphics tools with image processing techniques. In order to trade off between accuracy and efficiency, we choose wireframe model which provides automatic face generation in real time. The goal of this chapter is to provide a standalone and comprehensive framework to extract useful multi-feature from a 3D model. Such features due to their wide range of information and less computational power, finds their applications in several advanced camera mounted technical systems. Although this chapter focuses on multi-feature extraction approach for human faces in interactive applications with intelligent systems, however the scope of this chapter is equally useful for researchers and industrial practitioner working in the modeling of 3D deformable

DOI: 10.4018/978-1-60960-024-2.ch005

objects. The chapter mainly specified to human faces but can also be applied to other applications like medical imaging, industrial robot manipulation and action recognition.

INTRODUCTION

Human face image analysis has been one of the challenging fields over the last few years. Currently, many commercially available systems can interpret face images in an efficient way but are generally limited to only one specific application domain. For instance, face recognition systems focus on identifying the person by reducing the facial expressions and synthesizing the facial pose to frontal. As a general rule of thumb, they try to isolate the sources of variations and enable the system for one particular application. This approach is not quite useful for advanced intelligent systems. Currently, cameras are becoming a useful tool in human life and are the vital constituent of most of the intelligent systems. Over the availability of advanced hardware, better computational power and GPUs, graphics tools are being usefully embedded in the computer vision applications to enhance the system performance. This resulted in development of the systems with underlying 3D computer vision applications which provide even more details than the conventional 3D methods for object reconstruction, analysis and manipulation. Image textures on the other hands provide a wide range of information for object analysis. A well-realized graphic object provides detailed configuration of the objects in 3D. Such realization provides sufficient information about shape, pose, light source and textures in an image. Moreover these attributes could be synthesized over time to get detailed dynamics and improved realization with additional temporal information. In this regard, we present a technique to develop a unified set of features extracted from a 3D face model. These features are successfully used for higher level facial image interpretation in different application domains. These features are extracted with the help of a coarse 3D wireframe model.

We also study current outstanding issues in human face realizations and information interpretation. These issues are head pose, lighting conditions, facial expressions and real time rendering. The extracted features are made stable over these variations and are capable to be used in different applications. The structural hierarchy of this chapter leads towards multi-feature extraction. We proceed step-by-step by providing essential knowledge about the topic. Some sections also provide generic examples which are not only the key constituent of our model based approach but also equally useful for computer vision object modeling.

These applications not only apply to the face image analysis in challenging environments but also emphasize on insufficiency of the traditional approaches for face image analysis. For instance, traditional face recognition systems have the abilities to recognize the human using various techniques like feature based recognition, face geometry based recognition, classifier design and model based methods (Zhao, Chellappa, Phillips, & Rosenfeld, 2003) but on the other hand similar features are not sufficient for gender recognition or facial expressions recognition. Models due to their wide range of information in minimum parameter descriptors provide a better solution. In this regard, model based approaches have been very successful over last few years. Currently the available models used by the researchers are deformable models, point distribution models, rigid models, morphable models and wireframe models (Zhao W. & Chellapa, 2006).

BACKGROUND

In the recent decade advancement in the field of camera technology, their mountability on mobiles and availability of high computational powers in personal computers have increased the demand of the user to extract more information from the images for higher applications. For instance, face detection cameras, smile-capture cameras and face recognition in notebooks. Future systems will be relying more on the facial image analysis, especially socially inspired robots need to know about the behavior of interacting person at a very first glance. In this manner robots can get friendly with the humans in the very first meeting and can adapt themselves easily to the interacting person's habits. The applications of such system can further be extended to intelligent nurses for patients and assistive robots for elders.

In this section we study the background knowledge required to describe the role of model based approaches in intelligent interaction. We subdivide this section in two parts. In the first part we briefly describe the face modeling in computer vision. Intention of this part is to provide the reader basic knowledge of human face modeling. The second part of this section contains a brief survey of the recent work and results by the other researchers. We address mainly state of the art approaches. (For readers not familiar with the topic, this section is useful).

MODELING OBJECTS IN COMPUTER VISION

Human face modeling has been one of the widely studied topics over the last couple of decades. By the development in the field of algorithm, availability of better hardware and their capability to deal with the real world scenarios, currently it is one of the challenging fields in computer vision. After the failure of Bertillon system (System, 2009) in face recognition application, researchers started to pay attention to develop a reliable system to recognize the humans from their faces. This followed several year research and efforts in face recognition which resulted in commercially avail-

able systems (Zhao, et al., 2003). Face modeling started roughly in mid eighties (Wen & Huang, 2004). A face model in general comprise of the structure of the face. This structure can either be defined using contours (Gupta, Roychowdhury, & Chellappa, 2004) or anatomical landmarks (T. F. Cootes, Taylor, C.J., 1992). This structure defines the shape representation of the local facial features, which can vary from person to person and under varying factors. Another important part of the models is the color information. Color information can be defined as simple gray values (Lanitis, Taylor, & Cootes, 1995), face texture (Riaz, Mayer, Wimmer, Beetz, & Radig, 2008) or detailed texture map in computer graphics and games applications (Buss, 2003). The model of an object is generally a small set of parameters to control the variations of this particular object in a relatively low dimensional subspace. The set of parameters is constrained to the degrees of freedoms of the object. This causes to filter out unrealistic and hallucinated views of the object. For example, a simple model can be represented by:

$$p = (s, r, t, x, g) \qquad (1)$$

where, the components of the models are the parameters showing different variations. For instance, s is a vector of parameters controlling scaling, r and t are rotation and translation vectors respectively and x and g are shape and textural parameters. These parameters can be varied over a constrained span in order to observe deformation in the object in any sense. The set of these parameters which perfectly defines the object in the image are the optimal parameters p* and referred as "ground truth" for that image.

OVERVIEW OF FACE MODELING

Before we proceed further, we provide sufficient background about face modeling by discussing state-of-the-art approaches. This sub-section gives surface knowledge about these models, their applications, advantages and challenges. Active shape model (ASM) was first devised by Cootes et. al. (T. F. Cootes, Taylor, C.J., 1992) which was followed by active contour snakes (Kass, Witkin, & Terzopoulos, 2004), consisting of distribution of points in 2D space. ASM is widely used by different researchers (Pietzsch, Wimmer, Stulp, & Radig, 2008; Stegmann, 2004; M. Wimmer, Riaz, Mayer, & Radig, 2008). This type of model is useful for studying facial structural deformations and shapes changes. One of their useful applications is facial expressions recognition (M. Wimmer, et al., 2008). However, additional texture information is necessary when person identity or gender classification is required. Active appearance model (AAM) devised by Cootes et. al. (T. F. Cootes, Edwards, G.J., Taylor C. J., 2001) is an extension of ASM with texture as an embedded component in model parameters. AAM is the landmark in the area of object modeling in 2D and used for several applications like medical imaging (Stegmann, 2004) and face modeling (Matthews & Baker, November, 2004). AAM is a 2D parameterized, generative and deformable model which finds its extension in 3D. Model parameters are extracted linearly using principal components analysis (PCA). Although AAM contains sufficient information in 2D, some work has been performed by the researcher to their 3D extension in real time (Xiao, Baker, Matthews, & Kanade, 2004).

Wireframe models are similar to point distribution models but defined over 3D space. They are surface models consisting of different landmarks. Candide models series is a good example of wireframe model. Candide-I was devised by Rydk (Rydfalk, 1987) consisting of 110 points. Three different versions of Candide model are available. Candide-III is the final modification of previous versions consisting of 113 points (Ahlberg, 2001). The model is a coarser than morphable models (Blanz V. & Vetter, 2003). It provides better control over facial features motion using facial action

coding system (FACS) (Ekman & Friesen, 1978). It is parameterized differently than the previous versions by adding shape modes to animation modes. We will study this model in more detail later in this chapter. Other 3D realistic models are photorealistic models (Park, Zhang, Vezhnevet, & Choh, 2004) and 3D morphable models (Blanz V. & Vetter, 2003). A photorealistic model in (Park, et al., 2004) is developed using two images, frontal and profile face views. Original image texture and synthesized texture is projected to the 3D head with improved model for hair and ears. 3D morphable models are famous realistic models and use laser scanner data for generation of the model. They are more detailed because of the dense point distribution from scanner data. This chapter focuses to get comparable results as that of the 3D morphable models but with a coarser wireframe model. The results are compared both in the sense of better visualization and diverse applicability of the realistic 3D wireframe model.

MAIN FOCUS OF THE CHAPTER

The main goal of this chapter is to extract useful multi-feature for different applications at the same time providing an overview of the model based approaches for face images and provide the reader with a simple and useful platform to develop such system and understanding of the applications of this task. We split our approach explicitly in problem statement and proposed solution.

Problem Statement: Face-at-a-Glance Scenario

In the recent decade, model based approaches have attained a huge attention of the research community owing to their compactness and detailed description over the other techniques. Models described a large size image in small set of parameters. These few descriptors are called model parameters. Further they narrow the search domain in an image and precisely look for the object of interest for which they are designed. This reduces false alarms in finding an object. We address the problem in which a robotic system is able to extract a common feature set automatically from face images and capable to classify gender, person identity and facial behavior. In such applications an automatic and efficient feature extraction technique is necessary to be developed which can interpret any possible face information. Currently available systems lack this property. A major reason is that researchers focus on isolating the sources of variations while focusing on a particular application. For example, in face recognition application, many researchers normalize face in order to remove facial expressions variations to improve face recognition results. So the extracted features do not contain facial expressions information. We address an idea to develop a unified feature set which is used for different applications like face recognition, facial expressions and behavior and gender classification. Since, humans can get this information at a very first glance, so we term this problem as face-at-a-glance problem in human robot interaction domain. Further, in such scenarios faces are seen from different views under varying facial deformations and lightings. It is hard to find any solution in such case where a robot can find different information from the faces at the same time. Since 3D modeling can deal mostly with these challenges so we can propose a solution of finding useful features called multi-feature extraction for this problem.

Proposed Solution: Multi-Feature Extraction

We propose multi-feature extraction as a recommended solution to this problem with some experimental evidence. Model parameters are obtained in an optimal way to maximize information from face region under various factors like facial pose, expressions, and illuminations. We use a wireframe 3D face model known as Candide-III (Ahlberg, 2001). The model is fitted to the face image by learning robust objective functions. Model fitting provides the optimal set of parameters describing structure of the face in the given image. Texture information is mapped from the example image to a reference shape which is the mean shape of all the shapes available in database. However the texture is not well defined on face edges where the triangles are tilted. We apply transformation of texture from image plane to frontal texture patches. This is achieved by comparatively applying affine and perspective transformation. With the best of two we choose perspective transformation. This undistorted texture is stored in a texture map which is an image with blocks where each block represents a triangle. Texture is warped from given image to a reference shape, which is the mean shape in our case. However the choice of mean shape is arbitrary. Image texture is extracted using planar subdivisions of the reference and the example shapes. We use model triangulation which is the Delaunay triangulation. Principal Component Analysis (PCA) is used to obtain the texture and shape parameters of the example image. The shape parameters additionally contain action unit activation levels. In addition to shape and texture parameters, temporal features of the facial changes are also calculated. Local motion of the feature points is observed using optical flow. We use reduced descriptors by trading of between accuracy and run time performance. These features are then used for classification. Our approach achieves real-time performance and provides robustness against facial expressions in real-world scenarios. Currently the system finds the pose information implicitly in structural parameters whereas illuminations changes are dealt in appearance parameters. This computer vision task comprises of various phases shown in Figure 1 for which it exploits model-based techniques that accurately localize facial features, seamlessly track them through image sequences, and finally infer facial features. We specifically adopt state-of-the-

Figure 1. Different modules of our proposed system

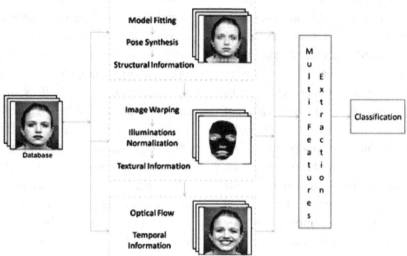

art techniques in conjunction with our approach to solve challenging HRI problem.

MULTI-FEATURE EXTRACTION

In this section we explain our approach in different modules including shape model fitting, image warping, texture extraction, varying poses and expressions normalizations and finally synthesizing the image to extract model parameters.

The proposed framework initializes with a coarse localization of the face image. If the robot is unable to find a person then cameras keep on finding a person unless they locate a face. Any coarse localization algorithm can be used for this purpose which can be refined in later stages of the system. We initialize by applying the algorithm of Viola et al. (Viola & Jones, 2004) to roughly detect the face position within the image. There could be false positive case where a face can be falsely found in an image. In this case model fitting approach diverges and losses the control on the face image in few frame. Under this condition algorithm re-initializes itself for face search. In

this section, we explain step-by-step our method towards *multi-feature* extraction and their fusion.

Model Fitting

Initial localization of the face image is used for model fitting. If the face is located near to real face in the image then model is capable to quickly adapt to the face. In other case it needs some images to adapt to the model. If face locator fails due to any reason, the system stops proceeding unless it finds an image with a face. A realistic face model relies strongly on model fitting. We use shape model to fit to the face image as contrary to AAM and other model fitting approaches. The reason behind is the efficiency and robustness of the fitting algorithm. Local objective functions are calculated using haar-like features. Face locator localizes the face region with a box. Probability of skin color is computed and local facial features like eyes and lip are obtained. We use a state-of-the-art approach towards model fitting using best objective functions. This approach is less prone to errors because of better quality of annotated images which are to be provided to the system for training. Further it is less laborious because the objective function design is replaced with automated learning. An objective function is defined as a cost function *f(I,p)*, where *I* is image and *p* is the best set of parameters defining the fitted model. Figure 2 shows the model fitting approach. An objective function is subjected to few conditions for robustness. For further details we refer to (Pietzsch, et al., 2008; Matthias Wimmer, Stulp, Pietzsch, & Radig, 2008). Figure 2 shows the learning of objective function approach and Figure 3 shows the divergence case. In such case system keeps on searching face.

To extract descriptive features, the model parameters are exploited. The model configuration represents information about various facial features, such as lips, eye brows or eyes and therefore contributes to the extracted features. These structural features include information about the person's face structure that helps to determine person-specific information such as face deformations and facial expression generation. Furthermore, changes in these features indicate shape changes

and therefore contribute to the recognition of facial expressions.

Structural Features

Candide-III model consists of 113 vertices forming 184 non-overlapping triangles to define a wireframe model in 3D. As compared to AAM, this is a shape model whose geometry is controlled by set of action units and animation units. The difference between these parameters is shape parameters control static deformation whereas animation parameters control facial expressions.

Any shape *s* can be written as a sum of mean shape $\bar{s}$ and a set of action units and shape units.

$$s\left(\alpha, \sigma\right) = \bar{s} + \varnothing_a \alpha + \varnothing_s \sigma \qquad (2)$$

where $\varnothing_a$ is the matrix of action unit vectors and $\varnothing_s$ is the matrix of shape vectors. Whereas α

Figure 2. Learn approach for objective function

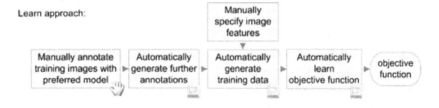

Figure 3 Model Fitting, (left) model fitted to the face image (right) failure case, model diverges and then re-initializes face search

Figure 4. Shape variations generated before texture extraction using FACS coding and global rotations

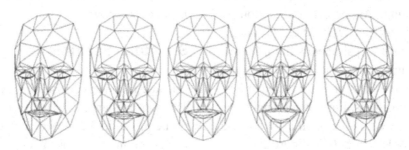

denotes action units parameters and σ denotes shape parameters (Li & Jain, 2005).

The scaling, rotation and translation of the model is described by

$$s(\alpha,\sigma,\pi)=mRs(\alpha,\sigma)+t \qquad (3)$$

where R and t are rotation and translation matrices respectively, m is the scaling factor and π contains six pose parameters plus a scaling factor. By changing the model parameters, it is possible to generate some global rotations and translations. Figure 4 shows some global rotations of the model.

Facial Action Coding System (FACS)

Candied-III supports facial action coding system (FACS) by Ekmann and Freisen (Ekman & Friesen, 1978). Facial actions arise from the muscle movements inside the facial skins. They are direct reflection of these motions. Figure 5 shows Candied-III model with global rotations

and opened mouth face mesh generate using action AU13/15.

Textural Features

We study texture in two different approaches. Extracted facial texture is representative of different facial features. Low frequency texture information corresponds to gender and aging information. While global texture is a key constituent for person identification. We take benefit of the 3D model to get texture projected to 3D surface and store undistorted texture in the form of texture map. On the other hand a simple way is to apply PCA after texture mapping and parameterize the extracted texture. The approach is different to AAM texture extraction where texture is extracted using affine transformation between the triangles using interpolation. We use undistorted texture in our case. Before we proceed to texture parameters, we explain two different texture mappings approaches comparatively.

Figure 5. Example original texture image, frontal triangle and tilted triangle with texture

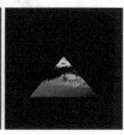

Once we have the shape information, the texture can be extracted after perspective correction from the image. This texture information can either be parameterized using standard PCA or PCA over discrete cosine transform (DCT) coefficients of the texture image. Since the DCT coefficients of the lower frequencies contain the major information and remove the noise of the texture, in combination with the PCA we get robust and reliable texture parameters. However, the robustness of these parameters hardly depends upon the input texture image. For example, the affine warping of the rendered triangle is not invariant to 3D rigid transformations of this triangle as can be seen in Figure 6. It can be seen in Figure 6 (top row), the affine warping works only, if the triangle is not tilted in respect to the camera coordinate frame. If the triangle is tilted, as can be seen in Figure 6 (bottom row), the extracted texture is distorted.

Since, the 3D position of each triangle vertex as well as the camera parameters are known, we can determine the homogeneous mapping between the image plane and the texture coordinates. This mapping which is usually known as Homography is given by following formula:

$$H = K. \begin{bmatrix} r_1 & r_2 & -R.t \end{bmatrix} \qquad (4)$$

where K denotes the camera matrix, R denotes the rotation and t denotes the translation vector. It can easily be shown, that the formula above maps a 2D point of the texture image to the corresponding 2D point of the rendered image of the triangle.

Since the 2D projection q of a general 3D point p in homogeneous coordinates can be written as following

$$q = K. \begin{bmatrix} R & -R.t \end{bmatrix}.p \qquad (5)$$

Figure 6. Affine transformation of the triangles in Figure 5. (top row) results for frontal triangle texture projected to upper triangular area of texture map block, right image shows difference texture of this extracted texture with original texture, (bottom row) similar result for tilted triangle. It shows that in case of titled triangle texture is distorted badly

It can be seen, that each homogeneous 3D point lying on a plane with *z = 0*, i.e. *p = (x y 0 1)* leads to above Equation (5).

$$q = K. \begin{bmatrix} r_1 & r_2 & r_3 & -R.t \end{bmatrix}. \begin{bmatrix} x \\ y \\ 0 \\ 1 \end{bmatrix} = K. \begin{bmatrix} r_1 & r_2 & -R.t \end{bmatrix}. \begin{bmatrix} x \\ y \\ 1 \end{bmatrix} = H.p'$$

(6)

with *p'* being the homogeneous 2D point in texture coordinates. Since the camera parameters are known beforehand, the only values to be obtained are the rotation matrix *R* and the translation vector *t*. Since we use the upper triangle of a rectangular image for the texture values, and the triangles rarely fit this shape, we use an additional affine transformation *A*. The final homogeneous transformation *M* is the given by

$$M = A.K. \begin{bmatrix} R & -R.t \end{bmatrix} = A.H \qquad (7)$$

and is determined in two steps. First we find the Homography *H*, by obtaining the rotation and transformation of the triangle, by supposing that the initial triangle lies on the texture plane, the first vertex lies on the origin (0, 0, 1) and the first edge lies on the x-axis. The affine transformation *A* is then calculated, so that the mapped triangle on the texture plane fits the upper triangle of the rectangular texture.

Figure 7 shows the same examples as for the affine warping. As can be seen, the extracted texture is not distorted anymore. Besides the effects caused by the discretization of the image in pixels, the texture extraction is invariant against rigid transformations.

In case of 2D textures, once we have shape information of the image, we extract texture from

Figure 7. Perspective transformation of the triangles in Figure 5. (top row) results for frontal triangle texture projected to upper triangular area of texture map block, right image shows difference texture of this extracted texture with original texture, (bottom row) similar result for tilted triangle. In this case extracted texture is much better and comparable to original texture which can be seen from the difference image

the face region by mapping it to a reference shape. A reference shape is extracted by finding the mean shape over the dataset. Image texture is extracted using planar subdivisions of the reference and the example shapes. The planar subdivision used is normally Delaunay triangulation. Texture warping between the subdivisions is performed using affine transformation. This extracted texture is parameterized using PCA and discrete cosine transform (DCT). An advantage of using DCT over PCA is its better performance against lighting variations (Ekenel & Stiefelhagen, 2009).

The extracted texture is parameterized using PCA by using mean texture $\overline{g}$ and matrix of eigenvectors P_g to obtain the parameter vector b_g (Li & Jain, 2005).

$$g = \overline{g} + P_g b_g \qquad (8)$$

where g is a vector of gray values.

Face Synthesis and Texture Extraction

We use perspective distortion free texture for each triangle and store the texture in a texture map. Our texture map consists of blocks where each block represents a triangle. Undistorted texture is stored as upper left triangle (as shown in Figure 7) and used for later purposes. This texture map can be used for two different purposes at this stage. Firstly, we can synthesize different views of a person at this level. Since we already have shape and texture information in the form of parameters, it is quite simple to synthesize different views of a person. By changing rotation, scaling and translation vector we can generate some global motion. This can be seen in Figure 9 where half profile view of an example face (Figure 8, last row) is synthesized for rotation across vertical axis. Texture from one view is projected to other views after removing perspective distortions. An interesting result can be seen from synthesized views that mouth is open or closed in some images, which differs from original images. Images are taken from PIE-database (Sim, Baker, & Bsat, 2002).

Texture map is stored for each view seen and further views can be synthesized. In order to find textural parameters, we use Equation (8). This is simple PCA projection which provides *eigenfaces* for the persons in the dataset.

Figure 8. Model Fitting to any example image and Texture projection on 3D surface after perspective correction (© images from PIE-database)

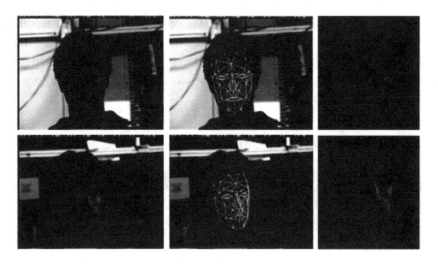

Figure 9. Synthesized poses from Figure 8 (bottom row) by changing global rotation and FACS units. Mouth opened and closed can be produced with FACS coding

Figure 10. Texture Map and synthesized novel view from Figure 8

Since Candide-III supports FACS, it is quite useful to synthesize facial motions especially during training phase. This can help in learning person independent features and learning the faces with novel views. For example, laugh is synthesized from the neutral face by mainly varying action unit "AU13/15" as sehown in Figure 10.

Temporal Features

Further, temporal features of the facial changes are also calculated that take movement over time into consideration. Local motion of feature points is observed using optical flow. We do not specify the location of these feature points manually but distribute equally in the whole face region. The number of feature points is chosen in a way that the system is still capable of performing in real time and therefore inherits a tradeoff between accuracy and runtime performance. Since the motion of the feature points are relative so we choose 140 points in total to observe the optical flow. We again use PCA over the motion vectors to reduce the descriptors. Figure 11 shows motion patterns for some of the images from images used in experiments. Images are taken from Cohn-Kanade facial expression database (Kanade, Cohn, & Tian, 2000).

Feature Fusion

We combine all extracted features into a single feature vector. Single image information is considered by the structural and textural features whereas image sequence information is consid-

Figure 11. Optical flow using Locas-Kanade pyramidal algorithm (Bouguet, 2000)

ered by the temporal features. The overall feature vector becomes:

$$u=(b_{s,1},\ldots,b_{s,m},b_{g,1},\ldots,b_{g,n},b_{t,1},\ldots,b_{t,p}) \qquad (9)$$

where b_s, b_g and b_t are shape, textural and temporal parameters respectively with m, n and p being the number of parameters retained from subspace in each case. Equation (9) is called *multi-feature*.

We extract 85 structural features, 74 textural features and 12 temporal features textural parameters to form a combined feature vector for each image. These features are then used for binary decision tree (BDT) and bayesian network (BN) for different classifications.

The face feature vector consists of the shape, texture and temporal variations, which sufficiently defines global and local variations of the face. All the subjects in the database are labeled for classification. Since features arise from different sources, it is not quite obvious to fuse them together to get a feature set. This can cause the dominance of the features with higher values and ones with low values are ignored (Fu, Cao, Guo, & Huang, 2008). We use simple scaling of the features in [0,1]. However, any suitable method for feature fusion can be applied here.

EXPERIMENTATIONAL EVALUATION

For experimentation purposes, we benchmark our results on Cohn Kanade Facial Expression (CKFE) database (Kanade, et al., 2000).The database contains image sequences with facial expression variations. Some faces are also rotated to a small angle in upright position. The reason to choose this database is the similarity with the application domain of our system. In HRI scenarios faces are seen with varying facial expressions and multi-feature also requires temporal information.

In order to experiment feature versatility we use two different classifiers with same feature set on three different applications: face recognition,

facial expressions recognition and gender classification. The results are evaluated using classifiers from Weka (Witten & Frank, 2005) with 10-fold cross validation. Table 1 shows different recognition rates achieved during experimentations. This can be analyzed from receiver operating characteristics (ROC) curves. Figure 12 shows receiver ROC curves for six different facial expressions. Since laugh and fear are often confused facial expressions, it can be analyzed from the curves that there exists some confusion between these two expressions for BN classifier, which is improved using BDT classifier. This shows the role of classifier for *multi-feature*. Figure 13 shows gender classification results for these classifiers.

APPLICATIONS

This work is intended for robots designed for elderly people working in an assistive environment. This can help people to perform their activities safely and freely in the presence of an intelligent assistant. This kind of application is useful in house based robot (some examples are shown in Figure 14) (Beetz, 2009). By the rapid grow in the field of robotic technology it is quite possible to get a personal robot as like personal computer in past days. Beside this, such system can be applied to any robotic guided environment. For example, in medical imaging where the objects under treatment are deformable during surgeries. Further applications include action recognition, driver fatigue analysis, stress analysis and behavioral

Table 1. Comparison of results

	Binary Decision Tree (BDT)	Bayesian Network (BN)
Face Recognition	98.49%	90.67%
Facial Expressions Recognition	85.70%	80.57%
Gender classification	99.08%	89.70%

Figure 12. ROC for expressions (anger, disgust, fear, laugh, sadness, surprise)

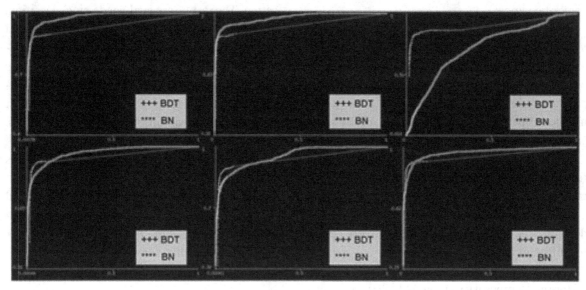

Figure 13. ROC for gender classification (female, male)

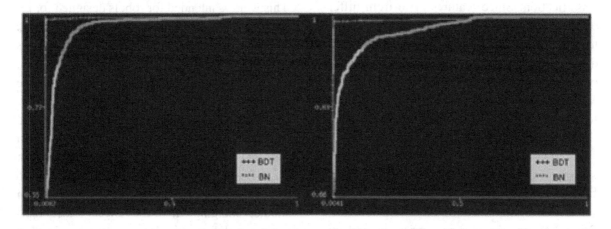

Figure 14. Assistive robots (Beetz, 2009)

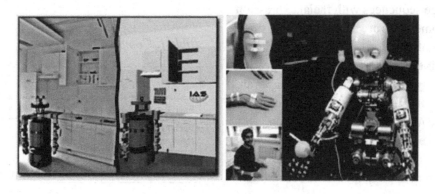

analysis of patients during treatment. The system takes input from camera sensors only, however the areas of application domain mostly consist of the system with multi-sensory data. The current system can be enhanced and configured according to its application with different sensory data. Due to its efficiency it can be integrated with other modalities like human voice, body language analysis, psychological analysis with fMRI or other modalities in parallel.

FUTURE WORK

Multi-feature has been extracted from subspace learning however it is required to study non-linear behavior of these parameters. Further, face-at-a-glance problem is studies for three applications but other factors like age estimation and ethnical background can be implemented very well inside this framework and can increase the performance of the system to understand different behaviors. For example, behaviors can be understood using ethnic origin of the person under certain context based applications. A near future extension of this work which we suggest the reader is to experiment this system in different real time applications. Further possibilities are for the researchers in the area of psychology and neurosciences to study social behavior of humans by facial visualization. This will help to learn more intuitive features from human brain studies.

CONCLUSION

This chapter concludes a full platform to develop a system for human robot interaction scenario with diverse applications. The proposed technique to develop a set of feature vectors consists of three types of facial information. The feature set is applied to three different applications: face recognition, facial expressions recognition and gender classification, which produced the reasonable

results in all three cases. We currently considered two different classifiers for checking the versatility of our extracted features. However there are still open doors towards research in machine learning and pattern classification.

REFERENCES

Ahlberg, J. (2001). *CANDIDE-3 -- an updated parameterized face* (No. LiTH-ISY-R-2326).

Beetz, M. (2009). Retrieved from http://ias.in.tum.de/research/awarekitchen

Blanz, V., & Vetter, T. (2003). Face Recognition Based on Fitting a 3D Morphable Model. *IEEE Transactions on Pattern Analysis and Machine Intelligence*, 25(9), 1063–1074. doi:10.1109/TPAMI.2003.1227983

Bouguet, J.-Y. (2000). Pyramidal Implementation of the Lucas Kanade Feature Tracker Description of the algorithm: Intel Corporation Microprocessor Research Labs.

Buss, S. (2003). *3D Computer Graphics: A mathematical approach with OpenGL*. Cambridge University Press.

Cootes, T. F., Edwards, G. J., & Taylor, C. J. (2001). *Active Appearance model*. IEEE Transaction of Pattern Analysis and Machine Intelligence.

Cootes, T. F., & Taylor, C. J. (1992). *Active shape models–smart snakes*. Paper presented at the British Machine Vision Conference.

Ekenel, H. K., & Stiefelhagen, R. (2009). *Generic versus Salient Region-Based Partitioning for Local Appearance Face Recognition*. Paper presented at the 3rd International Conference on Biometrics.

Ekman, P., & Friesen, W. (1978). *The Facial Action Coding System: A Technique for The Measurement of Facial Movement*.

Fu, Y., Cao, L., Guo, G., & Huang, T. S. (2008). *Multiple Feature Fusion by Subspace Learning.* Paper presented at the ACM International Conference on Image and Video Retrieval.

Gupta, H., Roychowdhury, A. K., & Chellappa, R. (2004). *Contour-based 3D Face Modeling from a Monocular Video.* Paper presented at the British Machine Vision Conference.

Kanade, T., Cohn, J. F., & Tian, Y. (2000). *Comprehensive Database for Facial Expression Analysis.* Paper presented at the IEEE International Conference on Automatic Face and Gesture Recognition (FGR00).

Kass, M., Witkin, A., & Terzopoulos, D. (2004). Snakes: Active contour models. *International Journal of Computer Vision*, 321–331.

Lanitis, A., Taylor, C. J., & Cootes, T. F. (1995). *A unified approach to coding and interpreting face images.* Paper presented at the Proceedings of the Fifth International Conference on Computer Vision.

Li, S. Z., & Jain, A. K. (2005). *Handbook of Face Recognition.* Springer.

Matthews, I., & Baker, S. (2004, November). Active Appearance Model - Revisited. *International Journal of Computer Vision*, *60*(2), 135–164. doi:10.1023/B:VISI.0000029666.37597.d3

Park, I. K., Zhang, H., Vezhnevet, V., & Choh, H., K. (2004). *Image-based Photorealistic 3-D Face Modeling.* Paper presented at the 6th IEEE Conference on Automatic Face and Gesture Recognition.

Pietzsch, S., Wimmer, M., Stulp, F., & Radig, B. (2008). *Face Model Fitting with Generic, Group-specific, and Person-specific Objective Functions.* Paper presented at the 3rd International Conference on Computer Vision Theory and Applications (VISAPP).

Riaz, Z., Mayer, C., Wimmer, M., Beetz, M., & Radig, B. (2008). *A Model Based Approach for Expression Invariant Face Recognition.* Paper presented at the 3rd International Conference on Biometrics.

Rydfalk, M. (1987). *CANDIDE, a parameterized face* (No. LiTH-ISY-I-866).

Sim, T., Baker, S., & Bsat, M. (2002). *The CMU Pose, Illumination, and Expression (PIE) Database.* Paper presented at the Proceedings of the Fifth IEEE International Conference on Automatic Face and Gesture Recognition.

Stegmann, M. (2004). *Generative Interpretation of Medical Images: Automated Segmentation and Analysis of Cardiac MRI using Statistical Image Analysis.* TU Denmark.

System, B. (Ed.). (2009) Encyclopædia Britannica. Retrieved November 06, 2009, from Encyclopædia Britannica Online.

Viola, P., & Jones, M. J. (2004). Robust real-time face detection. *International Journal of Computer Vision*, *57*(2), 137–154. doi:10.1023/B:VISI.0000013087.49260.fb

Wen, Z., & Huang, T. S. (2004). *3D Face Processing: Modeling, Analysis and Synthesis.* Kulwer Academic Publisher.

Wimmer, M., Riaz, Z., Mayer, C., & Radig, B. (2008). Recognizing Facial Expressions Using Model-based Image Interpretation [-Tech Publisher.]. *Advances in Human-Computer Interaction*, I.

Wimmer, M., Stulp, F., Pietzsch, S., & Radig, B. (2008). Learning Local Objective Functions for Robust Face Model Fitting. *IEEE Transactions on Pattern Analysis and Machine Intelligence*, *30*(8), 1357–1370. doi:10.1109/TPAMI.2007.70793

Witten, I. H., & Frank, E. (2005). *Data Mining: Practical Machine Learning Tools and Techniques* (2nd ed.). San Francisco: Morgan Kaufmann.

Xiao, J., Baker, S., Matthews, I., & Kanade, T. (2004). *Real-Time Combined 2D+3D Active Appearance Models*. Paper presented at the IEEE Conference on Computer Vision and Pattern Recognition.

Zhao, W., & Chellapa, R. (Eds.). (2006). *Face Processing: Advanced Modeling and Methods*. Elsevier.

Zhao, W., Chellappa, R., Phillips, P. J., & Rosenfeld, A. (2003). Face recognition: A literature survey. *ACM Computing Surveys*, *35*(4), 399–458. doi:10.1145/954339.954342

Section 2
Computer Vision for Multimedia Content Summary and Retrieval

Chapter 6
Video Summarization by Redundancy Removing and Content Ranking

Tao Wang
Intel Labs China, China

Yue Gao
Intel Labs China, China & Tsinghua University, China

Patricia P. Wang
Intel Labs China, China

Wei Hu
Intel Labs China, China

Jianguo Li
Intel Labs China, China

Yangzhou Du
Intel Labs China, China

Yimin Zhang
Intel Labs China, China

ABSTRACT

Video summary is very important for users to grasp a whole video's content quickly for efficient browsing and editing. In this chapter, we propose a novel video summarization approach based on redundancy removing and content ranking. Firstly, by video parsing and cast indexing, the approach constructs a story board to let user know about the main scenes and the main actors in the video. Then it removes redundant frames to generate a "story-constraint summary" by key frame clustering and repetitive segment detection. To shorten the video summary length to a target length, "time-constraint summary" is constructed by important factor based content ranking. Extensive experiments are carried out on TV series, movies, and cartoons. Good results demonstrate the effectiveness of the proposed method.

DOI: 10.4018/978-1-60960-024-2.ch006

INTRODUCTION

Rapid advances in the technology of media capture, storage and network have contributed to an amazing growth of digital video content. Existing so many and long videos, it is very time-consuming for us to know the video content before we browse them and decide which part to watch. To deal with the problem, video summarization becomes very important to help users to grasp the video content efficiently.

Video summarization is generally a condensed sequence of still or moving images, which provide the essential content of a video in a general, logical, and connected way. According to the summary mode, summarization approaches can be categorized into "story board" and "video skimming". Story board is a collection of still images, such as a key frame list of important shots or scenes (Uchihashi, 1999). Story board can be constructed fast with small storage but their descriptive ability is limited since they lose lots of dynamic audiovisual content in the original video. Compared with story board, video skimming is made up of video clips which show important scenes, actors, objects and events for efficient browsing, e.g. highlights of a Hollywood movie. Based on the information theory, Gong and Liu (2001) proposed a video skimming approach with minimal visual content redundancies. They first cluster key frames and then concatenate short video segments of representative key frames to construct a video skimming. Li and Schuster (2005) formulated the optimal video summarization problem as finding a predetermined number of frames that minimize the temporal constraint. Otsuka and Nakane (2005) proposed a highlights summarization approach. They use audio feature to detect sports highlights as the video skimming.

Video summarization is so active research field that the National Institute of Standards and Technology (NIST) hold the evaluation of rushes video summarization in both 2007 and 2008 (Paul Over, 2007 and 2008). Rushes are the raw material (extra video, B-rolls footage) used to produce a video. The rushes summarization task is to automatically create a MPEG-1 summary clip less than or equal to a maximum duration (e.g. 2%) that shows the main objects and events of the rushes videos. Since there are many redundant, repeated, unstructured and bad video clips, e.g. color bar, near uniform-color, abrupt and clapboard frames etc, rushes video summarization is more challengeable than summarization of teleplays and movies. There are about 30 teams to join in the evaluation including Carnegie Mellon University, Dublin City University, City University of Hong Kong, National Institute of Informatics, FX Palo Alto Laboratory Inc., AT&T Labs, and Intel etc. In rushes summarization of TRECVID, the popular approaches are video sampling, key frame clustering and iteratively selecting video clips. For video sampling, the CMU team's baseline1 approach selects 1-second video segments from every 25 seconds of an original video (Alexander, 2007). The 1-second segments are then concatenated to generate the summary video. Sampling approach is very simple but hard to beat other methods due to losing analysis of video structure and content. For key frame based clustering, many teams employ the approach to find representative video clips and remove redundant clips, e.g. k-means clustering of CMU-baseline2 (Alexander, 2007) and UCAL (Anindya, 2007), and hierarchical clustering of JOANNEUM(Werner, 2007) and THU-ICRC(Wang, 2007) etc. After key frame clustering, the representative key frames (which are near to cluster center, last appeared or longest in duration) are selected and concatenated into the summary video by their temporal order. Key frame clustering approach is effective, but how to automatically select the most representative clips and decide their concatenated order are the main problems. Different from clustering approaches, the greedy method of iteratively selecting video clips divides a video into 1-second video clips and generate the video summary by iteratively selecting the clips with the highest representative score (Wang, 2007). This greedy approach can quickly select representative video clips and easily control the summary length by stopping the iterative selection but may be not good enough for the global optimization.

To generate a perfect video summary, it requires good understanding of the video structure and semantic content in order to select the most representative or important/exciting video clips. Motivated by this criterion, this chapter proposes a novel video summarization approach based on video parsing, cast indexing, repetitive segment detection and content ranking. Our video summarization approach has two main advantages: (1) Shorten the original video to the target length or as short as possible by redundancy removing. (2) Reserve the main objects and events in the video by content ranking. In detail, by video parsing of shot detection, scene segmentation and cast indexing, the approach first constructs story boards to let user know about the main scenes and the main actors in the video. Then it removes redundant video clips to generate a "story-constraint summary" by key frame clustering and repetitive segment detection. Finally, to shorten the video summary length to the target length, e.g. 1 minute summary, our approach constructs a "time-constraint summary" by important factor based content ranking.

THE PROPOSED METHOD

Video summary generates a condensed sequence of still or moving images while keeping main objects and events with pleasant tempo, logical and connected way. According to the information theory, video summarization can be looked as the following problem: Cluster video frames into M video segments and then select N video segments to construct a video summary with the maximum information and pleasant tempo. Figure 1 illustrates the framework of the video summarization system. In the video parsing modules, it first parses a video into shots, key frames, and scenes and then discovers main actors by face tracking and face clustering. Then story boards are constructed to

let user know about the main scenes and the main actors in the video. Secondly, the redundancy removing modules remove similar key frames and repetitive segments to generate a *story-constraint summary*. Finally, to shorten the summary to the target length, content ranking modules calculate the important factors of key frames and scenes and then selects out ranked important video segments to construct a *time-constraint summary*.

Low Level Feature Extraction

Video content of actors/objects, scenes and events generally change the frame images in both spatial and temporal aspects. In preprocessing step, low-level audiovisual features are first extracted from the input video. For visual features, a 48bins RGB color histogram (48RGB_hist) with 16 bins for each channel is extracted. To characterize image content in different spatial regions, we extract color layout features (2x2_48RGB_hist and 4x4_RGB48_hist) which are color histogram features in 2x2 and 4x4 blocks of an image. A 36 bins edge histogram (edge_hist) is extracted on canny edge image to describe the shape property. A 320 bins GridHog (Histograms of Oriented

Figure 1. Framework of the video summary system

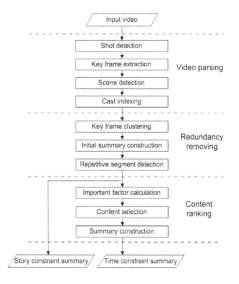

93

Gradient) feature (Dalai, 2005) is extracted in 2x2 blocks+1 center regions of a gradient image to characterize the fine-scale structure info. For the camera/object motion, we use a multi-resolution gradient-based alignment approach (Park, 1994) to estimate the dominant motion $[x, y, s]$, where x, y, s is the motion in x, y, and scale directions respectively.

Besides visual features, main objects and events generally happen with particular sounds, e.g. talking, music, explosion, shooting and car running etc. For audio features, Mel Frequency Cepstral Coefficients (MFCC), Energy and pitch features are extracted to detect speech, music, and explosion etc. To reserve intact speech in video clips, the speech segment boundaries are further used to adjust the boundaries of video clips.

Video Parsing

Similar to text summary based on word, sentence, paragraph and document, video summary can be analyzed from four granularity levels, i.e., key frame, shot, scene and the whole video. A shot is a set of video frames captured by a single camera in one consecutive recording action. A scene is one of subdivisions of a video in which the setting is fixed and time continuous, or when it presents the continuous action in one place.

Video parsing divides a whole video into shots, key frames and scenes to analyze video content in different granularity. Shot boundaries are detected by color histogram and camera motion features (Yuan, 2004). Then the key frames in each shot are extracted by a leader-follower clustering algorithm (Rasheed, 2003). Based on detected shots, we segment temporal-spatial coherent shots into scenes by NCuts algorithm (Rasheed, 2005; Zhao, 2007). Finally, a representative key frame in each scene is selected to construct a story board of the main scene list at the beginning of the video summary.

Cast Indexing

Based on face tracking and clustering, cast indexing discovers main actors and retrieve their associated video clips for efficient browsing. As shown in Figure 2, face tracking first detects and track faces in each shot and outputs face sets of continuous faces belonging to the same person (Li, 2006). Each face set contains a few face exemplars of the same person with different pose, expression and lighting to increase the clustering samples and accuracy. Then local SIFT features (Lowe, 1999) are extracted in five local regions of a normalized

Figure 2. Cast indexing by face tracking and clustering

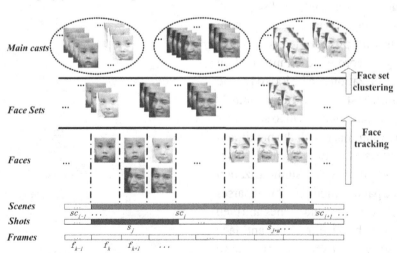

Figure 3. Local SIFT feature extraction. (a) The original face image; (b) Detected landmarks by face alignment; (c) SIFT feature extraction in five local regions of the normalized face

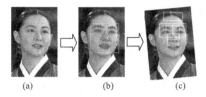

face image as shown in Figure 3. Secondly, face clustering discovers main actors by clustering similar face sets on the local SIFT features (Gao, 2007). Finally, Cast ranking module ranks actors by their importance factor (IF) of appeared time length and co-appeared frequency with others. A representative face image of each main actor is selected to construct a story board of the main cast list as shown in Figure 6.

Redundancy Removing

There are many redundant contents in a video. For example, a dialog scene has many similar shots of talking persons. By clustering similar frames and removing repetitive segments, the video length can be shortened a lot without losing the main objects and events in the video.

Key Frame Clustering

To shorten the video length, we first use hierarchical agglomerative clustering (HAC) to cluster similar key frames. In each scene, HAC iteratively merges the most similar key frames until the intra-cluster distance between any pair of key frames exceeds a pre-selected threshold. The distance threshold makes sure that the two merged key frames are similar to each other, e.g. the similarity score of RGB color histogram is above 0.85. After key frames clustering, the key frames located in each cluster center are reserved and other redundant key frames are removed.

Initial Summary Construction

Cognitive experiments show that the ideal playback length for each video segment is between 2.0~3.0 seconds (Gong, 2001). A playback time shorter than 2 seconds may result in a non-smooth and choppy video show, while a playback time longer than 3.0 seconds yields a lengthy and slow-paced one. According to this rule, we extend each reserved key frame to a 2 seconds video segment and adjust the video segment boundary not to cross the shot boundaries and speech boundary. By concatenating these video segments in the

Figure 4. Face clustering on face sets. (a) Representative face images of four face sets of two actors. (b) Corresponding manifolds are visualized by first two dimensions of PCA subspace where face clustering categorizes face set 1,4 and face set 2,3 as two actors

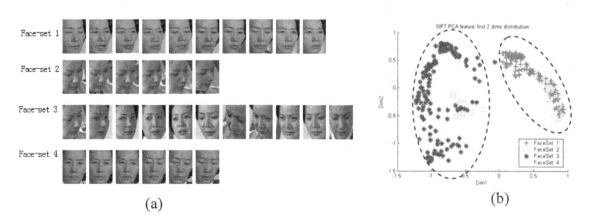

(a)   (b)

original video's temporal order, it generates an initial video summary for further processing.

Repetitive Segment Detection

Although key frame clustering in each scene removes similar key frames, the concatenated initial video summary may have some repetitive segments due to extending key frames to continuous video segments. To further remove redundant contents in the initial video summary, we employ "Smith-Waterman" local alignment algorithm to identify the similar segments. For two string sequences S_1 and S_2 with length l_1 and l_2, the Smith-Waterman algorithm (Temple, 1981) computes the similarity matrix $H(i, j)$ to identify the common subsequences, i.e. similar segments, by Equation (1):

$$
H(i, j) = \max \begin{cases} 0 \\ E(i, j) \\ F(i, j) \\ H(i-1, j-1) + sbt(S_{1i}, S_{2j}) \end{cases}
$$

$$
E(i, j) = \max \begin{cases} H(i, j-1) - \alpha \\ E(i, j-1) - \beta \end{cases}
$$

$$
F(i, j) = \max \begin{cases} H(i-1, j) - \alpha \\ F(i-1, j) - \beta \end{cases}
$$

$$
with \quad H(i, 0) = E(i, 0) = 0, \quad 0 \le i \le l_1
$$
$$
H(0, j) = F(0, j) = 0, \quad 0 \le j \le l_2
$$

$$(1)$$

where $sbt(S_{1i}, S_{2j})$ is the similarity value between character S_{1i}, and S_{2j}. Affine gap costs are defined as follows: α is the cost of the first gap; β is the cost of the following gaps. Each element $H(i, j)$ of the matrix H is a similarity value ending local alignment at the position (i, j). The common subsequence of S_1 and S_2 producing this value can be determined by a tracing-back procedure.

To find repetitive segments in the initial video summary sequence, we only trace back the positions in the upper triangle matrix of H because H is

a symmetrical matrix when $S_1 = S_2$. Then we merge matched blocks located in the same horizontal, or vertical strip regions and output long repetitive segments satisfying its average similarity score (*similarity score/matching length*) > *threshold*. Figure 5 illustrates an example to find repetitive segments in a video sequence "*ABCDEFBCD-JBCD*". The matrix H is shown for the computation with gap costs $\alpha = 2$ and $\beta = 2$, and a substitution cost of $+2$ if the characters are identical and -2 otherwise. The arrows illustrated the trace-backed path. If the tracked path ends at the diagonal, the matching path is invalid since two repetitive segments cannot start or end at the same position (i, i). By tracking all paths of the matrix H, it finds two similar blocks ($H_{1, 6\sim8}$, $H_{2, 1\sim3}$) and ($H_{1, 10\sim12}$, $H_{2, 1\sim3}$). Since the two blocks locate in the same horizontal strip region $1\sim3$, we merge them and output detected three repetitive segments s1$\sim$3, s6$\sim$8 and s10$\sim$12. After repetitive segment detection, we reserve the first appeared segments (e.g. s1$\sim$3) and remove repetitive segments to output the "*story-constraint video summary*".

Figure 5. Smith-Waterman local alignment to find repetitive segments "BCD" in a sequence "ABCDEFBCDJBCD". Gray arrows show invalid matching paths and red arrows illustrate valid matching paths

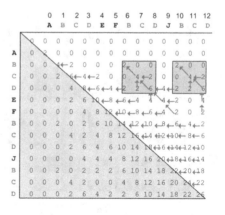

Content Ranking

Although "story-constraint summary" shortens the video length a lot, it may still be very long due to the complex video content. Like paper abstracts which have almost equal length (e.g. 120 words), users more prefer a "time-constraint summary" whose length is limited in a target length while containing as more as possible important contents. In this section, we propose content ranking to construct *"time-constraint summary"*.

Important Factor Calculation

Generally, key frames with people, sound, moving objects and high repetitive frequency bring user more information and are important to be reserved in the video summary. Therefore, the important factor (IF_{key}) of the kth key frame is calculated according to the number of appeared faces, audio energy, motion magnitude and repetitive number as Equation (2):

$$IF_{key}(k) = w_f I_f(k) + w_a I_a(k) + w_m I_m(k) + w_r I_r(k) \tag{2}$$

where I_f, I_a, I_m, I_r are the face number, audio's MFCC feature energy, motion magnitude and repetitive number (the key frame's cluster size) respectively. w_f, w_a, w_m, w_r are their corresponding weights.

A scene consists of shots and key frames. More important key frames and shot numbers, more important the scene will be. Therefore the scene important factor (IF_{sc}) of the ith scene is calculated by important factors of its key frames and shot number as Equation (3):

$$IF_{sc}(i) = w_k \sum_{k=k_1...k_{m_i}} IF_{key}(k) + w_s \cdot sh_i \tag{3}$$

where m_i and sh_i are the ith scene's key frame number and shot number respectively. $IF_{key}(k)$ is the important factor of the kth key frame

Time-Constraint Summary Construction

Assuming the length of required video summary is T, e.g. 60 seconds and each video segment is 2 seconds. For reserving intact speech to achieve better pleasant tempo, each video clip's boundary is adjusted by the corresponding speech segment's boundary. Based on ranked important factors, our approach selects 56/2=28 (the two story boards take 2+2=4 seconds in the 60 seconds) important video segments to construct a time-constraint summary by following steps:

Algorithm of time-constraint video summary

```
Input: a video
Output: story boards and time-con-
straint video summary
1.       Parse the video into
shots, key frames and scenes.
2.       Discover main actors by
cast indexing.
3.       Remove redundant key
frames by key frame clustering and
repetitive segment detection to
construct a "story-constraint video
summary".
4.       Calculate the important
factors of each key frame, and each
scene by Equation (2) and Equa-
tion(3).
5.       According to the con-
straint summary length T, decide the
number n_i of selected video segments
in each scene_i, where n_i ∝ IF_sc(i)
satisfying ∑ n_i = T. The rule is
that a scene with a higher important
factor IF_sc will be assigned more
video segments to show.
6.       In each scene_i, select n_i
key frames according to their ranked
IF_key order. A key frame with higher
importance factor IF_key will be se-
```

lected to show with higher priority.

7.   Extend selected key frames to short video segments and adjust the extended video segment's boundary not to cross the shot and speech boundaries.

8.   Generate the *story boards* of the main scene list and main cast lists and then concatenate selected important video segments by original temporal order to output the *"time-constraint video summary"*.

EXPERIMENTS

To demonstrate the performance of the proposed video summary approach, extensive experiments were conducted on 5 videos including a Korea TV series *"DaChangJin"*, a US soap opera *"Friends"*, a famous action movie *"007-die another day"*, a romantic Hollywood movie *"Sleepless in seattle"*, and a cartoon *"Shrek II"*. The details of testing videos are listed in Table 1, where L, N_{Sc}, N_{Sh}, N_{Kf} are the video length (seconds), scene number, shot number, and key frame number of original videos respectively. Five human observers watch these videos and manually summarized their contents which are used as the ground truth.

For each video, the system generates a story-constraint summary and a time-constraint sum-mary with time length 60s. After watching the original videos and the summarized videos, each reviewer gives three evaluation scores: Compression ratio (Cr), Informativeness (Im) and Satisfaction (Sa). Compression ratio is the ratio of summarized video length L' divided by the original video length L. Informativeness score evaluates how many objects/events of the original video are included in the summarized video. Satisfaction score indicates how satisfied the reviewers understand and prefer the summarized video. For I_m and S_a scores, the best score is 10 and the lowest score is 0.

The video summary first shows the generated story boards for 4 seconds to let user know about the main scenes and main actors and then playback the constructed video skimming. Figure 6 illustrates generated story boards of the TV series "DaChangJin", in which the main scenes and actors are well detected. Table 1 compares the performance of the story-constraint summary and the time-constraint summary. It can be observed that the averaged performance of the story-constraint summary with both story board and video skimming achieves good compress ratio Cr=6.4% and very high informativeness Im=9.3 and high satisfaction Sa=8.8. For different video types, the compress ratio changes significantly. The "007" movie contains many repetitive and short shots and is compressed better Cr=2.9% than other videos. However, since the shots of "shrek

Table 1. Performance comparison between the story-constraint and the time-constraint summary

Details of testing videos					Redundancy removing		Story-constraint summary				Time-constraint summary of 60s			
Video	$L(s)$	N_{Sc}	N_{Sh}	N_{Kf}	KeyCr	RepCr	$L'(s)$	$Cr(\%)$	Im	Sa	$L'(s)$	$Cr(\%)$	Im	Sa
DaChangJin	2650	23	597	766	8.4	92.8	216	8.2	10	9.5	60	2.3	8.5	8
Friends	1366	21	369	421	7.1	73.2	77	5.6	9	9	60	4.4	8.5	9
007	4018	23	1110	1651	2.9	78.9	103	2.6	8.5	8	60	1.5	8	7.5
Sleepless	5434	11	545	950	7.2	94.9	389	7.2	9.5	8.5	60	1.1	7.5	7
Shrek	5053	20	1142	2386	9.2	84.7	427	8.5	9.5	9	60	1.2	7.5	8
Average	3704	20	753	1235	7.0	84.9	242	6.4	9.3	8.8	60	2.1	8	7.9

Figure 6. Story boards of main scene list and main cast list

II" are long and independent, its compression ratio is a little bigger Cr=8.5%. Due to the time constraint of 60 seconds, the average performance of time-constraint summary has higher compress ratio Cr=2.1% but it still keeps good informativeness Im=8 and good satisfaction Sa=7.9. We also evaluate the performance of the redundancy removing modules. As the key frame clustering could remove most of the similar frames, the initial video summary shortens the original video length to $KeyCr$=7.0%. The repetitive segment detection further shortens the initial video summary length to $RepCr$=84.9%.

CONCLUSION AND FUTURE RESEARCH DIRECTIONS

Video summarization is a process of removing redundant contents and selecting important video segments to construct a shortened, logical and connected video. Different from traditional methods which have little processing on the video structure and semantic contents, this chapter proposes a novel video summarization approach based on video parsing, cast indexing, repetitive segment detection and content ranking. By video parsing and face analysis, the approach first constructs story boards to let user know about the main scenes and main actors. Then it constructs the story constraint and time-constraint video skimming by key frame clustering, repetitive segment detection, and content ranking. Extensive experiments are tested on TV series, movie, and cartoons.

The experimental results demonstrate the good performance of the proposed summary method.

Video summary has widespread application in video search, video browsing, personalized TV, and video editing etc. Although there is lots of literature in video summary research, automatic video summary is still not good enough at pleasant tempo, logical and connected property among concatenated video clips. For future research directions, the camera motion (zoom in/out, pan, tilt etc.) and audio categorization (music tempo, laughing, crying, shooting etc.) should be used to make the video summarization better in audiovisual characteristic. In addition, advanced event and highlight detection approaches can be employed to make personalized video summarization to reserve more impressive and exciting segments than the representative summarization of the whole video.

REFERENCES

Bailer, W., Lee, F., & Thallinger, G. (2007). Skimming Rushes Video Using Retake Detection. In *Proc. of the TRECVID Workshop on Video Summarization (TVS'07)*. ACM Multimedia.

Dalai, N., & Triggs, B. (2005). *Histograms of oriented gradients for human detection* (pp. 886–893). CVPR.

Gao, Y., Wang, T., Li, J.G., et al. (2007). *Cast Indexing for Videos by NCuts and Page Ranking*. ACM CIVR 2007.

Gong, Y. H., & Liu, X. (2001). *Video Summarization with Minimal Visual Content Redundancies.* IEEE Proc. of ICIP.

Hauptmann, A. G., Christel, M. G., Lin, W., et al. (2007). Clever Clustering vs. Simple Speed-Up for Summarizing BBC Rushes. In *Proc. of the TRECVID Workshop on Video Summarization (TVS'07).* ACM Multimedia.

Kleban, J., Sarkar, A., Moxley, E., et al. (2007). Feature Fusion and Redundancy Pruning for Rush Video Summarization. In *Proc. of the TRECVID Workshop on Video Summarization (TVS'07).* ACM Multimedia.

Li, C., Ou, Z. J., Hu, W., Wang, T., & Zhang, Y. (2008). Caption-aided speech detection in videos. *ICASSP, 2008,* 141–144.

Li, Y., Ai, H.Z., Huang, C., et al. (2006). *Robust Head Tracking with Particles Based on Multiple Cues Fusion.* ECCV 2006.

Li, Z., Schuster, G. M., & Katsaggelos, A. K. (2005). Rate-Distortion Optimial Video Summary Generation. *IEEE Transactions on Image Processing, 14*(10).

Lowe, D. (1999). Object recognition from local scale-invariant features.In *Proceedings of the 7th International Conference on Computer Vision (ICCV99),* (pp. 1150–1157). Corfu, Greece, September 1999.

Otsuka, I., Nakane, K., & Divakaran, A. (2005). A Highlight Scene Detection and Video Summarization System using Audio Feature for a Personal Video Recorder. *IEEE Transactions on Consumer Electronics, 51*(1), 112–116. doi:10.1109/TCE.2005.1405707

Over, P., Smeaton, A. F., & Awad, G. M. (2007). The TRECVID 2007 BBC Rushes Summarization Evaluation Pilot. In *Proc. of the TRECVID Workshop on Video Summarization (TVS'07).* ACM Multimedia.

Over, P., Smeaton, A. F., & Awad, G. M. (2008). The TRECVID 2008 BBC rushes summarization evaluation. In *Proc of the International Workshop on TRECVID Video Summarization(TVS '08).* ACM Multimedia.

Park, J. I., Yagi, N., Enami, K., Aizawa, K., & Hatori, M. (1994). Estimation of camera parameters from image sequence for model-based video coding. *CirSysVideo, 4*(3), 288–296.

Rasheed, Z., & Shah, M. (2003). Scene Detection in Hollywood Movies and TV shows. *IEEE Proc. of CVPR.*

Rasheed, Z., & Shah, M. (2005). Detection and Representation of Scenes in Videos. *IEEE Transactions on Multimedia, 7*(6), 1097–1105. doi:10.1109/TMM.2005.858392

Smith, T. F., & Waterman, M. S. (1981). Identification of Common Molecular Subsequences. *Journal of Molecular Biology,* 195–197. doi:10.1016/0022-2836(81)90087-5

Uchihashi, S., Foote, J., Girgensohn, A., & Boreczky, J. (1999). *Video Manga: Generating Semantically Meaningful Video Summaries.* ACM Multimedia.

Wang, F., & Ngo, C. W. (2007). Rushes Video Summarization by Object and Event Understanding. In *Proc. of the TRECVID Workshop on Video Summarization (TVS'07).* ACM Multimedia.

Wang, T., Gao, Y., Li, J. G., et al. (2007). THU-ICRC at Rush Summarization of TRECVID 2007. In *Proc. of the TRECVID Workshop on Video Summarization (TVS'07).* ACM Multimedia.

Yuan, J. H., Zheng, W. J., & Chen, L. (2004). 2004: shot boundary detection and high-level feature extraction. In *NIST workshop of TRECVID 2004.* Tsinghua University at TRECVID.

Zhao, Y.J., Wang, T., Wang, P., et al. (2007). Scene Segmentation and Categorization Using NCuts. *IEEE SLAM workshop of CVPR07.*

ADDITIONAL READING

Benini, S., Bianchetti, A., Leonardi, R., & Migliorati, P. (2006). Extraction of Significant Video Summaries by Dendrogram Analysis. *ICIP, 2006*, 133–136.

Ciocca, G., & Schettini, R. (2006). Supervised and unsupervised classification post-processing for visual video summaries. *IEEE Transactions on Consumer Electronics, 52*(2), 630–638. doi:10.1109/TCE.2006.1649689

Li, Z., Schuster, G. M., & Katsaggelos, A. K. (2005). Rate-Distortion Optimal Video Summary Generation. *IEEE Transactions on Image Processing, 14*(10).

Luo, J., Papin, C., & Costello, K. (2009). Towards Extracting Semantically Meaningful Key Frames From Personal Video Clips: From Humans to Computers. *IEEE Transactions on Circuits and Systems for Video Technology, 19*(2), 289–301. doi:10.1109/TCSVT.2008.2009241

Pan, C., Chuang, Y., & Hsu, W. H. (2007). NTU TRECVID-2007 Fast Rushes Summarization System. In *Proc. of the TRECVID Workshop on Video Summarization (TVS'07)*. ACM Multimedia.

Qiu, X.K., Jinag, S.Q., & Huang, Q.M. (2009). *Spatial-temporal video browsing for mobile environment based on visual attention analysis*. ICME 2009.

Ren, K., Fernando, W. A. C., & Calic, J. (2008). Optimising video summaries using unsupervised clustering. *50th International Symposium, ELMAR 2008* (pp. 451-454).

Taskiran, C. M., Pizlo, Z., & Amir, A. (2006). Automated video program summarization using speech transcripts. *IEEE Transactions on Multimedia, 8*(4), 775–791. doi:10.1109/TMM.2006.876282

Truong, B. T., & Venkatesh, S. (2007). Generating Comprehensible Summaries of Rushes Sequences Based on Robust Feature Matching. In *Proc. of the TRECVID Workshop on Video Summarization (TVS'07)*. ACM Multimedia.

Tsai, C., Chung, C., & Huang, Y. T. (2007). VCSR: Video Content Summarization for Recommendation. *ICALT, 2007*, 862–864.

You, J., Hannuksela, M. M., & Gabbouj, M. (2009). Semantic audiovisual analysis for video summarization. *IEEE EUROCON, 2009*, 1358–1363.

KEY TERMS AND DEFINITIONS

Cast Indexing: Discovers main actors and retrieve their associated video clips by face tracking, face clustering and face recognition.

Content Ranking: Ranks video clips by their important factors of the number of appeared faces, audio energy, motion magnitude and repetitive number as equation.

Redundancy Removing: Remove similar frames to reserve the main objects and events in the video.

Scene Segmentation: One of the subdivisions of a video in which the setting is fixed and time continuous, or when it presents the continuous action in one place.

Video Parsing: Divides a whole video into shots, key frames and scenes in order to analyze video content from different granularity levels.

Video Summarization: Generally a condensed sequence of still or moving images, which provide the essential content of a video in a general, logical, and connected way.

Chapter 7
Multi–Sensored Vision for Autonomous Production of Personalized Video Summary

Fan Chen
Université Catholique de Louvain, Belgium

Damien Delannay
Université Catholique de Louvain, Belgium

Christophe De Vleeschouwer
Université Catholique de Louvain, Belgium

Pascaline Parisot
Université Catholique de Louvain, Belgium

ABSTRACT

This chapter provides a survey of the major research efforts that have exploited computer vision tools to extend the content production industry towards automated infrastructures allowing contents to be produced, stored, and accessed at low cost and in a personalized and dedicated way.

INTRODUCTION

Today's media consumption evolves towards increased user-centric adaptation of contents, to meet the requirements of users having different expectations in terms of story-telling and heterogeneous constraints in terms of access devices. Individuals and organizations want to access dedicated contents through a personalized service that is able to provide what they are interested in, at the time when they want it and through the distribution channel of their choice.

Hence, democratic and personalized production of multimedia content is one of the most exciting challenges that content providers will have to face in the near future. In this chapter, we explain how it is possible to address this challenge by building on computer vision tools to automate the collection and distribution of audiovisual contents.

In a typical application scenario, as depicted in Figure 1, the sensor network for media acquisi-

DOI: 10.4018/978-1-60960-024-2.ch007

tion is composed of (microphones and) cameras, which, for example, cover a basket-ball field. Distributed analysis and interpretation of the scene are exploited to decide what to show or not to show about the event, so as to produce a video composed of a valuable subset from the streams provided by each individual camera, or interpolated from multiple cameras. The process involves numerous integrated technologies and methodologies, including but not limited to automatic scene analysis, camera viewpoint selection and control, and generation of summaries through automatic organization of stories. Considering the problem in a multi-camera environment not only mitigates the difficulty of scene understanding caused by reflection, occlusion and shadow in the single view case, but also offers higher flexibility in producing visually pleasant video reports. In final, multi-camera autonomous production/summarization can provide practical solutions to a wide range of applications, such as personalized access to local sport events through a web portal or a mobile hand-set (APIDIS, 2008; Papaoulakis, 2008), cost-effective and fully automated production of content dedicated to small-audience, e.g. souvenirs DVD, university lectures, conference (Rui, 2001; Al-Hames, 2007), etc, and interactive

browsing and automated summarization for video surveillance (Yamasaki, 2008).

From a technical perspective, this chapter will present a unified framework for cost-effective and autonomous generation of video contents from multi-sensored data. It will first investigate the automatic extraction of intelligent contents from a network of sensors distributed around the scene at hand. Here, intelligence refers to the identification of salient segments within the audiovisual content, using distributed scene analysis algorithms. Second, it will explain how that knowledge can be exploited to automate the production and personalize the summarization of video contents.

In more details, to identify salient segments in the raw video content, multi-camera analysis is considered, with an emphasis on people detection methods relying on the fusion of the foreground likelihood information computed in each view. We will observe that multi-view analysis can overcome traditional hurdles such as occlusions, shadows and changing illumination. This is in contrast with single sensor signal analysis, which is often subject to interpretation ambiguities, due to the lack of accurate model of the scene,

Figure 1. Vision of autonomous production of personalized video summaries

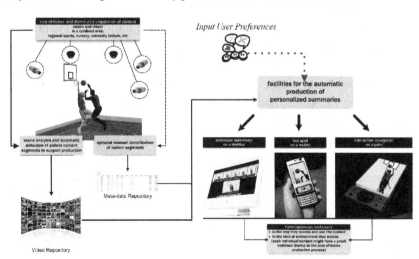

and to coincidental adverse scene configurations (Delannay, 2009).

To produce semantically meaningful and perceptually comfortable video summaries based on the extraction or interpolation of images from the raw content, our proposed framework introduces three fundamental concepts, i.e. "completeness", "smoothness" and "fineness", to abstract the semantic and narrative requirement of video contents. Based on those concepts, as a key contribution, we formulate the selection of camera viewpoints and that of temporal segments in the summary as two independent optimization problems. In short, those problems define and trade-off the above concepts as a function of the computer vision analysis outcomes, in a way that is easily parameterized by individual user preferences. Interestingly, the solution to the viewpoint selection problem is augmented by Markov regularization mechanisms (Chen, 2009a; Chen, 2010), while the formulation of the summarization problem builds on a generic resource allocation framework (Chen, 2009b).

Note that end-users do not have to access the multiple camera feeds in our application scenario. Those feeds are only exploited by the local server to create the video stream that is forwarded to the user. Moreover, to avoid repeating complex video production and compression operations for each user request, the timeline is divided into non-overlapping periods, and one or several video segments are produced for each period. Personalization is then achieved by selecting a subset of the pre-computed segments.

To demonstrate our framework, we consider both basket-ball and soccer use cases, and rely on some of the latest research outputs of the FP7 APIDIS research project (APIDIS, 2008). These methods presented here might be able to be extended to other controlled scenarios, such as conferences, lectures, and news with proper modifications. In this chapter, we will only focus on sport videos.

BACKGROUND

In this section, we survey the main achievements related to distributed video analysis, and to autonomous production of personalized video summaries. In the meantime, we position our contributions with respect to previous works in those fields, to highlight the originality of the approaches presented in subsequent sections.

Related Works in Autonomous Distributed Video Analysis

Tracking multiple people in cluttered and crowded scenes is a challenging task, primarily due to occlusion between people. The problem has been extensively studied, mainly because it is common to numerous applications, ranging from (sport) event reporting to surveillance in public space. Detailed reviews of tracking research in monocular or multi-view contexts are for example provided in (Yilmaz, 2006) or (Khan, 2009). In the context of team sport event monitoring, all players have similar appearance. For this reason, in this chapter, we focus on a particular subset of methods that do not use color models or shape cues of individual people, but instead rely on the distinction of foreground from background in each individual view to infer the ground plane locations that are occupied by people.

Detection of people from the foreground likelihood information, i.e. the probability that a pixel in an image belongs to the foreground, computed in multiple views has been investigated in details in the past few years. We differentiate two classes of approaches.

On the one hand, the authors in (Khan, 2006; Lanza, 2007; Khan, 2009; Delannay, 2009) adopt a bottom-up approach, and project the points of the foreground likelihood (background subtracted silhouettes) of each view to define a ground plane occupancy mask. Specifically, the change probability maps computed in each view are warped to (a set of planes that are parallel to) the ground plane based on homographies that have been computed off-line, e.g. based on reference points calibration. The projected maps are then merged to define the patches of the ground plane for which the appearance has changed compared to the background model and according to the single-view change detection algorithm.

On the other hand, the works in (Berclaz, 2008; Fleuret, 2008; Alahi, 2009) adopt a top-down approach. They consider a grid of points on the ground plane, and estimate the probabilities of occupancy of each point in the grid based on the back-projection of some kind of generative model in each one of the calibrated multiple views. Hence, they all start from the ground plane, and validate occupancy hypothesis based on associated appearance model in each one of the views. The approaches proposed in this second category mainly differ based on the kind of generative model they consider (rectangle or learned dictionary), and on the way they decide about occupancy in each point of the grid (combination of multiple view-based classifiers in (Berclaz, 2008), probabilistic occupancy grid inferred from background subtraction masks in (Fleuret, 2008), and sparsely constrained binary occupancy map for (Alahi, 2009)).

The first category of methods has the advantage to be computationally efficient, since the decision about ground plane occupancy is directly taken from the observation of the projection(s) of the change detection masks of the different views. In contrast, the complexity of the second category of algorithms depends on the number of ground plane points to be investigated (chosen to limit the area to be monitored), and on the computational load associated to the validation of each occupancy hypothesis. This validation process generally involves back-projection of a 3D-world template in each one of the views. Hence, in most practical cases, the first kind of approach is significantly less complex than the second one.

Moreover, in the particular case for which the objects to detect are vertical, the methods from the first category can also exploit the entire silhouette of the object to decide about ground occupancy. This is done by projecting the foreground silhouettes on multiple parallel planes instead of on the ground plane only (Delannay, 2009; Khan, 2009). Thereby, methods from the first category become able to achieve similar performances to the ones of the second category.

Later in this chapter, we present a player detection method that brings two fundamental improvements to methods from the first category. First, it computes the ground occupancy mask in a computationally efficient way, based on the implementation of integral image techniques on a well-chosen transformed version of the foreground silhouettes. Second, it proposes an original and simple greedy heuristic to handle occlusions, and alleviate the false detections occurring at the intersection of the masks projected from distinct players' silhouettes by distinct views. Until now, this phenomenon had only been taken into account by the method from the second category described in (Fleuret, 2008), through a complex iterative approximation of the joint posterior probabilities of occupancy. In contrast, whilst approximate, our approach appears to be both efficient and effective.

Related Works in Autonomous Production

Regarding the camerawork planning, we interpret the planning of "virtual" camera actions as selecting a camera view and its in-frame viewpoint, as depicted in Figure 2, rather than synthesizing a free-viewpoint scene. The related previous works are roughly classified into three major categories:

- **Event-triggered selection.** Camera switching or viewpoint movements are triggered by certain activities detected in the scene from audiovisual clues, such as an object entering the field of view or an audio event happening. (Kubicek, 2005) and (Rui, 2001) consider a meeting room

Figure 2. Two key tasks in automatic video editing: Camera selection and viewpoint selection

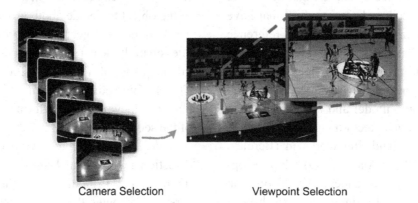

Camera Selection   Viewpoint Selection

scenario, and switch to the camera that displays the speaker. Event-triggered systems usually target at people-sparse and low-activity scenarios, and perform selection based on naive but explicit rules.

- **Rule-based selection.** More complicated conditions of camera switching can be achieved by introducing semantic or cinematic rules, relying on the analysis of objects, events and other contextual information. (Kubicek, 2005) used decaying curves to avoid fast camera switching and suppress too long shots in multimodal meetings. (Vronay, 2006a; Vronay, 2006b) selected a best shot from a list of candidate shots of each scene for a video conference or a multiplayer game TV show, according to pre-defined cinematic rules. (Papaoulakis, 2008) studied camera selection for athletic videos based on rules explicitly defined on user preferences and the characteristics of athletic events. The most challenge task is to extract explicit rules based on the integrated knowledge derived from scene understanding algorithms. For conference or athletic videos, it is possible to identify the dominant object of the scene, such as the speaker or the leading runner. Following this dominant object provides a reasonable

and effective base to those rules. However, it is difficult to guide all camera/viewpoint selection with pre-defined rules for people-dense scenarios, such as basketball, where players change their speeds and directions all the time and the ball is passing rapidly between players.

- **Data-driven selection.** Rather than defining explicit rules, methods in this category adaptively adjust camera and viewpoints by evaluating some criteria defined on the current contextual configuration. There are some methods proposed in the literature for selecting the most representative area from a standalone image (Suh, 2003; Xie, 2006), based on some visual attention model (Itti, 1998). In contrast, we presented an automatic video production system in (Chen, 2009a), where the optimal camera/viewpoint is found by evaluating some global metrics about the completeness, fineness and occlusion of the scene, under the specified user preference. Compared to event-triggered or rule-based methods, data-driven selection is able to deal with people-dense, high activity scenarios, such as team-sports, in a flexible and efficient manner.

Related Works in Personalized Video Summaries

Summarization implies selection of temporal segments and local stories organization. Here, we identify two classes of automatic methods that have addressed this problem in previous literature:

- **Methods targeting clustering of visual stimuli.** Many works interpreted video summarization as extracting a short video sequence of a desired length from native video content, in a way that minimizes the loss resulting from the skipped frames and/or segments. Those methods differ in their various definition of the similarity between the summary and the original video, and in their diversified techniques to maximize this similarity. They cluster similar frames/shots into so called key frames (Tseng, 2003; Ferman, 2003), or solve constrained optimization of objective functions (Li, 2005; Pahalawatta, 2005). Since they attempt to preserve as much as possible of the initial content, all those methods are well suited to support efficient browsing applications.

- **Methods targeting story-telling and semantic relevance.** End-users' motivation in viewing summaries is not limited to fast browsing of all clips in the whole video content. It also includes the intention to enjoy a concise video with well-organized story-telling and retrieval of semantically meaningful events that best satisfy users' interest. Regarding semantic relevance, we observe that many works have been devoted to the automatic detection of key actions in sport events, especially for football games (Qian, 2004; Ekin, 2003; Murphy, 2005; Jung, 2006; Pan, 2004; Gong, 2004). However, when addressing the problem of summary organization from actions, all

those methods just implement pre-defined filtering or ranking procedures to extract the actions of interest from the original audiovisual stream. Typically, it just arbitrarily extracts a pre-defined fraction of the scene, e.g. 15 or 30 seconds prior the end of the last live action segment preceding the replay (Gong, 2004), without taking care of story-telling artifacts. In contrast, (Albanese, 2006) considers the continuity of the clips included in the generated summary to improve story-telling, and (Chen B.W., 2009) organizes stories by considering a graph model for managing semantic relations among concept entities. Compared to general videos, stories in sport videos have much simpler structures and a limited set of possible events, which allows for both local and global control of story-telling without the need for sophisticated ontology or semantic graph models, as demonstrated by our work (Chen, 2009b) in the context of soccer summarization. It unifies all previous works, in the sense of exploiting all kind of available knowledge, related to either production principles or the semantic of events. It goes beyond previous works by offering a flexible and generic resource allocation framework to adaptively select audio-visual segments into the summary according to user preferences. By evaluating the benefit of segments from both the content and the presentation style of the summary, our framework is able to balance the semantic (what is included in the summary) and narrative (how it is presented to the user) aspects of the summary in a natural and personal way, which is the fundamental difference of our method to filtering based approaches.

AUTONOMOUS PRODUCTION OF PERSONALIZED VIDEO SUMMARIES

To produce condensed video reports of a (sport) event, the temporal segments corresponding to actions that are worth being included in the summary have to be selected. For each segment, local story organization and production of associated content are also essential. In an autonomous system, all those steps have to be run in an integrated manner, independently of any human intervention. This section describes the first attempt to integrate video analysis, production, and summarization technologies to automatically produce content, according to individual user preferences. We first present an overview of the proposed integrated automatic production and summarization framework. We then illustrate in details two of its main components, namely people detection from multiple views and automatic camerawork planning, in a team sport environment covered by a distributed set of still cameras.

Problem and Solution Overview

Although good production strategy and story organization are relative to a person's perspective, there are certain general principles whose implementation results in improved understanding of the scene, with a more enjoyable viewing experience.

In our proposed framework, we identify three major factors affecting the quality of the produced summary, namely the "completeness", the "fineness" and the "smoothness", and interpret production and summarization as optimization processes that trade-off among these three factors.

In more details, the factors are defined as follows:

- **Completeness** stands for both the integrity of view rendering in camera/viewpoint selection, and that of story-telling in summarization. A viewpoint of high completeness includes more salient objects, while a story of high completeness consists of more key actions.

- **Smoothness** refers to the graceful displacement of the virtual camera viewpoint, and to the continuous story-telling resulting from the selection of contiguous temporal segments. Preserving smoothness is important to avoid distracting the viewer from the story by abrupt changes of viewpoints or constant temporal jumps (Owen, 2007).

- **Fineness** refers to the amount of details provided about the rendered action. Spatially, it favors close views. Temporally, it implies redundant story-telling, including replays. Increasing the fineness of a video does not only improve the viewing experience, but is also essential in guiding the emotional involvement of viewers by close-up shots.

Obviously, those three concepts have to be maximized to produce a meaningful and visually pleasant content. In practice however, maximization of the three concepts often results in antagonist decisions, under some limited resource constraints, typically expressed in terms of the spatial resolution and temporal duration of the produced content. For example, at fixed output video resolution, increasing completeness generally induces larger viewpoints, which in turns decreases fineness of salient objects. Similarly, increased smoothness of viewpoint movement prevents accurate pursuit of actions of interest along the time. The same observations hold regarding the selection of segments and the organization of stories along the time, under some global duration constraints.

Hence, our production/summarization system turns to search for a good balance between the three major factors. It first defines quantitative metrics to reflect completeness, fineness, and closeness. It then formulates constrained optimization problems to balance those concepts. Interestingly, it appears that both the metrics and the problem can be formulated as a function of individual user preferences, typically expressed in terms of output video resolution, or preferred camera or players' actions, so that it becomes possible to personalize the produced content.

In addition, for improved computational efficiency, both production and summarization are envisioned in the divide and conquer paradigm. This especially makes sense since video contents intrinsically have a hierarchical structure, starting from each frame, shots (set of consecutive frames created by similar camerawork), to semantic segments (consecutive shots logically related to the identical action), and ending with the overall sequence.

Figure 3 summarizes the framework resulting from the above considerations. The event time-frame is first cut into semantically meaningful temporal segments, such as an offense/defense round of team sports, or an entry in news. For each segment, several narrative options are considered. Each option defines a local story, which consists of multiple shots with different camera coverage. A local story not only includes shots to render the global action at hand, but also shots for explanative and decorative purposes, e.g., replays and close-up views in sports or graph data in news. Given the timestamps and the production

strategy (close-up view, replay, etc) of the shots composing a narrative option, the camerawork associated to each shot is planned automatically, taking into account the knowledge inferred about the scene by video analysis modules.

Benefits and costs are then assigned to each local story. The cost simply corresponds to the duration of the summary. The benefit reflects user satisfaction (under some individual preferences[1]), and measures how some general requirements, e.g., the continuity and completeness of the story, are fulfilled. Those pairs of benefits and costs are then fed into the summarization engine, which solves a conventional resource allocation problem (Everett, 1963) to find the organization of local stories that achieves the highest benefit under the constrained summary length.

In the sequel, our framework for automatic planning of camerawork is described in details and demonstrated in the context of basket-ball production. Since our production framework relies on the knowledge of players' positions, we also derive an original multi-view algorithm that detects people from their background-subtracted silhouettes.

Due to space limitation, we omit the description of the summarization resource allocation framework, but refer interested readers to our

Figure 3. Automatic production in divide-and-conquer paradigm

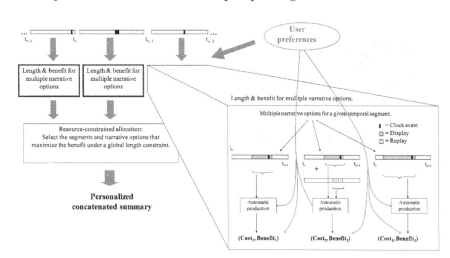

paper (Chen, 2009b) for a detailed description and a study of the football use case.

Camerawork Planning for Team Sport Videos

In this section, we develop an algorithm for basketball video production, as a realistic implementation of the above integrated framework for content production. Whilst extendable to other contexts (e.g. PTZ camera control), the process has been designed to select which fraction of which camera view should be cropped in a distributed set of still cameras to render the scene at hand in a semantically meaningful and visually pleasant way by assuming the knowledge of players' positions in (Chen, 2009a; Chen 2010). In Figure 4, we schematically depict the three steps composing the process, and describe them as follows.

Step 1: Camera-Wise Viewpoint Selection

At each time instant and in each view, we assume that the players' supports are known, and select the

cropping parameters that optimize the trade-off between completeness and fineness.

Formally, a viewpoint $\mathbf{v}_{ki}$ in the kth camera view of the ith frame is defined by the size S_{ki} and the center $\mathbf{c}_{ki}$ of the window that is cropped in the kth view for actual display. It has to be selected to include the objects of interest, and provide a fine, i.e. high resolution, description of those objects. If there are N salient objects in this frame, and the location of the nth object in the kth view is denoted by $\mathbf{x}_{nki}$, we select the optimal viewpoint $\mathbf{v}_{ki}{}^*$, by maximizing a weighted sum of object interests as follows:

$$\mathbf{v}_{ki}^{\,*} = \underset{\{S_{ki},\mathbf{c}_{ki}\}}{\arg\max} \sum_{n=1}^{N} I_n \cdot \beta(S_{ki},\mathbf{u}) \cdot \alpha\left(\frac{\left\|\mathbf{x}_{nki}-\mathbf{c}_{ki}\right\|}{S_{ki}}\right)$$

(1)

In the above equation:

- I_n denotes the level of interest assigned to the nth object detected in the scene. Note that assigning distinct weights to team sport players allows focusing on a pre-

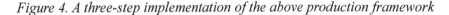

Figure 4. A three-step implementation of the above production framework

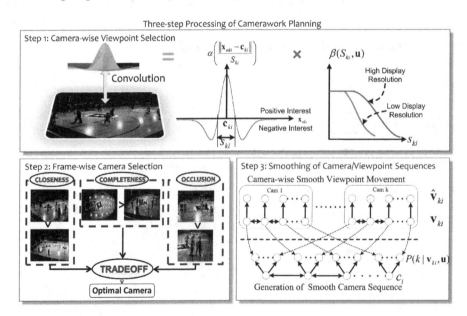

ferred player, but also implies recognition of each player. Player digit recognition is for example considered in (Delannay, 2009). In the rest of the chapter, we assign a unit weight to all players, thereby producing a video that renders the global team sport action.

- The vector **u** reflects the user constraints and preferences in terms of viewpoint resolution and camera view, $\mathbf{u}=[u^{close}\ u^{res}\ \{u_k\}]$. In particular, its component u^{res} defines the resolution of the output stream, which is generally constrained by the transmission bandwidth or end-user device resolution. Its component u^{close} is set to a value larger than 1, and increases to favor close viewpoints compared to large zoom-out views. The other components of **u** are dealing with camera preferences, and are defined in the second step below.

- The function $\alpha(.)$ modulates the weights of the objects according to their distance to the center of the viewpoint, compared to the size of this window. Intuitively, the weight should be high and positive when the object-of-interest is located in the center of the display window, and should be negative or zero when the object lies outside the viewing area. Many instances are appropriate (Chen, 2009-1), among which the well-known Mexican Hat function.

- The function $\beta(.)$ reflects the penalty induced by the fact that the native signal captured by the kth camera has to be subsampled once the size of the viewpoint becomes larger than the maximal resolution u^{res} allowed by the user. This function typically decreases with S_{ki}. An appropriate choice consists in setting the function equal to one when $S_{ki} < u^{res}$, and in making it decrease afterwards. An example of $\beta(.)$ is defined by:

$$\beta\left(S_{ki}, \mathbf{u}\right) = \left[\min\left(\frac{u^{res}}{S_{ki}}, 1\right)\right]^{u^{close}}, \qquad (2)$$

where $u^{close} > 1$ increases to favor close viewpoints compared to large zoom-out views.

Step 2: Frame-Wise Camera Selection

We rate the viewpoint selected in each view according to the quality of its completeness/closeness trade-off, and to its degree of occlusions. The highest rate should correspond to a view that (1) makes most object of interest visible, and (2) is close to the action, meaning that it presents important objects with lots of details, i.e. a high resolution.

Formally, given the interest I_n of each player, the rate $I_{ki}(\mathbf{v}_{ki}, \mathbf{u})$ associated to each camera view is defined as follows:

$$I_{ki}(\mathbf{v}_{ki}, \mathbf{u}) = u_k \cdot \sum_{n=1}^{N} I_n \cdot o_k\left(\mathbf{x}_{nki} | \overline{\mathbf{x}}\right) \cdot h_k\left(\mathbf{x}_{nki}\right) \cdot \beta\left(S_{ki}, \mathbf{u}\right) \cdot \alpha\left(\frac{\|\mathbf{x}_{nki} - \mathbf{c}_{ki}\|}{S_{ki}}\right)$$
$$(3)$$

In the above equation:

- u_k denotes the weight assigned to the kth camera, while α and β are defined as in the first step above.

- $\mathbf{o}_k(\mathbf{x}_{nki} | \overline{x})$ measures the occlusion ratio of the nth object in camera view k, knowing the position of all other objects. The occlusion ratio of an object is defined to be the fraction of pixels of the object that are hidden by other objects when projected on the camera sensor.

- The height $h_k(\mathbf{x}_{nki})$ is defined to be the height in pixels of the projection in view k of a six feet tall vertical object located in $\mathbf{x}_{nki}$. Six feet is the average height of the players. The value of $h_k(\mathbf{x}_{nki})$ is directly computed based on camera calibration. When calibration is not available, it can be estimated based on the height of the object detected in view k.

Step 3: Smoothing of Camera/ Viewpoint Sequences

For the temporal segment at hand, we then compute the parameters of an optimal virtual camera that pans, zooms and switches across views to preserve high ratings of selected viewpoints while minimizing the amount of virtual camera movements.

The smoothing process is implemented based on the definition of two Markov Random Fields, as shown in Figure 4. At first, we take $\hat{\mathbf{v}}_{ki}$ as observed data on the ith image, and assume that they are noise-distorted outputs of some underlying smooth results $\mathbf{v}_{ki}$. Given the smooth viewpoint sequence recovered for each camera, we then compute camera-gains $I_{ki}(\mathbf{v}_{ki}, \mathbf{u})$ of those derived viewpoints, and infer a smooth camera sequence from the second Markov field, by making the probabilities $P(k|\mathbf{v}_{ki}, \mathbf{u})$ of each camera proportional to the gains $I_{ki}(\mathbf{v}_{ki}, \mathbf{u})$.

More details about the smoothing process are available in (Chen, 2009a).

Compared to simple Gaussian smoothing filters, the depicted model enables adaptive smoothing by setting different smoothing strength on each individual frame. Furthermore, iterative slight smoothing in our method is able to achieve softer results than one-pass strong smoothing.

Multi-View Player Detection and Recognition

As explained above, autonomous production of visual content relies on the detection (and recognition) of object-of-interest in the scene. In this section, we explain how players can be detected based on joint processing of multiple views.

The method is depicted in Figure 5. Similar to (Khan, 2009) or (Fleuret, 2008), our approach computes foreground likelihood independently on each view, using standard background modeling techniques. Our method then fusions those likelihoods by projecting them on the ground plane, thereby defining a set of so-called ground occupancy masks. The originality of our method compared to (Khan, 2009) comes both from the efficient computation of the ground occupancy mask associated to each view, and from the way those masks are combined and processed to infer the actual position of players. In final, our method appears to improve the state of the art both in terms of computational efficiency and detection reliability.

Formally, the computation of the ground occupancy mask G_k associated to the kth view is described as follows. At a given time, the kth view is the source of a foreground likelihood image $F_k \in [0,1]^{Mk}$, where M_k is the number of pixels of camera k, $0 < k < C$. Due to the player verticality assumption, vertical line segments anchored in occupied positions on the ground plane support a part of the detected object, and thus back-project on foreground silhouettes in each camera view. Hence, to reflect ground occupancy in x, the value of G_k in x is defined to be the integration of the (forward-)projection of F_k on a vertical segment anchored in x. Obviously, this integration can equivalently be computed in F_k, along the back-projection of the vertical segment anchored in x. This is in contrast with (Khan, 2009), which computes the mask by aggregating the projections of the foreground likelihood on a set of planes that are parallel to the ground.

To speed up the computations associated to our formulation, we observe that, through appropriate transformation of F_k, it is possible to shape the back-projected integration domain so that it also corresponds to a vertical segment in the transformed view, thereby making the computation of integrals particularly efficient through the principle of integral images. Figure 6 illustrates that specific transformation for one particular view. The transformation has been designed to address a double objective. First, points of the 3D

Figure 5. Multi-view people detection. Foreground masks are projected and aggregated to define a ground plane occupancy map, from which players' positions are directly inferred

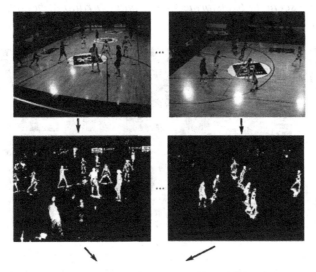

Aggregated ground occupancy mask (half of field)

space located on the same vertical line have to be projected on the same column in the transformed view (vertical vanishing point at infinity). Second, vertical objects that stand on the ground and whose feet are projected on the same horizontal line of the transformed view have to keep same projected heights ratios. Once the first property is met, the 3D points belonging to the vertical line standing above a given point from the ground plane simply project on the column of the transformed view that stands above the projection of the 3D ground plane point. Hence, $G_k(x)$ is simply computed

as the integral of the transformed view over this vertical back-projected segment. Preservation of height along the lines of the transformed view even further simplifies computations.

For side views, these two properties can be achieved by virtually moving (through homography transforms) the camera viewing direction (principal axis) so as to bring the vertical vanishing point at infinity and ensure horizon line is horizontal. For top views, the principal axis is set perpendicular to the ground and a polar mapping is performed to achieve the same properties. Note

113

Figure 6. Efficient computation of the ground occupancy mask: the original view (on the left) is mapped to a plane through a combination of homographies that are chosen so that (1) verticality is preserved during projection from 3D scene to transformed view, and (2) ratio of heights between 3D scene and projected view is preserved for objects that lies on the same line in the transformed view

that in some geometrical configurations, these transformations can induce severe skewing of the views.

Given the ground occupancy masks G_k for all views, we now explain how to infer the position of the people standing on the ground. A priori, in a team sport context, we know that (i) each player induces a dense cluster on the sum of ground occupancy masks, and (ii) the number of people to detect is equal to a known value N, e.g. N = 12 for basket-ball (10 players + 2 referees).

For this reason, in each ground location x, we consider the sum of all projections -normalized by the number of views that actually cover x-, and look for the higher intensity spots in this aggregated ground occupancy mask. To locate those spots, we have first considered a naive greedy approach that is equivalent to an iterative matching pursuit procedure. At each step, the matching pursuit process maximizes the inner product between a translated Gaussian kernel, and the aggregated ground occupancy mask. The position of the kernel which induces the larger inner-product defines the player position. Before running the next iteration, the contribution of the Gaussian kernel is subtracted from the aggregated mask to produce a residual mask. The process iterates until sufficient players have been located.

This approach is simple, but suffers from many false detections at the intersection of the projections of distinct players silhouettes from different views. This is due to the fact that occlusions induce non-linearities in the definition of the ground occupancy mask[2]. Hence, knowledge about the presence of some people on the ground field affects the informative value of the foreground masks in these locations. In particular, if the vertical line associated to a position x is occluded by/occludes another player whose presence is very likely, this particular view should not be exploited to decide whether there is a player in x or not.

For this reason, we propose to refine our naive approach as follows. To initialize the process, we define $G_k^1(x) = G_k(x)$ to be the ground occupancy mask associated to the kth view, and set $w_k^1(x)$ to 1 when x is covered by the kth view, and to 0 otherwise.

Each iteration is then run in two steps. At iteration n, the first step searches for the most likely position of the nth player, knowing the position of the $(n-1)$ players located in previous iterations. The second step updates the ground occupancy masks of all views to remove the contribution of the newly located player.

Formally, the first step of iteration n aggregates the ground occupancy mask from all views, and then searches for the denser cluster in this mask. Hence, it computes the aggregated mask as:

$$G^n\left(x\right) = \frac{\sum_{k=1}^{C} w_k^n\left(x\right).G_k^n\left(x\right)}{\sum_{k=1}^{C} w_k^n\left(x\right)}, \qquad (4)$$

and then defines the most likely position x_n for the nth player by

$$x_n = \underset{y}{\mathrm{argmax}} < G^n, \psi(y) > \qquad (5)$$

where $\psi(y)$ denotes a Gaussian kernel centered in y, and whose spatial support corresponds to the typical width of a player.

In the second step, the ground occupancy mask of each view is updated to account for the presence of the nth player. In the ground position x, we consider that the typical support of a player silhouette in view k is a rectangular box of width W and height H, and observe that the part of the silhouette that occludes or is occluded by the newly detected player does not bring any information about the potential presence of a player in position x. In (Delannay, 2009), we estimate the fraction $\varphi_k(x, x_n)$ of the silhouette in ground position x that becomes non-informative in the kth view, as a consequence of the presence of a player in x_n. We then propose to update the ground occupancy mask and aggregation weight of the kth camera in position x as follows:

$$G_k^{n+1}\left(x\right) = \max\left(0, G_k^n\left(x\right) - \varphi_k\left(x, x_n\right).G_k^1\left(x_n\right)\right), \qquad (6)$$

$$w_k^{n+1}\left(x\right) = \max\left(0, w_k^n\left(x\right) - \varphi_k\left(x, x_n\right)\right). \qquad (7)$$

For improved computational efficiency, we limit the positions x investigated in the refined approach to the 30 local maxima that have been detected by the naive approach.

For completeness, we note that the above described update procedure omit the potential interference between occlusions caused by distinct players in the same view. However, the consequence of this approximation is far from being dramatic, since it ends up in omitting part of the information that was meaningful to assess the occupancy in occluded positions, without affecting the information that is actually exploited. Taking those interferences into account would require to back-project the player silhouettes in each view, thereby tending towards a computationally and memory expensive top-down approach such as the one presented in (Fleuret, 2008) and (Alahi, 2009). In these approaches, the authors propose formulations that simultaneously search for the N positions that best explain the multiple foreground masks observations. However, jointly considering all positions increases the dimensionality of the problem, and dramatically impacts the computational load. Since our experimental results show that our proposed method does not suffer from the usual weaknesses of greedy algorithms, such as a tendency to get caught in bad local minima, we believe that it compares very favorably to any joint formulation of the problem, typically solved based on iterative proximal optimization techniques. This statement is for example confirmed when comparing the results reported in (Delannay, 2009) and (Alahi, 2009).

Experimental Results

In Figure 7, we plotted the average missed detection and false detection rates that are achieved by our method on a 3 minutes-long segment of the APIDIS basket ball dataset. Distinction is made between the performance of our basic approach - which can be related to the approach proposed by (Khan, 2009) - and the improvement brought by our refined approach. We also plotted the results that we obtained when projecting the foreground masks on the ground plane only, similar to the approach described in (Khan, 2006). The achieved performance is quite satisfying with respect to the automatic production process requirements. Using these results as input, a tracking algorithm can further improve the performance assuming temporal consistency of player tracks. Combined with a number recognition (OCR) algorithm(Delannay, 2009), one can track individual players from the time they enter until they exit the court. This knowledge can then be used to infer the valuable information about the ongoing events to feed the personalized summarization process.

Figure 8 gives the thumbnails of the videos produced under three different display resolutions, based on the above player detection performance. When the resolution is low, the selected viewpoint will focus on less objects or more condensed area, e.g. side view from the far end as shown in the first column. When the resolution gets higher, the selected viewpoint will include more objects and favor wide views. Readers are invited to visit the website of APIDIS project (Apidis, 2008), to view more video results and forge their own opinions.

Extensive quantitative results on system behavior and subjective evaluation can be found in (Chen, 2009a~2009b, 2010).

FUTURE RESEARCH DIRECTIONS

The technology presented in this chapter paves the way for a novel discipline, with numerous applications ranging from coaching assistance to sport event production and summarization. Practical deployment of commercially viable systems would however benefit from advances related to:

- **Improved computational efficiency.** Real-time and low latency implementation of the players' detection algorithms would allow to control the parameters of a (set of) dynamic pan-tilt-zoom camera(s), by using the autonomous production principles to select appropriate PTZ parameters to render the scene. This would dramatically

Figure 7. ROC analysis of player detection performance

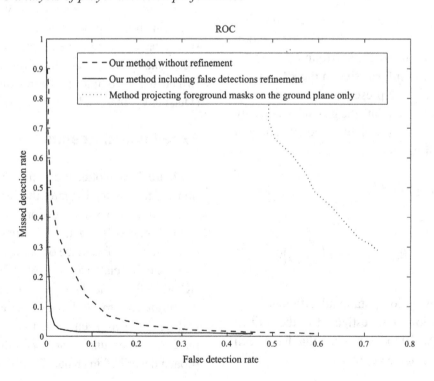

Figure 8. Results of automatic video production

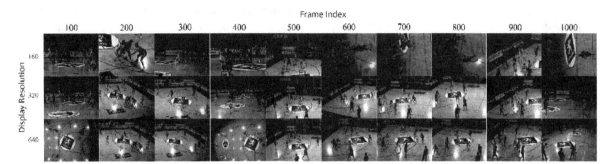

improve the quality of images compared to the ones generated based on still image cropping, which in turns would open TV broadcast markets.

- **Improved story organization.** The mechanisms controlling camerawork planning and local/global story organization are quite flexible in the way they integrate the user preferences and the applicative context. In particular, the importance assigned to a particular salient object or the benefit resulting from a local story can be arbitrarily chosen. This opens the door for a wide range of application scenarios, both within and outside sport environment.
- **Automatic collection of meta-data.** Although our frameworks of video production and summarization can live with few semantic meta-data (Chen, 2009b; Chen, 2010), their personalization capabilities can be significantly refined by integrating more abundant and accurate meta-data. We expect improved automatic collection of meta-data, by making further progress on player recognition (see Delannay, 2009), ball tracking, and event recognition. Being able to generate those metadata automatically could also open perspectives in terms of annotation of content resulting from conventional human-made production.
- **Inclusion of audio information.** Synthesis of audio commentary from the knowledge

collected about the action is certainly a central task to consider in a near future. It brings benefits in terms of user experience, but also multimodal challenges related to the definition of audiovisual completeness, smoothness, and fineness.

CONCLUSION

It appears from this chapter that our method for producing personalized video summaries has four major advantages. Namely, it offers (1) Strong personalization opportunities. Semantic clues about the events detected in the scene can easily be taken into account to adapt camerawork or story organization to the needs of the users. (2) Improved story-telling complying with production principles. On the one hand, production cares about smooth camera movement while focusing on semantically meaningful actions. On the other hand, summarization naturally favors continuous and complete local stories. (3) Computational efficiency. We adopt a divide-and-conquer strategy and consider a hierarchical processing, from frames to segments. (4) Generic and flexible deployment capabilities. The proposed framework balances the benefits and costs of different production strategies, where benefits and other narrative options can be defined in many ways, depending on the application context.

ACKNOWLEDGMENT

This work has been partly funded by FP7 Apidis European Project, DGTRE Walcomo project, and Belgium NSF.

REFERENCES

Al-Hames, M., Hornler, B., Muller, R., Schenk, J., & Rigoll, G. (2007). Automatic multi-modal meeting camera selection for video-conferences and meeting browsers. In *Proceedings of the 2007 IEEE International Conference on Multimedia and Expo* (pp. 2074-2077). Beijing, China: IEEE.

Alahi, A., Boursier, Y., Jacques, L., & Vandergheynst, P. (2009). A sparsity constrained inverse problem to locate people in a network of cameras. In *Proceedings of the 16th International Conference on Digital Signal Processing (DSP)*, Santorini, Greece.

Albanese, M., Fayzullin, M., Picariello, A., & Subrahmanian, V. S. (2006). The priority curve algorithm for video summarization. *Information Systems*, *31*(7), 679–695. doi:10.1016/j. is.2005.12.003

APIDIS. (2008). Autonomous Production of Images Based on Distributed and Intelligent Sensing. Homepage of the APIDIS project. http://www.apidis.org/ Demo videos related to this paper. http://www.apidis.org/InitialResults/APIDIS%20Initial%20Results.htm

Berclaz, J., Fleuret, F., & Fua, P. (2008). Principled detection-by-classification from multiple views. In [VISAPP]. *Proceedings of the International Conference on Computer Vision Theory and Application*, *2*, 375–382.

Chen, B. W., Wang, J. C., & Wang, J. F. (2009). A novel video summarization based on mining the story-structure and semantic relations among concept entities. *IEEE Transactions on Multimedia*, *11*(2), 295–312. doi:10.1109/TMM.2008.2009703

Chen, F., & De Vleeschouwer, C. (2009a). *Autonomous production of basket-ball videos from multi-sensored data with personalized viewpoints*. The 10th international workshop for multimedia interactive services (pp. 81–84). London, UK: IEEE.

Chen, F., & De Vleeschouwer, C. (2009b). A resource allocation framework for summarizing team sport videos. *2009 IEEE International Conference on Image Processing*, (Vol. 1, pp.4349-4352), Cairo, Egypt: IEEE.

Chen, F., & De Vleeschouwer, C. (2010). Personalized production of team sport videos from multi-sensored data under limited display resolution. *Computer Vision and Image Understanding. Special Issue on Sensor Fusion*, *114*(6), 667–680.

Delannay, D., Danhier, N., & De Vleeschouwer, C. (2009). Detection and recognition of sports (wo)men from multiple views. *The 3rd ACM/IEEE International Conference on Distributed Smart Cameras*. Como, Italia: IEEE.

Ekin, A., & Tekalp, M. (2003). Automatic soccer video analysis and summarization. *IEEE Transactions on Image Processing*, *12*(7), 796–807. doi:10.1109/TIP.2003.812758

Everett, H. (1963). Generalized lagrange multiplier method for solving problems of optimum Allocation of Resources. *Operations Research*, *11*(3), 399–417. doi:10.1287/opre.11.3.399

Ferman, A. M., & Tekalp, A. M. (2003). Two-stage hierarchical video summary extraction to match low-level user browsing preferences. *IEEE Transactions on Multimedia*, *5*(2), 244–256. doi:10.1109/TMM.2003.811617

Fleuret, F., Berclaz, J., Lengagne, R., & Fua, P. (2008). Multi-camera people tracking with a probabilistic occupancy map. *IEEE Transactions on Pattern Analysis and Machine Intelligence*, *30*(2), 267–282. doi:10.1109/TPAMI.2007.1174

Gong Y. (2004). Method and apparatus for personalized multimedia summarization based upon user specified theme. Nippon Electric Co [JP], US6751776 (B1).

Itti, L., Koch, C., & Niebur, E. (1998). A model of saliency-based visual attention for rapid scene analysis. *IEEE Transactions on Pattern Analysis and Machine Intelligence*, 20(11), 1254–1259. doi:10.1109/34.730558

Jung C., Kin C., Kim S.K., Lee G., Kim W.Y., & Hwang S., (2006). Method and Apparatus for Summarizing Sports Moving Picture. Samsung Electronics Co Ltd, JP2006148932.

Khan, S., & Shah, M. (2006). A multiview approach to tracing people in crowded scenes using a planar homography constraint. In *Proceedings of the 9th European Conference on Computer Vision (ECCV)* (Vol. 4, pp. 133-146).

Khan, S. M., & Shah, M. (2009). Tracking multiple occluding people by localizing on multiple scene planes. *IEEE Transactions on Pattern Analysis and Machine Intelligence*, 31(3), 505–519. doi:10.1109/TPAMI.2008.102

Kubicek, R., Zak, P., Zemcik, P., & Herout, A. (2008). Automatic video editing for multimodal meetings, *International Conference on Computer Vision and Graphics 2008* (pp. 1-12), Warsaw, Poland: Springer.

Lanza, A., Di Stefano, L., Berclaz, J., Fleuret, F., & Fua, P. (2007). Robust multiview change detection, *British Machine Vision Conference (BMVC)*, Warwick, UK.

Li, Z., Schuster, G. M., & Katsaggelos, A. K. (2005). MINMAX optimal video summarization. *IEEE Transactions on Circuits and Systems for Video Technology*, 15(10), 1245–1256. doi:10.1109/TCSVT.2005.854230

Murphy N., & Smeaton A., (2005). Audio-visual sequence analysis, WO2005124686 A1, Univ Dublin City, Publication info: IE20040412 (A1).

Owens, J. (2007). *Television sports production* (4th ed.). Burlington, MA: Focal Press.

Pahalawatta, P. V., Zhu, L., Zhai, F., & Katsaggelos, A. K. (2005). Rate-distortion optimization for internet video summarization and transmission. *IEEE 7th Workshop on Multimedia Signal Processing* (pp. 1-4). Shanghai, China: IEEE.

Pan, H., & Li, B.X., (2004). Summarization of soccer video content, US20040017389A1.

Papaoulakis, N., Doulamis, N., Patrikakis, C., Soldatos, J., Pnevmatikakis, A., & Protonotarios, E. (2008). Real-time video analysis and personalized media streaming environments for large scale athletic events. In *Proceeding of the 1st ACM Workshop on Analysis and Retrieval of Events/Actions and Workflows in Video Streams* (pp.105-112). Vancouver, Canada: ACM.

Qian, R., & Haering, N. (2004). Method for automatic extraction of semantically significant events from video, US6721454 (B1), Sharp Lab Of America Inc.

Rui, Y., Gupta, A., & Cadiz, J. J. (2001). Viewing meetings captured by an omni-directional camera. In *Proceedings of the SIGCHI Conference on Human Factors in Computing Systems* (pp. 450-457). Seattle, USA: ACM.

Suh, B., Ling, H., Bederson, B. B., & Jacobs, D. W. (2003). Automatic thumbnail cropping and its effectiveness. In *Proceedings of the 16th Annual ACM Symposium on User interface Software and Technology* (pp. 95-104). Vancouver, Canada: ACM.

Tseng, B. L., & Smith, J. R. (2003). Hierarchical video summarization based on context clustering. In Smith, J. R., Panchanathan, S., & Zhang, T. (Eds.), *Internet Multimedia Management Systems IV: Proceedings of SPIE* (pp. 14–25). Orlando, USA: SPIE-International Society for Optical Engine.

Vronay, D., Wang, S., Zhang, D., & Zhang, W. (2006a). Automatic video editing for real-time multi-point video conferencing. *US Patent 20060251384*.

Vronay, D., Wang, S., Zhang, D., & Zhang, W. (2006b). Automatic video editing for real-time generation of multiplayer game show videos. *US Patent 20060251383*.

Xie, X., Liu, H., Ma, W. Y., & Zhang, H. J. (2006). Browsing large pictures under limited display sizes. *IEEE Transactions on Multimedia, 8*(4), 707–715. doi:10.1109/TMM.2006.876294

Yamasaki, T., Nishioka, Y., & Aizawa, K. (2008). Interactive retrieval for multi-camera surveillance systems featuring spatio-temporal summarization. In *Proceedings of the 16th ACM international Conference on Multimedia: MM '08* (pp.797-800). New York: ACM.

Yilmaz, A., Javed, O., & Shah, M. (2006). *Object tracking: a survey*. ACM J. Computing Surveys.

ENDNOTES

[1]   Note that this might involve video analysis, to measure the consistency between the preferences of the users, and the actual content of the scene.

[2]   In other words, the ground occupancy mask of a group of players is not equal to the sum of ground occupancy masks projected by each individual player.

Chapter 8
A Perceptual Approach for Image Representation and Retrieval:
The Case of Textures

Noureddine Abbadeni
King Saud University, Saudi Arabia

ABSTRACT

This chapter describes an approach based on human perception to content-based image representation and retrieval. We consider textured images and propose to model the textural content of images by a set of features having a perceptual meaning and their application to content-based image retrieval. We present a new method to estimate a set of perceptual textural features, namely coarseness, directionality, contrast and busyness. The proposed computational measures are based on two representations: the original images representation and the autocovariance function (associated with images) representation. The correspondence of the proposed computational measures to human judgments is shown using a psychometric method based on the Spearman rank-correlation coefficient. The set of computational measures is applied to content-based image retrieval on a large image data set, the well-known Brodatz database. Experimental results show a strong correlation between the proposed computational textural measures and human perceptual judgments. The benchmarking of retrieval performance, done using the recall measure, shows interesting results. Furthermore, results merging/fusion returned by each of the two representations is shown to allow significant improvement in retrieval effectiveness.

1. INTRODUCTION

Texture has been extensively studied and used in literature as it plays a very important role in human visual perception. Defining texture is not that easy; however some intuitive concepts can be defined about texture. Texture refers to the spatial distribution of grey-levels and can be defined as the repetition of one or several primitives in an image, in a deterministic or random way. Microtextures refer to textures with small primitives while macrotextures refer to textures with large primitives (Tomita & Tsuji, 1990; Tuceryan & Jain, 1993; Van Gool, Dewaele, &

DOI: 10.4018/978-1-60960-024-2.ch008

Oosterlinck, 1985). Texture analysis techniques have been used in several domains such as classification, segmentation, shape from texture, and image retrieval. In a general way, texture analysis techniques can be divided into two main categories: spatial techniques and frequency-based techniques. Generally, the frequency-based methods are based on the analysis of the spectral density function in the frequency-based domain. Such methods include the Fourier transform and the wavelet-based methods such as the Gabor model. Spatial texture analysis methods fall in one of the following classes: statistical methods and structural methods (Haralick, Shanmugam, & Dinstein, 1973; Haralick 1979; Jain, Kasturi, & Schunck, 1995; Solberg & Jain 1997; Tuceryan & Jian, 1993).

The majority of the existing methods applied on textures have many drawbacks. In fact, statistical methods seem to give results better in the case of microtextures while structural methods give better results in the case of macrotextures. These methods, whether they are statistical, structural or hybrid, have another drawback not less significant: the computational cost. In fact, most of these methods necessitate a very significant computation cost. At the opposite, the human visual perception seems to work perfectly for almost all types of textures (Amadasun & King, 1989). The differences between textures are usually easily visible for the human eye while the automatic processing of these textures is very complex. One reason for this mismatch between human vision and computational models proposed in literature is the fact that the majority of computational methods use mathematical features that have no perceptual meaning easily comprehensible by users. In this paper, we are interested in textural features that have a perceptual meaning for users. It is widely admitted that there is a set of textural features that human beings use to recognize and categorize textures. Among these features, we can mention coarseness, contrast and directionality (Amadasun & King, 1989; Tamura, Mori, & Yamawaki,

1978). In such a perceptual approach, and in order to simulate the human visual perception system, we must dispose of computational techniques that allow a quantitative and computational estimation of the mentioned perceptual textural features. This is exactly the problem we are tackling in this paper: given a set of perceptual textural features, namely coarseness, contrast, directionality and busyness, that humans use to distinguish between textures, how can one simulate them with quantitative and computational measures that correspond, to an acceptable degree, to human perception? Then, how such perceptual features perform when applied in texture retrieval?

There are some works published in literature on the subject of human visual perception since the early studies done by Julesz (1976) and Bergen et al. (1988). However, there are two main works that are closely related to our. The first work is done by Tamura et al. (1978) and the second work is done by Amadasun et al. (1989). Each of the two has for a set of textural features. The work of Tamura et al. (1978) was based on the co-occurrence matrix and the work of Amadasun et al. (1989) was based on a variant of the co-occurrence matrix called NGTDM (neighborhood grey-tone difference matrix). The results obtained by both of them were good compared to the human perception. Another work done by Ravishankar et al. (1996) in which the authors present what they call a texture naming system: they have made an attempt to determine the relevant dimensions of the texture, as in the case of color (RGB, HSI, etc).

The objective we are following in this work falls into this global framework. We propose, however, a new method to estimate a set of perceptual textural features. The perceptual model proposed is evaluated using a psychometric method (based on rank-correlation) and found to correspond better to human judgments compared to related works (Tamura et al. (1978); Amadasun et al. (1989)). We apply the proposed perceptual model to texture retrieval and show interesting results. Furthermore, to improve retrieval efficiency, we propose to use two representations: the original images representation and the autocovariance function representation. The fusion of their results is shown to improve performance in an important way.

2. PERCEPTUAL TEXTURAL FEATURES

We can find a long list of perceptual textural features in literature. However, only a small list of features is considered as the most important ones. This list comprises coarseness, contrast and directionality. Other features of less importance are busyness, complexity, roughness and line-likeness (Tamura et al. (1989); Amadasun et al. (1978)). In this study, we have considered four perceptual features, namely coarseness, directionality, contrast and busyness.

Coarseness is the most important feature and, in a certain sense, it is coarseness that determines the existence of texture in an image. Coarseness measures the size of the primitives that constitute the texture. A coarse texture is composed of large primitives and is characterized by a high degree of local uniformity of grey-levels. A fine texture is constituted by small primitives and is characterized by a high degree of local variations of grey-levels.

Directionality is a global property in an image. It measures the degree of visible dominant orientation in an image. An image can have one or several dominant orientation(s) or no dominant orientation at all. In the latter case, it is said isotropic. The orientation is influenced by the shape of primitives as well as by their placement rules.

Contrast measures the degree of clarity with which one can distinguish between different primitives in a texture. A well-contrasted image is an image in which primitives are clearly visible and separable. Among the factors that influence contrast, we cite: the grey-levels in the image; the ratio of white and black in the image; and the intensity change frequency of grey-levels.

Busyness refers to the intensity changes from a pixel to its neighborhood: a busy texture is a texture in which the intensity changes are quick and rush; a non-busy texture is a texture in which the intensity changes are slow and gradual. One can say, therefore, that busyness is related to spatial frequency of the intensity changes in an image. If these intensity changes are very small, they will be invisible. Consequently, the amplitude of the intensity changes has also an influence on busyness. We must note also that busyness has an inverse relationship with coarseness.

3. COMPUTATIONAL MEASURES FOR TEXTURAL FEATURES

3.1. The Autocovariance Function

The set of computational measures simulating perceptual textural features that we will define in the next section can be based on two representations (or representations): original images or the autocovariance function associated with images. Applying computational measures on one or the other of the two representations did not give the same results. We will show at the end of this paper that, in the framework of content-based image retrieval, adopting multiple representations will allow significant improvement in retrieval performance.

The autocovariance function, denoted $f(\delta_i, \delta_j)$, for an $n \times m$ image I is defined as follows (Jain, Kasturi, & Schunck, 1995):

$$f(\delta_i, \delta_j) = \frac{1}{(n - \delta_i)(m - \delta_j)} \sum_{i=0}^{n-\delta_i-1} \sum_{j=0}^{m-\delta_j-1} I(i, j) I(i + \delta_i, j + \delta_j)$$

(1)

where $0 \le \delta_i \le n-1$ and $0 \le \delta_j \le m-1$. $\delta_i = i$ and δ_j represent shift on rows and columns respectively.

The autocovariance function was chosen as a second representation because it presents some very desirable characteristics. For images containing repetitive primitives, the corresponding autocovariance function presents an equivalent periodicity. For images with a high degree of coarseness, the autocovariance function decreases slowly and presents few variations, while for images with a fine degree of coarseness, it decreases quickly and presents a lot of variations. For oriented images, the autocovariance function keeps the same orientation as in the original image and, in addition, if we compare the method that applies the gradient on the autocovariance function with the method that applies the gradient on the original image, we can see that the former method saves the global orientation in the image rather than the local orientation as is the case with the latter method.

Finally, let us mention again that using directly original images or the autocovariance function associated with images does not give the same results for the different features, and this is the main secret behind the potential of their results merging as we will see in experimental results later in this paper. In this work, we adopt this multiple representations approach and we will show in the benchmarking section related to image retrieval presented at the end of this paper how this approach can improve search results in an important way. However, when studying the correspondence between the computational measures and the perceptual features, we will only use the autocovariance function representation since the differences in results between the two representations are not significant.

In order to simplify the presentation, we will base the computational features only on the autocovariance function. Similar reasoning holds in the case when we use the original images representation. In the section on image retrieval, we will use the two representations.

3.2. Coarseness Estimation

When we consider the autocovariance function, one can notice two phenomena related to coarse-ness: (1) Coarseness is saved in the corresponding autocovariance function; (2) For fine textures, the autocovariance function presents a lot of local variations, and, for coarse textures, it presents few local variations. Therefore, we can deduce that the number of extrema in the autocovariance function determines coarseness of a texture (we can use either maxima or minima). First, we compute the first derivatives of the autocovariance function, $f(i,j)$ in a separable way according to rows and columns respectively. Two functions $C_x(i,j)$ and $C_y(i,j)$ are then obtained:

$$\begin{cases} C_x(i,j) = f(i,j) - f(i+1,j) \\ C_y(i,j) = f(i,j) - f(i,j+1) \end{cases} \tag{2}$$

Second, we compute the first derivatives of the obtained functions $C_x(i,j)$ and $C_y(i,j)$ in a separable way according to rows and columns. Two functions $C_{xx}(i,j)$ et $C_{yy}(i,j)$ are then obtained:

$$\begin{cases} C_{xx}(i,j) = C_x(i,j) - C_x(i+1,j) \\ C_{yy}(i,j) = C_y(i,j) - C_y(i,j+1) \end{cases} \tag{3}$$

To detect extrema, we use the following equations (according to rows and columns respectively):

$$\begin{cases} C_x(i,j) = 0 \\ C_{xx}(i,j) < 0 \end{cases} \tag{4}$$

$$\begin{cases} C_y(i,j) = 0 \\ C_{yy}(i,j) < 0 \end{cases} \tag{5}$$

Coarseness, denoted C_s, is estimated as the average number of maxima in the autocovariance function: a coarse texture will have a small number of maxima and a fine texture will have a large number of maxima. Let $Max(i,j)=1$ if pixel (i,j) is a maximum (a maximum line or column) and *Max(i,j)*=0 if pixel (i, j) is not a maximum. Coarseness C_s can be expressed by the following equation:

$$C_s = \cfrac{1}{\cfrac{1}{2} \times \left(\cfrac{\sum_{i=0}^{n-1} \sum_{j=0}^{m-1} Max(i, j)}{n} + \cfrac{\sum_{j=0}^{m-1} \sum_{i=0}^{n-1} Max(i, j)}{m} \right)} \quad (6)$$

The denominator gives the number of maxima according to lines and columns. To have C_s between 0 and 1, we put this number in denominator. A value of C_s close to 1 means that the image contains, in average, few maxima and, therefore, it is a very coarse texture. If coarseness C_s equals or is very close to 1, we can consider that the image contains object forms rather than texture. A value of C_s close to 0 means that the image contains, in average, a high number of maxima and, therefore, it is a very fine texture. If coarseness C_s is very close to 0, we can consider that the image contains noise data rather than texture.

3.3. Contrast Estimation

When considering the autocovariance function, we can notice that the value of this function decreases quickly for well- contrasted images and it decreases slowly for non-well-contrasted images. Therefore, we can say that the amplitude *M* of the gradient of the autocovariance function according to the lines *G'x* and according to the columns *G'y* can be used to estimate contrast. There are two main parameters related to the amplitude: 1. we compute the average amplitude in the image by considering only pixels with significant amplitude and, therefore, superior to a certain threshold *t*; 2. we consider also the number of pixels (i, j) that have significant amplitude:

$$\begin{cases} C_x = f * G'_x \\ C_y = f * G'_y \end{cases} \quad (7)$$

$$M = \sqrt{C_x^2 + C_y^2} \quad (8)$$

where G'_x and G'_y are partial derivatives of the Gaussian according to rows and columns, respectively. Let $t(i, j)$=1 if pixel (i, j) has an amplitude superior than threshold t, and let $t(i, j)$=0 if pixel (i, j) has an amplitude inferior than threshold t. Let N_t the number of pixels having an amplitude superior to threshold t:

$$N_t = \sum_{i=t}^{n-1} \sum_{j=0}^{m-1} t(i, j) \quad (9)$$

The average amplitude M_a is given by:

$$M_a = \frac{\sum_{i=0}^{n-1} \sum_{j=0}^{m-1} M(i, j) \times t(i, j)}{N_t} \quad (10)$$

Coarseness plays an important role to determine if an image is well contrasted or not. In fact, an image with a high degree of coarseness tends to be perceived as being more contrasted than the one with a fine coarseness. Since images with high degree of coarseness have weak amplitudes, it is interesting to introduce the coarseness in the computation of contrast in order to compensate this inconvenience.

Considering all these factors, we propose the following equation to estimate contrast C_t:

$$C_t = \frac{M_a \times N_t \times C_s^{\frac{1}{\alpha}}}{n \times m} \quad (11)$$

where M_a represents the average amplitude, $\dfrac{N_t}{n \times m}$ represents percentage of pixels having an amplitude superior than threshold t, and C_s is the computational measure of coarseness ($\dfrac{1}{\alpha}$ is parameter used to make C_s significant against the quantity $\frac{M_a \times N_t}{n \times m}$).

3.4. Directionality Estimation

Regarding directionality, we want to estimate two parameters: the dominant orientation(s) and the degree of directionality. Orientation refers to the global orientation of primitives that constitute the texture. The degree of directionality is related to the visibility of the dominant orientation(s) in an image, and refers to the number of pixels having the dominant orientation(s).

1) Orientation Estimation: When considering the autocovariance function, one can notice two phenomena concerning the orientation: (1) existing orientation in the original image is saved in the corresponding autocovariance function; (2) the usage of the autocovariance function instead of the original image allows keeping the global orientation rather than the local orientation when one uses the original image. It follows that the global orientation of the image can be estimated by applying the gradient on the autocovariance function of the original image according to the lines C_x and according to the columns C_y. The orientation Θ is given then by:

$$\Theta = \arctan C_y / C_x \qquad (12)$$

Note that we consider only pixels with a significant orientation. A pixel is considered as oriented if its amplitude $M = \sqrt{C_x^2 + C_y^2}$ is superior to a certain threshold t. The same threshold as in the case of contrast was used for orientation.

2) Directionality Estimation: For directionality, we consider the number of pixels N_{Θ_d} having dominant orientation(s) Θ_d. Let $\Theta_d(i,j)=1$ if pixel (i, j) has a dominant orientation Θ_d and $\Theta_d(i,j)=0$ if pixel (i, j) does not have a dominant orientation Θ_d. We consider only dominant orientations Θ_d that are present in a sufficient number

of pixels, and then more than a threshold t_Θ so that orientation becomes visible. Let us denote N_{Θ_d} the number of non-oriented pixels. The degree of directionality N_{Θ_d} of an image can be expressed by the following equation:

$$N_{\Theta_d} = \frac{\sum_{i=0}^{n-1} \sum_{j=0}^{m-1} \Theta_d(i,j)}{(n \times m) - N_{\Theta_{nd}}} \qquad (13)$$

The more N_{Θ_d} is large, the more the image is directional. The more N_{Θ_d} is small, the more the image is non-directional.

3.5. Busyness Estimation

Busyness is related to coarseness in the reverse order. We propose the following equation, based on the computational measure of coarseness, to estimate busyness:

$$B_s = 1 - C_s^{\frac{1}{\alpha}} \qquad (14)$$

where C_s represents the computational measure of coarseness ($\frac{1}{\alpha}$ is a quantity used to make C_s significant against 1).

Note that busyness is not necessary and can be omitted. However we keep it because, depending on applications, users might want to use it in their queries.

Note. The threshold t, used for different measures, namely directionality and contrast, was chosen as dynamic. Several thresholds were tested, and we found that the threshold which consists in taking the average number of oriented pixels across all orientations present in an image is the best one. So, this is the threshold used with the different computational measures. Parameter α was set to 4 in experimentations for both contrast and busyness.

4. THE PSYCHOMETRIC METHOD

The psychometric method we used to evaluate the correspondence between our proposed computational texture features and human perceptual judgments was inspired from the work done by Guildford (1954) and was used also by Tamura et al. (1978) and Amadasun et al. (1989) in their respective works. This method consists in the following major steps:

- Conceptual and intuitive definitions of the different perceptual textural features were given to human subjects participating in experimentations. Then, a series of textures was presented to these human subjects. Each of them ranked images according to each perceptual textural feature. We obtained one ranking of images per perceptual textural feature and per human subject.
- For each perceptual feature, a consolidation of the rankings obtained by human subjects in one ranking was realized through the computation of the sum of rank values. We obtained one consolidated ranking per each perceptual textural feature.
- Considering the consolidated human rankings of textures according to each textural feature and the computational rankings obtained for each textural feature, we compute the rank-correlation between the two rankings for each textural feature. The computation of this rank-correlation is based on Spearman's coefficient of rank-correlation.

4.1. Sum of Rank Values

Suppose that n images were ranked in r different rankings, each performed by a human subject, according to a given perceptual textural feature. A quantity s_i, called the sum of rank values is computed using the following equation (Guildford, 1954):

$$S_i = \sum_{k=1}^{n} f_{ik} R_k \tag{15}$$

where i represents the ith image and varies between 1 and n; k represents the rank given to image i and varies between 1 and n; f_{ik} represents the number of human subjects that gave rank k to image i (the frequency to attribute rank k to image i); R_k is a quantity allowing to give more importance to images ranked at top positions and is given by the following equation (Guildford, 1954)

$$R_k = n - k + 1 \tag{16}$$

Once the sums of rank values S_i are computed for images i (i varying from 1 to n), they are ordered in the decreasing order: image i that has the sum of rank values S_i the most important is classified at the first position, image j that has the second most important sum of rank values S_j is classified at the second position, etc., image l with the lowest sum of rank values S_l is classified at the last position.

4.2. Spearman Coefficient of Rank-Correlation

Once the different consolidated human rankings are obtained for each textural feature, and considering the computational ranking for the same textural feature, we compute the rank-correlation between the two rankings. Doing so, we can judge the correspondence between the computational measures and the human vision. One of the most known methods to compute this rank-correlation is the Spearman coefficient of rank-correlation. There are two different techniques, depending if there is a significant number of images ranked at the same rank or not.

The value of Spearman coefficient r_s is between 1 and -1. A value close to 1 indicates that there is an almost perfect correlation between the compared rankings. A value close to -1 indicates that there is a very strong correlation between the two compared rankings but in the inverse order. A value close to 0 indicates that the compared rankings are almost orthogonal.

Case 1. In the case where no significant number of images is classified in the same rank, Spearman coefficient of rank-correlation r_s can be computed using the following equation (Guildford, 1954):

$$r_s = 1 - \frac{6D}{n(n^2 - 1)} \tag{17}$$

where D is the squared sum and is defined by (Guildford, 1954):

$$D = \sum_{i=1}^{n} d_i^2 \tag{18}$$

where d_i is the difference between ranks given to image i in the two rankings m and l and is defined as follows (Guildford, 1954):

$$d_i = (k_{mi} - k_{li}) \tag{19}$$

Case 2. In the case where there is a significant number of images classified in the same rank, we give to each of the images the average row (let us suppose that two images were given rank 10; we will attribute to them the rank 10.5). If the proportion of the classified images in the same rank is not large, t heir effect of the coefficient of Spearman rs is negligible and Equation (17) can still be used (Guildford, 1954). Nevertheless, if the proportion of the classified images in the same rank is important, a correction factor must be introduced in the computation of the Spearman coefficient rs. In this case, the equation becomes more complex and the Spearman coefficient of rank-correlation is given by (Guildford, 1954):

$$r_s = \frac{\sum_{i=1}^{n} x^2 + \sum_{i=1}^{n} y^2 - \sum_{i=1}^{n} d_i^2}{2\sqrt{\sum_{i=1}^{n} x^2 \sum_{i=1}^{n} y^2}} \tag{20}$$

where x and y are two variables corresponding to the two rankings to be compared and are defined as follows (Guildford, 1954):

$$\sum_{i=1}^{n} x^2 = \frac{n^3 - n}{12} - \sum_{i=1}^{n} T_x \tag{21}$$

$$\sum_{i=1}^{n} y^2 = \frac{n^3 - n}{12} - \sum_{i=1}^{n} T_y \tag{22}$$

where T_x and T_y are the correction factors of x and y respectively. To simplify, let us denote T_x and T_y by T. T is given by (Guildford, 1954):

$$T = \frac{t^3 - t}{12} \tag{23}$$

where t is the number of images classified at a given rank.

5. EXPERIMENTAL RESULTS AND PSYCHOMETRIC EVALUATION

Psychological experimentations were conducted with human subjects in order to evaluate the correspondence between computational results obtained by applying the proposed computational measures and those obtained with human subjects. Thirty human subjects participated in these experimentations. Two principal objectives were targeted:

- The first objective was to determine the degree of correspondence between results obtained by the computational measures and those obtained by human subjects, and thus, to be able to judge the validity of the proposed computational measures.

- The second objective was to determine the relatedness relationships between the different textural features, both the perceptual and the computational ones.

To reach these objectives, we have used the psychometric method described in the precedent section.

5.1. Computational and Consolidated Human Rankings

Figure 2 summarizes the computational rankings for each of the four textural features and Figure 3 summarizes the consolidated human rankings for each of the four textural features for textures given in Figure 1.

5.2. Correspondence between Human and Computational Rankings

Figure 4 gives the Spearman coefficient of rank-correlation between the two rankings, consolidated human ranking and computational ranking, computed using Equation (17) and taking into account the case where several images are given the same rank. A quick examination of the results

shown in this table allows us to say that there is a very strong correlation between the two ranking in the case of coarseness (r_s=0.913), a strong correlation between the two rankings in the case of contrast (r_s=0.755), directionality (r_s=0.841) and busyness (r_s=0.774). According to these results, every computational measure is correlated with the corresponding textural feature more than the remaining features.

The main discrepancies that can be observed from those results between consolidated human rankings and computational ones are summarized as follows:

- For Coarseness, the correspondence is very good (r_s = 0.913) and the most important difference between the two rankings is the rank given to image L: it was given rank k = 2 in the consolidated human ranking and rank k = 5 in the computational ranking (d_i = 3). The other differences are not significant (d_i = 1).

- For the degree of directionality, the correspondence is very good (r_s = 0.841). The main differences happen for images G (d_i = 4) and E (d_i = 2). This is essentially due to the fact that, in human ranking, some images were not considered as directional. For

Figure 1. Sample of test images from Brodatz database used in the psychometric evaluation

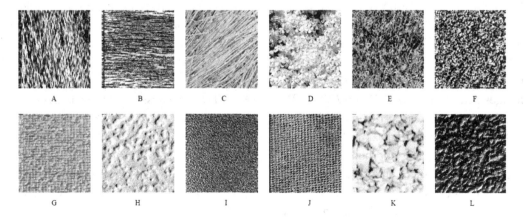

Figure 2. Computational rankings of textures according to each of the four perceptual textural features

Rank (k)	C_s	N_{Θ_d}	C_t	B_s
1	K	G	J	I
2	H	C	B	B
3	D	B	F	E
4	C	A	A	F
5	L, G	J	L	J
6	-	L	I	A
7	A	D	G	G, L
8	F, J	F	E	-
9	-	E	C	C
10	E	I	D	D
11	B	K, H	H	H
12	I	-	K	K

Figure 3. Consolidated human rankings of textures according to each of the four perceptual textural features

Rank (k)	Coars.	Cont.	Direct.	Bus.
1	K	F	C	F
2	L	J	B	E
3	H	A	A	A
4	D	L	J	B
5	G	B	G	I
6	C	D	L	D
7	F	C	E	J
8	J	E	I	L
9	A	G	F	G
10	E	K	D, H, K	C
11	B	I	-	K
12	I	H	-	H

Figure 4. Spearman coefficient of rank -correlation r_s between the consolidated human ranking and the computational ranking for each textural feature

r_s	Coars.	Direct.	Cont.	Bus.
C_s	**0.913**	-0.388	-0.290	-0.748
N_{Θ_d}	-0.201	**0.841**	0.435	0.082
C_t	-0.587	0.573	**0.755**	0.601
B_s	-0.904	0.390	0.299	**0.774**

example, only 7 human subjects, among 30, classified image *E* as directional.

- For contrast, correlation is smaller compared to the cases of coarseness and directionality, but it remains very good (r_s =0.755). The differences between the two rankings happen especially in the case of images *I* ($d_i = 5$), *D* ($d_i = 4$) and *F* ($d_i = 2$). For image *I*, the reason of this difference is that image *I* has high amplitude and a very weak coarseness and human subjects tend to classify such images as not very contrasted. For image *F*, the reason of the difference between the two rankings lies

in the fact that this image has practically the same amplitude and the same degree of coarseness as images *H*, *B* and *J*, and, therefore, they have practically the same degree of contrast. For image *D*, the difference is due to the weak amplitude of this image.

- For busyness, the correspondence is very good (r_s= 0.774). The principal differences happen for images *I* (d_i=4) and *D*(d_i=4).

Finally, we can say that the four proposed computational measures C_s, C_t, N_{Θ_d} and B_s have a very good correspondence with the rankings done by human subjects and, thus, these computational measures simulate to a very good level the human visual perception.

5.3. Features Relatedness

Figure 5 summarizes rank-correlation between consolidated human rankings and Figure 6 summarizes rank-correlation between computational rankings for each of the four textural features. From these two figures, we can make the following remarks: on one side, there is a quite small correlation between coarseness and contrast (human: −0.174; computational: −0.731) in the inverse order as well as a very small correlation, if not an orthogonality, between coarseness and directionality (human: −0.290; computational: −0.159); on the other side, there is an average correlation between contrast and directionality (human: 0.430; computational: 0.460). In fact, in the last case, when contrast is low, directionality

will not be visible. We can also notice that there is an important correlation between busyness and coarseness in the inverse order (human: −0.706; computational: -0.987), which is normal since busyness is estimated exclusively from coarseness. Finally, we can point out a good correlation between contrast and busyness (human: 0.566; computational: 0.729) and a very small correlation, if not an orthogonality, between directionality and busyness (human: 0.185; computational: 0.175).

5.4. Comparison

A comparison between the results we obtained and the results obtained by the two main related works, namely Tamura et al. (30) and Amadasun et al. (11), is given below. Let us mention first that Tamura et al. (30) did not consider busyness in his work and Amadasun et al. (11) did not consider directionality in his work.

Figure 5. Spearman coefficient of rank -correlation **rs** *between the consolidated human rankings*

r_s	Coars.	Cont.	Direct.	Bus.
Coars.	1	-0.174	-0.290	-0.706
Cont.	–	1	0.430	0.566
Direct.	–	–	1	0.185
Bus.	–	–	–	1

Figure 6. Spearman coefficient of rank-correlation **rs** *between the computational rankings*

r_s	C_s	N_{Θ_d}	C_t	B_s
C_s'	1	-0.159	-0.731	-0.987
N_{Θ_d}	–	1	0.460	0.175
C_t'	–	–	1	0.729
B_s	–	–	–	1

1) ***Correspondence between human and computational rankings:*** When we compare our results with those obtained by Tamura et al. (30) as well as Amadasun et al. (11) we can state the followings:

   ◦ Compared to the results obtained by Amadasun et al. (11), our results are more satisfactory. Regarding coarseness, we have obtained is 0.913 against 0.856; regarding contrast, we have obtained is 0.755 against 0.685; regarding busyness, we have obtained is 0.774 against 0.782.

   ◦ Compared to the results obtained by Tamura et al. (30), our results are also more satisfactory. Regarding coarseness, we have obtained is 0.913 against 0.831; regarding contrast, we have obtained is 0.755 against 0.904; regarding directionality, we have obtained is 0.841 against 0.823.

2) ***Feature relatedness:*** When we compare our results to the results of Tamura et al. (30) as well as Amadasun et al. (11) concerning the relatedness and dependence that may exist between textural features, we can state the following:

   ◦ We found that there is a relatively average correlation between coarseness and contrast in the inverse order (human: −0.174; computational: −0.731) while Amadasun et al. (11) found an average correlation between coarseness and contrast in the same order (human: 0.079; computational: 0.539).

   ◦ We found that there is an average correlation between contrast and directionality (human: 0.430; computational: 0.460) while Tamura et al. (30) found a small correlation between directionality and contrast in the inverse order (human: not provided; computational: −0.250).

   ◦ Finally, we also found an important correlation, in the inverse order, between coarseness and busyness (human: −0.706; computational: −0.987). This result was also found by Amadasun et al. (11) (human: −0.855; computational: −0.939).

6. APPLICATION TO CONTENT-BASED IMAGE RETRIEVAL

Computational measures proposed in this paper, based on the two considered representations, were applied in content-based image retrieval. For each of two representations, we considered two variants of the perceptual model: 1. In the first variant, we weighted each feature with the inverse of its variance, that is a feature with the smallest variance is the one which has the most important weight; 2. In the second variant, we used the Spearman coefficient of rank-correlation, found when the correspondence of computational measures and perceptual features was studied, as weight for the corresponding feature. Note that in the first approach, weighted are dependent on the data set considered in experiences while in the second approach, weights are independent from the considered data set.

In the rest of this chapter, the following notations are used:

- **PCP-COV-V:** Perceptual model based on the autocovariance representation in which each feature is weighted with the inverse of its variance.
- **PCP-COV-S:** Perceptual model based on the autocovariance representation in which each feature is weighted with the Spearman coefficient of rank-correlation.
- **PCP-V:** Perceptual model based on the original images representation in which each feature is weighted with the inverse of its variance.

- **PCP-S**: Perceptual model based on the original images representation in which each feature is weighted with the Spearman coefficient of rank-correlation.
- In the next subsections, we will briefly define the similarity measure and the results merging model used before presenting experimental results and benchmarking using the recall graph.

6.1. Similarity Measure

The similarity measure used is based on the Gower coefficient of similarity we have developed in our earlier work (Abbadeni, 2003). The non-weighted similarity measure, denoted *GS*, can be defined as follows:

$$GS_{ij} = \frac{\sum_{k=1}^{n} S_{ij}^{(k)}}{\sum_{k=1}^{n} \delta_{ij}^{(k)}} \tag{24}$$

where $S_{ij}^{(k)}$ is the partial similarity between images i and j according to feature k, $S_{ij}^{(k)}$ represents the ability to compare two images i and j on feature k ($S_{ij}^{(k)} = 1$ if images i and j can be compared on feature k and $S_{ij}^{(k)} = 0$ if not. $\sum_{k=1}^{n} \delta_{ij}^{(k)} = n$ if image i and j can be compared on all features k, k = 1,…,n).

Quantity $S_{ij}^{(k)}$ is defined as follows:

$$S_{ij}^{(k)} = 1 - \frac{|x_{ik} - x_{jk}|}{R_k} \tag{25}$$

where R_k represents a normalization factor. R_k is computed on the database considered for experimentations and is defined as follows:

$$R_k = \max(x_{ik}) - \min(x_{ik}) \tag{26}$$

The weighted version of the similarity measure can be defined as follows:

$$GS_{ij} = \frac{\sum_{k=1}^{n} w_k S_{ij}^{(k)}}{\sum_{k=1}^{n} w_k \delta_{ij}^{(k)}} \tag{27}$$

where w_k corresponds to the weight associated with feature k. As mentioned, w_k can be either the inverse of variance of feature k or the Spearman coefficient of rank-correlation. For more details on the similarity measure, please refer to (Abbadeni, 2003).

6.2. Results Fusion

In order to merge the results returned by each of the two representations, we have tested several results merging models. The model which gives the best results, denoted FusCL, can be defined as follows:

$$FusCL_{ij} = \frac{\sum_{k=1}^{K} GS_{M_{ij}^k}}{K} \tag{28}$$

Equation (28) is based on the similarity value (score) returned by the similarity measure and expresses the merging of results returned by different representations as an average of the scores obtained by an image in its different rankings corresponding to these different representations.

The FusCL model exploits two effects, known as the chorus effect and the dark horse effect in the information retrieval community (French, Chapin, & Martin, 2003):

- The chorus effect concerns the case when an image is returned as relevant to a query by several representations. This is considered as a stronger evidence of relevance than if it is returned as relevant by only one representation.

- The dark horse effect concerns the case when a representation ranks, exceptionally, an image, which is not relevant to a query, in top positions. This can be attenuated by the fused model if the other representations do not rank that image in top positions. Actually, it is very rare for a non-relevant image to be ranked at top positions by several representations.

Note that experimental results show that **PCP-COV-V** gives the best results when using the autocovariance function representation and **PCP-S** gives the best results when using the original images representation. Therefore, these are the two models that will be considered for results fusion.

6.3. Brodatz Database

We have applied the computational features presented in this paper in a large image retrieval experience on Brodatz database (Brodatz, 1966). Each of the 112 images of Brodatz database was divided into 9 tiles to obtain 1008 128x128 images (112 images x 9 tiles per image). For each query, we will be searching for 9 images (including the query itself since the query is in the database and it will be always returned at the first position with a score of 1). For benchmarking purposes, we have considered 112 queries, each from a different class (we have taken the first image of each class corresponding to the top left corner tile). Creating a class of images from an original image by dividing it into tiles and considering them as similar is a questionable procedure. In fact, when the original image is non homogeneous, the resulting tiles are not visually similar (see Figure 7). Brodatz database contains an important number of images presenting a medium to high degree of non-homogeneity. As a result, when creating tiles from a non-homogeneous image, the resulting tiles are very dissimilar. Considering such tiles in one class will have a negative influence on recall. The list of highly non-homogeneous images is as follows: D2, D5, D7, D13, D19, D23, D30, D31, D36, D41, D42, D43, D44, D45, D58, D59, D61, D63, D67, D73, D74, D88, D89, D90, D97, D98, D99, D100, and D108. Figure 7 gives an example of such images. Also, some images are very similar in Brodatz. Considering such images in different classes will also have a negative influence on recall. Figure 8 gives some examples of such images.

Figure 7. An example of a highly non-homogeneous image: D59 (D59-1 is the query image)

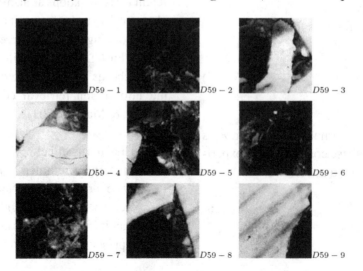

6.4. Experimental Results

Figures 9 and 10 give examples of computational features values from Brodatz database based on the autocovariance function and the original images representations respectively. We can see in these figures that feature values are not the same from a representation to another as we have discussed earlier in this chapter.

Figures 11 and 12 give normalization factors and weights used in the case of the original images and in the case of the autocovariance function

representations respectively. We can point out the differences between the two representations in both the normalization factors and the weights. In this latter case, and with the original images representation, the importance of perceptual features is, in a decreasing order, busyness, coarseness, directionality and contrast whether with the autocovariance function representation, the importance of perceptual features is, in a decreasing order, coarseness, contrast, busyness and directionality. Also, with the autocovariance represen-

Figure 8. Examples of visually similar images in Brodatz database (although they belong to different classes)

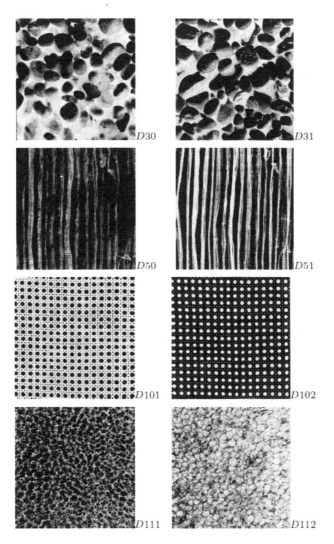

Figure 9. Example of computational features (after normalization) based on the auto covariance function

Image	C_s	N_{Θ_d}	C_t	B_s
D1	.068	.648	.053	2.137
D2	.127	.302	.023	1.981
D3	.077	.443	.046	2.11
D4	.071	.365	.025	2.128
D5	.135	.374	.034	1.964
D6	.08	.584	.105	2.099
D7	.145	.443	.041	1.945
D8	.446	.711	.095	1.581
D9	.067	.268	.022	2.143
D10	.076	.274	.016	2.113

Figure 10. Examples of computational features (after normalization) based on original images

Image	C_s	N_{Θ_d}	C_t	B_s
D1	1.198	.486	.309	15.277
D2	1.363	.460	.357	15.096
D3	1.377	.506	.603	15.081
D4	1.528	.686	.629	14.930
D5	1.591	.424	.352	14.870
D6	1.486	.364	.322	14.971
D7	1.356	.282	.285	15.103
D8	1.191	.171	.071	15.286
D9	1.380	.467	.720	15.078
D10	1.336	.262	.372	15.124

tation, coarseness takes much more importance than the other features.

Figure 13 shows search results obtained for query image D110-1 using the **PCP–S** model. Figure 14 shows search results obtained for query image D96-1 using the **PC P–S** model. Results are presented in a decreasing order based on the score of similarity to the query image.

These results show that the considered models give interesting results. The returned images, when they are not in the same class as the query image, generally, present a good visual similarity with the query image with respect to some aspects.

Figure 11. Normalization factors and weights used in the case of the original images representation

Feature	Normalization Factor	Spearman Coef.	Inv. Variance
Coarseness	.022	.913	32.558
Directionality	.748	.841	29.785
Contrast	17.410	.755	23.751
Busyness	.077	.774	34.143

Figure 12. Normalization factors and weights used in the case of the Auto covariance function representation

Feature	Normalization Factor	Spearman Coef.	Inv. Variance
Coarseness	.860	.913	157.474
Directionality	.948	.841	41.7801
Contrast	605.627	.755	66.0817
Busyness	.575	.774	56.5337

6.5. Retrieval Effectiveness

The recall measure is widely accepted and used to benchmark search relevance (effectiveness) in information retrieval systems in general even if they are not perfect. Recall, which can be defined as the number of relevant and retrieved images divided by the number of relevant images in the database for the considered query, measures the ability of a model to retrieve all relevant images. The recall is computed for each query at each position. Then, the average recall is computed as an average across a set of representative queries. The average recall shows the ability of the model to retrieve all relevant images as the model retrieves more images.

Figure 15 shows the recall graph for different perceptual models and for the fused model

Figure 13. Search results returned for query image D110-1 using the **PCP − S** *model*

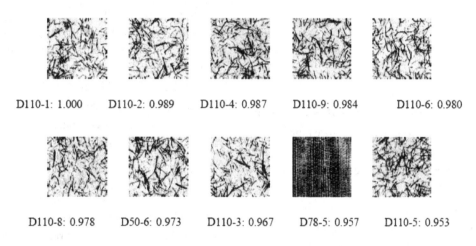

D110-1: 1.000   D110-2: 0.989   D110-4: 0.987   D110-9: 0.984   D110-6: 0.980

D110-8: 0.978   D50-6: 0.973   D110-3: 0.967   D78-5: 0.957   D110-5: 0.953

Figure 14. Search results returned for query image D96-1 using the **PCP−S** *model*

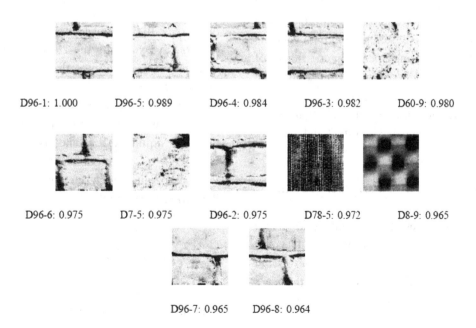

D96-1: 1.000   D96-5: 0.989   D96-4: 0.984   D96-3: 0.982   D60-9: 0.980

D96-6: 0.975   D7-5: 0.975   D96-2: 0.975   D78-5: 0.972   D8-9: 0.965

D96-7: 0.965   D96-8: 0.964

Figure 15. Recall graph for different perceptual models (separated and fused): Recall= f(Retrieved images)

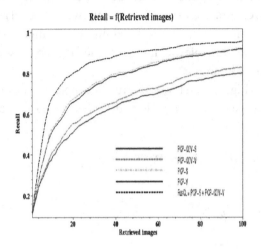

(considering ***PCP−COV−V*** and ***PCP−S*** separated models). The recall plotted in this figure is an average computed over 83 classes among 112 classes in Brodatz database. That is, we have rejected the 29 highly non homogeneous classes, since images within such classes are not visually similar as discussed earlier, in order to avoid misleading conclusions. One can point out from this graph that the perceptual model based on the original images representation gives better performance than the perceptual model based on the autocovariance function representation in both variants (weighted variant using Spearman coefficient of correlation and weighted variant using the inverse of variance). The fused model allows significant improvement compared to the separated model by exploiting both the chorus effect and the dark horse effect as mentioned earlier.

6.6. Comparison to Related Works

Comparing one's results to other works is not an easy task. In fact, in order to do so, all works must use the same database, the same queries and the same evaluation criteria. In practice, these are rarely available. In our case, there are different versions of Brodatz database that are used by different works. These different versions differ in acquisition conditions of images. For example, in our work we used a 640x640 Brodatz version and we have taken 9 non-overlapping 128x128 tiles from each image to obtain 1008 images divided by 112 classes of 9 images each. In Liu & Picard (1996), a 384x384 version of Brodatz database was used, each image was divided into 9 128x128 non-overlapping tiles to obtain 1008 images divided into 112 classes of 9 images each. In Manjunath & Ma (1996), a 512x512 version of Brodatz database was used, excluding 2 images (D30 and D31) and including 6 other images from the USC database, each image was divided into 16 128x128 non-overlapping tiles to obtain 1856 images divided into 116 classes of 16 images each.

Despite these differences and difficulties, we will give, however, a comparison with *Tamura*'s model (Tamura et al., 1978), which is the main work published in literature that is closely related to our work and which was used in image retrieval in the well-known QBIC system (Ashley et al., 1995; Flickner et al., 1995) as benchmarked in (Liu & Picard, 1996) using recall measure only. This benchmark used also the Brodatz database of textures.

Figure 16 gives the average recall rate computed over all of the 112 classes and over only 83 classes (by excluding the 29 highly non homogeneous classes). It gives also the average recall rate for *Tamura*'s model. From this table, it is clear that our model, in almost all of its variants, outperforms *Tamura*'s model. The only variant that has a similar performance as *Tamura*'s model is the *PCP-COV-V* model. When we consider the fused model, its search relevance is largely better than *Tamura*'s model.

7. CONCLUSION

A perceptual model based on a set of computational measures corresponding to perceptual textural

Figure 16. Average retrieval rate at positions 9, 18, 50, and 100 using different separated perceptual models and the fused model compared to Tamura's model

	P9	P18	P50	P100
Tamura's model	.32	.46	.65	.75
PCP-COV-V (112 classes)	.328	.451	.626	.765
PCP-S (112 classes)	.417	.551	.73	.842
FusCL (112 classes)	.549	.677	.806	.894
PCP-COV-V (83 classes)	.377	.529	.71	.831
PCP-S (83 classes)	.493	.648	.825	.924
FusCL (83 classes)	.644	.783	.906	.959

features, namely coarseness, directionality, contrast and busyness, was described in this chapter. Computational measures were estimated based on two different representations: original images and the autocovariance function associated with images. Coarseness was estimated as an average of the number of extrema. Contrast was estimated as a combination of the average amplitude of the gradient, the percentage of pixels having the amplitude superior to a certain threshold and coarseness itself. Directionality was estimated as the average number of pixels having the dominant orientation(s). Busyness was estimated based on coarseness. The computational measures proposed for each perceptual textural feature were evaluated, based on a psychometric method, by conducting a set of experimentations taking into account human judgments. The psychometric method used is based on the sum of rank values and the Spearman coefficient of rank-correlation. Experimental results show an appreciable correspondence between the proposed computational measures and human judgments. Compared to related works, our results are better. In order to validate the proposed set of computational measures, we applied them in a content-based image retrieval experimentation using a large image database, the well-known Brodatz database, which contains 112 classes of 9 images each class for a total of 1008 images. Experimental results show

very good results and benchmarking based on the recall measure shows a significant improvement in retrieval performance, especially when fusing results returned by different representations.

AUTHOR'S NOTE

Part of this work was done while the author was with Abu Dhabi University (UAE) and University of Sherbrooke (Canada).

REFERENCES

Abbadeni, N. (2003). A New Similarity Matching Measure: Application to Texture-Based Image Retrieval. In *Proceedings of the Third International Workshop on Texture Analysis and Synthesis (Joint with ICCV'03)*, Nice, France (pp. 1-5).

Abbadeni, N. (2003). Content representation and similarity matching for texture-based image retrieval. *Proceedings of the Fifth ACM International Workshop on Multimedia Information Retrieval (Joint with ACM Multimedia'03)*, Berkeley, CA, USA (pp. 63-70).

Abbadeni, N. (2005). Multiple representations, similarity matching, and results fusion for content-based image retrieval. *ACM/Springer Multimedia Systems Journal, 10*(5), 444-456.

Abbadeni, N. (2005). Perceptual Image Retrieval. In *Proceedings of the international conference on visual information systems (VISUAL '05)*, Amsterdam, Netherlands (pp. 259-268).

Abbadeni, N. (2011). Computational Perceptual Features for Texture Representation and Retrieval. To Appear in *IEEE Transactions on Image Processing*, 20(1), January 2011.

Abbadeni, N., Ziou, D., & Wang, S. (2000). Autocovariance-based Perceptual Textural Features Corresponding to Human Visual Perception. In *Proceedings of the Fifteenth IAPR/IEEE International Conference on Pattern Recognition* (Vol. 3, pp. 901-904). Barcelona, Spain.

Abbadeni, N., Ziou, D., & Wang, S. (2000). Computational measures corresponding to perceptual textural features. *Proceedings of the Seventh IEEE International Conference on Image Processing* (Vol. 3, pp. 897-900). Vancouver, BC.

Abbadeni, N., Ziou, D., & Wang, S. (2000). Perceptual Textural Features Corresponding to Human Visual Perception. In *Proceedings of the Thirteenth Vision Interface Conference* (pp. 365-372). Montreal, QC.

Amadasun, M., & King, R. (1989). Textural Features corresponding to textural properties. *IEEE Transactions on Systems, Man, and Cybernetics, 19*(5), 1264–1274. doi:10.1109/21.44046

Ashley, J., Barber, R., Flickner, M., Hafner, J., Lee, D., Niblack, W., & Petkovic, D. (1995). Automatic and Semi-Automatic Methods for Image Annotation and Retrieval in QBIC. In. *Proceedings of the SPIE Conference on Storage and Retrieval for Image and Video Databases, 2420*, 24–35.

Bergen, J. R., & Adelson, E. H. (1988). Early Vision and Texture Perception. *Nature, 333*(6171), 363–364. doi:10.1038/333363a0

Brodatz, P. (1966). *Textures: A Photographic Album for Artists and Designers*. New York: Dover.

Datta, R., Joshi, D., Li, J., & Wang, J. Z. (2008). Image Retrieval: Ideas, Influences, and Trends of the New Age. *ACM Transactions on Computing Surveys, 40*(2), 1–60. doi:10.1145/1348246.1348248

Flickner, M., Sawhney, H., Niblack, W., Ashley, J., Huang, Q., & Dom, B. (1995). Query by Image and Video Content: The QBIC System. *IEEE Computer, 28*(9), 23–32.

French, J. C., Chapin, A. C., & Martin, W. N. (2003). An Application of Multiple Viewpoints to Content-based Image Retrieval. In *Proceedings of the ACM/IEEE Joint Conference on Digital Libraries* (pp. 128-130).

Guildford, J. P. (1954). *Psychometric Methods*. New York: McGraw-Hill.

Haralick, R. M. (1979). Statistical and Structural Approaches to Texture. *Proceedings of the IEEE, 67*(5), 786–804. doi:10.1109/PROC.1979.11328

Haralick, R. M., Shanmugam, K., & Dinstein, I. (1973). Textural Features for Image Classification. *IEEE Transactions on Systems, Man, and Cybernetics, 3*(6), 610–621. doi:10.1109/TSMC.1973.4309314

Haralick, R. M., & Shapiro, L. G. (1992). *Computer and Robot Vision (Vol. 1)*. USA: Addison-Wesley.

Jain, R., Kasturi, R., & Schunck, B. G. (1995). *Machine Vision*. USA: McGraw-Hill.

Julesz, B. (1976). Experiments in the Visual Perception of Texture. *Scientific American, 232*(4), 34–44. doi:10.1038/scientificamerican0475-34

Karu, R., Jain, A. K., & Bolle, R. M. (1996). Is there any Texture in the Image? *Pattern Recognition*, *29*(9), 1437–1466. doi:10.1016/0031-3203(96)00004-0

Lazebnik, S., Schmid, C., & Ponce, J. (2004). *A Sparse Texture Representation Using Local Affine Regions* (Beckman CVR Technical Report, NO 2004-01). University of Illinois at Urbana Champaign. UIUC.

Lew, M., Sebe, N., Djeraba, C., & Jain, R. (2006). Content-Based Multimedia Information Retrieval: State of the art and challenges. *ACM Transactions on Multimedia Computing, Communications, and Applications*, *2*(1), 1–19. doi:10.1145/1126004.1126005

Liu, F., & Picard, R. W. (1996). Periodicity, Directionality and Randomness: Wold Features for Image Modeling and Retrieval. *IEEE Transactions on Pattern Analysis and Machine Intelligence*, *18*(7), 722–733. doi:10.1109/34.506794

Manjunath, B. S., & Ma, W. Y. (1996). Texture Features for Browsing and Retrieval of Image Data. *IEEE Transactions on Pattern Analysis and Machine Intelligence*, *18*(8), 837–842. doi:10.1109/34.531803

Ravishankar Rao, A. (1990). *A Taxonomy for Texture Description and Identification*. New York: Springer-Verlag.

Ravishankar Rao, A., & Lohse, G. L. (1996). Towards a Texture Naming System: Identifying Relevant Dimensions of Texture. *Vision Research*, *36*(11), 1649–1669. doi:10.1016/0042-6989(95)00202-2

Solberg, A. H. S., & Jain, A. K. (1997). Texture Analysis of SAR Images: A Comparative Study. Research Report. Norwegian Computing Center and Michigan State University.

Tamura, H., Mori, S., & Yamawaki, T. (1978). Textural Features Corresponding to Visual Perception. *IEEE Transactions on Systems, Man, and Cybernetics*, *8*(6), 460–472. doi:10.1109/TSMC.1978.4309999

Tomita, F., & Tsuji, S. (1990). *Computer Analysis of Visual Textures*. USA: Kluwer Academic Publishers.

Tuceryan, M., & Jain, A. K. (1993). Texture Analysis. In Chen, C. H., Pau, L. F., & Wang, P. S. P. (Eds.), *Handbook of Pattern Recognition and Computer Vision* (pp. 235–276). River Edge, NY: World Scientific.

Van Gool, L., Dewaele, P., & Oosterlinck, A. (1985). Texture Analysis Anno 1983. *Computer Vision, Graphics, and Image Processing Journal*, *29*(3), 336–357. doi:10.1016/0734-189X(85)90130-6

Vogt, C. C., & Cottrell, G. W. (1999). Fusion Via a Linear Combination of Scores. *Information Retrieval Journal*, *1*, 151–173. doi:10.1023/A:1009980820262

Zhang, J., & Tan, T. (2002). Brief Review of Invariant Texture Analysis Methods. *Pattern Recognition*, *35*(3), 735–747. doi:10.1016/S0031-3203(01)00074-7

Section 3
Computer Vision for Multimedia Content Analysis

Chapter 9

Event Detection in Sports Video Based on Generative-Discriminative Models

Guoliang Fan
Oklahoma State University, USA

Yi Ding
Oklahoma State University, USA

ABSTRACT

Semantic event detection is an active and interesting research topic in the field of video mining. The major challenge is the semantic gap between low-level features and high-level semantics. In this chapter, we will advance a new sports video mining framework where a hybrid generative-discriminative approach is used for event detection. Specifically, we propose a three-layer semantic space by which event detection is converted into two inter-related statistical inference procedures that involve semantic analysis at different levels. The first is to infer the mid-level semantic structures from the low-level visual features via generative models, which can serve as building blocks of high-level semantic analysis. The second is to detect high-level semantics from mid-level semantic structures using discriminative models, which are of direct interests to users. In this framework we can explicitly represent and detect semantics at different levels. The use of generative and discriminative approaches in two different stages is proved to be effective and appropriate for event detection in sports video. The experimental results from a set of American football video data demonstrate that the proposed framework offers promising results compared with traditional approaches.

INTRODUCTION

The goal of video mining is to discover knowledge, patterns, and events in the video data stored either in databases, data warehouses, or other online repositories (S.-F. Chang, 2002; Mei, Ma,

Zhou, Ma, & Zhang, 2005). Specifically, semantic event detection is an active research field driven by the ever increasing needs of numerous multimedia and online database applications. Its benefits range from efficient browsing and summarization of video content to facilitating video access and retrieval. According to different production and edition styles, videos can be

DOI: 10.4018/978-1-60960-024-2.ch009

classified into two major categories: *scripted* and *non-scripted* (Xiong, Zhou, Tian, Rui, & Huang, 2006), which are usually associated with different video mining tasks. *Scripted videos* (e.g., news and movies) are produced or edited according to a pre-defined script or plan, for which we can build a Table-of-Content (TOC) to facilitate the viewing or editing of the video data (Rui, Huang, & Mehrotra, 1998). In *Non-scripted videos* (e.g., sports), events usually occur spontaneously in a relatively fixed setting, such as meetings, sports, and surveillances. Therefore, how to detecting the highlights or events of interests is of great interest for non-scripted videos. In our research, we focus on sports video and use the American football video as a case study.

Sports video mining has been widely studied due to its great commercial value (L. Duan, Xu, Tian, Xu, & Jin, 2005; Gong, Sin, Chuan, Zhang, & Sakauchi, 1995; Kokaram, et al., 2006; Xie, Chang, Divakaran, & Sun, 2002). Although the sports video is considered non-scripted, they usually have a relatively well-defined structure (such as the field scene) or repetitive patterns (such as a certain play type), which could help us enhance its "*scriptedness*" and develop effective tools for retrieval, searching, browsing and indexing. Currently, there are two kinds of approaches for sports video mining: *structure-based* (Kokaram, et al., 2006; Xie, Chang, Divakaran, & Sun, 2004) and *event-based* (Assfalg, Bertini, Colombo, Bimbo, & Nunziati, 2003; T. Wang, et al., 2006). The former one uses either supervised or unsupervised learning methods to recognize some basic semantic structures (such as the canonical view in a baseball game or the play/break in a soccer game). This can serve as an intermediate representation to support semantics-oriented video retrieval, but usually cannot deliver high-level semantics directly. The latter one provides a better understanding of the video content by detecting and extracting the events-of-interest or highlights, which could be very specific and task-dependent and usually requires sufficient and representative training data.

Because these two approaches are complementary in nature, researchers have investigated how to integrate both of them in one unified computational framework. For example, a mid-level representation framework was proposed for semantic sports video analysis involving both temporal structures and events hierarchy (L. Y. Duan, Xu, Chua, Q. Tian, & Xu, 2003) and a mosaic-based generic scene representation was developed from video shots and used to mine both events and structures (Mei, et al., 2005). The advantage of this kind of video representation lies in its expandability and openness to support versatile and flexible video mining tasks.

Inspired by previous efforts, the goal of our research is to develop an integrated video mining framework that offers both structure analysis (at the mid-level) and event analysis (at the high-level) in a systematic way. Specifically, we promote a collaborative use of two different statistical models, i.e., generative and discriminative, for event detection in sports video. The major challenge of our research is the semantic gap between the understandable high-level semantics and computable low-level features. In this chapter, we will propose a hybrid generative-discriminative model based approach that supports explicit semantic modeling and direct semantic computing and bridges the semantic gap via two inference processes. Specifically, we addressed the following three technical issues: (1) to represent sports video data by a three-layer semantic space that involves low-level visual features, mid-level semantic structures, and high-level semantics; (2) to formulate the issue of semantic event detection as two related statistical inference problems, i.e., the inference from low-level visual features to mid-level semantic structures and the inference from the mid-level semantic structure to the high-level semantic events; (3) to employ appropriate statistical tools to tackle the two inference problems of different nature, i.e., the generative models for the first one and the discriminative models for the second one.

This chapter is organized as follows. We will first review the recent work on semantic video analysis, followed by a detailed discussion of the recent progress on statistical model-based video analysis approaches. Thirdly, we present the problem formulation where we introduce the three-layer semantic space, and we convert event detection as two sequent inference problems with different purposes. Then we discuss feature extraction and two inference problems in details, where we present several generative and discriminative models used in our research. In the experiment, we will compare various statistical models in terms of their modeling capability, efficiency and applicability for specific video mining tasks, especially their suitability for different inference problems. Finally, we conclude this chapter by providing some discussion for future research.

RELATED WORK

The sports video mining research could be roughly divided into two groups, *structure-based* (Kokaram, et al., 2006; Xie, et al., 2004) and *event-based* (Assfalg, et al., 2003; T. Wang, et al., 2006).

Structure-based approaches usually attempt to parse a long video sequence into individual segments by detecting scene changes or the boundaries between camera shots in a video stream. For example, in (Xie, et al., 2002), a soccer video sequence can be segmented into plays and breaks, and in (Pan, Beek, & Sezan, 2001), the authors classify a video sequence into plays and replays. Both works focused on the detection of general semantic structures in the video data and treated them as the basic semantic components. Event-based approaches aim to summarize the video data by highlights or specific events of interest. Event detection in sports video can be done at both the object level (Koubaroulis, Matas, & Kittler, 2002; Xu, G. Zhu, Zhang, Huang, & Lu, 2008; Yu, et al., 2003) and the scene level (L. Duan, et al., 2005; Li & Sezan, 2002; Naphade & Huang,

2002). Object-level event detection approaches usually associate semantic events with the appearance or behavior of some specific objects. For example, in (Xu, et al., 2008), the author employed object-based features such as the trajectory of a ball and players to detect goals in a soccer game. However, most of semantic events are typically defined on the complex collections of multiple objects. In some cases, the object of interest may not always be available. Instead of focusing on objects, scene-level event detection algorithms, i.e., (L. Duan, et al., 2005), utilize various visual cues in the video data, including color distribution, specific landmarks, camera motion, and even caption information to detect semantic events. Usually, feature extraction at the scene-level is more robust and efficient compared with the feature extration at the object-level.

There are two major kinds of approaches for event detection, one is the rule-based approaches (Lazarescu & Venkatesh, 2003; W. Zhou, Vellaikal, & Kuo, 2000) and the other is the statistical model based approaches (Naphade & Huang, 2002; Sadlier & Connor, 2005). The major advantages of rule based methods are that they are usually goal-oriented and can support specific video search tasks effectively. In (Lazarescu & Venkatesh, 2003), camera motion is used to classify each play shot into one of seven different plays. However, in general, the rule-based approaches may not be effective to deal with the uncertainty and ambiguity of the visual features for high-level semantic analysis, and the task-specificity limits their flexibilities and expandability.

In contrast, the statistical model-based approaches are usually more flexible and general to discover underlying structures or events in video data, such as recurrent events or highlights (Naphade & Huang, 2002). Recently, two types of statistical models are intensively studied for semantic video analysis: the generative models (Y. Wang, Liu, & Huang, 2000; Xie, et al., 2002) and the discriminative models (Sadlier & Connor, 2005; T. Wang, et al., 2006). Similarly, some hybrid approaches that combine both generative and discriminative models were advanced, which are either to enhance data classification (Raina, Shen, NG, & Mccallum, 2003) or to detect semantic events in video data (X. Zhou, et al., 2008). Compared with rule-based approaches, statistical model-based approaches have the potential to offer better capabilities, flexibility, and generality to handle a large volume of video data with high complexity and diverse nature.

STATISTICAL MODEL BASED APPROACHES

In this section, we will introduce and compare two types of important statistical models, i.e., the generative and the discriminative models, in terms of their mechanisms, functionalities, and applications.

Generative Models

Figure 1 shows several typical generative models used for content-based and semantic-based video analysis, including the prototype hidden Markov model (HMM), coupled HMM (CHMM), Factorial HMM (FHMM), and Hierarchical HMM (HHMM). These models involve specific state dynamics and an observation likelihood function. The expectation maximization (EM) algorithm is usually used for model learning and Bayesian inference is involved for decision making given an observation sequence. The Dynamic Bayesian Network (DBN) (Murphy, 2002) provides a unified probabilistic framework to represent various graphical structures with direct dependency, and the HMM is considered the simplest DBN that has been widely used in many video analysis applications (P. Chang, Han, & Gong, 2002). Recently, there have been intensive efforts to enhance HMMs for semantic video analysis, and the recent studies mainly focus on two issues, i.e., *structuring* and *learning*.

There are usually two types of dynamic structure involved for semantic video analysis, i.e., parallel and hierarchical structures. A parallel structure involves information fusion at either the decision-level or the feature-level. For example, when there are two parallel semantic structures involved in a video sequence, the Coupled HMM (CHMM) (M. Brand, Oliver, & Pentland, 1997) and the Influence Model (Zhang, Gatica-Perez, Bengio, & Roy, 2005) were proposed to capture the interaction between two Markov processes via decision-level fusion. In contrast, the Factorial HMM (FHMM) includes multiple uncoupled state transitions that share the same observation sequence (feature-level fusion) (P. Wang & Ji, 2005) or where observation vectors are obtained by the concatenation of low-level features from different modalities or sources (Nefian, Liang, Pi, Liu, & Murphy, 2002). On the other hand, the hierarchical structure usually imposes a multi-layer representation where semantic event analysis can be accomplished by two steps, *recognition of primitives* and *recognition of structures*. For example, the Hierarchical HMM (HHMM) is able to capture low-level primitives based on which we can represent some mid-level structures, e.g., plays and breaks (Xie, et al., 2004; Xie, Chang, Divakaran, & Sun, 2003). Furthermore, some signal processing applications may desire a more effective observation model that can represent variable-length observations for state estimation. The segmental HMM (SHMM) was proposed for speech recognition that effectively handle variable-length observations by involving segmental observation models (Gales & Young, 1993). The key idea in the SHMM is a two-layer observation model that captures feature variability both within a segment and across segments.

Model learning is another important issue, especially for HMMs with a complex state space or variable-length observations. Generally, there are two issues, one is *structure learning* (Friedman & Koller, 2003), another is *parameter learning* (Ghahramani, 2002). The former tries to provide

Figure 1. Generative models: variations of the DBN: Hidden Markov Model (HMM), Coupled HMM (CHMM), Factorial HMM (FHMM), and Hierarchical HMM (HHMM). The white and black nodes represent the state and observations, respectively

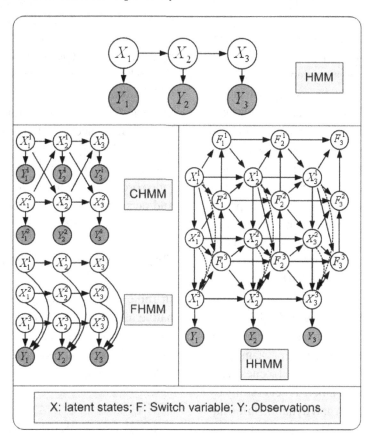

compact and effective model representations by condensing state space and eliminating unnecessary state dynamics. The latter aims at estimating model parameters given certain model structure. In (Matthew Brand, 1999), concepts of entropic prior and parameter extinction were proposed to optimize the model structure by a state trimming process. Another example is the reverse-jump Markov chain Monte Carlo (RJMCMC) that was used to learn an online adaptive HHMM for break-play video analysis (Xie, et al., 2003).

Discriminative Models

Discriminative models, like support vector machines (SVMs) (Sadlier & Connor, 2005), conditional random fields (CRFs) (Lafferty, McCallum, & Pereira, 2001), and neural networks (Arbib, 2002), directly compute the posterior probability given an observation sequence for learning and classification.

The SVM approaches focus on structural risk minimization by maximizing the decision margin. The SVM-based approach is sensitive to the noise or limited in some cases where a large and complex data set is involved. However, it directly models the decision boundary, therefore, it is efficient to separate two sets of data when the data set is small or not much prior knowledge is available. In (Sadlier & Connor, 2005), a SVM-based approach is proposed to detect events in field sports video by using audio-visual features. In (Ayache,

Quénot, Gensel, & Satoh, 2006), the SVM was used to classify video shots into certain high-level semantic concepts, such as sports, buildings, or intermediate topic concepts.

Compared with DBNs, the CRF and its variations are more expressive due to the fact that it allows more flexible statistical dependency structures on observations and states, as shown in Figure 2. The traditional CRF is an undirected conditional probabilistic graphical model for segmenting and labeling sequential data. In order to handle complex dependencies with no clear prior knowledge, (T. Wang, et al., 2006) proposed a CRF-based method that employs the Markov blanket to specify the dependency among observations and states. To label sequential data in an interactive way, in (McCallum, Rohanimanesh, & Sutton, 2003), the authors proposed the dynamic CRF (DCRF) for part-of-speech tagging and noun-phrase segmentation. Due to its unique structure, the DCRF is able to accomplish several labeling tasks at once by sharing information between them. For example, in (Wojek & Schiele, 2008), objects and scenes in the video sequence are jointly labeled successfully by integrating the interaction and dynamic information between them via DCRF. To handle the long range dependencies as well as the latent structure, in (S. B. Wang, Quattoni, Morency, Demirdjian, & Darrell, 2006), the authors proposed the hidden CRF (HCRF) for gesture recognition. Different

from the traditional CRF where a label is assigned to a single observation, the HCRF incorporates the sub-sequence of hidden state variables in the CRF to assign a label for an entire observation sequence. The proposed HCRF extends the spatial relationship in the CRF into a joint spatial-temporal way, where the labels of individual observations are optimized and incorporated into a sequence classifier for the recognition task. CRFs have been widely used in video mining research, i.e., highlight detection (T. Wang, et al., 2006), human tracking and analysis (Y. Wang & Mori, 2009), video browsing (Reiter, Schuller, & Rigoll, 2007) and personalized content-based retrieval (Jiang, Chang, & Loui, 2007).

Generative vs. Discriminative

In Table 1, we compare generative and discriminative models in terms of several aspects. In this table, six key issues are considered that will help us to choose an appropriate one for a specific video mining task.

PROBLEM FORMULATION

We believe that explicit semantic modeling and direct semantic computing are effective to bridge the semantic gap and reduce the ambiguity and

Figure 2. Discriminative Models: variations of the conditional random field (CRF): the Conditional Random Field (CRF), the Dynamic CRF (DCRF), and the Hidden CRF (HCRF)

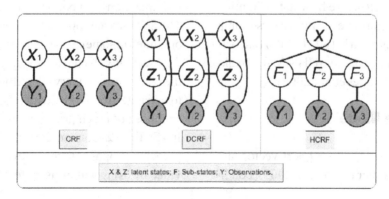

Table 1. Comparison of generative models and discriminative models

	Generative Models	Discriminative Models
Objective	To infer the latent states by learning the statistical distribution of each class.	To infer the latent states by learning the statistical difference between different classes.
Observations	Discrete or continuous, Dependent on current states, conditionally independent to observations from other states.	Mostly discrete, dependent on any other observations or states.
Latent states	Discrete; directed dependent, Markovian chain.	Discrete, undirected dependent.
Inference	To build a probability density function over all observations for each state, and to compute the posterior probability via Bayesian theorem.	To directly map the observation and latent states by potential functions, and estimate the posterior probabilities directly.
Learning	Could handle less training data, and constrain the training process by using the prior knowledge about the observation distribution o and the dependency among states.	Requires more training data, and attempts to map observations and states directly without underlying distribution.
Example Models	Naive Bayes, GMMs, HMMs, Markov random fields.	Logistic regression, SVMs, Neural Networks, CRFs.

uncertainty in sports video mining. Therefore, we propose a three-layer semantic space that includes *low-level visual features*, a set of *mid-level semantic structures* and desired *high-level semantics*. We then convert the issue of event detection into two statistical inference problems with different levels of semantic analysis. This approach supports not only event detection but also customized events-of-interest, increasing the usability and interactivity of video data. Additionally, in this work, we assume that a video sequence is composed of a set of pre-segmented consecutive shots with all breaks and commercials removed, and each shot can be characterized by multiple mid-level semantic structures that can be used to specify high-level semantics, such as highlights, as shown in Figure 3.

Semantic Space

We want to advocate the concept of a three-layer semantic space to facilitate the semantic understanding of video content and to support effective user queries. It is our belief that the exploration of high-level semantics from mid-level semantic structures is more reliable and feasible than from the low-level features directly. Our main reasoning is that mid-level semantic structures have relatively stable and repeatable patterns, and they can be more useful and expressive to represent high-level semantics than low-level visual features. Similar video mining paradigms can be found in recent literature (L. Y. Duan, et al., 2003; T. Wang, et al., 2006). However, it is our attempt to provide a unified machine learning paradigm

Figure 3. From low-level visual features to high-level semantic events

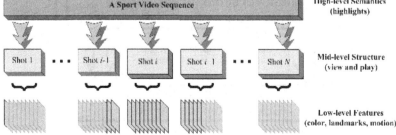

where semantic video analysis is formulated as two related statistical inference problems, i.e., we want to infer mid-level semantic structures from low-level visual features by generative models, and then we can further infer high-level semantics from mid-level semantic structures via discriminative models.

- *Low-level visual features:* At the first layer of the semantic space, relevant low-level visual features are needed to represent different mid-level semantic structures, i.e., views and plays. In this work, three types of visual features in field-based sport videos are used, i.e. the color distribution and landmarks for the view information, and the camera motion for the play information;
- *Mid-level semantic structures:* In this work, the mid-level semantic structure serves as rudimentary semantic building blocks for high-level semantic analysis. These building blocks are frequent, repeatable and relatively well-defined, and their transition can be governed by certain dynamics, and a combination of several semantic structures can be used to specify some high-

level semantics. Therefore, we choose two common structures in most field sports to represent the mid-level semantic structures, i.e., *play types* (what happened) and *camera views* (where it happened), both of which are defined at the shot-level and can be specified by a set of frame-wise visual features in a shot;

- *High-level semantics: Compared* with the mid-level semantic structure, the high-level semantics are immediately useful to viewers and quite specific (user or content dependent), i.e., the *touchdown, turnover,* and other user-specified events of interests. They can hardly be defined directly from low-level visual features. Therefore, we want to represent the high-level semantics based on available informative mid-level semantic structures.

Two Inference Problems

We formulate the issue of event detection in sports video as two inference problems. The first one is from low-level visual features to mid-level semantic structures, and the other is from mid-

Figure 4. The semantic space in football video

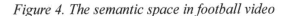
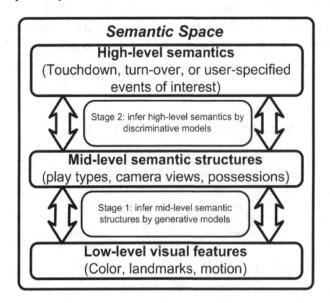

level semantic structures to high-level semantics. We expect to have three major advantages in this framework that are featured with explicit semantic modeling and direct semantic computing. First, we can fully take advantage of the available semantics and prior knowledge about a sport game that makes the video mining problem well structured and formulated. Second, it provides both structure analysis (at the mid-level) and event analysis (at the high-level) that are complementary in nature for semantic video analysis. Third, it not only supports highlight detection but also is able to deliver customized events-of-interest, increasing the usability and interactivity of video data.

Inference problem 1: Mid-level semantic structures are the building blocks for high-level semantic analysis that are governed by certain underlying dynamics and can be specified by low-level frame-wise features in each shot. We consider the generative model for this inference problem where rich prior knowledge is available, such as the conditional distributions of visual observations with respect to different mid-level semantic structures. Specifically, we can regard the low-level frame-wise visual features as observations and the mid-level semantic structures as shot-wise hidden states. Two issues are involved in this inference problem. The first is how to find an effective observation model that can take advantage of the rich statistics of frame-wise features for shot-wise state estimation, and the second is to find the optimal dynamic structure among hidden stages for mid-level semantic modeling.

Inference problem 2: Different from the first inference problem, the prior knowledge may not be sufficient or not well defined in the second inference problem. It is mainly because that high-level semantics have more ambiguities compared with mid-level semantic structures. For example, in American football, the touchdown could happen during either a short play or a long play. High-level semantic analysis usually involves multiple

mid-level semantic structures from several shots. Therefore, it is important for us to find a more flexible statistical model to represent and detect these complex high-level semantics from mid-level semantic structures. The discriminative model provides a feasible way to directly map the observation and hidden states that relaxes some strong dependency assumptions and prior knowledge usually required in generative models. This motivates us to use discriminative models for the second inference problem.

Comparisons

In Table 2, we summarize and compare the two inference problems according to the objective, available prior knowledge, properties of the input, output, and their relationship. By comparing with Table 1, we choose the generative and discriminative models to tackle inference problems 1 and 2 respectively.

Using hybrid generative/discriminative models together has been advocated by several researchers to improve the classification performance. On one hand, the generative model can be used to generate more training data to boost the performance of the discriminative model when training data is limited (Enzweiler & Gavrila, 2008; Raina, et al., 2003). On the other hand, the generative model can be used to extract more meaningful features or key words from low-level features that can help the discriminative model to detect high-level semantic events in the video data more effectively (T. Wang, et al., 2006; X. Zhou, et al., 2008). Inspired by these recent hybrid approaches, we will propose a new hybrid generative-discriminative approach for semantic event detection in sports video where two inference problems are involved. In the following sections, we will introduce three levels of the semantic space along with two statistical modeling approaches used for two inference problems.

Table 2. Comparison between two inference problems

	Inference Problem 1	Inference Problem 2
Objective	To infer the mid-level semantic structure from the low-level visual features.	To infer the high-level semantic events from mid-level semantic structures.
Inputs (observations)	Low-level visual features, frame-wise, continuous, strong temporal dependencies within each shot, conditional independent across shots.	Multiple mid-level semantic structures; shot-wise; temporal dependency across shots.
Outputs (latent states)	Mid-level semantic structure, discrete, relatively well-defined, repeatable, high recurrence.	High-level semantic events, discrete, specific, rare.
Prior knowledge	Conditional distributions of observations and the dynamics of latent states.	The distributions of observation and latent state are lacking.

FEATURE EXTRACTION: VISUAL OBSERVATIONS

At the first layer of the semantic space, relevant low-level visual features are needed to specify the two mid-level semantic structures involved in this work, i.e., play types and camera views. Specifically, there are four play types, i.e., *long play*, *short play*, *field goal*, and *kick off*, and four camera views, i.e., *left view*, *central view*, *right view*, and *end-zone view*. Correspondingly, we define two sets of visual features in the following.

Play types are largely dependent on camera motion that is characterized by two patterns, panning and tilting, as shown in Figure 5 (right). To estimate camera motion, we can use the optical flow based method (Srinivasan, Venkatesh,

& Hosie, 1997) to qualitatively compute motion parameters between two adjacent frames. Also, the frame indices are included as an additional temporal feature to distinguish long plays and short plays. Therefore, a 3-D feature vector is used to represent the play type in each shot.

In Figure 5 (left), we illustrate typical scenes for four different camera views where spatial color distribution and the yard line angle are the two major visual features. Specifically, we employ the robust dominant color region detection algorithm (Ekin, Tekalp, & Mehrotra, 2003) to extract the dominant color region, i.e., the play ground. Then we use Canny edge detection and the Hough transform to detect the yard lines in the region of the playing field. Based on the detected playing field and yard lines, we extract a 6-D feature vec-

Figure 5. Basic visual features: color distribution, yard line angle, camera motion

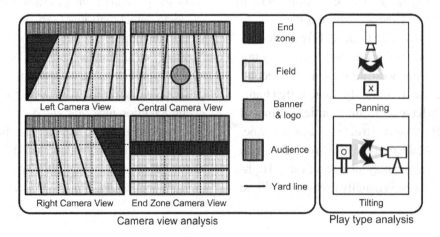

Camera view analysis — Play type analysis

tor composed by the following (1) the ratio of the dominant color region; (2) the ratio difference of dominant color between the left/right and center parts; (3) the ratio difference of dominant color between the left and right parts; (4) the ratio difference of dominant color between the top and bottom parts; (5) the average angle of all yard lines; (6) the angle difference between the first and last frames in a shot (Ding & Fan, 2006).

INFERENCE PROBLEM 1: MID-LEVEL SEMANTIC STRUCTURES

To detect the mid-level semantic structures, we chose the generative model that is preferred for a large data set due to their better generality and the availability of sufficient prior knowledge. In sports video, different mid-level semantic structures will be visualized statistically by visual features and the multiple mid-level semantic structures exist in parallel, such as play types and camera

views as shown in Figure 6. More interestingly, it was observed that camera views and play types are quite related to each other during the game. Therefore, our work will be focused on three issues in generative approaches: how to find an accurate statistical distribution of the observation from hidden states, how to define the dynamic relationship between hidden states in each mid-level semantic structure or multiples, and how to learn the model effectively.

Hidden Markov models (HMMs)

A typical HMM as shown in Figure 7 assumes the underlying system is a Markov process with unknown parameter including a state transition matrix:

$$A = \{a_{k,j} = p(S_t = j \mid S_{t-1} = k) \mid t = 1, \dots, T; j, k = 1, 2, 3, 4\}, \quad (1)$$

Figure 6. Two representative mid-level semantic structures: camera view and play type

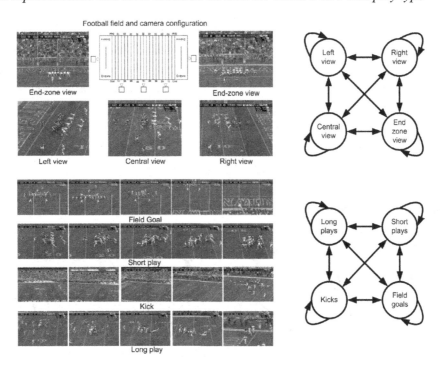

and a probabilistic observation model that we choose Gaussian or Gaussian mixture model as show in (2) and (3)

$$p(o_t \mid S_t = k) = N(o_t \mid \mu_k, \Sigma_k), \qquad (2)$$

$$p(o_t \mid S_t = k) = \sum_{n=1}^{N} \alpha_n N(o_t \mid \mu_{nk}, \Sigma_{nk}), \qquad (3)$$

where k is the number of components in each mid-level semantic structure. Then, the former one captures the underlying state dynamics, and the latter one characterizes observations pertaining to the hidden states either as probability density functions. After EM training (Bilmes, 1997), we can obtain the optimized parameter set,

$$\Gamma^* = \arg \max_{\Gamma} p(o_{1:T} \mid \Gamma), \qquad (4)$$

where

$$p(o_{1:T} \mid \Gamma) = \sum_k \pi_k \prod_{t=1}^{T} p(S_{t+1} \mid S_t) p(o_t \mid S_t = k). \qquad (5)$$

Then the Viterbi algorithm can help us find the optimized state sequences, i.e., the mid-level semantic structure sequences.

$$S_{1:T}^* = \arg \max_{S_{1:T}} P(S_{1:T} \mid o_{1:T}, \Gamma^*). \qquad (6)$$

The basic HMM-based approach is able to infer mid-level semantic structures from low-level visual features. However, the major limitation of the HMM is that each shot is represented by an averaged feature vector that is less representative and informative. This fact motivates us to improve the observation model in the HMM, i.e., we are expecting to explore the frame-wise features and the temporal dependency across frames in a shot.

Segmental Hidden Markov Models

To fully utilize frame-wise visual features and temporal dependency across frames in a shot, we invoke a segmental HMM (SHMM) (Gales & Young, 1993) that is able to handle variable-length observations to attack this problem. Instead of generating one observation by each hidden state in the traditional HMM, each hidden state of the SHMM can emit a sequence of observations, which can be called a segment. In the SHMM as shown in Figure 7, observations in a given segment are assumed to be independent to the observations belonging to other segments. In addition, in each segment all observations are conditionally independent given the mean of that segment. Thus a closed form likelihood function is attainable that can capture rich statistics of frame-wise features. Here, we can regard a segment as a shot and observations in a segment as frame-wise features in a shot.

A SHMM of M states can be characterized by a set of parameters

Figure 7. Generative model based approaches: (a) HMM; (b) SHMM; (c) MCSHMM

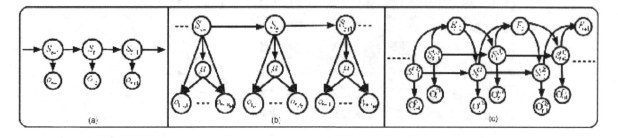

$$\Gamma = \{\pi_k, a_{k,j}, \mu_{\mu,k}, \Sigma_{\mu,k}, \Sigma_k \mid k, j = 1, ..., K\},$$
(7)

where π_k is the initial probability, $a_{k,j}$ the transition probability, $\mu_{\mu,k}$ characterize the mean of the each segment of state m, and $\Sigma\mu_k$ the variance of the segment. Given a shot in time t with n_t observations, i.e., $O_{1:T} = \{O_t | t = 1, ..., T\}$, under the conditionally independent assumption, the conditional likelihood of O_t is defined as:

$$p(\mathbf{O}_t \mid S_t = k, \Gamma) = \int p(\mu \mid S_t = k, \Gamma) \prod_{i=1}^{n_t} p(o_{t,i} \mid \mu, S_t = k, \Gamma) d\mu,$$
(8)

where

$$p(\mu \mid S_t = k, \Gamma) = N(\mu \mid \mu_{\mu,k}, \Sigma_{\mu,k}),$$
(9)

and

$$p(o_{t,i} \mid \mu, S_t = k, \Gamma) = N(o_{t,i} \mid \mu, \Sigma_k),$$
(10)

which are both specified by Gaussian model. This likelihood function describes the probability distribution of a semantic unit which generates multiple observations, i.e., visual features distribution for a specific camera view within a shot with length n_t. Then, similar as HMMs, by using a new EM algorithm and Viterbi algorithm introduced in (Ding & Fan, 2007a), we can estimate all model parameters using the optimal state sequence:

$$S_{1:T}^* = \arg\max_{S_{1:T}} P(S_{1:T} \mid o_{1:T}, \Gamma^*),$$
(11)

i.e., the mid-level semantic structures. However, the SHMM including the HMM based approaches can only detect a single semantic structure and model structure, e.g., the state space, is pre-defined, which cannot capture the interaction between different mid-level semantic structures

with a flexible manner. Therefore, we expect a new model that can have these capabilities.

Multi-Channel Hidden Markov Models (MCSHMM)

We expect a new model to inherent the merits of the SHMM, i.e., handle multiple observations tied with each semantic structure, and to explore the interaction between different semantic structures. In (Ding & Fan, 2008, 2009b), we advance a new multi-channel SHMM model (MCSHMM) that involves two *parallel* SHMMs and a two-layer *hierarchical* Markovian structure, as shown in Figure 7. In this model, each channel is a single SHMM and they are connected by a hybrid parallel-hierarchical structure, we also developed a new learning algorithm that can learn a model with compact structure and optimized parameters simultaneously.

In the view of generative models, both the dynamic model (among hidden states) and the observation model (between hidden states and observations) in the MCSHMM have a two-layered structure that greatly enhances its capability of learning and inference. Specifically, at the first layer of the dynamic model,

$$\mathbf{S} = \{S_t^{(j)} \mid t = 1, ..., T; j = 1, 2\},$$
(12)

which denotes the state sequence of two channels where $S_t^{(j)}$ denotes the state of shot t in channel j, and at the second-layer of the dynamic model,

$$\mathbf{F} = \{F_t = (S_t^{(1)}, S_t^{(2)}) \mid t = 1, ..., T\},$$
(13)

which represents the state sequence at the second layer where each state consists of two current states at the first layer. At the observation layer,

$$\mathbf{O} = \{o_{t,i}^{(j)} \mid t = 1, ..., T; i = 1, ..., n_t; j = 1, 2\},$$
(14)

in which, $o_{t,i}^{(j)}$ indicates observations of shot t with n_t frames in channel j. Therefore, the MCSHMM's parameter set $\Gamma=\{\mathbf{A},\Pi,\Omega\}$ includes following components:

- Initial probabilities:

$$\Pi = \{P(S_t^{(1)}), P(S_t^{(2)}), P(F_t \mid S_t^{(1)}, S_t^{(2)})\}. \tag{15}$$

- Transition probabilities:

$$\mathbf{A}=\{A_w, w=1,2,3\} \tag{16}$$

where

$$
\begin{aligned}
A_1 &= \{P(S_t^{(1)}=m \mid S_{t-1}^{(1)}=n, F_{t-1}=l) \mid m,n=1,...,4, l=1,...,16\}, \\
A_2 &= \{P(S_t^{(2)}=m \mid S_{t-1}^{(2)}=n, F_{t-1}=l) \mid m,n=1,...,4, l=1,...,16\}, \\
A_3 &= \{P(F_t=l \mid S_t^{(1)}=m, S_t^{(2)}=n) \mid m,n=1,...,4, l=1,...,16\}.
\end{aligned}
\tag{17}
$$

- Observation density functions:

$$p(\mathbf{O}_t^{(j)} \mid S_i^{(j)}=m, \Omega) = \int N(\mu \mid \mu_{\mu,m}^{(j)}, \Sigma_{\mu,m}^{(j)}) \prod_{i=1}^{n_t} N(o_{t,i}^{(j)} \mid \mu, \Sigma_m^{(j)}) d\mu, \tag{18}$$

where

$$\Omega = \{\mu_{\mu,m}^{(j)}, \Sigma_{\mu,m}^{(j)}, \Sigma_m^{(j)} \mid j=1,2; m=1,...,4\}$$

specifies two segmental models, and $o_{t,i}^{(j)}$ denotes the observation from the ith frame in shot t of channel j. Then, given the dual-channel observations $\mathbf{O}$ of T shots, the joint likelihood is defined as

$$
\begin{aligned}
p(\mathbf{S},\mathbf{F},\mathbf{O} \mid \Gamma) = {} & P(S_1^{(1)})P(S_1^{(2)})P(F_1 \mid S_1^{(1)}, S_1^{(2)}) \\
& \prod_{t=1}^{T} P(F_t \mid S_t^{(1)}, S_t^{(2)}) \prod_{t=2}^{T}\prod_{j=1}^{2} P(S_t^{(j)} \mid S_{t-1}^{(j)}, F_{t-1}) \prod_{t=1}^{T}\prod_{j=1}^{2} p(o_{t,i}^{(j)} \mid S_t^{(j)}).
\end{aligned}
\tag{19}
$$

We refer the reader to (Ding & Fan, 2008, 2009b) for more details, where a new unsupervised learning algorithm was proposed to learn the model structure and parameters simultaneously. The key idea is to find a compact model structure that has good determinism and minimal ambiguity. We first pre-define a coarse model structure that includes every possible configuration of the semantic structure, then we use the ideas of entropic prior and parameter extinction proposed in (Matthew Brand, 1999) to trim the weakly supported parameters and states, leading to a compact and concise model with good determinism. Then, by using the Viterbi decoding algorithm, we can estimate multiple semantic structures at the same time. MCSHMM can provide more accurate mid-level semantic analysis compared with SHMM and HMMs.

INFERENCE PROBLEM 2: HIGH-LEVEL SEMANTICS ANALYSIS

As aforementioned, the mid-level semantic structures deliver the rudimentary building blocks for high-level semantic analysis because they can be used to represent high-level semantics (i.e., events) effectively. Particularly, in addition to the play type and camera view, we also introduce another mid-level structure, i.e., *the possession*, which indicates the team holding the ball and can be easily detected by using the initial camera motion direction in the beginning of a shot. Thus, given the three kinds of mid-level semantic structures of all shots, the second inference problem aims at detecting the interesting events, such as highlights (or the touchdown plays a football game) (Ding & Fan, 2009a).

Event Detection Example

Unlike the first inference problem that is well supported by the generative models, the second inference problem, also referred to as event detection in this work, is very different in nature. We use one example below for discussion.

We show three play drives that lead to scoring in Figure 8, each of which includes four shots and the three mid-level structures are also given for each shot. Among the three drives, the first two results in a touch-down followed by a field goal and the third one is only a field goal. We can have a few important observations.

- There are strong temporal dependencies across shots with respect to each mid-level structure and an evident semantic correlation between multiple mid-level structures in each shot.
- A touch-down play cannot be determined from a single shot, and its determination requires multiple semantic mid-level structures from several shots.
- There is some uncertainty of the definition of a touch-down play as well as ambiguity between the touch-down play and the field goal.

Moreover, the events of interest, such as touch-downs or field goals, are usually relative rare and unbalanced compared to other non-specific events in a game. This is in contrast with the mid-level semantic structures. A supervised learning method is more appropriate for high-level semantic analysis due to a very small portion of events of interest. Therefore, it is important for us to find an effective statistical model to address the above characteristics of high-level semantic analysis. Particularly, we are interested in developing a discriminative model based approach for event detection. The discriminative model provides a flexible and plausible way to capture the complex dependency among multiple mid-level semantic structures both within and across shots.

Conditional Random Fields

The conditional random fields (CRFs) as shown in Figure 9 were first introduced in (Lafferty, et al., 2001) and provide an undirected probabilistic model to directly compute the statistical mapping relationship between the input (observations) and the output (states) for classification and regression purposes. Compared with the HMMs, CRFs do not involve the conditional distributions of observations, and the state variable in CRFs can be related to multiple observations from different time slices. Compared with SVM, CRFs are more appropriate to capture the temporal dependencies both among observations and states for sequential data analysis. Specifically, the Markov blanket in a CRF defines the set of neighboring nodes that specifies the potential functions from both states

Figure 8. Three touch-down drives of four consecutive shots in the football game

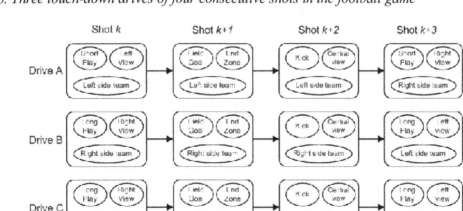

and observations and simplifies the factorization of joint distribution in the CRF.

A general random field, as shown in Figure 9, can be characterized by the parameter set

$$\Theta = (\lambda_1, \ldots, \lambda_n; \mu_1, \ldots, \mu_m) \qquad (20)$$

which specifies the *feature functions* between observations and hidden states as

$$p_\Theta(\mathbf{S} \mid \mathbf{O}) = \frac{1}{Z(\mathbf{O})} \exp\{\sum_t (\sum_i \lambda_i f_i(S_{t-1}, S_t) + \sum_j \mu_j g_j(S_t, \mathbf{O}))\}, \qquad (21)$$

where $Z(\mathbf{O})$ is a normalization over the data sequence $\mathbf{O}$, $f_i(\cdot)$ and $g_j(\cdot)$ are *transition feature functions* and *state feature functions* respectively. In different applications, we can choose different type of feature functions in terms of the prior knowledge about the temporal or spatial relationship among states and observations, which provides us the flexibility to effectively formulate arbitrary dependencies that can hardly be described in generative models. Then, by maximum likelihood (ML) estimation, we can obtain the CRF by maximize conditional probabilities as

$$\Theta^* = \arg\max_\Theta p_\theta(\mathbf{S} \mid \mathbf{O}). \qquad (22)$$

Then, for a new data sequence $\mathbf{O}$, we can predict the label $\mathbf{S}$ that can maximize $p(\mathbf{S} \mid \mathbf{O}, \Theta^*)$, i.e.,

$$\mathbf{S}^* = \arg\max_\mathbf{S} p(\mathbf{S} \mid \mathbf{O}, \Theta^*). \qquad (23)$$

In this work, $\mathbf{O}$ is the mid-level semantic structure sequences for all shots and $\mathbf{S}$ as the corresponding high-level events, i.e., touch-down plays or non-touchdown plays. Therefore, we can formulate the second inference problem as (22) and (23) based on the trained CRF.

In practice, we need to define possible transition and state feature functions, then utilize dynamic programming algorithms, e.g., gradient based approaches (Lecun, Bottou, Bengio, & Haffner, 1998), to optimize the model parameter. Then the classification task is straightforward according to (23). Especially, we employ the first order Markov chain to define the transition function, and the Markov blanket (Pearl, 1988; T. Wang, et al., 2006) to formulate feature functions that determine the conditional relationship between the state and observation as well as the relationship among observations. As shown in Figure 9, for each time slice, we set a Markov blanket that involves the current high-level semantic event and neighboring mid-level semantic structures to define the state feature functions. In this work, we

Figure 9. (a) A typical CRF; (b) CRF-based event detection. (CV: central view; RV: right view; LV: left view; EZ: end-zone; LP: long play; SP: short play; FG: field goal; KP: kick/punt; LS: left-side team; RS: right-side team)

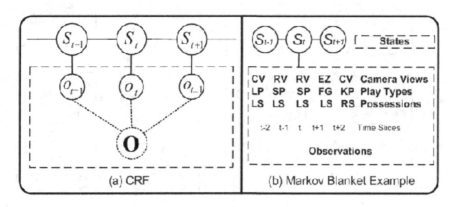

choose the Markov blanket with the width of 5, and construct the state feature function regarding all three types of mid-level semantic structures, i.e., play type, camera view, and possessions.

EXPERIMENTS AND DISCUSSION

In our experiments, the proposed framework is tested on 9 NFL football games (352×240, 30fps) that have been pre-segmented into a series of consecutive play shots by removing commercials and replays, and each game has 150-170 shots and each shot has 300-500 frames. Then, we use the Bayesian net and CRF toolkits from Murphy (Website) in Matlab 7.0 on a PC with dual-core 2.4G CPU and 2Gb memory for learning and inference of the GMM, HMMs, the SHMM, the MCSHMM, and CRFs respectively. To demonstrate the effectiveness of the proposed framework, we first manually annotate all ground truth of both mid-level semantic structures and high-level semantics, and then we compare experiment results based on mid-level semantic structure, i.e., camera views and play types, by generative and discriminative models respectively, and high-level semantics, i.e., touchdown, detection via rule-based, generative and discriminative models. In each set of experimental result, we show three criteria for the performance by using an "error bar" chart showing the average, the best, and the worst in each algorithm.

Mid-Level Semantic Structure Classification

Seven generative methods and one discriminative model are involved for comparison. Generative models include a supervised GMM (with order 3), the HMM with Gaussian emission (HMM[1]), the HMM with GMM emission (HMM[2]), the embedded GMM-HMM (HMM[3]) (Ding & Fan, 2007b) and the SHMM (Ding & Fan, 2007a), the CHMM with GMM observations (CHMM[1]), the CHMM with segmental observations (CHMM[2]), and the MCSHMM (Ding & Fan, 2008). The first five explore two semantic structures (plays and views) independently and separately, while the last three estimate both jointly. To improve the EM training, we adopted a coarse-to-fine learning strategy that uses the training result of a simpler model to initialize a more complex one. Specifically, we first use K-mean (4-class) to obtain a coarse classification, and this result can be utilized to initialize HMM[1] whose training result can be used to initialize HMM[2], and so on, also the training result of SHMM was used to initialize MCSHMM. For the discriminative model, we employ the CRF with shot-wise observations by averaging all frame-wise observations in one shot, which are then quantized as a discrete value in each dimension. Figure 10 shows the experimental results for mid-level semantic structure analysis. It is clearly shown that the MCSHMM outperforms all other algorithms with significant improvements, and the HMM-based generative approaches show clear advantages over the discriminative model, i.e., the CRF-based approach.

As shown in Figure 10, the performance is enhanced from HMMs to the MCSHMM. The reason that SHMM is better than other HMMs is because of the segmental observation model used. The improvement of MCSHMM over other HMMs and SHMM is owing to the hybrid hierarchical-parallel dynamic model involved. The MCSHMM can effectively capture the mutual interaction between two Markov chains by introducing the second-layer dynamics and decision-level fusion that are able to balance the dependency both within each channel and across the two channels. On the contrary, the CRF-based method is less effective than the HMM-based one when they are in same configuration. We expect it is due to the fact that the CRF may not take advantage of rich observation and the available prior knowledge about the distribution of observations and state dynamics during inference.

Figure 10. Classification results of mid-level semantic structures based on 9 different statistical models: (a). Camera view analysis results; (b). Play type analysis results

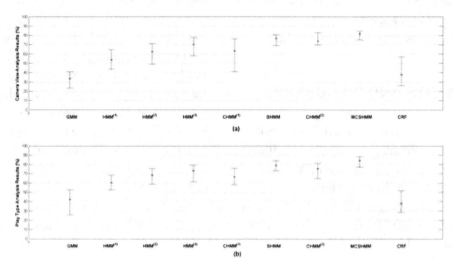

High-Level Semantic Event Detection

Three methods are tested here, each of which is examined by using the manually annotated ground truth and the MCSHMM outputs. In each game, there are usually 5-12 touchdowns out of 150-170 shots.

- *Rule-based approach* is simple but effective when the game is highly organized according to some rules. In our case, we find most touchdowns occur in either left or right camera views by a short or long play, and followed by an end zone camera view with a field goal, and then we use this rule to detect the touchdown.
- *CRF-based approach* takes available mid-level semantic structures as the observation along with the 5-order Markov blanket, and high-level semantics (touchdown) as the latent state for each shot. We employed the cross validation strategy in this experiment where, for each video sequence to be tested, all other video sequences are used as the training data.

- *HMM-based approach* is similar to the CRF based approach in terms of the definition of state and observation as well as the experimental setting. However, due to the underlying assumption of HMM, we cannot involve multiple observations from different shots for state estimation.

As shown in Figure 11, the rule-based approach can reach a higher recall score but a lower precision score, and the HMM-based approach shows more balanced precision and recall. The CRF-based approach achieves the best precision and F-measure, and the recall rate is slightly lower than that of the rule-based approach that over-detects touchdown highlights (low precision) due to the simple rules involved. In general, the CRF can detect the high-level semantics with high specificity (high precision) when the training data is sufficient and representative. It is mainly owing to the flexible dependency structure involved between states and observations, as shown in Figure 9(b). However, due to the ambiguities of the high level semantic events and less training data available, the traditional CRF may not be generalized

Figure 11. High-level event detection results for Rule-based, HMM-Based, and CRF-based algorithms: (a), (b), (c). Case 1 – ground truth data as the input; (d), (e), (f). Case 2 – MCSHMM outputs as the input

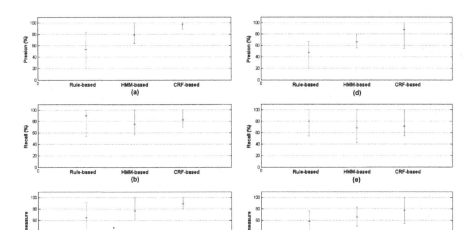

well (relatively low recall rate compared with the rule-based methods).

Comparing Case 1 (using the ground-truth mid-level structures as the input) with Case 2 (using the MCSHMM output as the input), we can see more than 10% improvement in both the precision and the F-measurement, showing the first inference problem is critical to the second inference problem, and the CRF-based algorithm can improve the detection results effectively. However, compared with the rule-based method, the CRF-based method is still not efficient in terms of the recall. So, there is still room for further improvement to better integrate two inference problems in a seamless way.

CONCLUSION AND FUTURE WORK

In this chapter, we have proposed a general video mining framework for event detection in the sports video, specifically, American football video. A three-level semantic space is presented that supports explicit semantic modeling and direct semantic computing. Under this semantic

space, event detection can be formulated as two inter-related statistical inference problems that have different nature and can be addressed by generative and discriminative models individually. Compared with other similar approaches, it is our attempt to provide a new perspective on the research of sport video mining, under which event detection can be formulated systematically and be addressed effectively by appropriate statistical modeling approaches. This framework can be extended to other sports video mining applications by incorporating new domain knowledge, a problem-oriented semantic space, and relevant visual features, as well as novel statistical modeling and learning techniques.

Our future work will be two-fold. One is that we want to incorporate more relevant mid-level semantic structures (as well as low-level features) that could enrich the expressiveness for high-level semantics. The other is that we will enhance the capability and generality of CRF for more effective and accurate event detection. Our ultimate goal is to automatically generate a complete game flow that can be used for various sports video mining applications.

ACKNOWLEDGMENT

This work is supported by the National Science Foundation (NSF) under Grant IIS-0347613 and a Oklahoma NASA EPSCoR Research Initiation Grant (2009). The authors also thank the reviewers for their valuable comments and suggestions that improved this paper.

REFERENCES

Arbib, M. A. (2002). *The handbook of Brain Theory and Neural Network*. Cambridge, MA: The MIT Press.

Assfalg, J., Bertini, M., Colombo, C., Bimbo, A. d., & Nunziati, W. (2003). Semantic annotation of soccer videos: automatic highlights identification. *Computer Vision and Image Understanding, 92*(2-3), 285–305. doi:10.1016/j.cviu.2003.06.004

Ayache, S., Quénot, G., Gensel, J., & Satoh, S. (2006). Using topic concepts for semantic video shots classification. In *Proc. 5th international conference on image and video retrieval*.

Bilmes, J. (1997). *A Gentle Tutorial on the EM Algorithm and its Application to Parameter Estimation for Gaussian Mixture and Hidden Markov Models* (ICSI-Report-97-021).

Brand, M. (1999). Structure Learning in Conditional Probability Models via an Entropic Prior and Parameter Extinction. *Neural Computation, 11*(5), 1155–1182. doi:10.1162/089976699300016395

Brand, M., Oliver, N., & Pentland, A. (1997). Coupled hidden Markov models for complex action recognition. In *Proc. IEEE International Conference on Computer Vision and Pattern Recognition*.

Chang, P., Han, M., & Gong, Y. (2002). Highlight detection and classification of baseball game video with Hidden Markov Models. In *Proc. IEEE International Conference on Image Processing, Rochester, NY*.

Chang, S.-F. (2002). The holy grail of content-based media analysis. *IEEE Multimedia Magazine, 9*(2), 6–10. doi:10.1109/93.998041

Ding, Y., & Fan, G. (2007a). Segmental Hidden Markov Models for View-based Sport Video Analysis. In *Proc. International Workshop on Semantic Learning Applications in Multimedia, in conjunction with IEEE International Conference on Computer Vision and Pattern Recognition*.

Ding, Y., & Fan, G. (2007b). Two-Layer Generative Models for Sport Video Mining. In *Proc. IEEE International Conference on Multimedia and Expo*.

Ding, Y., & Fan, G. (2008). Multi-channel Segmental Hidden Markov Models for Sports Video Mining. In *Proc. the ACM Multimedia Conference*.

Ding, Y., & Fan, G. (2009a). Event Detection in Sports Video based on Generative-Discriminative Models. In *Proc. the 1st ACM International Workshop on Events in Multimedia (EiMM09) in conjunction with the ACM Multimedia Conference*.

Ding, Y., & Fan, G. (2009b). Sports Video Mining via Multi-channel Segmental Hidden Markov Models. *IEEE Transactions on Multimedia, 11*(7), 1301–1309. doi:10.1109/TMM.2009.2030828

Duan, L., Xu, M., Tian, Q., Xu, C., & Jin, S. J. (2005). A unified framework for semantic shot classification in sports video. *IEEE Transactions on Multimedia, 7*(6), 1066–1083. doi:10.1109/TMM.2005.858395

Duan, L. Y., Xu, M., Chua, T. S., & Tian, Q. Q., & Xu, C. S. (2003). A Mid-level Representation Framework for Semantic Sports Video Analysis. In *Proc. the ACM Multimedia Conference*.

Ekin, A., Tekalp, A., & Mehrotra, R. (2003). Automatic soccer video analysis and summarization. *IEEE Transactions on Image Processing, 12*(7), 796–807. doi:10.1109/TIP.2003.812758

Friedman, N., & Koller, D. (2003). Being Bayesian About Network Structure. A Bayesian Approach to Structure Discovery in Bayesian Networks. *Machine Learning, 50*(1), 95–125. doi:10.1023/A:1020249912095

Gales, M., & Young, S. (1993). *The theory of segmental hidden Markov models* (Technical Report CUED/F-INFENG/TR 133). Cambridge University.

Ghahramani, Z. (2002). Graphical models: parameter learning. In Arbib, M. A. (Ed.), *The Handbook of Brain Theory and Neural Networks.* MIT Press.

Gong, Y., Sin, L. T., Chuan, C. H., Zhang, H. J., & Sakauchi, M. (1995). Automatic parsing of TV soccer programs. In *Proc. International Conference on Multimedia Computing and Systems.*

Jiang, W., Chang, S. F., & Loui, A. C. (2007). Context-based concept fusion with boosted conditional random fields. In *Proc. IEEE Conference on Computer Vision and Pattern Recognition.*

Kokaram, A., Rea, N., Dahyot, R., Tekalp, M., Bouthemy, P., & Gros, P. (2006). Browsing sports video: trends in sports-related indexing and retrieval work. *IEEE Signal Processing Magazine, 23*(2), 47–58. doi:10.1109/MSP.2006.1621448

Koubaroulis, D., Matas, J., & Kittler, J. (2002). Colour-based object recognition for video annotation. In *Proc. IEEE International Conference on Pattern Recognition.*

Lafferty, J., McCallum, A., & Pereira, F. (2001). Conditional Random Fields: Probabilistic Models for Segmenting and Labeling Sequence Data. In *Proc. the Eighteenth International Conference on Machine Learning (ICML).*

Lazarescu, M., & Venkatesh, S. (2003, July). Using camera motion to identify types of American football plays. In *Proc. International Conf. on Multimedia and Expo.*

Lecun, Y., Bottou, L., Bengio, Y., & Haffner, P. (1998). Gradient-based learning applied to document recognition. *Proceedings of the IEEE, 86*(11), 2278–2324. doi:10.1109/5.726791

Li, B., & Sezan, I. (2002). Event detection and summarization in American football brocast video. In *Proc. SPIE Storage and Retrieval for Media Database.*

McCallum, A., Rohanimanesh, K., & Sutton, C. (2003). Dynamic Conditional Random Fields for Jointly Labeling Multiple Sequences. In *Proc. 17th Annual Conference on Neural Information Processing Systems.*

Mei, T., Ma, Y., Zhou, H., Ma, W., & Zhang, H. (2005). Sports Video Mining with Mosaic. In *Proc. the 11th IEEE International Multimedia Modeling Conference.*

Murphy, K. (2002). *Dynamic Bayesian Networks: Representation, Inference and Learning.* UC Berkeley.

Murphy, K. (2007). *BNT Matlab Toolbox.* Retrieved from http://people.cs.ubc.ca/~murphyk/Software/

Naphade, M., & Huang, T. (2002). Discovering recurrent events in video using unsupervised methods. *Proc. IEEE International Conference on Image Processing, Rochester, NY.*

Nefian, A. V., Liang, L., Pi, X., Liu, X., & Murphy, K. (2002). Dynamic Bayesian Networks for Audio-Visual Speech Recognition. *EURASIP Journal on Applied Signal Processing, 11,* 1–15.

Pan, H., Beek, P., & Sezan, M. I. (2001). Detection of slow-motion replay segments in sports video for highlights generation. *IEEE International Conference on Acoustics Speech and Signal Processing.*

Pearl, J. (1988). *Probabilistic reasoning in intelligent systems: networks of plausible inference.* Morgan Kaufmann Publishers Inc.

Raina, R., & Shen, Y. NG, A. Y., & Mccallum, A. (2003). Classification with hybrid generative / discriminative models. In *Proc. Neural Information Processing Systems*.

Reiter, S., Schuller, B., & Rigoll, G. (2007). Hidden conditional random fields for meeting segmentation. In *Proc. IEEE international conference on multimedia and expo*.

Rui, Y., Huang, T., & Mehrotra, S. (1998). Constructing table-of-content for video. In *Proc. the ACM Multimedia conference*.

Sadlier, D., & Connor, N. (2005). Event detection in field-sports video using audio-visual features and a support vector machine. *IEEE Transactions on Circuits and Systems for Video Technology*, *15*(10), 1225–1233. doi:10.1109/TCSVT.2005.854237

Srinivasan, M., Venkatesh, S., & Hosie, R. (1997). Qualitative estimation of camera motion parameters from video sequences. *Pattern Recognition*, *30*, 593–606. doi:10.1016/S0031-3203(96)00106-9

Wang, P., & Ji, Q. (2005). Multi-view Face Tracking with Factorial and Switching HMM. In *Proc. IEEE Workshop on Applications of Computer Vision (WACV/MOTION05)*.

Wang, S. B., Quattoni, A., Morency, L.-P., Demirdjian, D., & Darrell, T. (2006). Hidden Conditional Random Fields for Gesture Recognition. In *Proc. IEEE Computer Society Conference on Computer Vision and Pattern Recognition*.

Wang, T., Li, J., Diao, Q., Hu, W., Zhang, Y., & Dulong, C. (2006). Semantic Event Detection using Conditional Random Fields. In *Proc. IEEE Conference on Computer Vision and Pattern Recognition*.

Wang, Y., Liu, Z., & Huang, J. (2000). Multimedia content analysis using both audio and visual clues. *IEEE Signal Processing Magazine*, *17*(6), 12–36. doi:10.1109/79.888862

Wang, Y., & Mori, G. (2009). Max-margin hidden conditional random fields for human action recognition. *Proc. IEEE Conference on Computer Vision and Pattern Recognition*.

Wojek, C., & Schiele, B. (2008). A dynamic conditional random field model for joint labeling of object and scene classes. In *Proc. the 10th European Conference on Computer Vision*.

Xie, L., Chang, S., Divakaran, A., & Sun, H. (2003). Unsupervised Mining of Staistical Temporal Structures in Video. In Rosenfeld, D. D. A. (Ed.), *Video Mining*. Kluwer Academi Publishers.

Xie, L., Chang, S.-F., Divakaran, A., & Sun, H. (2002). Structure Analysis of Soccer Video with Hidden Markov Models. In *Proc. Interational Conference on Acoustic, Speech and Signal Processing*.

Xie, L., Chang, S.-F., Divakaran, A., & Sun, H. (2004). Structure Analysis of Soccer Video with domain knowledge and Hidden Markov Models. *Pattern Recognition Letters*, *25*(7), 767–775. doi:10.1016/j.patrec.2004.01.005

Xiong, Z. Y., Zhou, X. S., Tian, Q., Rui, Y., & Huang, T. S. (2006). Semantic retrieval of video - review of research on video retrieval in meetings, movies and broadcast news, and sports. *IEEE Signal Processing Magazine*, *23*(2), 18–27. doi:10.1109/MSP.2006.1621445

Xu, C., Zhu, G., Zhang, Y., Huang, Q., & Lu, H. (2008). Event tactic analysis based on player and ball trajectory in broadcast video. In *Proc. International conference on Content-based image and video retrieval*.

Yu, X., Xu, C., Leong, H. W., Tian, Q., Tang, Q., & Wan, K. W. (2003). Trajectory-based ball detection and tracking with applications to semantic analysis of broadcast soccer video. In *Proc. the ACM Multimedia conference*.

Zhang, D., Gatica-Perez, D., Bengio, S., & Roy, D. (2005). *Learning influence among interacting Markov chains*. Proc. Neural Information Processing Systems.

Zhou, W., Vellaikal, A., & Kuo, C. C. J. (2000). Rule-based video classification system for basketball video indexing. In *Proc. the ACM Multimedia Conference*.

Zhou, X., Zhuang, X., Yan, S., Chang, S. F., Johnson, M., & Huang, T. S. (2008). SIFT-Bag Kernel for Video Event Analysis. In *Proc. the ACM Multimedia Conference*.

KEY TERMS AND DEFINITIONS

Conditional Random Field: An undirected graphical model in which the label sequence is defined by a single log-linear distribution given a particular observation sequence.

Discriminative Models: Are models used for modeling the dependence of an unobserved variables on an observed variables, which is done by modeling the conditional probability distribution.

Event Detection: To analyze and locate highlights, special patterns, or cases of interest in the video data.

Generative Models: Are models for randomly generating observable data given some hidden parameters, which specifies a joint probability distribution over observation and label sequences.

Hidden Markov Model: A directed graphical model in which the system being modeled is assumed to be a Markov process with unknown parameters.

Semantic Structures: An organization or a pattern that represents specific meaning.

Sports Video Analysis: To discover the meaningful structure or events of interest in the sports video.

Video Mining: The process of discovering knowledge, structures, patterns and events of interest in the video data.

Chapter 10
Content–Based Video Scene Clustering and Segmentation

Hong Lu
Fudan University, China

Xiangyang Xue
Fudan University, China

ABSTRACT

With the amount of video data increasing rapidly, automatic methods are needed to deal with large-scale video data sets in various applications. In content-based video analysis, a common and fundamental preprocess for these applications is video segmentation. Based on the segmentation results, video has a hierarchical representation structure of frames, shots, and scenes from the low level to high level. Due to the huge amount of video frames, it is not appropriate to represent video contents using frames. In the levels of video structure, shot is defined as an unbroken sequence of frames from one camera; however, the contents in shots are trivial and can hardly convey valuable semantic information. On the other hand, scene is a group of consecutive shots that focuses on an object or objects of interest. And a scene can represent a semantic unit for further processing such as story extraction, video summarization, etc. In this chapter, we will survey the methods on video scene segmentation. Specifically, there are two kinds of scenes. One kind of scene is to just consider the visual similarity of video shots and clustering methods are used for scene clustering. Another kind of scene is to consider both the visual similarity and temporal constraints of video shots, i.e., shots with similar contents and not lying too far in temporal order. Also, we will present our proposed methods on scene clustering and scene segmentation by using Gaussian mixture model, graph theory, sequential change detection, and spectral methods.

1. INTRODUCTION

In recent years, with the amount of video data increasing rapidly, automatic methods are needed to deal with large-scale video data sets in various applications. A common and fundamental preprocess for these applications is video segmentation. Based on the segmentation results, video has a hierarchical representation structure of frames, shots, and scenes from the low level to high level. And frames are not appropriate to represent video

DOI: 10.4018/978-1-60960-024-2.ch010

contents due to their huge amount. In the levels of video structure analysis, shot is defined as an unbroken sequence of frames from one camera; however, the contents in shots are trivial and can hardly convey valuable semantic information. Also, the number of shots is still large for analysis and processing. On the other hand, scene is a group of consecutive shots that focuses on an object or objects of interest. And a scene can represent a semantic unit. Therefore, the effectiveness of scene segmentation is crucial for further analyzing and understanding video content.

There are two types of scenes. The first type of scene is defined as shots having similar visual contents and can be obtained by *scene clustering*. The second type of scene is defined as a collection of consecutive shots featuring a dramatic event; such scene can be obtained by *scene segmentation* with the incorporation of suitable temporal correlation and prior knowledge.

In *scene clustering* work, much of the work has been done. Specifically, Yeung *et al.* (Yeung, 1998) proposed shot-based representation structure. And video can be represented as a scene transition graph (STG). In the graph, each node represents a shot and links between shots reflect transitions which are characterized by visual features and temporal characteristic of video. Then hierarchical clustering method is used to find out the closed subgraphs from the entire graph. These subgraphs are regarded as scenes. Rasheed *et al.* (Rasheed, 2005) constructed a weighted undirected graph, i.e. shot similarity graph, (SSG). In the graph, each node represents a shot while each edge between two nodes (shots) represent the similarity which is based on color and motion information. The SSG is split into subgraphs by using normalized cuts. Rasheed *et al.* (Rasheed, 2003) adopted a two-pass segmentation algorithm for scene boundary detection. Their work focuses on featured films and TV shows by utilizing the features of motion, shot length, and color similarity. The potential boundaries are first detected

based on color feature, then the over-segmented scenes are merged based on motion.

Also, some work has been done in *scene segmentation*. Specifically, Kender *et al.* (Kender, 1998) computed video coherence between shots using a short term memory-based model. In the processing, the local minimum is determined to permit robust and flexible scene segmentations. Due to the variance of shot length, the method is sensitive to the buffer size. Furthermore, to deal with different genres of videos, Li *et al.* (Li, 2004) adopted the method of sequential change detection to perform the video scene segmentation. To let the proposed method could be suitable for various genres of videos, nonparametric density estimation and adaptive threshold were employed. However, this method simply computes the log-likelihood for determining scene boundaries. Thus it may fall into some unsatisfied local minima which would lead to poor performance.

Hidden Markov Models (HMM) is well known for its ability of incorporating temporal information. Thus, in (Huang, 2005), an HMM is modeled for video classification and segmentation since video having spatial and temporal dimensions. By using audio and visual features, the segmentation performance is improved, but the method becomes more complicated. (Zhai, 2006) proposes a general framework of Markov Chain Monte Carlo (MCMC) to solve the issues of scene segmentation on different video genres. The posterior probabilities of the number of the scenes are first computed, then the corresponding boundaries are determined to complete segmentation based on the model priors and the data likelihood. The model parameters are updated by the hypothesis ratio test in the MCMC process and the samples are used to generate the final results. It could effectively solve the problems of processing different genres of videos. However, MCMC itself has some problems. Specifically, one problem is how to select the initial values for the parameters; the other is the convergence of the iteration process. To get a better result, multiple restarts are required. Therefore it has an expensive computational cost.

Although these methods could obtain promising segmentation results, there are some limitations in the methods. Specifically, in scene clustering, there still remains a problem of automatically determining the cluster number. And in scene segmentation, there is a limitation that they are much dependent on the specified grammar which is used to constitute videos. For example, in action movies, shots are usually short and motion energy is always high; while in sports videos, although motion energy is still high, shots are usually long. So these methods could not perform well in various genres of videos.

Thus in this chapter, we present our work on scene clustering and scene segmentation to solve these problems.

2. SCENE CLUSTERING AND SCENE SEGMENATION

2.1 Scene Clustering by Model-Based Method

For scene clustering, we presented a principled approach for clustering video scenes using a Gaussian mixture model. Specifically, the shot boundaries of the video under analysis are first obtained by a simple shot detection algorithm (Tan, 2000). For each detected video shot, the average HSV color histogram of all the frames in the shot is computed as the shot color histogram, where the HSV color coordinates are uniformly quantized into 12 (Hue), 4 (Saturation), and 4 (Value) bins, respectively, amounting to a total of 192 color bins. As the dimensionality of the shot color histograms is high and many of the color bins are practically null for most shots in a given video sequence, the feature dimensionality can be reduced by projecting the shot color histograms to a lower dimensional space using principal component analysis.

Let h_n be the r-dimensional shot color histogram of the n-th video shot. The first $d \leq r$ principal components of h_n, denoted as $\{x_{nk}\}_{k=1}^d$, can be computed as follows:

$$\{x_{nk}\}_{k=1}^d = u_k^T(h_n - m) \tag{1}$$

where $1 \leq k \leq d$. $u_{kk=1}^d$ are the d eigenvectors associated with the d largest eigenvalues of the scatter matrix

$$S = \sum_{n=1}^N (h_n - m)(h_n - m)^T \tag{2}$$

and m is the average color histogram of the N video shots. The reduced feature dimension d is determined by keeping 90% variance information.

Given a feature set X, the search for the optimal model starts by considering a model with one Gaussian density component, i.e., M_1. The ML (Maximum Likelihood) model parameters $\hat{\theta}_1^{ML} = \{\hat{\alpha}_{1,1}, \hat{\mu}_{1,1}, \hat{\Sigma}_{1,1}\}$ can be computed as follows:

$$\hat{\alpha}_{1,1} = 1; \hat{\mu}1.1 = \frac{\sum_{n=1}^N X_n}{N}; \hat{\Sigma}_{1,1} = \frac{\sum_{n=1}^N (X_n - \hat{\mu}_{1,1})(X_n - \hat{\mu}_{1,1})^T}{N-1} \tag{3}$$

To estimate the model parameters for a higher model dimension K, their initial estimate $\theta_K^{(0)}$ are derived from the ML parameters of model with dimension $K+1$, i.e., from $\hat{\Theta}_{K-1}^{ML} = \{\hat{\alpha}_{K-1,1}, \hat{\mu}_{K-1,1}, \hat{\Sigma}_{K-1,1}\}_{l=1}^{K-1}$. An initial estimate of parameters for model M_K is obtained by splitting an existing cluster $J \in \{1,2,\ldots,K-1\}$ in model M_{K-1} into two, each with its mean vector displaced by a standard deviation from $\hat{\mu}_{K-1,J}$ along the direction of the first principal component vector obtained from covariance matrix $\hat{\Sigma}_{K-1,J}$.

Specifically, an initial estimate of parameters $\Theta_K^{(0)}$ is computed as

$$\left\{\alpha_{K,l}^{(0)}, \Sigma_{K,l}^{(0)}\right\} = \begin{cases} \left\{\hat{\alpha}_{K-1,l}, \hat{\Sigma}_{K-1,l}\right\} & \text{if } l < J \\ \left\{\hat{\alpha}_{K-1,J}/2, \hat{\Sigma}_{K-1,J}\right\} & \text{if } l = J, J+1 \\ \left\{\hat{\alpha}_{K-1,l-1}, \hat{\Sigma}_{K-1,l-1}\right\} & \text{if } l > J+1 \end{cases}$$

(4)

$$\mu_{K,j}^{(0)} = \begin{cases} \hat{\mu}_{K-1,l} & \text{if } l < J \\ \hat{\mu}_{K=1,l} - \sigma U & \text{if } l = J \\ \hat{\mu}_{K=1,l} + \sigma U & \text{if } l = J+1 \\ \hat{\mu}_{K-1,l-1} & \text{if } l > J+1 \end{cases}$$

(5)

where U is the eigenvector associated with the largest eigenvalue λ_{max} of covariance matrix $\hat{\Sigma}_{K-1,J}$, and $\sigma = \sqrt{\lambda_{max}}$ is the standard deviation along the direction of eigenvector U. For each set of initial parameters, the EM algorithm is used to obtain a local ML-estimate of parameters, denoted as $\hat{\Theta}_{K,J}^{ML}$, Out of the $K-1$ estimates $\left\{\hat{\Theta}_{K,J}^{ML}\right\}_{J=1}^{K-1}$, the one which gives the largest BIC (Bayesian Information Criterion) is chosen as the ML parameters for model M_K, i.e., $\hat{\Theta}_K^{ML}$. The procedure is repeated until a large enough model dimension, denoted as K^* and set as $\sqrt{N}$ in our experiments, has been considered.

2.2 Scene Clustering by Graph Theory

In (Lu, 2003), a graph theoretic approach is presented for video scene clustering in sports and news videos. In the approach, video shots are grouped into clusters of similar scenes based on shot color attributes. First, the similarity between video shots is measured by shot color histogram intersection. To obtain scene likeness matrix in a maximum-a-posterior (MAP) probability manner, a thresholding method is proposed on shot similarity matrix. Then, a graph is constructed based on the scene likeness to connect shots with similar scenes. Based on the constructed graph, a graph partitioning method is proposed to cluster video shots into different scenes such that the connectivity of video shots within one cluster is higher than that between different clusters. The advantage of the graph partitioning method is that the cluster number need not be known as a *priori*. The graph partitioning method is introduced in detail below.

Given the shots S of a video, let $G=(V,E)$ be the graph induced by the scene likeness matrix L, where V is a set of nodes, each corresponding to a shot, and E is a set of edges, each connecting two shots with similar scenes; that is, the scene of shot s_i is considered similar to that of shot s_j if $(s_i, s_j) \in E$. Figure 1 shows the first 10 shots of a tennis and a football test videos where each edge connects two shots with scenes similar to each other. For example, in the test tennis video, shot #1 is similar to shots #3, #6, and #9, while shot #2 is similar to shots #5, #8, and #10, etc.; in the test soccer video, shot #1 is similar to shots #3, #5, #7, and #9, while shot #2 is similar to shots #4, #6, #8, and #10, etc.

Grouping the M shots of S into K scene clusters is equivalent to partitioning the graph G into K subgraphs $G_k = (V_k, E_k)(k=1,...,K)$, where each set V_k consists of shots of similar scenes, $U_{k=1}^K V_k = V$, $V_m \cap V_n = \emptyset$ for $m \neq n$ and set E_k comprises only those edges in E connecting nodes (shots) in V_k.

First, we define some measures used in the graph partitioning method.

Scene likeness of a shot to a set: Given a set of shots A, the scene likeness of a shot s_i to set $A(s_i A)$ is defined as

Figure 1. The graph induced for the first 10 shots of the (a) tennis and (b) soccer test videos

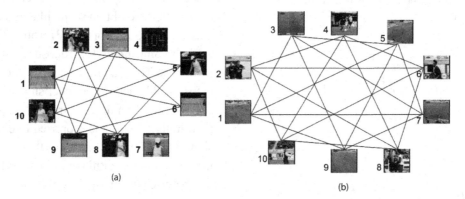

(a)   (b)

$$L\left(s_i, A\right) = \sum_{s_j \in A} \frac{L\left(s_i, s_j\right)}{|A|} \qquad (6)$$

where $|A|$ denotes the total number of shots in A. Figure 2 depicts how the scene likeness of a shot s_i to set $A(s_i \notin A)$ and that to set $B(s_i \notin B)$ are measured. Set A contains shots s_1 to s_7, and the scene likeness of shot s_i to set A is $L(s_i, A) = 3/7 = 0.43$. Set B contains shots s_8 to s_{11} and the scene likeness of shot s_i to set B is $L(s_i, B) = 4/4 = 1$.

It is easy to see that, by this definition, the larger the scene likeness of a shot to a shot set, the more number of shots in the set is similar to the given shot.

Scene likeness ratio: Given two shot sets, A and B. To determine whether the scene of a shot s_i is more similar to that of set A or set B, we compare the scene likeness ratio

$$\gamma\left(s_i; A, B\right) = \frac{L\left(s_i, A\right)}{L\left(s_i, B\right)} \qquad (7)$$

against a threshold that depends on the priors of set A and set B as well as the associated decision cost. As shown in Figure 2, the scene likeness ratio of shot s_i to set A and set B is equal to

$$\gamma(s_i; A, B) = \frac{3/7}{1} = 3/7.$$

Connectivity of a subgraph: To measure the overall scene likeness of all the shots within set V_k, we define the connectivity of subgraph G_k as

$$\phi\left(V_k\right) = \frac{1}{|V_k|} \sum_{s_i \notin V_k} L\left(s_i, V_k \setminus \{s_i\}\right) \qquad (8)$$

Note that $0 \le \varphi(V_k) \le 1$ and $\varphi(V_k) = 1$ if and only if $L(s_i, s_j) = 1$, for any $s_i, s_j \in V_k$. When $\varphi(V_k) = 1$, the corresponding graph is called a *clique* (O'Neil,

Figure 2. The scene likeness of a shot s_i to set $A(s_i \notin A)$ and that to set $B(s_i \notin B)$

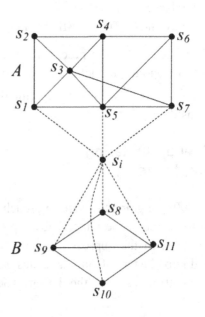

1990). Conversely, for a subgraph with only a single shot s_i, we have $\varphi(\{s_i\})=0$. Referring to Figure 2, the connectivity of set A is $\varphi(A)=0.62$ and that of set B is $\varphi(B)=0.83$.

Extending the block partitioning algorithm proposed in (O'Neil, 1990) for solving a system of linear equations and using the scene likeness of shots defined above, we have devised the following iterative procedure for partitioning the graph induced by the scene likeness matrix of a video into scene clusters in a way that maximizes the likeness of shots within a scene cluster and the distinction of shots between different scene clusters.

The proposed graph partitioning method works as follows. Let C_k be the set of shots under consideration for inclusion in cluster V_k and R be the set of shots that have not been assigned to any scene clusters.

Step 1: Set $k=1$ and $R=V$.

Step 2: Initialize V_k with shot s_1^k, where $s_1^k = \arg\max_{s_i \in R} L\left(s_i, R \backslash \{s_i\}\right)$; that is, $V_k \leftarrow s_1^k$ Set $R \leftarrow R \backslash \{s_1^k\}$, $C_k \leftarrow \{s_i | L\left(s_i, s_1^k\right) =1, s_i \in R\}$, and $R \leftarrow R \backslash C_k$.

Step 3: For each shot $s_i \in C_k$, if either one of the two following criteria:

i) $\varphi(V_k \cup \{s_i\}) \geq \alpha$, where $\alpha \geq 0$,

ii) $\gamma(s_i; V_k, R \cup C_k) \geq \beta$, where $\beta \geq 1$

is satisfied, move s_i from C_k to V_k and include in C_k all shots from R that are similar to s_i; that is, set $n \leftarrow n+1$, $s_n^k = s_i$, $V_k \leftarrow V_k \cup \{s_n^k\}$, $C_k = C_k \backslash \{s_i\}$, $C_k \leftarrow C_k \cup \{s_i | L\left(s_i, s_1^k\right)=1, s_i \in R\}$, and $R \leftarrow R \backslash \{s_i | L\left(s_i, s_1^k\right)=1, s_i \in R\}$ in turn. Otherwise, move s_i from C_k to R; that is, $R=R \cup \{s_i\}$ and $C_k = C_k \backslash \{s_i\}$.

Repeat Step 3 until C_k is empty.

Step 4: If $R \neq \phi$, set $k \leftarrow k + 1$ and go to Step 2.

Note that only those shots that are similar to at least one shot in V_k are eligible for inclusion in set C_k. In Step 3, the first criterion ensures that the connectivity of subgraph G_k remains high after the addition of a new shot, while the second criterion requires that the new shot is similar to more shots in V_k than the set of shots that have not been clustered.

Moreover, parameters α and β allow us to adjust the likeness or connectivity of shots within each scene cluster V_k, and hence the scene clustering result. The larger the value of α, the more small and highly similar scene clusters will be formed. By increasing the value of β, a new shot can be admitted to cluster V_k only if most of its similar shots are in V_k. Based on our empirical study, the values of α and β that can produce good clustering results lie between 0.6–0.9 and 2–5, respectively.

Figure 3 shows the scene likeness matrix of the Tennis test video, where the rows and columns of the matrix have been permuted according to the scene clusters obtained by the proposed method. It can be seen that shots of similar scenes are grouped as dense blocks along the diagonal of the permuted scene likeness matrix. In particular, the first three clusters cover the scenes that appear repeatedly over the test video: wide-angle views of the court (Scene 1), close-up views of the players (Scene 2), and medium views of the players and the court (Scene 3). The remaining clusters mainly consist of only one shot or two shots of transition scenes or commercials breaks (Scene 4 to Scene 49); which can be combined to form a miscellaneous scene.

2.3 Scene Segmentation by Spectral Method

We propose a novel spectral clustering method for scene segmentation based on video structure. First, we adopt the method that is similar to the idea of JSEG (Deng, 2001) for image segmentation to construct a pair-wise similarity matrix to exploit the underlying scene structure. The matrix is based on color similarity and temporal relations of shots. It can be regarded as a kind of video "texture". It

Figure 3. The permuted scene likeness matrix of the Tennis test video after scene clustering

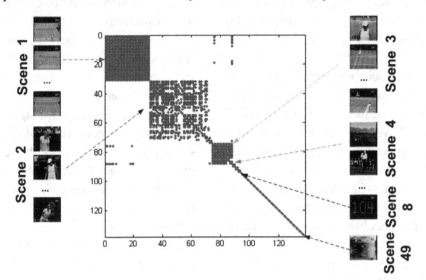

can adaptively reflect the structural characteristics of different videos and guarantee the effectiveness by avoiding the subjective affections. Second, the spectral method is used to cluster shots into scenes. By analyzing the eigenvalues obtained from spectral clustering, we can automatically determine the number of clusters.

Scene usually has a typical structure like AAAABBBB or ABABABAB, where A's (or B's) denote shots belonging to a same cluster by performing shot clustering. Here, the scene boundary for AAAABBBB is between A and B (two scenes in it) or for ABABABAB after AB (one scene in it), respectively. However, in real scenarios, the structures of video clips are usually more complex. Figure 4 shows the scene structure of Tennis1 video clip, where each shot is represented by one key frame. Although these shots are not ordered as well as the aforementioned two examples, they do exhibit some underlying scene structures. By computing the similarity between each pair of shots, we obtain a similarity (or affinity) matrix in Figure 5, where pure white means the similarity value is 1 and pure black means the value is 0.

It can be seen from Figure 5 that some kind of video "texture" does exist therein. Motivated by the idea of JSEG (Deng, 2001), we adopt J

value to exploit the underlying scene structures and measure this kind of local homogenous characteristics. We compute J value over all shots to detect scene changes, and the larger J value implies that it is more likely that a scene boundary exists. The homogenous measure in JSEG can take into account the local information that is important and suitable for scene segmentation. To make use of the temporal relations of shots, in our proposed method, a sliding window is also used. The details of similarity matrix construction are as follows:

Step 1: (Shot Representation) A 192-dimensional histogram feature in HSV color space is also used to represent a shot.

Step 2: (J Value Computation) We compute J value for each two consecutive shots. A sliding window with length of L is centered at the detecting point, i.e., $L/2$ shots before and $L/2$ shots after that point. The Euclidean distance between every pair of shots in the sliding window is then computed by using 192-dimensional HSV features and normalized to construct an $L{\times}L$ similarity matrix in which the element is $W_{ij}(i,j = 1,2,...,L)$. Two thresholds, ϕ_1, ϕ_2, are set such that $W_{ij}=1$ if $W_{ij}<\phi_1$; $W_{ij}=3$ if $W_{ij}<\phi_2$; and $W_{ij}=2$ otherwise. These new elements construct a quantization matrix $\overline{W}$ that is used to reflect the local information simply

Figure 4. One example of scene structure on Tennis1 video. The letters represent different views of scene structure such as wide-angle, close-up, score board, etc

Figure 5. Similarity matrix of (a) structure AAAABBBB, (b) structure ABABABAB

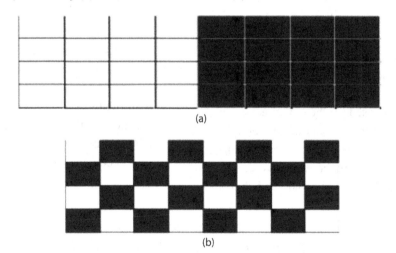

and intuitively. We set $L=10, \phi 1=0.3, \phi 2=0.6$ based on empirical study. Then we can obtain J value by using equations below:

$$m = \frac{1}{N} \sum_{z \in Z} z \tag{9}$$

$$m_i = \frac{1}{N_i} \sum_{z \in Z_i} z \tag{10}$$

$$S_T = \sum_{z \in Z} \left\| z - m \right\|^2 \tag{11}$$

$$S_W = \sum_{i=1}^{C} S_i = \sum_{i=1}^{C} \sum_{z \in Z_i} \left\| z - m_i \right\|^2 \tag{12}$$

$$J = (S_T - S_W)/S_W \tag{13}$$

where Z is the set of all N elements in $\overline{W}$, $z=(x,y),z\in Z$ denotes the element's location. Suppose Z is classified into C classes, $Z_i(i=1,2,\ldots,C)$ is the set of N_i elements which has the same value in $\overline{W}$.

We use two video clips to test the effectiveness of our method. Both of the videos include three scenes. One video is an artificial clip which has three scenes and each scene has 40 shots of the same image class. The other is an actual one which has sports scenes including tennis, basketball, and volleyball. The experimental results are in Figure 6, from which we can observe that the peaks of J values just correspond to the scene boundaries. Especially for the artificial one, our method can perform perfectly. Thus, we can conclude that J value can be used to exploit and describe the scene structure.

From Figure 6, we can only "see" the locations of peak values as scene boundaries subjectively. Therefore, we need a strategy to automatically determine the underlying boundaries. Spectral clustering has been widely applied in the field of the graph partition based on the eigenvectors of the pair-wise similarity matrix. In various methods, one popularity is to bi-partition the graph recursively until satisfying some convergence condition. On the other hand, Alpert showed that a direct K-way partition can provide a better result (Alpert, 1999). Consequently, (Ng, 2001) proposed a simple algorithm for graph clustering by simultaneously using K eigenvectors and demonstrated its effectiveness under some constrains. The algorithm could perform well in some complicated cases. In (Odobez, 2002), Odobez adopted the idea of (Ng, 2001) to segment home videos and used eigengap to determine the number of clusters. Motivated by (Ng, 2001; Odobez, 2001), we adopt the spectral method for our scene segmentation based on the obtained J values introduced in Section II. The algorithm consists of the following steps.

1. Construct the similarity matrix $A\in R^{N\times N}$ in the following way: $A_{ij} = \exp(-\dfrac{\sum_{k=i}^{j-1}J_k}{2\sigma^2})$, if $j>i$ and $A_{ii}=0, A_{ij}=A_{ji}$, where N is the number of shots, J the value for the *k-th* pair of consecutive shots, and σ^2 a controlling parameter and is set as $\sigma^2=0.05$ based on empirical study.

2. Define D as the diagonal matrix, whose i-th diagonal element is the sum of i-th row in A, and construct the matrix

Figure 6. (a) J values over one artificial video clip; (b) J values over an actual one including three scenes which has sports scenes of tennis (shot #1-40), basketball (shot # 41-78), and volleyball (shot # 79-118), respectively

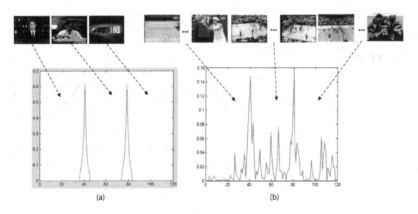

(a)   (b)

$L=D^{-1/2}AD^{-1/2}$ (14)

3. Find eigenvectors $x_1, x_2, ..., x_k$, corresponding to the k largest eigenvalues of L (chosen to be orthogonal to each other in the case of repeated eigenvalues), and form the matrix $X=[x_1 x_2 ... x_k]$ by stacking the eigenvectors in columns.

4. Form the matrix Y from X by renormalizing each row to have unit length. Then each row vector, Y_i, becomes the new feature corresponding to node i.

5. Treating each row of Y as a point in R^k, cluster them into k clusters via the K-means algorithm.

6. Finally, assign the cluster label to each node in the set S.

In our work, before applying k-means, we compute the eigenvalues of matrix L. According to the sorted eigenvalues, we adopt the top K eigenvalues to determine the number of clusters, i.e. to find an abrupt change among these eigenvalues by computing the difference between adjacent eigenvalues. Then we obtain a new eigenspace whose dimension is K. By Step 4 the row vectors in Y can be viewed as the points in the new feature space. By using k-means, we can obtain tight clusters due to the approximate orthogonal property of the larger eigenvectors which was explained in detail in (Ng, 2001; Odobez, 2001). To visualize the effectiveness of the spectral method in 3-D space, we select two videos. The two videos are the same as that for showing the J values. Specifically, each video has three scenes and the scenes are well clustered in the new feature space. Thus, the projection to the new k-dimensional space can theoretically obtain the best discriminative ability.

3. EXPERIMENTATION

In this section, we give the experiments on scene clustering by model-based method, graph partitioning method, and scene segmentation by spectral method.

3.1 Scene Clustering by Model-Based Method

As broadcast sports videos are mostly recorded by a limited number of cameras at fixed locations, the videos mainly consist of a few *dominant* scenes of different camera views. Here the term *dominant* refers to high coverage of video footage. To record as many actions of a sports game as possible, long shots with global views of the court/field are normally used when the game is in play. These long shots are often interrupted by close-up or medium-view shots, which are used to show clear view of a player (i.e., who just made a score or foul), the coach, the referee, the scoreboard, or the audience, especially when the game is not in play. In addition, commercials are also regularly inserted into these broadcast videos. Table 1 summarizes the test video clips used in our experiments. The video clips are digitized from a variety of sports games at 25 frames/sec. Most of them last from about 7 minutes to 20 minutes.

Table 1. Test sports videos

Sports type	Source	No of frames	No of shots	No of scenes
Tennis1	Wimbledon 2000	17981	137	4
Tennis2	Wimbledon 2000	24171	141	3
Basket-ball1	NBA 2000	22014	194	4
Basket-ball2	NBA 2000	24192	195	4
Volley-ball1	Montreux Masters 2000	31608	240	4
Volley-ball2	Montreux Masters 2000	11664	56	3
Soccer1	FC Cup 2000	32301	179	3
Soccer2	FC Cup 2000	12562	48	2

Table 2 shows the recall and precision for clustering the first two dominant scenes—global views of the court and close-up/medium views of the players/coaches/audience—by using the proposed model-based clustering method (MCM). To show the advantages of the proposed method, it also includes the performance of an average-linkage hierarchical clustering method (HCM), which also employs the Davies-Bouldin's Indexes (DBI) (Bezdek, 1998) to determine the appropriate number of scene clusters. The results show that the proposed MCM method performs consistently better than HCM in most of the test video clips. In particular, the HCM is rather sensitive to outlier or noise shots, which often come from the commercials and flash scenes in the test videos. To consider both recall and precision, the Harmonic Mean (HM) value is also measured (Shaw, 1997). HM measure is defined as

$$HM = \frac{2}{\frac{1}{Pr\,ecision} + \frac{1}{Re\,call}}.$$

3.2 Scene Clustering by Graph Theory

The experimental data include sports video as in Table 1, and news videos as in Table 3.

We have compared the proposed graph partitioning method with conventional k-means clustering method. We use k-means clustering instead of hierarchical clustering since, in general, the former requires less computational and storage space. Furthermore, the hierarchical clustering is rather sensitive to outliers. In our implementation of k-means clustering, random initialization is used. The maximum cluster number is set to $\sqrt{M}$, where M is the total number of shots.

In determining the optimal cluster number when using k-means clustering, the cluster validity measure of DBI (Bezdek, 1998) is also employed. Table 4 gives the clustering results by graph partitioning and k-means clustering. In the table, Θ_{G1} is the cluster number obtained by graph partitioning method, Θ_{G2} is the cluster number by combining all the small clusters (cluster with shot number less than 5) into one cluster, and Θ_K is the cluster number determined by the cluster

Table 3. Test videos

Video type	Source	No of frames	No of shots	No of scenes
News1	MPEG-7	71378	476	5
News2	MPEG-7	57462	342	5

Table 2. Performance of the proposed model-based clustering method (MCM) and a typical hierarchical clustering method (HCM)

Video data	MCM						HCM					
	R_1	P_1	R_2	P_2	HM1	HM2	R_1	P_1	R_2	P_2	HM1	HM2
Tns1	1.00	0.97	0.88	0.77	0.98	0.82	1.00	0.73	0.02	1.00	0.84	0.04
Tns2	1.00	0.93	0.98	0.95	0.96	0.96	1.00	0.60	0.02	1.00	0.75	0.04
Bkb1	1.00	0.70	0.91	0.97	0.82	0.94	1.00	0.46	0.02	1.00	0.63	0.04
Bkb2	0.82	0.91	0.83	0.70	0.86	0.76	1.00	0.48	0.01	1.00	0.65	0.02
Vlb1	0.95	0.97	0.72	0.74	0.96	0.73	1.00	0.66	0.02	1.00	0.80	0.04
Vlb2	0.96	0.86	0.87	0.96	0.91	0.91	1.00	0.36	0.03	1.00	0.53	0.06
Soc1	0.88	0.76	0.83	0.92	0.81	0.87	1.00	0.41	0.03	1.00	0.58	0.06
Soc2	0.96	0.96	0.96	1.00	0.96	0.98	1.00	0.91	0.93	1.00	0.95	0.96
Mean	0.94	0.88	0.87	0.87	0.90	0.86	1.00	0.57	0.13	1.00	0.68	0.04

Table 4. The number of scene clusters, obtained by the proposed graph partitioning method and the conventional k-means clustering method, as well as the recall and precision of the first two dominant scene clustering results

Video data	Graph partitioning								k-means						
	ΘG_1	ΘG_2	R_1	P_1	R_2	P_2	HM1	HM2	ΘK	R_1	P_1	R_2	P_2	HM1	HM2
Tns1	49	4	1.00	0.97	1.00	0.84	0.98	0.91	4	1.00	0.63	1.00	0.71	0.77	0.83
Tns2	30	6	1.00	0.71	0.76	0.98	0.83	0.86	2	1.00	0.46	0.76	0.54	0.63	0.63
Bkb1	38	5	1.00	0.81	0.92	0.86	0.90	0.89	2	1.00	0.21	0.02	0.01	0.35	0.01
Bkb2	47	9	1.00	0.57	0.82	0.87	0.73	0.84	2	1.00	0.20	0	0	0.33	NaN
Vlb1	36	10	1.00	0.75	0.50	1.00	0.86	0.67	2	1.00	0.31	0	0	0.47	NaN
Vlb2	8	4	1.00	0.81	0.38	1.00	0.90	0.55	2	1.00	0.52	0.62	1.00	0.68	0.77
Soc1	8	6	1.00	0.59	0.41	0.53	0.74	0.46	2	1.00	0.59	0.61	0.63	0.74	0.62
Soc2	4	3	1.00	0.96	0.96	1.00	0.98	0.98	2	1.00	0.96	0.96	0.92	0.98	0.94
News1	7	7	1.00	0.61	0.84	0.88	0.76	0.86	3	1.00	0.31	0.33	0.79	0.47	0.47
News2	10	5	0.85	0.70	0.92	0.97	0.77	0.94	2	0.85	0.32	0.89	0.96	0.46	0.92
Mean			0.99	0.75	0.85	0.90	0.85	0.94		0.99	0.45	0.52	0.56	0.62	0.54

validity measure in *k*-means clustering. Also, R_1, P_1, R_2, P_2, *HM1*, *HM2* are the recall, precision, and Harmonic Mean obtained for the first two dominant scenes of the clustering results.

It can be observed from Table 4 that the graph partitioning method can obtain better clustering results, i.e. higher recall and precision, than that of *k*-means clustering for most test videos except the Soccer1 test video. In Soccer1 video, the differences in recall and precision for the second dominant scene are 0.2 and 0.1 by using *k*-means clustering and our proposed graph theoretic approach, respectively. Furthermore, in Basketball1, Baksetball2, and Volleyball1 test videos, the cluster numbers obtained by using k-means clustering is 2, where the sports view shots form one cluster and the commercial shots from another cluster. We also observe that, compared with our proposed graph theoretic approach, the results of *k*-means clustering rely more on the initial prototypes.

It can also observed from Table 2 and Table 4, and by computing the mean of the recall and precision for the first two dominant scenes in sports videos and also in sports video and news videos, the proposed MCM and graph partitioning method performs better than HCM and *k*-means clustering method.

3.3 Scene Segmentation by Spectral Method

We evaluate the proposed method on various video sets, including cartoon, commercial, movie, and sports. The detail information about the experiment data is tabulated in Table 5. Three measures of recall, precision, and Harmonic Mean are also adopted for performance evaluation. Experimental results are tabulated in Table 6. Specifically, in the table, N_c is the number of the correctly detected scenes, N_d is the number of the all detected scenes, and N_{gt} is the number of the scenes in ground truth. And Precision $= \dfrac{N_c}{N_d}$ and

Recall $= \dfrac{N_c}{N_{gt}}$.

We have also compared the results by using our method with that of Kender *et al.*'s memory-based video coherence method (Kender, 1998)

Table 5. Summary of testing videos

Video type	No. of frames	No. of shots	No. of scenes (N_{gt})
Cartoon	16617	200	13
Commercial	12806	160	13
Movie	37262	250	15
Sports	44052	443	17

Table 6. Scene segmentation performance obtained by (Kender, 1998) (I), (Li, 2004) (II), and our method (III)

Video type	Method	$N_d N_c$	Precision	Recall	HM
Cartoon	I	15 11	0.73	0.73	0.73
	II	10 7	0.70	0.54	0.61
	III	11 9	0.82	0.70	0.76
Commercial	I	12 10	0.83	0.77	0.80
	II	9 7	0.78	0.54	0.64
	III	11 10	0.91	0.77	0.83
Movie	I	15 10	0.67	0.67	0.67
	II	15 12	0.80	0.80	0.80
	III	13 12	0.92	0.80	0.86
Sports	I	21 14	0.67	0.82	0.74
	II	17 11	0.65	0.65	0.65
	III	14 13	0.93	0.77	0.84

and the method based on sequential change detection (Li, 2004). From the results, one can see that the proposed algorithm outperforms (Kender, 1998; Li, 2004) and is especially suitable for applications which prefer higher precision.

It can be observed from Table 6, this spectral method can find the global optimal solution and get the number of scenes automatically which differs from the traditional approaches. Furthermore, spectral method can observably improve the performance.

4. FUTURE RESEARCH DIRECTIONS

Currently, the scene clustering methods are mainly focused on structured videos such as sports video, news, etc. And the methods on other types of video such as movie, sitcom, etc. and the methods not rely much on the domain knowledge are needed.

Also, for some applications, the speed but not the accuracy is more important. And in these kinds of applications, the fast methods or the speed up of the existing methods are needed.

5. CONCLUSION

In this chapter, we review the work on two types of scenes: scene clustering and scene segmentation. And our solutions on scene clustering by model-based method and graph theory, and on scene segmentation by spectral methods are presented. Also, some future research directions are discussed in the chapter.

ACKNOWLEDGMENT

This chapter is supported in part by 973 Program (Project No. 2010CB327900), Natural Science Foundation of China (No. 60875003 and 60873178), and Shanghai Committee of Science and Technology, China (No. 08DZ2271800 and 09DZ2272800).

REFERENCES

Alpert, C., Kahng, A., & Yao, S. (1999). Spectral partitioning: The more eigenvectors, the better. *Discrete Applied Mathematics, 90*, 3–26. doi:10.1016/S0166-218X(98)00083-3

Bezdek, J. C., & Pal, N. R. (1998). Some new indexes of cluster validity. *IEEE Transactions on Systems, Man, and Cybernetics, 28*(3), 301–315. doi:10.1109/3477.678624

Deng, Y., & Manjunath, B. S. (2001). Unsupervised Segmentation of Color-Texture Regions in Images and Video. *IEEE Transactions on Pattern Analysis and Machine Intelligence, 23*(8), 800–810. doi:10.1109/34.946985

Huang, J., Liu, Z., & Wang, Y. (2005). Joint Scene Classification and Segmentation Based on Hidden Markov Model. *IEEE Transactions on Multimedia, 7*(3), 538–550. doi:10.1109/TMM.2005.843346

Kender, J. R., & Yeo, B. (1998). Video scene segmentation via continuous video coherence. *IEEE Computer Society Conference on Computer Vision and Pattern Recognition* (pp. 367-373).

Li, Z. Y., Lu, H., & Tan, Y. P. (2004). Video Scene Segmentation Using Sequential Change Detection. *IEEE Pacific-Rim Conference on Multimedia* (pp. 575-582).

Ng, A. Y., Jordan, M. I., & Yair, W. (2001). *On spectral Clustering: Analysis and an algorithm.* Advances in Neural Information Processing Systems.

O'Neil, J., & Szyld, D. B. (1990). A block ordering method for sparse matrices. *SIAM Journal on Scientific and Statiscal Computing, 11*(5), 811–823. doi:10.1137/0911048

Odobez, J-M., & Gatica-Perez, D., & Guillemot, M. (2002). On Spectral Methods and the Structuring of Home Videos. *IDIAP-RR 02-55.*

Rasheed, Z., & Shah, M. (2003). Scene Detection In Hollywood Movies and TV Shows. *IEEE Computer Society Conference on Computer Vision and Pattern Recognition* (pp. II-343-348).

Rasheed, Z., & Shah, M. (2005). Detection and representation of scenes in videos. *IEEE Transactions on Multimedia, 7*(6), 1097–1105. doi:10.1109/TMM.2005.858392

Shaw, W. M. Jr, Buigin, R., & Howell, P. (1997). Performance standards and evaluation on IR test collections: Cluster-based retrieval models. *Information Processing & Management, 33*(1), 1–14. doi:10.1016/S0306-4573(96)00043-X

Tan, Y.-P., Saur, D. D., Kulkarni, S. R., & Ramadge, P. J. (2000). Rapid Estimation of Camera Motion from MPEG Video With Application to Video Annotation. *IEEE Trans. on Circuits and Systems for Video Technology, 10*(1), 133–146. doi:10.1109/76.825867

Yeung, M., Yeo, B., & Liu, B. (1998). Segmentation of video by clustering and graph Analysis. *Computer Vision and Image Understanding, 71*(1), 94–109. doi:10.1006/cviu.1997.0628

Zhai, Y., & Shah, M. (2006). Video Scene Segmentation Using Markov Chain Monte Carlo. *IEEE Transactions on Multimedia, 8*(4), 686–697. doi:10.1109/TMM.2006.876299

Chapter 11
Vision Based Hand Posture Recognition

Kongqiao Wang
Nokia Research Center, China

Yikai Fang
Nokia Research Center, China

Xiujuan Chai
Chinese Academy of Sciences, China

ABSTRACT

Vision based gesture recognition is a hot research topic in recent years. Many researchers focus on how to differentiate various hand shapes, e.g. the static hand gesture recognition or hand posture recognition. It is one of the fundamental problems in vision based gesture analysis. In general, most frequently used visual cues human uses to describe hand are appearance and structure information, while the recognition with such information is difficult due to variant hand shapes and subject differences. To have a good representation of hand area, methods based on local features and texture histograms are attempted to represent the hand. And a learning based classification strategy is designed with different descriptors or features. In this chapter, we mainly focus on 2D geometric and appearance models, the design of local texture descriptor and semi-supervised learning strategy with different features for hand posture recognition.

INTRODUCTION

As the prevalence of ubiquitous computing, traditional user interaction approaches with mouse, keyboard and touch pen are not convenient enough for them. In addition, many emerging applications such as augmented reality and interactive entertainments require natural and intuitive interface.

Moreover the limited input space on traditional mobile or hand held device leads to encumbered experience with tiny keyboard or touch screen. Hand gesture is frequently used in people's daily life. It's also an important component of body languages. So a natural interaction between humans and computing devices can be achieved if hand gestures can be used for communication between human and computing devices.

DOI: 10.4018/978-1-60960-024-2.ch011

Vision based hand gesture interface has been attracting more attentions due to no extra hardware requirement except camera, which is very suitable for ubiquitous computing and emerging applications.

In recent years, many researchers focus on how to differentiate various hand shapes, e.g. the static hand gesture recognition or hand posture recognition. It is one of the main problems in vision based gesture analysis. However, hand posture recognition is still an unresolved problem. Hand is an articulated object with variable configurations, shapes and structures. In addition, it's difficult to describe the texture in hand area. To have a good representation of hand area, we try to use local features such as rectangular features and local texture histograms to represent the hand. Besides, rule based and semi-supervised classification strategies are designed to differentiate various hand postures. The comparison between the methods in this chapter and other methods are carried out and the results show the effectiveness of the proposed methods in this chapter.

BACKGROUND

Methods for vision based hand gesture recognition fall into two categories: 3D model based methods and appearance model based methods. 3D model may exactly describe hand movement and its shape, but most of them are computational expensive to use. Recently there are some methods to obtain 3D model with 2D appearance model such as ISOSOM (Haiying, Rogerio & Matthew, 2006) and PCA-ICA (Makoto, Yenwei and Gang, 2006). For the consideration of easy implementation and non-intrusive characteristic, we prefer to use 2D model and appearance based methods for hand posture recognition in this chapter.

Freeman and Weissman (1995) recognized gestures for television control using normalized correlation. This technique is efficient but may be sensitive to different users, deformations of the pose and changes in scale, and background. Cui and Weng (1996) proposed a hand tracking and sign recognition method using appearance based method. Although its accuracy was satisfactory, the performance was far from real-time. Elastic graphs were applied to represent hands in different hand gestures in Triesch's work with local jets of Gabor filters (Triesch & Malsburg 1996). It locates hands without separate segmentation mechanism and the classifier is learned from a small set of image samples, so the generalization is very limited. These model based methods are intuitive for hand representation. With elaborate design of local features, it's not necessary to use complicated classification strategy. Bretzner, Laptev & Lindeberg (2002) use scale-space feature detection to decompose hand into palm and fingers. The decomposition is intuitive and effective. However, the detection involves lots of Gaussian convolution across images and brings high time consumption in practice.

Ong and Bowden (2004) distinguished hand postures with boosted classifier tree and obtained fairly good results. However, the classifier in their method too complicated and time-consuming. In addition, the samples are with simple and similar backgrounds and the training requires thousands of labeled samples. Kolsch (2006) employed fanned boosting detection for classification and got nearly real time results, while the training process is extremely time-exhausting. Just, Rodriguez and Marcel (2006) introduce modified census transform (MCT) into hand gesture classification. Their method gives fairly good average accuracy above 80 percent with the classifier trained with more than 2,000 samples per posture, while the performance in recognition experiments under complex background was not much satisfactory. These prevalent methods for recognition are learning based with specific features. Compared with model and rule based methods, learning mechanism make discriminative/generative classifiers that have strong adaptiveness to different set of examples. The training that converges on abundant examples usually has good generalization performance. Most of these methods use rather simple features like Haar (Kolsch 2004) or LBP(Local Binary Pattern) (Just et al. 2006). Recently there are some methods use SIFT and surf- like features in classifiers (Hailing, Lijun & Xuliang, 2007). Almost all the learning based methods are based on single kind of feature and they need thousands of labeled examples to obtain final classifiers. In some practical cases, it's a quite time-consuming work and places restricts on gesture applications.

Considering above issues, there are mainly 3 problem discussed in this chapter.

1. The speeding up of posture recognition with 2D geometric model.
2. Design local texture descriptor for hand posture recognition.
3. Combine different features with semi-supervised methods and improve performance of classifiers.

VISION BASED HAND POSTURE RECOGNITION

Problems and Related Work

As an articulated object, even one kind of hand posture has different shapes which are affected by subjects and viewpoint heavily. And these variations in different shapes are difficult to model or describe. In this chapter, our concerns mainly include the following points.

Each hand posture can be decomposed of palm and fingers. There have been some methods (Bretzner, Laptev & Lindeberg, 2002) give instance of implementing the decomposition. The decomposition is simple and intuitive for hand posture recognition, while the Gaussian convolution that is used in feature detection brings the unfavorable situation that the decomposition leads to computational burden for practical applications. With computational efficiency in consideration,

it's significant to find the approach to describe hand structures accurately and efficiently. Especially on devices that has limited computation power. Inspired by SURF in (Herbert, Tinnee & Luc, 2006), an integral image based multi-scale feature detection method are used to find hand structures. With speeded feature description, computation cost are dramatically cut off. And the accuracy of feature description is comparable. The speeding up is significant for platforms with limited competencies such as hand held and future wearable devices.

Although the 2D geometric model built by palm finger decomposition is simple and intuitive, it obtains quite good performance with limited hand configurations and viewpoint variations. Usually the decomposable hand postures have rich meaning for command input in application. Some of these examples are shown in Figure 1(a). However, there are still many hand shapes that cannot be decomposed into palm and fingers. Such model based method cannot deal with postures in those indecomposable configurations or with viewpoint changes as shown in this Figure 1(b).

For the purpose of recognizing more kinds of hand postures, appearance based method have been used and become an important category for hand posture recognition. There have been many visual methods such as edge (Freeman & Weissman 1995, Zhou et al 2004), image transformation (Triesch & Malsburg 1996, Binh, Shuichi & Ejima 2005, Just et al. 2006) and texture (Chai, Fang & Wang 2009) have been used to tackle the recognition. Among these methods, Local binary pattern (LBP) has been widely used in face recognition and texture classification and draws much attention in the field of target recognition and texture analysis. In this chapter, a patch based local texture representation is used for hand posture recognition. The spatial structure information along with the local texture information is well maintained by this feature representation.

Further, there are many research efforts using learning based appearance methods for posture

Figure 1. The example of hand postures

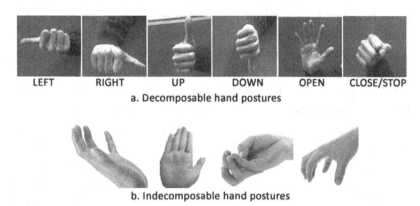

a. Decomposable hand postures

b. Indecomposable hand postures

classification to deal with more hand shapes and obtain tolerance to view point changes. Usually this training process needs thousands of labeled samples and is extremely time exhausting (Kolsch, 2005). Most of these methods convert or normalize a variety of features into a unified feature space, which ignores the distinct attributes of the different features. The combination of different features has draw lots of attention.

Semi-supervised method like co-training was proposed by Blum and Mitchell (1998) to train a pair of learning algorithms. The basic assumption is that the two learning algorithms use two different views of the data. The key property is that some examples which would have been confidently labeled using one classifier would be misclassified by the other classifier. The classifiers go through unlabeled examples, label them, and add the most confident predictions to the labeled set of the other classifier. Therefore the classifiers train each other by providing additional informative examples from unlabeled data. After co-training, the final classifiers, which are trained on labeled and unlabeled data, are significantly improved.

There have been research recently in object detection and tracking (Javed, Ali & Shah, 2005, Feng, Shane, Qi & Hai, 2007) which utilize the complementation of different features and acquire improved results compared with single feature, even using basic classifiers. Levin, Viola & Freund

(2003) trains two classifiers to detect vehicles with the same feature of grey and background subtracted images. Javed (2005) improves the performance of two boosting classifiers with co-training, in which the based classifiers are Bayes classifiers and features are derived from PCA of training samples. Feng et.al (2007) obtains two SVM classifiers with color histogram and HOG (histogram of oriented gradient) as two independent views of object. The two SVM classifiers are combined to get the location of object in video and new samples are generated to update the SVMs online.

In this chapter, a hand posture recognition approach with co-training strategy is described for the same purpose. The main idea is to train two disparate classifiers with each other and improve the performance of both classifiers with unlabeled samples. This method improves the recognition performance with less labeled data in a semi-supervised way based on a co-training framework.

Fast Multi-Scale Analysis for Posture Analysis

Multi-Scale Feature Detection

Since Lindberg made seminal work on scale-space framework for geometric features detection (Lindeberg, 2004), scale-space feature detection has been widely applied in object recognition, image registering etc. Bretzner, Laptev &Lindeberg (2002) uses scale-space feature detection to detect blob and ridge structures of hand, i.e. palm and finger structures. Blobs are detected as local maxima or minima in scale-space of the square of the normalized Laplacian operator.

$$\nabla^2_{norm} L = t \left(L_{xx} + L_{yy} \right) \tag{1}$$

L_{xx} and L_{yy} are Gaussian derivative operators at scale t along two dimensions of image. Elongated ridge structures usually represented as ellipses are localized where the ridge detector.

$$\mathcal{R}^2_{norm} L = t^{\frac{3}{2}} \left(\left(L_{xx} - L_{yy} \right)^2 + 4 L_{xy}^2 \right) \tag{2}$$

assumes a local maximum in scale-space[4]. Ellipse parameters such as orientation and axis length are defined by a windowed second moment matrix in (3) as described in Lindeberg's work (2004). L_x and L_y are Gaussian mixture derivative operator and g is Gaussian kernel at a certain integration scale t_{int}.

$$\Sigma = \int_{\eta \in R^2} \begin{pmatrix} L_x^2 & L_x L_y \\ L_x L_y & L_y^2 \end{pmatrix} g \left(\eta; t_{int} \right) \tag{3}$$

Gaussian derivatives in blob and ridge detector involve a great deal of large-scale image convolution in implementation. The computation cost of the detectors is expensive for real-time gesture interaction.

Fast Feature Detection and Description

As shown by Lindberg, Gaussian is optimal for scale-space analysis. However, the Gaussian needs to be discrete and cropped in practice. So aliasing still occurs as long as the resulting

images are sub-sampled (Herbert, Tinne & Luc, 2006). Lindberg shows that the property that no new structures can appear while going to lower resolutions have been proven in the 1D case, but it is still unknown in the 2D case. In practice, the Gaussian may not be necessarily indispensable as described in Lindeberg's work (2004). David Lowe (2004) shows the LoG approximation is effective in SIFT. Further approximation (Herbert, Tinne & Luc, 2006) with box filters get comparable performance with discrete and cropped Gaussians. Moreover the box filters can be computed much faster with integral images.

Gaussian derivatives and the corresponding box filters used in our method are shown in Figure2 The 9x9 filters in the first row are Gaussian derivates withσ=1.2. The second row gives corresponding box filters. Derivates and box filters at other scales are similar. Speed performance is improved just with these box filters. In Lindeberg's work, scale-space is usually imagined as image pyramids. A series of Gaussian filters at different scales repeatedly smooth the images, which are down-sampled in a higher level of the pyramid. It has disadvantages of iteratively image smoothing prevalent floating-point operations. In consideration of speed performance, we don't directly apply Gaussian derivatives to smoothed images, but instead apply rectangle filters at different sizes on original images and avoid floating-point operations. Thus the computation cost of scale space implementation is significantly reduced.

Figure 2. (a) Discrete Gaussian derivative templates. (b) Rectangular features

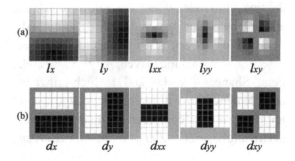

Laplacian detector (Bretzner, Laptev &Lindeberg, 2002) locates geometric blob feature points both in spatial and scale space. L_{xx} and L_{yy} are the convolution of the second order Gaussian derivatives with the image I at point x. We denote D_{xx} and D_{yy} as approximated second order Gaussian derivatives and D_{xy} as mixture partial Gaussian derivative. Then we extend rectangle filter to first order Gaussian derivatives denoted by D_x and D_y and apply them in multi-scale geometric feature detection.

With these approximated Gaussian derivatives, we construct a fast Laplacian detector for blob structures. The detector for blobs is

$$\nabla^2_{norm} D = t \left(D_{xx} + D_{yy} \right) \qquad (4)$$

For the elongated ridge structures represented as ellipses, the fast ridge detectors turn into

$$\mathcal{R}^2_{norm} D = t^{\frac{3}{2}} \left(\left(D_{xx} - D_{yy} \right)^2 + 4 D_{xy}^2 \right) \qquad (5)$$

The matrix that defines orientation and axis length of ellipses corresponding to ridges becomes

$$\Sigma = \int_{\eta \in R^2} \begin{pmatrix} D_x^2 & D_x D_y \\ D_x L_y & D_y^2 \end{pmatrix} g \left(\eta; t_{int} \right) \qquad (6)$$

Results

Both the standard Jochen Triesch database and customized database are used in this section to show fast scale-space feature detection results. The standard database consists of 10 hand gestures in ASL (American Sign Language) performed by 24 different people against different backgrounds. To validate our method, we select the images of 8 hand gestures which denote 8 letters as shown in Figure 3 because these 8 gestures are decomposable with geometric features representation. The

Figure 3. Results on Triesch dataset

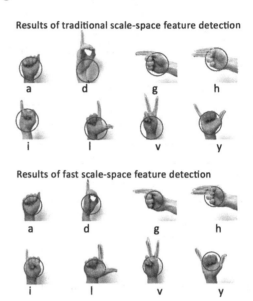

backgrounds in selected images are of two types: uniform light and uniform dark.

Palm and finger structures can be accurately detected with fast multi-scale analysis. Compared with traditional scale-space methods, we have less feature detected in images. The reduction of features is caused by the approximation with rectangular features. So the fast analysis method is not sensitive to noises and artifacts in images, while the competence of detect small structures is degraded at the same time. As finger and palm are usually distinctive structures in hand posture images, the degradation for small structures does not lead to missing detection of hand structures. Figure 3. shows the results of fast multi-scale space method and traditional method. The dark circle denotes palm structure and lighter ellipse denotes finger structure detected in hand posture image.

As for the time consumption of feature detection, the fast method takes 30~35ms to get palm and fingers across images at QVGA resolution(320x240) at our platform (Pentium 2.8Ghz, 512M RAM). The consumption is less

Table 1. The comparison time consumption and accuracy (8 letters)

posture	Time cost		Accuracy	
	Fast method (ms)	Traditional method(ms)	Fast method (%)	Traditional method(%)
a	30	67	83.33	81.25
d	33	70	85.42	62.50
g	34	71	85.42	79.17
h	35	72	91.67	87.50
i	32	67	89.58	85.42
l	33	70	85.42	91.67
v	32	71	93.75	91.67
y	33	68	87.50	89.58

than half of the traditional methods. Table 1 shows the speeding up and accuracy quantitatively.

The customized database contains video clips captured in experiments. The hand shapes included in the video clips are shown in Figure 1(a). These postures are for navigation interface. These gestures execute operations like shifting focus. LEFT, RIGHT, UP and DOWN are for shifting focus in four directions; OPEN and CLOSE are used to open and close the selected item. Usually CLOSE is also interpreted as STOP when shifting focus. The features are detected across a total of 2596 frames. Figure 4 gives some detection results with both methods. The comparison of time consumption and detection accuracy of hand structures are shown in Table 2.

Patch Based Local Texture Description

Recently, Local Binary Patterns (LBP) is widely used in texture classification, image matching and retrieval fields for its powerful texture description ability (Ojala, Pietikainen & Harwood, 1996, Ojala, Pietikainen & Maenpaa, 2002, Zhang, Shan, Gao, Chen & Zhang, 2005). In this section, a patch-based local texture representation for the hand posture recognition is proposed. Although hand image looks very smooth in color space, it

indeed contains enough texture information in gray level. LBP is suitable for extracting the local feature by comparing the intensity variation within its neighborhood. Considering the large structural diversity among these different postures, the global histogram for the LBP image is obviously less reasonable. Therefore, a patch-based strategy is used to maintain the spatial structure relation of each hand posture. Finally, the whole feature vector is achieved by concatenating all the small histogram vectors.

Figure 4. Comparison of features by two methods on customized dataset

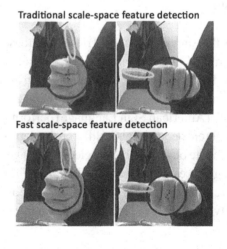

Traditional scale-space feature detection

Fast scale-space feature detection

Table 2. Recognition results on customized dataset

	LEFT	RIGHT	UP	DOWN	OPEN	CLOSE
Frames	438	387	400	438	433	500
Correct recognized frames by fast method (accuracy)	403(0.92)	340(0.879)	375(0.936)	403(0.974)	408(0.942)	475(0.950)
Average time consumption by fast method (ms)	36	35	37	36	40	36
Correct recognized frames by traditional method (accuracy)	410(0.936)	347(0.896)	378(0.945)	413(0.987)	413(0.954)	475(0.950)
Average time consumption by traditional method (ms)	84	83	86	84	91	84

Local Texture Description

The original Local Binary Pattern operator measures the variation of local image texture. For each pixel in the image, label it by a binary string, which is obtained by thresholding the 8-neighbourhood pixels $p(x_p, y_p)$ with $c(x_c, y_c)$ as Equation(7) shows:

$$s(p,c) = \begin{cases} 1, & f_p \geq f_c \\ 0, & f_p < f_c \end{cases} \qquad (7)$$

Here, f denotes the corresponding gray value of pixel. For the binary string, performing the convolution with a transform coefficients matrix the final decimal value corresponding to pixel is computed according to Equation(8).

$$LBP(c) = \sum_{i=0}^{7} s(p_i, c) \cdot 2^i \qquad (8)$$

Some LBP filtered images on different hand postures are shown in Figure 5(a). The first row comes from the Jochen Triesch database (Triesch & Malsburg, 1996) and the second row is the corresponding LBP filtered images. From this figure, it can be seen that LBP operator can extract many image details. Although the complex background affects the transform results, the similarity within

Figure 5. Sketch map of the patch-based local texture feature representation

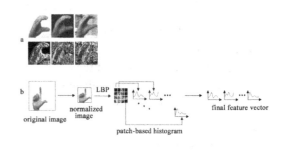

one posture class is always higher than the extra-class condition.

Patch-Based Local Texture Feature

With gray-level LBP texture description, the histogram is used as the feature vector by counting the appearance times of each gray-level pixel. However, a drawback of histogram is the loss of spatial structure relation, which leads to some false matching

To maintain the spatial structure relation of the histogram feature vector, a natural way is patch-based strategy. For the LBP filtered image, first, partition it into small patches. Histogram is counted within each local patch and the final feature vector is formed by concatenating all the small histograms based on local regions. f10 gives the sketch map of the patch-based local texture feature representation.

Recognition Scheme

To perform the recognition of hand postures, here we only select the simple histogram intersection as the similarity measurement, and the nearest neighbor principle is used to give the final recognition result.

The similarity between two images ($\mathbf{I}_1$ and $\mathbf{I}_2$) is defined as Equation(9):

$$d(\mathbf{I_1},\mathbf{I_2}) = \sum_{i=0}^{M \cdot Bin} \min\left(\mathbf{H}_i^{\mathbf{I}_1}, \mathbf{H}_i^{\mathbf{I}_2}\right) \Big/ (W \times H) \tag{9}$$

Here, the M is the total patch number and Bin is the category number we classify the gray value. W and H are the width and height of the normalized image respectively. Comparing all the similarities between the probe image and each image in the gallery, the final recognition result is gotten according to the largest similarity:

$$Identity = \arg\max_j d(\mathbf{I_p},\mathbf{I_{G_j}}) \tag{10}$$

where, j ranges over the whole gallery.

Recognition Results

Experiment is conducted on the Jochen Triesch dataset, which includes 10 different hand postures provided in the dataset. Each posture is recorded by 24 persons under three backgrounds (light, dark, complex). Due to the missing of two images, the database totally has 718 images.

In this recognition task, the performance is closely related with some parameters, especially the histogram bin and patch size. Intuitively, if the number of histogram bin is too small, such as 2, then the 256 gray levels can only be classified into 2 bins. The statistical histogram is meaningless.

With the increasing of the histogram bins, more information of the original image is maintained along with higher computation cost. As for the patch size, the larger size will induce the loss of the spatial information, while the smaller size will dramatically increase the dimension of the final feature vector.

The results using different histogram bins and different patch sizes are shown in Figure 6. Different histogram bins affect lightly on recognition rate under one same patch size. While for one fixed histogram bin, the variation of the patch size causes dramatically changes of the recognition rate. Considering the balance of the accuracy and efficiency, the number of bins is selected as 128 and the patch size is 8×8.

The recognition accuracy for gesture recognition is shown in Table 3.

Co-Training Framework for Hand Posture Classification

In this section, the co-training strategy uses two different views of samples: haar and histogram of oriented gradients (Hog) features. These features describe different type of information in samples. If the two views are just simply combined using disparate classifiers, the complementation characteristics of different features is ignored. In the co-training framework, the disparate classifiers of the two features are trained together in a uniform

Figure 6. Recognition results comparison with different parameters

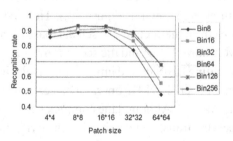

Table 3. comparison between patch based texture descriptor and MCT method

	Uniform background		Complex background	
	MCT	Patch texture	MCT	Patch texture
A	100	97.5	100	100
B	93.75	97.5	93.75	95.0
C	93.75	92.5	93.75	100
D	84.38	95.0	81.25	100
G	100	97.5	68.75	100
H	90.63	80.0	87.5	80.0
I	90.63	97.5	62.5	80.0
L	96.88	100	75.0	95.0
V	96.77	89.7	87.5	78.9
Y	81.25	94.7	62.5	100
Average	92.79	**94.2**	81.25	**92.9**

cooperation process and improved performance is acquired with less labeled examples.

Multiviews

One approach for object representation is to use haar features. The advantage of using the haar features is that they can be calculated very efficiently. And the boosting learning based on haar features has many successful applications in face detection and recognition. Histogram of oriented gradients (or Hog) is another feature for object representation and is frequently used in pedestrian detection (Dalal & Triggs, 2005). Since this feature descriptor operates on a dense grid of localized cells and reflects the shape or appearance information of object, we apply it in hand posture recognition with LDA(linear discriminant analysis) as weak classifiers.

The Training of Classifiers

There are totally two boosting based classifiers trained to differentiate one hand posture against others. One classifier uses haar features and the other use Hog feature.

In the training process, one important aspect to keep the co-training effective is that each classifier labels only those unlabeled samples on which it can make a confident prediction and add them to the training data of the other classifier. So the additional samples should have large margins on one classifier. In our method, the sequential logistic regression algorithm (Collins, Schapire & Singer, 2000) is used to obtain the boosting classifiers. Denote the outputs from the weak classifiers by the vector $\vec{h} \in [-1,1]^n$ and the weights associated with these classifiers by

$$\vec{\alpha} \in [-1,1]^n, \sum_{j=1}^{n} \vec{\alpha}_j = 1,$$ n is the number of weak

classifiers. According to Schapire, Freund, Bartlett & Lee (1998), large margins on the training set imply correct classification on test data both experimentally and theoretically. That is, if there is some real number $\theta_L > 0$ such that the probability that $\vec{h} \cdot \vec{\alpha} > \theta_L$ is significant and the conditional probability that $\vec{h}$ corresponds to a confident prediction given that $\vec{h} \cdot \vec{\alpha} > \theta_L$ is close to 1. Schapire et. al (1998) conclude that there exists θ_L estimated on the training or validation set, for which the risk of misclassification on test data is very low. So the samples confidently labeled with threshold criteria can be added to the training data of another classifier.

However, it would be inefficient to add each confidently labeled sample to training data of the other classifier. The samples labeled during co-training improve the performance of the boosted classifier only if the samples have small or negative margin. If the samples have been labeled confidently by the boosted classifier with large margin, add it to training will have little effect on the final classifier. Thus the unlabeled samples which are confidently labeled by current classifier and have a small margin simultaneously are indispensable. The threshold θ_S on the score of the boosted classifier can also be established through the training or validation set. Once a sample has been labeled and if it has a small margin, it's used for updating the boosting classifiers.

The co-training and classifier update algorithm is shown in Figure 7. C_{HOG} and C_{Haar} are classifiers with HOG and haar respectively. The number of classes is denoted with N_c. The function SeqLogBoost implements the sequential logistic regression algorithm.

The update of classifier C_{Haar} and C_{HOG} is shown in Figure 7. To simplify the threshold selection, the threshold θ_L for the large margin is selected

Figure 7. The training process of classifiers

Given initial classifiers C_{HOG} and C_{Haar} trained with labeled data x_L

while new samples are available, *do*

If current classifier C_{HOG} confidently predicts incoming sample x the label c_i with score above $\omega_1 \theta_L^{HOG}$, $i \in \{1, \ldots N_c\}$ and current C_{Haar} predicts incoming sample x the label c_i with score below $\omega_2 \theta_S^{Haar}$, *then*

New classifier $C_{Haar}^{new} = SeqLogBoost_{Haar}(x_L, x, c_i)$;

If current classifier C_{Haar} confidently predicts incoming sample x the label c_i with score above $\omega_1 \theta_L^{Haar}$, $i \in \{1, \ldots N_c\}$ and current C_{HOG} predicts incoming sample x the label c_i with score below $\omega_2 \theta_S^{HOG}$, *then*

New classifier $C_{HOG}^{new} = SeqLogBoost_{HOG}(x_L, x, c_i)$;

Update thresholds θ_L^{Haar}, θ_S^{Haar} for classifier C_{Haar}, and θ_L^{HOG}, θ_S^{HOG} for C_{HOG};

Replace C_{HOG} and C_{Haar} with C_{Hog}^{new} and C_{Haar}^{new};

as the highest score achieved by negative examples in labeled and unlabeled data, and θ_S for the small margin is the lowest score achieved. To be more conservative, ω_1 and ω_2 are set to 1.5 and 2 in the following section.

Classification Results

The dataset used to validate the co-training classifier is the benchmark dataset Triesch dataset (Triesch & Malsburg, 1996). It consists of 10 hand signs performed by 24 different people against different backgrounds. The backgrounds are of three types: uniform light, uniform dark and complex. In this section, examples of all the 10 gestures are included.

To train classifiers and test the method with these images, they are cropped and resized to 128x128, followed by histogram normalization. As the samples of each posture contain only 72 images, which is insufficient for the training of boosting based classifier. So it's necessary to increase the available number of samples. Here some little perturbations are added to the initial images. The images are shifted, scaled and rotated. Then 35 images are generated for each original image. Thus there are totally 25200 images, 2520 images for each hand posture.

The dataset is divided into 2 subsets: training set, and test set. For each hand posture, there are 1050 images in training set and 1470 images in test set. One classifier is trained for each posture. For a given posture test image, all classifiers are applied and the classifier giving the highest score is selected to label the test posture. The negative samples which are necessary to each posture classifier comprise samples of nine other postures and have equivalent number of images with positive samples.

The initial two classifiers of haar and Hog feature are trained with 150 positive samples. Then in each step of classifier update, 300 samples are added to training set as unlabeled data, which

Figure 8. Accuracy of hand posture recognition

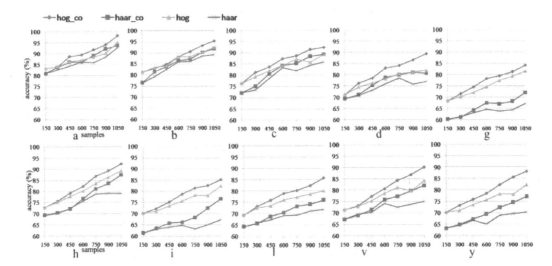

contains 150 positive samples mixed with the same amount of negative samples, until the 1050 positive samples for each posture are used up. The recognition accuracies for 10 postures are shown in Figure 8. Each plot in Figure 8 gives recognition accuracy on one posture.

As is shown in Figure 8, co-training based classifiers (hog_co and haar_co) obtain better results than single classifiers (hog and haar) in general. For the postures difficult to recognize, such as d, g, i and y, recognition accuracy is improved by 5~9 percent with co-training for both classifiers with haar and Hog The most significant improvement appears on posture d with Hog and posture *i* with haar. While for the easier postures a, b and c, the improvement by co- training is 2~4 percent, not as significant as difficult postures, as the accuracy of a, b and c are rather high (above 85%) by single classifiers without co-training with little space for improvement by simple boosting training. For all postures, Hog is a more effective feature descriptor than haar. The average accuracy on the dataset by independent classifiers with Hog and haar is 85.3% and 77.4%. After co-training, the accuracy is 90.1% with Hog and 82.7% with haar. Both the co-trained classifiers outperform the MCT classifiers (Just, Rodriguez & Marcel, 2006) with the amount of labeled data decreased by more than 80%.

CONCLUSION AND FUTURE RESEARCH DIRECTIONS

Hand posture recognition is an important problem in vision based gesture recognition. We have described geometric model based method and appearance based methods. Fast multi-scale feature detection is used to obtain palm and finger structure in hand images. Thus the geometric structure of hand configuration can give recognition results. This method is intuitive and simple to implement. With extended rectangular feature included, the time consumption of fast analysis is reduced greatly compared with traditional scale-space methods. In appearance based methods, firstly the patch based local texture representation is introduced to reserve spatial cues for the LBP like representation. With spatial information included in the representation, the patch based local texture description achieves higher accuracy compared with former methods. We have the other focus in appearance based methods on co-training based methods, which utilize the complementation of different features such as Haar and Hog. For each feature, the disparate classifiers are trained together in a uniform cooperation process and improved performance is acquired with less labeled examples.

Fast multi-scale analysis for feature detection is effective to speed up the detection process of scale-space features. However in current implementation, it cannot deal with small structures in images which may lead to degradation of generalization performance when it is applied for feature detection in general sense. And the computation cost of obtaining the descriptor of scale-space features needs further simplification.

Local texture descriptor using patch based LBP achieves high recognition accuracy for standard hand gesture database. Yet the measure of features and classifiers used here is the simple histogram intersection and nearest neighbor classifier. For the hand postures in practical application, we should have more elaborate designed measures and classifiers.

The semi-supervised co-training framework in this chapter acquires disparate classifiers with less labeled examples in an off-line mode. The future work should be revising the learning process into an online mode and make practical application with the co-training strategy.

REFERENCES

Bay, H., Tuytelaars, T., & Van Gool, L. (2006). Surf: Speeded up robust feature. In *Proceedings of European Conference on Computer Vision* (pp.404-417).

Binh, N., Shuichi, E., & Ejima, T. (2005). Real-Time Hand Tracking and Gesture Recognition System. In *Proceedings of International Conference on Graphics, Vision and Image Processing* (pp. 362-368).

Blum, A., & Mitchell, T. (1998). Combining labeled and unlabeled data with co-training. In *Proceedings of 11th Annual Conference on Computational Learning Theory* (pp. 92-100).

Bradski, G., Yeo, B. L., & Yeung, M. M. (1999). Gesture for Video Content Navigation. In *Proceedings of the IS&T/SPIE Conferene on Storage and Retrieval for Image and Video Database VII* (pp.230-242).

Bretzner, L., Laptev, I., & Lindeberg, T. (2002). Hand gesture recognition using multi-scale colour features, hierarchical models and particle filtering. In *Proceedings of International Conference on Automatic Face and Gesture Recognition* (pp. 423-428).

Chai, X., Fang, Y., & Wang, K. (2009). Robust hand gesture analysis and application in gallery browsing. In *Proceedings of International Conference on Multimedia and Expo* (pp.938-941).

Collins, M., Schapire, R. E., & Singer, Y. (2000). Logistic Regression, Adaboost and Bregman distances. In *Proceedings of 13th Annual Conference on Computational Learning Theory* (pp.158-169).

Cui, Y., & Weng, J. (1996). View-based hand segmentation and hand sequence recognition with complex backgrounds. In R. Dienstbier (Ed.), *Proceedings of International Conference on Pattern Recognition* (pp. 617-621).

Dalal, N., & Triggs, B. (2005). Histograms of oriented gradients for human detection. In *Proceedings of Computer Vision and Pattern Recognition* (pp.886-893).

Freeman, W. T., & Weissman, C. (1995). Television control by hand gestures. In *Proceedings of International Conference on Automatic Face and Gesture Recognition* (pp.197-183).

Guan, H., Rogerio, S., & Turk, M. (2006). The isometric self-organizing map for 3d hand pose estimation. In *Proceedings of International Conference on Automatic Face and Gesture Recognition* (pp. 263-268).

Javed, O., Ali, S., & Shah, M. (2005). Online detection and classification of moving objects using progressively improving detectors. In *Proceedings of Computer Vision and Pattern Recognition* (pp. 696-701).

Jones, M., & Viola, P. (2003). *Fast multi-view face detection* (Technical Report TR2003-96). Mitsubishi Electric Research Laboratories.

Just, A., Rodriguez, Y., & Marcel, S. (2006). Hand posture classification and recognition using the modified census transform. In R. Dienstbier (Ed.), In *Proceedings of International Conference on Automatic Face and Gesture Recognition* (pp. 351-356).

Kato, M., Chen, Y.-W., & Xu, G. (2006). Articulated hand tracking by pca-ica approach. I In proceedings of *International Conference on Automatic Face and Gesture Recognition* (pp. 329-334).

Kolsch, M. (2005). *Vision based hand gesture interfaces for wearable computing and virtual environments*. Doctoral dissertation, University of California, Santa Barbara.

Kolsch, M., & Turk, M. (2004). Fast 2D Hand Tracking with Flocks of Features and Multi-cue Integration. In *Proceedings of Computer Vision and Pattern Recognition Workshop on Real-Time Vision for HCI*.

Kolsch, M., & Turk, M. (2004). Robust hand detection. in Proceedings of *International Conference on Automatic Face and Gesture Recognition* (pp.614- 619).

Letessier, J., & Berard, F. Visual tracking of bare fingers for interactive surfaces(2004). In *Proceedings of 17th ACM Symposium on User Interface Software and Technology* (pp.119-122).

Levin, A., Viola, P., & Freund, Y. (2003). Unsupervised improvement of visual detectors using co-training. In *Proceedings of International Conference on Computer Vision* (pp. 626-633).

Lindeberg, T. (2004). Feature detection with automatic scale selection. *International Journal of Computer Vision, 30*(6), 77–116.

Lowe, D. G. (2004). Distinctive image features from scale-invariant key points. *International Journal of Computer Vision, 60*(2), 91–110. doi:10.1023/B:VISI.0000029664.99615.94

Ojala, T., Pietikainen, M., & Harwood, D. (1996). A Comparative Study of Texture Measures with Classification based on Feature Distribution. *Pattern Recognition, 29*(1), 51–59. doi:10.1016/0031-3203(95)00067-4

Ojala, T., Pietikainen, M., & Maenpaa, T. (2002). Multiresolution Gray-Scale and Rotation Invariant Texture Classification with Local Binary Patterns. *IEEE Transactions on Pattern Analysis and Machine Intelligence, 24*(7), 971–987. doi:10.1109/TPAMI.2002.1017623

Ong, E.-J., & Bowden, R. (2004). A boosted classifier tree for hand shape detection. In *Proceedings of International Conference on Automatic Face and Gesture Recognition* (pp. 889-894).

Pavlovic, V. I., Sharma, R., & Huang, T. S. (1997). Visual Interpretation of Hand Gestures for Human-Computer Interaction: A Review. *IEEE Transactions on Pattern Analysis and Machine Intelligence, 19*(7), 677–696. doi:10.1109/34.598226

Sato, Y., Kobayashi, Y., & Koike, H. (2000). Fast tracking of hands and fingertips in infrared images for augmented desk interface. In *Proceedings of International Conference on Automatic Face and Gesture Recognition* (pp. 462-467).

Schapire, R. E., Freund, Y., Bartlett, P., & Lee, W. S. (1998). Boosting the margin: A new explanation for the effectiveness of voting methods. *Annals of Statistics, 26*(5), 1651–1686. doi:10.1214/aos/1024691352

Tang, F., Brennan, S., Zhao, Q., & Tao, H. (2007). Co-Tracking Using Semi-Supervised Support Vector Machines. In *Proceedings of International Conference on Computer Vision* (pp.1-8)

Triesch, J., & von der Malsburg, C. (1996). Robust classification of hand posture against complex background. In *Proceedings of International Conference on Automatic Face and Gesture Recognition* (pp. 170-175).

Zhang, W., Shan, S., Gao, W., Chen, X., & Zhang, H. (2005). Local Gabor Binary Histogram Sequence: A Novel Non-Statistical Model for Face Representation and Recognition. In *Proceedings of International Conference on Computer Vision* (pp.786-791).

Zhou, H., Lin, D. J., & Huang, T. S. (2004). Static hand gesture recognition based on local orientation histogram feature distribution. In *Proceedings of Computer Vision and Pattern Recognition* (pp. 161-169).

Zhou, H., Xie, L., & Fang, X. (2007). Visual Mouse: SIFT Detection and PCA Recognition. In *Proceedings of International Conference on Computational Intelligence and Security Workshops* (pp. 263-266).

ADDITIONAL READING

Athitsos, V., & Sclarok, S. (2003). Estimating 3d hand pose from a cluttered image. In *Proceedings of International Conference on Computer Vision and Pattern Recognition* (pp.432-439).

Belongie, S., Malik, J., & Puzicha, J. (2000). Shape context: A new descriptor for shape matching and object recognition. In *Proceedings of Neural Information Processing Systems* (pp. 831-837).

Cheng, J., & Wang, K. (2006). Multi-view sampling for relevance feedback in image retrieval. In *Proceedings of International Conference on Pattern Recognition* (pp.881-884).

Cheng, J., & Wang, K. (2007). Active learning for image retrieval with co-svm. *Pattern Recognition, 40*(1), 330–334. doi:10.1016/j.patcog.2006.06.005

Jin, H., Liu, Q., Tang, X., & Lu, H. (2005). Learning local descriptors for face detection. In *Proceedings of International Conference on Multimedia and Expo* (pp.928-931).

Jones, M. J., & Regh, J. M. (2002). Statistical color models with application to skin detection. *International Journal of Computer Vision, 46*(1), 81–96. doi:10.1023/A:1013200319198

Li, S., Zhang, Z., Li, M., & Zhang, H. (2002). Multi-view face detection with floatboost. In *Proceedings of IEEE Workshop on Applications of Computer Vision* (pp.184-188).

Li, S. Z., & Zhang, Z. (2004). Float boost learning and statistical face detection. *IEEE Transactions on Pattern Analysis and Machine Intelligence, 26*(9), 1112–1123. doi:10.1109/TPAMI.2004.68

Malik, J., Belongie, S., & Puzicha, J. (2002). Shape matching and object recognition using shape contexts. *IEEE Transactions on Pattern Analysis and Machine Intelligence, 24*(4), 509–522. doi:10.1109/34.993558

McNeill, D. (1996). *Hand and mind: What gestures reveal about thoughts*. University of Chicago Press.

Muslea, I., Minton, S., & Knoblock, C. (2003). Active learning with strong and weak views: A case study on wrapper induction. In *Proceedings of 18th International Joint Conference on Artificial Intelligence* (pp.415-420).

Park, S.-B., & Zhang, B.-T. (2004). Co-trained support vector machines for large scale unstructured document classification using unlabeled data and syntactic information. *Information Processing & Management, 40*(3), 421–439. doi:10.1016/j.ipm.2003.09.003

Pavlovic, V. I., & Garg, A. (2001). Boosted detection of objects and attributes. In *Proceedings of International Conference on Computer Vision and Pattern Recognition*.

Pierce, D., & Cardie, C. (2001). Limitations of co-training for natural language learning from large datasets. In *Proceedings of the Conference on Empirical Methods in Natural Language Processing*.

Quek, F. K. H. (1995). Eyes in the interface. *Image and Vision Computing, 12*(6), 511–525. doi:10.1016/0262-8856(95)94384-C

Quek, F. K. H. (1996). Unencumbered gestural interaction. *IEEE MultiMedia, 4*(3), 36–47. doi:10.1109/93.556459

Thayananthan, A., Stenger, B., Torr, P. H. S., & Cipolla, R. (2003). Shape context and chamfer matching in cluttered scenes. In *Proceedings of International Conference on Computer Vision and Pattern Recognition* (pp.127-133).

Toews, M., & Arbel, T. (2003). Entropy-of-likelihood feature selection for image correspondence. In *Proceedings of International Conference on Computer Vision* (pp.1041-1048).

Topi, M., Timo, O., Matti, P., & Maricor, S. (2000). Robust texture classification by subsets of local binary patterns. In *Proceedings of 15th International Conference on pattern recognition* (pp. 935-938).

Turk, M., Hong, P., & Huang, T. S. (2000). Gesture modeling and recognition using finite state machines. In *Proceedings of International Conference on Automatic Face and Gesture Recognition* (pp. 410-415).

Viola, P., & Jones, M. (2001). *Fast and robust classification using asymmetric adaboost and detector cascade* (pp. 1311–1318). Neural Information Processing Systems.

Wu, Y., & Huang, T. S. (2000). View-independent recognition of hand postures. In *Proceedings of International Conference on Computer Vision and Pattern Recognition* (pp. 84-94).

Wu, Y., Lin, J., & Huang, T. S. (2005). Analyzing and capturing articulated hand motion in image sequences. *IEEE Transactions on Pattern Analysis and Machine Intelligence, 27*(12), 1910–1922. doi:10.1109/TPAMI.2005.233

Wu, Y. & Huang, T. (1999). Vision-based gesture recognition: A review (LNAI 1739).

Zhang, H., Hou, X., Li, S. Z., & Cheng, Q. (2001). Direct appearance models. In *Proceedings of International Conference on Computer Vision and Pattern Recognition* (pp.828-833).

Section 4
Multimedia Authentication

Chapter 12
Detecting Image Forgeries Using Geometric Cues

Lin Wu
Tianjin University, China

Yang Wang
Tianjin University, China

ABSTRACT

This chapter presents a framework for detecting fake regions by using various methods including watermarking technique and blind approaches. In particular, we describe current categories on blind approaches which can be divided into five: pixel-based techniques, format-based techniques, camera-based techniques, physically-based techniques and geometric-based techniques. Then we take a second look on the geometric-based techniques and further categorize them in detail. In the following section, the state-of-the-art methods involved in the geometric technique are elaborated.

INTRODUCTION

Today's digital technology has begun to erode our trust on the integrity of the visual imagery since image editing software can generate highly photorealistic images (Farid, 2009). Doctored photographs are appearing with a growing frequency and sophistication in tabloid magazines, mainstream media outlets, political campaigns, photo hoaxes, evidences in a courtroom, insurance claims, and cases involving scientific fraud (Farid, 2009). With the rapid advancement in image editing software, photorealistic images will

become increasingly easier to be generated and it becomes difficult for people to differentiate them from photographic images (Lyu & Farid, 2005). If we are to have any hope that photographs can hold the unique stature of being a definitive recording of events, we must develop technologies that can detect the tampered images. Therefore, authenticating the integrity of digital image's content has become particularly important when images are used as critical evidence in journalism and security surveillance applications.

Over the past several years, the field of digital forensics has emerged to authenticate digital images by enforcing several authentication methods. The presence or absence of the watermark in in-

DOI: 10.4018/978-1-60960-024-2.ch012

terpolated images captured by the camera can be employed to establish the authenticity of digital color images. Digital watermarking (I.J. Cox & M.L. Miller & J.A. Bloom, 2002; H. Liu & J. Rao & X. Yao, 2008) has been proposed as a means to authenticate an image. However, a watermarking must be inserted at the time of recording, which would limit this approach to specially equipped digital cameras having no capabilities to add a watermarking at the time of image capture. Furthermore, the watermarking would be destroyed if the image is compressed and the ruin of watermark would make the method failed.

Passive (nonintrusive) image forensics is regarded as the future direction. In contrast to the active methods, blind approaches need no prior information that is used in the absence of any digital watermarking or signature. Blind approaches can be roughly grouped into five categories (Farid, 2009):

1. pixel-based techniques that analyze pixel-level correlations arising from tampering. Efficient algorithms based on pixels have been proposed to detect cloned (B. Mahdian & S. Saic, 2007; A. Popescu & H. Farid, 2004; J. Fridrich & D. Soukal & J. Lukas, 2003), re-sampled (A. C. Popescu & H. Farid, 2005), spliced (T. T. Ng & S. F. Chang, 2004; T. T. Ng & S. F. Chang & Q. Sun, 2004; W. Chen, & Y. Shi, & W. Su, 2007) images.Statistical properties (H. Farid & S. Lyu, 2003; S. Bayram, & N. Memon, & M. Ramkumar, & B. Sankur, 2004) in natural images are also utilized;

2. format-based techniques detect tampering in lossy image compression: unique properties of lossy compression such as JPEG can be exploited for forensic analysis (H. Farid, 2008; J. Lukas & J. Fridrich, 2003; T. Pevny & J. Fridrich, 2008).

3. camera-based techniques exploit artifacts introduced by the camera lens, sensor or on-chip post-processing (J. Lukas, & J. Fridrich

& M. Goljan, 2005; A. Swaminathan & M. Wu & K. J. Ray Liu, 2008). Models of color filter array (A. C. Popescu & H. Farid, 2005; S. Bayram & H. T. Sencar & N. Memon, 2005), camera response (Y. F. Hsu & S. F. Chang, 2007; Z. Lin & R. Wang & X. Tang & H.Y. Shum, 2005) and sensor noise (H. Gou & A. Swaminathan & M. Wu, 2007; M. Chen & J. Fridrich &M. Goljan & J. Lukas, 2008; J. Lukas, & J. Fridrich & M. Goljan, 2005) are estimated to infer the source digital cameras and reveal digitally altered images. Other work such as (A. Swaminathan & M. Wu & K. J. Ray Liu, 2008) trace the entire in-camera and post-camera processing operations to identify the source digital cameras and reveal digitally altered images using the intrinsic traces.

4. physically-based techniques model and detect anomalies using physical rules. For example, three dimensional interaction between physical objects, light, and the camera can be used as evidence of tampering (M.K. Johnson & H. Farid, 2005; M. K. Johnson & H. Farid, 2007).

5. geometric-based techniques make use of geometric constraints that are preserved or recovered from perspective views (M. K. Johnson & H. Farid, 2006; M. K. Johnson, 2007; W. Wang & H. Farid, 2008; W. Zhang & X. Cao & Z. Feng & J. Zhang & P. Wang, 2009; W. Zhang & X. Cao & J. Zhang & J.Zhu.&P. Wang, 2009).

Several geometric-based techniques (M. K. Johnson & H. Farid, 2007; W. Wang & H. Farid, 2008; W. Zhang & X. Cao & Z. Feng & J. Zhang & P. Wang, 2009; M. K. Johnson & H. Farid, 2006) have been proposed in the field of image forgery detection. The estimation of internal camera parameters including principal point (M. K. Johnson & H. Farid, 2007) and skew (W. Wang & H. Farid, 2008) can be used as evidence of tampering. In (M. K. Johnson & H. Farid, 2007) the authors showed how translation in the image plane is equivalent to a shift of the principal point and differences in which can therefore be used as evidence of forgery. Wang and Farid (W. Wang & H. Farid, 2008) argued that the skew of the re-projected video is inconsistent with the expected parameter of an authentic video. The approach has the advantage that the re-projection can cause a non-zero skew in the camera intrinsic parameters, but there are also some drawbacks that it only applies to frames that contain a planar surface. Zhang et al. (W. Zhang & X. Cao & Z. Feng & J. Zhang & P. Wang, 2009) described a technique for detecting image composites by enforcing two-view geometrical constraints. The approach can detect fake regions efficiently on pictures at the same scene but requires two images correlated with **H** (planar homography) or **F** (fundamental matrix) constraints.

Metric measurements can be made from a planar surface after rectifying the image. In (M. K. Johnson & H. Farid, 2006), the authors reviewed three techniques for the rectification of planar surfaces under perspective projection. They argued that knowledge of polygons of known shape, two or more vanishing points, and two or more coplanar circles can be used to recover the image to world transformation of the planar surface, thereby allowing metric measurements to be achieved on the plane. Each method in (M. K. Johnson & H. Farid, 2006) requires only one single image but fails in measurements for objects out of the reference plane.

Wang et al. (G. Wang & Z. Hu & F. Wu & H. T. Tsui, 2005) show how to use the camera matrix and some available scene constraints to retrieve geometrical entities of the scene, such as height of an object on the reference plane, measurements on a vertical or arbitrary plane with respect to the reference plane, etc.

The single view metrology using geometric constraints has been addressed in (A. Criminisi & I. Reid & A. Zisserman, 1999). The authors demonstrated that the affine 3D geometry of a scene may be measured from a single perspective image using the vanishing line of a reference plane and the vertical vanishing point. However, they are only concerned with measurements of the distance between the plane which is parallel to the reference plane and measurements on this plane.

This chapter is organized as follows. After reviewing the background in section 2, the involved methods based on geometric technique are described in sections 3. The future research direction is given in section 4 and the final conclusions are drawn in section 5.

BACKGROUND

Photographic alterations have existed about as long as photography itself. However, before the digital age, such deceptions required mastery of complex and time-consuming darkroom techniques. Nowadays, anyone who has a little of computer skill can use powerful and inexpensive editing software to create tampered images as he or she likes. Therefore, as sophisticated forgeries appear with fast and alarming frequency, people's belief in what they see has been eroded (H. Farid, 2009).

A more recent example of photo tampering came to light in July 2008. Sepah News, the media arm of Iran's Revolutionary Guard, celebrated the country's military prowess by releasing a photo showing the simultaneous launch of four missiles. But only three of those rockets actually left the ground, a fourth was digitally added. The truth emerged after Sepah circulated the original photo showing three missiles in flight—but not before the faked image appeared on the front pages of the Chicago Tribune, the Financial Times, and the Los Angeles Times.

Over the past few years, the field of digital-image forensics has emerged to challenge this growing problem and return some level of trust in photographs. Nearly every digital forgery starts out as a photo taken by a digital camera. The camera's image sensor acts as the film. By using

Figure 1. A July 2008 photo shows four Iranian missiles streaking skyward. The right is the true image Sepah News replaced the faux photo with the original without explanation

computer methods to look at the underlying patterns of pixels that make up a digital image, specialists can detect the often-subtle signatures of manipulated images that are invisible to the naked eye.

Traditionally, watermarking is added into the images or video to give the validating information for image authentication. However, the watermarking can be easily destroyed in the process of image compression. Recently, digital blind techniques emerge in the field of image forgery detection. These techniques work on the assumption that although digital forgeries may leave no visual clues that indicate tampering, they may alter the underlying statistics of an image.

MAIN FOCUS AND CONTRIBUTION OF THE CHAPTER

In this chapter, we focus on the category on the geometric-based techniques in image forgery detection. Geometric techniques, which appear as a new application: the nonintrusive digital image forensic can be further divided into four categories: (1) techniques based on the camera's intrinsic parameters; (2) techniques based on metric measurement; (3) techniques based on multiple view geometry; (4) techniques based on other geometrical constraints.

After reviewing the literature in the field, we propose a potential solution for image integrity's authentication, which is based on the published geometric method on 3D height measurement, measurements on the vertical or an arbitrary plane with respect to a reference plane. Our proposed solution enriches the detecting methods for image forgery, which provides a prospect to build a integrated framework incorporating various methods for fake region detection.

Solutions and Recommendations

Preliminary

Camera model. The general pinhole camera can also be written as:

$$\mathbf{P} = \begin{bmatrix} \mathbf{r_1} & \mathbf{r_2} & \mathbf{r_3} & \mathbf{t} \end{bmatrix}, \mathbf{K} = \begin{bmatrix} f & \gamma & u_0 \\ 0 & \lambda f & v_0 \\ 0 & 0 & 1 \end{bmatrix} \quad (1)$$

where $\mathbf{r}_i$ is the ith column of the rotation matrix $\mathbf{R}$, $\mathbf{t}$ is the translation vector, and $\mathbf{K}$ is a non-singular 3×3 upper triangular matrix known as the camera calibration matrix including five parameters, i.e. the focal length f, the skew γ, the aspect ratio λ and the principal point at (u_0, v_0).

Planar homography. Suppose there is a plane in the scene, without loss of generality, we define the origin of the coordinate frame lie on this plane (i.e. reference plane), with the X and Y- axes spanning the plane. The Z-axis is the reference direction, which is any direction not parallel to the plane. A 3D point $\mathbf{M}=[x\,y\,0\,w]^T$ and its corresponding image projection $\mathbf{m}=[u\,v\,1]^T$ are related via a 3×4 matrix $\mathbf{P}$ by:

$$\mathbf{m} \sim \mathbf{PM} = \mathbf{P}\begin{bmatrix} x & y & 0 & w \end{bmatrix}^T = \underbrace{\begin{bmatrix} \mathbf{p_1} & \mathbf{p_2} & \mathbf{p_4} \end{bmatrix}}_{\mathbf{H}}\begin{bmatrix} x & y & w \end{bmatrix}^T = \begin{bmatrix} h_{11} & h_{12} & h_{13} \\ h_{21} & h_{22} & h_{23} \\ h_{31} & h_{32} & h_{33} \end{bmatrix}\begin{bmatrix} x \\ y \\ w \end{bmatrix}$$

$$(2)$$

where $\sim$ indicates equality up to multiplication by a non-zero scale factor, h_{ij} is the component of $\mathbf{H}$, and $\mathbf{p}_i$ is the ith column of $\mathbf{P}$. Hence, the projection from a point on the plane to its image is simplified as

$$\mathbf{m} \sim \mathbf{HM'} \qquad (3)$$

where, $\mathbf{H}=[\mathbf{p_1 p_2 p_4}]$ is called plane to plane homography, $\mathbf{M'}=[x\,y\,w]^T$ is a homogeneous vector for a point on the reference plane. Usually, $\mathbf{H}$ is a 3×3 homogeneous matrix with 8 degrees of freedom (*dof*).

Here, for generality, we introduce an approach to estimate the transformation from 2D points in image to metric rectification of world coordinates up to similarity's ambiguity. This transformation, $\mathbf{H}$, can be decomposed into the multiplication of two matrices:

$$\mathbf{H}=\mathbf{H_A H_P} \qquad (4)$$

where $\mathbf{H_A}$ and $\mathbf{H_P}$ represent affine and pure projective transformations respectively:

$$\mathbf{H_P} = \begin{pmatrix} 1 & 0 & 0 \\ 0 & 1 & 0 \\ l_1 & l_2 & l_3 \end{pmatrix} \qquad (5)$$

$$\mathbf{H_A} = \begin{pmatrix} \dfrac{1}{\beta} & \dfrac{\alpha}{\beta} & 0 \\ 0 & 1 & 0 \\ 0 & 0 & 1 \end{pmatrix} \qquad (6)$$

where $\mathbf{l}_\infty = (l_1, l_2, l_3)^T$ is the vanishing line of the reference plane that is determined by two vanishing points, the coefficients α and β are estimated as follows. Given a known angle θ on the world plane between two lines $\mathbf{m}=(m_1, m_2, m_3)^T$ and $\mathbf{n}=(n_1, n_2, n_3)^T$ (parameterized as homogeneous vectors), it can be shown in (D. Liebowitz & A. Zisserman, 1998) that α and β lie on a circle with center:

$$(c_\alpha, c_\beta) = (\frac{a+b}{2}, \frac{a-b}{2}\cot(\theta)) \qquad (7)$$

with radius:

$$r = \left| \frac{(a-b)}{2\sin(\theta)} \right| \qquad (8)$$

where $a=-m_2/m_1$, $b=-n_2/n_1$.

Alternatively, two equal but unknown angles on the world plane between two lines imaged with directions a_1, b_1 and a_2, b_2 also provide a constraint circle with center:

$$(c_\alpha, c_\beta) = (\frac{a_1 b_2 - b_1 a_2}{a_1 - b_1 - a_2 + b_2}, 0) \qquad (9)$$

and radius:

$$r^2 = (\frac{a_1 b_2 - b_1 a_2}{a_1 - b_1 - a_2 + b_2})^2 + \frac{(a_1 - b_1)(a_1 b_1 - a_2 b_2)}{a_1 - b_1 - a_2 + b_2} \qquad (10)$$

Thereby, two pairs of equal but unknown angles can provide two circles, and α, β will be obtained from the intersection of such two circles.

Besides, a known length ratio between two non-parallel line segments **i** and **j** on the world plane can provide another constraint circle with center:

$$(c_\alpha, c_\beta) = (\frac{\Delta i_1 \Delta i_2 - \rho^2 \Delta j_1 \Delta j_2}{\Delta i_2^2 - \rho \Delta j_2^2}, 0) \qquad (11)$$

and with radius:

$$r = \left| \frac{\rho(\Delta j_1 \Delta i_2 - \Delta i_1 \Delta j_2)}{\Delta i_2^2 - \rho \Delta j_2^2} \right| \qquad (12)$$

where ρ is the known length ratio between **i** and **j**, and $\Delta i_1 \Delta i_2$ are the differences between the first and second coordinates of the line segment **i**. We can also use another combination: length ratio and a known angle to obtain the affine transformation $\mathbf{H}_A$.

Fundamental matrix. The fundamental matrix **F** encapsulates the intrinsic projective geometry between two views which only depends on the camera's internal parameters and relative pose. F is a 3×3 matrix of rank 2. If a point in 3-space is imaged as x in the first view, and **x'** in the second, then the image points satisfy the relation **x'Fx**=0.

If points x and **x'** correspond, then **x'** lies on the epipolar line **l'**=**Fx** corresponding to the point x. In other words **x'FX**=**x'^{T}l**=0.

Solutions

Image Forgery Detection Based on Camera Internal Parameters

The internal parameters in the camera matrix (Equation (1)) are focal length, skew, aspect ratio and principal point. The estimated internal parameters recovered from a non-tampered image should be inconsistent across the image. Therefore, Differences in these parameters across the image are used as evidence of tampering

Using principal point. It is a common thing that a single image is composited of two or more people, for example, Figure 2, is a composite of actress Marilyn Monroe (1926-1962) and President Abraham Lincoln (1809-1865).

Estimating a camera's principal point from the image of a person's eyes is a feasible approach to authenticate an image's integrity. Inconsistencies in the principal point can be used as evidence of tampering. In authentic images, the principal point is near the center of the image. In (M. K. Johnson & H. Farid, 2007), the authors stated that the principal point is moved proportionally when a person is translated in the image as part of creating a composite.

This section first describes how the planar homography **H** can be estimated from an image of a person's eyes and show how this transform can be factored into a product of matrices that embody the camera's intrinsic and extrinsic parameters. Then it will be shown how translation in the image plane can be detected from inconsistencies in the estimated camera's intrinsic parameters.

Since the world points lie on a single plane, **H** can be decomposed in terms of the intrinsic and extrinsic parameters:

Figure 2. Composite of Marilyn Monroe and Abraham Lincoln

$$\mathbf{H}=[\mathbf{h}_1 \mathbf{h}_2 \mathbf{h}_3]=s\mathbf{K}(\mathbf{r}_1 \mathbf{r}_2 \mathbf{t}) \tag{13}$$

where s is a scale factor and $\mathbf{K}$ is the camera calibration matrix. For simplicity, it is assumed that the skew is zero and the aspect ratio is 1. Under these assumptions, the matrix $\mathbf{K}$ is:

$$\mathbf{K} = \begin{bmatrix} f & 0 & u_0 \\ 0 & f & v_0 \\ 0 & 0 & 1 \end{bmatrix} \tag{14}$$

The camera's intrinsic components can be estimated by decomposing $\mathbf{H}$ according to Equation (13). It is evident to show that $\mathbf{r}_1 = \dfrac{1}{s}\mathbf{K}^{-1}\mathbf{h}_1$ and $\mathbf{r}_2 = \dfrac{1}{s}\mathbf{K}^{-1}\mathbf{h}_2$. The constraints that are orthogonal and have the same norm yield two constraints on the matrix K:

$$\mathbf{r}_1^T \mathbf{r}_2 = \mathbf{h}_1^T (\mathbf{K}^{-T}\mathbf{K}^{-1})\mathbf{h}_2 = 0 \tag{15}$$

$$\mathbf{r}_1^T \mathbf{r}_1 - \mathbf{r}_2^T \mathbf{r}_2 = \mathbf{h}_1^T (\mathbf{K}^{-T}\mathbf{K}^{-1})\mathbf{h}_1 - \mathbf{h}_2^T (\mathbf{K}^{-T}\mathbf{K}^{-1})\mathbf{h}_2 = 0 \tag{16}$$

It is possible to estimate the principal point (u_0, v_0) or the focal length f, but not the both with only two constraints. As such, the authors assumed a known focal length. Therefore, the homography H can be achieved from image of people's eyes.

The translation of two circles (eyes) in the image is equivalent to translating the camera's principal point. In homogeneous coordinates, translations are represented by multiplication with a translation matrix T:

$$\mathbf{y}=\mathbf{Tx} \tag{17}$$

where:

$$\mathbf{T} = \begin{bmatrix} 1 & 0 & d_1 \\ 0 & 1 & d_2 \\ 0 & 0 & 1 \end{bmatrix} \tag{18}$$

and the amount of translation is (d_1, d_2). The mapping from world X to image coordinates y is:

$$\mathbf{y} = \mathbf{THx} = s\mathbf{TK}(\mathbf{r}_1 \quad \mathbf{r}_2 \quad \mathbf{t})\mathbf{X} = s\hat{\mathbf{K}}(\mathbf{r}_1 \quad \mathbf{r}_2 \quad \mathbf{t})\mathbf{X} \tag{19}$$

where

$$\hat{\mathbf{K}} = \begin{bmatrix} f & 0 & u_0 + d_1 \\ 0 & f & v_0 + d_2 \\ 0 & 0 & 1 \end{bmatrix} \tag{20}$$

Therefore, translation in image coordinates is equivalent to translating the principal point. If the principal point in an authentic image is near the origin which has large deviations from the image center, or inconsistencies in the estimated principal point across the image, can be used as the evidence of tampering.

Using skew. Another camera internal parameter, the skew, can also be used as the evidence of tampering. In Figure 3, the right is a re-projected frame of a movie, the left is the same scene as viewed on a movie screen.

The author in (W. Wang & H. Farid, 2008) described an automatic technique for detecting a video that was recorded from a screen. It is ready to show that the internal camera parameters of such video are inconsistent with the expected parameters of an authentic video. Due to the angle of the video camera relative to the screen in the re-projected process, a perspective distortion has been introduced into this second recording. It can introduce a distortion into the intrinsic camera parameters the camera skew which depends on the angle between the horizontal and

Figure 3. Projected movie introduces distortions that can be used to detect re-projected video

vertical pixel axes. In (W. Wang & H. Farid, 2008), the authors demonstrated that re-projection can cause a non-zero skew in the camera's intrinsic parameters. Now we review two approaches for estimating camera skew from a video sequence.

Skew estimation I. The projection of a planar surface is given by:

$$\mathbf{y} = s\mathbf{KPY} = s\mathbf{HY} \tag{21}$$

where $\mathbf{K}$ and $\mathbf{P}$ are the intrinsic and extrinsic matrices, $\mathbf{y}$ is the 2-D projected point in homogeneous coordinates, and $\mathbf{Y}$, in the appropriate coordinate system, is specified by 2-D coordinates in homogeneous coordinates. The 3×3 matrix $\mathbf{H}$ is a non-singular matrix referred to as a homography. Given the above equality, the left- and right-hand sides of this homography satisfy the following:

$$\mathbf{y} \times (\mathbf{HY}) = 0$$

$$\begin{pmatrix} y_1 \\ y_2 \\ y_3 \end{pmatrix} \left(\begin{pmatrix} h_{11} & h_{21} & h_{31} \\ h_{12} & h_{22} & h_{32} \\ h_{13} & h_{23} & h_{33} \end{pmatrix} \begin{pmatrix} Y_1 \\ Y_2 \\ Y_3 \end{pmatrix} \right) = 0 \tag{22}$$

A matched set of points y and Y appear to provide three constraints on the eight unknown elements of H which is defined only up to an unknown scale factor.

Next we describe how to estimate the camera skew from the estimated homography $\mathbf{H}$. Since $\mathbf{H}$ can be expressed as:

$$\mathbf{H} = \mathbf{KP} = \mathbf{K}(\mathbf{p}_1 \mathbf{p}_2 \ | \mathbf{t}) \tag{23}$$

The orthonormality of $\mathbf{p}_1$ and $\mathbf{p}_2$, yields the following two constraints:

$$\mathbf{p}_1^T \mathbf{p}_2 = 0 \text{ and } \mathbf{p}_1^T \mathbf{p}_1 = \mathbf{p}_2^T \mathbf{p}_2 \tag{24}$$

which in turn imposes the following constraints on H and K:

$$\begin{pmatrix} h_{11} \\ h_{12} \\ h_{13} \end{pmatrix}^T K^{-T} K^{-1} \begin{pmatrix} h_{21} \\ h_{22} \\ h_{23} \end{pmatrix} = 0 \tag{25}$$

$$\begin{pmatrix} h_{11} \\ h_{12} \\ h_{13} \end{pmatrix}^T K^{-T} K^{-1} \begin{pmatrix} h_{11} \\ h_{12} \\ h_{13} \end{pmatrix} = \begin{pmatrix} h_{21} \\ h_{22} \\ h_{23} \end{pmatrix}^T K^{-T} K^{-1} \begin{pmatrix} h_{21} \\ h_{22} \\ h_{23} \end{pmatrix} \tag{26}$$

Denote $\mathbf{B} = \mathbf{K}^{-T}\mathbf{K}^{-1}$, where B is a symmetric matrix parameterized with three degrees of freedom:

$$\mathbf{B} = \begin{pmatrix} b_{11} & b_{12} & 0 \\ b_{12} & b_{22} & 0 \\ 0 & 0 & 1 \end{pmatrix} \tag{27}$$

Each image of a planar surface enforces two constraints on the three unknowns b_{ij} The matrix

$\mathbf{B} = \mathbf{K}^{-T}\mathbf{K}^{-1}$ can, therefore, be estimated from two or more views of the same planar surface using standard least-square estimation. The desired skew can be then determined from the estimated matrix B as:

$$s = -f\frac{b_{12}}{b_{11}} \tag{28}$$

Skew estimation II. Here we review an approach that does not require any known world geometry, but requires a non-linear minimization. Suppose two frames of a video sequence with corresponding image points given by u and v. The corresponding points satisfy the following relationship:

$$\mathbf{V}^T\mathbf{Fu} = 0 \tag{29}$$

The above relationship can yield:

$$\begin{pmatrix} v_1 & v_2 & 1 \end{pmatrix} \begin{pmatrix} f_{11} & f_{21} & f_{31} \\ f_{12} & f_{22} & f_{32} \\ f_{13} & f_{23} & f_{33} \end{pmatrix} \begin{pmatrix} u_1 \\ u_2 \\ 1 \end{pmatrix} = 0 \tag{30}$$

Each pair of matched points u and v provides one constraint for the eight unknown elements. Therefore, eight or more matched pairs of points are required to solve for the components of the fundamental matrix.

It then will be described how to estimate the camera skew from the estimated fundamental matrix **F**. Assume the intrinsic camera matrix **K**, is the same across the views containing the matched image points. The essential matrix E is defined as:

$$\mathbf{E} = \mathbf{K}^T\mathbf{FK} \tag{31}$$

The essential matrix E has rank 2 and the two non-zero singular values of E are equal. This property will be exploited to estimate the camera

skew. The cost function that is minimized in terms of the camera focal length f and skew s:

$$C(f,s) = \sum_{i=1}^{n} \frac{\sigma_{i1} - \sigma_{i2}}{\sigma_{i2}} \tag{32}$$

where σ_{i1} and σ_{i2} are the non-zero singular values of E from n estimated fundamental matrices, and K is parameterized as:

$$\mathbf{K} = \begin{pmatrix} f & s & 0 \\ 0 & f & 0 \\ 0 & 0 & 1 \end{pmatrix} \tag{33}$$

Image forgery detection based on metric measurement. Obtaining metric measurement from a single image is proved useful in forensic settings where real-world measurements are required. Three techniques for making metric measurements on planar surfaces from a single image are reviewed here. In (M. K. Johnson & H. Farid, 2006), the authors surveyed three techniques for the rectification of planar surfaces imaged under perspective projection. Each method requires only a single image. Three methods exploit knowledge of polygons of known shape, two or more vanishing points on a plane, two or more coplanar circles, respectively. In each case, the world to image transformation of the planar surface can be recovered, thereby allowing metric measurements to be made on the plane.

Polygons. Under an ideal pinhole camera model, points on a plane, **X**, in the world coordinate system are imaged to the image plane with coordinates **x**, given by:

$$\mathbf{x} = \mathbf{HX} \tag{34}$$

where both points are homogeneous 3-vectors in their respective coordinate systems. In order to solve for the projective transformation matrix **H**, four or more points with known coordinates

X and **x** are required. The estimation of **H** is determined up to an unknown scale factor. From a single image, a known length on the world plane is required to determine this scale factor. With a known **H**, the image is warped according to **H**$^{-1}$ to yield a rectified image, from which measurements can be made.

Shown in Figure 4 is a tampered image – two boxes of Marlboro cigarettes were doctored to read "Marlboro kids" with an image of the cartoon character Tweety Bird. The center and right of Figure 4 are the results of planar rectification based on the known shape of the rectangle on the front of the box. It is obvious that after rectification the text and character on the boxes are inconsistent with another, clearly revealing them to be fakes.

Vanishing points. Here, we review how two or more vanishing points can be used to make metric measurements on a planar surface in the world. Consider the inverse mapping:

$$\mathbf{X} = \mathbf{H}^{-1}\mathbf{x} = (\mathbf{H}_S\mathbf{H}_A\mathbf{H}_P)\mathbf{x} \qquad (35)$$

The projective transformation matrix **H**$^{-1}$ is uniquely decomposed into a product of three matrices: a similarity matrix **H**$_S$, an affine matrix **H**$_A$ and a pure projective matrix **H**$_P$. The final similarity matrix **H**$_S$ is given by:

$$\mathbf{H}_s = \begin{pmatrix} sr_1 & sr_2 & t_x \\ sr_3 & sr_4 & t_y \\ 0 & 0 & 1 \end{pmatrix} = \begin{pmatrix} s\mathbf{R} & \mathbf{t} \\ 0^T & 1 \end{pmatrix} \qquad (36)$$

where s is an isotropic scaling, R is a rotation matrix, and t is a translation vector. Only the scale factor s is required in order to make absolute Euclidean measurements on a world plane. From a single image, a known length on the world plane is required in order to determine this scale factor. The image is then warped according to **H**$^{-1}$ to yield a rectified image, from which measurements can be made.

Figure 5 is an image of two people standing outside of a store. Also shown in this figure is a rectified version of this image. The lines along the building face were used to find vanishing points. Since the two people are standing in a plane that is approximately parallel to the plane of the store front, their relative heights can be measured after rectification. Using the height of the person on the left as a reference (64.75 inches), the height of the person on the right was estimated to be 69.3 inches. This person's actual height is 68.75 inches, yielding an error of 0.55 inches or 0.8%.

Circles. The circular points **I**=$(1\ i\ 0)^T$ and **J**=$(1\ -i\ 0)^T$ lie on every circle in a plane. Consider the effect of the projective transform **H** on the circular points **I** and **J**. The mapping from world to image coordinates is:

Figure 4. The face of each cigarette box is rectified using the known shape of the box face. The center and right panels are the rectified images, clearly showing an inconsistency in the cartoon character and text

Figure 5. The wall was rectified using vanishing lines, a known angle and length ratio. The right is the rectified image, from which measurements of the two people can be made

$$\mathbf{H} = (\mathbf{H_S H_A H_P})^{-1} = \mathbf{H_P^{-1} H_A^{-1} H_S^{-1}} \qquad (37)$$

The circular points are mapped under this projective transform $\mathbf{H}$: $\mathbf{HI}$ and $\mathbf{HJ}$. The similarity matrix $\mathbf{H}_S^{-1}$ can be ignored because the circular points are either invariant or are swapped under this transformation. Therefore, without loss of generality, it can be assumed that the circular points are invariant to $\mathbf{H}_S^{-1}$, in which:

$$\mathbf{HI} = \mathbf{H_P^{-1} H_A^{-1} I} = \mathbf{H_P^{-1}} \begin{pmatrix} \beta + i\alpha \\ i \\ 0 \end{pmatrix} = \begin{pmatrix} \beta + i\alpha \\ i \\ -l_1/l_3(\beta + i\alpha) - il_2/l_3 \end{pmatrix} \qquad (38)$$

The projection of $\mathbf{J}$ is the complex conjugate of $\mathbf{HI}$. $\mathbf{HI}$ and $\mathbf{HJ}$ contain the required coefficients of the desired matrices $\mathbf{H}_P$ and $\mathbf{H}_A$. Under the projective transform, the intersections of any two coplanar circles are preserved, while these circles are projected to ellipse in the image. As a result, it is important to compute the intersection of these ellipses, two of which correspond to $\mathbf{HI}$ and $\mathbf{HJ}$.

Image forgery detection based on multiple view geometry. W. Zhang & X. Cao & Z. Feng & J. Zhang & P. Wang(2009) stated a technique for detecting image composites by enforcing two-view geometrical constrains: $\mathbf{H}$ and $\mathbf{F}$ constraints on image pairs, where $\mathbf{H}$ denotes the planar homography matrix and $\mathbf{F}$ the fundamental matrix.

H constraint When a camera rotates for an angle, corresponding points $\mathbf{x}_1$ and $\mathbf{x}_2$ on two image planes are related by:

$$\mathbf{x}_2 = \mathbf{K[R|0]X} = \mathbf{KRK^{-1}x}_1 \qquad (37)$$

while in case of pure zooming, corresponding points hold:

$$\mathbf{x}_2 = \mathbf{K'[R|0]X} = \mathbf{K'RK^{-1}x}_1 \qquad (38)$$

where $\mathbf{K}$ and $\mathbf{K'}$ are two internal parameter matrices.

Pictures taken before and after camera motion are constrained by a planar homography, $\mathbf{H}$, if any of the assumptions holds: (1) camera does not change its position; (2) scenes viewed are locally coplanar.

F constraint. When a camera moves generally and points are not coplanar, they still can be related with a Fundamental Matrix, $\mathbf{F}$, which maps a point $\mathbf{x}_1$ on one image to a line $\mathbf{l}_1$ on the other image:

$$\mathbf{x}_2^T \mathbf{l}_1 = \mathbf{x}_2^T \mathbf{F} \mathbf{x}_1 = 0 \qquad (39)$$

where $\mathbf{x}_2$ is the corresponding point of $\mathbf{x}_1$.

For $\mathbf{H}$ constraint, the authors combine bucketing technique and RANSAC for the estimation of $\mathbf{H}$, since SIFT fails to find initial matches for the estimation of $\mathbf{H}$ and $\mathbf{F}$. After the estimation of H, the rectified image $\mathbf{l}_2$ can be recovered from the original image $\mathbf{l}_1$. The difference matrix $\mathbf{D}$

is introduced to evaluate the similarity of the image l_1 and l_2. Regions with high difference **D** are selected to produce the binary map, which highlights fake regions. The threshold of cutting the difference is given by:

$$t = \max(\mathbf{D}) - c \qquad (40)$$

where **D** denotes the difference of image l_1 and l_2, at every pixel, and the constant value c locates in [0.3, 0.6].

For detecting composites using **F** constraint, "Gold Standard" algorithm (R. Hartley & A. Zisserman, 2004)is applied to estimate **F**. The point x_1 from frame l_1 maps to an epipolar line on image l_2. Distance between x_2 and epipolar line $l = Fx_1$ is used as the metric,

$$d(\mathbf{x}_2, \mathbf{Fx}_1) = \sqrt{(\mathbf{x}_2^T \mathbf{Fx}_1)^2 / ((\mathbf{Fx}_1)_x^2 + (\mathbf{Fx}_1)_y^2)} \qquad (41)$$

The distance measurement provides a candidate set, $\Psi = \{(\mathbf{x}_{1i}, \mathbf{x}_{2i}) | d(\mathbf{x}_{2i}, \mathbf{Fx}_{1i}) > t\}$, of features inside the potential fake regions. Morphological operation is used to dilate the points in Ψ to highlight a region including dense fake points.

Image Forgery Detection Using Other Geometrical Constraints

Shadow Geometry. Shadow compositing must be taken into account in some target scenes when there presents shadow projection from the sun. In (W. Zhang & X. Cao & J. Zhang & J.Zhu.&P. Wang,2009) the authors utilize the planar homology (C. E. Springer, 1964) that encompasses the imaged shadow relationship as shown in Figure 7 to detect photo composites. Note that the light source is not necessarily to be at infinity to keep the model by a planar homology, provided that the light source is a point light source, i.e. all light rays are concurrent.

As shown in Figure 8, a planar homology is a planar projective transformation **H** which has a line l of fixed points, called the *axis*, and a distinct fixed point v, not on the axis l, called the *vertex* of the homology, **H**,

$$\mathbf{H} = \mathbf{I} + (\mu - 1) \frac{\mathbf{v}\mathbf{l}^T}{\mathbf{v}^T\mathbf{l}} \qquad (42)$$

where α is the cross ratio that will be discussed later. In our case, the vertex **v** is the image of the

*Figure 6. Detecting composites by enforing the **H** constraint. (a, b) Original image pairs. (c) Images rectified from (a) using the estimated **H**. (d) Difference maps between (b) and (c) based on correlation. (e) Binary masks with fake regions. Rows 1 and 2 are images taken with rotation, and row 3 is a zooming case*

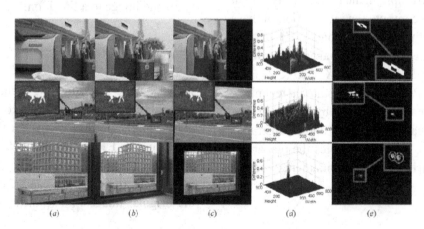

Figure 7. Detecting composites by enforcing the F constraint. (a) Two natural image pairs with visually plausible fake regions. (b) Points with large distance to their corresponding epipolar lines. Some examples are highlighted with larger size. (c) Binary map highlighting the fake regions

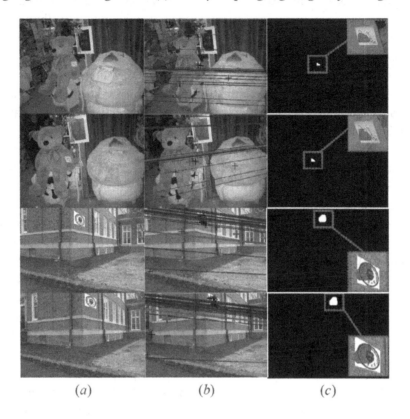

(a)   (b)   (c)

Figure 8. Geometry of a planar homology. A plane π1, and its shadow, illuminated by a point light source v and cast on a ground plane π, are related by a planar homology

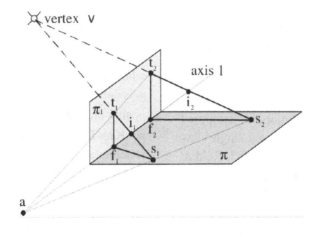

light source, and the axis, **l**, is the image of the intersection between planes π_1 and π. Each point off the axis, e.g. $\mathbf{t}_2$, lies on a fixed line $\mathbf{t}_2\mathbf{s}_2$ through **v** intersecting the axis at $\mathbf{i}_2$ and is mapped to another point s_2 on the line. Note that i_2 is the intersection in the image plane, although the light ray $t_2 s_2$ and the axis, l, are unlikely to intersect in 3D real world.

One important property of a planar homology is that the corresponding lines intersect with the axis, e.g. the lines $t_1 t_2$ and $s_1 s_2$ intersect at a on l. Another important property of a planar homology is that the cross ratio, μ, defined by the vertex, v, the corresponding points, t_i and s_i, and the intersection point, i_i, is the characteristic invariance of the homology, and thus is the same for all corresponding points. For example, the cross ratios $\{v, t_1; s_1, i_1\}$ and $\{v, t_2; s_2, i_2\}$ are equal. The two constraints can be expressed as:

$$((t_2 \times t_1) \times (s_2 \times s_1)) \cdot (f_2 \times f_1) = 0 \qquad (43)$$

$$\{v, t_1; s_1, i_1\} = \{v, t_2; s_2, i_2\} \qquad (44)$$

where

$$v = (t_2 \times s_2) \times (t_1 \times s_1) \qquad (45)$$

Therefore, these two constraints can be used to detect composites in a nature image. Notice that t_1, f_1, t_2, f_2 have to be coplanar and f_1, f_2 on the intersection of plane π_1 and π. In real world, vertical objects standing on the ground satisfy this assumption, such as standing people, street lamps, trees and buildings. In addition, people usually are interested in inserting a new actor, which is mostly standing and vertical, into some target scene.

As another potential solution for tampered region authentication, we can leverage single view geometric constraints (A. Criminisi & I. Reid & A. Zisserman, 1999) to detect composited regions. General methods (A. Criminisi & I. Reid & A. Zisserman, 1999; G. Wang & Z. Hu & F. Wu & H. T. Tsui, 2005) try to compute the camera matrix P induced by rigid constraints to achieve metric rectification. However, we can use minimal geometric constraints including known angles,

equal but known angles or length ratios to obtain the planar homography H. In the following, we will first show that P may be derived from H and then, we demonstrate that various geometric combinations can derive the planar homography. After metric rectification is implemented, we present the 3D metric measurement and measurements on the vertical plane or arbitrary plane.

Metric rectification. The camera matrix P can be retrieved from H up to 3 degrees of freedom's ambiguities since P is 11 *dof* while H is 8. Typically, the skew γ of the COTS camera is zero, which provides one constraint. The remaining two ambiguities can be relieved by the availability of vertical vanishing point (G. Wang & Z. Hu & F. Wu & H. T. Tsui, 2005), which needs restricted scene to provide the vertical direction. Here, the principal point is instead used since it can provide two independent constraints on P, and it is known to be approximately at the center of a natural image (M. K. Johnson & H. Farid, 2007; X. Cao & H. Foroosh, 2006). Therefore, in our implementation, the principal point is assumed as the center of the image and P can be determined from H. When H is determined by using the geometric constraints, then the Image of Absolute Conic (IAC) i.e. ω can be determined by the orthogonal vanishing points satisfying the following relationship:

$$h_1^T \omega h_2 = 0 \qquad (46)$$

where h_i is the ith column of H, $\omega = (KK^T)^{-1}$. After ω is determined, K may be computed by decomposing the IAC. Since $h_1^T = Kr_1$, $h_2^T = Kr_2$ and $p_3 = Kr_3 = K(r_1 \times r_2)$. Thereby, the camera matrix P is achieved from H.

Simply and particularly, ω may be directly retrieved from the orthogonal relationship provided by two orthogonal vanishing points which may be available from some scene.

$$v_x^T \omega v_y = 0 \qquad (47)$$

Figure 9. Composite detection based on shadow geometry. **Top row**: *Two nature images with composited regions.* **Middle row**: *The corresponding lines that involve composited regions (R1 and R6) don't intersect on the axis. In addition, they dissatisfy the characteristic invariance constraint in Equation (44) (see Table 1).* **Bottom row**: *The imaged shadow relationship of authentic objects can be modeled by a planar homology. Black squares, crosses and circles denote the locations of* **t**, **f** *and* **s** *in Figure 8 respectively*

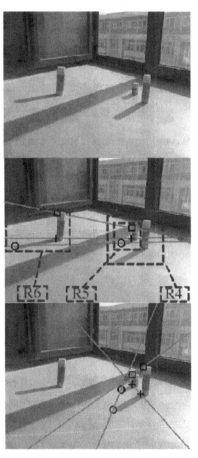

Table 1. Cross ratios of planar homologies in Figure 9

Region A	Region B	μ_A	μ_B	Diff Ratio
R1	R2	0.1741	0.1231	29.2589%
R2	R3	0.1587	0.1573	0.8794%
R1	R3	0.4454	0.4966	11.5145%
R4	R5	0.6298	0.6352	0.8647%
R4	R6	0.4473	0.3384	24.3526%
R5	R6	0.3237	0.2625	18.9191%

where $\mathbf{v}_x$ and $\mathbf{v}_y$ are two vanishing points which are perpendicular to each other. And then, **H** may be computed from such geometric constraints.

Height measurement. We wish to measure the object's 3D height which can be treated as the distance between two parallel planes. The distance between scene planes is specified by a base point on the reference plane and top point in the scene (A. Criminisi & I. Reid & A. Zisserman, 1999). The image containing such planes is illustrated in Figure 10.

Suppose the base and the top points can be specified as $\mathbf{X}=[X,Y,0]^T$ and $\mathbf{X'}=[X,Y,0]^T$ respectively, and their images are $\mathbf{x}$ and $\mathbf{x'}$. Then the image coordinates are:

$$\mathbf{x}=\mathbf{PX}=\mathbf{P}[X,Y,0]^T, \quad \mathbf{x'}=\mathbf{PX'}=\mathbf{P}[X,Y,Z]^T,$$

which can be written as

$$\mathbf{x}=\rho(X\mathbf{p}_1+Y\mathbf{p}_2+\mathbf{p}_4) \tag{48}$$

$$\mathbf{x'}=\mu(X\mathbf{p}_1+Y\mathbf{p}_2+Z\mathbf{p}_3+\mathbf{p}_4) \tag{49}$$

where ρ and are two unknown scalar factors and $\mathbf{p}_i$ is the ith column of $\mathbf{P}$. We set it to be $\mathbf{p}_4=\mathbf{l}/\|\mathbf{l}\|$ for linear independence, and $\mathbf{p}_3=\alpha\mathbf{v}_z$, where α is scale factor (A. Criminisi & I. Reid & A. Zisserman, 1999). Taking the scalar product of Equation (13) with $\overline{\mathbf{l}}$ yields $\rho=\overline{\mathbf{l}}\cdot\mathbf{x}$, and combining it with Eq. (14), we obtain

$$\alpha Z=-\frac{\|\mathbf{x}\times\mathbf{x'}\|}{(\overline{\mathbf{l}}\cdot\mathbf{x})\|\mathbf{v}_z\times\mathbf{x'}\|} \tag{50}$$

Consequently, if α is known, then a metric value for Z can be easily computed out and conversely, α can be obtained from a reference value Z_r. Note that the metric value Z_r defined by $\mathbf{x'}_r$ and $\mathbf{x'}$ also satisfy the Equation (15).

Thereby, the metric value Z for target can be obtained by the following equation in algebraic representation:

$$Z=\frac{\|\mathbf{x}\times\mathbf{x'}\|}{(\overline{\mathbf{l}}\cdot\mathbf{x})\|\mathbf{v}_z\times\mathbf{x'}\|}Z_r\frac{(\overline{\mathbf{l}}\cdot\mathbf{x}_r)\|\mathbf{v}_z\times\mathbf{x'}_r\|}{\|\mathbf{x}\times\mathbf{x'}_r\|} \tag{51}$$

where Z_r is the referred object's metric value.

Herein, the vertical vanishing point Z_r in Equation (51) is not required in our method which can be obtained from

$$\mathbf{l}=\omega\mathbf{v}_z \tag{52}$$

where $\mathbf{l}$ is the horizon line.

Consequently, the method based on single view metrology only requires two sets of parallel

Figure 10. Height measurement, measurement on vertical plane π_1 and arbitrary plane π_2, π_0 is the reference plane. The point x_r and x on the reference plane π_0 correspond to the point $\mathbf{x'}_r$ and $\mathbf{x'}$. $\mathbf{l}$ is the horizon line, the vertical vanishing point $\mathbf{v}_z$, $\mathbf{i}_r$, $\mathbf{x'}_r$ and $\mathbf{x'}$ can define a cross ratio: $\{\mathbf{v}_z, \mathbf{i}_r; \mathbf{x'}_r, \mathbf{x'}\}$. The same situation holds true for $\{\mathbf{v}_z, \mathbf{i}; \mathbf{x'}, \mathbf{x}\}$. The three planes intersect on line L, and L_1, L_2 are parallel lines on π_2

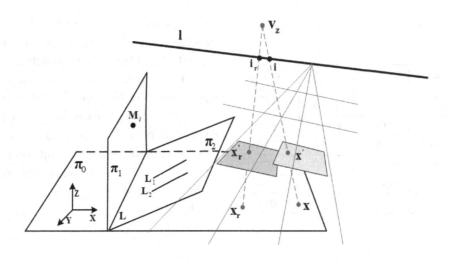

lines to obtain the vanishing line and different combinations of geometric constraints to achieve metric rectification.

Measurement on vertical and arbitrary plane. In this section, we show that scene measurements on vertical or arbitrary plane can also be retrieved from the camera projection matrix and some scene constraints.

Suppose π_0 is the reference plane, π_1 is the vertical plane perpendicular to π_0 and intersects π_0 at line **L** seeing Figure 2. We denote π_1 as $\Pi_1 = [a_1, b_1, c_1 d_1]^T$, and the point $\mathbf{M}_i$ is in π_1 if and only if $\pi_1^T \mathbf{M}_i = 0$. Let **l** is the corresponding image of **L**, and **H** is the planar homography, then $a_1 = (\mathbf{H^T l})_1$, $b_1 = (\mathbf{H^T l})_2$, $c_1 = 0$, π_1 (G. Wang & Z. Hu & F. Wu & H. T. Tsui, 2005). For a point $\mathbf{M}_i$ on the vertical plane π_1, its coordinates can be retrieved by the intersection of the back-projected ray of image point $\mathbf{m}_i$ and the plane π_1, i.e.

$$\begin{cases} s_i \mathbf{m}_i = \mathbf{P M}_i \\ \Pi_1^T \mathbf{M}_i = 0 \end{cases} \tag{53}$$

where s_i is a scalar factor.

For the measurement on an arbitrary plane, we assume that an arbitrary plane π_2 intersect the reference plane at line **L** then all the plane passing through **L** can form a pencil which may be expressed as $\Pi_2 = \Pi_1 + \lambda \Pi_0 = [(\mathbf{H^T l})_1, (\mathbf{H^T l})_2, \lambda, (\mathbf{H^T l})_3]^T$, where $\Pi_0 = [0,0,1,0]^T$ is the reference plane and $\Pi_1 = [(\mathbf{H^T l})_1, (\mathbf{H^T l})_2, 0, (\mathbf{H^T l})_3]^T$ is the vertical plane. Therefore, the arbitrary plane is defined up to a unknown parameter λ which can be determined from a pair of imaged parallel lines in the plane (G. Wang & Z. Hu & F. Wu & H. T. Tsui, 2005). Once the plane π_2 is determined, we can take measurements on the plane in a similar way like the vertical plane, using the following equations.

$$\begin{cases} s_j \mathbf{n}_j = \mathbf{P N}_i \\ \Pi_2^T \mathbf{N}_i = 0 \end{cases} \tag{54}$$

where s_j is a scalar factor, $\mathbf{N}_j$ is a 3D point in π_2 and $\mathbf{n}_j$ is its corresponding image point.

FUTURE RESEARCH DIRECTIONS

Image forgeries detection is a comprehensive problem involving computer vision, signal process, machine learning, pattern recognition, to name a few. Future research directions in the field can be concentrated on the two following aspects:

1. It is necessary to build a consistent model and select the authenticated features for an image to be authenticated, since different features induce diverse authenticating results. The consistent model can be built based on the quality of a natural image, consistency in lighting or imaging, color period and so on.
2. Object-oriented forensics technology. Images possess not only digital signals but also contexts on human vision and space architecture. Efforts should be made on the changes of an image's context such as appending, removing or modification.

The methods reviewed in this chapter use geometric information to detect tampered regions. In the field of image forgeries detection, traditional methods perform well in some particular circumstances. As a new direction, geometric methods give better detecting results when geometric constraints are available. However, like other algorithms, it also fails when geometric constraints are not at hand. In the future work, it is important to detect the fake regions using less geometric information and make the detecting process automatic.

CONCLUSION

This chapter presents a new framework for detecting image forgery based on geometrical cues such as cross ratio constraint and shadow geometry constraint. Algorithms have been introduced to obtain different kinds of measurements for fake region detection: 3D height measurement requiring a reference distance; measurements on a vertical or arbitrary plane with respect to the reference plane. The experimental results demonstrate that this method is efficient and can be applied to a variety of target scenes. As a pragmatic and flexible framework, it is also simple and easy to implement. However, it is evident that the problem of detecting digital image forgeries is complicated one with no universally applicable solution. Indeed, it may be easier to undergo forgery processing operations as the editing software improves. The rapid advancements in image editing software make the images undetectable using individual method, and what we need is a large set of methods based on different principles that can be applied to all tampered images. This accumulative evidence may provide a convincing proof that each individual method can not carry out.

REFERENCES

Bayram, S., Memon, N., Ramkumar, M., & Sankur, B. (2004). A classifier design for detecting image manipulations. In *Proc. IEEE Int. Conf. on Image Processing, Singapore, 4,* 2645-2648.

Bayram, S., Sencar, H. T., & Memon, N. (2005). Source camera identification based on CFA interpolation. *IEEE International Conference on Image Processing, Genoa, Italy, Sep* (Vol. 3, pp. 69-72).

Cao, X., & Foroosh, H. (2006). Camera Calibration using Symmetric Objects. *IEEE Transactions on Image Processing, 15*(11), 3614–3619. doi:10.1109/TIP.2006.881940

Chen, M., Fridrich, J., Goljan, M., & Lukas, J. (2008). Determining Image Origin and Integrity Using Sensor Noise. *IEEE Transactions on Information Forensics and Security, 3*(1), 74–90. doi:10.1109/TIFS.2007.916285

Chen, W., Shi, Y., & Su, W. (2007). Image splicing detection using 2D phase congruency and statistical moments of characteristic function. In *Proc. SPIE, Electronic Imaging, Security, Steganography, Watermarking of Multimedia Contents IX, San Jose, CA, J 29 January-1 February, 6505,* 65050R.1-65050R.8.

Cox, I. J., Miller, M. L., & Bloom, J. A. (2002). *Digital Watermarking*. Morgan Kaufmann Publishers.

Criminisi, A., Reid, I., & Zisserman, A. (1999). Single View Metrology. *International Conference on Computer Vision* (pp. 434-441).

Farid, H. (2008). *Digital ballistic from jpeg quantization: A follow study* (Technical Report TR2008-638). Department of Computer Science, Dartmouth College.

Farid, H. (2009). A Survey of Image Forgery Detection. *IEEE Signal Processing Magazine, 26*(2), 16–25. doi:10.1109/MSP.2008.931079

Farid, H. (2009). Seeing is not believing. *IEEE Spectrum, 46*(8), 44–48. doi:10.1109/MSPEC.2009.5186556

Farid, H., & Lyu, S. (2003). *Higher-order wavelet statistics and their application to digital forensics*. IEEE Workshop on Statistical Analysis in Computer Vision.

Fridrich, J., Soukal, D., & Lukas, J. (2003, August). *Detection of Copy-Move Forgery in Digital Images*. Pro. Digital Forensic Research Workshop, Cleveland, OH.

Gou, H., Swaminathan, A., & Wu, M. (2007). Noise features for image tampering detection and steganalysis. *IEEE International Conference on Image Processing, San Antonio, TX, 2007* (Vol. 3, pp. 97-100).

Hartley, R., & Zisserman, A. (2004). *Multiple View Geometry in Computer Vision*. Cambridge University Press.

Hsu, Y. F., & Chang, S. F. (2007). Image splicing detection using camera response function consistency and automatic segmentation. *IEEE International Conference on Multimedia and Expo.*

Johnson, M. K., & Farid, H. (2005). *Exposing digital forgeries by detecting inconsistencies in lighting.* New York, NY: ACM Multimedia and Security Workshop.

Johnson, M.K., & Farid, H. (2006). *Metric Measurements on a Plane from a Single Image* (Technical Report, TR2006-579).

Johnson, M. K., & Farid, H. (2007). Exposing Digital Forgeries in Complex Lighting Environments. *IEEE Transactions on Information Forensics and Security, 2,* 450–461. doi:10.1109/TIFS.2007.903848

Johnson, M. K., & Farid, H. (2007). Detecting Photographic Composites of People. *Proc. IWDW.*

Kersten, D., Mamassian, P., & Knill, D. C. (1997). Moving cast shadows induce apparent motion in depth. *Perception, 26,* 171–192. doi:10.1068/p260171

Liebowitz, D., & Zisserman, A. (1998). Metric Rectification for Perspective Images of Planes. *IEEE Computer Society Conference on Computer Vision and Pattern Recognition.*

Lin, Z., Wang, R., Tang, X., & Shum, H. Y. (2005). Detecting doctored images using camera response normality and consistency. *IEEE Computer Society Conference on Computer Vision and Pattern Recognition* (Vol. 1, pp. 1087- 1092).

Liu, H., Rao, J., & Yao, X. (2008). Feature based watermarking scheme for image authentication. In *Proceedings of the 2007 IEEE International Conference on Multimedia and Expo* (pp. 229-232).

Lukas, J., & Fridrich, J. (2003). *Estimation of primary quantization matrix in double compressed JPEG images.* Digital Forensic Research Workshop.

Lukas, J., Fridrich, J., & Goljan, M. (2005). Determining Digital Image Origin Using Sensor Imperfections. In *Proc. SPIE Electronic Imaging, Image and Video Communication and Processing, San Jose, California., 5685*(2), 249-260.

Lyu & Farid. (2005). How Realistic is Photorealistic? *IEEE Transactions on Signal Processing, 53*(2), 845–850. doi:10.1109/TSP.2004.839896

Mahdian, B., & Saic, S. (2007). Detection of copy-move forgery using a method based on blur moment invariants. *Forensic Science International, 171*(2), 180–189. doi:10.1016/j.forsciint.2006.11.002

Ng, T. T., & Chang, S. F. (2004). A model for image splicing. *IEEE International Conference on Image Processing* (pp. 1169-1172).

Ng, T. T., Chang, S. F., & Sun, Q. (2004). Blind detection of photomontage using higher order statistics. In *Proceedings of the 2004 International Symposium on Circuits and Systems, 5,* 688-691.

Pevny, T., & Fridrich, J. (2008). Detection of Double-Compression in JPEG Images for Applications in Steganography. *IEEE Transactions on Information Forensics and Security, 3*(2), 247–258. doi:10.1109/TIFS.2008.922456

Popescu, A., & Farid, H. (2004). *Exposing digital forgeries by detecting duplicated image regions (Technical Report TR2004-515).* Department of Computer Science, Dartmouth College.

Popescu, A. C., & Farid, H. (2005). Exposing digital forgeries by detecting traces of re-sampling. *IEEE Signal Processing Magazine, 53*(2), 758–767.

Popescu, A. C., & Farid, H. (2005). Exposing digital forgeries in color filter array interpolated images. *IEEE Signal Processing Magazine, 53*(10), 3948–3959.

Springer, C. E. (1964). *Geometry and Analysis of Projective Spaces.* Freeman.

Swaminathan, A., Wu, M., & Ray Liu, K. J. (2008). Digital Image Forensics via Intrinsic Fingerprints. *IEEE Transactions on Information Forensics and Security, 3*(1), 101–117. doi:10.1109/TIFS.2007.916010

Wang, G., Hu, Z., Wu, F., & Tsui, H. T. (2005). Single view metrology from scene constraints. *Image and Vision Computing, 23*(9), 831–840. doi:10.1016/j.imavis.2005.04.002

Wang, W., & Farid, H. (2008). *Detecting Re-Projected Video*. International Workshop on Information Hiding.

Zhang, W., Cao, X., Feng, Z., Zhang, J., & Wang, P. (2009). Detecting Photographic Composites Using Two-View Geometrical. *IEEE International Conference on Multimedia and Expo.*

Zhang, W., Cao, X., Zhang, J., Zhu, J., & Wang, P. (2009). Detecting Photographic Composites Using Shadows. *IEEE International Conference on Multimedia and Expo.*

ADDITIONAL READING

Bravo, M. J., & Farid, H. (2008). A Scale Invariant Measure of Image Clutter. *Journal of Vision (Charlottesville, Va.), 8*(1), 1–9. doi:10.1167/8.1.23

Bravo, M. J., & Farid, H. (2009). The Specificity of the Search Template. *Journal of Vision (Charlottesville, Va.), 9*(1), 1–9. doi:10.1167/9.1.34

Bravo, M. J., & Farid, H. (2009). *Training Determines the Target Representation for Search. Vision Sciences*. Naples, FL: VSS.

Cao, X., & Foroosh, H. (2006). Camera Calibration using Symmetric Objects. *IEEE Transactions on Image Processing, 15*(11), 3614–3619. doi:10.1109/TIP.2006.881940

Cao, X., & Foroosh, H. (2007). Camera Calibration and Light Source Orientation from Solar Shadows. *Computer Vision and Image Understanding, 105,* 60–72. doi:10.1016/j.cviu.2006.08.003

Cao, X., Shen, Y., Shah, M., & Foroosh, H. (2005). Single View Compositing with Shadows. *The Visual Computer, 21*(8-10), 639-648. Also in Pacific Graphics 2005.

Cao, X., Wu, L., Xiao, J., Foroosh, H., Zhu, J., & Li, X. (2009). (in press). Video Synchronization and Its Application on Object Transfer. *Image and Vision Computing.*

Farid, H. (2008). *Digital Image Forensics*. Washington, DC: American Academy of Forensic Sciences.

Farid, H. (2008). *Photography Changes What We Are Willing To Believe*. Smithsonian Photography Initiative.

Farid, H. (2009). Digital Doctoring: can we trust photographs? In *Deception: Methods, Motives, Contexts and Consequences.*

Farid, H. (2009). Digital Imaging. In *Encyclopedia of Perception.*

Farid, H. (2009). Exposing Digital Forgeries from JPEG Ghosts. *IEEE Transactions on Information Forensics and Security, 4*(1), 154–160. doi:10.1109/TIFS.2008.2012215

Farid, H. (2009). Photo Fakery and Forensics. *Advances in Computers, 77.*

Farid, H. (2009). Seeing Is Not Believing. *IEEE Spectrum, 46*(8), 44–48. doi:10.1109/MSPEC.2009.5186556

Farid, H., & Woodwoard, J. B. (2007). *Video Stabilization and Enhancement (Technical Report, TR2007-605)*. Dartmouth College, Computer Science.

Johnson, M. K. (2007). *Lighting and Optical Tools for Image Forensics*. Ph.D. Dissertation, Department of Computer Science, Dartmouth College.

McPeek, M. A., Shen, L., & Farid, H. (2009). The Correlated Evolution of 3-Dimensional Reproductive Structure Between Male and Female Damselflies. *Evolution; International Journal of Organic Evolution, 63*(1), 73–83. doi:10.1111/j.1558-5646.2008.00527.x

Shen, L., Farid, H., & McPeek, M. A. (2009). Modeling 3-Dimensional Morphological Structures using Spherical Harmonics. *Evolution; International Journal of Organic Evolution, 63*(4), 1003–1016. doi:10.1111/j.1558-5646.2008.00557.x

Wang, W. (2009). *Digital Video Forensics*. Ph.D. Dissertation, Department of Computer Science. Dartmouth College.

Wang, W., & Farid, H. (2009). *Exposing Digital Forgeries in Video by Detecting Double Quantization*. Princeton, NJ: ACM Multimedia and Security Workshop.

KEY TERMS AND DEFINITIONS

Digital Forensics: Authenticate a digital image's integrity.

Metric Measurement: Get the measurements in a metric rectified image.

Metric Rectification: Remove the projective distortion from a perspective image.

Planar Homology: A plane projective transformation is a planar homology if it has a line of fixed points together with a fixed point.

Region of Interest: The region in an image whose integrity is suspicious.

Shadow Geometry: The geometric relationship between the shadow point, the light source and the shadow casting object.

Single View Metrology: Get measurements in a single image.

Chapter 13
Salient Region Detection for Biometric Watermarking

Bin Ma
Beihang University, China

Chun-lei Li
Beihang University, China & Zhongyuan Institute of Technology, China

Yun-hong Wang
Beihang University, China

Xiao Bai
Beihang University, China

ABSTRACT

Visual saliency, namely the perceptual significance to human vision system (HVS), is a quality that differentiates an object from its neighbors. Detection of salient regions which contain prominent features and represent main contents of the visual scene, has obtained wide utilization among computer vision based applications, such as object tracking and classification, region-of-interest (ROI) based image compression, etc. Specially, as for biometric authentication system, whose objective is to distinguish the identification of people through biometric data (e.g. fingerprint, iris, face etc.), the most important metric is distinguishability. Consequently, in biometric watermarking fields, there has been a great need of good metrics for feature prominency. In this chapter, we present two salient-region-detection based biometric watermarking scenarios, in which robust annotation and fragile authentication watermark are respectively applied to biometric systems. Saliency map plays an important role of perceptual mask that adaptively select watermarking strength and position, therefore controls the distortion introduced by watermark and preserves the identification accuracy of biometric images.

1. INTRODUCTION

Nowadays, while the rapid development of multimedia and network technology greatly facilitates the creation and distribution of digital media contents, it also provides convenience for unauthorized manipulation and duplication of digital work, thus poses new challenges to multimedia security.

DOI: 10.4018/978-1-60960-024-2.ch013

Cryptography is a traditional tool to address security issues. It encrypts original content into incomprehensible cipher text, and only allows legitimate customers to decrypt them with provided secret keys. However, such strategy has two critical shortcomings. Firstly, the encrypted messages are conspicuous; the exposed cipher text could be examined by attackers and therefore poses a risk to the secret communication. Secondly, once intercepted and decrypted, the content will no longer have any protection.

Digital watermarking could be regarded as a complement to cryptography. It is one technique that embeds secret message named watermark into digital media by making non-perceptible slight change to the original host content. It is generally accepted that, digital watermarking was firstly described in (Van, 1994), and has received constant attention ever since (Cox, 1997; Bender, 1996; Miller, 2001). Embedded in digital media as secret information, the watermark can provide further protection even after decryption, and consequently be regarded as the last defensive line of multimedia security.

Existing digital watermarking methods can be classified into two categories: robust watermarking and fragile watermarking. The former can be applied to protect the copyright of digital multimedia (Pereira, 2000; Mohammad, 2008; Bi, 2007; Wang, 2004; Prayoth, 2005). And the latter is used to identify the integrity of media contents. It can be further separated into two classes: fragile watermarking and semi-fragile watermarking (Maeno, 2006; Yuan, 2006; Zhang, 2007; Li, 2007; Yu, 2006; Chang, 2006; Zhu, 2007; Thiemert, 2006). Fragile watermarking can detect any changes on the contents, and semi-fragile watermarking is used as detecting malicious manipulations performing on the contents while robust to natural operation, such as filtering, cropping, rotation and so on.

Digital watermarking is different from other techniques in some aspects. Firstly, watermarks are inseparable from the host contents in which they are embedded. Any attacks trying to remove the watermark, will destroy the contents as well. Secondly, watermarks are invisible, thus will not detract from the aesthetic of digital media. Furthermore, when transmitted over the Internet, such transparency makes the watermark inconspicuous to malicious attackers. In the end, watermarks can undergo the same transformations as the contents. The performance of watermarking technology can be evaluated on three features: robustness, fidelity, and embedding capacity. As a novel technology, digital watermarking has been applied in many fields, such as broadcast monitoring, owner identification, proof of ownership, transaction tracking, content authentication, copy control, device control and legacy enhancements (Cox, 2007).

Salient region detection plays an important role in many computer vision tasks, especially matching problems, such as tracking, object classification, and so forth. The detection result is a saliency map which represents the importance of the object in the scene that is projected into the visual field at that position. In a similar manner, saliency maps are useful in computer vision as they provide an efficient means of processing complex scenes by locating likely areas of interest for directing analysis (Rosin, 2009). Thus it has wide applicability: object extraction, content aware resizing, region-of-interest based compression, and so forth. Moreover, the characteristic of salient region can be applied into watermarking system. Firstly, the features of salient region have good invariance to geometric and some signal processing operations, they are already used by robust watermarking schemes to resist RST (rotation, scaling, and translation), compression (Bas, 2002; Tang, 2003; Zheng, 2009). Secondly, the salient regions can be used in determination of suitable locations for embedding watermarks (Birgit, 2005; Dom, 2005). The salient region of image contains more information. We should avoid these regions while embedding the watermark. Thus, the modification of image information can be reduced.

For the first scenario, many schemes have been proposed. In (Tang, 2003), the authors extracted salient region of the cover image and used these region for watermark embedding and extraction. Meanwhile, image normalization was applied in the scheme to make those regions invariant and scaling. It was stated that the extracted salient region can survive a variety of attacks. In (Zheng, 2009), the author extracted feature using Gaussian scale model, and generated salient region centered at the feature point. Each salient region is first rotated to align with the orientation of the feature point. Then the scaling invariant normalization is applied to transform the disk region to its compact size. (Bas, 2002) extracts feature points using Harris corner detector, and subsequently, apply Delaunay tessellation on the feature points set to divide image into triangle mesh, in which watermark embedding and extraction is implemented. (Fan, 2008) proposed a ROI-based watermarking scheme for JPEG2000. The watermark is embedded into the host image based on the characteristic of the ROI to protect rights to the images. The proposed watermark technique successfully survives JPEG2000 compression, progressive transmission, and principal attacks.

(Birgit, 2005) proposed a block-based medical image watermarking using a perceptual similarity metric. The medical image is partitioned different regions according to some features. Each region is then watermarked with a particular watermark method. ROB can be watermarked using more robust techniques and ROI can be watermarked using lighter or no embedding. (Dom, 2005) proposed a novel multiple watermarking techniques which can be used to verify the integrity of the ROI prior to diagnosis. This has the benefit of assuring that incidental degradation has not affected any of the crucial regions. This is made possible with extraction of DCT signature coefficients from the ROI and embedding multiply in the region of backgrounds (ROB).

Biometric authentication is defined as the technologies for automatically identifying individuals based on their distinct physical or behavioral characteristics, such as fingerprint, face, voice, iris, etc. Compared with traditional person identification technique such as passwords and PIN codes, biometrics is being increasingly used for accurate identification in diverse business (e.g., security, e-commerce, remote authentication) since they cannot be misplaced or forgotten. However, with the widely used of biometric verification systems, it creates a demand for ensuring the security and integrity of biometrics data. Cryptography, steganography and watermarking can be used to protect the security and secrecy of biometric data (Anil, 1999; Ratha, 2000; Yeung, 2000; Khan, 2007). And as another alternative or complement to cryptography, watermarking can be used as protecting the security and secrecy of biometrics data.

Nevertheless, distortion introduced by watermarking will decrease the recognition accuracy of biometric identification system. In order to control such effect, embedding position and strength should be chosen adaptively according to feature analysis. Salient region detection just provides an effective strategy to address such problem.

In this chapter, we present two biometric watermarking scenarios using salient region detection. Firstly, to protect the copyright of the database of biometric templates, we add notation for biometric images by means of robust watermark technique; secondly, fragile authentication watermark is embedded into biometric images to verify the integrity of biometric data. For the two scenarios, the watermarks are adaptively embedded into biometric image based on saliency map.

2. BACKGROUND

The application of salient region in digital watermarking has been a research focus for a few years. Many methods have been proposed as depicted in previous section. Meanwhile, as biometric data provide uniqueness, they do not provide secrecy themselves. The wide utilization of biometric verification system has created a great demand for ensuring the security and integrity of biometric data.

Traditional digital watermarking methods that developed for natural images, take no consideration of the prominent feature in biometric images. However, by applying high level vision characteristics, saliency for instance, the goal of content adaptive could be achieved in watermarking progress. Regarding salient region as ROI, and the rest as ROB, (Ahmed, 2008) proposed a phase-encoding-based digital watermarking for fingerprint template protection and verification. To minimize the degradation to important minutiae features of fingerprint, the author segmented the template into ROI and ROB, subsequently embedded the watermark adaptively into these two regions using an adaptive phase quantization method. However, the author only gave the performance results for the template authentication test, not gave the effect on the recognition rate after embedding signatures. (Zebbiche, 2008) gave a novel scheme to watermark biometric image. It exploits the fact that biometric images, normally, have one region of interest (salient region), which represents the relevant part of information processable by most of the biometric-based authentication systems. Their proposed scheme only embeds the watermark into ROI, thus, preserve the hidden data from the segmentation process that removes the useless background and keeps the region of interest unaltered.

It should be noted that, the idea of salient region based watermarking is not only applicable to digital images. Furthermore, frequency peak based audio watermarking; key frame based video watermarking can also be regarded as extended applications of 'saliency'.

3. SALIENT REGION BASED WATERMARKING METHODS

Regarding salient regions as one kind of ROI, biometric images can be simply split into region of salient (ROI) and region of background (ROB) based on the result of salient region detection. As discussed earlier, we state that ROI of biometric image is more suitable for watermarking, for the following aspects:

- Permanent features are not sensitive to noise and will be little affected by watermarking;
- Salient region represents the main content of an image, whose copyright and integrity deserve close attention;
- For robust watermarking, the watermark should be embedded in perceptually significant components of original host media to achieve good robustness;
- For fragile watermarking, embedded within critical regions, the watermark can identify the manipulation on important components.

In this section, we present two salient-region-based biometric watermarking systems. Section 3.1 reviews the algorithm of salient region detection; Section 3.2 gives the first scenario: add annotation for face database using adaptive watermarking based on saliency map; Section 3.3 introduces a salient-region-segmentation based fragile watermarking scheme for biometric template protection.

3.1 Salient Region Detection

The computation model of human visual attention system is an important research issue in computer vision. Existing methods in such area can be categorized into two classes: task dependent top-down schemes based on prior knowledge of the scene, and task independent bottom-up schemes based on low-level visual features. In most cases, people do not have much pre-knowledge about the visual scene, besides any fixed hypothesis would decrease the applicability. Consequently, more research efforts are put on the bottom-up attention models, which encode saliency by generating a matrix, named 'saliency map', from basic sets of low-level visual features.

It is generally accepted that, the original idea of 'saliency map' comes from a 'master map of locations' in (Treisman, 1980). Such modal describes a general framework for visual attention simulation, which first extracts low-level features from the visual scene, and then combines them into a topographical representation of saliency. In later work (Koch, 1985), the combined topographical representation of saliency is firstly termed as 'saliency map', and is used to describe shifts of visual attention by selecting the peak values in such map. The work in (Itti, 1998) can be regard as an implementation of Koch's biological model. Distinct color, intensity and orientation features of the input image are extracted by a difference of Gaussian (DoG) filter, and subsequently merged into a unit saliency map.

Many state-of-the-art works have been performed following such research line. (Hou, 2007) hold the opinion that saliency detector should be implemented with least reference of statistical features. They extract the spectral residual of an image by subtracting the log spectrum of the original image and its blurred version. The final saliency map is obtained by transforming the spectral residual into spatial domain. It is claimed that, the information jumps out of the smooth log spectrum curve really deserves human attention.

In (Harel, 2007), firstly, initial feature maps on various feature channels are formed similar with Itti's method by a DoG filter. Afterward, they define Markov chains over these individual maps, and regard the equilibrium distribution over map locations as activation values. And finally, combine distinct activation maps into a single

saliency map. In (Achanta, 2009), a frequency-domain analysis of saliency is performed. They imply DoG filter bank in Lab color space to extract center-surround difference of color and luminance features, and use the Euclidean distance of pixel luminance as the measure of dissimilarity to generate a full resolution saliency map.

Detection results of the methods mentioned above are shown in Figure 1. Furthermore, since (Itti, 1998) is the most classic work that lays the foundation of such area, and is adopted in our watermarking applications, here we briefly review some related details. In such scheme, firstly, the distinct color, intensity and orientation features of the input image are obtained by linear filtering. Then, each feature channel is sub-sampled into a Gaussian pyramid, and "feature maps" are computed by a serial of center-surround differences between scales. Take intensity channel for instance, a Gaussian pyramid $I(\sigma)$, $\sigma \in [0,1,\ldots,8]$ is obtained by progressive low-pass filtering and down-sampling with a factor of 2 in each dimension. The intensity feature maps will be:

$$F_I(c,\ s) = N(|I(c) \ominus I(s)|)$$

where $c \in \{2, 3, 4\}$ denotes a center fine scale, and $s = c + \delta$, $\delta \in \{3, 4\}$, and "$\ominus$" here indicates a across-scale subtraction, which first interpolates scale s to c, and subsequently compute pixel-by-pixel difference. $N(\cdot)$ is an predefined normalization operator. And finally, feature maps are combined into "conspicuity map" through across-scale addition:

$$\bar{I} = \overset{4}{\underset{c=2}{\oplus}} \ \overset{c+4}{\underset{s=c+3}{\oplus}} \ F_I(c,s)$$

Trough a similar progress, conspicuity maps of color $\bar{C}$ and orientation $\bar{O}$ are obtained (see Itti, 1998). And finally these three conspicuity maps are normalized and averaged to form the output saliency map S:

Figure 1. The compassion of saliency maps on natural images and face images. From 1ˢᵗ to 5ᵗʰ columns are original images, saliency maps of (Itti, 1998), spectral residual maps (Hou, 2007), graphic-based maps (Harel, 2007), and frequency-tuned maps (Achanta, 2009). Original face images are selected from FERET database (Phillips, 2000)

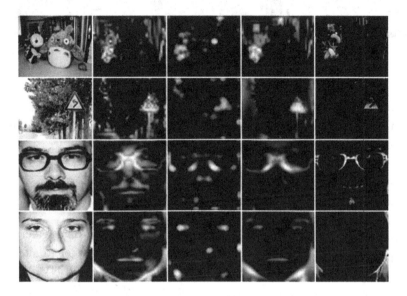

$$S = \frac{1}{3}\left(N(\bar{I}) + N(\bar{C}) + N(\bar{O}) \right)$$

3.2 Face Database Annotation

Robust watermarking is designed to survive general processing of digital media, and thus can be accurately extracted even after moderate distortion. On account of this good property, robust watermarking has been involved in image annotation application.

In this section, we present a biometric image database annotation scenario. A 32-bytes metadata containing associate information of one individual such as name, gender, age etc., is embedded into each person's face image by robust watermarking method.

Since the face images are used for biometric identification, visual quality along with the discriminating feature should be taken into consideration during watermark embedding. Here, saliency map is involved to generate a perceptual

mask named "watermarking map" which adaptively select watermarking position and strength in special domain, and thus limits the distortion made by watermark embedding.

Section 3.2.1 describes the generation of saliency based perceptual mask. Section 3.2.2 and Section 3.2.3 present the watermarking embedding and extraction method based on the proposed visual model. Section 3.2.4 demonstrates and discusses the experimental results.

3.2.1 Perceptual Mask Generation

A proper visual model is important to control the distortion introduced by embedded watermark. To achieve the high fidelity of the embedded image, we introduce Itti's saliency map to form a perception mask that aims at adaptively quantifying the local mean value of block wise luminance by the method of (He, 2009).

Since the size of Itti's saliency map is only 1/256 of the original image, we firstly up-sample the saliency map by bilinear interpolation to obtain

Figure 2. Perceptual mask and watermarking effect

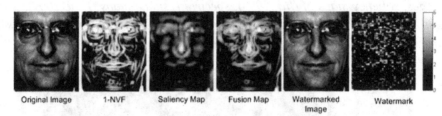

Original Image   1-NVF   Saliency Map   Fusion Map   Watermarked Image   Watermark

a one-to-one mapping between saliency values and image pixels. Each element of the saliency map is a float number ranges from 0 to 1. The higher the value, the more salient the corresponding pixel, and vice versa. Following the principles previously discussed, we should distribute more watermark energy to pixels with high saliency value.

However, it is worth noticing that, although saliency indicates prominence of features, it does not necessarily imply tolerance to noise. Actually, a considerable number of salient regions have smooth color and luminance, which is perceptually sensitive to noise.

In order to control embedding strength in salient regions, we take noise visibility function (NVF) into account. The most well known form of NVF is: (Voloshynvskiy, 2000)

$$NVF(i, j) = \frac{1}{1 + \theta \cdot \sigma_x^2(i, j)}, \left(\theta = \frac{D}{\sigma_{x\,max}^2}\right)$$

where $\sigma_x^2(i, j)$ denotes the local variance of a window centered at pixel(i, j), $\sigma_{x\,max}^2$ is the maximum local variance of the given image, D is an empirical scaling constant ranges from 50 to 100, which is set to 75 in our method.

Through the definition we may find that, the value of $NVF \in [0, 1]$. Small value indicates busy area with high variance, while high value denotes smooth area. Consequently, $1 - NVF$ will be an efficient descriptor of noise tolerance ability (see Figure 2).

Finally, we fuse the saliency map (SM) and NVF with a Gaussian mixing function as follow:

$$WM = \exp\left\{-\frac{(SM - 1)^2 + NVF^2}{2s^2}\right\}$$

where WM is the final watermarking map, and $s \in [0,1]$ is a parameter to alter the shape of the function. As SM and NVF are both within the range of [0,1], so WM is naturally normalized between 0 and 1, and only has high value at the pixels with high SM and low NVF, which indicates salient and noise tolerant regions.

3.2.2 Watermark Embedding

Once the perceptual watermarking map is generated, we performed HVS based watermark embedding in space domain. The result needs to be robust to JPEG compression and keep critical information for biometric identification. Considering the robustness..

The object of the data embedding is to add 32 bytes (256 bits) annotation into an image so that the detection is as robust as possible to JPEG compression and cropping. We apply the developed saliency map based perceptual model and build the system in one step.

A general problem of space domain watermarking is cropping. If one watermark bit is embedded within a space neighborhood, cropping of that area will result in a complete loss of the information bit. A typical solution to such problem is randomly select embedding position, distribute a watermark bit on the whole image.

So firstly, we separate the original image I into 4×4 pixels non-overlapped blocks, and use a secret key to mass them up, just like a jigsaw puzzle. Then, encrypted image I_r is separated into 256 distinctive blocks, each block is assigned to a single watermark bit. Subsequently, we perform the map based watermark embedding by means of first-order statics quantization scheme (He, 2009).

Let Λ_i indicate the corresponding block of a watermark bit b_i. The mean value of μ_i is quantized to an odd number of Q if $b_i =1$, or to an even number of Q if $b_i =$ Equation Section (Next) 0, where Q is the quantization step parameter. Obviously, the robustness of watermark increases with Q, while fidelity is just on the contrary.

$$\mu_i' = \left\lfloor \frac{\mu_i + Qb_i}{2Q} + 0.5 \right\rfloor \cdot 2Q - Qb_i$$

μ_i' is the mean value of Λ_i after watermark embedding. So the total change of Λ_i will be:

$$\Delta_i = \Delta\mu_i \cdot N$$

where N is the number of pixels in Λ_i. Finally the watermarking map WM is used to assign these modification to each pixel $P(j)$, $j \in \Lambda_i$:

$$\Delta_{P(j)} = \Delta_i \cdot \frac{WM(j)}{\sum\limits_{j \in \Lambda_i} WM(j)}$$

The whole progress of watermark embedding is summarized in Figure 3.

3.2.3 Watermark Extraction

In the extraction process, the detector firstly uses the secret key to identify the blocks corresponding to each watermark bit. Then, the mean value of each block, $\widehat{\mu_i'}$ is calculated. Since both normal image processing and malicious attacks are likely to occur between embedding and extraction, $\widehat{\mu_i'}$ is used as the estimated value of μ_i'.

The quantization step parameter Q is assumed to be shared by watermark embedder and extractor, so the watermark bit $\hat{b}_i$ can be extracted by quantizing $\widehat{\mu_i'}$ with Q, and examining the parity of the result as follows:

$$\hat{b}_i = \mathrm{mod}\left\{ \left\lfloor \left| \frac{\widehat{\mu_i'}}{Q} \right| + 0.5 \right\rfloor, 2 \right\}$$

3.2.4 Experimental Results

In the practical application, images are usually compressed by JPEG algorithm in order to save

Figure 3. Watermark embedding progress

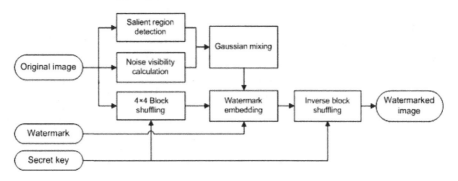

storage space. So our proposed scheme should be robust to JPEG compression. We evaluate the performance of our scheme on FERET face image database, which contains about 1200 face images, and each of them is normalized to the size of 152×128. We use bit accuracy rate (BAR) to evaluate the performance of watermark extraction after JPEG compression. The experiment result is shown in Figure 4.

From the above figure, we can conclude that WM based method have better performance over PM based method, where PM indicates a naive watermarking map named plain map, which has the same value at all positions, and WM is the proposed map, which considers both saliency and noise visibility.

Furthermore, in order to evaluate the "recognizing quality", we implement several experiments on a 600-individuals subset of FERET face database, which are divided into two sets. One is used as reference database; the other is used as query image set.

The annotation should be embedded into reference database. We watermark reference database using different watermarking schemes, and two watermarked database PM watermarked reference set and WM watermarked reference set are generated.

We compare the recognition performance of watermarked and non-watermarked image database with three typical methods in face authentication system: PCA, LBA and Gabor feature, and utilize recognition rate (RR) as evaluation metric. The results are show in Table 1.

Since PCA and Gabor methods are focusing on the global characteristics of biometric images, highly texture-like local features, will be filtered out during dimensionality reduction. So the watermark, a low-amplitude pseudorandom noise in nature, has little influence on the recognition performance.

On the contrary, LBP features only describe local texture pattern which is robust to illumination condition while sensitive to expression change. Since we introduce saliency map to avoid changing salient features, and adopt NVF to select abundant textures whose LBP feature can hardly be altered by noise, the WM-based method performs better that PM-based method. However, one surprising phenomenon is that both of the two watermarking methods increase the recognition performance of LBP based system. A speculative explanation is that, the change of expression change in query set can be regard as one kind of noise to LBP recognition algorithm. If we add moderate noise to the original reference set, to some extent, it will result in decreasing of the difference between reference and query set. Although the increase of recognition rate is not inevitable, the recognition performance that ROI >UNIFORM still verifies our previous statement.

Figure 4. Detection accuracy under different JPEG quality

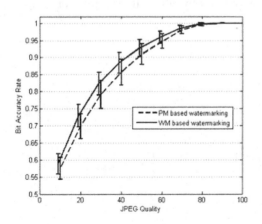

Table 1. Recognition performance using different reference sets

	ORIGINAL	PM(UNIFORM)	wm(ROI)
PCA	71.0%	70.7%	70.8%
LBP	81.7%	85. 5%	86.4%
Gabor	80.4%	80.2%	80.2%

3.3 Salient Region Based Authentication Watermarking

Authentication watermarking can be used as verifying the integrity of the contents and tamper-proof by detecting malicious manipulations without access to the original digital content. In this section, a novel scheme for protecting biometric image based on authentication watermarking is proposed. Firstly, the authentication watermark bits are generated from biometric images using MD5, and embedded into themselves, which can be used as verifying the integrity of biometric image. Secondly, the biometric features of these biometric images are redundancy embedded into them. When receiving the biometric images, the biometric authentication systems verifies the integrity of these images, if the watermarked biometric images suffer from modification, we can also recover the biometric feature using the hidden information. The novel scheme improves the security of the biometrics-based authentication systems, but it brings the possible quality degradation of the biometric images due to watermarking. In order to preserve the recognition quality, the watermarks are adaptively embedded the images based on salient region detection.

We segment the biometric image into region of salient (ROI) and region of background (ROB) based on salient region detection. While salient region (ROI) contains abundant information and is less sensitive to watermark, region of background (ROB) is susceptible to the effect of watermarks. The authentication watermark is spread over the biometric image for protecting the whole image. When embedding the biometric features, these features are embedded into ROI for preserving the "recognizing quality" of the biometric images. The watermark algorithm can be described as following.

3.3.1 Salient Region Map (SRM) Generation

In order to get the same SRM for the original image and the watermarked image, the salient region is generated for the contents (4MSBs) of the image. Firstly, we set the 4LSBs of the original image to zeros, and the salient region of the modified image is extracted according to the method described in Section 3.1. Figure 5 shows the salient-region of a face image.

At the same time, a salient region map $M_r=\{m_j|j=1,2,\cdots,N_p\}$ which is used as depicting whether a pixel is in salient region. If $m_j=1$, the pixel is in salient region; otherwise, this pixel is not in salient region.

Then the face image X can be split into the image block X_i with size 4×4. And the blocks are numbered from top-to-bottom and left-to-right. For an image block X_t, the number of pixels which located in salient region can be calculated according to the following equation:

$$N_{SR} = \sum_{j=1}^{m_b \times n_b} p_j$$

The number N_{SR} is above $(m_b \times n_b)/2$, which represent the block is in the region of salient (ROS), where $m_b \times n_b$ is the number of pixels in an image block. In the end, a salient map for image block $Mb_r=\{mb_j|j=1,2,\cdots nN_b\}$ is generated. If $mb_j=1$, the block is in salient region; otherwise, this block is not in salient region.

Figure 5. Salient region of a face image from FERET database

Original Image   GBVS Map   Salient Region (60%)

3.3.2 Watermark Algorithm

1. Watermark Generation

In order to detect tamper in an image and recover the features of the image, two kinds of watermark should embed into the original image. One is used as authentication watermark to detect and locate tamper in an image; the other is used as information watermark to recover the feature of the image. The cryptographic hash function MD5 is used to generate the hash code of block X_i.

$$H(m, n, \widetilde{X}_i) = (c_1, c_2, \cdots, c_h)$$

We take the first N_{bp} bits form C_i in the case where $h > N_{bp}$. The hash code C_i is used as authentication watermark to verify the integrity of the image.

As a kind of biometrics, Eigen-face coefficients can re-construct face image, it is used as information hidden. If the original image suffers from malicious tamper, the biometric feature hidden can be extracted, which can be used for verification system. The reconstructed face using the recovered coefficient will be used as a second source of authenticity, either automatically or by a human in a supervised biometric application (Jain, 2003). An Eigen-face coefficient B_m (m=1,2,… ,T) can be converted to a binary stream using 4 bytes per coefficient, corresponding 32 bits, where T is the number of the coefficient of a biometric image. For an image block X_i, an Eigen-face coefficient can be embedded into it according to two selected bit-planes. We extent the Eigen-face coefficients periodically to a number stream with size $Q = \left\lfloor \widetilde{N}_b / T \right\rfloor \times T$, where $\widetilde{N}_b$ is the number of blocks located in the ROI. Then the block information watermark B_l(l=1,2,…,Q) is obtained. For any B_l, it is converted to a binary stream $b_{l'}(l' = 1, 2, …, 32)$, and redundancy embedded into the ROI of the original image. The embedded Eigen-face coefficient of a face image has $\left\lfloor \widetilde{N}_b / T \right\rfloor$ copies. Therefore, if one or more copies are tempered, we have any chance to recover the feature of a face image from the other copies.

2. Block Watermark Embedding

Firstly, the authentication watermarking scheme proposed by (He, 2008) is adopted to verify the integrity of the biometric image. In order to recover the biometric feature, it is redundancy embedded into the image. The embedding process can be described as the follows.

Step 1. Compute the salient map MB_r for image $\widehat{X}$ which 4LSBs is set to zeros as described in section 3.3.1.

Step 2. The random matrix M of size $N_p \times r$ is generated based on the secret key k_1, where r = 3, N_p is the number of pixels in the image. Each element in M is an integer in interval [1, 4], and the elements among the same column are not equal; Partition the random matrix M into non-overlapping blocks M_i of the size $N_{bp} \times r$.

Step 3. Compute hash-code C_i of block X_i according to MD5 hashes function.

Step 4. In order to resist vector quantization (VQ) codebook attack and collage attack, our method is block-wise dependency by embedding the hash-code of an image block into another block image.

Step 4.1. The authentication watermark embedded position sequence $f^1 = (I_1^1, I_2^1, \cdots, I_{N_b}^1)$ is generated using k_2.

Step 4.2. Embed the authentication watermark C_i (He, 2008), and get $\widetilde{X}_i$ ($i' = 1, 2, \cdots, N_b$), where i' is decided by the position sequence f^1. For each pixel x_j^i in the image block $x_{i'}$, the position at which C_j^i is hidden is decided by the value of the corresponding $M[k][1]$ (k=1,2,$\cdots$,N_{bp}). This process can be described using the following equation.

$$\tilde{x}^{i}_{j} = \left\lfloor x^{i}_{j} / t_{1} \right\rfloor \times 2t_{1} + C^{i}_{j} \times t_{1} + \mathrm{mod}(x^{i}_{j}, t_{1})$$

where $t_1 = 2^{M[j][1]}$, and symbol $\lfloor x \rfloor$ represents the largest integer less than or equal to x.

Step 5. Generate the Eigen-face coefficient embedding position sequence $f^2 = (I^2_1, I^2_2, \cdots, I^2_{N_{ROI}})$ is generated using k_3, where N_{ROI} is the number of non-zero element in MB_r. Embed the Eigen-face coefficients into $\widetilde{X}$ which is obtained after embedding the authentication watermark, and the final watermarked face image Y. An Eigen-face coefficient is embedded into an image block selected by the position sequence f^2, and the block locate the region of background (ROI). For each pixel $\tilde{x}^{i}_{j}$ in the block $\widetilde{X}_i$, two bits of biometric feature are embedded into the pixel, the position at which b_l, b_{l+1} are hidden is decided by the value of the corresponding $M[k][2], M[k][3] (k=1,2,\cdots,N_{bp})$.

$$\tilde{x}^{*i}_{j} = \left\lfloor \tilde{x}^{i}_{j} / t_{2} \right\rfloor \times 2t_{2} + b_{l} \times t_{2} + \mathrm{mod}(\tilde{x}^{i}_{j}, t_{2})$$

$$Y^{i}_{j} = \left\lfloor \tilde{x}^{*i}_{j} / t_{3} \right\rfloor \times 2t_{3} + b_{l+1} \times t_{3} + \mathrm{mod}(\tilde{x}^{*i}_{j}, t_{3})$$

where $t_2 = 2^{M[j][2]}$,, $t_3 = 2^{M[j][3]}$,.

3.3.3 Tamper Detection and Recovery of Biometric Feature

The authentication watermark is embedded into the other image block depend on a secret key, which can resist the VQ attack and collage attack. And the process of image verification will give us the result of tamper. When the biometric image keeps unaltered, it can be directly used for the biometric authentication system. And if the biometric image suffers malicious tamper, we can recover the biometric feature using the information hidden in the original biometric image. And the recovery biometric image feature can also used for identification or authentication. Firstly, we give the process of tamper detection and localization. It is briefly described as follows.

Step 1. Split the test image Y^* into image block. For each image block Y_i, find the embedding position of its corresponding authentication watermark C_i and extract it using k_1 and k_2

Step 2. Followed by the step4 in watermark embedding algorithm, the value of C'_i is obtained using MD5 Hash function for the image block Y_i.

Step 3. Get the block mark $D\{d_i|i=1.2.\cdots,N_b\}$ according to comparing the authentication watermark generated by step2 with the extract one.

$$d_{i} = \begin{cases} 1, & C'_{i} \neq C_{i} \\ 0 & C'_{i} = C_{i} \end{cases}$$

If $d_i=1$, we suppose the image block X_i suffer from tampering. Otherwise, it is a valid image block.

Step 4. Traversal the block mark D, if $d_i=1$, mark this block invalid by denoting $r_i=1$ if there are two or more neighboring blocks in its 3×3 block-neighborhood that are invalid, otherwise, $r_i=0$. Then a binary sequence $R=\{r_i|i=1,2,\cdots,N_b\}$ is obtained, which is used as depicting the validity of each image block.

According to the result of tamper detection, we can get whether the image suffer from malicious tamper. If the biometric image keeps unaltered, it can be directly used for the biometric authentication system. And if the biometric image suffers malicious tamper, we can use the following process to recover the biometric feature using the information hidden in the original biometric image.

Step 1. Get MB_r for the image $\widehat{Y}$ which 4LSBs is set to zeros according to the method described in section3.3.1.

Table 2. Watermarked image quality (PSNR in dB)

1-layer watermark	2-layer watermark	Spread over	ROB	ROI
37.43	35.39	35.49	37.45	35.21

Step 2. Split the whole image Y into image block $Y=\{Y_i|i=1,2,\cdots,N_b\}$. Then, partition these blocks into two sets: tempered blocks and un-tampered blocks.

Step 3. For the tampered image blocks which locate in the ROB, we abandon the hidden information. And extract the hidden information from un-tampered blocks.

Step 4. Recover the embedded coefficients according to the result of tamper detection. If an image block suffers from malicious tampering, we discard the extracted coefficient from the tampered image block. Voting-scheme is adopted to reduce the probabilities of false recover using the coefficient mark as un-tampered.

3.3.4 Experimental Results

In this section, we give the simulation results. Firstly, we use the metric Peak signal-to-noise ratio (PSNR) as a measure of how the quality of the biometric images is affected by watermark. The size of biometric image is152×128, and authentication watermark payload is 19456 bits, information watermark is 7680bits. The result is given in talbe2. The first column gives 1-layer watermarked image using authentication watermark; the second column gives 2-layer watermarked image using authentication watermark and information watermark, and information watermark is all embedded into ROI; the third column gives 2-layer watermarked image using authentication watermark and information watermark, but information watermark is spread over the whole image; the last two columns give the PSNR of ROB and ROI.

In order to reduce the effect which caused by watermark, we should adaptively embed watermark into region of salient (ROI) and region of background (ROB) of biometric images. Figure 6 and Figure 7 give the experimental results for recognition rate of the biometric image watermarked with different methods. In these figures, 'Original' represents the recognition rate of the original biometric image; 'Wm1' represents the recognition rate of the biometric image embedded into information bits over the whole image; 'Wm2' represents the recognition rate of the biometric image embedded information bits into ROB of the biometric images; 'Wm3' represents the recognition rate of the biometric image embedded information bits into ROI of the biometric images.

As for Figure 6, PCA and Gabor feature are adopted to evaluate our algorithm, the recognition rate of the four kind of biometric images nearly equal, which represents that the watermark has less affect on PCA and Gabor features of biometric image. PCA and Gabor features are the appearance of the biometric image, which are less affected by noise; watermark can be looked upon the noise added on the image. Thus, the recognition rate of the four kind of biometric images nearly equal based on PCA and Gabor feature. LBP which represents the local texture feature is affected by the watermark embedded into it. Thus, from Figure 7, the recognition rate of "Wm1", 'Wm2'and 'Wm3' is lower than 'Original'. 'Wm3' is higher than 'Wm1' and 'Wm2', which show our proposed scheme can keep "recognizing quality" to certain extent.

Eigen-face coefficients can re-construct face image, in this paper, it is used as information

Figure 6. Comparison of different watermarked image set using PCA (left) and Gabor (right)

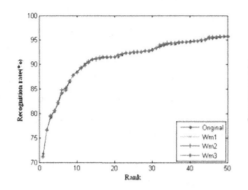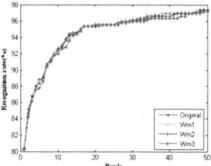

Figure 7. Comparison of different watermarked image set using LBP

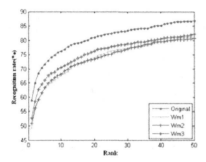

tamper ratio [0.1, 0.7], and the interval is 0.1, and the number of embedded coefficients is 128.

4. CONCLUSION

Compared with traditional personal identification techniques such as passwords and PIN codes, automatic biometric authentication system provides a convenient and reliable method in diverse applications, on condition that the security of biometric data is guaranteed. Watermarking technique is an efficient way to ensure the secrecy and integrity of biometrics. However, the distortion introduced by watermarking to the original biometric image will decrease the recognition performance of biometric authentication system. In this chapter, we introduce salient region detection methods for biometric watermarking to adaptively select watermark embedding position and strength. Two watermarking applications have been presented to discuss and illustrate the benefits of adopting computer vision methods. Firstly, to protect

hidden embedding the host biometric image. If the image suffers from malicious tamper, the face information hidden can be extracted.

As for Eigen-face coefficients, it can reconstruct the face image. Thus, the recovered Eigen-face can be used as a second source of authentication, either automatically or by a human in a supervised biometric application. In Figure 8, we give the reconstructed face images under

Figure 8. Results of face recovery

Original   10%   20%   30%   40%   50%   60%   70%

copyright of biometric database, we add robust notation into faces image using an adaptive quantization watermarking method. Saliency map plays an important part of perceptual masking which guarantees the robustness of watermark while keeping the quality of host biometrics; secondly, a fragile watermarking is applied to verify the integrity of biometric image by detecting malicious manipulations. Saliency map is utilized to segment original face image into ROI/ROB, and offers a basis for subsequent authentication and self-recovery. Experimental results demonstrate that embedding watermark into biometric image base on salient region detection can achieve better watermarking performance while preserving distinctive biometric features.

Furthermore, for salient region detection based applications, the overall system performance greatly relies on the quality of generated saliency map. In the future, we plan to investigate visual saliency by applying graph based methods (Bai, 2009a; Bai, 2009b).

5. ACKNOWLEDGMENT

This work was supported by the National Natural Science Foundation of China (Grant No.60873158).

6. REFERENCES

Achanta, R., Hemami, S., Estrada, F., & Susstrunk, S. (2009). Frequency-tuned salient region detection. *International Conference on Computer Vision and Pattern Recognition.*

Ahmed, F., & Marie, K. B. (2008). Fingerprint Reference Verification Method Using a Phase-encoding-based Watermarking Technique. *Journal of Electronic Image, 17*(1).

Bai, X., Wilson, R., & Hancock, E. (2009a). A Generative Model for Graph Matching and Embedding. *Computer Vision and Image Understanding, 113*, 777–789. doi:10.1016/j.cviu.2009.01.004

Bai, X., Wilson, R., & Hancock, E. (2009b). Graph Characteristics from the Heat Kernel Trace. *Pattern Recognition, 42*, 2589–2606. doi:10.1016/j.patcog.2008.12.029

Bas, P., Chassery, J. M., & Macq, B. (2002, September). Geometrically invariant watermarking using feature points. *IEEE Transactions on Image Processing, 11*(9), 1014–1028. doi:10.1109/TIP.2002.801587

Bender, W. D., Morimoto, G. N., & Lu, A. (1996). Techniques for data hiding. *IBM Systems Journal, 35*(3/4), 313–316. doi:10.1147/sj.353.0313

Bi, N., Sun, Q., & Huang, D. (2007). Robust Image Watermarking Based on Multiband Wavelets and Empirical Mode Decomposition. *IEEE Transactions on Image Processing, 16*(8), 1956–1966. doi:10.1109/TIP.2007.901206

Birgit, M., & Maeder, J. (2005). A study of block-based medical image watermarking using a perceptual similarity metric. *Digital Imaging Computing: Techniques and Applications (DICTA)*, 1-8.

Chang, C. C., Hu, Y. S., & Lu, T. C. (2006). A watermarking-based image ownership and tampering authentication scheme. *Pattern Recognition Letters, 27*(5), 439–446. doi:10.1016/j.patrec.2005.09.006

Cox, I. J., & Miller, M. L. (1997). Secure spread spectrum watermarking for multimedia. *IEEE Transactions on Image Processing, 6*(12), 1673–1687. doi:10.1109/83.650120

Cox, I. J., Miller, M. L., Bloom, J. A., Fridrich, J., & Kalker, T. (2008). *Digital Watermarking and Steganography* (2nd ed.). Morgan Kaufmann.

Dom, O., Derek, R., & Matthew, S. (2005). Multiple medical image ROI authentication schemes using watermarking. *Biomedical Applications of Micro- and Nanoengineering II*, 221-231.

Fan, Y. C., Chiang, A., & Shen, J. H. (2008). ROI-based watermarking scheme for JPEG2000. *Circuits Syst Signal Process*, *27*, 763–774. doi:10.1007/s00034-008-9055-6

Harel, J., Koch, C., & Perona, P. (2007). Graph-based visual saliency. *Advances in Neural Information Processing Systems*, *19*, 545–552.

He, H. J., Zhang, J. S., & Tai, H. M. (2008). Block-Chain based watermarking scheme with superior localization, *IHW 2008* (. *LNCS*, *5284*, 147–160.

He, S., Kirovski, D., & Wu, M. (2009). High-fidelity data embedding for image annotation. *IEEE Transactions on Image Processing*, *18*(2), 429–435. doi:10.1109/TIP.2008.2008733

Hou, X., & Zhang, L. (2007). Saliency detection: a spectral residual approach. *IEEE Conference on Computer Vision and Pattern Recognition*.

Itti, L., Koch, C., & Niebur, E. (1998). A model of saliency-based visual attention for rapid scene analysis. *IEEE Transaction on PAMI.*, *20*(11), 1254–1258.

Jain, A. K., Pankanti, S., & Boll, R. (1999). *Biometrics: personal identification in networked society*. Kluwer.

Jain, A. K., & Uludag, U. (2003). Hiding biometric data. *IEEE Transactions on Pattern Analysis and Machine Intelligence*, *25*(11), 1494–1498. doi:10.1109/TPAMI.2003.1240122

Khan, M. K., Zhang, J. s., & Tian, L. (2007). Chaotic Secure Content-based Hidden Transmission of Biometric Templates. *Chaos, Solitons, and Fractals*, *32*(5), 1749–1759. doi:10.1016/j.chaos.2005.12.015

Koch, C., & Ullman, S. (1985). Shifts in selective visual attention: towards the underlying neural circuitry. *Human Neurobiology*, *4*, 219–227.

Li, C. T., & Si, H. (2007). Wavelet-based fragile watermarking scheme for image authentication. *Journal of Electronic Imaging*, *16*(1). doi:10.1117/1.2712445

Maeno, K., Sun, Q. B., Chang, S. F., & Suto, M. (2006). New semi-fragile image authentication watermarking techniques using random bias and nonuniform quantization. *IEEE Transactions on Multimedia*, 32–45. doi:10.1109/TMM.2005.861293

Miller, M. L. (2001). Watermarking with dirty-paper codes. *International conference on image processing*, May 15-18, Thessaloniki, Greece.

Mohammad, A., & Lu, G. (2008). A robust content-based watermarking technique. *MMSP*, *2008*, 713–718.

Pereira, S., & Pun, T. (2000). Robust template matching for affine resistant image watermarks. *IEEE Transactions on Image Processing*, *9*(6), 303–317. doi:10.1109/83.846253

Phillips, P. J., Moon, H., Rizvi, S. A., & Rauss, P. J. (2000). The FERET evaluation methodology for face recognition algorithms. *IEEE Transactions on Pattern Analysis and Machine Intelligence*, *22*(10), 1090–1104. doi:10.1109/34.879790

Prayoth, K. A., Kitti, & Arthit, S. (2005, December). A new approach for optimization in image watermarking by using genetic algorithms. *IEEE Transactions on Signal Processing*, *12*(12), 4707–4719.

Ratha, N. K., Connell, J. H., & Bolle, R. M. (2000). Secure data hiding in wavelet compressed fingerprint images. In *Proc. ACM Multimedia 2000 Workshops* (pp. 127-130). Los Angeles, CA.

Rosin, P. L. (2009). A simple method for detecting salient regions. *Journal of Pattern Recognition*, *42*, 2362–2371.

Tang, C. W., & Hang, H. M. (2003). A feature-based robust digital image watermarking scheme. *IEEE Transactions on Image Processing, 13*(2), 145–153.

Thiemert, S., Sahbi, H., & Steinebach, M. (2006). *Using entropy for image and video authentication watermarks* (*Vol. 6072*, pp. 607218–1, 607218–10). Security, Steganography, and Watermarking of Multimedia Contents VIII.

Treisman, A., & Glade, G. (1980). A feature-integration theory of attention. *Cognitive Psychology, 12*, 97–136. doi:10.1016/0010-0285(80)90005-5

Van, S. R. G., Tirkel, A. Z., & Osborne, C. F. (1994). A digital watermark [C]. *Proceedings of International Conference on Image Process, 94*(2), 86–90.

Voloshynvskiy, S., Pereira, S., Herrigel, A., Baumgartner, N., & Pun, T. (2000). A generalized watermark attack based on stochastic watermark estimation and perceptual remodulation. *Electronic Image 2000: Security and Watermarking of Multimedia Content II.* (Vol. 3971).

Wang, S. H., & Lin, Y. P. (2004, February). Wavelet tree quantization for copyright protection watermarking. *IEEE Transactions on Image Processing, 13*(2), 154–165. doi:10.1109/TIP.2004.823822

Yeung, M. M., & Pankanti, S. (2000). Vertification watermarks on fingerprint recognition and retrieval, *Electron imaging*, 468-476.

Yu, D., Sattar, F., & Barkat, B. (2006). Multi-resolution fragile watermarking using complex chirp signals for content authentication. *Pattern Recognition, 39*(5), 935–952. doi:10.1016/j.patcog.2005.11.023

Yuan, H., & Zhang, X. P. (2006). Multiscale fragile watermarking based on the Gaussian Mixture Model. *IEEE Transactions on Image Processing, 15*(10), 3189–3200. doi:10.1109/TIP.2006.877310

Zebbiche, K., & Khelifi, F. (2008). Region-Based Watermarking of Biometric Images: Case Study in Fingerprint Images. *International Journal of Digital Multimedia Broadcasting*, 1-13.

Zhang, X. P., & Wang, S. Z. (2007). Statistical Fragile Watermarking Capable Of Locating Individual Tampered Pixels. *Signal Processing Letters, 14*(10), 727–730. doi:10.1109/LSP.2007.896436

Zheng, D., Wang, S., & Zhao, J. (2009). RST invariant image watermarking algorithm with mathematical modeling and analysis of the watermarking processes. *IEEE Transactions on Image Processing, 18*(5), 1055–1068. doi:10.1109/TIP.2009.2014807

Zhu, X. Z., Anthony, T. S. H., & Pina, M. (2007). A new semi-fragile image watermarking with robust tampering restoration using irregular sampling. *Signal Processing Image Communication, 22*(5), 515–528. doi:10.1016/j.image.2007.03.004

ADDITIONAL READING*

Altun, O., Sharma, Celik, G. M., & Bocko, M. (2006). A Set Theoretic Framework for Watermarking and Its Application to Semifragile Tamper Detection. *IEEE Transactions on Information Forensics and Security, 1*(4), 479-492.

Anold, M., Schomucker, M., & Wolthusen, S. D. (2003). *Techniques and Applications of Digital Watermarking and Content Protection*. London: Artech House.

Bruce, N. D. B. (2005). Features that draw visual attention: An information theoretic perspective. *Neurocomputing, 65-66*, 125–133. doi:10.1016/j.neucom.2004.10.065

Bruce, N. D. B., & Tsotsos, J. K. (2006). Saliency based on information maximization. *Advances in Neural Information Processing Systems, 18,* 155–162.

Bruce, N. D. B., & Tsotsos, K. (2009). Saliency, attention, and visual search: An information theoretic approach. *Journal of Vision (Charlottesville, Va.), 9*(3), 1–24. doi:10.1167/9.3.5

Chang, C. C., Lin, P. Y., & Chuang, J. C. (2007). Fragile Watermarking Scheme for Digital Image Authentication Using Pixel Difference. *The Imaging Science Journal, 55*(3), 140–147.

Cox, I. J., Miller, M. L., Bloom, J. A., Fridrich, J., & Kalker, T. (2008). *Digital Watermarking and Steganography* (2nd ed.). Burlington, US: Morgan Kaufmann.

Evans, K. K., & Treisman, A. (2005). Perception of objects in natural scenes: Is it really attention free? *Journal of Experimental Psychology. Human Perception and Performance, 31,* 1476–1492. doi:10.1037/0096-1523.31.6.1476

Fei, C. H., Kundur, D., & Kwong, R. H. (2006). Analysis and Design of Secure Watermark-Based Authentication Systems. *IEEE Transactions on Information Forensics and Security, 1*(1), 43–55. doi:10.1109/TIFS.2005.863505

He, H. J., Zhang, J. S., & Tai, H. M. (2006). A Wavelet-Based Fragile Watermarking Scheme for Secure Image Authentication. In *Proc. 5th Int. Workshop Digital Watermarking* (Vol. 4283, pp. 422-432).

Hershler, O., & Hochstein, S. (2005). At first sight: A high-level pop out effect for faces. *Vision Research, 45,* 1707–1724. doi:10.1016/j.visres.2004.12.021

Itti, L., & Koch, C. (2001). Computational modelling of visual attention. *Nature Reviews. Neuroscience, 2*(3), 194–203. doi:10.1038/35058500

Itti, L., Koch, C., & Niebur, C. E. (1998). A model of saliency-based visual attention for rapid scene analysis. *IEEE Trans. PAMI., 20,* 1254–1259.

Jain, A. K., Flynn, P., & Ross, A. A. (Eds.). (2008). *Handbook of biometrics.* New York: Springer. doi:10.1007/978-0-387-71041-9

Jain, A. K., Ross, A. A., & Prabhakar, S. (2004). An introduction to biometric recognition. *IEEE Transactions on Circuits and Systems for Video Technology, 14*(1), 4–20. doi:10.1109/TCSVT.2003.818349

Kadir, T., & Brady, M. (2001). Saliency, scale and image description. *International Journal of Computer Vision, 45*(2), 83–105. doi:10.1023/A:1012460413855

Laurent, I., & Christof, K. (2001). Computational modeling of visual attention. *Macmillan Magazines Ltd,* 194-203.

Li, S. Z., & Jain, A. K. (2005). (Ed.). *Handbook of face recognition.* New York: Springer.

Li, Z. (2002). A saliency map in primary visual cortex. *Trends in Cognitive Sciences, 6,* 9–16. doi:10.1016/S1364-6613(00)01817-9

Liao, K. C., Lee, W. B., & Liao, C. W. (2006). Security of fragile watermarking scheme for image authentication. *Imaging Science Journal, 54*(3), 129–133. doi:10.1179/174313106X106278

Liu, S. H., Yao, H. X., & Gao, W. (2006). An image fragile watermark scheme based on chaotic image pattern and pixel-pairs. *Applied Mathematics and Computation, 185*(2), 869–882. doi:10.1016/j.amc.2006.07.036

Lu, Z. M., Zheng, W. M., Pan, J. S. & Sun, Z. (2006). Multipurpose Image Watermarking Method Based on Mean-removed Vector Quantization. *Journal of Information Assurance and Security,* 33-42.

Maeno, K., Sun, Q. B., Chang, S., & Suto, F. M. (2006). New semi-fragile image authentication watermarking techniques using random bias and nonuniform quantization. *IEEE Transactions on Multimedia*, 32–45. doi:10.1109/TMM.2005.861293

Sang, J., & Alam, M. S. (2008). Fragility and Robustness of Binary Phase Only Filter Based Fragile/Semifragile Digital Image Watermarking. *IEEE Transactions on Instrumentation and Measurement*, 57(3), 595–606. doi:10.1109/TIM.2007.911585

Yeh, F. H., & Lee,G. C.(2006). Content-based watermarking in image authentication allowing remedying of tampered images. *Optical Engineering, 45*(7), 077004-1-07700410.

Yuan, H., & Zhang, X. P. (2006). Multiscale fragile watermarking based on the Gaussian Mixture Model. *IEEE Transactions on Image Processing, 15*(10), 3189–3200. doi:10.1109/TIP.2006.877310

Zhang, L., Tong, M. H., Marks, T. K., Shan, H., & Cottrell, G. W. (2008). SUN: A Bayesian framework for saliency using natural statistics. *Journal of Vision (Charlottesville, Va.), 8*(7), 1–20. doi:10.1167/8.7.32

Zhua, X. Z., Anthony, T. S., & Pina, H. M. (2007). A new semi-fragile image watermarking with robust tampering restoration using irregular sampling. *Signal Processing Image Communication, 22*(5), 515–528. doi:10.1016/j.image.2007.03.004

KEY TERMS AND DEFINITIONS

Biometric Authentication: The technologies for automatically identifying individuals according to their distinct physical (e.g. face, fingerprint, etc.) or behavioral (e.g. signature, gait, etc.) characteristics.

Digital Qatermarking: The technologies that embed non-perceptual secret message, named watermark, into host digital media as ancillary information for copyright protection, integrity authentication or other application specific purposes.

Integrity Authentication: The technologies to identify the source of incoming data, and detect fortuitous or (and) malicious distortion.

Perceptual Mask: One metric that reflects the relatively perceptual importance of media components such as, image pixels, audio frequency coefficients, etc.

Saliency Map: One normalized 2D matrix has the same size of (or smaller than) a visual scene, with each element indicates the saliency of a corresponding pixel (or region).

Salient Region: 'Meaningful region' in a visual scene, which achieves high visual saliency and contains prominent features.

Visual Saliency: The perceptual significance to human vision system (HVS), which enables an object to stick out from its neighbors, and thus attracts visual attention.

ENDNOTE

*   In this section, many additional readings are recommended to readers who are interested in relative research issues.

Section 5
Biologically Inspired Multimedia Computing

Chapter 14
Bio-Inspired Scheme for Classification of Visual Information

Le Dong
University of Electronic Science and Technology of China, China

Ebroul Izquierdo
University of London, UK

Shuzhi Sam Ge
University of Electronic Science and Technology of China, China

ABSTRACT

In this chapter, research on visual information classification based on biologically inspired visually selective attention with knowledge structuring is presented. The research objective is to develop visual models and corresponding algorithms to automatically extract features from selective essential areas of natural images, and finally, to achieve knowledge structuring and classification within a structural description scheme. The proposed scheme consists of three main aspects: biologically inspired visually selective attention, knowledge structuring and classification of visual information. Biologically inspired visually selective attention closely follow the mechanisms of the visual "what" and "where" pathways in the human brain. The proposed visually selective attention model uses a bottom-up approach to generate essential areas based on low-level features extracted from natural images. This model also exploits a low-level top-down selective attention mechanism which performs decisions on interesting objects by human interaction with preference or refusal inclination. Knowledge structuring automatically creates a relevance map from essential areas generated by visually selective attention. The developed algorithms derive a set of well-structured representations from low-level description to drive the final classification. The knowledge structuring relays on human knowledge to produce suitable links between low-level descriptions and high-level representation on a limited training set. The backbone is a distribution mapping strategy involving two novel modules: structured low-level feature extraction using convolution neural network and topology preservation based on sparse representation and unsupervised learning algorithm. Classification is achieved by simulating high-level top-down visual

DOI: 10.4018/978-1-60960-024-2.ch014

information perception and classification using an incremental Bayesian parameter estimation method. The utility of the proposed scheme for solving relevant research problems is validated. The proposed modular architecture offers straightforward expansion to include user relevance feedback, contextual input, and multimodal information if available.

INTRODUCTION

In this chapter, the well-established attention models are exploited to build a model for image analysis and classification following human perception and interpretation of natural images. The proposed approach aims at, to some extent, mimicking the human visual system and to use it to achieve higher accuracy in image classification. Low-level features are used to generate an essential area in the image of concern. A method to generate a topology representation based on the structured low-level features is developed. Using this method, the preservation of new objects from a previously perceived ontology in conjunction with the color and texture perceptions can be processed autonomously and incrementally. The topology representation network structure consists of the posterior probability and the prior frequency distribution map of each image cluster conveying a given semantic concept. The proposed framework uses a biologically inspired visually selective attention model and knowledge structuring techniques to approximate human-like inference.

Contrasting related works from the conventional literature, the proposed framework exploits known fundamental properties of biologic visual systems and a suitable knowledge structuring model to achieve classification of natural images.

Based upon the roles of the brain structures related with visual information processing, a biologically inspired framework for visually selective attention has been developed. The developed system is implemented by mimicking the functions and the connection of the brain structures including the visual pathway in the human brain. The developed system has human-like mechanisms such as incremental learning, a social function

with human interaction processing, autonomous mechanism for visually selective attention, and low-level visual information perception.

An object non-specific perception model is used in the knowledge structuring that can make a representation of an arbitrary object by using the sparse coded features of a convolution neural network (CNN). A generative model based upon Bayes' theorem using Gaussian mixtures, can classify an arbitrary object in a feature space that is generated by a CNN [Vailaya and Jain 1999]. Moreover, the developed model plays a role in perceiving an arbitrary object in a natural scene, by recognizing an object category based upon the maximum likelihood (ML) method in a natural scene. It is one of the most important thing in the proposed biologically inspired framework, whereby the training object area is automatically decided by the proposed selective attention model and not by hand, which is a very important feature.

An important contribution of the presented work is the dynamic preservation of high-level representation of visual information based on the visually selective attention of a natural scene.

Another important feature of the proposed framework is the constant evaluation of the involved confidence and support measures used in the classification of visual information. As a result, continually changing associations and frequencies for each class according to the inference rules is achieved.

The last but not the least, the presented ingenious framework integrates visually selective attention model with graphical model-based topology representation, thus rendering favorable low- and high-level features and reasonable premise to drive the final classification.

These main novel features of the framework together with an open and modular architecture enable important extensions to include user relevance feedback, contextual input, and multimodal information if available. These important features are the scope of ongoing implementations and system extensions targeting enhanced robustness and classification accuracy.

BACKGROUND

A quick overview of the state of the art is given in this section. Due to the explosive growth of digital content, automatic classification of images has become one of the most critical challenges in visual information indexing and retrieval systems. Despite great research efforts dedicated to overcome this problem, so far the outcome has been confined to very specialized systems mostly based on the analysis of low-level image primitives [Jing et al. 2004, Wallraven et al. 2003, Tang et al. 2003]. Relying on low-level features only, it is possible to automatically extract important relationships between images. However, such an approach lacks the potential to achieve accurate semantic-based image classification for generic automatic annotation and retrieval. The last few years have witnessed an increased research effort towards automatic generation of links between low- and high-level features for semantic-based image classification. For instance, in [Sethi et al. 2001] an approach based on classification trees and conventional k-means clustering is used to identify appropriate relations between low-level features and semantic concepts represented by key-words. In [Assfalg et al. 2001] several different low-level visual primitives are combined together by domain-specific rules in order to capture relevant semantics encapsulated in natural images. Based on a better understanding of visual information elements and their role in synthesis and manipulation of their content, an approach called "computational media aesthetics" studies

the dynamic nature of the narrative via analysis of the integration and sequencing of audio and video [Dorai and Venkatesh 2003]. An important aspect that adds complexity to the problem is the high dimensionality of low-level feature spaces used for classification. Since the dimensionality and size of the feature space bring high computational cost and make algorithms prone to fail, it is crucial to find low-dimensional but meaningful feature representations. This problem was addressed in [Dorado *et al.* 2006]. In that paper the authors introduced a system that exploits the ability of support vector classifiers to learn from relatively small number of patterns. Selected descriptors in low dimensionality spaces are used to process high dimensional feature spaces. A two-layered Bayesian network integrating multimodal features was proposed in [Jasinschi *et al.* 2002]. Semantic extraction using fuzzy inference rules has been used in [Dorado *et al.* 2004]. These approaches are based on the premise that the rules needed to infer a set of high-level concepts from low-level descriptors cannot be defined a priori. Rather, knowledge embedded in the database and interaction with an expert user is exploited to enable learning.

Closer to the models described in this chapter, knowledge- and feature-based clustering as well as topology representation are important aspects that can be used to improve classification and annotation performance. Within these fields, attention mechanisms have been widely exploited by the image processing and computer vision communities. Several works related to attention models can be highlighted. In [Treisman and Gelade 1980], an approach called "feature integration" was proposed for the theory of visual attention. The same model is exploited by Itti et al. to achieve rapid scene analysis on saliency-based visual attention [Itti et al. 1998]. In that work the authors use color, intensity and orientation as basis to generate the saliency map. Tsotsos et al. proposed a biologically motivated attention model for motion [Tsotsos et al. 1995]. Sun and Fisher use hierarchical selectivity for object-based visual attention integrating visual salience from bottom-up groupings and top-down attention setting [Sun and Fisher 2002]. Bottom-up or saliency-based visual attention allows primates to detect unspecific conspicuous targets in cluttered scenes [Itti and Koch 2001b]. Mundhenk et al. developed a method for clustering features into objects using intensity, orientations and colors from the most salient points in an image [Mundhenk et al. 2004]. Several other computational architectures serving this bottom-up, stimulus-driven, spatiotemporal deployment of attention are reviewed in [Itti 2005]. The resulting computational models have applications not only to the prediction of visual search psychophysics, but also, in the domain of machine vision, e.g., for the rapid selection of regions of interest in complex, cluttered environments [Itti 2005]. Recently, Navalpakkam and Itti also presented a combined model of bottom-up and top-down visual attention in [Navalpakkam and Itti 2006].

Biological research [Edelman, Intrator et al. 2002] shows that unsupervised methods are essential for visual information processing in the primate's brain, and thus, can be used as computational strategies for developing advanced visual modeling that is both highly sophisticated and versatile. In this chapter, the presented models were developed by unsupervised learning based on biologically inspired theory and statistical properties. Biologically based principles, such as sparse coding, will likely have the information processing capabilities as well as huge payoffs in power/energy minimization and optimal resource management [Barlow 1994]. Sparse coding has been proved to provide superior information storage capacity compared to local (grandmother cell theory or Gnostic representations) or fully distributed information representation [Attwell & Laughlin, 2001]. Because only a very few cells need to be activated and there are only a few cells encoding an event, sparse coding constraints used in our modeling work can bring fault-tolerance

and low-power implementation [Jabri, 2000] to the physical realization of computational models.

The retina is the light-sensitive portion of the eye, containing the cones, which are responsible for color vision, and the rods, which are mainly responsible for vision in the dark. When the rods and cones are excited, signals are transmitted through successive neurons in the retina itself and finally into the optic nerve fibers and cerebral cortex [Guyton 1991, Goldstein 1995, Kuffler et al. 1984, Majani et al. 1984, Bear et al. 2001]. The visual pathways can be divided roughly into an old system to the midbrain and base of the forebrain and a new system for direct transmission into the visual cortex. The new system is responsible in man for the perception of virtually all aspects of visual form, colors, and other conscious vision [Guyton 1991]. The overall visual pathway from the retina to the secondary visual cortex covers several parts. Each part will be described in detail in the following subsections.

The visual pathway in the human brain, from the retina and LGN to the primary visual cortex, is considered to be a factor in bottom-up processing part. The roles of the retina are determined by extracting low- level features of the input images such as edges, intensity, and color opponency. The LGN and the V1 are considered when modeling the on-centre and off-surround mechanism and feature integration, respectively. The hypothalamus and the hippocampus in the limbic system are considered when developing a low-level top-down preference attention model. The reward and punishment functions of the hypothalamus are regarded when developing a low-level top-down visual attention model so that an interesting area as an attentive area can be reinforced and an uninteresting area can be inhibited. Moreover, the LIP is taken into consideration in integrating attentive features for deciding the attention area based on several different sources. The PFC is simply reflected in order to mimic human interaction and store simple knowledge.

In a primate's retina, three types of cells are the important processing elements for performing edge extraction. They are photoreceptors, horizontal and bipolar cells, respectively [Kuffler *et al.* 1984]. According to these well-known facts, the edge information is obtained by the role of cells in the visual receptor and it is delivered to the visual cortex through the LGN and the ganglion cells. The edge signal is detected by the output signal of the bipolar cell. In parallel, a neural circuit in the retina creates opponent cells from the signals generated by three types of cone receptors: M, L, and S. The R+G- cell receives inhibitory input from the M cone and excitatory input from the L cone. The opponent response of the R+G- cell occurs because of the opposing inputs from the M and L cones. The B+Y- cell receives inhibitory input by adding the inputs from the M and L cones and excitatory input from the S cone. Those pre-processed signal are transmitted to the LGN through the ganglion cell and the on-centre and off-surround mechanism of the LGN and the visual cortex intensifies the opponency phenomena. Moreover, the LGN and the primary visual cortex also play a role for detecting the shape and patterns in an object. In general, the shape of an object has symmetrical information. Consequently, the symmetrical information becomes an important feature for constructing a essential map. Even though the role of the visual cortex for finding an essential area is important, it is very difficult to model the detailed and complex function of the visual cortex. Thus, suitable assumptions leading to model simplifications are needed. Following Barlow's hypothesis, we simply consider the role of the visual cortex as a redundancy reduction mechanism [Barlow and Tolhust 1992]. The LIP also plays a role to provide a retinotopic spatio-featural map that is used to control the spatial focus of attention and fixation. This mechanism enables the integration of feature information in its spatial map. As an integrator of spatial and feature information, the LIP provides the inhibition of return (IOR) mechanism required to prevent the scan path returning to previously inspected sites. Furthermore, it is clear that several limbic structures, including the hypothalamus, are particularly concerned with the affective nature of a sensation. These affective qualities are also called reward and punishment, or satisfaction and aversion. The reward and punishment centers are undoubtedly one of the most important controllers in biologic systems. They drive aversions and motivations. According to Guyton's studies, the limbic system for reward and punishment has much to do with selecting the information that we learn. Finally, the frontal lobe integrates information from the "what" pathway and "where" pathway. Then, it generates not only an inference to construct knowledge but also feedback signals to the parietal cortex area including the LIP area [Guyton 1991].

The selected object information is transmitted to the PFC through V4 and IT areas. On the other hand, the low-level top-down selective attention uses the fuzzy adaptive resonance theory (ART) to explore the "what" path and "where" path in the primate's brain functions. The hypothalamus function, which is implemented by the fuzzy ART, generates a modified scan path by reflecting reward and punishment in the low-level top-down selective attention. The reward and punishment is realized via the preference and refusal mechanism which is associated with the role of the limbic system and especially related with the function of the hypothalamus.

The biologically inspired visually selective attention model integrates a low-level top-down selective attention module into a bottom-up essential map module to generate essential areas related with human interest. This may lead to a sequence of essential areas according to visual stimuli using the bottom-up essential map. However, the bottom-up essential map may select an unwanted area and generate an unreasonable scan path because it just generates the essential sequence based on low-level features. On the other hand, a human being can learn and memorize the characteristics of the unwanted area, and also inhibits or reinforces attention to that area in subsequent visual search by low-level top-down selective attention mechanisms. The proposed model can generate a more intentional scan path like the human visual attention system and reflects the relative importance of different feature maps in consideration of human supervisor interest.

FRAMEWORK OVERVIEW

The framework consists of three main aspects: biologically inspired visually selective attention, knowledge structuring, and classification of visual information. For the sake of clarity, the biological background of the proposed models is already given in the previous section. The single modules making up the overall framework are then elaborated in the subsequent sections. To assess the performance of the proposed system, a comprehensive experimental evaluation was conducted. The obtained results show high classification accuracy in databases with a small number of semantic classes. A comparative analysis with other clustering methods was also conducted to validate robustness and generalization capability of the proposed framework. Selected results of experimental evaluation are given in this chapter. The chapter closes with summary and an outlook of ongoing extensions.

The proposed system classifies visual information automatically using extracted knowledge from a pre-annotated dataset. It creates relevance

map from a set of low-level visual information features and infers the associations between low-level features and high-level semantic-based classification. The flowchart of the proposed system is depicted in Figure 1. As shown in Figure 1, the bottom-up essential map and the low-level top-down selective attention modules are integrated in the same processing unit. As a consequence, the knowledge structuring model can be derived seamlessly. Based on the information from the knowledge structuring model, the clusters of specific group can be generated by the last unit of the system. The underlining sequential processes outlined in Figure 1 are elaborated in the remaining of this section.

Initially, a set of low-level features is extracted from the pre-annotated dataset. These low-level features are used to generate the essential map in natural image by the biologically inspired model. The output from the biologically inspired model is then used as an input base in the knowledge structuring model. The knowledge structuring model starts with the extraction of the structured low-level features in the essential map, and then dynamically assigns high-level knowledge based on the extracted structured low-level features to any new visual information added to the database. Using the semantic concept defined beforehand by the expert user in the training stage, the new visual information is mapped into the corresponding feature-related relevance maps by a neural network learning process. Thus, the knowledge structuring model generates the pattern

Figure 1. System framework

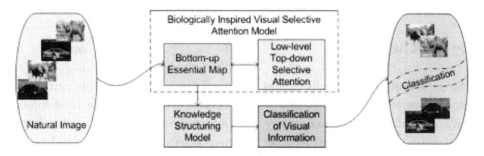

of assigned labels and outputs a set of high-level representation from the relevance map. In this process, new knowledge can be created and added to the knowledge structuring chains. Finally, the classification of visual information will generate distinct clusters for specific image groups based on the output of the knowledge structuring model.

Biologically Inspired Visually Selective Attention

The biologically inspired visually selective attention consists of two modules: bottom-up essential map and low-level top-down visually selective attention. These two modules are related with the function of the PFC and have close relationship with the working memory. These two modules closely follow the mechanisms of the visual "what" pathway and "where" pathway in the human brain. The biologically inspired visually selective attention can autonomously decide the focus areas based on bottom-up essential of input visual features as well as top-down preference of a supervisor who interacts with the attention model. The bottom-up essential map selects candidates for interesting regions from the visual information using low-level features [Kuffler et al. 1984]. The first module generates an essential area based on low-level features extracted from natural images. The second module, i.e., low-level top-down selective attention, performs decisions on interesting objects by human interaction. Here, a preference/refusal mechanism is exploited. A detailed description of these two modules making up the proposed biologically inspired visually selective attention is given in the latter part of the chapter.

Knowledge Structuring

The knowledge structuring automatically creates a relevant map from essential areas generated by the biologically inspired model. It also derives a set of high-level representations from a low-level

description to drive the classification. This model relies on human knowledge to produce suitable links between low-level descriptions and high-level representation on a small number of training set. Using initial representations generated from low-level descriptions, the knowledge structuring model identifies whether a relationship between the low- and high-level representations exists. Afterwards, it unifies these relationships into a set of rules expressing the underlying context. The backbone of this model is a distribution mapping strategy involving two basic modules: structured low-level feature extraction using convolution neural network (CNN) and topology representation based on neural network structure. In the first module, the structured low-level color and texture information is obtained using CNN, which is based on the sparse coding scheme. In the second module, the topology structure of the extracted feature information is generated through neural network, which uses the structured low-level features to make a topology map and dynamical network structures to reflect two-dimensional maps. Explorative results related to the functions of the brain showed that the color perception and the texture perception can be used for object representation and knowledge structuring. The knowledge structuring model uses pre-annotated visual content to generate information that link a particular low-level description of the visual information with a high-level representation. Then, it automatically infers knowledge and preserves them for the following classification process. A detailed description of these modules is given in the latter section.

Classification

In the third framework aspect, the output from the knowledge structuring is used to drive the final classification. In this part, a classification approach based on high-level top-down visual information perception is used. Its implementation uses a generative approach based on an incremental

Bayesian parameter estimation method. In this model, the probability density function (PDF) is represented in the color and texture integrated feature space generated from CNN. This kind of hybrid structure can play a key role in modeling an autonomous visual information classification and retrieval system. A detailed description of the methods and functionalities of the classification is given in the latter domain.

Implementation of the Framework

The framework is mainly implemented using Matlab and C. Our current implementation is capable of processing images at various pixel resolutions on a 3.4 GHz Pentium 4 CPU. Ground truth for all experiments is established manually. This is done by displaying every match between images and classes established by the algorithm to a human subject, who has to rate it as either correct or incorrect based on whether the image and the category or the test image and the training image have any significant overlap/similarity. The false positive rate is derived from the number of images that were incorrectly associated with one another.

Experiment Setup

Given a collection of completely unlabelled images, the goal is to automatically discover the visual categories present in the data and localize them in the topology representation of the image. To this end, a set of quantitative experiments with progressively increasing level of topology representation complexity was conducted. The databases used in the reported experimental evaluation are described in the sequel, along with the evaluation metrics. The actual experiments and selected results are given in the latter part of this chapter, respectively.

Two different datasets have been mainly used in the experimental evaluation: Corel database and Caltech101 database [www.vision.caltech.edu/feifeili/101 ObjectCategories]. Some other per-

sonal images are also used to test the biologically inspired visually selective attention model. Experimental evidence to evaluate the performance of the topology representation and preservation modules is presented, which includes knowledge inference, topology representation and knowledge preservation. The evaluation of the classification result and a comparative analysis of the proposed approach with other existing methods are given, along with the analysis on parameter determination and influence on classification results.

COREL Database

A small dataset consisting of 700 images extracted from the Corel database was used. The small dataset was labeled manually with eight predefined concepts. The concepts are "building"(100), "car"(100), "autumn"(56), "rural"(44), "cloud"(100), "elephant"(100), "lion"(100), and "tiger"(100). Here, the number in parentheses is the number of relevant images for each concept in the database. The vigilance threshold and the learning rate in the system are set as 0.97 and 0.95, respectively. The process involved in the estimation of these parameters and the influence on the final classification result are discussed.

CALTECH101 Database

For the Caltech101 database, two datasets were used to evaluate the efficiency and complexity of the proposed system. The small dataset consists of eleven categories: "airplane"(800), "butterfly"(91), "Dalmatian"(67), "elephant"(64), "Joshua tree"(64), "leopard"(200), "lotus"(66), "minaret"(76), "motorbike"(798), "starfish"(86), and "sunflower" (85). Here, the number in parentheses is the number of relevant images for each concept in the database. The large dataset is the whole Caltech101 database, with total of 9144 images. Ten images were chosen randomly from each of the 101 object and background classes and used as for training, that is, a total 1020 exemplar images were used for training. Since the cardinality of different classes in the testing set is not the same, the obtained results were normalized. Thus, no bias toward a specific class with more or less images could influence the final experimental outcome. The spatial support of objects of interest in the training exemplars was acquired by a human annotator.

Evaluation Metrics

In order to assess the accuracy of the knowledge structuring and classification procedure, a statistical performance evaluation based on the amount of missed detections (MD) and false alarm (FA) for each class from the database was conducted. In this evaluation the best-known and most widely used measures of recall and precision values were estimated and used:

$$recall=D/(D+MD), \qquad (1)$$

$$precision=D/(D+FA), \qquad (2)$$

where D is a sum of true memberships for the corresponding recognized class, MD is a sum of the complement of the full true memberships and FA is a sum of false memberships.

To some extent, these two measures are opposed to each other as precision is usually higher in the beginning of a query and it deteriorates as more items are returned. On the other hand, if the whole database is returned, recall reaches one, but precision is low i.e., the a priori probability of relevant items. As a result, both precision and recall are insufficient measures when used alone and should either be used together, e.g., precision when recall attains a certain value, or at a fixed cut off point, i.e., when a fixed number of database items have been returned. Precision and recall are also commonly represented as a recall-precision graph, in which precision values are plotted against values of recall. Both precision and recall can also be plotted against the number of

target images. These graphs are very informative methods for illustrating system performance and e.g., show clearly the effect of relevance feedback. Comparing two graphs is, however, more difficult than comparing scalars, so interpreting recall-precision graphs requires some experience. In the experiments performed in this chapter, the recall-precision graph was used as one of the performance evaluation measures. Still, due to the difficulties in dealing with two evaluation parameters, several methods for combining precision and recall to a single measure have been proposed, although none of these measures contain as much information as recall-precision graphs. For example, average precision is obtained by computing precision at each point when a relevant item is found and then averaging these precision values.

F-measure is an appropriate measure used to attach degrees of importance to precision and recall [Van Rijsbergen 1979]. A single measure is obtained with deciding the most appropriate parameters, i.e., vigilance threshold value, which is defined as:

$$F\text{-}measure=2 \cdot recall \cdot precision/ \\ (recall+precision) \qquad (3)$$

Bottom-Up Essential Map

Five features of intensity (I), edge (E), colour (C), orientation (O), and symmetry (S) are used to model the human-like bottom-up visual attention mechanism [Goldstein 1995], as shown in Figure 2. The roles of retina and LGN are reflected in previously proposed attention models [Park *et al.* 2002]. The feature maps are constructed by the centre-surround difference and normalisation (CSD&N) of the five bases. This mimics the on-centre and off-surround mechanism in the human brain. Subsequently, they are integrated using a conventional ICA algorithm [Bell and Sejnowski 1997]. The symmetry information is used as a joint basis to consider shape primitives in objects [Li 2001], which is obtained by the noise tolerant general symmetry transform (NTGST) method [Park *et al.* 2002]. The ICA can be used for modelling the role of the primary visual cortex for the redundancy reduction according to Barlow's hypothesis and Sejnowski's results [Bell and Sejnowski 1997]. Barlow's hypothesis is that human visual cortical feature detectors might be the end result of a redundancy reduction process [Barlow and Tolhust 1992]. Sejnowski's result states that the ICA is the best way to reduce redundancy [Bell and Sejnowski 1997].

Using a similar notation to that used in [Itti *et al.* 1998], and after the convolution between the channel of feature maps and filters obtained by ICA, the essential map is computed by the summation of all feature maps for every location [Ratnaparkhi 1998]. In the course of pre-processing, a Gaussian pyramid with different scales from 0 to n levels is used [Park *et al.* 2002]. Each level is obtained by subsampling of 2^n, thus constructing five feature maps. Subsequently, the centre-surround mechanism is implemented in the model as the difference between the fine and coarse scales of Gaussian pyramid images [Park *et al.* 2002]. Consequently, five feature maps are obtained by the following equations.

$$I(c,\tilde{s}) =\mid I(c) \circ I(\tilde{s}) \mid, \tag{4}$$

$$E(c,\tilde{s}) =\mid E(c) \circ E(\tilde{s}) \mid, \tag{5}$$

$$S(c,\tilde{s}) =\mid S(c) \circ S(\tilde{s}) \mid, \tag{6}$$

$$O(c,\tilde{s}) =\mid O(c) \circ O(\tilde{s}) \mid, \tag{7}$$

$$C(c,\tilde{s}) =\mid C(c) \circ C(\tilde{s}) \mid. \tag{8}$$

Here, $\circ$ represents interpolation to the finer scale and point-by-point subtraction, *Nor* stands for the normalization operation, c and $\tilde{s}$ are indices of the finer scale and the coarse scale, respectively. Feature maps are combined into five characteristic maps.

$$\bar{I} = \overset{4}{\underset{c=2}{\oplus}} \overset{c+4}{\underset{\tilde{s}=c+3}{\oplus}} Nor(I(c,\tilde{s})), \tag{9}$$

$$\bar{E} = \overset{4}{\underset{c=2}{\oplus}} \overset{c+4}{\underset{\tilde{s}=c+3}{\oplus}} Nor(E(c,\tilde{s})), \tag{10}$$

$$\bar{S} = \overset{4}{\underset{c=2}{\oplus}} \overset{c+4}{\underset{\tilde{s}=c+3}{\oplus}} Nor(S(c,\tilde{s})), \tag{11}$$

$$\bar{O} = \overset{4}{\underset{c=2}{\oplus}} \overset{c+4}{\underset{\tilde{s}=c+3}{\oplus}} Nor(O(c,\tilde{s})), \tag{12}$$

Figure 2. The architecture of essential map model. $\bar{I}$: normalized intensity feature map, $\bar{E}$: normalized edge feature map, $\bar{S}$: normalized symmetry feature map, $\bar{O}$: normalized orientation feature map, $\bar{C}$: normalized colour feature map, EP: essential point

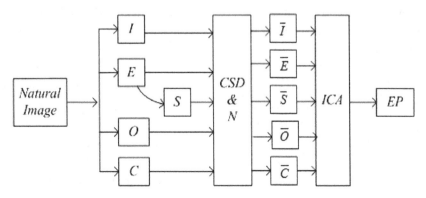

$$\bar{C} = \bigoplus_{c=2}^{4} \bigoplus_{\tilde{s}=c+3}^{c+4} Nor(RG(c,\tilde{s}) + BY(c,\tilde{s})).$$

$$(13)$$

Here, $\bar{I}, \bar{E}, \bar{S}, \bar{O}$ and $\bar{C}$, are obtained through across-scale addition "$\bigoplus$". To obtain ICA filters, the five feature maps are used for input patches of the ICA. The basic functions are determined using the extended infomax algorithm [Jasinschi *et al.* 2002]. Each row of the basic functions represents an independent filter and that is ordered according to the length of the filter vector. The resulting ICA filters are then applied to the five feature maps to obtain the essence map according to [Park *et al.* 2002]:

$$EM_{qi} = FM_q * ICs_{qi}, \qquad (14)$$

where $i=1,\cdots,M$, $q=1,\cdots,5$.

$$EM(\alpha,\beta) = \sum_i EM_{qi}(\alpha,\beta). \qquad (15)$$

Here, M denotes the number of filters; FM_q denotes feature maps, ICs_{qi} denotes each independent component accounting for the number of filters and feature maps, $EM(\alpha,\beta)$ denotes the essence map, in which α and β represent the horizontal and vertical coordinates, respectively. The convolution result EM_{qi} represents the influences of the five feature maps on each independent component and the most essential point is computed by maximum operator, then an appropriate essential area centred by the most essential location is masked off and the next essential location in the input visual information is calculated using the essence map model. The generic symmetrical property of the object is used as a guideline to determine the suitable size and shape of the masking area. This kind of inhibition of return (IOR) mechanism indicates that a previously selected essential location is not duplicated in the analysis.

Low-Level Top-Down Selective Attention

Although the bottom-up essential map generates essential areas and scan paths, the selected areas may not be interesting because the essential map generation only involves low-level analysis. To develop a more plausible selective attention model, an interactive procedure with a human supervisor is used along the bottom-up information processing. Here a new selective attention model that mimics the human-like selective attention mechanism is proposed. It embraces not only low-level analysis but also high-level human interaction attempting to model the way the human brain learns and memorize new things without completely forgetting existing ones.

Figure 3 shows the architecture of the low-level top-down selective attention during the training step. The core of the approach is a fuzzy ART network. It is well-known that fuzzy ART network can easily be trained for additional input patterns and it can solve the stability-plasticity dilemma in a conventional multi-layer neural network [Carpenter *et al.* 1992]. The corresponding feature map information of the attention area obtained from essential map is used as an input pattern for a fuzzy ART network. A human supervisor then provides information on whether it is a preference area or a refusal area. If the selected area is marked as an uninteresting area, even though it has conspicuous features, the refusal part trains and memorizes that area to be ignored in later processing stages. If the supervisor decides that the selected area should be preferred, that area is trained by the preference part. After the training step is successfully finished, it memorizes the characteristics of unwanted and desired areas.

The fuzzy ART architecture consists of two layers of nodes, designated F_1 and F_2. Inputs are presented at the F_1 layer. The F_2 layer is usually referred to as the category representation layer because its nodes denote the categories to which the input patterns belong.

Figure 3. The architecture of the low-level top-down visually selective attention during the training step

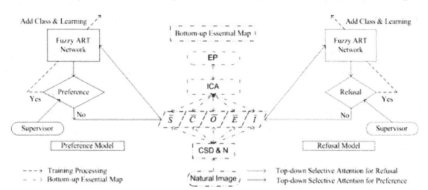

The feature maps, which are used as input of the fuzzy ART network, have continuous real values. Thus, a fuzzy ART network that can process real values like an ART 2 network is used. The used fuzzy ART network has a simpler structure than an ART 2 network and shows suitable performance for analogue pattern clustering. The corresponding feature maps from the attended area obtained from the essential map are normalized and then represented as one dimensional array X. This array consists of every pixel value a_i of the feature maps and each complement a_i^c computed by $1-a_i$. The fuzzy ART network consecutively follows the three processing steps: choice, match and adaptation. During the choice process, for every node Y_j in the F_2 layer, a net activity y_j is calculated using a fuzzy conjunction operator ($\wedge$) as:

$$y_j = |X \wedge W_{ji}|/(\varepsilon + |W_{ji}|). \qquad (16)$$

y_j can be seen as the degree of prototype bottom-up weight vector W_{ji}, being a fuzzy subset of the input pattern X where the fuzzy conjunction $\wedge$ is computed by component wise min operator and the magnitude operator $|\cdot|$ of a vector is calculated by its L1-norm defined by the sum of its components. The parameter ε in Equation (16) is used to avoid divisions by zero. Node Y_j in the F_2 layer with the highest value y_j is chosen as the winner node. After selecting the winner node for input

pattern X, the fuzzy ART checks the similarity of input pattern X and the top-down weight vector W_j of the winner node Y_j using:

$$\rho \le |X \wedge W_j|/|X|, \qquad (17)$$

where the vigilance parameter ρ defines the minimum similarity between input pattern and the prototype of the winner node. The synaptic top-down weight vector W_j is the same bottom-up weight vector W_{ji} in Equation (16). If the similarity is larger than the vigilance value, then the vector W_j is adapted by moving its values toward the common MIN vector of X and W_j according to:

$$W_J^{(new)} = \eta(X \wedge W_J^{(old)}) + (1 - \eta)W_J^{(old)}, \qquad (18)$$

where η is a learning rate. When Equation (18) is satisfied, then resonance occurs. However, if the similarity is less than the vigilance, the current winning F_2 node is removed from the competition by a reset signal. The fuzzy ART searches again a node with the next most similar weight vector with the input pattern X before an uncommitted prototype is chosen. If none of the committed nodes matches the input pattern well enough, the search is stopped and an uncommitted prototype is taken. Clearly, as the number of training patterns increases, the fuzzy ART network requires more time to reinforce or inhibit some selected areas. For faster analysis in finding an inhibition or reinforcement area, the hierarchical structure of this network can be used.

Knowledge Structuring with Convolution Neural Network

The CNN architecture is capable to characterize and recognize variable object patterns directly from images free of pre-processing, by automatically synthesizing its own feature extractors from a large data set [Lawrence *et al.* 1997, Delakis and Garcia 2002]. Moreover, the use of RFs, shared weights, and spatial subsampling in such a neural model provides some degrees of partial invariance to translation, rotation, scale, and deformation. CNN has been applied to object detection and face recognition when sophisticated pre-processing is to be avoided and raw visual information are to be processed directly [Lawrence *et al.* 1997, Delakis and Garcia 2002]. The CNN extracts successively large volume of features in a hierarchical set of layers. Furthermore, the convolution network topology is more similar to biological networks based on RFs and improves tolerance to local distortions. A framework is set up to extract and build structured low-level features of an object via CNN architecture in this chapter. A sparse coding scheme is considered in order to extract and represent structured low-level features of an arbitrary object using CNN.

As shown in Figure 4, a CNN for structured low-level feature extraction consists of a subsequent processing such as convolutional operation, local sampling, further convolutional operation and subsampling. Each processing contains one or more levels. Multi-levels are usually used in each processing in order to detect multi-features. The input of the CNN is essential areas detected by the aforementioned biologically inspired visually selective attention model described in the aforementioned part. In the illustrated CNN architecture shown in Figure 4, color and texture features extracted from essential areas are used as parallel detailed information. The convolutional operation is typically followed by the local sampling that makes normalization and sampling around the considered neighborhood. Technically, further convolutional operation and subsampling are necessary for the well represented feature maps. Finally, the structured low-level feature can be extracted using such kind of CNN architecture.

The color/texture feature for the detected essential area is represented by a certain dimensional vector including specific feature maps. In our implementation, the initial colour feature components contain hue, saturation and intensity. This kind of colour space is used as a better representation for clustering than RGB space, which was validated experimentally. After the first convolutional operation, we have a 192-dimensional vector with feature map size of 8x8 for each component. Then a 48-dimensional vector is remained on local sampling, with feature map size of 4x4 for each component. Following the second convolutional operation, we get a 96-dimensional vector with feature map size of 4x4. The final structured colour feature vector is generated after the subsampling, 24-dimentional vector with feature map size of 2x2. The eight directional Gabor filter is used to generate the initial texture

Figure 4. The architecture of CNN

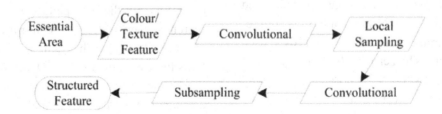

features. After the first convolutional operation, we have a 512-dimensional vector with feature map size of 8x8 for each direction. Then a 128-dimensional vector is remained on local sampling, with feature map size of 4x4 for each direction. Following the second convolutional operation, we get a 576-dimensional vector with feature map size of 4x4. The final structured texture feature vector is generated after the subsampling, 144-dimentional vector with feature map size of 2x2. Therefore, each area is totally represented by a 168-dimensional vector containing colour and texture features, with each feature map size of 2x2. The dimension and the size of feature map are set experimentally. These kind of structured features outweigh simplex low-level features in representation and application for the further clustering.

Clustering with Growing Cell Structure Network

The topology representation based on the GCS algorithmic steps are summarized below:

Step 1. Create initial network topology; initialize node parameters $\Gamma(i)$, for $i=1,\cdots,k+1$, with small values.

Step 2. Repeat steps 3-5 for $t=1,\cdots,L$, where t denotes the number of presentation epochs.

Step 3. Randomly select input vector V, and find the winner node w. Move the winner node towards the input $X_{\Gamma w}=h_w(V-\Gamma_w)$, where h_w denotes a learning rate of the winner node, Γ_w denotes the parameter of the winner node.

Step 4. Increase the frequency counter of the winner node by a fixed value Δ, where Δ is set 1 in our experiments.

Step 5. Correct parameters of its direct neighbours $X_{\Gamma k}=h_k(V-\Gamma_k)$, where h_k denotes a learning rate of the neighbour node, Γ_k denotes the parameter of the neighbour node.

Step 6. After L epochs calculate renormalized frequency for each node.

Step 7. Find node with highest frequency Γ_1; find direct neighbour Γ_2 with largest distance $\|\Gamma_1-\Gamma_2\|$; add new node $\Gamma_n=(\Gamma_1+\Gamma_2)/2$ in between, link Γ_1, Γ_2, and Γ_n.

Step 8. Stop if total number of epochs is too large; otherwise go to step 2.

The input of the algorithm is a set of extracted structured low-level features generated by CNN. Various topology maps subtly reflect the characteristics of distinct image groups which are closely related to the order of the forthcoming visual information. Furthermore, the extracted information from perceptions in colour and texture domains can also be used to represent objects.

Topology Representation

The topology representation for visual information processing is illustrated in Figure 5.

The input of the topology representation module is a set of extracted structured low-level features of essential areas in the visual information. The essential areas are selected by the biologically inspired visually selective attention model and the structured low-level features are generated by the CNN. The various unsupervised learning algorithms are also integrated into the mechanism of topology preserving to maintain the gracious network structure. Thus, the chain of the topology preservation of the visual information can be established with the interaction of the topology representation process. Various topology maps subtly reflect the characteristics of distinct visual information categories which are closely related to the order of the forthcoming visual information. In the proposed system, the total topology preservation can be induced from the learned information. The extracted information from perceptions in colour and texture domains can also be used to represent objects, while the labelling can be designated by the human supervisor or suitable reasoning rules. Furthermore, ontology maps can be generated through the

Figure 5. Topology representation for visual information processing

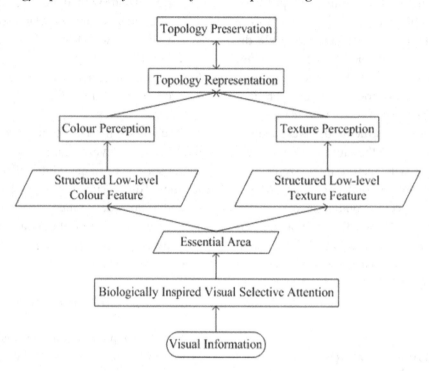

conceptual scheme by the given relevance between the represented object and its components. The dynamical mechanism can be enhanced by full integrations with other hierarchical frameworks. It can also be extended to many other applications such as inference, reasoning, and forecasting.

Classification of Visual Information

A proposed high-level top-down visual information perception and classification model uses a generative approach based on an incremental Bayesian parameter estimation method. The input features of this generative object representation are the structured low-level feature information generated by CNN. In general, generative models can handle missing data or partially labelled data, and can augment small quantities of expensive labelled data with large quantities raw data. A new class can be added incrementally by learning its class-conditional density independently of all the previous classes. Moreover, generative models can

readily handle compositionality whereas standard discriminative models need to see all combinations of possibilities during training [Ulusoy and Bishop 2005].

On independently learning the conditional density of the pattern with all other existing patterns, the novel pattern might be added dynamically into the current pattern setting. Considering n training data samples from a pattern ω, with each pattern featured by $f(f<n)$ codebook vectors, learning is progressing with updating the corresponding codebook vectors whenever a novel feature vector v is enrolled. The prior probabilities $p(\omega)$ and the conditional densities $p(v\square\omega)$ of the pattern can be learned independently by generative approach. Furthermore, the posterior probabilities are obtained using the Bayes' theorem:

$$p(\omega \mid v) = \frac{p(v \mid \omega)p(\omega)}{p(v)} = \frac{p(v \mid \omega)p(\omega)}{\sum_j p(v \mid j)p(j)}.$$

(19)

Following Vailaya *et al.* in [Vailaya *et al.* 2001], a vector quantizer is used to extract codebook vectors from training samples in order to estimate the conditional density of the feature vector v given the pattern ω. The conditional densities of the pattern are approximated using a mixture of Gaussians, assuming identity covariance matrices, with each centred at a codebook vector. The reason the variance is set to unity in the Gaussian mixture is that the mean square error criterion is the sum of the Euclidean distances of each training sample from its closest codebook vector. From a mixture point of view, this is equivalent to assuming covariance matrices of the form $\sigma^2 I$ (where I is the identity). This leads to:

$$p(v^{(i)} \mid \omega, \theta_{(f)}) \propto \sum_{j=1}^{f} m_j^{(i)} \exp\left(-\frac{\parallel v^{(i)} - v_j^{(i)} \parallel^2}{2\sigma^2}\right)$$

(20)

where $\theta_{(f)}^{(i)} = \left\{ v_1^{(i)}, \cdots, v_f^{(i)}, m_1^{(i)}, \cdots, m_{f-1}^{(i)} \right\}$, (note that $\sum_j m_j^{(i)} = 1$) [Vailaya *et al.* 2001]. Notice that, the value of σ is empirically estimated for each feature. Alternatively, the expectation maximization algorithm could be used to directly find the ML estimates of the mixture parameters, under a diagonal covariance constraint. This option is however computationally more demanding [Vailaya *et al.* 2001]. It is observed that the value of σ is not crucial as it only affects the number of codebook vectors that influence classification. Thus, unless σ is exceptionally large, only a few codebook vectors close to the input pattern influence the class-conditional probabilities. Finally, the conditional densities of the pattern can be represented as [Vailaya *et al.* 2001]:

$$p_V(v \mid \omega) \propto \sum_{j=1}^{f} m_j * \exp\left(- \parallel v - \hat{v}_j \parallel^2 / 2\right),$$

(21)

where $\hat{v}_j (1 \leq j \leq f)$ denotes the codebook vectors, m_j is the proportion of training samples assigned to $\hat{v}_j$.

A task for target visual information detection activates a visual information non-specific representation model for a desired target visual information area. Then, the high-level visual information perception and classification model just computes the similarity of the statistical properties for candidate attended regions. This process is based on the visual information non-specific representation model and the visual information detection model using ML. Finally, an integrated essential map for the specific target visual information is generated.

According to human perception, the inferior temporal (IT) area plays a role in understanding visual information with invariant representation mechanism based on the received bias signals. Indeed, when human beings focus their attention in a given image area, the PFC gives a competition bias related to the target object in the IT area [Lanyon and Denham 2004]. Then, the IT area generates specific information and transmits it to the high level attention generator which conducts a biased competition. Thus, the high-level visual information perception and classification model can assign a specific class to a target visual information area, which gives the ML.

Assuming the prior density is essentially uniform, the posterior probability can be estimated as follows [Vailaya *et al.* 2001, Duda *et al.* 2001]:

$$\arg\max_{\omega \in \Omega} \left\{ p(\omega \mid v) \right\} = \arg\max_{\omega \in \Omega} \left\{ p_V(v \mid \omega) p(\omega) \right\}$$

(22)

where Ω is the set of pattern classes.

In addition, the high-level visual information perception and classification model can generate a visual information specific attention based on the visual information class indication ability. Moreover, it may provide informative control signals to the internal effectors. This in turn can be seen as an incremental framework for knowledge structuring with human interaction.

EXPERIMENTAL RESULTS

Topology Representation

Simulation results of the topology representation and preservation on the clustering of the visual information are presented in Figure 6.

In this case the posterior probability of each class is represented by the different colour regions corresponding to the spatial location. In this representation the colour reflect the probability of the occurrence of the specific class. According to the simulation results, distinct classes can be detected by the configuration of the distribution map. The location of each class is exactly recorded in the structure of the topographic network, which further stresses the relevance between adjacent clusters such as the class "autumn" and the class "rural". Clearly, these two classes have common features in general.

Finally, the proposed knowledge structuring model can successfully generate new object clusters by interaction with the inference procedure.

Figure 6. Simulation results of the posterior probability of each class in the Corel database. The left column from the top to the down: "building", "autumn", "car", and "cloud". The right column from the top to the down: "tiger", "rural", "elephant", and "lion"

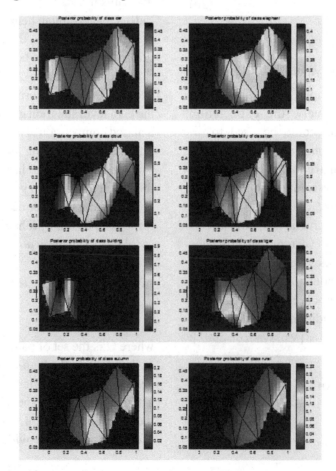

The distribution of different clusters indicates the effectiveness of knowledge representation and inference, while the total incremental structure suggests the knowledge restoration mechanism.

The experiments are carried out based on the database and evaluation metrics given in this chapter. The proposed technique based on different neural network algorithms was also compared with an approach based on multi-objective optimization (MOO) [Zhang & Izquierdo 2006; Jaszkiewicz 2001] and another using Bayesian networks for concept propagation [Li *et al.* 2003]. The selection of the subset depends on the common categories among fairly comparable approaches. The obtained results based on various neural network algorithms are given in the following subsections, respectively.

Comparison and Analysis of Classification Results

It can be observed that the proposed technique outperforms the other two approaches. Even though MOO can be optimized for a given concept, the result of the proposed technique performs better in general. Except for the class lion, in which the Bayesian approach delivers the highest accuracy, the proposed technique performs substantially better in other cases. The exception of the lion is due to the interference from complex background environment, while there is more larruping color and texture information in other categories. It could be compensated by considering the prior information between affiliated features and semantic meaning. This summary of results truly represents the observed outcomes with other classes and datasets used in the experimental evaluation and validates our claim that the proposed technique has good discriminative power and it is suitable for retrieving natural images in large database.

COREL Database

The classification result based on the GCS algorithm is given in Table 1. Table 2 shows a summary

of results on some subsets of the image categories coming out from the comparative evaluation with the Bayesian approach and MOO.

CALTECH101 Database

In the following a series of experiments on the small Caltech101 dataset was used with varying number of images and concepts with different degrees of difficulty. Observe that the Caltech101 database offers a well established platform for classification containing images with significant texture and clutter. In each case images were pooled out from the original datasets, and the proposed technique trained for a specified number of concepts. Selected results showing the number of outliers or wrong classifications for each concept are summarized in the "confusion" tables showed as Table 3. In these experiments it is necessary to specify the number of categories. Moreover, it is

Table 1. Image classification and retrieval based on GCS

Class	D	MD	FA	recall (%)	precision (%)
building	83	17	10	83	89
autumn	46	10	8	82	85
car	84	16	12	84	88
cloud	92	8	6	92	94
tiger	88	12	16	88	85
rural	36	8	6	82	86
elephant	94	6	14	94	87
lion	85	15	12	85	88

Table 2. GCS-based precision comparison with other approaches

(%)	GCS	Bayesian	MOO
building	89	72	70
cloud	94	84	79
lion	88	92	88
tiger	85	60	60

Table 3. (I) Confusion table for categories "airplane", "motorbike", and "minaret"

True Class→	airplane	motorbike	minaret
airplane	94.76	2.95	4.34
motorbike	0.88	95.24	3.53
minaret	4.36	1.80	92.13

Table 3. (II) Confusion table for categories "butterfly", "Dalmatian", "elephant", and "leopard"

True Class→	butterfly	Dalmatian	elephant	leopard
butterfly	98.82	0.45	0.20	0.38
dalmatian	0.34	96.50	1.44	1.75
elephant	0.42	2.86	95.89	4.96
leopard	0.42	0.19	2.46	92.90

important to find a collection of images containing objects of the same category that is large enough, with good intra-class variation between objects. Here, intra-class variation is based on appearance, not semantics or concepts. Dealing with realistic backgrounds presents another challenge for the system.

Another experiment was conducted using the large Caltech101 database. Each experiment was carried out under identical conditions. First, for each category, K training images were selected randomly. All the remaining images were then used for testing. Training was performed using both the proposed Incremental mode and a Batch mode to evaluate the system performance. For each category, K takes the values 1, 3, 5, 8 and 10. The experiments are then repeated 15 times for each value using randomly chosen K training images each time. Figure 7 illustrates the performance for the algorithms using Incremental and Batch modes. Despite the rudimentary prior, a strong performance gain is observed for the majority of the 101 categories. Even when only a

few training examples were used. For instance using a single training example (K=1), an average performance of 86% is achieved, with the best results being over 90%. For K = 3, both modes achieve a performance close to 86%. For K = 10, the average Incremental mode is not as reliable as the Batch mode. In general the Incremental mode is much more sensitive to the quality of the training images and to the order in which they are presented to the algorithm. Therefore it is more likely to form suboptimal models. Figure 7 shows the comparative results between Batch mode and Incremental mode.

It is obvious that both modes allow category learning from small training sets and the desirable Incremental mode leads to much faster learning speed. However, this also results in a worse performance for larger training set sizes. This is due to the fact that less information is carried along by the Incremental mode from one learning epoch to the next, while the Batch mode has all training

Figure 7. Comparison results of using Incremental mode and Batch mode over all Caltech101 categories: (a) Average learning time for two modes, (b) Performance error for two modes

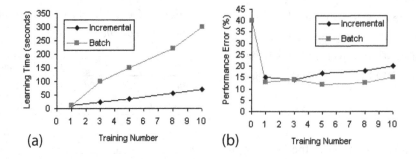

Table 3. (III) Confusion table for categories "Joshua tree", "lotus", "starfish", and "sunflower"

True Class→	Joshua tree	llepic 3 - mopicstext.he images, relevant image. classification rather than binary classification.otus	starfish	sunflower
Joshua tree	96.56	0.68	2.84	4.09
lotus	0.83	95.45	1.03	1.26
starfish	1.94	0.99	94.71	2.33
sunflower	0.66	2.88	1.42	92.32

images available at the same time thus allowing to test a larger number of hypotheses on how image features should be assigned for each training image. Further strategies should be explored to optimize the trade-off between these two modes. While performance is a key measurement for classification algorithms, efficiency in training and learning are also important. One big advantage that we have gained from the Incremental mode is its fast speed in training. Figure 7(a) shows the comparison of average learning time across all 101 categories between these two modes. Both modes show approximately linear increase in learning time as the number of training images increases. The Incremental mode, particularly, shows a very small slope. A great source of improvement could potentially come from prior model information. However, the performance could be degraded if the model was to incorporate misleading information. The choice of prior for this chapter is kept as simple as possible to facilitate the experiments. It is expected that further studies in this direction will help to improve the overall performance of the system.

Parameter Determination and Influence on Classification Result

It is necessary to consider the issue of the parameter determination and its influence on the classification result. The learning rate and the vigilance threshold in the fuzzy ART network play an important role. If the learning rate η is small then the algorithm learns the weights very slowly, while if η is large then the fast changes of the weights

may cause an unstable behavior with oscillations of the weight values. the value of learning rates is varied to observe the influence on the classification results. Table 4 gives the summary of this variation. Here, the categories of "car" and "lion" were used respectively from the Corel database. The vigilance threshold was set as 0.97. Points of the highest recall, the highest precision, and the highest F-measure are shown in bold in Table 4. We always take the highest value of F-measure to optimize the performance of the system. It can be observed that the performance of the proposed system achieves the balance between the recall and precision value when learning rate is 0.95. To further investigate the role of determination parameters in the classification process, the performance of classification was studied by varying the vigilance threshold value. Results obtained for the concept "elephant" from the Corel database are reported in Table 5. R denotes recall, P denotes precision. This concept was used to find the appropriate vigilance threshold, with the learning rate 0.95 as verified before. The performance for this concept is given in Table 5 with a variation of the vigilance threshold value. The initial vigilance threshold value was set as 0.97.

From the F-measure value in Table 5 it can be observed that the optimal vigilance threshold is 0.97, which means reasonable numbers of records distributed in the corresponding clusters. If the threshold is higher, the number of records in a cluster is less, and more outliers are within the total set.

Finally, Figure 8 shows a Recall-Precision Curve based on Table 5, where few sample results

Table 4. Accuracy on the category of "car" and "lion" under the different learning rate value

Learning Rate	D		FA		R (%)		P (%)		F-measure (%)	
	car	lion	car	lion	car	lion	car	lion	car	lion
0.90	91	88	43	39	**91.00**	**88.00**	67.91	69.29	77.78	77.53
0.92	86	85	37	32	86.00	85.00	69.92	72.65	77.13	78.34
0.95	81	82	23	22	81.00	82.00	77.88	78.85	**79.41**	**80.39**
0.97	77	78	17	18	77.00	78.00	81.91	81.25	79.38	79.59
0.99	70	74	14	13	70.00	74.00	**83.33**	**85.06**	76.09	79.15

Table 5. Accuracy of "raising" (↑) and "lowering" (↓) the vigilance threshold value

Threshold		D		FA		R (%)		P (%)		F-measure (%)	
↑	↓	↑	↓	↑	↓	↑	↓	↑	↓	↑	↓
0.97	0.97	92	92	19	19	**92.00**	**92.00**	82.88	82.88	**87.20**	**87.20**
0.98	0.96	85	83	16	14	85.00	83.00	84.16	85.57	84.58	84.27
0.99	0.95	64	61	6	5	64.00	61.00	91.43	92.42	75.29	73.49
0.995	0.93	42	34	3	1	42.00	34.00	93.33	97.14	57.93	50.37
0.997	0.90	24	15	1	0	24.00	15.00	96.00	100.00	38.40	26.09
0.999	0.85	10	4	0	0	10.00	4.00	**100.00**	**100.00**	18.18	7.69

for recall, precision and F-measure are depicted. These results indicate that the used vigilance threshold is in fact optimal for the learning algorithm. Lowering the vigilance threshold value leads to dissimilar categories being assigned to the same cluster. On the other hand, raising the vigilance threshold value causes categories that actually represent the same object, but do not cross the high cluster threshold, to be assigned to different clusters. Both cases lead to poorer generalization. From the aforementioned analysis, it is clear that the parameter determination, i.e., learning rate and vigilance threshold, is critical for the performance of the proposed framework.

FUTURE RESEARCH DIRECTIONS

As consequence of the constant evaluation of the rule confidence and support measure, the presented

Figure 8. Recall-Precision Curve on the "elephant" category with variation of the vigilance threshold value: (a) raising the vigilance threshold value; (b) lowering the vigilance threshold value

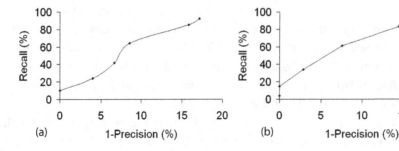

framework can learn and update topology representation using relevance feedback information. This is part of ongoing work. Additional ongoing work considers a hierarchical representation framework taking into account the ontology, which can be developed with a hierarchical neural network structure. This dynamically growing architecture can be embedded in a hierarchical network structure according to the characteristics of the input data. This will provide a new perception of the visual space. A graphical approach to construct a relevance map in topology representation is part of future developments. Furthermore, relying upon the relevance information, the topology representation model can be redesigned in a self-adaptive manner using soft computing techniques. Additional expansion capabilities include learning from semantics and annotation-based approach and the use of multimodal information. Although the performed experimental evaluation shows high accuracy in the results of classification, the computational complexity and the scalability of the proposed system need to be improved, the conducted research also shows that there is plenty of room for improvement and that the high-level classification and annotation task remains open and will be a subject of study for years to come.

CONCLUSION

An approach for classification of visual information based on a biologically inspired knowledge structuring technique is presented. Exploiting the constantly updating knowledge based on the essential map of visual information, the knowledge structuring approach automatically annotates new visual information added to the database. By utilizing biologically inspired theory and knowledge structuring approach, the framework simulates the human-like image classification and inference. The knowledge structuring approach automatically creates a relevance map from essential regions of visual information. It also derives a set of well-organized representations from low-level description to drive the final classification. Classification is achieved by simulating high-level top-down visual information perception and classifying using an incremental Bayesian parameter estimation method. Since the knowledge structuring base creation depends on information provided by expert users, the framework can be easily extended to support intelligent retrieval wit enabled user relevance feedback. The proposed modular framework architecture offers straightforward expansion to include user relevance feedback, contextual input, and multimodal information if available.

The proposed framework was motivated by human visual perception with regard to social functioning, selective processing and incremental learning. In order to develop such an autonomous model, the author tried to understand the brain mechanism and acquire insight from it. Based upon the brain mechanism, several cooperative models were developed for visual scene perception in a complex natural visual environment. A visually selective attention model was developed, which can autonomously decide the direction of sight based upon the bottom-up essential map model, in conjunction with the low-level top-down selective attention model. The bottom-up essential map model reflects the relativity of primitive visual features and the low-level top-down selective attention model reflects human preference through human interaction on the visual information.

The main contribution of this work is the biologically motivated integration of a number of existing approaches, e.g., unsupervised learning and sparse representation, into the hierarchical network architecture. These models yield better performance than many existing algorithms and represent biologically plausible mechanisms, and therefore, may provide a platform from where to further explore the mechanisms of visual information processing both in biological and robotic settings.

Overall, a biologically inspired framework for classification of visual information is presented in this chapter. Initially, it extracts features from the images in the dataset to generate an essential map for each image. Exploiting the constantly updating knowledge based on the essential map of natural images, the knowledge structuring automatically annotates new visual information added to the database. By utilizing biologically inspired theory and knowledge structuring, this framework simulates the human-like image classification and inference. Although the framework can be extended to other types of low-level visual information and abstraction levels, the evaluation of the proposed approach has focused on a few selected features extracted from still images. Since the knowledge structuring base creation depends on information provided by expert users, the system can be easily extended to support intelligent retrieval wit enabled user relevance feedback. The proposed knowledge structuring based on the biologically inspired visually selective attention model can be regarded as a framework for autonomous visual information classification and retrieval system through human interaction. The whole framework can automatically generate relevance maps from the visual information and clustering the visual information using learned information. The proposed framework is modular and easily expandable to allow additional functionalities as user relevance feedback in image retrieval scenarios.

REFERENCES

Assfalg, J., Bertini, M., Colombo, C., & Del Bimbo, A. (2001). Semantic characterization of visual content for sports videos annotation. In *Proc. 2nd Int. Workshop Multimedia Databases and Image Communication* (LNCS 2184, pp. 179-191).

Attwell, D., & Laughlin, S. (2001). An energy budget for signaling in the grey matter of the brain. *Journal of Cerebral Blood Flow and Metabolism, 21*, 1133–1145. doi:10.1097/00004647-200110000-00001

Barlow, H. (1994). What is the computational goal of the Neocortex? In Koch, C., & Davis, J. (Eds.), *Large-Scale Neuronal Theories of the Brain* (pp. 553–561). Oxford: Oxford University Press.

Barlow, H., & Tolhust, D. (1992). Why do you have edge detectors? *Optical Society of America Technical Digest, 23*(172).

Bear, M. F., Connors, B. W., & Paradiso, M. A. (2001). *Neuroscience Exploring the Brain*. Lippincott Williams & Wilkins Co.

Bell, A. J., & Sejnowski, T. (1997). The independent components of natural scenes are edge filters. *Vision Research, 37*(23), 3327–3338. doi:10.1016/S0042-6989(97)00121-1

Caltech 101 dataset (n.d.). Retrieved from www.vision.caltech.edu/feifeili/101 ObjectCategories

Carpenter, G. A., Grossberg, S., Markuzon, N., Reynolds, J. H., & Rosen, D. B. (1992). Fuzzy ARTMAP: A neural network architecture for incremental supervised learning of analog multi-dimensional maps. *IEEE Transactions on Neural Networks, 3*(5), 698–713. doi:10.1109/72.159059

Delakis, M., & Garcia, C. (2002). Robust face detection based on convolutional neural networks. In *Proc. of 2nd Hellenic Conf. on Artificial Intelligence* (pp. 367-378).

Dorado, A., Calic, J., & Izquierdo, E. (2004). A rule-based video annotation system. *IEEE Trans. on Circuits and Systems for Video Technology, 14*(5), 622–633. doi:10.1109/TCSVT.2004.826764

Dorado, A., Djordjevic, D., Pedrycz, W., & Izquierdo, E. (2006). Efficient image selection for concept learning. *IEE Proceedings. Vision Image and Signal Processing, 153*(3), 263–273. doi:10.1049/ip-vis:20050057

Dorai, C., & Venkatesh, S. (2003). Bridging the semantic gap with computational media aesthetics. *IEEE MultiMedia, 10*, 15–17. doi:10.1109/MMUL.2003.1195157

Duda, R. O., Hart, P. E., & Stork, D. G. (2001). *Pattern Classification.* John Wiley & Sons, Inc.

Edelman, S., & Intrator, N. (2002). *Unsupervised learning of visual structure* (pp. 629–642). Biologically Motivated Computer Vision.

Goldstein, E. B. (1995). *Sensation and Perception* (4th ed.). Thomson Publishing Company.

Guyton, A. C. (1991). *Textbook of medical physiology* (8th ed.). USA: W.B. Saunders Company.

Itti, L. (2005). *Models of bottom-up attention and saliency. Neurobiology of Attention* (pp. 576–582). San Diego, CA: Elsevier.

Itti, L., & Koch, C. (2001). Feature combination strategies for saliency-based visual attention systems. *Journal of Electronic Imaging, 10*(1), 161–169. doi:10.1117/1.1333677

Itti, L., Koch, C., & Niebur, E. (1998). A model of saliency-based visual attention for rapid scene analysis. *IEEE Transactions on Pattern Analysis and Machine Intelligence, 20*(11), 1254–1259. doi:10.1109/34.730558

Jabri, M. (2000). *Biological computing for robot navigation and control. NRA2-37143.* Beaverton, OR: OGI School of Science and Engineering at OHSU.

Jasinschi, R. S., Dimitrova, N., McGee, T., Agnihotri, L., Zimmerman, J., Li, D., & Louie, J. (2002). A probabilistic layered framework for integrating multimedia content and context information. In *Proc. IEEE Int. Conf. Acoustics, Speech, and Signal Processing: Vol.* 2 (pp. 2057–2060).

Jing, F., Li, M., Zhang, H.-J., & Zhang, B. (2004). Relevance feedback in region-based image retrieval. *IEEE Trans. on Circuits and Systems for Video Technology, 14*(5), 672–681. doi:10.1109/TCSVT.2004.826775

Kuffler, S. W., Nicholls, J. G., & Martin, J. G. (1984). *From Neuron to Brain.* Sunderland, UK: Sinauer Associates.

Lanyon, L. J., & Denham, S. L. (2004). A model of active visual search with object-based attention guiding scan paths. *Neural Networks, 17*(5-6), 873–897. doi:10.1016/j.neunet.2004.03.012

Lawrence, S., Giles, C. L., Tsoi, A. C., & Back, A. D. (1997). Face recognition: A convolutional neural-network approach. *IEEE Transactions on Neural Networks, 8*(1), 98–113. doi:10.1109/72.554195

Li, F.-F., Fergus, R., & Perona, P. (2003). A bayesian approach to unsupervised one-shot learning of object categories. In *Proc. of the 9th IEEE International Conference on Computer Vision* (Vol. 2., pp. 1134-1141).

Li, Z. (2001). Computational design and nonlinear dynamics of a recurrent network model of the primary visual cortex. *Neural Computation, 13*(8), 1749–1780. doi:10.1162/08997660152469332

Majani, E., Erlanson, R., & Abu-Mostafa, Y. (Eds.). (1984). *The Eye.* New York: Academic.

Mundhenk, T. N., Navalpakkam, V., Makaliwe, H., Vasudevan, S., & Itti, L. (2004). Biologically inspired feature based categorization of objects. In *Proc. SPIE Human Vision and Electronic Imaging IX* (Vol. 5292). San Jose, CA: Bellingham, WA, SPIE Press.

Navalpakkam, V., & Itti, L. (2006). Bottom-up and top-down influences on visual scanpaths. In *Proc. SPIE Human Vision and Electronic Imaging XI* (Vol. 6057). San Jose, CA: Bellingham, WA, SPIE Press.

Park, S. J., An, K. H., & Lee, M. (2002). Saliency map model with adaptive masking based on independent component analysis. *Neurocomputing, 49*, 417–422. doi:10.1016/S0925-2312(02)00637-9

Ratnaparkhi, A. (1998). *Maximum entropy models for natural language ambiguity resolution*. Ph.D. Dissertation. Computer and Information Science, Univ. of Pennsylvania, USA.

Sethi, I. K., Coman, I. L., & Stan, D. (2001). Mining association rules between low-level features and high-level concepts. In *Proc. SPIE Int. Soc. Opt. Eng.* (Vol. 4384, pp. 279-290).

Sun, Y., & Fisher, R. (2002). Hierarchical selectivity for object-based visual attention (LNCS 2525, pp. 427-438). Heidelberg: Springer-Verlag.

Tang, H. L., Hanka, R., & Ip, H. H. S. (2003). Histological image retrieval based on semantic content analysis. *IEEE Transactions on Information Technology in Biomedicine*, 7(1), 26–36. doi:10.1109/TITB.2003.808500

Treisman, A. M., & Gelade, G. (1980). A feature-integrations theory of attention. *Cognitive Psychology*, 12(1), 97–136. doi:10.1016/0010-0285(80)90005-5

Tsotsos, J. K., Culhane, S. M., Wai, W. Y. K., Lai, Y. H., Davis, N., & Nuflo, F. (1995). Modelling visual attention via selective tuning. *Artificial Intelligence*, 78, 507–545. doi:10.1016/0004-3702(95)00025-9

Ulusoy, I., & Bishop, C. M. (2005). Generative versus discriminative methods for object recognition. In *Proc. of IEEE Computer Vision and Pattern Recognition* (Vol. 2, pp. 258-265).

Vailaya, A., Figueiredo, M. A. T., Jain, A. K., & Zhang, H. J. (2001). Image classification for content-based indexing. *IEEE Transactions on Image Processing*, 10(1), 117–130. doi:10.1109/83.892448

Vailaya, A., & Jain, A. (1999). Incremental learning for Bayesian classification of images. In *Proc. of the International Conf. Image Processing*.

Van Rijsbergen, C. J. (1979). *Heavy emphasis on probabilistic models*. Information Retrieval.

Wallraven, C., Caputo, B., & Graf, A. (2003). Recognition with local features: the kernel recipe. In *IEEE International Conference on Computer Vision* (pp. 257-264).

Zhang, Q., & Izquierdo, E. (2006). A multi-feature optimization approach to object-based image classification. In *Proc. of International Conference on Image and Video Retrieval* (pp. 310-319).

Chapter 15
Ant–Inspired Visual Saliency Detection in Image

Jing Tian
South China University of Technology, China

Weiyu Yu
South China University of Technology, China

ABSTRACT

Visual saliency detection aims to produce saliency map of images via simulating the behavior of the human visual system (HVS). An ant-inspired approach is proposed in this chapter. The proposed approach is inspired by the ant's behavior to find the most saliency regions in image, by depositing the pheromone information (through ant's movements) on the image to measure its saliency. Furthermore, the ant's movements are steered by the local phase coherence of the image. Experimental results are presented to demonstrate the superior performance of the proposed approach.

INTRODUCTION

Visual saliency detection has been of great research interest in recent years, since it is potential for a wide range of applications, such as object detection, content-based image retrieval and perceptual image compression. Human perceptual attention usually tends to firstly pick attended regions, which correspond to prominent objects in an image, rather than the whole image (Jams, 1890; Itti, 2000). Visual saliency detection aims to simulate the behavior of the human visual system (HVS) by automatically producing saliency maps of the

image. Much research has been done on modeling visual attention; they can be classified into the following two categories: bottom-up and top-down. The first approach is an image-driven approach to select visual information based on saliency in the image itself, while the second one is a goal-driven approach based on both a user-defined task and the image itself.

This chapter is focused on the first kind of approach. In general, it uses certain means of determining local contrast of image regions with their surroundings using one or more of the features of color, intensity, and orientation. Usually, separate feature maps are created for each of the features used and then combined to obtain the final saliency

DOI: 10.4018/978-1-60960-024-2.ch015

map. Itti (1998) introduced a biologically-inspired saliency model. They proposed to use a set of feature maps from three complementary channels as intensity, color, and orientation. The normalized feature maps from each channel were then sent into a Winner-Take-All competition to select the most conspicuous image locations as attended points (i.e., the overall saliency map). Ma (2003) proposed a local contrast-based saliency model, which is obtained from summing up differences of image pixels with their respective surrounding pixels in a small neighborhood. A fuzzy-growing method then segments salient regions from the saliency map. Hu (2004) proposed to produce saliency maps by thresholding the color, intensity, and orientation maps using histogram entropy thresholding analysis instead of a scale space approach. They then use a spatial compactness measure, computed as the area of the convex hull encompassing the salient region, and saliency density, which is a function of the magnitudes of saliency values in the saliency feature maps, to weigh the individual saliency maps before combining them. Wu (2009) proposed to determine the saliency map using low-level features, including luminance, color and region information, then thresholding these feature maps using a just noticeable difference (JND) model and integrating them to a final saliency map.

The major challenges in visual saliency detection are (i) image features extracted and (ii) mechanisms of saliency measure. To tackle the above challenge, a new bottom-up approach, called an ant-inspired visual saliency detection approach, is proposed in this chapter. The proposed visual saliency detection approach exploits the ant colony optimization (ACO) (Dorigo, 2004; Dorigo, 2006) technique to establish a pheromone information matrix that represents the saliency information presented at each pixel position of the image. The proposed approach is inspired by the natural collective foraging behavior of ant species, which guides ants on short paths to their food sources, since ants can deposit pheromone on the ground

in order to mark some favorable path that should be followed by other members of the colony. The pheromone information matrix is estimated via the movements of a number of ants which are dispatched to move on the image. Furthermore, the ant's movement is steered by the local feature coherence (Morrone, 1988; Kovesi, 1999) of the image, which is able to provide a perceptual image representation that is fairly consistent to the human visual system.

This chapter is organized as follows. Section 2 provides a brief introduction to ant colony optimization. Section 3 presents the proposed approach, followed by the experimental results presented in Section 4. Furthermore, Section 5 provides some insightful comments to point out several promising research directions for future research. Finally, Section 6 concludes this chapter.

ANT COLONY OPTIMIZATION

Ant colony optimization (ACO) is a nature-inspired optimization algorithm (Dorigo, 2004; Dorigo, 2006) motivated by the natural collective behavior of real-world ant colonies. The major collective behavior is the foraging behavior that guides ants on short paths to their food sources. More specifically, it is achieved by a deposited and accumulated chemical substance called pheromone by the passing ant which moves towards the food. In its searching the ant uses its own knowledge of where the smell of the food comes from (called heuristic information) and the other ants' decision of the path toward the food (called pheromone information). After it decides its own path, it confirms the path by depositing its own pheromone making the pheromone trail denser and more probable to be chosen by other ants. This is a learning mechanism ants possess besides their own recognition of the path. Despite that ACO has been widely applied to tackle numerous optimization problems, its application in image processing is quite a few (Tian 2008).

ACO aims to iteratively find the optimal solution of the target problem through a guided search (i.e., the movements of a number of ants) over the solution space, by constructing the *pheromone information*. To be more specific, suppose totally K ants are applied to find the optimal solution in a space χ that consists of $M_1 \times M_2$ nodes, the procedure of ACO can be summarized as follows (Dorigo, 2006).

- Initialize the positions of each ant, as well as the pheromone matrix $\tau^{(0)}$.
- For the construction-step index $n=1{:}N$,
  - Consecutively move each ant for L steps, according to a probabilistic transition matrix $\mathbf{p}^{(n)}$ (with a size of $M_1 M_2 \times M_1 M_2$).
  - Update the pheromone information matrix $\tau^{(n)}$.
- Make the solution decision according to the final pheromone information matrix $\tau^{(N)}$.

There are two fundamental issues in the above ACO process; that is, the establishment of the probabilistic transition matrix $\mathbf{p}^{(n)}$ and the update of the pheromone information matrix $\tau^{(n)}$., each of which is presented in detail as follow, respectively.

First, at the n-th construction-step of ACO, each ant moves from the node i to the node j according to a probabilistic action rule, which is determined by (Dorigo, 2006)

$$p_{i,j}^{(n)} = \frac{\left(\tau_{i,j}^{(n-1)}\right)^{\alpha} \left(\eta_{i,j}\right)^{\beta}}{\sum_{j \in \Omega_i} \left(\tau_{i,j}^{(n-1)}\right)^{\alpha} \left(\eta_{i,j}\right)^{\beta}}$$

where $\tau_{i,j}^{(n-1)}$ is the pheromone information value of the arc linking the node i to the node j; Ω_i is the neighborhood nodes for the ant given that it is on the node i; the constants α and β represent the influence of pheromone information and

heuristic information, respectively; $\eta_{i,j}$ represents the heuristic information for going from node I to node j, which is fixed to be same for each construction-step.

Second, the pheromone information matrix needs to be updated twice during the ACO procedure. The first update is performed after the movement of each ant within each construction-step. More specifically, after the movement of each ant within the n-th construction-step, the pheromone information matrix is updated as (Dorigo, 2006)

$$\tau_{i,j}^{(n-1)} = \begin{cases} \tau_{i,j}^{(n-1)} + \Delta_{i,j}^{(k)}, & \text{if } (i,j) \text{ belongs to the } \textit{best tour}; \\ \tau_{i,j}^{(n-1)}, & \text{otherwise.} \end{cases}$$

Furthermore, the determination of the best tour is subject to the user-defined criterion, it could be either the best tour found in the current construction-step, or the best solution found since the start of the algorithm, or a combination of both of the above two (Dorigo, 2006). The second update is performed after the move of all K ants within each construction-step; and the pheromone information matrix is updated as (Dorigo, 2006)

$$\tau^{(n)} = (1-\varphi)\tau^{(n-1)} + \varphi\tau^{(0)}$$

where φ is the pheromone decay coefficient.

PROPOSED APPROACH

The idea of the proposed approach is to utilize a number of ants to move on a 2-D image for constructing a pheromone information matrix, each entry of which represents certain feature at each pixel location of the image. Furthermore, the movements of the ants are steered by the local feature of the image; that is the phase coherence used in our proposed approach. More conceptually, the visual saliency detection problem is formulated in this chapter as following. Given a function to maximize (the visual saliency information in the image), different solutions are examined (ant exploration), each of which is memorized (thanks to the pheromone deposit) depending on its quality, and then guide the search (driven by the local phase coherence of the image) of the next solutions until convergence (final visual saliency of the image is detected).

The proposed approach starts from assigning one ant on an image with a size of $M_1 \times M_2$, each pixel of which can be viewed as a node. Furthermore, the initial value of each component of the pheromone matrix $\tau^{(0)}$ is set to be a constant τ_{init}. Then the proposed algorithm runs for N iterations, in each iteration, each ant moves to neighboring coefficients and the pheromone content of the coefficient on the ant's path are updated. There are two issues need to be addressed; they are (i) how to move ants on the images and (ii) how to update the pheromone information. Both of these two are discussed in the following sections in detail.

Ant Movement

At the n-th iteration, one ant is randomly selected, and this ant will consecutively move on the image for L movement-steps. This ant moves from the node $(l.m)$ to its neighboring node (i,j) according to a transition probability that is defined as

$$p_{(l,m),(i,j)}^{(n)} = \frac{\left(\tau_{i,j}^{(n-1)}\right)^{\alpha} \left(\eta_{i,j}\right)^{\beta}}{\sum_{(i,j)\in\Omega_{(l,m)}} \left(\tau_{i,j}^{(n-1)}\right)^{\alpha} \left(\eta_{i,j}\right)^{\beta}}$$

where $\tau_{i,j}^{(n-1)}$ is the pheromone value of the node (i,j), $\Omega_{(l,m)}$ is the neighborhood nodes of the node (l,m), $\eta_{i,j}$ represents the heuristic information at the node (i,j). The constants α and β represent the influence of the pheromone matrix and the heuristic matrix, respectively. Furthermore, the permissible range of the ant's movement (i.e., $\Omega_{(l,m)}$) is proposed to be 8-connectivity neighborhood.

There is one crucial issue to determine the heuristic information $\eta_{i,j}$. In this chpater, it is proposed to be determined by the local statistics at the pixel position (i,j). The local statistics need to be adaptively adjusted according to the human perception system; therefore, it is necessary to determine a quantifiable measure for perceptual sensitivity to signal characteristics. An effective method for measuring human perceptual sensitivity that has been proposed in recent years is the use of local phase coherence (Morrone, 1988). Local phase coherence approaches are based on the theory that local phase coherence increases as the perceptual significance of signal characteristics increases. This has been supported by physiological evidence that showed high human perception response to signal characteristics with high local phase coherence (Morrone, 1988). Another advantage to the use of local phase coherence is the fact that it is insensitive magnitude variations caused by illumination conditions or noise incurred in image signals.

The proposed technique measures local phase coherence based on the method proposed in (Kovesi, 1999). Localized frequency information is extracted using a Log-Gabor filter bank. Local phase coherence at the position $\mathbf{x}$ and the orientation θ is formulated as follows:

$$c(\mathbf{x},\theta) = \frac{\sum_n W(\mathbf{x},\theta) \mid A_n(\mathbf{x},\theta)\Delta\varphi_n(\mathbf{x},\theta) \mid}{\sum_n A_n(\mathbf{x},\theta) + \xi}$$
$$\Delta\varphi_n(\mathbf{x},\theta) = \cos(\varphi_n(\mathbf{x},\theta) - \overline{\varphi}(\mathbf{x},\theta)) - \mid \sin(\varphi_n(\mathbf{x},\theta) - \overline{\varphi}(\mathbf{x},\theta)) \mid$$

where W represents the frequency spread weighting factor, A_n and φ_n represent the amplitude and phase at wavelet scale n, respectively, $\overline{\varphi}_n$ represents the weighted mean phase, ξ is a small constant used to avoid the division by zero. All of these parameters are as same as that used in (Kovesi, 1999).

Based on the local phase coherence at different orientations, the perceptual significance of the image at a particular position $\mathbf{x}$ can be determined as the maximum moment of phase coherence by aggregating the local phase coherence at all orientations into a single measure (denoted as $c_{total}(\mathbf{x})$) as below

$$c_{total}(\mathbf{x}) = \tfrac{1}{2} \sum_\theta \left[\left(c(\mathbf{x},\theta)\sin(\theta) \right)^2 + \left(c(\mathbf{x},\theta)\cos(\theta) \right)^2 \right] + \tfrac{1}{2}\sqrt{4\left(\sum_\theta \left(c(\mathbf{x},\theta)\sin(\theta)c(\mathbf{x},\theta)\cos(\theta) \right) \right)^2 + \left(\sum_\theta \left[\left(c(\mathbf{x},\theta)\cos(\theta) \right)^2 - \left(c(\mathbf{x},\theta)\sin(\theta) \right)^2 \right] \right)^2}$$

where $c(\mathbf{x},\theta)$ is the local phase coherence at orientation θ. The maximum moment of phase coherence at a particular point in the signal is proportional to the sensitivity of the human perception system at that point.

Pheromone Update

The proposed approach performs two updates operations for updating the pheromone matrix.

- The first update is performed after the movement of each ant *within* each construction-step. Each component of the pheromone matrix is updated according to

$$\tau_{i,j}^{(n-1)} = \begin{cases} (1-\rho) \times \tau_{i,j}^{(n-1)} + \rho \times \Delta_{i,j}^{(k)}, & \text{if } (i,j) \text{ is visted by the current } k\text{-th ant}; \\ \tau_{i,j}^{(n-1)}, & \text{otherwise}. \end{cases}$$

where ρ controls the degree of the updating of $\tau_{i,j}^{(n-1)}$, $\Delta_{i,j}^{(k)}$ is determined by the heuristic matrix; that is, $\Delta_{i,j}^{(k)} = \frac{1}{\eta_{i,j}}$.

- The second update is carried out after the movement of all ants within each construction-step according to $\tau^{(n)} = (1-\varphi)\tau^{(n-1)} + \varphi\tau^{(0)}$ where φ is the pheromone decay coefficient.

Summary of the Proposed Approach

A summary of the implementation of the proposed approach is presented in Figure 1. The proposed

approach starts from the initialization process, and then runs for N iterations to construct the pheromone matrix by performing both the construction process and the update process. Finally, the pheromone matrix, which has a same size with that of the image, represents the saliency information at each pixel position of the image.

Experimental Results

Experiments are conducted to demonstrate the performance of the proposed approach. Test images are obtained from MSRA Salient Object Database. Furthermore, the parameters of the proposed ACO-based approach are experimentally set as follows: $\tau_{init}=0.001$, $\alpha=1$, $\beta=2$, $L=15$, $\rho=0.1$, and $\varphi=0.3$. The Gabor filter used for computing the phase coherence is implemented using three scales (i.e., $n=3$) and four orientations (i.e., $o=4$). The above parameters are experimentally selected and applied on all test images.

Figure 1. An overview of the proposed ant-based visual saliency detection approach

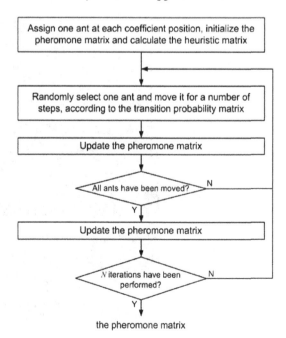

The first experiment is to compare the saliency map produced by the proposed approach with that of Harel *et al.*'s approach (Harel 2006), Tsapatsoulis *et al.*'s approach (Tsapatsoulis, 2006), Hou and Zhang's approach (Hou 2008), plus Zhang *et al.*'s approach (Zhang 2008). All of the above-mentioned four approaches are implemented using their respective softwares provided by authors online. The obtained saliency maps are presented in Figures 2-4, where the white pixels represent the positions with more important visual saliency information. As seen from Figures 2-4, the result of the proposed approach is more consistent to the human visual system.

The second experiment is to explore the computational complexity of the proposed approach. The above approaches are implemented using the *Matlab* programming language and run on a PC with a Intel Core2 1.67 GHz CPU and a 4096 MB RAM. One hundred experiments are conducted for each of the above-mentioned approaches. The computational complexity (in terms of the run time) of the proposed approach is compared with that of the above four approaches and their respective average run-times are presented in Table 1. As seen from this Table, the computational complexity of the proposed approach is fairly large compared with that of other four approaches. This is due to the fact that the proposed approach needs to exploit the ant's movement throughout the whole image to find the pheromone information matrix (i.e., saliency information).

FUTURE RESEARCH DIRECTIONS

There are several issues need to be further investigated for future research works. The first issue is to investigate the video data. Currently, only the image data is considered in this chapter. However,

Figure 2. Various visual saliency maps (white pixels represent positions with more important visual saliency information). (a) the test image Board; (b) Harel et al.'s approach (Harel 2006); (c) Tsapatsoulis et al.'s approach (Tsapatsoulis, 2006), (d) Hou and Zhang's approach (Hou 2008); (e) Zhang et al.'s approach. (Zhang 2008); and (f) our proposed approach

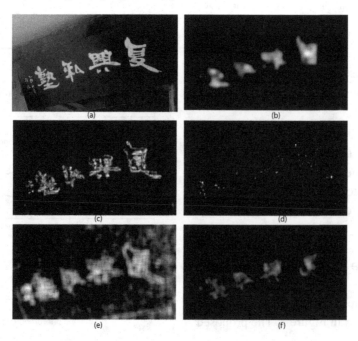

Figure 4. Various visual saliency maps (white pixels represent positions with more important visual saliency information). (a) the test image Stone; (b) Harel et al.'s approach (Harel 2006); (c) Tsapatsoulis et al.'s approach (Tsapatsoulis, 2006), (d) Hou and Zhang's approach (Hou 2008); (e) Zhang et al.'s approach. (Zhang 2008); and (f) our proposed approach

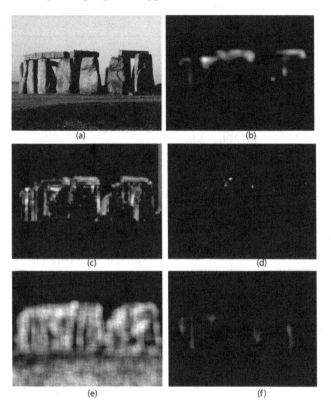

Figure 3. Various visual saliency maps (white pixels represent positions with more important visual saliency information). (a) the test image Flower; (b) Harel et al.'s approach (Harel 2006); (c) Tsapatsoulis et al.'s approach (Tsapatsoulis, 2006), (d) Hou and Zhang's approach (Hou 2008); (e) Zhang et al.'s approach. (Zhang 2008); and (f) our proposed approach

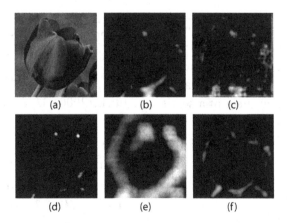

Table 1. The run-time comparison (in seconds)

Test image	Harel *et al.*'s approach (Harel 2006)	Tsapatsoulis *et al*'s approach (Tsapatsoulis, 2006)	Hou and Zhang's approach (Hou 2008)	Zhang *et al.*'s approach (Zhang 2008)	Our proposed approach
Board	11.81	6.72	0.83	28.94	26.39
Flower	5.44	0.89	0.23	1.89	7.53
Stone	7.16	2.95	0.56	12.17	17.90

one needs to consider the temporal aspects of the human visual system (Liu, 2007; Ma, 2002; Ma, 2005; Cheng, 2005). Second, the parallel ACO algorithm (Randall, 2002) can be exploited to further reduce the computational load of the proposed approach; consequently, shorten the execution time of the proposed approach. Third, only the monotone image data is considered in this chapter. Therefore, an interesting issue is how to address the color image data. The saliency maps produced from different color components need to be aggregated to a single map by considering the correlations among the color components. Fourth, more efficient and robust phase coherence model needs to be developed to be robust to noisy image, since the noiseless data is assumed in the most literature of visual saliency detection research (including the approach proposed in this chapter).

CONCLUSION

An ant-inspired approach has been proposed in this chapter to perform visual saliency detection with attractive performance. The proposed approach exploits the local phase coherence information of the image to guide the movement of a set of ants, which deposit the pheromone information on the image to measure its saliency. The proposed approach is able to produce saliency map that is more consistent with the human visual system, as verified in our experiments.

REFERENCES

Cheng, W.-H., Chua, W.-T., & Wu, J.-L. (2005). A visual attention based region-of-interest determination framework for video sequences. *IEICE Transactions on Information and Systems, E88*(7), 1578–1586. doi:10.1093/ietisy/e88-d.7.1578

Dorigo, M., Birattari, M., & Stutzle, T. (2006). Ant colony optimization. *IEEE Computational Intelligence Magazine, 1*(4), 28–39.

Dorigo, M., & Thomas, S. (2004). *Ant Colony Optimization*. Cambridge: MIT Press.

Harel, J., Koch, C., & Perona, P. (2006). Graph-based visual saliency. In *Proc. of Neural Information Processing Systems*. MIT Press.

Hou, X., & Zhang, L. (2008). Saliency detection: A spectral residual approach. In *Proc. IEEE Conf. on Computer Vision and Pattern Recognition* (pp. 1-8).

Hu, Y., Xie, X., Ma, W.-Y., Chia, L.-T., & Rajan, D. (2004). Salient region detection using weighted feature maps based on the human visual attention model (LNCS 3332, pp. 993-1000).

Itti, L. (2000). *Models of Bottom-up and Top-down Visual Attention*. Unpublished doctoral dissertation, California institute of Technology.

Itti, L., Koch, C., & Niebur, E. (1998). A model of saliency-based visual attention for rapid scene analysis. *IEEE Transactions on Pattern Analysis and Machine Intelligence, 20*(11), 1254–1259. doi:10.1109/34.730558

Jams, W. (1890). *The Principles of Psychology.* Oxford: Pergamon Press. doi:10.1037/10538-000

Kovesi, P. (1999). Image features from phase congruency. *Videre: A Journal of Computer Vision Research, 1*(3), 2-27.

Liu, T., Sun, J., Zheng, N.-N., Tang, X., & Shum, H.-Y. (2007). Learning to detect a salient object. In *Proc. IEEE Cont. on Computer Vision and pattern Recognition*, Minneapolis, Minnesota (pp. 1-8).

Ma, Y.-F., Hua, X.-S., Lu, L., & Zhang, H.-J. (2005). A generic framework of user attention model and its application in video summarization. *IEEE Transactions on Multimedia, 7*(5), 907–919. doi:10.1109/TMM.2005.854410

Ma, Y.-F., & Zhang, H.-J. (2002). A model of motion attention for video skimming. In *Proc. IEEE Int. Conf. on Image Processing* (pp. 129-132). Rochester, New York

Ma, Y.-F., & Zhang, H.-J. (2003). Contrast-based image attention analysis by using fuzzy growing. In *Proc. ACM Int. Conf. on Multimedia*. Berkeley, CA (pp. 374-381).

Morrone, M., & Burr, D. (1988). *Feature detection in human vision: A phase-dependent energy model* (pp. 221–245). Proc. Roy. Soc. London B.

Randall, M., & Lewis, A. (2002). A parallel implementation of ant colony optimization. *Journal of Parallel and Distributed Computing, 62*(9), 1421–1432. doi:10.1006/jpdc.2002.1854

Tian, J., Yu, W., & Xie, S. (2008). An ant colony optimization algorithm for image edge detection. In *Proc. IEEE Congress on Evolutionary Computation* (pp. 751-756). Hongkong, China.

Tsapatsoulis, N., Pattichis, C., Kounoudes, A., Loizou, C., Constantinides, A., & Taylor, J. G. (2006). Visual attention based region of interest coding for video-telephony applications. In *Proc. IEEE Int. Symp. on Communication Systems, Networks and Digital Signal Processing*.

Wu, C.-Y., Leou, J.-L., & Chen, H.-Y. (2009). Visual attention region determination using low-level features. In *Proc. International Symposium on Circuits and Systems* (pp. 3178-3181). Taiwan

Zhang, L., Tong, M., Marks, T., Shan, H., & Cottrell, G. (2008). SUN: A Bayesian framework for saliency using natural statistics. *Journal of Vision (Charlottesville, Va.), 8*(7), 1–20. doi:10.1167/8.7.32

ADDITIONAL READING

Bovik, A. C. (2000). *Handbook of Image and Video Processing.* Academic Press.

Cordon, O., Herrera, F., & Stutzle, T. (2002). Special Issue on Ant Colony Optimization: Models and Applications. *Mathware and Soft Computing, 9.*

Dorigo, M., Caro, G. D., & Stutzle, T. (2000). Special Issue on Ant Algorithms. *Future Generation Computer Systems, 16.*

Dorigo, M., Gambardella, L. M., Middendorf, M., & Stutzle, T. (2002). Special Issue on Ant Colony Optimization. *IEEE Transactions on Evolutionary Computation, 6*(7).

Dorigo, M., Maniezzo, V., & Colorni, A. (1996). Ant system: Optimization by a colony of cooperating agents. *IEEE Trans. on Systems, Man and Cybernetics. Part B, 26*(1), 29–41.

Ghanbarian, A. T., Kabir, E., & Charkari, N. M. (2007). Color reduction based on ant colony. *Pattern Recognition Letters, 28*(7), 1383–1390. doi:10.1016/j.patrec.2007.01.019

Gonzalez, R. C., & Woods, R. E. (2007). *Digital image processing.* Harlow: Prentice Hall.

Hegarat-Mascle, S. L., Kallel, A., & Descombes, X. (2007). Ant colony optimization for image regularization based on a nonstationary Markov modeling. *IEEE Transactions on Image Processing, 16*(3), 865–878. doi:10.1109/TIP.2007.891150

Malisia, A. R., & Tizhoosh, H. R. (2006). Image thresholding using ant colony optimization. In *Proc. Canadian Conf. on Computer and Robot Vision*, Quebec, Canada (p. 26).

Ouadfel, S., & Batouche, M. (2003). Ant colony system with local search for Markov random field image segmentation. In *Proc. IEEE Int. Conf. on Image Processing*, Barcelona, Spain (pp. 133-136).

Wang, Z., & Bovik, A. C. (2006). *Modern Image Quality Assessment*. Morgan & Claypool Publishers.

Wang, Z., & Simoncelli, E. P. (2004). Local phase coherence and the perception of blur. In *Proc. of Neural Information Processing Systems*. MIT Press.

Chapter 16
Modeling Visual Saliency in Images and Videos

Yiqun Hu
Nanyang Technological University, Singapore

Viswanath Gopalakrishnan
Nanyang Technological University, Singapore

Deepu Rajan
Nanyang Technological University, Singapore

ABSTRACT

Visual saliency, which distinguishes "interesting" visual content from others, plays an important role in multimedia and computer vision applications. This chapter starts with a brief overview of visual saliency as well as the literature of some popular models to detect salient regions. We describe two methods to model visual saliency – one in images and the other in videos. Specifically, we introduce a graph-based method to model salient region in images in a bottom-up manner. For videos, we introduce a factorization based method to model attention object in motion, which utilizes the top-down knowledge of cameraman for model saliency. Finally, future directions for visual saliency modeling and additional reading materials are highlighted to familiarize readers with the research on visual saliency modeling for multimedia applications.

INTRODUCTION

Visual saliency refers to the ability of any vision system to select a certain subset of visual information for further processing (Itti & Koch, 2001). This mechanism serves as the information processing bottleneck to allow only the "interesting" information related to current behaviors or tasks and ignores irrelevant information (Desimone &

Duncan, 1995). Only the visual information in the "fovea" region is analyzed and processed while other information outside this field is suppressed (Eriksen & Yeh, 1985; Eriksen & St James, 1986). This ability is of evolutionary significance because it allows an organism to detect quickly possible prey, mates or predators in the visual world. Visual saliency is a complex concept and has diverse interpretations in psychology, neuroscience and vision research, leading to different research

DOI: 10.4018/978-1-60960-024-2.ch016

methodologies as well as the evaluation criteria in these communities.

Visual saliency can be categorized based on taxonomies which are derived from different aspects of this mechanism. According to the target of saliency deployment, visual saliency has three forms: (i) feature-based saliency (Treisman, 1980) where saliency is attributed to different features; (ii) space-based saliency (Wolfe, 1994; Tsotsos et al., 1995) where saliency is deployed at different locations; (iii) object-based saliency (Scholl, 2001; Grossberg & Raizada, 2000) where saliency is deployed on different objects/groups. According to the control of saliency deployment, visual saliency can be driven in either bottom-up or top-down manner (Itti & Koch, 2001). In the bottom-up manner, visual saliency is purely driven by visual data itself. In top-down manner, high-level information like the goal and preferences of the observers can modulate and guide the deployment of saliency.

APPLICATIONS IN MULTIMEDIA

The two issues that limit the even more widespread use of multimedia content than in the present situation are their huge capacity and their high complexity. The use of visual saliency is a natural way to overcome these limitations by selecting relevant visual information and processing only the visual attention region. This mechanism can simultaneously improve the efficiency and robustness of various multimedia applications. In multimedia adaptation, images can be adapted (Chen et al., 2003) and browsed (Xie et al., 2006) or video sequences can be progressively transmitted for display (Hu et al., 2004) on small screen devices by preserving salient content. For Content-based Image Retrieval (CBIR) systems, detecting salient regions can improve the system performance by reducing the influence of cluttered background (Bamidele et al., 2004; Wang et al., 2004). Modeling visual saliency can also

facilitate visual tracking due to the common issues that they address: salient content can be used to initialize, detect as well as recover tracking target (Brajovic & Kanade, 1998; Toyama & Hager, 1999; Yang et al.. 2007). Recently, media retargeting techniques (Shamir & Avidan, 2009; Wolf et al., 2007) have been reported that rely on visual saliency modeling to indicate important information that needs to be preserved. As digital cameras become ubiquitous, their technology aims to help the amateur photographer to capture pictures that are aesthetically much superior than before. Face detection is already available in many such digital cameras. Clearly, there is a role for visual attention that can improve the performance of this task, as also in others such as automatically focusing on a certain area of the scene that is visually salient and in automatic zooming into salient regions.

The remainder of this chapter is organized as follows. We first briefly review the related work about visual saliency modeling. From this review, two important issues about visual saliency modeling for multimedia and computer vision applications are defined. We introduce two methods in this chapter to target these two issues. First, we introduce a graph-based method for modeling spatial saliency in images. This method provides a possible solution to integrate both global and local information to detect visual saliency. Next, we formulate the problem of Attention-from-Motion (AFM) to detect Attention Object in Motion (AOM) from videos and propose a factorization based method to solve it. This method decodes the subjective attention of the cameraman from video content and uses this top-down knowledge to model spatial-temporal visual saliency. Finally, we highlight the directions and open issues for the future research in visual saliency modeling.

LITERATURE REVIEW

In the literature on visual saliency modeling, researchers have proposed different ideas for detecting salient content in images. For space-based visual saliency, Feature Integration Model (Treisman, 1980) is the most successful conceptual framework, which states that different features contribute to visual saliency according to their own characteristics and a unique saliency map integrates all the salient features. Based on this theory, a number of feature contrast based methods (Itti et al., 1998; Ma & Zhang, 2003; Walther & Koch, 2006; Liu et al., 2007) defined visual saliency using different forms of feature contrast. Itti et al. (Itti et al., 1998) compute the center-surround difference across different scales on the color/orientation features to compute a saliency map. Walther and Koch extended Itti's model to infer the extent of a proto-object from the feature maps (Walther & Koch, 2006), leading to the creation of a saliency toolbox. Different from (Itti et al., 1998), Ma and Zhang (Ma & Zhang, 2003) only used center-surround contrast between image patches in the same scale to indicate visual saliency. Liu et al. (Liu et al., 2007) applied center-surround operator on histogram as the regional feature and further defined a multi-scale contrast as local feature and color spatial variance as the global feature. Conditional Random fields (CRF) is used for learning these features. Despite their popularity, all feature contrast based methods inherit the same disadvantage: the visual saliency is only defined locally such that the salient content cannot be directly link to semantic meaningful region/object. When applying in different applications of multimedia and computer vision, these methods are not optimal for further processing.

Some other methods (Kadir & Brady, 2001; Bruce & Tsotsos, 2006; Gao & Vasconcelos, 2005; Gao & Vasconcelos, 2007) also attempted to define visual saliency based on information theory. For example, Kadir et al. (Kadir & Brady, 2001) considered the local entropy as a clue to saliency while a self-information measure was used to compute saliency from local contrast in

(Bruce & Tsotsos, 2006). Note that these two methods also defined visual saliency in a local way. Recently, some new ideas about visual saliency are also proposed. For example, visual saliency is equated to discrimination (Gao & Vasconcelos, 2005) and extended to bottom-up mechanism in the pre-attentive biological vision (Gao & Vasconcelos, 2007). Spectral components in an image have been explored to detect visual saliency (Hou & Zhang, 2007; Guo et al., 2008). In (Hou & Zhang, 2007), the gist of the scene is represented with the averaged Fourier envelope and the differential spectral components are used to extract salient regions, which is replaced by the phrase spectrum of the Fourier transform in (Guo et al., 2008) because it is more effective and computationally efficient. These two methods model visual saliency using global information in the frequency domain.

In the case of video sequences, it has been shown in cognition science and neuroscience that motion is one of the most important information for modeling visual saliency in spatial-temporal domain. However, what constitutes salient motion is yet to be defined. Previous research on modeling spatial-temporal saliency proposed different definitions of salient motion. For example, Ma et al. (Ma et al., 2005) used motion vector fields to compute the motion energy to identify salient motion regions. In (Tian & Hampapur, 2005), the consistency of motion is used to discriminate salient motion from unimportant motion. By accumulating directionally consistent flow, Wixson (Wixson, 2000) also used the consistency to define the saliency of motion. All these definitions about salient motion are often invalid in different videos. For example, visual attention will be only drawn on one of the objects although the motions of all objects are consistent. Also, the motion energy of an object does not have any direct indication of visual attention.

RANDOM WALK FOR IMAGE SALIENCY

Graph based approaches for salient object detection have not been explored much though such methods have the advantage of capturing the geometric structure of the image. Previous works on detecting salient regions from images represented as graphs include (Costa, 2006) and (Harel et al., 2006). In (Costa, 2006) the frequency of node visits during random walks on graphs is used to identify salient regions. Similarly (Harel et al., 2006) also uses frequency of node visits on graph models in which the strength of edges represent the dissimilarity between two nodes. Here, the most frequently visited node will be most dissimilar in a local context. Such local dissimilarities of features can favor cluttered backgrounds with local contrasts while looking for salient regions. The proposed graph based random walk method evaluates the 'isolation' of nodes in a global sense and identifies nodes corresponding to 'compact' regions in a local sense (Gopalakrishnan et al., 2009b). A robust feature set based on color and orientation is used to create a fully connected graph and a k-regular sparse graph to model the global and local characteristics, respectively, of the random walks. The behaviors of random walks on the two separate graphs are used to identify the most salient node of the image along with some background nodes. The final stage of seeded salient region identification uses information about the salient and the background nodes in an accurate extraction of the salient part in the image.

Hitting Time in a Random Walk

In this section, we review some of the fundamental results from the theory of Markov chains (Aldous & Fill, 1999) and hitting time calculation based on Markov chains. A Markov chain with N states is fully characterized by an initial probability distribution on the states and by an $N \times N$ transition

matrix P, where P_{ij} is the probability of moving from state i to state j.

A random walk starting from any given state of a Markov chain with transition matrix P can be considered analogous to a random walk starting on some given node of a graph $G(V,E)$, where V is the set of vertices and E is the set of edges in the graph. The graph $G(V,E)$ is fully characterized by the affinity matrix A, where A is defined as

$$A_{ij} = \begin{Bmatrix} w_{ij} & i \neq j \\ 0 & i = j \end{Bmatrix} \tag{1}$$

and w_{ij} is the weight between node i and node j based on the affinity of features on the respective nodes defined as

$$w_{ij} = e^{\left\| f_i - f_j \right\|^2 / \sigma^2} \tag{2}$$

where f_i and f_j are feature vectors defined on node i and node j respectively.

The affinity matrix A of the graph $G(V,E)$ and the transition matrix P of the respective Markov chain are related as

$$P = D^{-1}A \quad \text{where} \quad D = diag(d_1, d_2, ...d_N), \quad d_i = \sum_j w_{ij} \tag{3}$$

and d_i is the total weight connected to node i known as the degree of node i.

The fundamental matrix Z of the Markov chain is an important quantity while calculating the hitting times between nodes. The $N \times N$ matrix Z can be calculated as

$$Z = (I - P + W)^{-1} \tag{4}$$

where I is the $N \times N$ identity matrix and W is an $N \times N$ matrix obtained by stacking the $1 \times N$ equilibrium distribution row vector π of the Markov chain, N times. We define $E_i(T_i)$ as the expected number of steps taken to return to state i if the Markov chain is started in state i at time t=0. Similarly, $E_i(T_j)$ is the expected number of steps taken to reach state j if the Markov chain is started in state i at time t=0. $E_{\pi(}Ti_j$ is the expected number of steps taken to reach state i if the Markov chain is started in the equilibrium distribution π at time t =0. (Aldous & Fill, 1999) computes the hitting times based on the entries of fundamental matrix Z as follows:

$$
\begin{aligned}
E_i(T_i) &= \pi^{-1} \\
E_i(T_j) &= E_j(T_j) \times (Z_{jj} - Z_{ij}) \\
E_\pi(T_i) &= E_i(T_i) \times Z_{ii}
\end{aligned}
\tag{5}
$$

Graph Representation

The image is represented as a graph $G(V,E)$, where V is the set of vertices or nodes and E is the set of edges. The vertices (nodes), are patches of size 8×8 on the image while the edges represent the connection between the nodes with weights w_{ij} showing the affinity between node i and node j. The seven dimensional vector f=$[C_b, C_r, E_{\rho 1}, E_{\rho 2,...}, E_{\rho 5}]$ represents the feature vector associated with a node on the graph. C_b and C_r represent the chrominance values when the image is represented in YCbCr format. $\{E_{\rho 1, ..., } E_{\rho 5}\}$ represents the orientation entropy of the node calculated in five different scales ρ=$[0.5,1,1.5,2,2.5]$ to capture the multiscale structures. Orientation entropy indicates the complexity of orientation histogram of the patch which is calculated as (Gopalakrishnan et al., 2009a)

$$
E_\rho = -\sum_i H_\rho(\theta_i) \log(H_\rho(\theta_i))
\tag{6}
$$

where $H\rho(\theta_i)$ represents the histogram value of ith orientation evaluated on a scale ρ. A salient region can be highly textured or smooth and the saliency is indicated by how its complexity is different with respect to the rest of the image. Hence, it is more useful to consider the contrast in complexity of orientations rather than the orientations itself.

In the new random walk framework, the detection of salient regions is initiated by the identification of the most 'salient' node in the graph by considering both global as well as local information. Clearly, such a technique is better compared to considering either global or local information only. The image is represented as a fully connected (complete) graph and a sparse k-regular graph to capture the global and local characteristics, respectively, of the random walk. In the complete graph, every node is connected to every other node so that there is no restriction on the movement of the random walker as long as the strength of the edge allows it. Hence, it is possible for the random walker to move from one corner of the image to the other corner in one step depending on the strength of the edge between the nodes. Spatial neighborhood of the nodes is given no preference and this manifests the global aspect of features in the image. The characteristics of the features in a local area in the image are encoded into the k-regular graph where every node is connected to k other nodes. A particular patch is chosen with the 8 patches in its spatial neighborhood to study the local properties of the random walk so that k = 8. Thus, the random walker is restricted to a local region in the image while its path is determined by the features in that region. In this configuration, therefore, a random walker at one corner of the image cannot jump to the opposite corner, but has to traverse through the image according to the strengths of the edges. Such random walks capture the properties of the local features of the image.

A^g denotes the affinity matrix of the global graph which is defined as

$$
A^g{}_{ij} = \begin{bmatrix} w_{ij} & i \neq j \\ 0 & i = j \end{bmatrix}
\tag{7}
$$

Similarly A^l denotes the affinity matrix of the local graph which is defined as

$$A^l_{ij} = \begin{bmatrix} w_{ij} & j \in N(i) \\ 0 & i = j \end{bmatrix} \qquad (8)$$

where $N(i)$ is the set of nodes in the spatial neighborhood of node i. The hitting times on the global graph, $E^g_i(T_i)$, $E^g_i(T_j)$, $E^g_\pi(T_i)$, and the hitting times on the local graph, $E^l_i(T_i)$, $E^l_i(T_j)$, $E^l_\pi(T_i)$, can be calculated from the affinity matrices A^g and A^l respectively.

Most Salient Node

The most salient node in the image should globally pop out in the image when compared to other competing nodes. At the same time it should fall on a compact object in the image in some local sense. The global pop-out and compactness properties are reflected in the random walks performed on the complete graph and the k-regular graph, respectively. When a node is globally a pop-out node, what it essentially means is that it is isolated from the other nodes so that a random walker takes more time to reach such a node in the global graph. On the other hand, if a node is to lie on a locally compact object, a random walker should take less time to reach it on a local k-regular graph.

We calculate the global isolation of a node i by the time taken to access the node i in the global graph when the Markov chain starts from equilibrium. The global isolation measure on node i will be more accurate if the hitting times from the most frequently visited nodes are given priority over hitting times from less frequently visited nodes. This property is inherent in $E^g_\pi(T_i)$, which is the time taken to access the node i when the Markov chain starts from equilibrium. The equilibrium distribution directly depends on the frequency of access to different nodes, and hence $E^g_\pi(T_i)$ gives priority to hitting times from most frequently visited nodes over hitting time from less frequently visited nodes. Next, we ensure that the most isolated node falls on a compact object by looking at the equilibrium access time of nodes in the k-regular graph. The local random walk under Markov equilibrium will reach the nodes corresponding to compact structures faster as it is guided by strong edge strengths from the neighborhoods. Hence a low value of local random walk equilibrium access time $E^l_\pi(T_i)$ ensures that the respective node falls on a compact surface. Considering both the global and local aspects, saliency of node i, $NSal_i$ is defined as (Gopalakrishnan et al., 2009b)

$$NSal_i = \frac{E^g_\pi(T_i)}{E^l_\pi(T_i)} \qquad (9)$$

The most salient node, N_s is identified as the node that maximizes $NSal_i$, i.e.,

$$N_s = \arg \max_i NSal_i \qquad (10)$$

Background Nodes

After identifying the most salient node in the image we move on to identify certain nodes in the background. This is to facilitate the extraction of the salient regions using the most salient node and the background nodes as seeds. The most important feature of a background node is obviously the less saliency of the node. Moreover, the background nodes have the property that it is at a large distance from the most salient node, N_s. The distance from node N_s to some node j is measured as the hitting time, $E^g_{N_s}(T_j)$, which is the average time taken to reach node j if the random walk starts from node N_s. We use the complete graph to calculate the hitting times since a global view of the image has to be taken in order to identify the background. Hence the first background node, N_{b1} is calculated as

$$N_{b1} = \arg\max_j \frac{E^g{}_{Ns}(T_j)}{NSal_j} \qquad (11)$$

The background in an image is, more often than not, inhomogeneous, e.g. due to clutter or due to regions having different feature values. Our goal is to capture as much of these variations as possible by locating at least one background node in each of such regions. Hence, while maximizing the distance of a node to the maximum salient node, we impose an additional condition of maximizing the distance to all background nodes identified so far. This will ensure that the newly found background node falls on a new region. Even if there are no multiple backgrounds, i.e. the background is relatively homogeneous, the algorithm will only place the new node in the same background region. Thus, the nth background node, N_{bn}, is identified as

$$N_{bn} = \arg\max_j \frac{E^g{}_{Ns}(T_j).E^g{}_{N_{b1}}(T_j)......E^g{}_{N_{b(N-1)}}(T_j)}{(NSal_j)^n}. \qquad (12)$$

The above equation can be viewed as a product of n terms, where each term is of the form $E^g_n(T_j) \,/\, NSal_j$. In our experiments the value of n is fixed to 4 but it can be increased to improve the accuracy of the algorithm at the cost of increased computational complexity.

Seeded Salient Region Extraction

The identification of the most salient node and the background nodes enables the extraction of the salient regions. The most salient node and the background nodes act as seeds and the problem now is to find the most probable seed that can be reached for a random walk starting from a particular node. If the hitting time from a node to the most salient node is less compared to hitting times to all the background nodes, then that node is deemed to be part of the salient object.

This process is repeated for the rest of the nodes in the graph so that at the end of the process, the salient region is extracted.

In the seeded segmentation process, using only the global graph or only the k-regular local graph put forwards separate challenges. In a global random walk it may turn out that a node that is far from a salient node in the spatial domain, but close to it in the feature domain (as indicated by the edge weights) may be erroneously classified as belonging to the salient region. On the other hand, a local random walk may treat a background region that is spatially close to a salient node as part of the salient object, since the random walk is restricted to a smaller area. Hence, we propose a linear combination of the global and local attributes of a random walk by defining a new affinity matrix for the image given by

$$A^c = \lambda A^g + A^l \qquad (13)$$

where A^c is the combined affinity matrix and λ is a constant that decides the mixing ratio of global and local matrices.

Experimental Results

The experiments are conducted on a database of about 5,000 images available from (Liu et al., 2007). The database used in this work contains the ground truth of the salient region marked as bounding boxes by nine different users. The median of the nine boxes is selected as the final salient region. The robustness of the detection of the most salient node is evaluated by calculating the percentage of images in which it falls inside the user annotated box. In 89.6% of cases on a database of 5000 images, the most salient node falls inside user annotated box. Figure 1 shows examples of the saliency map extracted using the proposed algorithm. Figure 1 (a) shows the original images and Figure 1 (b) shows the most salient node marked as the red region in the respective

Figure 1. Results of seeded salient region extraction. (a) Original image (b) Most salient node marked with a red spot (c) The final binary saliency map

images. The result of the seeded salient region extraction is shown in Figure 1 (c).

The saliency map of the proposed random walk based method is compared with the saliency maps generated by the saliency toolbox (STB) (Itti et al., 1998), the spectral residual method based on (Hou & Zhang, 2007). and the phase spectrum based on (Guo et al., 2008). The evaluation of the algorithms is carried out based on Precision, Recall and F-Measure. Precision is calculated as ratio of the total saliency, i.e., sum of intensities in the saliency map captured inside the user annotated rectangle to the total saliency computed for the image. Recall is calculated as the ratio of the total saliency captured inside the user annotated window to the area of the user annotated window. F-Measure is the overall performance measurement and is computed as the harmonic mean between the precision and recall values. Figure 2 shows the F-measure for the proposed method as well as for the other methods. The proposed method shows better objective measure among all competing methods.

ATTENTION-FROM-MOTION IN VIDEOS

Problem Definition

Figure 2. Comparison of f-Measure values of 1) Spectral Residual Method Hou X., & Zhang L. (2007), 2) Saliency Tool Box Itti L., & Koch C., & Niebur E. (1998), 3) Phase spectrum method Guo C., & Ma Q., & Zhang L. (2008), 4) the proposed method. Vertical axis shows F-Measure values while horizontal axis shows different methods in the order

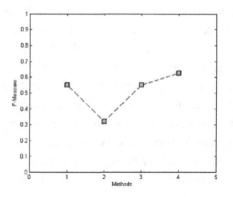

In the previous sections, we described a method for detecting saliency in images. Next, we focus on videos. While it is difficult to define motion saliency in a bottom-up manner, the shooting patterns during video creation and editing actually provide hints for modeling motion saliency. In video production manuals, one of the most important shot "tracking shot" actually encodes the subjective attention of cameraman. The cameraman focuses the viewer's attention on some object(s) by making the camera to follow one or more moving objects(s). Those moving object(s) which is followed by the camera is defined as the Attention Object in Motion (AOM). The problem of modeling motion saliency is then converted to detecting the "following" relationship between camera and object(s) in the video sequence. By successfully detecting the "tracking shot" pattern, we can easily discriminate the AOM(s) from others and hence model the motion saliency by focusing the attention only on AOM(s). We define the problem of Attention-from-Motion (AFM) as detecting AOMs from motion information in a video sequence (Hu et al., 2009). Compared to other heuristic definitions, this problem formulation is generally applicable on different types of videos.

To solve the problem of AFM, we propose a factorization based method to detect AOM from the measurement matrix of P feature points across F frames, under the assumption of orthographic projection and rigid body motion. Through the factorization analysis of AOM in the dynamic scene, we discover a special structure in the factorization of AOM. Single AOM analysis is conducted by identifying this structure without carrying out the complete factorization. In the situation of multiple AOMs, an iterative framework is proposed to extract multiple AOMs. This solution of AFM directly identifies the "following" relationship between camera motion and object motion without estimating either of them. It can detect AOMs even when the motion of camera/object is degenerate/dependent as well as when only partial data is available.

Factorization Analysis for AOM

In this section, we analyze the property of single AOM through its factorization. Different from the factorization analysis for structure-from-motion problem (Tomasi & Kanade, 1992; Costeira & Kanade, 1998) where either camera or object is static, we generalize the factorization analysis for dynamic scene where both camera and object are moving.

Dynamic Scene Factorization

The measurement matrix W consists of 2 parts: a F ×P submatrix X recording the horizontal coordinates x_{fp} and a F ×P submatrix Y recoding the vertical coordinates y_{fp} of P feature points across F frames. Under the assumption of rigid-body motion, we can represent the 3D coordinates of the pth feature points of the object at the fth frame as

$$s_{fp} = R_{o,f} s_{1p} + T_{o,f}, p=1,\ldots,P \text{ and } f=1,\ldots,F \qquad (14)$$

where $R_{o,f}$ and $T_{o,f}$ represent the rotation matrix and translation vector of the object at the fth frame, respectively. By defining the origin of the world coordinates at the center of all feature points at the 1st frame, the following equation is satisfied:

$$\frac{1}{P} \sum_{p=1}^{P} s_{1p} = 0 \qquad (15)$$

By combining (14) and (15), we will obtain

$$\frac{1}{P} \sum_{p=1}^{P} s_{fp} = \frac{1}{P} \sum_{p=1}^{P} (R_{o,f} s_{1p} + T_{o,f}) = T_{o,f} \qquad (16)$$

If we model the camera using orthography, the image coordinates (x_{fp}, y_{fp}) of s_{fp} can be given as

$$x_{fp} = i_f^T (s_{fp} - T_{c,f}), \quad y_{fp} = j_f^T (s_{fp} - T_{c,f}) \qquad (17)$$

where i_f and j_f define the image coordinate system at the fth frame w.r.t the world reference coordinate system. $R_{c,f}$ and $T_{c,f}$ are the rotation matrix and translation vector of the camera at the fth frame respectively. We also have the following relationships between i_f/j_f and $R_{c,f} T_{c,f}$

$$i_f = R_{c,f} i_0 + T_{c,f} - T_{c,f} = R_{c,f} i_0,$$
$$j_f = R_{c,f} j_0 + T_{c,f} - T_{c,f} = R_{c,f} j_0 \qquad (18)$$

where $i_0 = [1,0,0]^T$ and $j_0 = [0,1,0]^T$ are two axes of the canonical world coordinate system as shown in Figure 3. Note that the choice of i_0 and j_0 will not affect the subsequent analysis. Using (14) and (18), the entries of X and Y can be derived as

$$x_{fp} = i_0^T R_{c,f}^T R_{o,f} s_{1p} + i_0^T R_{c,f}^T (T_{o,f} - T_{c,f}),$$
$$y_{fp} = j_0^T R_{c,f}^T R_{o,f} s_{1p} + j_0^T R_{c,f}^T (T_{o,f} - T_{c,f}) \qquad (19)$$

Hence, the measurement matrix W can be factorized into $W = M \times S$ in the dynamic scene as (Hu et al., 2009)

$$W = \begin{bmatrix} X \\ Y \end{bmatrix} = \underbrace{\begin{bmatrix} i_0^T R_{c,1}^T R_{o,1} & i_0^T R_{c,1}^T (T_{o,1} - T_{c,1}) \\ i_0^T R_{c,2}^T R_{o,2} & i_0^T R_{c,2}^T (T_{o,2} - T_{c,2}) \\ \vdots & \vdots \\ i_0^T R_{c,F}^T R_{o,F} & i_0^T R_{c,F}^T (T_{o,F} - T_{c,F}) \\ j_0^T R_{c,1}^T R_{o,1} & j_0^T R_{c,1}^T (T_{o,1} - T_{c,1}) \\ j_0^T R_{c,2}^T R_{o,2} & j_0^T R_{c,2}^T (T_{o,2} - T_{c,2}) \\ \vdots & \vdots \\ j_0^T R_{c,F}^T R_{o,F} & j_0^T R_{c,F}^T (T_{o,F} - T_{c,F}) \end{bmatrix}}_{M(2F\times 4)} \underbrace{\begin{bmatrix} s_{11} & s_{12} & \cdots & s_{1P} \\ 1 & 1 & \cdots & 1 \end{bmatrix}}_{S(4\times P)} \qquad (20)$$

The matrix M contains the motion information of both camera and object while the matrix S contains the 3D world coordinates of the feature points. Such factorization yields the Rank Theorem for dynamic scene:

Without noise, the measurement matrix W of a moving object observed by a moving camera is at most of rank four.

Factorization of AOM

If the object is an AOM, which is followed by the camera, the following relationship between the object and the camera can be represented as, in the absence of noise,

Figure 3. The reference world coordinate system used in the factorization of dynamic scene. (Figure taken from (Hu et al., 2009))

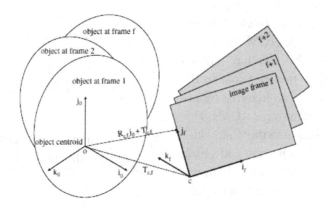

$$\frac{1}{P}\sum_{p=1}^{P} x_{fp} = \frac{1}{P}\sum_{p=1}^{P} x_{1p} \quad \forall f \in \{1,...,F\},$$

$$\frac{1}{P}\sum_{p=1}^{P} y_{fp} = \frac{1}{P}\sum_{p=1}^{P} y_{1p} \quad \forall f \in \{1,...,F\}. \tag{21}$$

Only during this condition is true, the moving object contains all these feature points are defined as an AOM. Using (14), (17) and (18), we can rewrite (21) as follows (Hu et al., 2009)

$$\frac{1}{P}\sum_{p=1}^{P} i_f^T(s_{fp} - T_{c,f}) = \frac{1}{P}\sum_{p=1}^{P} i_1^T(s_{1p} - T_{c,1})$$

$$\Rightarrow \frac{1}{P}\sum_{p=1}^{P} i_f^T(R_{o,f}s_{1p} + T_{o,f} - T_{c,f}) = \frac{1}{P}\sum_{p=1}^{P} i_0^T R_{c,1}^T(s_{1p} - T_{c,1})$$

$$\Rightarrow i_0^T R_{c,f}^T R_{o,f} \underbrace{\frac{1}{P}\sum_{p=1}^{P} s_{1p}}_{=0} + i_0^T R_{c,f}^T(T_{o,f} - T_{c,f}) = i_0^T R_{c,1}^T \underbrace{\frac{1}{P}\sum_{p=1}^{P} s_{1p}}_{=0} - i_0^T R_{c,1}^T T_{c,1}$$

$$\Rightarrow i_0^T R_{c,f}^T(T_{o,f} - T_{c,f}) = -i_0^T R_{c,1}^T T_{c,1} \quad \forall f \in \{1,...,F\} \tag{22}$$

Similarly, it can also be shown that

$$j_0^T R_{c,f}^T(T_{o,f} - T_{c,f}) = -j_0^T R_{c,1}^T T_{c,1} \quad \forall f \in \{1,...,F\} \tag{23}$$

Hence, for an AOM, the motion matrix M of its factorization can be represented as:

$$M = \begin{bmatrix} i_0^T R_{c,1}^T R_{o,1} & -i_0^T R_{c,1}^T T_{c,1} \\ i_0^T R_{c,2}^T R_{o,2} & -i_0^T R_{c,2}^T T_{c,2} \\ \vdots & \vdots \\ i_0^T R_{c,F}^T R_{o,F} & -i_0^T R_{c,F}^T T_{c,F} \\ \hline j_0^T R_{c,1}^T R_{o,1} & -j_0^T R_{c,1}^T T_{c,1} \\ j_0^T R_{c,2}^T R_{o,2} & -j_0^T R_{c,2}^T T_{c,2} \\ \vdots & \vdots \\ j_0^T R_{c,F}^T R_{o,F} & -j_0^T R_{c,F}^T T_{c,F} \end{bmatrix} \tag{24}$$

In the above matrix, the first 3 columns relate to the rotation component while the last column relates to the translation component of the dynamic scene. Two motion constraints can be derived from this matrix:

- Rotation constraint: Each pair row of first 3 columns of M are the rotations of two reference orthonormal basis (e.g. $[1,0,0]^T$ and $[0,1,0]^T$) of M. It is because $R_{c,f}^T R_{o,f}$ is a rotation matrix such that $i_0^T R_{c,f}^T R_{o,f}$ and $j_0^T R_{c,f}^T R_{o,f}$ are the rotations of i_0 and j_0, respectively.

- Translation constraint: The two halves of the last column of the matrix M are individually constant.

AOM Analysis Based on Factorization

In this section, we first study the case where all feature points of the measurement matrix W belongs to single object using factorization analysis. Note that we can factorize W using *Singular Value Decomposition (SVD)*, which gives the following factorization:

$$W = U\sum V^T = (U\sum{}^{1/2}) \cdot (\sum{}^{1/2} V^T) = \hat{M}\hat{S} \tag{25}$$

We call this factorization as the affine solution because by multiplying any 4×4 invertible matrix Q, it forms another valid factorization of W, i.e.,

$$(\hat{M}Q)(Q^{-1}\hat{S}) = \hat{M}(QQ^{-1})\hat{S} = \hat{M}\hat{S} = W \tag{26}$$

Instead of computing the exact solution of the factorization, we will analyze the whether the feature points of the measurement matrix W belongs to an AOM or not by only using the affine version of the factorization. Specifically, we will estimate the probability that there exists a Q that transforms $\hat{M}$ to M which has the special structure (i.e. two halves of last column of M are constant) of AOM. If such Q exists, those feature points of the measurement matrix belongs to an

AOM. The probability of Q existing can be used to define an attention measure to identify an AOM.

Factorization Constraints on $\hat{M}$ and Q

We can represent the matrix M as $M = \hat{M}Q = [\hat{M}Q_R \mid \hat{M}Q_T]$ when Q is decomposed into two parts: Q_R as the first 3 columns and Q_T as the last column. $\hat{M}Q_R$ satisfies the rotation constraint because it corresponds to the first 3 columns of M and $\hat{M}Q_T$ will satisfy the translation constraint when the measurement matrix W belongs to an AOM because it corresponds to the last column of M.

For rotation constraint, each of the 2F rows of matrix $\hat{M}Q_R$ is a unit norm vector. Also, the first and second set of F rows are pairwise orthogonal. These constraints can be represented as

$$
\begin{aligned}
\hat{M}_i Q_R Q_R^T \hat{M}_i^T &= 1, \quad \forall i = 1,...,F \\
\hat{M}_j Q_R Q_R^T \hat{M}_j^T &= 1, \quad \forall j = F+1,...,2F \\
\hat{M}_i Q_R Q_R^T \hat{M}_j^T &= 0, \quad \forall i = 1,...,F, j = i + F
\end{aligned}
\tag{27}
$$

Traditional factorization method solve the above equations by adding additional constraints about the reference coordinate system (e.g. $[1,0,0]^T$ and $[0,1,0]^T$). For our purpose to estimate the existence of Q, we only need to solve the entries of $Q_R Q_R^T$ which form a matrix

$$
Q_R Q_R^T =
\begin{bmatrix}
\xi_1 & \xi_5 & \xi_6 & \xi_7 \\
\xi_5 & \xi_2 & \xi_8 & \xi_9 \\
\xi_6 & \xi_8 & \xi_3 & \xi_{10} \\
\xi_7 & \xi_9 & \xi_{10} & \xi_4
\end{bmatrix}
\tag{28}
$$

whose elements are

$$
\begin{bmatrix}
\xi_1 \\
\xi_2 \\
\xi_3 \\
\xi_4 \\
\xi_5 \\
\xi_6 \\
\xi_7 \\
\xi_8 \\
\xi_9 \\
\xi_{10}
\end{bmatrix}
=
\begin{bmatrix}
Q_{11}^2 + Q_{12}^2 + Q_{13}^2 \\
Q_{21}^2 + Q_{22}^2 + Q_{23}^2 \\
Q_{31}^2 + Q_{32}^2 + Q_{33}^2 \\
Q_{41}^2 + Q_{42}^2 + Q_{43}^2 \\
Q_{11}Q_{21} + Q_{12}Q_{22} + Q_{13}Q_{23} \\
Q_{11}Q_{31} + Q_{12}Q_{32} + Q_{13}Q_{33} \\
Q_{11}Q_{41} + Q_{12}Q_{42} + Q_{13}Q_{43} \\
Q_{21}Q_{31} + Q_{22}Q_{32} + Q_{23}Q_{33} \\
Q_{21}Q_{41} + Q_{22}Q_{42} + Q_{23}Q_{43} \\
Q_{31}Q_{41} + Q_{32}Q_{42} + Q_{33}Q_{43}
\end{bmatrix}
\tag{29}
$$

Although (27) is a nonlinear system about Q_R, it is a linear system about the 10 unique entities of $Q_R Q_R^T$. We can solve ξ by minimizing the sum of least square errors.

For translation constraint, we have

$$
\begin{aligned}
\hat{M}_1 Q_T = \hat{M}_2 Q_T = \cdots = \hat{M}_F Q_T, \\
\hat{M}_{F+1} Q_T = \hat{M}_{F+2} Q_T = \cdots = \hat{M}_{2F} Q_T.
\end{aligned}
\tag{30}
$$

where $\hat{M}_i$ indicates the ith row of $\hat{M}$. These set of constraints form a linear system:

$$
\underbrace{
\begin{bmatrix}
\hat{M}_1 - \hat{M}_2 \\
\vdots \\
\hat{M}_{F-1} - \hat{M}_F \\
\hline
\hat{M}_{F+1} - \hat{M}_{F+2} \\
\vdots \\
\hat{M}_{2F-1} - \hat{M}_{2F}
\end{bmatrix}
}_{P_T((2F-2)\times 4)}
\begin{bmatrix}
Q_{14} \\
Q_{24} \\
Q_{34} \\
Q_{44}
\end{bmatrix}
=
\begin{bmatrix}
0 \\
0 \\
0 \\
0
\end{bmatrix}
\tag{31}
$$

We only obtain a normalized version $\bar{Q}_T$ of Q_T by fixing $Q_{44}=1$ from least square estimation. Note that this normalization will not affect the later analysis about the singularity of Q.

Attention Estimation from Factorization

Instead of computing the exact solution of the factorization, we will analyze whether the feature points of the measurement matrix W belongs to an AOM by only using the affine version of the factorization. It can be shown that both the existence and the non-singularity of a matrix Q to transform from affine version to the actual factorization can be estimated from $\bar{Q}_T$ and $Q_R Q_R^T$.

First, let's consider the existence of Q. It is ensured by the existences of $\bar{Q}_T$ which is computed from the linear system of (2.31). If the corresponding null space is not empty, $\bar{Q}_T$ can be computed. In the absence of noise, we can directly measure the smallest singular value of P_T. If the smallest singular value is equal to 0, the solution for $\bar{Q}_T$ exists. However, the smallest singular value is not robust to the noise and it is always not zero when the measurement matrix contains any error. We design another measure to check the existence of $\bar{Q}_T$ by utilizing the constant property of $\tilde{Q}_T = \hat{M} \times \bar{Q}_T$ as follows

$$S_q = \max(M_c(1) \cdot R_c(1), M_c(2) \cdot R_c(2)),$$
$$M_c(i) = \mathrm{var}(\tilde{Q}_T^i), \quad i = 1, 2, \qquad (32)$$
$$R_c(i) = \frac{\max(\tilde{Q}_T^i) - \min(\tilde{Q}_T^i)}{1 + \sum_{k=2}^{F} | \tilde{Q}_T^i(k) - \tilde{Q}_T^i(k-1) |}.$$

This measure takes into account two factors: $M_c(i)$ measures the variance of two halves of $\tilde{Q}_T$ and $R_c(i)$ measures the randomness in the change of $\tilde{Q}_T$. If $R_c(i)$ is close to 1, the randomness of the variation of $\tilde{Q}_T$ is small. Otherwise, the randomness of variation of $\tilde{Q}_T$ is large. With $R_c(i)$, this measure can better handle imperfect followed AOM.

Another requirement of Q is the non-singularity. We use the linear dependence in the columns of Q to measure its singularity. Only given $\bar{Q}_T$ and $Q_R Q_R^T$, we can estimate the linear dependence among the columns of Q in the following way. For Q to be non-singular, we have

$$rank(Q) = rank([Q_R \mid \bar{Q}_T]) = 4 \qquad (33)$$

Since $rank([Q_R \mid \bar{Q}_T]^T) = rank([Q_R \mid \bar{Q}_T])$, we also have

$$rank([Q_R \mid \bar{Q}_T] \cdot [Q_R \mid \bar{Q}_T]^T) = rank([Q_R \mid \bar{Q}_T]) = 4 \qquad (34)$$

This matrix can be directly calculated from $\bar{Q}_T$ and $Q_R Q_R^T$ without knowing Q:

$$[Q_R \mid \bar{Q}_T] \cdot [Q_R \mid \bar{Q}_T]^T = Q_R Q_R^T + \bar{Q}_T \bar{Q}_T^T \qquad (35)$$

The measure about linear dependence of Q denoted by L_q is then defined as $L_q = \sigma_4$ where σ_4 is the smallest singular value of $[Q_R \mid \bar{Q}_T] \cdot [Q_R \mid \bar{Q}_T]^T$. When L_q is close to 0, the matrix Q is singular. Otherwise, it is non-singular. The final attention measure for the group of feature points forming a measurement matrix is determined by L_q / S_q. If this ratio is large, there is much possible for a Q to exist, which can transfer the affine factorization to a factorization with constant column in the motion matrix. Note that for the degenerate motion, it is impossible to exactly compute Q from the factorization while the proposed method still can estimate its existence based on the available information.

In the situation that there are multiple moving objects in the scene, the measurement matrix will contain feature points from all moving objects. The feature points belonging to different objects will be first grouped first by applying some multibody motion segmentation (Hu et al., 2009). The measurement matrix formed by only the feature points belonging to individual object is analyzed by the introduced method based on the factorization.

EXPERIMENTAL EVALUATION

We test the designed method for the problem of attention-from-motion on both synthetic and real video sequences. Because the attention-from-motion is a new problem, we do not have any related work to compare with. However, the promising results have been obtained from both synthetic and real data and it empirically illustrates how the factorization based method can solve the problem of attention-from-motion.

Evaluation on Synthetic Data

Different number of synthetic video sequences are generate for test. Each synthetic sequence contains different number of synthetic objects e.g. cube, sphere and pyramid. The input measurement matrix is generated by selecting different number of feature points from every object including static background: 20 points from background, 7 points from pyramid, 12 from cube and 20 from sphere. We synthesize both camera motion and object motion according to the orthographic model. We synthesize the following relationship between the camera and some object(s) to define AOM. The 2D coordinates of every feature point in every frame are calculated with round-off errors to form the measurement matrix. The synthetic sequences introduce different challenges for the problem of attention-from-motion:

- The number of moving objects and AOM(s) are different in different sequences;
- There is no restriction on either object motion or camera motion. They can be (partial) dependent to each other, and even degenerated;

- Only partial feature points of the object are detected;

Figure 4 shows 3 exemplar sequences for experiment evaluation, where the top row shows the sequence and the bottom row shows the detected AOM (marked in red). The first sequence (shown in top row) containing a cube and a pyramid. Although the motion of camera and the cube are synthesized to undergo different 3D motion, the cube is followed by the camera and thus an AOM. Because the pyramid is not followed by the camera, it is not an AOM. We can see that the factorization based method succeeds to detect the cube as an AOM. The motion of cube and truncated pyramid in the second sequence is different from those in the first sequence. The motion of the truncated pyramid is degenerated because it is pure translation. In this sequence, both two objects are followed by the camera and they are all AOMs. The correct detection of both objects as AOM shows the ability of the factorization based method to handle degenerated motion. The third sequence introduces another challenge for AOM detection. We can see that the sphere is an AOM but only half of the sphere is observable and hence only feature points of this half are included in the measurement matrix. Another object pyramid is also an AOM but undergoes a different 3D motion. Note that we synthesize a degenerated motion for the camera in this sequence. Because of the factorization method can estimate the existence of special structure in the factorization from only partial data, it can successfully detect both AOMs in this sequence.

Evaluation on Real Data

We also apply the proposed factorization based method to solve the problem of attention-from-motion for real video sequences. The input measurement matrix is built by first detecting corner points in the first frame and then tracking them in the subsequent frames. Because the limita-

Figure 4. Examples of synthetic video sequences and AOM detection results. Top rows show synthetic objects in the 4 keyframes of every synthetic sequence. Bottom rows show detected AOMs (filled in red) in every sequence. (Figure taken from (Hu et al., 2009))

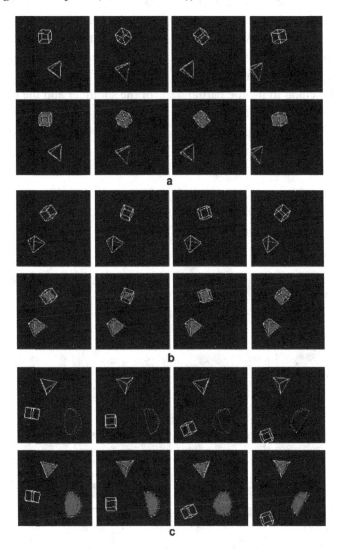

tions of the used tracking algorithm (Georgescu & Meer, 2004), some feature points are removed from forming the measurement matrix because they cannot be correctly tracked. If there are not enough feature points covering the AOM(s), we manually label some feature points to cover them.

Figure 5 shows the attention-from-motion results for 3 real video sequences. For the first sequence shown in Figure 5 (a), 70 feature points from 2 objects (yellow car and time stamp) as well as background are detected and tracked.

Note that in this sequence both the yellow car and the time stamp are followed by the camera and hence the AOMs. We can see that the feature points are successfully segmented into 3 groups (shown in the second row) and two AOMs are successfully detected as shown in the third row. The second tested sequence shown in Figure 5 (b) is the standard MPEG-2 sequence "mobile-and-calendar". There are totally 4 objects including static background. Different numbers of points belonging to these 4 objects are used to form the measurement matrix. In this sequence, the ball undergoes a degenerated rotation motion and the train undergoes a degenerated translation motion. The motions of these two objects are partial dependent while both are AOMs. The successful AOM detection results shown on the second and third rows illustrate the capability of the factorization based method to handle partial dependent/degenerated motion. Figure 5 (c) shows the third sequence used for experiment, where the whole walking person himself does not satisfy

rigid-body assumption. Interestingly, the proposed method still can be applied on detect different parts of the walking person: the head, the arm and the leg. Although both the arm and the leg are not stationary, they are recognized as partial feature points of a stationary object and detected as AOMs. It is because they belong to the joint of the shoulder and the knee which are followed by the camera. The result shown in the third row is a successful example of handling partial data.

Figure 5. Examples of real video sequences and AOM detection results. Top rows show all feature points in 4 keyframes of every video. Bottom rows show feature points belonging to detected AOMs in corresponding frames. (Figure taken from (Hu et al., 2009))

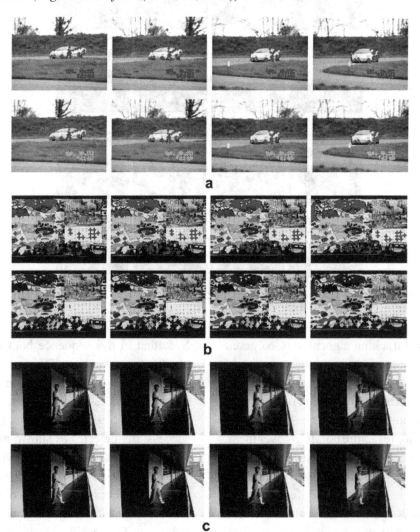

FUTURE RESEARCH

The research about visual saliency modeling is still ongoing. With the progress in understanding the attention mechanism of vision system from psychology and neuroscience, new theories about visual saliency need to be proposed and new computational methods will be developed. Here we illustrate some possible future directions of visual saliency modeling research. One interesting direction is how to model visual saliency using sparse coding. Sparsity is related to visual saliency such as feature/spatial rarity is a good clue to indicate saliency. Although theoretic results for sparse coding have been established, several issues are still unsolved yet about how to formulate the visual saliency modeling as a sparsity detection problem. For example, how to design a "good" dictionary to encode the visual saliency? What sparse property characterizes the saliency is another interest question. Is it feature sparsity, spatial sparsity or group sparsity? With the development of new applications e.g. media retargeting, new modeling techniques for the specific application need to be designed. Instead of assigning saliency on every pixel, new saliency measure can be proposed for the new representation e.g. seam-based saliency map. Currently, almost every retargeting algorithm relies on a pre-computed saliency map. How to refine the pre-computed saliency map by utilizing the retargeting information is another interesting problem. Motivated from the proposed AFM, we believe that detecting specific motion pattern related to camera which can indicate a top-down saliency of cameraman is useful in many applications.

CONCLUSION

In this chapter, we discuss about the modeling of visual saliency for multimedia and vision application. Specifically, we introduce one method to model spatial saliency in images and another to model motion saliency in videos. For images, we use a graph-based approach. The global dependency of image content is encoded in a globally connected graph while a local k-regular graph encodes the local dependency in spatial neighbors. We formulate the visual saliency as Markov random walks and use the equilibrium hitting times of the ergodic Markov chain for identifying the most salient node as well as background nodes. In videos, a new problem Attention-From-Motion (AFM) is defined where Attention Object in Motions (AOM) is defined as the moving object which is followed by the camera. A factorization based method is introduced to solve AFM, which estimates the existence of a special factorization in the motion matrix. This method can detect AOM(s) only from the affine version of the factorization. It can handle partial feature points, degenerated motion as well as partial dependent motion.

REFERENCES

Aldous, D., & Fill, J. A. (1999). Reversible Markov Chains and Random Walks on Graphs. Retrieved from http://stat-www.berkeley.edu/users/aldous/RWG/book.html

Bamidele, A., Stentiford, F. W. M., & Morphett, J. (2004). An Attention-based Approach to Content based Image Retrieval. [Pervasive Computing]. *British Telecommunications Advanced Research Technology Journal on Intelligent Spaces, 22*(3), 151–160.

Brajovic, V., & Kanade, T. (1998). Computational Sensor for Visual Tracking with Attention. *IEEE Journal of Solid-state Circuits, 33*(8), 1199–1207. doi:10.1109/4.705358

Bruce, N., & Tsotsos, J. (2006). Saliency based on Information Maximization. In Weiss, Y., Schölkopf, B., & Platt, J. (Eds.), *Advances in Neural Information Processing Systems 18* (*Vol. 1*, pp. 155–162). MIT Press.

Chen, L.-Q., Xie, X., Fan, X., Ma, W.-Y., & Zhang, H.-J. (2003). A Visual Attention Model for Adapting Images on Small Displays. *ACM Multimedia Systems Journal*, *9*(4), 353–364. doi:10.1007/s00530-003-0105-4

Costa, L. F. (2006). Visual Saliency and Attention as Random Walks on Complex Networks. *arXiv*:physics/0603025 eprint.

Costeira, J. P., & Kanade, T. (1998). A Multibody Factorization Method for Independently Moving Objects. *International Journal of Computer Vision*, *29*(3), 159–179. doi:10.1023/A:1008000628999

Desimone, R., & Duncan, J. (1995). Neural Mechanisms of Selective Visual Attention. *Annual Review of Neuroscience*, *18*, 193–222. doi:10.1146/annurev.ne.18.030195.001205

Eriksen, C. W., & St James, J. D. (1986). Visual Attention Within and Around the Field of Focus Attention: A Zoom Lens Model. *Perception & Psychophysics*, *40*(5), 225–240.

Eriksen, C. W., & Yeh, Y. Y. (1985). Allocation of Attention in the Visual Field. *Journal of Experimental Psychology. Human Perception and Performance*, *11*(5), 583–597. doi:10.1037/0096-1523.11.5.583

Gao, D., & Vasconcelos, N. (2005). Integrated Learning of Saliency, Complex Features, and Object Detectors from Cluttered Scenes. In. *Proceedings of the IEEE Conference on Computer Vision and Pattern Recognition*, *2*, 282–287.

Gao, D., & Vasconcelos, N. (2007). Bottom-up Saliency is a Discriminant Process. In *Proceedings of the IEEE Conference on Computer Vision*.

Goplakrishnan, V., Hu, Y., & Rajan, D. (2009a). Salient region detection by modeling distributions of color and orientation. *IEEE Transactions on Multimedia*, *11*(5), 892–905. doi:10.1109/TMM.2009.2021726

Goplakrishnan, V., Hu, Y., & Rajan, D. (2009b). Random walks on graphs to model saliency in images. In *Proceedings of the IEEE Conference on Computer Vision and Pattern Recognition*.

Grossberg, S., & Raizada, R. D. (2000). Contrast-Sensitive Persceptual Grouping and Object-based Attention in the Laminar Circuits of Primary Visual Cortex. *Vision Research*, *40*(10-12), 1413–1432. doi:10.1016/S0042-6989(99)00229-1

Guo, C., Ma, Q., & Zhang, L. (2008). Spatial-temporal Saliency Detection using Phrase Spectrum of Quaternion Fourier Transform. In *Proceedings of the IEEE Conference on Computer Vision and Pattern Recognition*.

Harel, J., Koch, C., & Perona, P. (2006). Graph-based Visual Saliency. In Weiss, Y., Schölkopf, B., & Platt, J. (Eds.), *Advances in Neural Information Processing Systems 18* (*Vol. 1*, pp. 545–552). MIT Press.

Hou, X., & Zhang, L. (2007). Saliency Detection: A Spectral Residual Approach. In *Proceedings of the IEEE Conference on Computer Vision and Pattern Recognition*.

Hu, Y., Rajan, D., & Chia, L.-T. (2009). Attention-from-Motion: A Factorization Approach for Detecting Attention Objects in Motion. *Computer Vision and Image Understanding*, *113*, 319–331. doi:10.1016/j.cviu.2008.08.010

Hu, Y., Xie, X., Chen, Z., & Ma, W.-Y. (2004). Attention Model based Progressive Image Transmission. In Proceedings of the *2004 International Conference on Multimedia and Expo* (Vol. 2, pp. 1079-1082).

Itti, L., & Koch, C. (2001). Computational Modeling of Visual Attention. *Nature Neuroscience Review*, *2*(3), 194–203. doi:10.1038/35058500

Itti, L., Koch, C., & Niebur, E. (1998). A Model of Saliency-based Visual Attention for Rapid Scene Analysis. *IEEE Transactions on Pattern Analysis and Machine Intelligence, 20*(11), 1254–1259. doi:10.1109/34.730558

Kadir, T., & Brady, M. (2001). Scale, Saliency and Image Description. *International Journal of Computer Vision, 45*(2), 83–105. doi:10.1023/A:1012460413855

Liu, T., Sun, J., Tang, X., & Zheng, N.-N. (2007). Learning to Detect a Salient Object. In *Proceedings of the IEEE Conference on Computer Vision and Pattern Recognition.*

Ma, Y.-F., Hua, X.-S., Lu, L., & Zhang, H.-J. (2005). A Generic Framework of User Attention Model and Its Application in Video Summarization. *IEEE Transactions on Multimedia, 7*(5), 907–919. doi:10.1109/TMM.2005.854410

Ma, Y.-F., & Zhang, H.-J. (2003). Contrast-based Image Attention Analysis by Using Fuzzy Growing. In *Proceedings of the eleventh ACM International Conference on Multimedia* (Vol. 1, pp. 228-241).

Scholl, B. J. (2001). Objects and Attention: The State of the Art. *Cognition, 80*(1-2), 1–46. doi:10.1016/S0010-0277(00)00152-9

Shamir, A., & Avidan, S. (2009). Seam Carving for Media Retargeting. *Communications of the ACM, 52*(1), 77–85. doi:10.1145/1435417.1435437

Tian, Y.-L., & Hampapur, A. (2005). Robust Salient Motion Detection with Complex Background for Real-time Video Surveillance. In *Proceedings of the IEEE Computer Society Workshop on Motion and Video Computing* (Vol. 2, pp. 30-35).

Tomasi, C., & Kanade, T. (1992). Shape and Motion from Image Streams under Orthography: A Factorization Method. *International Journal of Computer Vision, 9*(2), 137–154. doi:10.1007/BF00129684

Toyama, K., & Hager, G. D. (1999). Incremental Focus of Attention for Robust Vision-based Tracking. *International Journal of Computer Vision, 35*(1), 45–63. doi:10.1023/A:1008159011682

Treisman, A. (1980). A Feature Integration Theory of Attention. *Cognitive Psychology, 12*(1), 97–136. doi:10.1016/0010-0285(80)90005-5

Tsotsos, J. K., Culhane, S. M., Winky, Y. K. W., Yuzhong, L., Davis, N., & Nuflo, F. (1995). Modeling Visual Attention via Selective Tuning. *Artificial Intelligence, 78*(1), 507–545. doi:10.1016/0004-3702(95)00025-9

Walther, D., & Koch, C. (2006). Modeling Attention to Salient Photo-objects. *Neural Networks, 19*(1), 1395–1407. doi:10.1016/j.neunet.2006.10.001

Wang, X.-J., Ma, W.-Y., & Li, X. (2004). Data-driven Approach for Bridging the Cognitive Gap in Image Retrieval. In *Proceedings of the 2004 International Conference on Multimedia and Expo* (Vol 3, pp. 2231-2234).

Wixson, L. (2000). Detecting Salient Motion by Accumulating Directionally-Consistent Flow. *IEEE Transactions on Pattern Analysis and Machine Intelligence, 22*(8), 774–780. doi:10.1109/34.868680

Wolf, L., Guttmann, M., & Cohen-Or, D. (2007). Non-homogeneous Content-driven Video-retargeting. In *Proceedings of the Eleventh IEEE International Conference on Computer Vision.*

Wolfe, J. M. (1994). Guided Search 2.0: A Revised Model of Visual Search. *Psychonomic Bulletin & Review, 1*(2), 202–238.

Xie, X., Liu, H., Ma, W.-Y., & Zhang, H.-J. (2006). Browsing Large Pictures Under Limited Display Sizes. *IEEE Transactions on Multimedia, 8*(4), 707–715. doi:10.1109/TMM.2006.876294

Yang, M., Yan, J., & Wu, Y. (2007). Spatial Selection for Attentional Visual Tracking. In *Proceedings of the IEEE International Conference on Computer Vision and Pattern Recognition*.

ADDITIONAL READING

Avraham, T., & Lindenbaum, M. (2009). Esaliency: Meaningful Attention using Stochastic Image Modeling. *IEEE Transactions on Pattern Analysis and Machine Intelligence, 99*(1).

Boccignone, G., Chianese, A., Moscato, V., & Picariello, A. (2005). Foveated Shot Detection for Video Segmentation. *IEEE Transactions on Circuits and Systems for Video Technology, 15*(3), 365–377. doi:10.1109/TCSVT.2004.842603

Gao, D., Han, S., & Vasconcelos, N. (2009). Discriminant Saliency, The Detection of Suspicious Coincidences, and Applications to Visual Recognition. *IEEE Transactions on Pattern Analysis and Machine Intelligence, 31*(6), 989–1005. doi:10.1109/TPAMI.2009.27

Gao, D., & Mahadevan, V., & Vasconcelos, N. (2008). On The Plausibility of the Discriminant Center-Surround Hypothesis for Visual Saliency. *Journal of Vision, 8*(7), 13, 1-18.

Gao, D., & Vasconcelos, N. (2009). Decision-theoretic Saliency: Computational Principles, Biological Plausibility, and Implications for Neurophysiology and Psychophysics. *Neural Computation, 21*, 239–271. doi:10.1162/neco.2009.11-06-391

Georgescu, B., & Meer, P. (2004). Point Matching under Large Image Deformations and Illumination Changes. *IEEE Transactions on Pattern Analysis and Machine Intelligence, 26*(6), 674–688. doi:10.1109/TPAMI.2004.2

Hoffman, J. E. (1998). *Attention*. Psychology Press.

Horaud, R. P., Knossow, D., & Michaelis, M. (2006). Camera Cooperation for Achieving Visual Attention. *Machine Vision and Applications, 16*(6), 331–342. doi:10.1007/s00138-005-0182-9

Hou, X., & Zhang, L. (2008). Dynamic Visual Attention: Searching for Coding Length Increments. In *Advances in Neural Information Processing Systems 18*. MIT Press.

Itti, L., & Koch, C. (2000). A Saliency-based Search Mechanism for Overt and Covert Shifts of Visual Attention. *Vision Research, 40*, 1489–1506. doi:10.1016/S0042-6989(99)00163-7

Itti, L., Rees, G., & Tsotsos, J. (Eds.). (2005). *Neurobiology of Attention*. Academic Press.

Jägersand, M. (1995). Saliency Maps and Attention Selection in Scale and Spatial coordinates: An Information Theoretic Approach. In. *Proceedings of the IEEE International Conference on Computer Vision, 1*, 195–202.

Judd, T., Ehinger, K., Durand, F., & Torralba, A. (2009). Learning to Predict Where Humans Look. In *Proceedings of the IEEE International Conference on Computer Vision*.

Kienzle, W., Wichmann, F. A., Schölkopf, B., & Franz, M. O. (2006). A Nonparametric Approach to Bottom-up Visual Saliency. In Schölkopf, B., Platt, J., & Hoffman, T. (Eds.), *Advances in Neural Information Processing Systems 18* (Vol. 1, pp. 689–696). MIT Press.

Lindeberg, T. (1993). Detecting Salient Blob-like Image Structures and Their Sacles with a Scale-space Primal Sketch: A Method for Focus-of-Attention. *International Journal of Computer Vision, 45*(2), 83–105.

López, M. T., Femández, M. A., Femández-Caballero, A., Mira, A., & Delgado, A. E. (2007). Dynamic Visual Attention Model in Image Sequence. *Image and Vision Computing, 25*(5), 597–613. doi:10.1016/j.imavis.2006.05.004

Park, K. T., & Moon, Y. S. (2007). Automatic Extraction of Salient Objects using Feature Maps. In *Proceedings of the IEEE International Conference on Acoustics, Speech and Signal Processing* (Vol 1, pp. 617-620).

Rosenholtz, R. (1999). A Simple Saliency Model Predicts A Number of Motion Popout Phenomena. *Vision Research*, *39*(19), 3157–3163. doi:10.1016/S0042-6989(99)00077-2

Sun, Y., & Fisher, R. (2003). Object-based Visual Attention for Computer Vision. *Artificial Intelligence*, *146*(1), 77–123. doi:10.1016/S0004-3702(02)00399-5

Torralba, A. (2003). Modeling Global Scene Factors in Attention. *Journal of the Optical Society of America. A, Optics, Image Science, and Vision*, *20*(7), 1407–1418. doi:10.1364/JOSAA.20.001407

Tsotsos, J. K., Liu, Y., Martinez-Trujillo, J. C., Pomplun, M., Simine, E., & Zhou, K. (2005). Attention to Visual Motion. *Computer Vision and Image Understanding*, *100*(1-2), 3–40. doi:10.1016/j.cviu.2004.10.011

Ullman, S., & Shaashua, A. (1988). Structural Saliency: The Detection of Globally Salient Structures using A Locally Connected Network. In. *Proceedings of the IEEE International Conference on Computer Vision*, *1*, 321–327.

Wang, S., Kubota, T., Siskind, J. M., & Wang, J. (2005). Salient Closed Boundary Extraction with Ratio Contour. *IEEE Transactions on Pattern Analysis and Machine Intelligence*, *27*(4), 546–561. doi:10.1109/TPAMI.2005.84

Zelnik-Manor, L., Machline, M., & Irani, M. (2006). Multi-body Factorization with Uncertainty: Revisiting Motion Consistency. *International Journal of Computer Vision*, *68*(1), 27–41. doi:10.1007/s11263-005-4840-1

Zhang, L., Tong, M. H., Marks, T. K., Shan, H., & Cottrell, G. W. (2008). SUN: A Bayesian Framework for Saliency using Natural Statistics. *Journal of Vision (Charlottesville, Va.)*, *8*(7), 1–20. doi:10.1167/8.7.32

KEY TERMS AND DEFINITIONS

Attention Object in Motion (AOM): In a video sequence, an object that is in motion while being tracked by the camera.

Attention-from-Motion: The procedure of identifying attention objects in motion.

Entropy: A characteristic of a random variable that provides a measure of uncertainty about the random variable. It is also the average amount of information contained in a group of entities, e.g. pixels.

Markov Chain: A random (stochastic) process in which only the present state, and not the past states, influences the future states. The transition between states is probabilistic in nature.

Null Space: A vector space associated with a matrix A, in which all the vectors x cause the product Ax to be 0.

Orthographic Projection: A transformation of a 3D co-ordinate point to a point in the image plane by projecting rays from the 3D point parallel to the optical axis.

Random Walk: The path traced out while taking random steps on a structured pathway like a line, a plane, a graph etc.

Visual Saliency: The occurrence of regions in multimedia content, e.g., images and videos, which capture the attention of the human visual system. The stimulus for capturing the attention could be, for instance, rarity of features in images or motion in videos.

294

Compilation of References

Abbadeni, N. (2003). A New Similarity Matching Measure: Application to Texture-Based Image Retrieval. In *Proceedings of the Third International Workshop on Texture Analysis and Synthesis (Joint with ICCV '03)*, Nice, France (pp. 1-5).

Abbadeni, N. (2003). Content representation and similarity matching for texture-based image retrieval. *Proceedings of the Fifth ACM International Workshop on Multimedia Information Retrieval (Joint with ACM Multimedia '03)*, Berkeley, CA, USA (pp. 63-70).

Abbadeni, N. (2005). Multiple representations, similarity matching, and results fusion for content-based image retrieval. *ACM/Springer Multimedia Systems Journal, 10*(5), 444-456.

Abbadeni, N. (2005). Perceptual Image Retrieval. In *Proceedings of the international conference on visual information systems (VISUAL '05)*, Amsterdam, Netherlands (pp. 259-268).

Abbadeni, N. (2011). Computational Perceptual Features for Texture Representation and Retrieval. To Appear in *IEEE Transactions on Image Processing, 20*(1), January 2011.

Abbadeni, N., Ziou, D., & Wang, S. (2000). Autocovariance-based Perceptual Textural Features Corresponding to Human Visual Perception. In *Proceedings of the Fifteenth IAPR/IEEE International Conference on Pattern Recognition* (Vol. 3, pp. 901-904). Barcelona, Spain.

Abbadeni, N., Ziou, D., & Wang, S. (2000). Computational measures corresponding to perceptual textural features. *Proceedings of the Seventh IEEE International Conference on Image Processing* (Vol. 3, pp. 897-900). Vancouver, BC.

Abbadeni, N., Ziou, D., & Wang, S. (2000). Perceptual Textural Features Corresponding to Human Visual Perception. In *Proceedings of the Thirteenth Vision Interface Conference* (pp. 365-372). Montreal, QC.

Abrantes, G. A., & Pereira, F. (1999). MPEG-4 Facial Animation Technology: Survey, Implementation, and Results. *IEEE Transactions on Circuits and Systems for Video Technology, 9*(2), 290–305. doi:10.1109/76.752096

Ahlberg, J. (2002). An active model for facial feature tracking. *EURASIP Journal on Applied Signal Processing*, (6): 566–571. doi:10.1155/S1110865702203078

Ahlberg, J., & Li, H. (1999). Representation and Compressing Facial Animation Parameters Using Facial Action Basis Functions. *IEEE Transactions on Circuits and Systems for Video Technology, 9*(3), 405–410. doi:10.1109/76.754768

Ahlberg, J. (2001). *CANDIDE-3 -- an updated parameterized face* (No. LiTH-ISY-R-2326).

Alahi, A., Boursier, Y., Jacques, L., & Vandergheynst, P. (2009). A sparsity constrained inverse problem to locate people in a network of cameras. In *Proceedings of the 16th International Conference on Digital Signal Processing (DSP)*, Santorini, Greece.

Alam, M. S., & Bal, A. (2007). Improved multiple target tracking via global motion compensation and optoelectronic correlation. *IEEE Transactions on Industrial Electronics*, *54*(1), 522. doi:10.1109/TIE.2006.885513

Albanese, M., Fayzullin, M., Picariello, A., & Subrahmanian, V. S. (2006). The priority curve algorithm for video summarization. *Information Systems*, *31*(7), 679–695. doi:10.1016/j.is.2005.12.003

Aldous, D., & Fill, J. A. (1999). Reversible Markov Chains and Random Walks on Graphs. Retrieved from http://stat-www.berkeley.edu/users/aldous/RWG/book.html

Al-Hames, M., Hornler, B., Muller, R., Schenk, J., & Rigoll, G. (2007). Automatic multi-modal meeting camera selection for video-conferences and meeting browsers. In *Proceedings of the 2007 IEEE International Conference on Multimedia and Expo* (pp. 2074-2077). Beijing, China: IEEE.

Allman, J., Cacioppo, J. T., Davidson, R. J., Ekman, P., Friesen, W. V., Lzard, C. E., & Phillips, M. (1992). *NSF Report - Facial Expression Understanding*. San Francisco: University of California.

Alpert, C., Kahng, A., & Yao, S. (1999). Spectral partitioning: The more eigenvectors, the better. *Discrete Applied Mathematics*, *90*, 3–26. doi:10.1016/S0166-218X(98)00083-3

Amadasun, M., & King, R. (1989). Textural Features corresponding to textural properties. *IEEE Transactions on Systems, Man, and Cybernetics*, *19*(5), 1264–1274. doi:10.1109/21.44046

APIDIS. (2008). Autonomous Production of Images Based on Distributed and Intelligent Sensing. Homepage of the APIDIS project. http://www.apidis.org/ Demo videos related to this paper. http://www.apidis.org/Initial Results/APIDIS%20*Initial*%20*Results.htm*

Arbib, M. A. (2002). *The handbook of Brain Theory and Neural Network*. Cambridge, MA: The MIT Press.

Ashley, J., Barber, R., Flickner, M., Hafner, J., Lee, D., Niblack, W., & Petkovic, D. (1995). Automatic and Semi-Automatic Methods for Image Annotation and Retrieval in QBIC. In *Proceedings of the SPIE Conference on Storage and Retrieval for Image and Video Databases*, *2420*, 24–35.

Assfalg, J., Bertini, M., Colombo, C., Bimbo, A. d., & Nunziati, W. (2003). Semantic annotation of soccer videos: automatic highlights identification. *Computer Vision and Image Understanding*, *92*(2-3), 285–305. doi:10.1016/j.cviu.2003.06.004

Assfalg, J., Bertini, M., Colombo, C., & Del Bimbo, A. (2001). Semantic characterization of visual content for sports videos annotation. In *Proc. 2nd Int. Workshop Multimedia Databases and Image Communication* (LNCS 2184, pp. 179-191).

Attwell, D., & Laughlin, S. (2001). An energy budget for signaling in the grey matter of the brain. *Journal of Cerebral Blood Flow and Metabolism*, *21*, 1133–1145. doi:10.1097/00004647-200110000-00001

Ayache, S., & Qunot, G. (2007). Evaluation of active learning strategies for video indexing. *Signal Processing Image Communication*, *22*(7-8), 692–704. doi:10.1016/j.image.2007.05.010

Ayache, S., Quénot, G., Gensel, J., & Satoh, S. (2006). Using topic concepts for semantic video shots classification. In *Proc. 5th international conference on image and video retrieval*.

Bailer, W., Lee, F., & Thallinger, G. (2007). Skimming Rushes Video Using Retake Detection. In *Proc. of the TRECVID Workshop on Video Summarization (TVS'07)*. ACM Multimedia.

Baldauf, M., & Frohlich, P. (2009). Supporting Hand Gesture Manipulation of Projected Content with Mobile Phones. In *Proceedings of the Workshop on Mobile Interaction with the Real World*. New York: ACM Press.

Bamidele, A., Stentiford, F. W. M., & Morphett, J. (2004). An Attention-based Approach to Content based Image Retrieval. [Pervasive Computing]. *British Telecommunications Advanced Research Technology Journal on Intelligent Spaces*, *22*(3), 151–160.

Barlow, H. (1994). What is the computational goal of the Neocortex? In Koch, C., & Davis, J. (Eds.), *Large-Scale Neuronal Theories of the Brain* (pp. 553–561). Oxford: Oxford University Press.

Barlow, H., & Tolhust, D. (1992). Why do you have edge detectors? *Optical Society of America Technical Digest, 23*(172).

Bartlett, M. S., Littlewort, G. C., Frank, M. G., Lainscsek, C., Fasel, I. R., & Movellan, J. R. (2006). Automatic recognition of facial actions in spontaneous expressions. *J. Multimedia, 1*(6), 22–35.

Bay, H., Tuytelaars, T., & Van Gool, L. (2006). Surf: Speeded up robust feature. In *Proceedings of European Conference on Computer Vision* (pp.404-417).

Bayram, S., Memon, N., Ramkumar, M., & Sankur, B. (2004). A classifier design for detecting image manipulations. In *Proc. IEEE Int. Conf. on Image Processing, Singapore, 4*, 2645-2648.

Bayram, S., Sencar, H. T., & Memon, N. (2005). Source camera identification based on CFA interpolation. *IEEE International Conference on Image Processing, Genoa, Italy, Sep* (Vol. 3, pp. 69-72).

Bear, M. F., Connors, B. W., & Paradiso, M. A. (2001). *Neuroscience Exploring the Brain*. Lippincott Williams & Wilkins Co.

Beetz, M. (2009). Retrieved from http://ias.in.tum.de/research/awarekitchen

Bell, A. J., & Sejnowski, T. (1997). The independent components of natural scenes are edge filters. *Vision Research, 37*(23), 3327–3338. doi:10.1016/S0042-6989(97)00121-1

Bellotti, V., Back, M., Edwards, W. K., Grinter, R. E., Henderson, A., & Lopes, C. (2002). Making sense of sensing systems: five questions for designers and researchers. In *Proceedings of the SIGCHI Conference on Human Factors in Computing Systems: Changing Our World, Changing Ourselves* (pp. 415-422). New York: ACM Press.

Benford, S., Schnädelbach, H., Koleva, B., Anastasi, R., Greenhalgh, C., & Rodden, T. (2005). Expected, sensed, and desired: A framework for designing sensing-based interaction. *ACM Transactions on Computer-Human Interaction, 12*(1), 3–30. doi:10.1145/1057237.1057239

Berclaz, J., Fleuret, F., & Fua, P. (2008). Principled detection-by-classification from multiple views. In [VISAPP]. *Proceedings of the International Conference on Computer Vision Theory and Application, 2*, 375–382.

Bergen, J. R., & Adelson, E. H. (1988). Early Vision and Texture Perception. *Nature, 333*(6171), 363–364. doi:10.1038/333363a0

Bezdek, J. C., & Pal, N. R. (1998). Some new indexes of cluster validity. *IEEE Transactions on Systems, Man, and Cybernetics, 28*(3), 301–315. doi:10.1109/3477.678624

Bilmes, J. (1997). *A Gentle Tutorial on the EM Algorithm and its Application to Parameter Estimation for Gaussian Mixture and Hidden Markov Models* (ICSI-Report-97-021).

Binh, N., Shuichi, E., & Ejima, T. (2005). Real-Time Hand Tracking and Gesture Recognition System. In *Proceedings of International Conference on Graphics, Vision and Image Processing* (pp. 362-368).

Black, M. J., & Yacoob, Y. (1997). Recognizing Facial Expression in Image Sequences Using Local Parameterized Models of Image Motion. *International Journal of Computer Vision, 25*(1), 23–48. doi:10.1023/A:1007977618277

Blake, A., Curwen, R., & Zisserman, A. (1994). A framework for Spatio-Temporal Control in the Tracking of Visual Contours. In Brown, C. M., & Terzopoulos, D. (Eds.), *Real-Time Computer Vision*. Cambridge: Cambridge University Press.

Blanz, V., & Vetter, T. (2003). Face Recognition Based on Fitting a 3D Morphable Model. *IEEE Transactions on Pattern Analysis and Machine Intelligence, 25*(9), 1063–1074. doi:10.1109/TPAMI.2003.1227983

Blum, A., & Mitchell, T. (1998). Combining labeled and unlabeled data with co-training. In *Proceedings of 11th Annual Conference on Computational Learning Theory* (pp. 92-100).

Böhme, H. J., Braumann, U. D., Brakensiek, A., Corradini, A., Krabbes, M., & Gross, H. M. (1998). User localisation for visually-based human–machine interaction. In *Proceedings of the 1998 IEEE International Conference on Face and Gesture Recognition*, Nara, Japan (pp. 486–491).

Bouguet, J.-Y. (2000). Pyramidal Implementation of the Lucas Kanade Feature Tracker Description of the algorithm: Intel Corporation Microprocessor Research Labs.

Bradski, G., & Kaehler, A. (2008). *Learning OpenCV: Computer Vision with the OpenCV Library* (1st ed.). O'Reilly Media, Inc.

Bradski, G., Yeo, B. L., & Yeung, M. M. (1999). Gesture for Video Content Navigation. In *Proceedings of the IS&T/SPIE Conferene on Storage and Retrieval for Image and Video Database VII* (pp.230-242).

Brajovic, V., & Kanade, T. (1998). Computational Sensor for Visual Tracking with Attention. *IEEE Journal of Solid-state Circuits, 33*(8), 1199–1207. doi:10.1109/4.705358

Brand, M. (1999). Structure Learning in Conditional Probability Models via an Entropic Prior and Parameter Extinction. *Neural Computation, 11*(5), 1155–1182. doi:10.1162/089976699300016395

Brand, M., Oliver, N., & Pentland, A. (1997). Coupled hidden Markov models for complex action recognition. In *Proc. IEEE International Conference on Computer Vision and Pattern Recognition.*

Bretzner, L., & Laptev, I. Lindeberg. T., Lenman. S., & Sundblad, Y. (2001). *A prototype system for computer vision based human computer interaction* (Tech. Report, KTH University, Stockholm, Sweden).

Bretzner, L., Laptev, I., & Lindeberg, T. (2002). Hand gesture recognition using multi-scale colour features, hierarchical models and particle filtering. In *Proceedings of International Conference on Automatic Face and Gesture Recognition* (pp. 423-428).

Brodatz, P. (1966). *Textures: A Photographic Album for Artists and Designers*. New York: Dover.

Bruce, N., & Tsotsos, J. (2006). Saliency based on Information Maximization. In Weiss, Y., Schölkopf, B., & Platt, J. (Eds.), *Advances in Neural Information Processing Systems 18* (*Vol. 1*, pp. 155–162). MIT Press.

Bucher, T., Curio, C., Edelbrunner, J., Igel, C., Kastrup, D., & Leefken, I. (2003). Image processing and behavior planning for intelligent vehicles. *IEEE Transactions on Industrial Electronics, 50*(1), 62–75. doi:10.1109/TIE.2002.807650

Burnett, G. E. (1998). "Turn right at the King's Head": drivers' requirements for route guidance information. PhD thesis, Loughborough University, UK.

Buss, S. (2003). *3D Computer Graphics: A mathematical approach with OpenGL*. Cambridge University Press.

Caltech 101 dataset (n.d.). Retrieved from www.vision.caltech.edu/feifeili/101 ObjectCategories

Cao, X., & Foroosh, H. (2006). Camera Calibration using Symmetric Objects. *IEEE Transactions on Image Processing, 15*(11), 3614–3619. doi:10.1109/TIP.2006.881940

Carpenter, G. A., Grossberg, S., Markuzon, N., Reynolds, J. H., & Rosen, D. B. (1992). Fuzzy ARTMAP: A neural network architecture for incremental supervised learning of analog multidimensional maps. *IEEE Transactions on Neural Networks, 3*(5), 698–713. doi:10.1109/72.159059

Chai, X., Fang, Y., & Wang, K. (2009). Robust hand gesture analysis and application in gallery browsing. In *Proceedings of International Conference on Multimedia and Expo* (pp.938-941).

Chang, S.-F. (2002). The holy grail of content-based media analysis. *IEEE Multimedia Magazine, 9*(2), 6–10. doi:10.1109/93.998041

Chang, P., Han, M., & Gong, Y. (2002). Highlight detection and classification of baseball game video with Hidden Markov Models. In *Proc. IEEE International Conference on Image Processing, Rochester, NY*.

Chen, X., Yang, J., Zhang, J., & Waibel, A. (2004). Automatic detection and recognition of signs from natural scenes. *IEEE Transactions on Image Processing, 13*(1), 87–99. doi:10.1109/TIP.2003.819223

Chen, B. W., Wang, J. C., & Wang, J. F. (2009). A novel video summarization based on mining the story-structure and semantic relations among concept entities. *IEEE Transactions on Multimedia, 11*(2), 295–312. doi:10.1109/TMM.2008.2009703

Chen, F., & De Vleeschouwer, C. (2009a). *Autonomous production of basket-ball videos from multi-sensored data with personalized viewpoints. The 10th international workshop for multimedia interactive services* (pp. 81–84). London, UK: IEEE.

Chen, F., & De Vleeschouwer, C. (2010). Personalized production of team sport videos from multi-sensored data under limited display resolution. *Computer Vision and Image Understanding. Special Issue on Sensor Fusion, 114*(6), 667–680.

Chen, M., Fridrich, J., Goljan, M., & Lukas, J. (2008). Determining Image Origin and Integrity Using Sensor Noise. *IEEE Transactions on Information Forensics and Security, 3*(1), 74–90. doi:10.1109/TIFS.2007.916285

Chen, L.-Q., Xie, X., Fan, X., Ma, W.-Y., & Zhang, H.-J. (2003). A Visual Attention Model for Adapting Images on Small Displays. *ACM Multimedia Systems Journal, 9*(4), 353–364. doi:10.1007/s00530-003-0105-4

Chen, F., & De Vleeschouwer, C. (2009b). A resource allocation framework for summarizing team sport videos. *2009 IEEE International Conference on Image Processing*, (Vol. 1, pp.4349-4352), Cairo, Egypt: IEEE.

Chen, W., Shi, Y., & Su, W. (2007). Image splicing detection using 2D phase congruency and statistical moments of characteristic function. In *Proc. SPIE, Electronic Imaging, Security, Steganography, Watermarking of Multimedia Contents IX, San Jose, CA, J 29 January-1 February, 6505*, 65050R.1-65050R.8.

Chen, X., Yang, J., Zhang, J., & Waibel, A. (2002). Automatic detection of signs with affine transformation. In *Proceedings of the IEEE Workshop on Applications of Computer Vision* (pp. 32–36).

Cheng, W.-H., Chua, W.-T., & Wu, J.-L. (2005). A visual attention based region-of-interest determination framework for video sequences. *IEICE Transactions on Information and Systems, E88*(7), 1578–1586. doi:10.1093/ietisy/e88-d.7.1578

Chou, J., & Chang, Y. Y. & Chen, Y. (2001) Facial feature point tracking and expression analysis for virtual conferencing systems, *IEEE International Conference on Multimedia and Expo*, 24–27.

Cohn, J. F., & Schmidt, K. (2004). The Timing of Facial Motion in Posed and Spontaneous Smiles. *International Journal of Wavelets, Multresolution, and Information Processing, 2*, 1–12. doi:10.1142/S021969130400041X

Collins, M., Schapire, R. E., & Singer, Y. (2000). Logistic Regression, Adaboost and Bregman distances. In *Proceedings of 13th Annual Conference on Computational Learning Theory* (pp.158-169).

Cootes, T., Edwards, G., & Taylor, C. (2001). Active appearance models. *IEEE Transactions on Pattern Analysis and Machine Intelligence, 23*(6), 681–685. doi:10.1109/34.927467

Cootes, T. F., Taylor, C. J., Cooper, D. H., & Graham, J. (1995). Active shape models—their training and application. *Computer Vision and Image Understanding, 61*(1), 38–59. doi:10.1006/cviu.1995.1004

Costa, L. F. (2006). Visual Saliency and Attention as Random Walks on Complex Networks. *arXiv*:physics/0603025 eprint.

Costanzo, C., La Rosa, F., & Iannizzotto, G. (2003). VirtualBoard: Real-Time Visual Gesture Recognition for Natural Human-Computer Interaction. In. *Proceedings of IPDPS, 2003*, 112–119.

Costeira, J. P., & Kanade, T. (1998). A Multibody Factorization Method for Independently Moving Objects. *International Journal of Computer Vision, 29*(3), 159–179. doi:10.1023/A:1008000628999

Cowie, R. (2001). D-Cowie, E., Tsapatsoulis, N., Votsis, G., Kollias, S., Fellenz, W., & Taylor, J. G. (2001) Emotion recognition in human computer interaction. *IEEE Signal Processing Magazine*, (1): 33–80.

Cox, I. J., Miller, M. L., & Bloom, J. A. (2002). *Digital Watermarking*. Morgan Kaufmann Publishers.

Criminisi, A., Reid, I., & Zisserman, A. (1999). Single View Metrology. *International Conference on Computer Vision* (pp. 434-441).

Crowley, J., Coutaz, J., & Berard, F. (2000). Things That See. *Communications of the ACM, 43*(3), 54–64. doi:10.1145/330534.330540

Crowley, J. L. (1997). Vision for man-machine interaction. *Robotics and Autonomous Systems, 19*, 347–358. doi:10.1016/S0921-8890(96)00061-9

Cui, Y., & Weng, J. (1996). View-based hand segmentation and hand sequence recognition with complex backgrounds. In R. Dienstbier (Ed.), *Proceedings of International Conference on Pattern Recognition* (pp. 617-621).

Dalai, N., & Triggs, B. (2005). *Histograms of oriented gradients for human detection* (pp. 886–893). CVPR.

Dalal, N., & Triggs, B. (2005). Histograms of oriented gradients for human detection. In *Proceedings of Computer Vision and Pattern Recognition* (pp.886-893).

Datta, R., Joshi, D., Li, J., & Wang, J. Z. (2008). Image Retrieval: Ideas, Influences, and Trends of the New Age. *ACM Transactions on Computing Surveys, 40*(2), 1–60. doi:10.1145/1348246.1348248

Delakis, M., & Garcia, C. (2002). Robust face detection based on convolutional neural networks. In *Proc. of 2nd Hellenic Conf. on Artificial Intelligence* (pp. 367-378).

Delannay, D., Danhier, N., & De Vleeschouwer, C. (2009). Detection and recognition of sports (wo)men from multiple views. *The 3rd ACM/IEEE International Conference on Distributed Smart Cameras*. Como, Italia: IEEE.

Deng, Y., & Manjunath, B. S. (2001). Unsupervised Segmentation of Color-Texture Regions in Images and Video. *IEEE Transactions on Pattern Analysis and Machine Intelligence, 23*(8), 800–810. doi:10.1109/34.946985

Desimone, R., & Duncan, J. (1995). Neural Mechanisms of Selective Visual Attention. *Annual Review of Neuroscience, 18*, 193–222. doi:10.1146/annurev.ne.18.030195.001205

Di Bernardo, E., Goncalves, L., Perona, P., & Ursella, E. (1995). Monocular Tracking of the Human Arm in 3-D. In *Proceedings of the Fifth International Conference on Computer Vision* (pp. 764a). Washington: IEEE Computer Society.

Ding, Y., & Fan, G. (2009b). Sports Video Mining via Multi-channel Segmental Hidden Markov Models. *IEEE Transactions on Multimedia, 11*(7), 1301–1309. doi:10.1109/TMM.2009.2030828

Ding, Y., & Fan, G. (2007a). Segmental Hidden Markov Models for View-based Sport Video Analysis. In *Proc. International Workshop on Semantic Learning Applications in Multimedia, in conjunction with IEEE International Conference on Computer Vision and Pattern Recognition*.

Ding, Y., & Fan, G. (2007b). Two-Layer Generative Models for Sport Video Mining. In *Proc. IEEE International Conference on Multimedia and Expo*.

Ding, Y., & Fan, G. (2008). Multi-channel Segmental Hidden Markov Models for Sports Video Mining. In *Proc. the ACM Multimedia Conference*.

Ding, Y., & Fan, G. (2009a). Event Detection in Sports Video based on Generative-Discriminative Models. In *Proc. the 1st ACM International Workshop on Events in Multimedia (EiMM09) in conjunction with the ACM Multimedia Conference*.

Dorado, A., Calic, J., & Izquierdo, E. (2004). A rule-based video annotation system. *IEEE Trans. on Circuits and Systems for Video Technology, 14*(5), 622–633. doi:10.1109/TCSVT.2004.826764

Dorado, A., Djordjevic, D., Pedrycz, W., & Izquierdo, E. (2006). Efficient image selection for concept learning. *IEE Proceedings. Vision Image and Signal Processing, 153*(3), 263–273. doi:10.1049/ip-vis:20050057

Dorai, C., & Venkatesh, S. (2003). Bridging the semantic gap with computational media aesthetics. *IEEE MultiMedia, 10*, 15–17. doi:10.1109/MMUL.2003.1195157

Dorfmuller, K., & Wirth, H. (1998). Real-Time Hand and Head Tracking for Virtual Environments Using Infrared Beacons. In *Proceedings of the International Workshop on Modelling and Motion Capture Techniques for Virtual Environments* (pp. 113-127). London: Springer-Verlag.

Dorigo, M., Birattari, M., & Stutzle, T. (2006). Ant colony optimization. *IEEE Computational Intelligence Magazine, 1*(4), 28–39.

Dorigo, M., & Thomas, S. (2004). *Ant Colony Optimization*. Cambridge: MIT Press.

Duan, L., Xu, M., Tian, Q., Xu, C., & Jin, S. J. (2005). A unified framework for semantic shot classification in sports video. *IEEE Transactions on Multimedia, 7*(6), 1066–1083. doi:10.1109/TMM.2005.858395

Duan, L. Y., Xu, M., Chua, T. S., & Tian, Q. Q., & Xu, C. S. (2003). A Mid-level Representation Framework for Semantic Sports Video Analysis. In *Proc. the ACM Multimedia Conference.*

Duda, R. O., Hart, P. E., & Stork, D. G. (2001). *Pattern Classification*. John Wiley & Sons, Inc.

Edelman, S., & Intrator, N. (2002). *Unsupervised learning of visual structure* (pp. 629–642). Biologically Motivated Computer Vision.

Eister, S., & Girod, B. (1998). Analyzing Facial Expressions for Virtual Conferencing. *IEEE Computer Graphics and Applications, 18*(5), 70–79. doi:10.1109/38.708562

Ekenel, H. K., & Stiefelhagen, R. (2009). *Generic versus Salient Region-Based Partitioning for Local Appearance Face Recognition*. Paper presented at the 3rd International Conference on Biometrics.

Ekin, A., & Tekalp, M. (2003). Automatic soccer video analysis and summarization. *IEEE Transactions on Image Processing, 12*(7), 796–807. doi:10.1109/TIP.2003.812758

Ekman, P., & Friesen, V. (1978). *Facial Action Coding System (FACS): Manual*. Palo Alto, CA: Consulting Psychologists Press.

Elmezian, M., Al-Hamadi, A., Appenrodt, J., & Michaelis, B. (2008). A Hidden Markov model-based isolated and meaningful hand gesture recognition. In *Proceedings of World Academy of Science, Engineering and Technology* (pp. 394-401). World Academy of Science, Engineering and Technology.

Eriksen, C. W., & St James, J. D. (1986). Visual Attention Within and Around the Field of Focus Attention: A Zoom Lens Model. *Perception & Psychophysics, 40*(5), 225–240.

Eriksen, C. W., & Yeh, Y. Y. (1985). Allocation of Attention in the Visual Field. *Journal of Experimental Psychology. Human Perception and Performance, 11*(5), 583–597. doi:10.1037/0096-1523.11.5.583

Erol, A., Bebis, G., Nicolescu, M., Boyle, R. D., & Twombly, X. (2007). Vision-based hand pose estimation: A review. *Computer Vision and Image Understanding, 108*(1-2), 52–73. doi:10.1016/j.cviu.2006.10.012

Essa, I. A., & Pentland, A. P. (1997). Coding, Analysis, Interpretation, and Recognition of Facial Expressions. *IEEE Transactions on Pattern Analysis and Machine Intelligence, 19*(7), 757–763. doi:10.1109/34.598232

Everett, H. (1963). Generalized lagrange multiplier method for solving problems of optimum Allocation of Resources. *Operations Research, 11*(3), 399–417. doi:10.1287/opre.11.3.399

Fang, C.-Y., Chen, S.-W., & Fuh, C.-S. (2003). Road-sign detection and tracking. *IEEE Transactions on Vehicular Technology, 52*, 1329–1341. doi:10.1109/TVT.2003.810999

Farid, H. (2009). A Survey of Image Forgery Detection. *IEEE Signal Processing Magazine, 26*(2), 16–25. doi:10.1109/MSP.2008.931079

Farid, H. (2009). Seeing is not believing. *IEEE Spectrum, 46*(8), 44–48. doi:10.1109/MSPEC.2009.5186556

Farid, H. (2008). *Digital ballistic from jpeg quantization: A follow study* (Technical Report TR2008-638). Department of Computer Science, Dartmouth College.

Farid, H., & Lyu, S. (2003). *Higher-order wavelet statistics and their application to digital forensics.* IEEE Workshop on Statistical Analysis in Computer Vision.

Feraud, R., & Bernier, O. J. (2001). A Fast and Accurate Face Detection based on Neural Network. *IEEE Transactions on Pattern Analysis and Machine Intelligence, 23*(1), 42. doi:10.1109/34.899945

Ferman, A. M., & Tekalp, A. M. (2003). Two-stage hierarchical video summary extraction to match low-level user browsing preferences. *IEEE Transactions on Multimedia, 5*(2), 244–256. doi:10.1109/TMM.2003.811617

Feyrer, S., & Zell, A. (1999). Detection, tracking, and pursuit of humans with an autonomous mobile robot. In *Proceedings of the International Conference on Intelligent Robots and Systems* (pp.864–869).

FHWA. (2003). Manual on uniform traffic control devices (MUTCD) for streets and highways. In *The Federal Highway Administration (FHWA), U.S. Dept. Transp.* Retrieved from http://www.fhwa.dot.gov/

Finkel, R., & Bentley, J. L. (1974). Quad trees: A data structure for retrieval on composite keys. *Acta Informatica, 4*, 1–9. doi:10.1007/BF00288933

Fleuret, F., Berclaz, J., Lengagne, R., & Fua, P. (2008). Multi-camera people tracking with a probabilistic occupancy map. *IEEE Transactions on Pattern Analysis and Machine Intelligence, 30*(2), 267–282. doi:10.1109/TPAMI.2007.1174

Flickner, M., Sawhney, H., Niblack, W., Ashley, J., Huang, Q., & Dom, B. (1995). Query by Image and Video Content: The QBIC System. *IEEE Computer, 28*(9), 23–32.

Forlines, C., Vogel, D., & Balakrishnan, R. (2006). Hybridpointing: fluid switching between absolute and relative pointing with a direct input device. In *Proceedings of the 19th ACM symposium on User interface software and technology* (pp. 211-220). New York: ACM Press.

Freeman, W. T., & Weissman, C. (1995). Television control by hand gestures. In *Proceedings of International Conference on Automatic Face and Gesture Recognition* (pp.197-183).

French, J. C., Chapin, A. C., & Martin, W. N. (2003). An Application of Multiple Viewpoints to Content-based Image Retrieval. In *Proceedings of the ACM/IEEE Joint Conference on Digital Libraries* (pp. 128-130).

Fridrich, J., Soukal, D., & Lukas, J. (2003, August). *Detection of Copy-Move Forgery in Digital Images.* Pro. Digital Forensic Research Workshop, Cleveland, OH.

Friedman, N., & Koller, D. (2003). Being Bayesian About Network Structure. A Bayesian Approach to Structure Discovery in Bayesian Networks. *Machine Learning, 50*(1), 95–125. doi:10.1023/A:1020249912095

Fröba, B., & Küblbeck, C. (2001). Face detection and tracking using edge orientation information. *SPIE Visual Communications and Image Processing*, 583-594.

Fu, Y., Cao, L., Guo, G., & Huang, T. S. (2008). *Multiple Feature Fusion by Subspace Learning.* Paper presented at the ACM International Conference on Image and Video Retrieval.

Funt, B., Barnard, K. & Martin L. (1998). Is machine colour constancy good enough (LNCS 1406, pp. 445-459).

Gales, M., & Young, S. (1993). *The theory of segmental hidden Markov models* (Technical Report CUED/F-INFENG/TR 133). Cambridge University.

Gandy, M., Starner, T., Auxier, J., & Ashbrook, D. (2000). The Gesture Pendant: A Self-illuminating, Wearable, Infrared Computer Vision System for Home Automation Control and Medical Monitoring. In *Proceedings of the Fourth International Symposium on Wearable Computers* (pp. 87-94).

Gao, D., & Vasconcelos, N. (2005). Integrated Learning of Saliency, Complex Features, and Object Detectors from Cluttered Scenes. In *Proceedings of the IEEE Conference on Computer Vision and Pattern Recognition, 2,* 282–287.

Gao, D., & Vasconcelos, N. (2007). Bottom-up Saliency is a Discriminant Process. In *Proceedings of the IEEE Conference on Computer Vision.*

Gao, Y., Wang, T., Li, J.G., et al. (2007). *Cast Indexing for Videos by NCuts and Page Ranking.* ACM CIVR 2007.

Gavrila, D. M., & Davis, L. S. (1995). Towards 3D model-based tracking and recognition of human movement: A Multi-View Approach. In *Proceedings of the International Conference on Automatic Face and Gesture Recognition* (pp. 272-277). Los Alamitos: IEEE CS Press.

Ghahramani, Z. (2002). Graphical models: parameter learning. In Arbib, M. A. (Ed.), *The Handbook of Brain Theory and Neural Networks.* MIT Press.

Goldstein, E. B. (1995). *Sensation and Perception* (4th ed.). Thomson Publishing Company.

Gong Y. (2004). Method and apparatus for personalized multimedia summarization based upon user specified theme. Nippon Electric Co [JP], US6751776 (B1).

Gong, Y. H., & Liu, X. (2001). *Video Summarization with Minimal Visual Content Redundancies.* IEEE Proc. of ICIP.

Gong, Y., Sin, L. T., Chuan, C. H., Zhang, H. J., & Sakauchi, M. (1995). Automatic parsing of TV soccer programs. In *Proc. International Conference on Multimedia Computing and Systems.*

Goplakrishnan, V., Hu, Y., & Rajan, D. (2009a). Salient region detection by modeling distributions of color and orientation. *IEEE Transactions on Multimedia, 11*(5), 892–905. doi:10.1109/TMM.2009.2021726

Goplakrishnan, V., Hu, Y., & Rajan, D. (2009b). Random walks on graphs to model saliency in images. In *Proceedings of the IEEE Conference on Computer Vision and Pattern Recognition.*

Goto, T., Escher, M., Zanardi, C., & Thalmann, N. M. (1999). LAFTER: Lips and face real time tracker with facial expression recognition. In *Proceedings of IEEE Conf. on Erographics Workshop Computer Animation and Simulation.*

Gou, H., Swaminathan, A., & Wu, M. (2007). Noise features for image tampering detection and steganalysis. *IEEE International Conference on Image Processing, San Antonio, TX, 2007* (Vol. 3, pp. 97-100).

Grossberg, S., & Raizada, R. D. (2000). Constrast-Sensitive Persceptual Grouping and Object-based Attention in the Laminar Circuits of Primary Visual Cortex. *Vision Research, 40*(10-12), 1413–1432. doi:10.1016/S0042-6989(99)00229-1

Grzeszczuk, R., Bradski, G., Chu, M. H., & Bouguet, J. Y. (2000). Stereo Based Gesture Recognition Invariant to 3D Pose and Lighting. *In Proceedings of the International Conference on Computer Vision and Pattern Recognition* (pp. 1826a). Los Alamitos: IEEE CS Press.

Guan, H., Rogerio, S., & Turk, M. (2006). The isometric self-organizing map for 3d hand pose estimation. In *Proceedings of International Conference on Automatic Face and Gesture Recognition* (pp. 263-268).

Guildford, J. P. (1954). *Psychometric Methods.* New York: McGraw-Hill.

Guo, C., Ma, Q., & Zhang, L. (2008). Spatial-temporal Saliency Detection using Phrase Spectrum of Quaternion Fourier Transform. In *Proceedings of the IEEE Conference on Computer Vision and Pattern Recognition.*

Gupta, H., Roychowdhury, A. K., & Chellappa, R. (2004). *Contour-based 3D Face Modeling from a Monocular Video.* Paper presented at the British Machine Vision Conference.

Guyton, A. C. (1991). *Textbook of medical physiology* (8th ed.). USA: W.B. Saunders Company.

Haralick, R. M. (1979). Statistical and Structural Approaches to Texture. *Proceedings of the IEEE, 67*(5), 786–804. doi:10.1109/PROC.1979.11328

Haralick, R. M., Shanmugam, K., & Dinstein, I. (1973). Textural Features for Image Classification. *IEEE Transactions on Systems, Man, and Cybernetics*, 3(6), 610–621. doi:10.1109/TSMC.1973.4309314

Haralick, R. M., & Shapiro, L. G. (1992). *Computer and Robot Vision (Vol. 1)*. USA: Addison-Wesley.

Hardenberg, C., & Bérard, F. (2001). Bare-Hand Human Computer Interaction. In *Proceedings of the workshop on Perceptual User Interfaces* (pp. 1-8). New York: ACM Press.

Harel, J., Koch, C., & Perona, P. (2006). Graph-based Visual Saliency. In Weiss, Y., Schölkopf, B., & Platt, J. (Eds.), *Advances in Neural Information Processing Systems 18 (Vol. 1*, pp. 545–552). MIT Press.

Hartley, R., & Zisserman, A. (2004). *Multiple View Geometry in Computer Vision*. Cambridge University Press.

Hauptmann, A. G., Christel, M. G., Lin, W., et al. (2007). Clever Clustering vs. Simple Speed-Up for Summarizing BBC Rushes. In *Proc. of the TRECVID Workshop on Video Summarization* (TVS'07). ACM Multimedia.

Heuring, J. J., & Murray, D. W. (1999). Modeling and copying human face movements. *IEEE Transactions on Robotics and Automation*, 15(6), 1999. doi:10.1109/70.817672

Hong, L., & Jain, A. (1999). Multimodal biometrics. In *Biometrics: Personal Identification in Networked Society*. Kluwer.

Hou, X., & Zhang, L. (2008). Saliency detection: A spectral residual approach. In *Proc. IEEE Conf. on Computer Vision and Pattern Recognition* (pp. 1-8).

Hsu, R., Abdel-Mottaleb, M., & Jain, A. K. (2002). Face detection in colour images. *IEEE Transactions on Pattern Analysis and Machine Intelligence*, 24(5), 696. doi:10.1109/34.1000242

Hsu, Y. F., & Chang, S. F. (2007). Image splicing detection using camera response function consistency and automatic segmentation. *IEEE International Conference on Multimedia and Expo*.

Hu, Y., Rajan, D., & Chia, L.-T. (2009). Attention-from-Motion: A Factorization Approach for Detecting Attention Objects in Motion. *Computer Vision and Image Understanding*, 113, 319–331. doi:10.1016/j.cviu.2008.08.010

Hu, Y., Xie, X., Chen, Z., & Ma, W.-Y. (2004). Attention Model based Progressive Image Transmission. In Proceedings of the *2004 International Conference on Multimedia and Expo* (Vol. 2, pp. 1079-1082).

Hu, Y., Xie, X., Ma, W.-Y., Chia, L.-T., & Rajan, D. (2004). Salient region detection using weighted feature maps based on the human visual attention model (LNCS 3332, pp. 993-1000).

Huang, J., Liu, Z., & Wang, Y. (2005). Joint Scene Classification and Segmentation Based on Hidden Markov Model. *IEEE Transactions on Multimedia*, 7(3), 538–550. doi:10.1109/TMM.2005.843346

Iannizzotto, G., Costanzo, C., La Rosa, F., & Lanzafame, P. (2005). A Multimodal Perceptual User Interface for Collaborative Environments. In *Proceedings of the 13th International Conference on Image Analysis and Processing* (pp. 115-122). London: Springer-Verlag.

Iannizzotto, G., La Rosa, F., Costanzo, C., & Lanzafame, P. (2005). A Multimodal Perceptual User Interface for Video-Surveillance Environments. In *Proceedings of the 7th International Conference on Multimodal Interfaces* (pp. 45-52). New York: ACM Press.

Iannizzotto, G., Villari, M., & Vita, L. (2001). Hand Tracking for Human-Computer Interaction with Graylevel VisualGlove: Turning Back to the Simple Way. In *Proceedings of the workshop on Perceptual User Interfaces*. New York: ACM Press.

Isard, M., & Blake, A. (1998). Condensation – conditional density propagation for visual tracking. *International Journal of Computer Vision*, 29(1), 5–28. doi:10.1023/A:1008078328650

Itti, L., Koch, C., & Niebur, E. (1998). A model of saliency-based visual attention for rapid scene analysis. *IEEE Transactions on Pattern Analysis and Machine Intelligence*, 20(11), 1254–1259. doi:10.1109/34.730558

Itti, L. (2005). *Models of bottom-up attention and saliency. Neurobiology of Attention* (pp. 576–582). San Diego, CA: Elsevier.

Itti, L., & Koch, C. (2001). Feature combination strategies for saliency-based visual attention systems. *Journal of Electronic Imaging, 10*(1), 161–169. doi:10.1117/1.1333677

Itti, L., & Koch, C. (2001). Computational Modeling of Visual Attention. *Nature Neuroscience Review, 2*(3), 194–203. doi:10.1038/35058500

Itti, L. (2000). *Models of Bottom-up and Top-down Visual Attention*. Unpublished doctoral dissertation, California institute of Technology.

Jabri, M. (2000). *Biological computing for robot navigation and control. NRA2-37143*. Beaverton, OR: OGI School of Science and Engineering at OHSU.

Jain, A. K., & Yu, B. (1998). Automatic text location in images and video frames. *Pattern Recognition, 31*, 2055–2076. doi:10.1016/S0031-3203(98)00067-3

Jain, R., Kasturi, R., & Schunck, B. G. (1995). *Machine Vision*. USA: McGraw-Hill.

Jams, W. (1890). *The Principles of Psychology*. Oxford: Pergamon Press. doi:10.1037/10538-000

Jang, G. J., & Kweon, I. S. (2001). Robust object tracking using an adaptive color model. In *Proceedings of the IEEE International Conference on Robotics and Automation* (pp. 1677–1682).

Jasinschi, R. S., Dimitrova, N., McGee, T., Agnihotri, L., Zimmerman, J., Li, D., & Louie, J. (2002). A probabilistic layered framework for integrating multimedia content and context information. In *Proc. IEEE Int. Conf. Acoustics, Speech, and Signal Processing: Vol. 2* (pp. 2057–2060).

Javed, O., Ali, S., & Shah, M. (2005). Online detection and classification of moving objects using progressively improving detectors. In *Proceedings of Computer Vision and Pattern Recognition* (pp. 696-701).

Jensen, B., Tomatis, N., Mayor, L., Drygajlo, A., & Siegwart, R. (2005). Robots meet humans—Interaction in public spaces. *IEEE Transactions on Industrial Electronics, 52*(6), 1530–1546. doi:10.1109/TIE.2005.858730

Jiang, W., Chang, S. F., & Loui, A. C. (2007). Context-based concept fusion with boosted conditional random fields. In *Proc. IEEE Conference on Computer Vision and Pattern Recognition*.

Jing, F., Li, M., Zhang, H.-J., & Zhang, B. (2004). Relevance feedback in region-based image retrieval. *IEEE Trans. on Circuits and Systems for Video Technology, 14*(5), 672–681. doi:10.1109/TCSVT.2004.826775

Johnson, M. K., & Farid, H. (2005). *Exposing digital forgeries by detecting inconsistencies in lighting*. New York, NY: ACM Multimedia and Security Workshop.

Johnson, M. K., & Farid, H. (2007). Exposing Digital Forgeries in Complex Lighting Environments. *IEEE Transactions on Information Forensics and Security, 2*, 450–461. doi:10.1109/TIFS.2007.903848

Johnson, M. K., & Farid, H. (2007). Detecting Photographic Composites of People. *Proc. IWDW*.

Johnson, M.K., & Farid, H. (2006). *Metric Measurements on a Plane from a Single Image* (Technical Report, TR2006-579).

Jojic, N., Brumitt, B., Meyers, B., Harris, S., & Huang, T. (2000). Detection and Estimation of Pointing Parameters in Dense Disparity Maps. In *Proceedings of the Fourth International Conference on Automatic Face and Gesture Recognition*.

Jones, M., & Viola, P. (2003). *Fast multi-view face detection* (Technical Report TR2003-96). Mitsubishi Electric Research Laboratories.

Juang, C., Chiu, S., & Shiu, S. (2007). Fuzzy System Learned Through Fuzzy Clustering and Support Vector Machine for Human Skin Color Segmentation. *IEEE Transactions on Systems, Man, and Cybernetics, 37*(6), 1077. doi:10.1109/TSMCA.2007.904579

Julesz, B. (1976). Experiments in the Visual Perception of Texture. *Scientific American, 232*(4), 34–44. doi:10.1038/scientificamerican0475-34

Jung C., Kin C., Kim S.K., Lee G., Kim W.Y., & Hwang S., (2006). Method and Apparatus for Summarizing Sports Moving Picture. Samsung Electronics Co Ltd, JP2006148932.

Just, A., Rodriguez, Y., & Marcel, S. (2006). Hand posture classification and recognition using the modified census transform. In R. Dienstbier (Ed.), In *Proceedings of International Conference on Automatic Face and Gesture Recognition* (pp. 351-356).

Kadir, T., & Brady, M. (2001). Scale, Saliency and Image Description. *International Journal of Computer Vision, 45*(2), 83–105. doi:10.1023/A:1012460413855

Kanade, T., Cohn, J., & Tian, Y. (2000). Comprehensive Database for Facial Expression Analysis. In *Proceedings of International Conference on Automatic Face and Gesture Recognition.*

Kaplan, S. (1976). Adaption, structure and knowledge. In Golledge, R. G., & Moore, G. T. (Eds.), *Environmental Knowing: theories, research and methods.*

Karu, R., Jain, A. K., & Bolle, R. M. (1996). Is there any Texture in the Image? *Pattern Recognition, 29*(9), 1437–1466. doi:10.1016/0031-3203(96)00004-0

Kass, M., Witkin, A., & Terzopoulos, D. (2004). Snakes: Active contour models. *International Journal of Computer Vision*, 321–331.

Kato, M., Chen, Y.-W., & Xu, G. (2006). Articulated hand tracking by pca-ica approach. I In proceedings of *International Conference on Automatic Face and Gesture Recognition* (pp. 329-334).

Kender, J. R., & Yeo, B. (1998). Video scene segmentation via continuous video coherence. *IEEE Computer Society Conference on Computer Vision and Pattern Recognition* (pp. 367-373).

Kersten, D., Mamassian, P., & Knill, D. C. (1997). Moving cast shadows induce apparent motion in depth. *Perception, 26*, 171–192. doi:10.1068/p260171

Khan, S. M., & Shah, M. (2009). Tracking multiple occluding people by localizing on multiple scene planes. *IEEE Transactions on Pattern Analysis and Machine Intelligence, 31*(3), 505–519. doi:10.1109/TPAMI.2008.102

Khan, S., & Shah, M. (2006). A multiview approach to tracing people in crowded scenes using a planar homography constraint. In *Proceedings of the 9th European Conference on Computer Vision (ECCV)* (Vol. 4, pp. 133-146).

Kim, S., Park, S., & Kim, M. (2003). Central object extraction for object-based image retrieval. In *Proceedings of the ACM Intl. Conference on Image and Video Retrieval (CIVR).*

King, G. F. (1986). Driver performance in highway navigation tasks. *Transportation Research Record, 1093*, 1–11.

Kleban, J., Sarkar, A., Moxley, E., et al. (2007). Feature Fusion and Redundancy Pruning for Rush Video Summarization. In *Proc. of the TRECVID Workshop on Video Summarization (TVS'07).* ACM Multimedia.

Kokaram, A., Rea, N., Dahyot, R., Tekalp, M., Bouthemy, P., & Gros, P. (2006). Browsing sports video: trends in sports-related indexing and retrieval work. *IEEE Signal Processing Magazine, 23*(2), 47–58. doi:10.1109/MSP.2006.1621448

Kolsch, M. (2005). *Vision based hand gesture interfaces for wearable computing and virtual environments.* Doctoral dissertation, University of California, Santa Barbara.

Kolsch, M., & Turk, M. (2004). Fast 2D Hand Tracking with Flocks of Features and Multi-cue Integration. In *Proceedings of Computer Vision and Pattern Recognition Workshop on Real-Time Vision for HCI.*

Kolsch, M., & Turk, M. (2004). Robust hand detection. in Proceedings of *International Conference on Automatic Face and Gesture Recognition* (pp.614- 619).

Koubaroulis, D., Matas, J., & Kittler, J. (2002). Colour-based object recognition for video annotation. In *Proc. IEEE International Conference on Pattern Recognition.*

Kovesi, P. (1999). Image features from phase congruency. *Videre: A Journal of Computer Vision Research, 1*(3), 2-27.

Kshirsagar, S., Molet, T., & Magnenat-Thalmann, N. (2001). Principal Components of Expressive Speech Animation. In *Proceedings of International Conference on Computer Graphics.*

Kubicek, R., Zak, P., Zemcik, P., & Herout, A. (2008). Automatic video editing for multimodal meetings, *International Conference on Computer Vision and Graphics 2008* (pp. 1-12), Warsaw, Poland: Springer.

Kuffler, S. W., Nicholls, J. G., & Martin, J. G. (1984). *From Neuron to Brain.* Sunderland, UK: Sinauer Associates.

La Rosa, F., Costanzo, C., & Iannizzotto, G. (2003). VisualPen: A Physical Interface for natural human-computer interaction. *ACM MOBILE HCI'03, Physical Interaction (PI03) - Workshop on Real World User Interfaces.*

Lafferty, J., McCallum, A., & Pereira, F. (2001). Conditional Random Fields: Probabilistic Models for Segmenting and Labeling Sequence Data. In *Proc. the Eighteenth International Conference on Machine Learning (ICML).*

Lam, K., & Yan, H. (1996). An Analytic-to-Holistic Approach for Face Recognition Based on Single Frontal View. *IEEE Transactions on Pattern Analysis and Machine Intelligence, 29*(5), 1771.

Lang, S., Kleinehagenbrock, M., Hohenner, S., Fritsch, J., Fink, G. A., & Sagerer, G. (2003). Providing the basis for human–robot interaction: a multi-modal attention system for a mobile robot. In *Proceedings of the 2003 International Conference on Multimodal Interfaces*, Vancouver, Canada, 2003 (p. 28).

Lanitis, A., Taylor, C. J., & Cootes, T. F. (1995). *A unified approach to coding and interpreting face images.* Paper presented at the Proceedings of the Fifth International Conference on Computer Vision.

Lanyon, L. J., & Denham, S. L. (2004). A model of active visual search with object-based attention guiding scan paths. *Neural Networks, 17*(5-6), 873–897. doi:10.1016/j.neunet.2004.03.012

Lanza, A., Di Stefano, L., Berclaz, J., Fleuret, F., & Fua, P. (2007). Robust multiview change detection, *British Machine Vision Conference (BMVC),* Warwick, UK.

Lavagetto, & F., Pockaj, R. (1999). The facial Animation Engine: Toward a High-Level Interface for the Design of MPEG-4 Compliant Animation Faces. *IEEE Transaction on Circuits and Systems for Video Technology, 9*(2), 277-289.

Lawrence, S., Giles, C. L., Tsoi, A. C., & Back, A. D. (1997). Face recognition: A convolutional neural-network approach. *IEEE Transactions on Neural Networks, 8*(1), 98–113. doi:10.1109/72.554195

Lazarescu, M., & Venkatesh, S. (2003, July). Using camera motion to identify types of American football plays. In *Proc. International Conf. on Multimedia and Expo.*

Lazebnik, S., Schmid, C., & Ponce, J. (2004). *A Sparse Texture Representation Using Local Affine Regions* (Beckman CVR Technical Report, NO 2004-01). University of Illinois at Urbana Champaign. UIUC.

Lecun, Y., Bottou, L., Bengio, Y., & Haffner, P. (1998). Gradient-based learning applied to document recognition. *Proceedings of the IEEE, 86*(11), 2278–2324. doi:10.1109/5.726791

Leibe, B., Starner, T., Ribarsky, W., Wartell, Z., Krum, D., & Weeks, J. (2000). Toward Spontaneous Interaction with the Perceptive Workbench. *IEEE Computer Graphics and Applications, 20*(6), 54–65. doi:10.1109/38.888008

Letessier, J., & Berard, F. Visual tracking of bare fingers for interactive surfaces(2004). In *Proceedings of 17th ACM Symposium on User Interface Software and Technology* (pp.119-122).

Leung, T., Burl, M., & Perona, P. (1995). Finding Faces in cluttered scenes using labelled random graph matching. In *Proc. 5th Int. Conf. on Computer Vision* (p. 637). Boston, MA: MIT.

Levin, A., Viola, P., & Freund, Y. (2003). Unsupervised improvement of visual detectors using co-training. In *Proceedings of International Conference on Computer Vision* (pp. 626-633).

Lew, M., Sebe, N., Djeraba, C., & Jain, R. (2006). Content-Based Multimedia Information Retrieval: State of the art and challenges. *ACM Transactions on Multimedia Computing, Communications, and Applications, 2*(1), 1–19. doi:10.1145/1126004.1126005

Li, H., Doermann, D., & Kia, O. (2000). Automatic text detection and tracking in digital video. *IEEE Transactions on Image Processing, 1*(9), 147–156.

Li, S. Z., & Jain, A. K. (2005). *Handbook of Face Recognition*. Springer.

Li, C., Ou, Z. J., Hu, W., Wang, T., & Zhang, Y. (2008). Caption-aided speech detection in videos. *ICASSP, 2008*, 141–144.

Li, Z., Schuster, G. M., & Katsaggelos, A. K. (2005). Rate-Distortion Optimial Video Summary Generation. *IEEE Transactions on Image Processing, 14*(10).

Li, Z., Schuster, G. M., & Katsaggelos, A. K. (2005). MINMAX optimal video summarization. *IEEE Transactions on Circuits and Systems for Video Technology, 15*(10), 1245–1256. doi:10.1109/TCSVT.2005.854230

Li, Z. (2001). Computational design and nonlinear dynamics of a recurrent network model of the primary visual cortex. *Neural Computation, 13*(8), 1749–1780. doi:10.1162/08997660152469332

Li, B., & Sezan, I. (2002). Event detection and summarization in American football brocast video. In *Proc. SPIE Storage and Retrieval for Media Database.*

Li, F.-F., Fergus, R., & Perona, P. (2003). A bayesian approach to unsupervised one-shot learning of object categories. In *Proc. of the 9th IEEE International Conference on Computer Vision* (Vol. 2., pp. 1134-1141).

Li, Y., Ai, H.Z., Huang, C., et al. (2006). *Robust Head Tracking with Particles Based on Multiple Cues Fusion*. ECCV 2006.

Li, Z. Y., Lu, H., & Tan, Y. P. (2004). Video Scene Segmentation Using Sequential Change Detection. *IEEE Pacific-Rim Conference on Multimedia* (pp. 575-582).

Liebowitz, D., & Zisserman, A. (1998). Metric Rectification for Perspective Images of Planes. *IEEE Computer Society Conference on Computer Vision and Pattern Recognition.*

Lienhart, R. (1996). Automatic text recognition for video indexing. *In Proceedings of the ACM Intl. Conference on Multimedia (ACM MM)* (pp. 11–20).

Lin, Z., Wang, R., Tang, X., & Shum, H. Y. (2005). Detecting doctored images using camera response normality and consistency. *IEEE Computer Society Conference on Computer Vision and Pattern Recognition* (Vol. 1, pp. 1087- 1092).

Lindeberg, T. (2004). Feature detection with automatic scale selection. *International Journal of Computer Vision, 30*(6), 77–116.

Liu, F., & Picard, R. W. (1996). Periodicity, Directionality and Randomness: Wold Features for Image Modeling and Retrieval. *IEEE Transactions on Pattern Analysis and Machine Intelligence, 18*(7), 722–733. doi:10.1109/34.506794

Liu, H., Rao, J., & Yao, X. (2008). Feature based watermarking scheme for image authentication. In *Proceedings of the 2007 IEEE International Conference on Multimedia and Expo* (pp. 229-232).

Liu, T., Sun, J., Zheng, N.-N., Tang, X., & Shum, H.-Y. (2007). Learning to detect a salient object. In *Proc. IEEE Cont. on Computer Vision and pattern Recognition*, Minneapolis, Minnesota (pp. 1-8).

Lowe, D. G. (2004). Distinctive image features from scale-invariant key points. *International Journal of Computer Vision, 60*(2), 91–110. doi:10.1023/B:VISI.0000029664.99615.94

Lowe, D. (1999). Object recognition from local scale-invariant features. In *Proceedings of the 7th International Conference on Computer Vision (ICCV99),* (pp. 1150–1157). Corfu, Greece, September 1999.

Lukas, J., & Fridrich, J. (2003). *Estimation of primary quantization matrix in double compressed JPEG images.* Digital Forensic Research Workshop.

Lukas, J., Fridrich, J., & Goljan, M. (2005). Determining Digital Image Origin Using Sensor Imperfections. In *Proc. SPIE Electronic Imaging, Image and Video Communication and Processing, San Jose, California., 5685*(2), 249-260.

Lynch, K. (1960). *The Image of the City.* MIT Press.

Lyu & Farid. (2005). How Realistic is Photorealistic? *IEEE Transactions on Signal Processing, 53*(2), 845–850. doi:10.1109/TSP.2004.839896

Ma, Y.-F., Hua, X.-S., Lu, L., & Zhang, H.-J. (2005). A Generic Framework of User Attention Model and Its Application in Video Summarization. *IEEE Transactions on Multimedia, 7*(5), 907–919. doi:10.1109/TMM.2005.854410

Ma, Y.-F., & Zhang, H.-J. (2002). A model of motion attention for video skimming. In *Proc. IEEE Int. Conf. on Image Processing* (pp. 129-132). Rochester, New York

Ma, Y.-F., & Zhang, H.-J. (2003). Contrast-based Image Attention Analysis by Using Fuzzy Growing. In *Proceedings of the eleventh ACM International Conference on Multimedia* (Vol. 1, pp. 228-241).

Maggioni, C., & Kammerer, B. (1998). GestureComputer - history, design and applications. In Cipolla, R., & Pentland, A. (Eds.), *Computer Vision for Human-Machine Interaction.* Cambridge: Cambridge University Press.

Mahdian, B., & Saic, S. (2007). Detection of copy-move forgery using a method based on blur moment invariants. *Forensic Science International, 171*(2), 180–189. doi:10.1016/j.forsciint.2006.11.002

Majani, E., Erlanson, R., & Abu-Mostafa, Y. (Eds.). (1984). *The Eye.* New York: Academic.

Malciu, M. & F. Preteux, F. (2000) Tracking facial features in video sequences using a deformable model-based approach, *Proceding of SPIE International Society of Optical Engineering,* 4121, 51–62.

Manjunath, B. S., & Ma, W. Y. (1996). Texture Features for Browsing and Retrieval of Image Data. *IEEE Transactions on Pattern Analysis and Machine Intelligence, 18*(8), 837–842. doi:10.1109/34.531803

Matthews, I., & Baker, S. (2004, November). Active Appearance Model - Revisited. *International Journal of Computer Vision, 60*(2), 135–164. doi:10.1023/B:VISI.0000029666.37597.d3

May, A. J., & Ross, T. (2006). Presence and quality of navigational landmarks: Effect on driver performance and implications for design. *Human Factors: The Journal of the Human Factors and Ergonomics Society, 48*(2), 346–361. doi:10.1518/001872006777724453

McCallum, A., Rohanimanesh, K., & Sutton, C. (2003). Dynamic Conditional Random Fields for Jointly Labeling Multiple Sequences. In *Proc. 17th Annual Conference on Neural Information Processing Systems.*

Mei, T., Ma, Y., Zhou, H., Ma, W., & Zhang, H. (2005). Sports Video Mining with Mosaic. In *Proc. the 11th IEEE International Multimedia Modeling Conference.*

Menser, B., & Muller, F. (1999). Face detection in colour images using principal components analysis. In *Seventh International Conference on Image Processing and Its Applications* (Vol. 2, p. 620).

Meynet, J. (2007). *Information theoretic combination of classifiers with application to face detection,* PhD Thesis, EPFL, no 3951.

Mistry, P., Maes, P., & Chang, L. (2009). WUW - wear Ur world: a wearable gestural interface. In *Proceedings of the 27th International Conference on Human Factors in Computing Systems* (pp. 4111-4116). New York: ACM Press.

Morrone, M., & Burr, D. (1988). *Feature detection in human vision: A phase-dependent energy model* (pp. 221–245). Proc. Roy. Soc. London B.

MPEG4, & the Moving Picture Experts Group. (1998). *ISO/IEC 14496-MPEG-4 International Standard,* Tokyo.

Mundhenk, T. N., Navalpakkam, V., Makaliwe, H., Vasudevan, S., & Itti, L. (2004). Biologically inspired feature based categorization of objects. In *Proc. SPIE Human Vision and Electronic Imaging IX* (Vol. 5292). San Jose, CA: Bellingham, WA, SPIE Press.

Murphy, K. (2002). *Dynamic Bayesian Networks: Representation, Inference and Learning*. UC Berkeley.

Murphy N., & Smeaton A., (2005). Audio-visual sequence analysis, WO2005124686 A1, Univ Dublin City, Publication info: IE20040412 (A1).

Murphy, K. (2007). *BNT Matlab Toolbox*. Retrieved from http://people.cs.ubc.ca/~murphyk/Software/

Myers, G., Bolles, R., Luong, Q.-T., & Herson, J. (2001). Recognition of text in 3-D scenes. In *4th Symposium on Document Image Understanding Technology* (pp. 23–25).

Naphade, M., & Huang, T. (2002). Discovering recurrent events in video using unsupervised methods. *Proc. IEEE International Conference on Image Processing, Rochester, NY.*

Navalpakkam, V., & Itti, L. (2006). Bottom-up and top-down influences on visual scanpaths. In *Proc. SPIE Human Vision and Electronic Imaging XI* (Vol. 6057). San Jose, CA: Bellingham, WA, SPIE Press.

Nefian, A. V., Liang, L., Pi, X., Liu, X., & Murphy, K. (2002). Dynamic Bayesian Networks for Audio-Visual Speech Recognition. *EURASIP Journal on Applied Signal Processing, 11*, 1–15.

Ng, A. Y., Jordan, M. I., & Yair, W. (2001). *On spectral Clustering: Analysis and an algorithm*. Advances in Neural Information Processing Systems.

Ng, T. T., & Chang, S. F. (2004). A model for image splicing. *IEEE International Conference on Image Processing* (pp. 1169-1172).

Ng, T. T., Chang, S. F., & Sun, Q. (2004). Blind detection of photomontage using higher order statistics. In *Proceedings of the 2004 International Symposium on Circuits and Systems, 5,* 688-691.

Nielsen, F., & Nock, R. (2005). Clickremoval: Interactive pinpoint image object removal. In *Proceedings of the ACM Intl. Conference on Multimedia (ACM MM)*.

Norman, D. A. (1998). *The Invisible Computer*. Boston: MIT Press.

O'Neil, J., & Szyld, D. B. (1990). A block ordering method for sparse matrices. *SIAM Journal on Scientific and Statiscal Computing, 11*(5), 811–823. doi:10.1137/0911048

Odobez, J-M., & Gatica-Perez, D., & Guillemot, M. (2002). On Spectral Methods and the Structuring of Home Videos. *IDIAP-RR 02-55.*

Ojala, T., Pietikainen, M., & Harwood, D. (1996). A Comparative Study of Texture Measures with Classification based on Feature Distribution. *Pattern Recognition, 29*(1), 51–59. doi:10.1016/0031-3203(95)00067-4

Ojala, T., Pietikainen, M., & Maenpaa, T. (2002). Multiresolution Gray-Scale and Rotation Invariant Texture Classification with Local Binary Patterns. *IEEE Transactions on Pattern Analysis and Machine Intelligence, 24*(7), 971–987. doi:10.1109/TPAMI.2002.1017623

Oliver, N., Pentland, A., & Berard, F. (1997). LAFTER: Lips and face real time tracker with facial expression recognition. In *Proc. of IEEE Conf. on Computer Vision and Pattern Recognition*.

Ong, E.-J., & Bowden, R. (2004). A boosted classifier tree for hand shape detection. In *Proceedings of International Conference on Automatic Face and Gesture Recognition* (pp. 889-894).

Osuna, E., Freund, E., & Girosi, F. (1998). Training support vector machines: an application to face detection, *IEEE Conf. Computer Vision and Pattern Recognition* (p. 45).

Otsuka, I., Nakane, K., & Divakaran, A. (2005). A Highlight Scene Detection and Video Summarization System using Audio Feature for a Personal Video Recorder. *IEEE Transactions on Consumer Electronics, 51*(1), 112–116. doi:10.1109/TCE.2005.1405707

Over, P., Smeaton, A. F., & Awad, G. M. (2007). The TRECVID 2007 BBC Rushes Summarization Evaluation Pilot. In *Proc. of the TRECVID Workshop on Video Summarization (TVS'07)*. ACM Multimedia.

Over, P., Smeaton, A. F., & Awad, G. M. (2008). The TRECVID 2008 BBC rushes summarization evaluation. In *Proc of the International Workshop on TRECVID Video Summarization(TVS '08)*. ACM Multimedia.

Owens, J. (2007). *Television sports production* (4th ed.). Burlington, MA: Focal Press.

Pahalawatta, P. V., Zhu, L., Zhai, F., & Katsaggelos, A. K. (2005). Rate-distortion optimization for internet video summarization and transmission. *IEEE 7th Workshop on Multimedia Signal Processing* (pp. 1-4). Shanghai, China: IEEE.

Pan, H., & Li, B.X., (2004). Summarization of soccer video content, US20040017389A1.

Pan, H., Beek, P., & Sezan, M. I. (2001). Detection of slow-motion replay segments in sports video for highlights generation. *IEEE International Conference on Acoustics Speech and Signal Processing.*

Pantic, M., & Patras, I. (2006). Dynamics of Facial Expression: Recognition of Facial Actions and Their Temporal Segments from Face Profile Image Sequences. *IEEE Transactions on Systems, Man, and Cybernetics. Part B, Cybernetics, 36*(2), 433–449. doi:10.1109/TSMCB.2005.859075

Papaoulakis, N., Doulamis, N., Patrikakis, C., Soldatos, J., Pnevmatikakis, A., & Protonotarios, E. (2008). Real-time video analysis and personalized media streaming environments for large scale athletic events. In *Proceeding of the 1st ACM Workshop on Analysis and Retrieval of Events/Actions and Workflows in Video Streams* (pp.105-112). Vancouver, Canada: ACM.

Pardas, M., & Bonafonte, A., A. (2002). Facial animation parameters extraction and expression recognition using hidden markov models. *Signal Processing Image Communication, 17*, 675–688. doi:10.1016/S0923-5965(02)00078-4

Park, J. I., Yagi, N., Enami, K., Aizawa, K., & Hatori, M. (1994). Estimation of camera parameters from image sequence for model-based video coding. *CirSysVideo, 4*(3), 288–296.

Park, S. J., An, K. H., & Lee, M. (2002). Saliency map model with adaptive masking based on independent component analysis. *Neurocomputing, 49*, 417–422. doi:10.1016/S0925-2312(02)00637-9

Park, I. K., Zhang, H., Vezhnevet, V., & Choh, H., K. (2004). *Image-based Photorealistic 3-D Face Modeling.* Paper presented at the 6th IEEE Conference on Automatic Face and Gesture Recognition.

Pavlovic, V. I., Sharma, R., & Huang, T. S. (1997). Visual Interpretation of Hand Gestures for Human-Computer Interaction: a Review. *IEEE Transactions on Pattern Analysis and Machine Intelligence, 19*(7), 677–695. doi:10.1109/34.598226

Pavlovic, V., & Garg, A. (2001), Efficient Detection of Objects and Attributes using Boosting. *IEEE Conf. Computer Vision and Pattern Recognition. QMUL database* (n.d.). Retrieved from http://www.elec.qmul.ac.uk /mmv

Pearl, J. (1988). *Probabilistic reasoning in intelligent systems: networks of plausible inference.* Morgan Kaufmann Publishers Inc.

Pevny, T., & Fridrich, J. (2008). Detection of Double-Compression in JPEG Images for Applications in Steganography. *IEEE Transactions on Information Forensics and Security, 3*(2), 247–258. doi:10.1109/TIFS.2008.922456

Piekarski, W., Avery, B., Thomas, B. H., & Malbezin, P. (2004). Integrated Head and Hand Tracking for Indoor and Outdoor Augmented Reality. In *Proceedings of the IEEE Virtual Reality Conference* (p. 11). Los Alamitos: IEEE Computer Society.

Pietzsch, S., Wimmer, M., Stulp, F., & Radig, B. (2008). *Face Model Fitting with Generic, Group-specific, and Person-specific Objective Functions.* Paper presented at the 3rd International Conference on Computer Vision Theory and Applications (VISAPP).

Popescu, A. C., & Farid, H. (2005). Exposing digital forgeries by detecting traces of re-sampling. *IEEE Signal Processing Magazine*, *53*(2), 758–767.

Popescu, A., & Farid, H. (2004). *Exposing digital forgeries by detecting duplicated image regions* (*Technical Report TR2004-515*). Department of Computer Science, Dartmouth College.

Prante, T., Streitz, N. A., & Tandler, P. (2004). Roomware: Computers Disappear and Interaction Evolves. *IEEE Computer*, *37*(12), 47–54.

Qian, R., & Haering, N. (2004). Method for automatic extraction of semantically significant events from video, US6721454 (B1), Sharp Lab Of America Inc.

Raina, R., & Shen, Y. NG, A. Y., & Mccallum, A. (2003). Classification with hybrid generative / discriminative models. In *Proc. Neural Information Processing Systems*.

Randall, M., & Lewis, A. (2002). A parallel implementation of ant colony optimization. *Journal of Parallel and Distributed Computing*, *62*(9), 1421–1432. doi:10.1006/jpdc.2002.1854

Raouzaiou, A., Tsapatsoulis, N., Karpouzis, K., & Kollias, S. (2002). Parameterized Facial Expression Synthesis Based on MPEG-4. *EURASIP Journal on Applied Signal Processing*, (10): 1021–1038. doi:10.1155/S1110865702206149

Rasheed, Z., & Shah, M. (2005). Detection and Representation of Scenes in Videos. *IEEE Transactions on Multimedia*, *7*(6), 1097–1105. doi:10.1109/TMM.2005.858392

Rasheed, Z., & Shah, M. (2003). Scene Detection In Hollywood Movies and TV Shows. *IEEE Computer Society Conference on Computer Vision and Pattern Recognition* (pp. II-343-348).

Ratnaparkhi, A. (1998). *Maximum entropy models for natural language ambiguity resolution*. Ph.D. Dissertation. Computer and Information Science, Univ. of Pennsylvania, USA.

Ravishankar Rao, A. (1990). *A Taxonomy for Texture Description and Identification*. New York: Springer-Verlag.

Ravishankar Rao, A., & Lohse, G. L. (1996). Towards a Texture Naming System: Identifying Relevant Dimensions of Texture. *Vision Research*, *36*(11), 1649–1669. doi:10.1016/0042-6989(95)00202-2

Regh, J., & Kanade, T. (1994). DigitEyes: Vision-Based Hand Tracking for human-computer interaction. In *Proceedings of the Workshop on Motion of Non-Rigid and Articulated Objects* (pp. 16-22). Los Alamitos: IEEE Computer Society.

Reiter, S., Schuller, B., & Rigoll, G. (2007). Hidden conditional random fields for meeting segmentation. In *Proc. IEEE international conference on multimedia and expo*.

Rekimoto, J. (2001). GestureWrist and GesturePad: Unobtrusive Wearable Interaction Devices. In *Proceedings of the Fifth International Symposium on Wearable Computers* (pp. 21). Los Alamitos: IEEE Computer Society

Ren, X., & Malik, J. (2003). Learning a classification model for segmentation. In *Proceedings of the IEEE Intl. Conference on Computer Vision (ICCV)*.

Riaz, Z., Mayer, C., Wimmer, M., Beetz, M., & Radig, B. (2008). *A Model Based Approach for Expression Invariant Face Recognition*. Paper presented at the 3rd International Conference on Biometrics.

Ross, P. E. (2004). Managing Care Through the Air. *IEEE Spectrum*, *4*(12), 14–19. doi:10.1109/MSPEC.2004.1265120

Rother, C., Kolmogorov, V., & Blake, A. (2004). Grabcut: Interactive foreground extraction using iterated graph cuts. In *Proceedings of the ACM SIGGRAPH*.

Rowley, H. A., Baluja, S., & Kanade, T. (1998). Neural network-based face detection. *IEEE Transactions on Pattern Analysis and Machine Intelligence*, *20*(1), 23–38. doi:10.1109/34.655647

Rui, Y., & Huang, T. S. (1999). A novel relevance feedback technique in image retrieval. In *Proceedings of the ACM Intl. Conference on Multimedia (ACM MM)*.

Rui, Y., Gupta, A., & Cadiz, J. J. (2001). Viewing meetings captured by an omni-directional camera. In *Proceedings of the SIGCHI Conference on Human Factors in Computing Systems* (pp. 450-457). Seattle, USA: ACM.

Rui, Y., Huang, T., & Mehrotra, S. (1998). Constructing table-of-content for video. In *Proc. the ACM Multimedia conference*.

Russell, B. C., Torralba, A., Murphy, K. P., & Freeman, W. T. (2008). LabelMe: a database and web-based tool for image annotation. *International Journal of Computer Vision*, *77*(1-3), 157–173. doi:10.1007/s11263-007-0090-8

Rydfalk, M. (1987). *CANDIDE, a parameterized face* (No. LiTH-ISY-I-866).

Saber, E., & Tekalp, A. M. (1998). Frontal-view face detection and facial feature extraction using colour, shape and symmetry based cost functions. *Pattern Recognition Letters*, *19*(8), 669–680. doi:10.1016/S0167-8655(98)00044-0

Sadlier, D., & Connor, N. (2005). Event detection in field-sports video using audio-visual features and a support vector machine. *IEEE Transactions on Circuits and Systems for Video Technology*, *15*(10), 1225–1233. doi:10.1109/TCSVT.2005.854237

Sato, Y., Kobayashi, Y., & Koike, H. (2000). Fast tracking of hands and fingertips in infrared images for augmented desk interface. In *Proceedings of International Conference on Automatic Face and Gesture Recognition* (pp. 462-467).

Schapire, R. E., Freund, Y., Bartlett, P., & Lee, W. S. (1998). Boosting the margin: A new explanation for the effectiveness of voting methods. *Annals of Statistics*, *26*(5), 1651–1686. doi:10.1214/aos/1024691352

Scherer, K., & Ekman, P. (1982). *Handbook of Methods in Nonverbal Behavior Research*. Cambridge Univ. Press.

Schmidt, K., & Cohn, J. (2001). Dynamics of facial expression: Normative characteristics and individual differences. *IEEE Int'l Conf. on Multimedia and Expo* (pp. 728–731).

Scholl, B. J. (2001). Objects and Attention: The State of the Art. *Cognition*, *80*(1-2), 1–46. doi:10.1016/S0010-0277(00)00152-9

Schulz, D., Burgard, W., Fox, D., & Cremers, A. B. (2001). Tracking multiple moving targets with a mobile robot using particle filters and statistical data association. *IEEE International Conference on Robotics and Automation*.

Sethi, I. K., Coman, I. L., & Stan, D. (2001). Mining association rules between low-level features and high-level concepts. In *Proc. SPIE Int. Soc. Opt. Eng.* (Vol. 4384, pp. 279-290).

Shamir, A., & Avidan, S. (2009). Seam Carving for Media Retargeting. *Communications of the ACM*, *52*(1), 77–85. doi:10.1145/1435417.1435437

Shaw, W. M. Jr, Buigin, R., & Howell, P. (1997). Performance standards and evaluation on IR test collections: Cluster-based retrieval models. *Information Processing & Management*, *33*(1), 1–14. doi:10.1016/S0306-4573(96)00043-X

Shi, J., & Malik, J. (2000). Normalized cuts and image segmentation. *IEEE Transactions on Pattern Analysis and Machine Intelligence*, *22*(8), 888–905. doi:10.1109/34.868688

Shi, J., & Tomasi, C. (1994). Good features to track. In *Proceedings of the IEEE Conference on Computer Vision and Pattern Recognition (CVPR)* (pp. 593–600).

Sim, T., Baker, S., & Bsat, M. (2002). *The CMU Pose, Illumination, and Expression (PIE) Database*. Paper presented at the Proceedings of the Fifth IEEE International Conference on Automatic Face and Gesture Recognition.

Smeulders, A. W. M., Worring, M., Gupta, A., Santin, S., & Jain, R. (2000). Content-based image retrieval at the end of the early years. *IEEE Transactions on Pattern Analysis and Machine Intelligence*, *22*(12), 1349–1380. doi:10.1109/34.895972

Smith, T. F., & Waterman, M. S. (1981). Identification of Common Molecular Subsequences. *Journal of Molecular Biology*, 195–197. doi:10.1016/0022-2836(81)90087-5

Solberg, A. H. S., & Jain, A. K. (1997). Texture Analysis of SAR Images: A Comparative Study. Research Report. Norwegian Computing Center and Michigan State University.

Springer, C. E. (1964). *Geometry and Analysis of Projective Spaces*. Freeman.

Srinivasan, M., Venkatesh, S., & Hosie, R. (1997). Qualitative estimation of camera motion parameters from video sequences. *Pattern Recognition, 30*, 593–606. doi:10.1016/S0031-3203(96)00106-9

Starner, T., & Pentland, A. (1995). Visual Recognition of American Sign Language Using Hidden Markov Models. In *Proceedings of the International Workshop on Automatic Face and Gesture Recognition* (pp. 189-194).

Starner, T., Leibe, B., Singletary, B., & Pair, J. (2000). MIND-WARPING: towards creating a compelling collaborative augmented reality game. In *Proceedings of the International Conference on Intelligent User Interfaces Conference* (pp. 256-259).

Stegmann, M. (2004). *Generative Interpretation of Medical Images: Automated Segmentation and Analysis of Cardiac MRI using Statistical Image Analysis*. TU Denmark.

Suh, B., Ling, H., Bederson, B. B., & Jacobs, D. W. (2003). Automatic thumbnail cropping and its effectiveness. In *Proceedings of the 16th Annual ACM Symposium on User interface Software and Technology* (pp. 95-104). Vancouver, Canada: ACM.

Sun, Y., & Fisher, R. (2002). Hierarchical selectivity for object-based visual attention (LNCS 2525, pp. 427-438). Heidelberg: Springer-Verlag.

Sung, K. K. (1996). *Learning and Example Selection for Object and Pattern Detection*. PhD Thesis, Massachusetts Institute of Technology.

Swaminathan, A., Wu, M., & Ray Liu, K. J. (2008). Digital Image Forensics via Intrinsic Fingerprints. *IEEE Transactions on Information Forensics and Security, 3*(1), 101–117. doi:10.1109/TIFS.2007.916010

System, B. (Ed.). (2009) Encyclopædia Britannica. Retrieved November 06, 2009, from Encyclopædia Britannica Online.

Tamura, H., Mori, S., & Yamawaki, T. (1978). Textural Features Corresponding to Visual Perception. *IEEE Transactions on Systems, Man, and Cybernetics, 8*(6), 460–472. doi:10.1109/TSMC.1978.4309999

Tan, Y.-P., Saur, D. D., Kulkarni, S. R., & Ramadge, P. J. (2000). Rapid Estimation of Camera Motion from MPEG Video With Application to Video Annotation. *IEEE Trans. on Circuits and Systems for Video Technology, 10*(1), 133–146. doi:10.1109/76.825867

Tang, H. L., Hanka, R., & Ip, H. H. S. (2003). Histological image retrieval based on semantic content analysis. *IEEE Transactions on Information Technology in Biomedicine, 7*(1), 26–36. doi:10.1109/TITB.2003.808500

Tang, F., Brennan, S., Zhao, Q., & Tao, H. (2007). Co-Tracking Using Semi-Supervised Support Vector Machines. In *Proceedings of International Conference on Computer Vision* (pp.1-8)

Tao, H., Chen, H. H., Wu, W., & Huang, T. (1999). Compression of MPEG-4 Facial Animation Parameters for Transmission of Talking Heads. *IEEE Transactions on Circuits and Systems for Video Technology, 9*(2), 264–276. doi:10.1109/76.752094

Tao, H. & Huang, T. S. (1998) Facial animation and video tracking, *Workshop Modeling and Motion Capture Techniques for Virtual Environments*, 242–253, 1998.

Tian, Y., Kanade, T., & Cohn, J. F. (2001). Recognizing Action Units for Facial Expression Analysis. *IEEE Transactions on Pattern Analysis and Machine Intelligence, 23*(2), 97–115. doi:10.1109/34.908962

Tian, J., Yu, W., & Xie, S. (2008). An ant colony optimization algorithm for image edge detection. In *Proc. IEEE Congress on Evolutionary Computation* (pp. 751-756). Hongkong, China.

Tian, Y.-L., & Hampapur, A. (2005). Robust Salient Motion Detection with Complex Background for Real-time Video Surveillance. In *Proceedings of the IEEE Computer Society Workshop on Motion and Video Computing* (Vol. 2, pp. 30-35).

Tomasi, C., & Kanade, T. (1992). Shape and Motion from Image Streams under Orthography: A Factorization Method. *International Journal of Computer Vision, 9*(2), 137–154. doi:10.1007/BF00129684

Tomita, F., & Tsuji, S. (1990). *Computer Analysis of Visual Textures*. USA: Kluwer Academic Publishers.

Tong, Y., Chen, J., & Ji, Q. (2010). A Unified Probabilistic Framework for Spontaneous Facial Action Modeling and Understanding. *IEEE Transactions on Pattern Analysis and Machine Intelligence, 32*(2), 258–274. doi:10.1109/TPAMI.2008.293

Tong, Y., Liao, W., & Ji, Q. (2007). Facial Action Unit Recognition by Exploiting Their Dynamic and Semantic Relationships. *IEEE Transactions on Pattern Analysis and Machine Intelligence, 29*(10), 1683–1699. doi:10.1109/TPAMI.2007.1094

Tong, Y., Wang, Y., Zhu, Z., & Ji, Q. (2007). Robust Facial Feature Tracking under Varying Face Pose and Facial Expression. *Pattern Recognition Journal, 40*(11), 3195–3208. doi:10.1016/j.patcog.2007.02.021

Towles, H., Chen, W.-C., Yang, R., Kum, S.-U., Fuchs, H., Kelshikar, N., et al. (2002). 3D Tele-Collaboration Over Internet2. In *Proceedings of the International Workshop on Immersive Telepresence*.

Toyama, K., & Hager, G. D. (1999). Incremental Focus of Attention for Robust Vision-based Tracking. *International Journal of Computer Vision, 35*(1), 45–63. doi:10.1023/A:1008159011682

Treisman, A. (1980). A Feature Integration Theory of Attention. *Cognitive Psychology, 12*(1), 97–136. doi:10.1016/0010-0285(80)90005-5

Triesch, J., & von der Malsburg, C. (1996). Robust classification of hand posture against complex background. In *Proceedings of International Conference on Automatic Face and Gesture Recognition* (pp. 170-175).

Tsapatsoulis, N., Pattichis, C., Kounoudes, A., Loizou, C., Constantinides, A., & Taylor, J. G. (2006). Visual attention based region of interest coding for video-telephony applications. In *Proc. IEEE Int. Symp. on Communication Systems, Networks and Digital Signal Processing*.

Tseng, B. L., & Smith, J. R. (2003). Hierarchical video summarization based on context clustering. In Smith, J. R., Panchanathan, S., & Zhang, T. (Eds.), *Internet Multimedia Management Systems IV: Proceedings of SPIE* (pp. 14–25). Orlando, USA: SPIE-International Society for Optical Engine.

Tsotsos, J. K., Culhane, S. M., Winky, Y. K. W., Yuzhong, L., Davis, N., & Nuflo, F. (1995). Modeling Visual Attention via Selective Tuning. *Artificial Intelligence, 78*(1), 507–545. doi:10.1016/0004-3702(95)00025-9

Tuceryan, M., & Jain, A. K. (1993). Texture Analysis. In Chen, C. H., Pau, L. F., & Wang, P. S. P. (Eds.), *Handbook of Pattern Recognition and Computer Vision* (pp. 235–276). River Edge, NY: World Scientific.

Uchihashi, S., Foote, J., Girgensohn, A., & Boreczky, J. (1999). *Video Manga: Generating Semantically Meaningful Video Summaries*. ACM Multimedia.

Ulusoy, I., & Bishop, C. M. (2005). Generative versus discriminative methods for object recognition. In *Proc. of IEEE Computer Vision and Pattern Recognition* (Vol. 2, pp. 258-265).

Vadakkepat, P., Lim, P., Liyanage, C., Silva, D., Liu, J., & Ling, L. (2008). Multimodal Approach to Human-Face Detection and Tracking. *IEEE Transactions on Industrial Electronics, 55*(3), 1385. doi:10.1109/TIE.2007.903993

Vailaya, A., Figueiredo, M. A. T., Jain, A. K., & Zhang, H. J. (2001). Image classification for content-based indexing. *IEEE Transactions on Image Processing, 10*(1), 117–130. doi:10.1109/83.892448

Vailaya, A., & Jain, A. (1999). Incremental learning for Bayesian classification of images. In *Proc. of the International Conf. Image Processing*.

Valente, S., & Dougelay, J.-L. (2000). Face Tracking and Realistic Animations for Telecommunicate Clones. *IEEE MultiMedia*, *7*(1), 34–43. doi:10.1109/93.839309

Van Gool, L., Dewaele, P., & Oosterlinck, A. (1985). Texture Analysis Anno 1983. *Computer Vision, Graphics, and Image Processing Journal*, *29*(3), 336–357. doi:10.1016/0734-189X(85)90130-6

Van Rijsbergen, C. J. (1979). *Heavy emphasis on probabilistic models*. Information Retrieval.

Viola, P., & Jones, M. J. (2004). Robust real-time face detection. *International Journal of Computer Vision*, *57*(2), 137–154. doi:10.1023/B:VISI.0000013087.49260.fb

Viola, P., & Jones, M. (2001). Rapid object detection using a boosted cascade of simple features. In *Proceedings of the IEEE Conference on Computer Vision and Pattern Recognition* (CVPR).

Viola, P., & Jones, M. (2001). Robust real-time object detection. *Second International Workshop on Statistical Learning and Computational Theories of Vision Modeling, Learning, Computing and Sampling*, July 2001.

Vogt, C. C., & Cottrell, G. W. (1999). Fusion Via a Linear Combination of Scores. *Information Retrieval Journal*, *1*, 151–173. doi:10.1023/A:1009980820262

Volkmer, T., Smith, J. R., & Natsev, A. (2005). A web-based system for collaborative annotation of large image and video collections. In *Proceedings of the ACM Intl. Conference on Multimedia (ACM MM)*.

Vronay, D., Wang, S., Zhang, D., & Zhang, W. (2006a). Automatic video editing for real-time multi-point video conferencing. *US Patent 20060251384*.

Vronay, D., Wang, S., Zhang, D., & Zhang, W. (2006b). Automatic video editing for real-time generation of multiplayer game show videos. *US Patent 20060251383*.

Wallraven, C., Caputo, B., & Graf, A. (2003). Recognition with local features: the kernel recipe. In *IEEE International Conference on Computer Vision* (pp. 257-264).

Walther, D., & Koch, C. (2006). Modeling Attention to Salient Photo-objects. *Neural Networks*, *19*(1), 1395–1407. doi:10.1016/j.neunet.2006.10.001

Wang, P., & Ji, Q. (2007). Multi-View Face and Eye Detection Using Discriminant Features. *Computer Vision and Image Understanding*, *105*(2), 99–111. doi:10.1016/j.cviu.2006.08.008

Wang, Y., Liu, Z., & Huang, J. (2000). Multimedia content analysis using both audio and visual clues. *IEEE Signal Processing Magazine*, *17*(6), 12–36. doi:10.1109/79.888862

Wang, G., Hu, Z., Wu, F., & Tsui, H. T. (2005). Single view metrology from scene constraints. *Image and Vision Computing*, *23*(9), 831–840. doi:10.1016/j.imavis.2005.04.002

Wang, F., & Ngo, C. W. (2007). Rushes Video Summarization by Object and Event Understanding. In *Proc. of the TRECVID Workshop on Video Summarization (TVS'07)*. ACM Multimedia.

Wang, P., & Ji, Q. (2005). Multi-view Face Tracking with Factorial and Switching HMM. In *Proc. IEEE Workshop on Applications of Computer Vision (WACV/MOTION05)*.

Wang, S. B., Quattoni, A., Morency, L.-P., Demirdjian, D., & Darrell, T. (2006). Hidden Conditional Random Fields for Gesture Recognition. In *Proc. IEEE Computer Society Conference on Computer Vision and Pattern Recognition*.

Wang, T., Gao, Y., Li, J. G., et al. (2007). THU-ICRC at Rush Summarization of TRECVID 2007. In *Proc. of the TRECVID Workshop on Video Summarization (TVS'07)*. ACM Multimedia.

Wang, T., Li, J., Diao, Q., Hu, W., Zhang, Y., & Dulong, C. (2006). Semantic Event Detection using Conditional Random Fields. In *Proc. IEEE Conference on Computer Vision and Pattern Recognition*.

Wang, W., & Farid, H. (2008). *Detecting Re-Projected Video*. International Workshop on Information Hiding.

Wang, X.-J., Ma, W.-Y., & Li, X. (2004). Data-driven Approach for Bridging the Cognitive Gap in Image Retrieval. In *Proceedings of the 2004 International Conference on Multimedia and Expo* (Vol 3, pp. 2231-2234).

Wang, Y., & Mori, G. (2009). Max-margin hidden conditional random fields for human action recognition. *Proc. IEEE Conference on Computer Vision and Pattern Recognition.*

Want, R., Borriello, G., Pering, T., & Farkas, K. I. (2002). Disappearing Hardware. *IEEE Pervasive Computing / IEEE Computer Society [and] IEEE Communications Society, 1*(1), 36–47. doi:10.1109/MPRV.2002.993143

Wen, Z., & Huang, T. S. (2004). *3D Face Processing: Modeling, Analysis and Synthesis.* Kulwer Academic Publisher.

Wexelblat, A. (1995). An approach to natural gesture in virtual environments. *ACM TOCHI, 2*(3), 179–200. doi:10.1145/210079.210080

Wilhelm, T., Böhme, H. J., & Gross, H. M. (2004). A multi-modal system for tracking and analyzing faces on a mobile robot. *Robotics and Autonomous Systems, 48,* 31–40. doi:10.1016/j.robot.2004.05.004

Wimmer, M., Riaz, Z., Mayer, C., & Radig, B. (2008). Recognizing Facial Expressions Using Model-based Image Interpretation [-Tech Publisher.]. *Advances in Human-Computer Interaction,* I.

Wimmer, M., Stulp, F., Pietzsch, S., & Radig, B. (2008). Learning Local Objective Functions for Robust Face Model Fitting. *IEEE Transactions on Pattern Analysis and Machine Intelligence, 30*(8), 1357–1370. doi:10.1109/TPAMI.2007.70793

Witten, I. H., & Frank, E. (2005). *Data Mining: Practical Machine Learning Tools and Techniques* (2nd ed.). San Francisco: Morgan Kaufmann.

Wixson, L. (2000). Detecting Salient Motion by Accumulating Directionally-Consistent Flow. *IEEE Transactions on Pattern Analysis and Machine Intelligence, 22*(8), 774–780. doi:10.1109/34.868680

Wojek, C., & Schiele, B. (2008). A dynamic conditional random field model for joint labeling of object and scene classes. In *Proc. the 10th European Conference on Computer Vision.*

Wolf, L., Guttmann, M., & Cohen-Or, D. (2007). Non-homogeneous Content-driven Video-retargeting. In *Proceedings of the Eleventh IEEE International Conference on Computer Vision.*

Wolfe, J. M. (1994). Guided Search 2.0: A Revised Model of Visual Search. *Psychonomic Bulletin & Review, 1*(2), 202–238.

Wren, C. R., Azarbayejani, A., Darrell, T. J., & Pentland, A. P. (1997). Pfinder: Real-Time Tracking of the Human Body. *IEEE Transactions on Pattern Analysis and Machine Intelligence, 19*(7), 780–785. doi:10.1109/34.598236

Wu, W., Chen, X., & Yang, J. (2005). Detection of text on road signs from video. *IEEE Transactions on Intelligent Transportation Systems, 6*(4), 378–390. doi:10.1109/TITS.2005.858619

Wu, W., & Yang, J. (2009). Semi-automatically labeling objects in images. *IEEE Transactions on Image Processing, 18*(6), 1340–1349. doi:10.1109/TIP.2009.2017360

Wu, C.-Y., Leou, J.-L., & Chen, H.-Y. (2009). Visual attention region determination using low-level features. In *Proc. International Symposium on Circuits and Systems* (pp. 3178-3181).Taiwan

Wu, W. (2009). Multimedia Technologies for Landmark-Based Vehicle Navigation. Ph.D. thesis, CMU-LTI-09-014, Language Technologies Institute, School of Computer Science, Carnegie Mellon University, USA.

Wu, Y., & Huang, T. (1999). Vision-Based Gesture Recognition: A review. In *Proceedings of the International Gesture Workshop on Gesture-Based Communication in Human-Computer Interaction* (pp. 103-115). London: Springer-Verlag.

Xiao, J., Baker, S., Matthews, I., & Kanade, T. (2004). *Real-Time Combined 2D+3D Active Appearance Models.* Paper presented at the IEEE Conference on Computer Vision and Pattern Recognition.

Xie, L., Chang, S.-F., Divakaran, A., & Sun, H. (2004). Structure Analysis of Soccer Video with domain knowledge and Hidden Markov Models. *Pattern Recognition Letters, 25*(7), 767–775. doi:10.1016/j.patrec.2004.01.005

Xie, X., Liu, H., Ma, W.-Y., & Zhang, H.-J. (2006). Browsing Large Pictures Under Limited Display Sizes. *IEEE Transactions on Multimedia, 8*(4), 707–715. doi:10.1109/TMM.2006.876294

Xie, L., Chang, S., Divakaran, A., & Sun, H. (2003). Unsupervised Mining of Staistical Temporal Structures in Video. In Rosenfeld, D. D. A. (Ed.), *Video Mining*. Kluwer Academi Publishers.

Xie, L., Chang, S.-F., Divakaran, A., & Sun, H. (2002). Structure Analysis of Soccer Video with Hidden Markov Models. In *Proc. Interational Conference on Acoustic, Speech and Signal Processing*.

Xiong, Z. Y., Zhou, X. S., Tian, Q., Rui, Y., & Huang, T. S. (2006). Semantic retrieval of video - review of research on video retrieval in meetings, movies and broadcast news, and sports. *IEEE Signal Processing Magazine, 23*(2), 18–27. doi:10.1109/MSP.2006.1621445

Xu, C., Zhu, G., Zhang, Y., Huang, Q., & Lu, H. (2008). Event tactic analysis based on player and ball trajectory in broadcast video. In *Proc. International conference on Content-based image and video retrieval*.

Yamasaki, T., Nishioka, Y., & Aizawa, K. (2008). Interactive retrieval for multi-camera surveillance systems featuring spatio-temporal summarization. In *Proceedings of the 16th ACM international Conference on Multimedia: MM '08* (pp.797-800). New York: ACM.

Yang, J., & Waibel, A. (1998). Skin-color modeling and adaptation (LNCS 1352, pp. 687-694).

Yang, M., Yan, J., & Wu, Y. (2007). Spatial Selection for Attentional Visual Tracking. In *Proceedings of the IEEE International Conference on Computer Vision and Pattern Recognition*.

Ye, G., Corso, J., Burschka, D., & Hager, D. (2003). VICs: A Modular Vision-Based HCI Framework. In *Proceedings of the 3rd International Conference on Computer Vision Systems* (pp. 257-267).

Yeung, M., Yeo, B., & Liu, B. (1998). Segmentation of video by clustering and graph Analysis. *Computer Vision and Image Understanding, 71*(1), 94–109. doi:10.1006/cviu.1997.0628

Yilmaz, A., Javed, O., & Shah, M. (2006). *Object tracking: a survey*. ACM J. Computing Surveys.

Yip, A., & Sinha, P. (2001). Role of color in face recognition. *MIT tech report (ai.mit.com)*, AIM-2001-035 CBCL-212, 2001.

Yow, K. C., & Cipolla, R. (1996). Scale and orientation invariance in human face detection. In *Proc. British Machine Vision Conference* (p. 745).

Yu, X., Xu, C., Leong, H. W., Tian, Q., Tang, Q., & Wan, K. W. (2003). Trajectory-based ball detection and tracking with applications to semantic analysis of broadcast soccer video. In *Proc. the ACM Multimedia conference*.

Yuan, J. H., Zheng, W. J., & Chen, L. (2004). 2004: shot boundary detection and high-level feature extraction. In *NIST workshop of TRECVID 2004*. Tsinghua University at TRECVID.

Zhai, Y., & Shah, M. (2006). Video Scene Segmentation Using Markov Chain Monte Carlo. *IEEE Transactions on Multimedia, 8*(4), 686–697. doi:10.1109/TMM.2006.876299

Zhang, Y., & Ji, Q. (2005). Active and Dynamic Information Fusion for Facial Expression Understanding from Image Sequence. *IEEE Transactions on Pattern Analysis and Machine Intelligence, 27*(5), 699–714. doi:10.1109/TPAMI.2005.93

Zhang, Y., Ji, Q., Zhu, Z., & Yi, B. (2008). Dynamic Facial Expression Analysis and Synthesis with MPEG-4 Facial Animation Parameters. *IEEE Transactions on Circuits and Systems for Video Technology, 18*(10), 1383–1396. doi:10.1109/TCSVT.2008.928887

Zhang, J., & Tan, T. (2002). Brief Review of Invariant Texture Analysis Methods. *Pattern Recognition, 35*(3), 735–747. doi:10.1016/S0031-3203(01)00074-7

Zhang, D., Gatica-Perez, D., Bengio, S., & Roy, D. (2005). *Learning influence among interacting Markov chains.* Proc. Neural Information Processing Systems.

Zhang, L., Tong, M., Marks, T., Shan, H., & Cottrell, G. (2008). SUN: A Bayesian framework for saliency using natural statistics. *Journal of Vision (Charlottesville, Va.)*, *8*(7), 1–20. doi:10.1167/8.7.32

Zhang, Q., & Izquierdo, E. (2006). A multi-feature optimization approach to object-based image classification. In *Proc. of International Conference on Image and Video Retrieval* (pp. 310-319).

Zhang, W., Cao, X., Feng, Z., Zhang, J., & Wang, P. (2009). Detecting Photographic Composites Using Two-View Geometrical. *IEEE International Conference on Multimedia and Expo.*

Zhang, W., Shan, S., Gao, W., Chen, X., & Zhang, H. (2005). Local Gabor Binary Histogram Sequence: A Novel Non-Statistical Model for Face Representation and Recognition. In *Proceedings of International Conference on Computer Vision* (pp.786-791).

Zhao, W., & Chellapa, R. (Eds.). (2006). *Face Processing: Advanced Modeling and Methods.* Elsevier.

Zhao, W., Chellappa, R., Phillips, P. J., & Rosenfeld, A. (2003). Face recognition: A literature survey. *ACM Computing Surveys*, *35*(4), 399–458. doi:10.1145/954339.954342

Zhao, Y.J., Wang, T., Wang, P., et al. (2007). Scene Segmentation and Categorization Using NCuts. *IEEE SLAM workshop of CVPR07.*

Zhou, H., Taj, M., & Cavallaro, A. (2008). Target detection and tracking with heterogeneous sensors. *IEEE Journal of Selected Topics in Signal Processing*, *2*(4), 503–513. doi:10.1109/JSTSP.2008.2001429

Zhou, H., Lin, D. J., & Huang, T. S. (2004). Static hand gesture recognition based on local orientation histogram feature distribution. In *Proceedings of Computer Vision and Pattern Recognition* (pp. 161-169).

Zhou, H., Xie, L., & Fang, X. (2007). Visual Mouse: SIFT Detection and PCA Recognition. In *Proceedings of International Conference on Computational Intelligence and Security Workshops* (pp. 263-266).

Zhou, W., Vellaikal, A., & Kuo, C. C. J. (2000). Rule-based video classification system for basketball video indexing. In *Proc. the ACM Multimedia Conference.*

Zhou, X., Zhuang, X., Yan, S., Chang, S. F., Johnson, M., & Huang, T. S. (2008). SIFT-Bag Kernel for Video Event Analysis. In *Proc. the ACM Multimedia Conference.*

Zhu, X., Ghahramani, Z., & Lafferty, J. (2003). Semi-supervised learning using Gaussian fields and harmonic functions. In *Proceedings of the Intl. Conference on Machine Learning (ICML).*

About the Contributors

Jinjun Wang received the B.E. and M.E. degree from Huazhong University of Science and Technology, China, in 2000 and 2003. He received the Ph.D degree from Nanyang Technological University, Singapore, in 2006. From 2006 to 2009, Dr. Wang was with NEC Laboratories America, Inc. as a postdoctoral research scientist, and in 2010, he joined Epson Research and Development, Inc. as a seinor research scientist. His research interests include pattern classification, image/video enhancement and editing, content-based image/video annotation and retrieval, semantic event detection, etc. He has published over 30 journal and conference papers in those areas, and has six US patents pending. Dr. Wang served as Technical Program Committee Member of major international multimedia conferences, including ACM MM '08, IEEE PCM '09, IEEE MMM '09/'10, IEEE 3D-TV '09/'10, etc. He also served as peer reviewer of many journals and conferences.

Jian Cheng is currently an associate professor of Institute of Automation, Chinese Academy of Sciences. He received the B.S. and M.S. degrees in Mathematics from Wuhan University in 1998 and in 2001, respectively. In 2004, he got his Ph.D degree in pattern recognition and intelligent systems from Institute of Automation, Chinese Academy of Sciences. From 2004 to 2006, he has been working as postdoctoral in Nokia Research Center. Then he joined National Laboratory of Pattern Recognition, Institute of Automation. His current research interests include image and video search, machine learning, etc. He has authored or co-authored more than 40 academic papers in these areas. He was awarded LU JIAXi Young Talent Prize in 2010. Dr. Cheng served as Technical Program Committee member for some international conferences, such as ACM Multimedia 2009 (content), IEEE Conference on Computer Vision and Pattern Recognition (CVPR'08), IEEE International Conference on Multimedia and Expo (ICME'08), Pacific-Rim Conference on Multimedia (PCM'08), IEEE International Conference on Computer Vision (ICCV'07), etc. He has also co-organized one special issue on Pattern Recognition Journal, and several special sessions on PCM 2008, ICME 2009, PCM 2010.

Shuqiang Jiang, associate professor. He received the Ph.D degree from ICT CAS, China in 2005. He is currently a faculty member at Digital Media Research Center, Institute of Computing Technology, Chinese Academy of Sciences. He is also with the Key Laboratory of Intelligent Information Processing, Chinese Academy of Sciences. His research interests include multimedia processing and semantic understanding, pattern recognition, and computer vision. He has published over 60 technical papers in the area of multimedia. He is a Member of IEEE and ACM. He serves as General Special session Co-Chair of Pacific-Rim Conference on Multimedia (PCM2008). He also served as Technical Program Committee Member in many prestigious multimedia conferences including International conference on IEEE Conference on Computer Vision and Pattern Recognition, IEEE International Conference on Computer Vision, ACM Multimedia, International Conference on Multimedia and Expo (ICME), Pacific-Rim Conference on Multimedia (PCM).

* * *

Wen Wu received his B.S. degree in computer science and technology from Tsinghua University, China, in 2001, and M.Sc. degree in computer science from the National University of Singapore in 2003. After coming to USA, Wen obtained his M.Sc. and Ph.D. degrees in language and information technologies at the School of Computer Science, Carnegie Mellon University, Pittsburgh, Pennsylvania in 2005 and 2009. Wen's research experiences center around two themes real-world applications and high-performance systems. He has researched several problems in learning, multimedia and human-machine interface and published in various journals and conferences. Wen is currently working at Siemens Corporate Research in New Jersey, USA as a research scientist.

Xilin Chen received the BS, MS, and PhD degrees in computer science from the Harbin Institute of Technology (HIT), China, in 1988,1991, and 1994, respectively. He was a professor with HIT from 1999 to 2005 and was a visiting scholar with Carnegie Mellon University from 2001 to 2004. He was selected into the One Hundred Talent Program of the Chinese Academy of Sciences (CAS) in 2004, and as a professor with the Institute of Computing Technology (ICT), CAS. He is now the director of the Intelligent Information Processing Division, ICT, CAS, and the director of the Key Lab of Intelligent Information Processing, CAS. He also leads the ICT-ISVision Joint Lab for face recognition. He has served as a program committee member for more than 20 international conferences in these areas, including ICCV, CVPR, ICIP, ICPR, etc. His research interests are image understanding, computer vision, pattern recognition, image processing, multimodal interface, and digital video broadcasting. He received several awards, including China's State Scientific and Technological Progress Award in 2000, 2003, and 2005, respectively, for his academic researches. He is the (co)author of more than 150 papers.

Jie Yang received the Ph.D. degree from the University of Akron, Akron, OH, 1994. He is currently on leave from Carnegie Mellon University (CMU), Pittsburgh, PA, and serves as a Program Director in the Division of Information Intelligence Systems at the National Science Foundation. He pioneered hidden Markov models for human performance modeling in his Ph.D. dissertation research. He joined the Interactive Systems Laboratories of CMU in 1994, where he has been leading research efforts to develop visual tracking and recognition systems for multimodal human computer interaction. He has been involved in the development of many multimodal systems in both intelligent working spaces and mobile platforms. His current research interests include multimodal human computer interaction, computer vision, and pattern recognition.

Yongmian Zhang received the Ph.D degree in Computer Engineering from the University of Nevada, Reno in 2004. He held a Research position with the Department of electrical, Computer and Systems Engineering at Rensselaer Polytechnic Institute. His areas of research include information fusion, computer vision, Human ComputerInteractions. He is a member of the IEEE.

Jixu Chen received the BS and MS degrees in electrical engineering from the University of Science and Technology of China in 2003 and 2006, respectively. He is currently pursuing the PhD degree at

Rensselaer Polytechnic Institute, Troy, New York. His areas of research include computer vision, pattern recognition, and their applications in human-computer interaction. He is a student member of the IEEE and the IEEE Computer Society.

Yan Tong, General Electric, Ph.D. Rensselaer Polytechnic Institute. Dr. Tong received a B.S. degree in electrical engineering from Zhejiang University, Hangzhou, China, in 1997, an M.S. degree in computer engineering from University of Nevada, Reno, in 2004, and a Ph.D. degree in electrical engineering from Rensselaer Polytechnic Institute, Troy, NY, in 2007. Dr. Tong's Ph.D. thesis research focused on spontaneous facial activity modeling and understanding through the integration of a probabilistic model and computer vision techniques. At GE Global Research, she is active in biometrics fusion, face modeling and face alignment. She has 19 peer-reviewed publications and 4 book chapters.

Qiang Ji received his Ph.D degree in Electrical Engineering from the University of Washington. He is currently a Professor with the Department of Electrical, Computer, and Systems Engineering at Rensselaer Polytechnic Institute (RPI). He is also a program director at the National Science Foundation, managing NSF's computer vision and machine learning programs. He has also held teaching and research positions with the Beckman Institute at University of Illinois at Urbana-Champaign, the Robotics Institute at Carnegie Mellon University, the Dept. of Computer Science at University of Nevada at Reno, and the US Air Force Research Laboratory. Prof. Ji currently serves as the director of the Intelligent Systems Laboratory (ISL) at RPI. Prof. Ji's research interests are in computer vision and probabilistic machine learning and their applications in various fields. He has published over 150 papers in peer-reviewed journals and conferences. His research has been supported by major governmental agencies including NSF, NIH, DARPA, ONR, ARO, and AFOSR as well as by major companies including Honda and Boeing. Prof. Ji is an editor on several computer vision and pattern recognition related journals and he has served program chair, technical area chair, and program committee in numerous international conferences/workshops. Prof. Ji is a senior member of the IEEE.

Giancarlo Iannizzotto (M '99 - SM 2009) received the M.D. degree in Electronics Engineering from the University of Catania, Italy, in 1994 and the Ph.D. in Computer Science from the same University in February, 1998. From 1996 to 2006 he was Assistant Professor at the Faculty of Engineering, University of Messina, Italy. Since 2006 he is Associate Professor at the same Faculty. His research activity is in the field of image analysis and processing, as the leader of the VisiLAB at the University of Messina.

Francesco La Rosa received the M.D. degree in Electronics Engineering from the University of Messina, Italy, in 2001 and the Ph.D. in Computer Science from the same University in February, 2005. His research activity is in the field of image analysis and processing, and in particular on computer vision applications for Human-Computer Interaction (HCI). He is author and co-author of several publications in the cited fields.

Richard M. Jiang obtained his PhD in computer science from Queen's University Belfast, UK. He is currently with Computer Science, Loughborough University. His research interest includes content-based video retrieval, 3D computer vision, and VLSI vision processing.

Abdul H. Sadka obtained his PhD in Electrical and Electronic Engineering from the University of Surrey, UK, in 1997. He was appointed a Professor and the head of Electronic and Computer Engineering at Brunel University in 2004. His research interests include video coding and transcoding, video transmissions over networks, computer vision and content-based multimedia retrieval.

Zahid Riaz has received his B.Sc. degree in Physics and M.Sc. degree in Systems Engineering in 2002 and 2004 respectively. He is currently working as joint PhD student of Higher Education Commission (HEC), Pakistan and German Academic Exchange Service (DAAD), Germany in Computer Science Department at Technische Universität München, Germany. He has also worked as visiting researcher in computer vision laboratory at University of Central Florida, FL, USA in 2009-2010. His major areas of interest are 3D face modeling, human robot interaction and action recognition.

Suat Gedikli received a degree in informatics from 'Munich University of Applied Sciences' in 2002 and a doctoral degree in informatics from the University of Technology Munich in 2009. His research interests include artificial intelligence, computer vision, image understanding, and pattern recognition. Since 2010 he works as a research engineer for a research directed company in Silicon Valley, developing computer vision methods for personal robots.

Michael Beetz is working as professor in Computer Science at the Department at Technische Universität München. He is heading the Intelligent Autonomous Systems (IAS) group. He is also the vice coordinator of the German cluster of excellence CoTeSys (Cognition for Technical Systems).

Bernd Radig received a degree in physics from the University of Bonn in 1973 and a doctoral degree and a habilitation degree in informatics from the University of Hamburg in 1978 and 1982, respectively. Until 1986, he was an associate professor in the Department of Computer Science at the University of Hamburg, leading the Research Group Cognitive Systems. Since 1986, he has been a full professor in the Department of Computer Science at the Technische Universitaet Muenchen. His research interests include artificial intelligence, computer vision and image understanding, and pattern recognition. He is a senior member of the IEEE.

Tao Wang is a senior researcher in Intel Labs China. His research interests include multimedia mining, computer vision, pattern recognition, and computer graphics. Wang received his PhD in computer science from Tsinghua University.

Yue Gao is a PhD candidate student in Dept of Automation, Tsinghua university. His research interests include video summarization, multimedia information retrieval and 3D retrieval. Gao received his MS in computer science from Tsinghua University, China.

Patricia P. Wang is a researcher in Intel Labs China. Her interests focus on application research in visual computing and mobile platform. Wang received her PhD in computer science from Tsinghua University, China.

Wei Hu is a senior researcher in Intel Labs China. His research interests include advanced media mining, computer vision, machine learning, and 3D object modeling. Hu received his PhD in computer science from the Institute of Computing Technology, Chinese Academy of Sciences.

Jianguo Li is a researcher in Intel Labs China. His research interests include immersive visual computing, multimedia mining, and parallel algorithm design and analysis. Li received his PhD in electrical engineering from Tsinghua University.

Yangzhou Du is a researcher in Intel Labs China. His research interests include pattern recognition, computer vision, and graphics as well as optimization and parallelization of multimedia application in multicore processors. Du received his PhD in computer science from Tsinghua University, Beijing.

Yimin Zhang is a research manager and senior researcher in Intel Labs China. His research interests include developing advanced technology in the field of visual computing, media search and mining, and studying the performance implications for next-generation microprocessors and platforms. Zhang received his PhD in computer science from Shanghai Jiaotong University.

Fan Chen received the BS degree in computer science from Nanjing University in 2001. He received the MS degree in information science from Tohoku University in 2005 and Ph.D. from Japan Advanced Institute of Science and Technology in 2008. He was a post-doctoral researcher in TELE, UCL from 2008 to 2010. He is now an assistant professor in Japan Advanced Institute of Science and Technology. His research interests are focused on statistical inference and optimization techniques related to computer vision, pattern recognition and multimedia analysis.

Damien Delannay received the M.S. and Ph.D. degree in electrical engineering from the Universit"¦ catholique de Louvain (UCL), Belgium in 1998 and 2004 respectively. His first research activities dealt with digital watermarking of multimedia contents. Between 2004 and 2008, he has designed and developed stereo-vision systems for an industrial partner (ACIC), in the context of video-surveillance application such as people counting/detection. His current research interests are related to object detection and tracking in multiview scene analysis.

Christophe De Vleeschouwer is a permanent Research Associate of the Belgian NSF and an Assistant Professor at UCL. He was a senior research engineer with the IMEC Multimedia Information Compression Systems group (1999-2000), and contributed to projects with ERICSSON. He was also a post-doctoral Research Fellow at UC Berkeley (2001-2002) and EPFL (2004). His main interests concern video and image processing for communication and networking applications, including content management and security issues. He is also enthusiastic about non-linear signal expansion techniques, and their use for signal analysis and signal interpretation. He is the co-author of more than 20 journal papers or book chapters, and holds two patents. He serves as an Associate Editor for IEEE Transactions on Multimedia, has been a reviewer for most IEEE Transactions journals related to media and image processing, and has been a member of the (technical) program committee for several conferences, including ICIP, EUSIPCO, ICME, ICASSP, PacketVideo, ECCV, GLOBECOM, and ICC. He is the leading guest editor for the special issue on 'Multi-camera information processing: acquisition, collaboration, interpretation and production', for the EURASIP Journal on Image and Video Processing. He contributed to MPEG bodies, and several European projects. He now coordinates the FP7-216023 APIDIS European project (www.apidis.org), and several Walloon region projects, respectively dedicated to video analysis for autonomous content production, and to personalized and interactive mobile video streaming.

Pascaline Parisot received the M.S. degree in computer science and applied mathematics from ENSEEIHT, an engineering school, France in 2003. She received the PhD degree in computer science from the Universit"¦ de Toulouse, France in 2009. She is currently a post-doctoral researcher in TELE, Universit"¦ Catholique de Louvain (UCL), Belgium. Her research interests are video processing, computer vision and object tracking.

Noureddine Abbadeni is currently assistant professor in the college of computer and information sciences at KSU, Riyadh, KSA. He received the B.Eng. degree in Computer Science (Software Engineering) from USTHB-Algiers-Algeria, the M.Sc. degree in Computer Science and the M.Sc degree in Computational Linguistics, both from University of Grenoble-France, the DESS degree in Management from HEC Montreal-Canada, and the PhD degree in computer science from University of Sherbrooke-Canada. Dr. Abbadeni has an experience of more than 14 years in both academia and IT industry in Canada, USA, UAE, and KSA. On the academic side, Dr. Abbadeni conducted research in multimedia information retrieval and databases, image processing, and pattern recognition for several years and has several papers published in international refereed conferences and journals. Dr. Abbadeni has taught several courses related to computer science, information technology, software engineering, and information systems. On the IT industry and business sides, Dr. Abbadeni has an excellent experience of several years in Canada and USA. He was employed as a Database/Software architect, Data warehousing/Data mining/BI specialist, Project manager and Technical leader in several high-tech. companies. During his career, Dr. Abbadeni has gained extensive academic and industrial experiences in different fields including Multimedia Information Retrieval and Databases, Data Warehousing & Data Mining, Image Processing, Pattern Recognition, Information Systems, Software Engineering, Knowledge Engineering, and Automatic Language Processing as well as Project/Team Management and Leadership.

Yi Ding (S'06) received the B.S. degree in communication engineering from Xi'an University of Technology, China, and the M.S. degree in communication engineering from Xidian University, China, in 2002 and 2005 respectively. He is currently working toward the Ph.D. degree in the School of Electrical and Computer Engineering, Oklahoma State University, Stillwater, OK. His research interests include multimedia content analysis, pattern recognition, image processing, and computer vision. His current research focuses on generative and discriminative model based approaches for video mining.

Guoliang Fan (S'97, M'01, SM'05) received his B.S. degree in Automation Engineering from Xi'an University of Technology, Xi'an, China, M.S. degree in Computer Engineering from Xidian University, Xi'an, China, and Ph.D. degree in Electrical Engineering from University of Delaware, Newark, DE, USA, in 1993, 1996, and 2001, respectively. From 1996 to 1998, he was a graduate assistant in the Department of Electronic Engineering, Chinese University of Hong Kong. Since 2001, Dr. Fan has been with the School of Electrical and Computer Engineering, Oklahoma State University (OSU), Stillwater, OK, where he is currently an Associate Professor. He was awarded the First Prize in 1997 IEEE Hong Kong Section Postgraduate Student Paper Contest and the First Prize in 1997 IEEE Region 10 (Asia-Pacific) Postgraduate Paper Contest. Dr. Fan is a recipient of the National Science Foundation (NSF) CAREER award (2004). He received the Halliburton Excellent Young Teacher Award (2004) and Halliburton Outstanding Young Faculty award (2006) from OSU. His research interests are image processing, computer vision, biomedical imaging and remote sensing applications.

Hong Lu received the B.Eng. and M.Eng. degrees in computer science and technology from Xidian University, Xi'an, China, in 1993 and 1998, respectively, and the Ph.D. degree from Nanyang Technological University, Singapore, in 2005. From 1993 to 2000, she was a Lecturer and Researcher with the School of Computer Science and Technology, Xidian University. From 2000 to 2003, she was a Research Student with the School of Electrical and Electronic Engineering, Nanyang Technological University. Since 2004, she has been with School of Computer Science, Fudan University, Shanghai, China, where she is currently an Associate Processor. Her current research interests include image and video processing, computer vision, machine learning, and pattern recognition.

Xiangyang Xue received the B.S., M.S., and Ph.D. degrees in communication engineering from Xidian University, Xi'an, China in 1989, 1992 and 1995, respectively. Since 1995, he has been with School of Computer Science, Fudan University, Shanghai, China, where he is currently a Professor. His research interests include multimedia information processing, retrieval and filtering, pattern recognition and machine learning, etc.

Lin Wu received her B.E. in Software Engineering from Dalian University of Technology, Dalian, China in 2008. Since September 2008, she has been a graduate in Computer Science, Tianjin University. Her interests include camera calibration and multi-view geometry.

Xiaochun Cao received his B.E. and M.E. degrees both in Computer Science from Beihang University (BUAA), Beijing, China in 1999 and 2002, respectively. He received his Ph.D. degree in Computer Science from University of Central Florida, Orlando, FL in 206 with dissertation nominated for the university-level Outstanding Dissertation Award. After graduation, he spent about two and half years at ObjectVideo Inc. as a Research Scientist. Since August 2008, he has been with Tianjin University, where he is currently Professor of Computer Science and Adjunct Professor of Computer Software. He has authored and co-authored over 40 peer-reviewed journal and conference papers, and has been in the organizing and the technical committees of several international colloquia. In 2004, he was a recipient of the Pierro Zamperoni best paper award in the International Conf. on Pattern Recognition.

Bin Ma received the B.E. degree in Computer Science from Zhengzhou University, Zhengzhou, China, in 2008. He is currently pursuing the Ph.D degree in biometric information hiding area under the supervision of Professor Yunhong Wang, at School of Computer Science and Engineering, Beihang University (BUAA), Beijing, China. His research interests include digital watermarking, pattern recognition and computer vision.

Chunlei Li received the B.E. degree in Computer Science from Zhengzhou University, Zhengzhou, China, in 2001. He is currently pursuing the Ph.D degree in biometric information hiding area under the supervision of Professor Yunhong Wang, at School of Computer Science and Engineering, Beihang University (BUAA), Beijing, China. His research interests include digital watermarking, pattern recognition and computer vision.

Yunhong Wang received the B.Sc. degree in electronic engineering from Northwestern Polytechnical University, the M.S. degree (1995) and the Ph.D. degree (1998) in Electronic Engineering from Nanjing University of Science and Technology. She joined National Lab of Pattern Recognition, Institute of Automation, Chinese Academy of Sciences in 1998, where she has been an associate professor since 2000. Her research interests include biometrics, pattern recognition and image processing.

Xiao Bai received the BEng degree in Computer Science from Beihang University of China in 2001. From 2002 to 2006, he was a Ph.D. student at Computer Science Department, University of York, U.K. under the supervision of Professor Edwin R. Hancock. From Sep. 2006 to Dec. 2008, he was a Research Officer (Fellow, Scientist) at Computer Science Department, University of Bath. He is now an Associate Professor at Computer Science School, Beihang University (BUAA). He has published more than 30 papers in journals and refreed conferences. His current research interests include computer vision, pattern recognition and machine learning.

Le Dong, ACM Member, IEEE Member, IRSS Member, received the B.E. degree in telecommunication engineering and the M.E. degree in communications and information systems from Xidian University, Xi'an, China, in 2001 and 2004, respectively. She received the Ph.D. degree in Electronic Engineering from Queen Mary, University of London, London, U.K., in 2009. She is currently the Associate Professor of Institute of Intelligent Systems and Information Technology, School of Computer Science and Engineering, University of Electronic Science and Technology of China. She has served/ been serving as a reviewer for a number of flagship journals including IEEE Transactions on Circuits and Systems for Video Technology, IEEE Transactions on Neural Networks, and IEEE Transactions on Image Processing. She served as the Publicity Co-Chair of the 4th IEEE International Conference on Cybernetics and Intelligent Systems, Singapore 2010, the organizing committee of the 6th International Workshop on Content-Based Multimedia Indexing, London, U.K. 2008, the 5th IET Visual Information Engineering Conference, Xi'an, China 2008, and the Workshop in the 15th IEEE International Conference on Image Processing, San Diego, USA 2008. She was the recipient of Overseas Research Students Awards Scheme, U.K. 2006; The European Commission under the IST 6th Framework Program Fellowship, U.K. 2006; Royal Academy of Engineers Travel Grant, U.K. 2008; Sichuan High-level personnel, China 2009. Her current research interests include multimedia fusion, machine vision, knowledge representation, intelligent systems and artificial intelligence.

Ebroul Izquierdo is a full professor (chair) of multimedia and computer vision and head of the Multimedia and Vision Group at Queen Mary, University of London. For his thesis on the numerical approximation of algebraic-differential equations, he received the Dr. Rerun Naturalium (PhD) from the Humboldt University , Berlin, Germany, in 1993. From 1990 to 1992 he was a teaching assistant at the department of applied mathematics, Technical University Berlin. From 1993 to 1997 he was with the Heinrich-Hertz Institute for Communication Technology, Berlin , Germany, as associated researcher. From 1998 to 1999 he was with the Department of Electronic Systems Engineering of the University of Essex as a senior research officer. Since 2000 he has been with the Electronic Engineering department, Queen Mary, University of London. Prof. Izquierdo is an associate editor of the IEEE Transactions on Circuits and Systems for Video Technology (TCSVT) and the EURASIP journal on image and video processing. He has served as guest editor of three special issues of the IEEE TCSVT, several special issues of the journal Signal Processing: Image Communication and the EURASIP Journal on Applied Signal Processing. Prof. Izquierdo is a Chartered Engineer, a Fellow of the The Institution of Engineering and Technology (IET), past chairman of the Executive Group of the IET Visual Engineering Professional Network, a senior member of the IEEE, a member of the British Machine Vision Association and a member of the steering board of the Networked Audiovisual Media technology platform of the European Union. He is member of the programme committee of the IEEE conference on Information Visualization, the international program committee of EURASIP&IEEE conference on Video Processing and Multimedia Communication and the European Workshop on Image Analysis for Multimedia Interactive Services. Prof. Izquierdo has served as session chair and organiser of invited sessions at several conferences. Prof. Izquierdo coordinated the EU IST project BUSMAN on video annotation and retrieval. He was a main contributor to the IST integrated projects aceMedia and MESH on the convergence of knowledge, semantics and content for user-centred intelligent media services. Prof. Izquierdo coordinated the European project Cost292 and the FP6 network of excellence on semantic inference for automatic annotation and retrieval of multimedia content, K-Space. Currently, he coordinates the EU FP7 network of excellence on 3D Media, 3DLife. Prof. Izquierdo has published over 300 technical papers including chapters in books.

Shuzhi Sam Ge, IEEE Fellow, is the Director of Intelligent Systems and Information Technology (ISIT), University of Electronic Science and Technology of China. He received his BSc degree from the Beijing University of Aeronautics and Astronautics (BUAA) in 1986, and the Ph.D. degree and the Diploma of Imperial College (DIC) from the Imperial College of Science, Technology and Medicine in 1993. He has (co)-authored three books and over 300 international journal and conference papers, and co-invented 3 patents. He serves as a book Editor of the Taylor & Francis Automation and Control Engineering Series, and Editor in Chief of International Journal of Social Robotics. He has served/ been serving as an Associate Editor for a number of flagship journals including IEEE Transactions on Automatic Control, IEEE Transactions on Control Systems Technology, IEEE Transactions on Neural Networks, and Automatica. He provides technical consultancy to industrial and government agencies. His current research interests include social robotics, multimedia fusion, adaptive control, intelligent systems and artificial intelligence.

Jing Tian received his B.Eng. degree (Electronic and Information Engineering), from School of Electronic and Information Engineering, South China University of Technology, Guangzhou, China, M.Eng. degree (Electronic and Information Engineering), from School of Electronic and Information Engineering, South China University of Technology, Guangzhou, China, Ph.D. degree (Electrical and Electronic Engineering), from School of Electrical & Electronic Engineering, Nanyang Technological University, Singapore. His research interests include image processing, pattern recognition and computer vision.

Weiyu Yu received the B.Eng degree in Electronic Automation from Guangdong University of Technology, the M.Eng degree in Electronic and Information Engineering from South China University of Technology and the Ph.D. degree in Electrical and Electronic Engineering from South China University of Technology, Guangzhou, China. His research interests include image processing, video analysis and pattern recognition.

Yiqun Hu received the BS degree in computer science from Xiamen University, P.R.C in 2002 and the PhD degree in computer engineering from Nanyang Technological University Singapore in 2008. He is currently the research fellow in Nanyang Technological University Singapore. His research interest include pattern analysis, machine learning and their applications in computer vision and multimedia, especially computational attention detection and media retargeting.

Viswanath Gopalakrishnan received the B.Tech degree in Electronics and Communication Engineering from National Institute of Technology, Calicut (formerly REC Calicut) in 2001. From 2002 to 2006 he worked in Texas Instruments and Emuzed India, Bangalore, in the domain of image and video compression. He is currently pursuing the Ph.D. degree under School of Computer Engineering, Nanyang Technological University, Singapore. His research interests include visual attention in images/videos and graph based approaches in computer vision.

Deepu Rajan is an Associate Professor in the School of Computer Engineering at Nanyang Technological University. He received his Bachelor of Engineering degree in Electronics and Communication Engineering from Birla Institute of Technology, Ranchi (India), M.S. in Electrical Engineering from Clemson University, USA and Ph.D from Indian Institute of Technology, Bombay (India). From 1992 till 2002, he was a Lecturer in the Department of Electronics at Cochin University of Science and Technology, India. His research interests include image processing, computer vision and multimedia signal processing.

Kongqiao Wang received his Ph.D in 1999 in signal and information processing from University of Science and Technology of China. He then joined Nokia Research Center in December 1999. His research focus is mobile user interfaces and related enabling technologies research, e.g., mobile scanning by optical character recognition, Pen UI and continuous handwriting character recognition, face tracking and recognition, gestural UI, etc. Currently he is a research team leader of multimodal and multimedia user interactions in Nokia Research Center, Beijing laboratory. He is also an adjunct professor of University of Science and Technology of China (USTC) and Beijing University of Post and Telecommunication (BUPT). He has achieved more than 60 granted/pending family patents, published four book chapters and more than 50 conference and journal papers.

Yikai Fang received M.S. degree in control theory and control engineering in 2004 from Dalian University of Technology and Ph.D degree in pattern recognition and intelligent system in 2008 from Institute of Automation, Chinese Academy of Sciences. Then He joined Nokia Research Center in 2008. His research interests include pattern recognition, image processing and computer vision. In the past several years, he focused on vision based gesture interactions and has published more than ten research papers.

Xiujuan Chai received the B.S. M.S. and Ph.D degrees in computer science from the Harbin Institute of Technology, Harbin, China, in 2000, 2002 and 2007 respectively. She joined Nokia Research Center, Beijing in 2007 for her Post-doc research. From 2009, she is an assistant professor with Institute of Computing Technology, Chinese Academy of Sciences. Her research interests cover image analysis, pattern recognition, computer vision and multimodal interface, particularly focusing on gesture analysis and face recognition related research topics. She has published more than 20 technical articles in referred journals and proceedings.

Index